CW01096282

EMPERORS AND POLITICAL CULTURE IN CASSIUS DIO'S *ROMAN HISTORY*

The *Roman History* of Cassius Dio provides one of the most important continuous narratives of the early Roman empire, spanning the inception of the Principate under Augustus to the turbulent years of the Severan Dynasty. It has been a major influence on how scholars have thought about Roman imperial history, from the Byzantine period down to the present day, as well as being a work of considerable literary sophistication and merit. This book, the product of an international collaborative project, brings together thirteen chapters written by scholars based in Europe, North America, and Australia. They offer new approaches to Dio's representation of Roman emperors, their courtiers, and key political constituencies such as the army and the people, as well as the literary techniques he uses to illuminate his narrative, from speeches to wonder narratives.

CAILLAN DAVENPORT is Associate Professor in Roman History at Macquarie University and the author of *A History of the Roman Equestrian Order* (Cambridge, 2019), which won the Royal Historical Society's Gladstone Prize. He has received an Australian Research Council Discovery Early Career Researcher Award and an Alexander von Humboldt Fellowship.

CHRISTOPHER MALLAN is Senior Lecturer in Classics and Ancient History at the University of Western Australia. He is the author of *Cassius Dio. Roman History Books 57–58 (The Reign of Tiberius)* (2020).

EMPERORS AND POLITICAL CULTURE IN CASSIUS DIO'S *ROMAN HISTORY*

EDITED BY

CAILLAN DAVENPORT

Macquarie University

CHRISTOPHER MALLAN

University of Western Australia

CAMBRIDGE
UNIVERSITY PRESS

CAMBRIDGE
UNIVERSITY PRESS

University Printing House, Cambridge CB2 8BS, United Kingdom

One Liberty Plaza, 20th Floor, New York, NY 10006, USA

477 Williamstown Road, Port Melbourne, VIC 3207, Australia

314–321, 3rd Floor, Plot 3, Splendor Forum, Jasola District Centre,
New Delhi – 110025, India

103 Penang Road, #05–06/07, Visioncrest Commercial, Singapore 238467

Cambridge University Press is part of the University of Cambridge.

It furthers the University's mission by disseminating knowledge in the pursuit of
education, learning, and research at the highest international levels of excellence.

www.cambridge.org
Information on this title: www.cambridge.org/9781108831000
DOI: 10.1017/9781108923019

© Cambridge University Press 2021

First published 2021

A catalogue record for this publication is available from the British Library.

Library of Congress Cataloging-in-Publication Data
NAMES: Davenport, Caillan, 1981– editor, author. | Mallan, Christopher Thomas, 1986– editor,
author.
TITLE: Emperors and political culture in Cassius Dio's Roman history / edited by Caillan
Davenport, Macquarie University, Sydney, Christopher Mallan, University of Western
Australia, Perth.
DESCRIPTION: Cambridge ; New York : Cambridge University Press, 2021. | Includes
bibliographical references and index.
IDENTIFIERS: LCCN 2021025018 (print) | LCCN 2021025019 (ebook) | ISBN 9781108831000
(hardback) | ISBN 9781108923019 (ebook)
SUBJECTS: LCSH: Cassius Dio Cocceianus. Roman history. | Emperors – Rome – Historiography. |
Political culture – Rome – Historiography. | Rome – Politics and government – 30 B.C.-284 A.D. |
Rome – History – Empire, 30 B.C.-284 A.D. | BISAC: HISTORY / Ancient / General
CLASSIFICATION: LCC DG207.C373 E48 2021 (print) | LCC DG207.C373 (ebook) | DDC 937/
.05072–dc23
LC record available at https://lccn.loc.gov/2021025018
LC ebook record available at https://lccn.loc.gov/2021025019

ISBN 978-1-108-83100-0 Hardback

Contents

Figures

Contributors

RHIANNON ASH is Professor of Roman Historiography and Tutorial Fellow in Classics at Merton College, University of Oxford. She has written widely on Tacitus and other prose authors of the imperial period. Her publications include two 'Green and Yellow' commentaries on Tacitus *Histories* 2 (CUP, 2007) and Tacitus *Annals* 15 (CUP, 2018). Her latest research project involves Pliny the Elder's *Natural History* book nine, and his depictions of marine creatures and images of imperialism.

CAILLAN DAVENPORT is an associate professor in Roman history at Macquarie University (Sydney, Australia). He is the co-editor of *Fronto: Selected Letters* (Bloomsbury, 2014) and the author of *A History of the Roman Equestrian Order* (CUP, 2019), which won the Royal Historical Society's 2020 Gladstone Prize. He has received an Australian Research Council Discovery Early Career Researcher Award and an Alexander von Humboldt Fellowship for Experienced Researchers.

MONICA HELLSTRÖM is a departmental lecturer in ancient history at the University of Oxford. Her main interests are the history, historiography, art and architecture of the later Roman empire, from the Severans through the fourth century AD. A recurrent theme in her research is descriptions and representations of central power.

ADAM M. KEMEZIS is an associate professor in the Department of History and Classics at the University of Alberta (Edmonton, Canada). He specializes in the historiography, political culture and Greek literature of the high and late Roman Empire. He is the author of *Greek Narratives of the Roman Empire under the Severans: Cassius Dio, Philostratus and Herodian* (CUP, 2014) and articles on Dio, Philostratus, Tacitus and the *Historia Augusta*.

CHRISTINA T. KUHN is Associate Professor and Ttutorial Fellow in ancient history at the Faculty of Classics and Lady Margaret Hall of the University of Oxford. Her research centres on the political, social and cultural history of the Roman Empire, the epigraphy of the Graeco-Roman world, and the provincial administration and civic life of Roman Asia Minor.

MYLES LAVAN is Reader in Ancient History at the University of St. Andrews. He is the author of *Slaves to Rome: Paradigms of Empire in Roman Culture* (CUP, 2013) and co-editor of *Cosmopolitanism and Empire: Universal Rulers, Local Elites and Cultural Integration in the Ancient Near East and Mediterranean* (OUP, 2016). He has also published several articles on the history of Roman citizenship in the imperial period.

CESARE LETTA is a professor emeritus at the University of Pisa. From 1976 to 2014 he taught Roman History, from 1975 to 1989 he was director of the Pisan Archaeological Mission at Collelongo in the Abruzzi, and since 2005 has been chief editor of the journal *Studi Classici e Orientali*. He is author of many publications concerning Roman history and historiography, Latin and Italic epigraphy, and Roman archaeology.

SHUSHMA MALIK is Lecturer in Classics at the University of Roehampton, London. Her research interests include the role of Roman emperors in the classical tradition, Roman religions, and imperial historiography. She is author of *The Nero-Antichrist: Founding and Fashioning a Paradigm* (CUP, 2020).

CHRISTOPHER MALLAN is Senior Lecturer and Discipline Chair of Classics and Ancient History at the University of Western Australia, Perth. He is a Roman historian who works on the history and historiography of the Roman Empire and its reception in Byzantium. He has recently completed a commentary on Books 57 and 58 of Dio's *Roman History*, which was published by OUP in 2020.

CHRISTOPHER PELLING was Regius Professor of Greek at the University of Oxford from 2003 to 2015. Since his 'retirement', he has completed a commentary on Herodotus VI (with Simon Hornblower) for the Cambridge 'Green and Yellow' series and a further study on Herodotus, titled *Herodotus and the Question Why* (University of Texas Press, 2019).

BARBARA SAYLOR RODGERS is Professor Emerita of Classics at the University of Vermont. She is co-author (with Ted Nixon) of a translation and commentary on the *Panegyrici latini* and has written various works on historiography and rhetoric of the Roman Republic and late antiquity.

ALICIA SIMPSON is a lecturer in history and Classics at the American College of Greece. Her research interests focus on Middle Byzantine literature and culture and on the reception of the classics. She is the author of *Niketas Choniates. A Historiographical Study* (OUP, 2013).

Preface

How we make sense of our political leaders and the cultures they inhabit (and create) are questions of relevance for us in 2020 as they were for Cassius Dio in 220. The emperors of Rome remain, whether in academic circles or popular culture, common points of reference in such discussions. As such, the study of Roman emperors and the political culture of imperial Rome needs no special appeals for relevance. Nor is there need for an excuse to write a book about Cassius Dio. The consular historian from Nicaea has now entered the academic, if not (yet) popular, mainstream.

This volume had its genesis in a panel at the Classical Association conference in Edinburgh in 2016 featuring the editors of this volume, Adam Kemezis, and Verena Schulz. After this panel, we decided to bring together an international team comprising both early career academics and senior researchers in order to investigate questions around Dio's portrayals of emperors and his representation of Roman political culture in the *Roman History*. Between Easter 2016, when the outline of the volume was threshed out over coffee in the collegial atmosphere of the Wadham College SCR, and early 2020, when the final revisions were made in the isolation of lockdown during the COVID-19 pandemic, neither the world nor 'Dio Studies' has stood still. Even so, it is hoped that this volume will make contributions to the twin fields of Roman imperial history and historiography.

It has been a pleasure to work with our collaborators over these past four years. We would like also to take this opportunity to thank several individuals who have contributed to the making of this volume. Although Verena Schulz's contribution from the Classical Association conference does not appear in this volume, we would like to thank her for her contribution to the original panel in Edinburgh: the arguments that she presented there can now be found in her excellent 2019 monograph *Deconstructing Imperial Representation: Tacitus, Cassius Dio, and Suetonius on Nero and Domitian*. With characteristic generosity, Chris Pelling has read over the entire manuscript and offered feedback on several chapters at various stages. Rhiannon Ash, Cesare Letta, and Barbara Saylor Rodgers also provided valuable editorial feedback, not least by spotting typographical errors that had escaped our notice. Michael Sharp has been the model of professionalism at Cambridge University Press, and we are grateful for his support for this project from its inception. This volume benefitted from the advice of Cambridge's reviewers, who offered the best sort of critical feedback on the proposal and who helped shape the current structure of this volume.

Caillan Davenport would like to thank Nicola Linton for her research assistance, funded by a University of Queensland Summer Research Scholarship, and the Australian Research Council (Project DE15010III0) and the Alexander von Humboldt Foundation for funding his research into Roman emperors. He is particularly grateful to Hartmut Leppin for sponsoring his Humboldt Fellowship and for welcoming him so warmly as a guest researcher at the Johann Wolfgang Goethe-Universität in Frankfurt am Main. Caillan is indebted, as always, to Meaghan McEvoy for all her love and support and for keeping him grounded, and to their twins, Alaric and Hamish, whose arrival in April 2020 provided two wonderful lockdown playmates.

Finally, it seems only appropriate in a volume such as this that we acknowledge the scholarship of Sir Fergus Millar, who passed away in July 2019, and whose contributions to the study of Cassius Dio and to our understanding of Roman imperial culture continue to shape much of the current discussion.

Abbreviations

Abbreviations of ancient texts conform to those found in either *OCD³* or *LSJ*, except for those noted below. All references in this volume to Cassius Dio's *Roman History* are given by book, chapter, and section numbers. They are not prefaced by 'Cass. Dio' or 'Dio'. The 'reformed' book number of Boissevain's edition is given first, followed by the 'standard' numbering in brackets. Where the text derives from an epitome or collection from the *Excerpta Constantiniana* or another source, it is indicated in brackets following the reference.

Bekker	Bekker, I. (ed.) (1849), *Cassii Dionis Cocceiani rerum Romanarum libri octoginta*. Leipzig.
BMCRE	*Coins of the Roman Empire in the British Museum.*
Boissevain	Boissevain, U. P. (ed.) (1898–1931), *Cassii Dionis Historiarum Romanarum quae supersunt*, vols. 1–3 (text), 4 (*index historicus*, ed. H. Smilda), 5 (*index Graecitatis*, ed. W. Nawijn). Berlin.
Cary	Cary, E. (ed. and trans.) (1914–29), *Dio's Roman History*, vols. 1–9. London.
CIL	*Corpus Inscriptionum Latinarum.*
ELg	*Excerpta de Legationibus gentium ad Romanos* in Boor, C. de (ed.) (1904), *Excerpta de Legationibus*. Berlin.
ELr	*Excerpta de Legationibus Romanorum ad gentes* in Boor, C. de. (ed.) (1904), *Excerpta de Legationibus*. Berlin.
ES	Boissevain, U. P. (ed.) (1906), *Excerpta de Sententiis*. Berlin.
EV	Büttner-Wobst, T. and Roos, A. G. (eds.) (1906), *Excerpta de Virtutibus et Vitiis*. Berlin.
FGrH	Jacoby, F. (ed.) (1923–58), *Die Fragmente der griechischen Historiker*. Leiden.

FRHist	Cornell, T. J. *et al.* (eds.) (2013), *The Fragments of the Roman Historians*, 3 vols. Oxford.
IG	*Inscriptiones Graecae.*
ILS	*Inscriptiones Latinae Selectae.*
John Ant.	John of Antioch.
LSJ⁹	Liddell, H. G. and Scott, R. (rev. Jones, H. S. and McKenzie, R.) (eds.) (1996), *A Greek-English Lexicon*, 9th edition. Oxford.
OED	*Oxford English Dictionary.*
Pet. Pat.	Peter the Patrician.
P. Colon.	*Kölner Papyri.*
P. Giss.	*Griechische Papyri im Museum des Oberhessischen Geschichtsvereins zu Giessen.*
PIR²	Groag, E. *et al.* (eds.) (1933–2015), *Prosopographia Imperii Romani, saec. i, ii, iii*, 2nd edition. Berlin and Leipzig.
PLRE I	Jones, A. H. M., Martindale, J. R. and Morris, J. (eds.) (1971), *The Prosopography of the Later Roman Empire, Volume 1, AD 260–395*. Cambridge.
P. Oxy.	*The Oxyrhynchus Papyri.*
RE	Pauly, A. F. von, Wissowa, G. E. et al. (eds.) (1894–), *Paulys Realencyclopädie der classischen Altertumswissenschaft*. Berlin and Stuttgart.
RGDA	Cooley, A. E. (ed.) (2009), *Res Gestae Divi Augusti: Text, Translation, and Commentary*. Cambridge.
RIB	*Roman Inscriptions of Britain.*
RIC	*Roman Imperial Coinage.*
RPC	*Roman Provincial Coinage.*
Sherk, *Hadrian*	Sherk, R. (ed.) (1988), *The Roman Empire: From Augustus to Hadrian*. Cambridge.
TrGF	Snell, B., Kannicht, R., Radt, S. (eds.) (1971–85), *Tragicorum Graecorum Fragmenta*. Leipzig.
Xiph.	Xiphilinus, *Epitome.*
Zonar.	Zonaras, *Epitome of Histories.*

Cassius Dio
The Senator and His Caesars
Caillan Davenport and Christopher Mallan

I

The age of the Severan emperors (AD 193–235) was a period of exciting cultural, artistic, literary, and intellectual development in the Roman world.[1] Novels, poems, histories, dialogues, and treatises in both Greek and Latin on a range of topics from animals and wonder-workers to matters of religion, administration, and law attest to this flourishing. Most of these texts did not deal explicitly with emperors and politics, but it was rare for any literary work to entirely escape the spectre of Roman imperial power.[2] One small group of Roman intellectuals, however, endeavoured to explicitly define the political system in which they lived. Among these were three prominent jurists – Ulpian, Papinian, and Paul – who all served at the court of the Severan emperors. Their works do not survive as they were written, although copious fragments are preserved in the legal compendia of the age of Justinian.[3] Their titles, such as *De officio proconsulis* ('On the Office of Proconsul') and *Imperiales sententiae in cognitionibus prolatae* ('Imperial Decisions given in Official Hearings'), tell us much about the ways in which these men tried to explain the constitutional framework of their world. But this attempt to analyse the evolution and functioning of the Roman empire was not confined to the technical works of jurists. The eighty-book *Roman History* of the Bithynian senator Cassius Dio, completed some-time after AD 229, likewise attempted to articulate what the imperial system actually was in both idea and in practice.[4]

The title of this chapter deliberately echoes that of Wallace-Hadrill 1983, which deals with Suetonius, another important witness to the Roman imperial system. All translations come from E. Cary's Loeb Classical Library edition, with some tacit modifications.
[1] See the papers collected in Swain, Harrison and Elsner 2007.
[2] This is a central theme of Swain 1997. Note, for example, Smith 2014 on the work of Aelian.
[3] For an overview of these individuals and their work, see Ibbetson 2005.
[4] A few preliminary attempts to reconcile the worlds of Dio and Ulpian have been made: Millar 2005; Christol 2016. A full-length study may prove illuminating.

The ideal came first. In Books 52 and 53, Dio presented an outline of how the Roman imperial government should operate.[5] Prior to this point in the narrative, Dio devoted serious attention to the corruption of the Republican system (*demokratia*), both in terms of the institutions of government and the ambitions of generals which were inimical to the order of the state.[6] The new monarchical *res publica* was a means to harmonise the discordant elements in Roman society (44.1–2). Provided that the state did not descend into a tyranny of the sort outlined by Agrippa in his defence of democracy at the start of Book 52, the monarchical system would provide a place for everyone and would endure so long as everyone knew their place.[7] Perhaps more significantly, the importance of the personality or individual character of the *princeps* is peripheral to the discussion.

For the remainder of Dio's imperial narrative (Books 53–80[80]) the reality appears, at least on first inspection, to play out differently from the ideal. Dio's narrative is focussed tightly on the emperor and his immediate associates. Although the picture is exaggerated by the editorial choices of Dio's epitomators,[8] Dio seems to show little interest in the history of the empire writ large, except as it affects the transformation of the Roman state and the conduct of its rulers and their associates. The men who inherit or seize the imperial purple are seldom model rulers of the sort found in panegyric or treatises *On Kingship*. They are men driven by human emotions and urges – fear, lust, jealousy.[9] Unlike the meditations on this theme found in Books 52 and 53, in his narrative of the Roman imperial monarchy, here we find that the character and behaviour of the emperors matter.[10] We are left with little doubt that life under Marcus Aurelius is very different from living under Caligula, at least for the senatorial and equestrian elite.[11] As for the emperor's associates, they too are seen to be products of the system. Dio's portrayal of these men provides us with a unique glimpse into the psychology of the ruled. Occasionally the

---

[5] The 'Agrippa–Maecenas' debate occupies the bulk of Book 52 and puts forward the case *contra* and *pro* monarchy. 53.12–18 provides an overview of the imperial system. For a discussion of the relationship between Books 52 and 53.12–18, see Kemezis 2014: 126–39.

[6] For Dio's approaches to this period, see now the collection of studies contained in Osgood and Baron 2019.

[7] Note the injunctions of 'Maecenas' at 53.37.5–11.

[8] On this point, note Brunt 1980: 488–93; Mallan 2013; Berbessou-Broustet 2016.

[9] For elements of Dio's ethical vocabulary, see Kuhn-Chen 2002.

[10] See the full analysis in Chapter 11 by Barbara Saylor Rodgers.

[11] Cf. Syme 1971: 146: 'As the imperial system developed, it disclosed its various *arcana* one by one. How much does the personality of the ruler matter? Less and less, it should seem.'

offhand comments are illuminating, as when Dio describes the impotent fury of senators under Tiberius just after the fall of Sejanus. These were men, according to our historian, who 'would have gladly eaten the flesh' (τῶν σαρκῶν ἂν αὐτοῦ ἡδέως ἐμφαγεῖν) of the emperor but instead voted him honours (58.17.1).

Thus, in Dio's mind, we are confronted with a twofold image of the imperial system. The *Roman History* shows that there was more to imperial history than the lives of emperors, but equally, the history of the Roman state cannot be written without emperors. To understand this, we need to acknowledge the fact that the figure of the emperor was perhaps the dominant motif in the political imagination of the inhabitants of the Roman empire. Historians could largely avoid emperors if one turned to the Republican past, or to Greek antiquities, as many authors did during the Antonine period.[12] But for writers of imperial history and biography, emperors were an inescapable reality. The extent of imperial influence can be seen even in the grammar and syntax of these works. In his discussion of Suetonius' *Lives of the Caesars*, Tristan Power has shown how Suetonius' emperors control the narrative, by looking at the proportion of sentences where the emperor is the grammatical subject.[13] Much the same observation holds for the imperial books of Cassius Dio. From the constitutional debate between Agrippa and Maecenas in Book 52 onwards, emperors and emperorship are Dio's joint points of focus. His concern is with what emperors did, the impact of their actions, and how others perceived them. The Roman Republican narrative of the *Roman History* shows that as a historian Dio was interested in sovereign power, and how power was used by the individuals or groups who held it.[14] Moreover, he possessed a palpable interest in the psychology of power – that is, how the possession of power influenced the actions of the possessor and those who were subject to his power. In Dio's mind this could be explained in terms of human nature. This aspect of his work has traditionally been seen to be Dio at his most Thucydidean. But there is much that is un-Thucydidean about Dio's imperial narrative and meditations on power: the narrow focus on individuals, the presence of women, the sometimes-gossipy tone of the contemporary books. This suggests a vastly different political world from that described by the historian of the Peloponnesian War.

In formulating and defining the term 'political culture', Gabriel Almond stated that '[e]very political system is embedded in a particular pattern of

---

[12] Kemezis 2010; Kemezis 2020.   [13] Power 2014b: 5–6.
[14] On the different forms of power possessed by emperors, see Harris 2016: 166–88.

orientations to political action'.[15] With the title of this book, *Emperors and Political Culture in Cassius Dio's Roman History*, we signal our intention to explore not only the centrality of emperors and the monarchical system of government to Dio, but also the historian's concern with the fundamental way emperors shaped individuals, groups, and communities.[16] For, as Lucian Pye has written, '[a] political culture is the product of both the collective history of a political system and the life histories of the individuals who currently make up the system; and thus it is rooted equally in public events and private experiences'.[17] The world inhabited by Dio and other Romans was both an explicit evolution and transformation of the Roman Republic into a new, monarchical form, as well as a lived experience, one that was often anxious and traumatic. We do acknowledge, as Emma Dench has recently explored, that the Roman world was home to a multiplicity of 'cultures' that can in various ways be considered political.[18] Our use of the singular here is designed to emphasise that we are discussing the vision of the empire as a political system in the mind of one man – Cassius Dio.

As editors, we have made no attempt to impose any orthodoxy on the chapters in this volume: indeed, contributors have been encouraged to approach their topics thorough whichever methodological or theoretical framework they choose to discuss Dio's (and his epitomators') representation of emperors and political culture in the *Roman History*. Thematically, these chapters fall into four sections: Dio's construction of political narratives under the Principate; his portrayals of individual emperors; his representations of political groups and their place in the wider political culture; and finally, the ways in which later generations of scholars in Late Antiquity and in the Byzantine Middle Ages engaged and reworked the imperial narrative of Dio's *Roman History* to suit the interests and political realities of their own times.

II

Dio's *Roman History* spans the period from the foundation of Rome to AD 229, the year of his own second consulship in the reign of Severus Alexander. According to the conventional periodisation of Roman history used by modern scholars, Books 1–2 covered the Regal Period, Books 3–51 the Republic (509 BC–29 BC), and Books 52–80 the Roman empire

[15] Almond 1956: 396.
[16] Thus, the definition of 'political' provided by the *OED* s.v. 'political' A. 1a: 'Of, belonging to, concerned with the form, organization, and administration of a state'.
[17] Pye 1965: 8.   [18] Dench 2018, esp. 16–17.

(28/27 BC–AD 229).[19] This is not quite the way that Dio conceived of the history of Rome in his own work, however. As the programmatic statement at the start of Book 52 shows, he considered the age of the kings as a separate period (*basileia*) but then divided the Republican government into *demokratia* and *dynasteiai* (52.1.1).[20] The latter period, roughly corresponding to the late Republican and triumviral periods (133–31 BC), represents a new stage of Rome's story in the *Roman History*, as the *demokratia* breaks down through the competition for power between great men, such as Marius and Sulla, Pompey and Caesar, and Octavian and Antony. Adam Kemezis has argued that this division corresponds to a transition between 'narrative modes' in the *Roman History*, as each period takes on distinct characteristics which reflect the political situation of the times.[21]

The transition to *monarchia* in the *Roman History* is marked both by the Battle of Actium in 31 BC in Book 52 and Octavian's assumption of the *cognomen* Augustus in 27 BC in Book 53 (52.1.1, 53.17.1). It is the second turning point which occasions Dio's famous methodological statement about how the history of the Roman imperial monarchy must be written in a different way from that of the Roman Republic:

> In this way the government was changed at that time for the better and in the interest of greater security; for it was no doubt quite impossible for the people to be saved under a republic. Nevertheless, the events occurring after this time cannot be recorded in the same manner as those of previous times. Formerly, as we know, all matters were reported to the senate and to the people, even if they happened at a distance; hence all learned of them and many recorded them, and consequently the truth regarding them, no matter to what extent fear or favour, friendship or enmity, coloured the reports of certain writers, was always to a certain extent to be found in the works of the other writers who wrote of the same events and in the public records. But after this time most things that happened began to be kept secret and concealed, and even though some things are perchance made public, they are distrusted just because they cannot be verified; for it is suspected that everything is said and done with reference to the wishes of the men in power at the time and of their associates. (53.19.1–3)[22]

---

[19] For the structure of Dio's early books, see Rich 2016. As Rich has shown, the conventional book divisions for Dio's early and mid Republican narrative are speculative.

[20] The decadic structure is noticed by Photius (*Bib. cod.* 71). On turning points occurring within the Republican narrative, see Millar 1964: 39; Simons 2009: 120–86. cf. Rich 2016: 276.

[21] Kemezis 2014: 94–104. Cf. Lindholmer 2018, whose argument does not undermine the distinct narrative modes discussed by Kemezis.

[22] ἡ μὲν οὖν πολιτεία οὕτω τότε πρός τε τὸ βέλτιον καὶ πρὸς τὸ σωτηριωδέστερον μετεκοσμήθη· καὶ γάρ που καὶ παντάπασιν ἀδύνατον ἦν δημοκρατουμένους αὐτοὺς σωθῆναι. οὐ μέντοι καὶ ὁμοίως τοῖς πρόθεν τὰ μετὰ ταῦτα πραχθέντα λεχθῆναι δύναται. πρότερον μὲν γὰρ ἔς τε τὴν βουλὴν καὶ ἐς

In this passage, Dio identifies a fundamental change in political culture. The *res publica* of the Republican period was characterised by accessibility and openness in the transmission of information, whereas the monarchy resisted such transparency, preferring to keep official news secret and concealed. He did not conceive of this change in terms of political debate or the capacity of the Roman people to influence laws or policies. The decline of popular sovereignty is not the issue, at this juncture (27 BC), in part, no doubt, because Dio believed that monarchy was the best form of government for Rome at this point in its development, given its geographical size and large population.[23] This is amply shown by Tiberius' funeral oration for Augustus, which establishes the parameters for good monarchical government for future *principes* to follow.[24] Instead, it is access to information about the deliberations of state which changes the political culture of the empire and thus the type of history Dio is able to write. In the words of Adam Kemezis, this passage shows 'Dio's explicit recognition that profound political changes call for a radically different kind of narrative'.[25]

The first two chapters of this volume, by Adam Kemezis and Caillan Davenport, offer different but complementary readings of this famous passage and its ramifications for understanding the depiction of the Roman imperial monarchy in Dio's work. In Chapter 1, Kemezis draws attention to Dio's solution to this methodological conundrum, namely his profession that he will describe all events as they were reported, regardless of how they actually happened (53.19.6). Kemezis explores Dio's use of information in terms established by anthropologist James Scott. These are the 'public transcript', or official version of events, and the 'hidden transcript', which offers a counterpoint (sometimes deliberately subversive) to the public one. Dio presents the 'public transcript' of imperial regimes and

τὸν δῆμον πάντα, καὶ εἰ πόρρω που συμβαίη, ἐσεφέρετο· καὶ διὰ τοῦτο πάντες τε αὐτὰ ἐμάνθανον καὶ πολλοὶ συνέγραφον, κἀκ τούτου καὶ ἀλήθεια αὐτῶν, εἰ καῖ τὰ μάλιστα καὶ φόβῳ τινὰ καὶ χάριτι φιλίᾳ τε καὶ ἔχθρᾳ τισὶν ἐρρήθη, παρά γοῦν τοῖς ἄλλοις τοῖς τὰ αὐτὰ γράψασι τοῖς τε ὑπομνήμασι τοῖς δημοσίοις τρόπον τινὰ εὑρίσκετο. ἐκ δὲ δὴ τοῦ χρόνου ἐκείνου τὰ μὲν πλείω κρύφα καὶ δι' ἀπορρήτων γίγνεσθαι ἤρξατο, εἰ δέ πού τινα καὶ δημοσιευθείη, ἀλλὰ ἀνεξέλεγκτά γε ὄντα ἀπιστεῖται· καὶ γὰρ λέγεσθαι καὶ πράττεσθαι πάντα πρὸς τὰ τῶν ἀεὶ κρατούντων τῶν τε παραδυναστευόντων σφίσι βουλήματα ὑποπτεύεται.

23 Millar 1964: 74–6; Aalders 1986: 297–9. Cf. Dio's comments about the decline of frank speech (sc. παρρησία) following the battle of Philippi (47.39.2–3), and the destruction of the democratic element within the state which came with the defeat of Brutus and Cassius. Manuwald (1979: 8–26) has shown that Dio does present negative aspects to monarchy. One key problem for Dio was hereditary succession, which did not always secure a good ruler: see further Davenport and Mallan 2014; Ando 2016; Madsen 2016; and Chapter 11 by Barbara Saylor Rodgers.
24 This crucial speech is discussed further below, and in Chapter 5 by Christina Kuhn.
25 Kemezis 2014: 96.

the behaviour of individual emperors, as he avows in 53.19, but he does set these beside alternate interpretations. He does not suggest that these different viewpoints, or 'hidden transcripts', are based on detailed historical investigation or research in the archives. But Dio nevertheless indicates that they represent contemporary evaluation of emperors, vocalised through specific groups, such as senators and the *populus Romanus*.

In Chapter 2, Caillan Davenport examines the tendency towards secrecy and the restriction of official information which Dio highlighted in 53.19. The lack of reliable news and information in the new monarchical regime resulted in the generation of rumours as a way for people to make sense of political happenings. Davenport shows how the presence of rumours in Dio's late Republican narrative increases as one comes closer to Octavian assuming sole rule, before becoming an integral part of the monarchical books. In the *Roman History*, the recourse to rumour and speculation in order to interpret the decisions of the emperor is not confined to people far away from the centre of power, but also affects those closest to the emperor at court. In historical terms, political rumours did exist and flourish under the Roman Republic, so the historicity of Dio's interpretation is certainly open to challenge. But by identifying rumour as a facet of monarchical political culture, Dio highlights the peculiarity of a system of government in which everything depended on the wishes and whims of one man, whose real thoughts and intentions usually remained opaque.

In seeking out the 'official transcript' of the imperial regime, Cassius Dio consulted a wide range of literary and documentary sources, as Cesare Letta proposes in Chapter 3. The historian rarely cites literary works and their authors by name in his imperial books, with only a few exceptions such as the autobiography of Hadrian (66.17.1 [Xiph.], 69.11.2 [Xiph.]). However, it remains the case that Dio used an extensive range of previous historical works for his account of the early Principate during his ten years of research (73[72].23.5 [Xiph.]). In a fragment which should be placed at the very beginning of the *Roman History*, Dio proclaims that he has read nearly everything that has ever been written about the Romans (F 1.2 [*ES*]). This extensive research thus represented a key part of Dio's credibility as a historian.[26] We cannot specifically identify these histories, not only because Dio does not cite them by name, but also because he reworks the material into his own original narrative of the Roman empire, as Letta argues in his chapter. Dio is much more extensive in his reference to documentary sources, such as *senatus consulta* ('senatorial decrees'),

[26] Millar 1964: 37–8; Marincola 1997: 105–6.

imperial letters and speeches, which he refers to or quotes directly. But we can also posit the use of these documents in interesting and original ways, which goes beyond mere namechecking. For example, in Chapter 5, Christina Kuhn shows how Tiberius' funeral oration for Augustus in Book 56 uses the *Res Gestae Divi Augusti* as a key point of reference. Kuhn demonstrates that that Dio reworks the themes of the *Res Gestae* to serve the themes of his portrayal of Augustus and Roman emperors in the *Roman History* at large, particularly in his desire to highlight the official view of Augustus' regime promulgated by the *domus Augusta* at his death.

The use and quotation of original documents increases in the contemporary portion of the *Roman History*, from Commodus to Severus Alexander. Indeed, Kemezis has proposed that this section of the work forms its own distinct 'narrative mode'.[27] Beginning in the reign of Commodus, Dio presents himself as a reliable eyewitness to events (73[72].4.1–2 [Xiph.]).[28] The most famous claim comes in Book 73(72):

> And, indeed, all the other events that took place in my lifetime I shall describe with more exactness and detail than earlier occurrences, for the reason that I was present when they happened and know no one else, among those who have any ability at writing a worthy record of events, who has so accurate a knowledge of them as I. (73[72].18.4 [Xiph.])[29]

The view that autopsy results in authenticity and reliability was a commonplace of ancient historians who wrote contemporary history.[30] But it is particularly interesting that Dio's programmatic statement quoted above emerges from his account of Commodus' outrageous and transgressive behaviour in the arena (73[72].16.1–18.4 [Xiph.]).[31] The theatre, circus, and arena were venues for entertainment, but they were also key political battlegrounds, in which the people could engage with and challenge the emperor. The emperor was always supposed to be a spectator, never a performer, at the games. Commodus' fighting as a gladiator and engaging in extravagant beast hunts were shocking to (at least some elite) Roman sensibilities, which did not expect emperors (or senators for that matter) to participate themselves. Dio vouched that he was present and witnessed this transgression of political and social norms first-hand.[32] The account of

---

[27] Kemezis 2014: 96–8, 141–5.   [28] Millar 1964: 120.

[29] καὶ μέντοι καὶ τἆλλα πάντα τὰ ἐπ' ἐμοῦ πραχθέντα καὶ λεπτουργήσω καὶ λεπτολογήσω μᾶλλον ἢ τὰ πρότερα, ὅτι τε συνεγενόμην αὐτοῖς, καὶ ὅτι μηδένα ἄλλον οἶδα τῶν τι δυναμένων ἐς συγγραφὴν ἀξίαν λόγου καταθέσθαι διηκριβωκότα αὐτὰ ὁμοίως ἐμοί.

[30] Marincola 1997: 79–81.

[31] For proper imperial behaviour in entertainment venues, see Wallace-Hadrill 1982: 42.

[32] See the discussions in Schmidt 1997: 2596–7; Scott 2018a: 231–3.

Commodus' gladiatorial antics thus takes the form of a 'wonder narrative', in which a historian recounts an event which might seem to be completely unbelievable. As Rhiannon Ash explores in Chapter 4, the wondrous and the incredible play a pivotal role in the *Roman History*, increasing as one enters the contemporary narrative, as Dio 'himself becomes one of the astonished internal viewers in his own text'.[33] It was standard practice for ancient historians to offer autopsy as a guarantee of the reliability of their own wonder narratives.[34] In the *Roman History*, this authorial strategy explicitly marks out Dio's account of the Commodan and Severan regimes as wondrous, but nevertheless completely true.

The extensive citation of documentary evidence in the contemporary narrative is a narrative strategy which serves to bolster Dio's authorial persona as a reliable witness and political insider. Readers might be amazed and horrified at Caracalla's massacre of the Alexandrians, emotions that would be amplified by Dio's pronouncement that Caracalla wrote to the senate to say that he did not care how many had died, for their fate was entirely deserved (78[77].22.3 [Xiph.]). But as Cesare Letta shows in Chapter 3, verbatim quotations from imperial letters are a feature of Dio's account of the reigns of Caracalla, Macrinus, and Elagabalus in particular, allowing the reader to experience the emperors in their own words. It is particularly fortunate that much of the original text of Dio's narrative of Macrinus survives in a manuscript, *Codex Vaticanus graecus* 1288, which covers 79(78).2.2–80(79).8.3.[35] Dio takes the reader into the senate house in Rome when letters arrive from the Macrinus in far-off Syria, allowing them to read the emperor's words and gauge contemporary senatorial reaction. An example of this is Macrinus' dispatch about Caracalla's failings and his own attempts to set matters right as emperor:

> Then he added in his letter something to the following effect: 'I realize that there are many who are more eager to see an emperor killed than they are to live themselves. But this I do not say with reference to myself, that anyone could either desire or pray that I should perish.' At which Fulvius Diogenianus exclaimed: 'We have all prayed for it.' (79[78].36.5)[36]

This passage demonstrates how Dio was able to make the transition from citation of documents to contemporary reactions. The witty apophthegm of Diogenianus provides the reader with amusement, as well as a sense of

---

[33] Section II.   [34] Marincola 1997: 82–3.   [35] Boissevain III.iii-ix; Scott 2018b: 2.

[36] ἔπειτα καὶ τοιόνδε τι προσενέγραψεν, ὅτι "πολλοὺς οἶδα μᾶλλον ἐπιθυμοῦντας αὐτοκράτορα σφαγῆναι ἢ αὐτοὺς βιῶναι. τοῦτο δὲ οὐ περὶ ἐμαυτοῦ λέγω, ὅτι τις ἢ ἐπιθυμήσειεν ἂν ἢ εὔξαιτό με ἀπολέσθαι". ἐφ' ᾧ δὴ Φούλουιος Διογενιανὸς ἐξεβόησεν ὅτι "πάντες εὐξάμεθα".

the senatorial disregard for Macrinus. Indeed, one of the features of Dio's contemporary books is the recounting of political events with a certain black humour.[37] In Chapter 4, Rhiannon Ash examines the arraignment of a bald-headed senator on a charge of treason during the reign of Septimius Severus, an incident which Dio describes as 'an extraordinary affair even in the hearing' (παράδοξα ὄντα καὶ ἀκουσθῆναι) (77[76].8.1 [Xiph.]). This story begins as a comical tale of senators feeling their own heads to make sure they cannot be identified as the culprit, but then takes a dark turn as the guilty man is dragged out of the senate to be beheaded. Here we have a story that reflects the incredible dangers in which senators found themselves under the Severan regime, coupled with the gratitude and guilt felt by those, such as Dio, who were fortunate enough to escape with their lives.

Dio's claim to being an eyewitness must be tempered by the fact that while he was sometimes present when events occurred (as in the case of the trial of the bald-headed man), very often he was not.[38] For example, Dio wintered with the court of Caracalla in Nicomedia (probably in 213/14), but after the emperor left in April 214, Dio never saw him again.[39] He also spent a considerable portion of the reign of Elagabalus outside Rome, an absence which does not reduce the level of scandalous detail in the *Roman History*.[40] As Kemezis points out in his chapter, 'Dio's final claim about his own worth as a historian is more about his social position and education than his personal experience'.[41] The reader is thus expected to respect Dio's position as a senator and his ability to be a reliable witness in the contemporary narrative. This is bolstered by a wealth of prosopographical detail about Dio's senatorial coevals, as Christopher Mallan explores in Chapter 12. The 'born prosopographer' creates a world full of distinguished nobles and generals, whose deserved promotions and unwarranted executions reflect on the emperors of the day.[42] Yet once again, caution is required. Dio presents himself as a spokesperson for the senatorial order as a whole, frequently using the first-person plural in the contemporary narrative to express the views and experiences of the *amplissimus ordo*.[43] Now, we know

---

[37] See Chapter 1 by Adam Kemezis in this volume and Osgood 2016 on the reign of Elagabalus.

[38] For Dio's career, which often took him away from Rome or other places where events were happening, see Millar 1964: 13–17; Chapter 12 by Christopher Mallan in this volume.

[39] Davenport 2017: 93–4. For the dating, see Molin 2016a: 441.   [40] Millar 1964: 168–9.

[41] See Chapter 1, Section VI by Kemezis in this volume. See also Chapter 5 by Christina Kuhn and Chapter 7 by Shushma Malik.

[42] The quotation is from Millar 1964: 164.

[43] Marincola 1997: 199–200. Whittaker (1969: xlvii) notes the necessity of comparing Dio and Herodian's accounts, for example, on Severus' return to Rome, which offers a 'salutary warning against assuming that Dio [. . .] speaks for the whole senate'.

that Dio was not the only writer of the Severan period interested in recent history.[44] But the *Roman History* is the only work that survives since the *Lives* of Marius Maximus have been lost, and Herodian was not a senator (or at least never presented himself as such).[45] Dio's criticisms of Septimius Severus' behaviour when he returned to Rome and his neglect of the senate must be tempered by the fact that Severus had many close senatorial advisors, but Dio was never part of this inner circle.[46] Furthermore, Dio resented the rise of men from the ranks of the army (below the centurionate) to high equestrian and senatorial office (52.25.6–7). These frequently come in for criticism as unworthy recipients of the emperor's attention, as seen in the case of Caracalla's new men, whose careers benefited from his patronage.[47] We believe, therefore, that Dio cannot be regarded as an authentic voice of all senators, but only of a segment of the *curia*.[48] Dio's own authorial strategy suggests that he is playing with the limits of knowledge and experience. For in Book 53, Dio sets up his account of the monarchical period as one in which the channels of political information are constrained, but then proceeds to portray himself in the contemporary narrative as *the* authoritative source of information on political events.

III

Dio's *Roman History* is fundamentally an annalistic work, structured by years and consular dates.[49] The naming of ordinary and sometimes suffect

---

[44] For a general discussion of historiography during the Severan period, see Sidebottom 2007; Zecchini 2016.

[45] For Herodian's lack of self-representation in his work, see Kemezis 2014: 304–8. There are circumstantial, but plausible, grounds for supposing that Marius Maximus' series of biographies offered a different perspective to Dio. See further Molinier Arbo 2009; Kemezis 2012.

[46] Davenport 2012a: 799–801. Cf. the opinions of Crook 1955: 82; Hose 2007: 462, who argued for Dio's intimacy with the emperor.

[47] Davenport 2012a: 808–11; Chapter 12 by Christopher Mallan in this volume.

[48] In dialogue with Davenport 2012a, Scott 2015 emphasises Dio's reliability as a guide to the experiences of senators, and argues that he did not judge emperors (such as Caracalla) according to how they treated him, but only how they measured up to the ideals demonstrated by Marcus Aurelius. While we would agree that Marcus is an idealised, almost model, figure in the *Roman History*, we have doubts that Dio was as dispassionate as Scott argues when it came to assessing emperors such as Caracalla. The fact remains that both Septimius Severus and Caracalla had loyal senatorial supporters who benefited personally from their regimes, and Dio's narrative does not present their point of view. Moreover, it is more realistic to conceive of the senate and the imperial court as institutions divided by ever-shifting alliances and factions than as monolithic bodies with one view.

[49] Millar 1964: 39–40. For further considerations on Dio's annalistic form, see Devillers 2016b; Rich 2016; Baron 2019.

consuls occurs even in the imperial books.[50] But the return of monarchy to Rome under Augustus still had profound implications for the structure of the *Roman History*. The dating by consuls co-exists with another chronological indication, Dio's precise reckoning of the regnal years of emperors.[51] The style of the narrative is adapted to the new form of government, as emperors are introduced with character sketches at the beginning of their reigns and necrologies at the end.[52] In the words of Christopher Pelling, this change represents a 'move towards biostructure', as events are shaped by individuals – the Roman emperors – to a greater extent than they were in the Republican books.[53] The centrality of the emperor in the second half of the *Roman History* may seem a prosaic and obvious development, but it mirrors wider changes in literature and historiography during the Principate, as all forms of writing addressed the new power structure of the Roman state.[54] The most noticeable result of this was the birth of imperial biography, in the form of 'sequential, linked biographies of dynastic rulers', which did not exist before Plutarch and Suetonius' *Lives of the Caesars* were written in the Flavian and Hadrianic periods, respectively.[55] Many aspects of Suetonius' *Lives* were completely original for the biographical genre, such as his emphasis on physiognomy and imperial character.[56] Suetonius' Latin biographies found an imitator in Dio's Severan coeval (and possible rival), L. Marius Maximus Perpetuus Aurelianus, who held the ordinary consulship for the second time in AD 223, six years before Dio obtained the same honour.[57] But it would be inappropriate to characterise Dio's imperial books as a poor imitation of Suetonian biography: in the *Roman History* the biographical and annalistic styles coexist and complement each other.[58] It was a feature of ancient historiography in general that genre was never fixed, but 'dynamic', as John Marincola has argued, and this was no less true of the annalistic format

---

[50] For Dio's methodological statement on consuls, see 43.46.6. For an example from the Severan books, see 79(78).26.8 (from *Codex Vaticanus graecus* 1288). Dio may have been the author of the consular *fasti* at the beginning of the books (as argued by Mallan 2017a: 714–18).

[51] See, for example, the length of Nerva's reign: one year, four months, and nine days (Dio 68.4.2 [Xiph.]).

[52] Questa 1957.   [53] Pelling 1997a: 117–22 (quotation from p. 121). See now also Devillers 2016b.

[54] Swain 1997: 1–9.

[55] Bowersock 1998: 193. For Suetonius, see Wallace-Hadrill 1983; Power and Gibson 2014.

[56] Hägg 2012: 228–9.

[57] For an overview of Marius Maximus and his work, see *PIR²* M308; *FRHist* (no. 101) I.602–11 (Levick and Cornell); cf. Syme 1968: 89–93; Syme 1971: 113–45 (comparing him with Dio).

[58] Pelling 1997a: 117–18. For comparison of the techniques of Suetonius and Dio, see Freyburger-Galland 2010.

than other styles.[59] We should thus not be surprised that Dio's annalistic history was heavily influenced by genres such as paradoxography (as shown by Rhiannon Ash in Chapter 4) and biography, thus producing a work that was uniquely his own.

Dio's representation of Roman emperors should thus be assessed on his own terms, for no one else in the Antonine or Severan periods produced a history of Rome with such scale and ambition.[60] Indeed, Antonine Rome witnessed a general aversion to writing contemporary history, as its practitioners turned to the age of Alexander and the Republic instead.[61] Dio, however, weaved Rome's Republican past and monarchical present into one historical continuum.[62] The reign of the first emperor Augustus acted as the fulcrum between these two phases, with his life and career dominating the narrative from Books 45 to 56. Any reader of these books is left in no doubt that Rome needed to become a monarchy to restore effective government. The summation of this narrative is the funeral oration of Augustus delivered by his adopted son and successor Tiberius, explored by Christina Kuhn in Chapter 5. Kuhn shows how this speech draws upon the themes and structure of Augustus' own *Res Gestae* to emphasise the legitimacy of the *princeps'* actions in seizing sole power. Dio wished to present his readers with the arguments that the *domus Augusta* would have made at this key turning point to justify their continued rule.

One of the problems of monarchy, which Dio does not shy away from in the *Roman History*, is that one could not guarantee that all emperors would be worthy of ruling the empire (as vividly demonstrated by Barbara Saylor Rodgers in Chapter 11). The funeral speech for Augustus may well leave the reader wondering whether its speaker, Tiberius, will manage to reach the same heights as his father. This is the problem which Christopher Mallan tackles in Chapter 6. He shows how Dio presents Tiberius as a man who is

---

[59] Marincola 1999: 282. On the adaption of the annalistic framework in Roman historiography, see Ginsburg 1981 on the *Annals* of Tacitus.

[60] Baldwin 1986's efforts to find precursors did not turn up similar histories.

[61] For example, Florus concluded his history with the victory of Augustus in the civil war. The bulk of Appian's history concluded with the annexation of Egypt following the defeat of Cleopatra and Mark Antony, although a few books were added to incorporate the wars in Arabia. Granius Licinianus seems to have written a history focussing on Republican history. For an overview of Antonine historiography, see Kemezis 2010.

[62] Thus, while this volume focuses on the imperial books of the *Roman History*, many chapters consider these books in dialogue with the Republican parts of the narrative (for example, Chapter 2 by Caillan Davenport, Chapter 9 by Monica Hellström, Chapter 10 by Myles Lavan, and Chapter 11 by Barbara Saylor Rodgers). There is considerable scholarly discussion about the extent to which the portrayal of emperors is anticipated by the great men of the late Republic (e.g. Coudry 2016b; Coudry 2019). Christopher Pelling returns to this theme in his Epilogue.

destined to be Augustus' successor, but nevertheless constantly fears imperial rivals, first Gaius and Lucius Caesar under Augustus, and later Germanicus and Sejanus during his own reign. Germanicus and Sejanus are particularly important characters in the Tiberian books, as their presence and rivalry with the emperor are fashioned to represent distinct 'phases' of Tiberius' principate. One way for historians to adapt the annalistic format for their own purposes was to 'focalise' the narrative through particular characters.[63] In Dio, the emperors themselves are key focalisers, but so are other figures such as wives, sons, and advisors.[64] Mallan shows how the Germanicus and Sejanus phases of the Tiberian narrative represent different manifestations of the emperor's fearful nature.

Virtues and vices were one way of assessing Roman emperors, most famously undertaken by the biographer Suetonius in his structuring of imperial lives *per species*.[65] Dio certainly characterises emperors in terms of their virtues and vices, both directly in his own authorial voice and through speeches delivered by characters in his history. It is interesting that most of the virtues ascribed to Augustus occur in speeches, namely the *princeps'* own address to the senate in Book 53 and in Tiberius' funeral oration in Book 56. Augustus emerges from these as an emperor who exhibits a host of valuable qualities, such as ἐπιείκεια ('reasonableness'), πραότης ('mildness'), φρόνιμος ('prudence'), φιλανθρωπία ('benevolence'), and εὐεργεσία ('kindness').[66] Although Augustus is not a perfect character in the *Roman History*, one cannot escape the impression that subsequent emperors are intended to be measured against him. Augustus' catalogue of virtues is exceeded only by two emperors of the second century AD, Marcus Aurelius and Pertinax.[67] Most emperors possess both virtues and vices, with the weight tending towards the latter (sometimes exclusively so) in typical 'bad' emperors, such as Caligula, Nero, Domitian, Commodus, and Caracalla (see particularly Chapter 7 by Shushma Malik and Chapter 11 by Barbara Saylor Rodgers).[68] Yet one should be wary of applying the Suetonian analytical framework directly to the *Roman History*. Dio often distinguishes between an emperor's

[63] Marincola 1999: 300–4.   [64] Pelling 1997a: 119–21.
[65] For discussion of this feature of Suetonius' compositional method, see now Hurley 2014 and Gunderson 2014.
[66] 53.6.1, 56.35.4, 56.37.2, 56.39.1, 56.60.4.
[67] See Chapter 8 by Caillan Davenport. For the characterisation of the early kings of Rome, whose portrayal forms an effective point of comparison with later emperors, see Schulz 2019b.
[68] For Nero and Domitian, see now Schulz 2014 and 2019a.

innate character (represented by virtues and vices) and his behaviour and conduct in office.[69] This can be seen in his portrait of Vitellius, the much-maligned emperor of AD 69 who receives a hostile treatment from Tacitus, and especially Suetonius. Dio recognised Vitellius' many vices, but praised him for showing mercy to supporters of his rivals, his legislation, and his relationship with the people and his fellow senators.[70] This approach to assessing emperors helps us to unravel the puzzling portrait of the emperor Tiberius, as Christopher Mallan argues. Tiberius does not have the many virtues of his predecessor Augustus, but on the other hand Dio does not indulge in the stories of sex and scandal familiar from Suetonius' *Life of Tiberius*. The 'ethical profile' of the emperor does not matter so much as his actual conduct of government – the account of Tiberius is an exercise in unravelling how kingship works. This makes Dio a more interesting and perceptive author than merely a 'Greek version' of Suetonius, but a historian interested in the functioning of the monarchical system.

Indeed, if there is one aspect of Dio's historical method which has been highlighted in recent years, it is that he sometimes chose to present emperors and their actions in a manner that encourages different interpretations from the reader.[71] This is most often apparent in imperial speeches, the sentiments of which are often problematised by the immediate context or the emperor's character.[72] Christina Kuhn, building on the work of Bernd Manuwald, shows how the sentiments of Tiberius' funeral oration for Augustus are often at odds with the emperor's conduct in the preceding narrative.[73] This, Kuhn contends, was an intentional strategy on Dio's part to show that he was not beholden to the official view of Augustus' reign, but could exercise his own critical judgement. The same degree of complexity is also exhibited in Dio's characterisation of some of Augustus' successors. Pertinax, who ruled only briefly following the assassination of Commodus, was an emperor whom Dio knew personally and admired

---

[69] Note the historian's comments on kingship, which he says, needs 'not only personal excellence, but also understanding and experience' (οὐκ ἀρετῆς μόνον ἀλλὰ καὶ ἐπιστήμης καὶ συνηθείας) (F 12.9). Schulz (2019b: 320–1) explores the ramifications of this statement in Dio's narratives of the kings and emperors.

[70] Davenport 2014, in which it is argued that this behaviour on Vitellius' part contrasted favourably with emperors of Dio's own day. Dio did not, and could not, make such a distinction in all his portraits of emperors, of course: some rulers were plagued by vices and their conduct as emperor offered no redeeming features. See the full discussion by Barbara Saylor Rodgers in Chapter 11.

[71] For the sophisticated level at which Dio was capable of operating, see Chapter 10 by Myles Lavan and the Epilogue by Christopher Pelling.

[72] Kemezis 2007; Adler 2011; Davenport and Mallan 2014.   [73] Manuwald 1979.

deeply. His own account of Pertinax's virtues is worthy of a panegyric, as he draws the picture of a man who is φοβερός ('formidable') in war and σοφός ('wise') in peace, epitomising the ideal of service to the state *domi militiaeque* (75[74].5.6 [*EV*]). Yet, as Caillan Davenport explores in Chapter 8, this laudatory judgement must be set against Pertinax's rapid demise. Pertinax did not realise the true threat which the praetorian guard posed to him, and despite all his virtues, he ultimately failed as a *princeps* because he could not adapt to the situation in which he found himself and appease the soldiery. The juxtaposition of Pertinax's career as a successful general and administrator with his unfortunate death in the palace highlights the problems with the distribution of power in the imperial monarchy, in which the military had the power to make and break emperors. Not all emperors or reigns in the *Roman History* receive this type of nuanced analysis. The overwhelmingly negative characterisation of Nero, for example, does not demand or encourage multiple interpretations from the reader. In these cases, our interest is drawn to Dio's techniques of criticism and invective, which, as Shushma Malik demonstrates in Chapter 7, mark him out as his own man rather than a slavish follower of the choices made by earlier historians and biographers.[74]

The emphasis on emperors both as characters and chronological markers still allows the development of what Christopher Pelling has aptly called 'trans-regnal themes' across imperial reigns and the *Roman History* at large.[75] One of these themes is the role of the emperor as a military leader. In the speech of Maecenas, Octavian's advisor urges the new *princeps* to be ready to deal with threats, but not to expand the limits of the empire (52.37.1). The same idea occurs in Tiberius' funeral oration for Augustus, which, as Christina Kuhn shows in Chapter 5, was at odds with the *princeps'* own self-presentation in the *Res Gestae*. This resistance to expansionism manifests itself in Dio's dislike of Septimius Severus' desire to extend the empire in the East, which he regarded as prompting further conflicts and financial losses (75(75).3.3 [Xiph.]). The early third century AD witnessed increases in army pay under Septimius Severus and his son Caracalla, the latter rise in particular stretching the imperial budget. Wars with Parthia took place under both these emperors, followed by a Persian campaign under Severus Alexander (though at least this was a defensive reaction to an unjustified attack).[76] Given this background, it is understandable that Dio did not approve of emperors who were

---

[74] These ideas are explored further in Section IV, below.   [75] Pelling 1997a: 125.
[76] For all these events, see the excellent summary of Severan history in Campbell 2005.

motivated by a desire for glory to expand the empire, as Caillan Davenport explores in Chapter 8.[77] For example, Dio's portrait of Trajan, as reconstructed from Xiphilinus and the *Excerpta Constantiniana*, shows an emperor who possessed a number of outstanding attributes, but whose ambition leads him into an unnecessary expansionistic war. Hadrian, on the other hand, acts as Trajan's counterpoint: he keeps the troops ready and disciplined, and uses them when necessary in a defensive war. The theme of discipline and warfare connects the early Principate with Dio's own contemporary narrative, enabling readers to see the historian's ideas unfold across multiple reigns and books. Tellingly, it also has points of connection with Dio's self-presentation in the *Roman History*, as he highlights his own behaviour as a stern disciplinarian of the troops when he was a provincial governor (80[80].4.2 [Xiph./*EV*]).

The intersection between imperial biographies and personal biography in the *Roman History* is symptomatic of the growing interest in 'the biographical' in different genres of writing under the Principate. Simon Swain has argued that this represented 'a fundamental transformation in the role of the person which placed the person at the centre of literary production'.[78] Dio's insertion of himself into his history might be compared with other authors such as Josephus and Ammianus Marcellinus.[79] We have already observed the key role played by Dio's authorial persona in guaranteeing the authenticity of his narrative, particularly in the contemporary books. But by the end of the *Roman History*, the autobiographical starts to supersede the biographical, as Christopher Mallan explores in Chapter 12.[80] The fact that the eighty-book work concludes in AD 229 with Severus Alexander awarding Dio his second consulship serves as an imperial mark of approval for Dio the senator, and by extension Dio the historian. This emphasises to Dio's readers that he was a suitable and reliable representative of the *amplissimus ordo* to pass judgement on emperors.

Dio's authority as a senatorial historian did not only depend on his public service, but also on his literary talent and erudition.[81] In a fragment from the start of the work, Dio explicitly made a connection between his style of writing and his trustworthiness (F 1.2 [*ES*]). Thucydides was

---

[77] On Dio and Roman imperialism, see Bertrand 2016b; Bertrand 2019.   [78] Swain 1997: 36.
[79] Scott (2018a: 234–7), in a stimulating discussion, also offers Cato the Elder and Sallust as points of comparison.
[80] See also Marincola 1997: 203–5; Scott 2018a: 232.
[81] See particularly Chapter 4 by Rhiannon Ash on Dio's narrative and artistic techniques. Appreciation of Dio's skill as a writer is raised by Christopher Pelling in the Epilogue.

a significant influence, as he was for most later classicising historians, but Dio also told the audience that he read the works of contemporary Atticising authors in order to familiarise himself with the style (55.12.4–5).[82] In this way, Dio emerges as a 'senatorial *pepaideumenos*', as Brandon Jones has argued, a man whose culture, education, and political career were intertwined.[83] This viewpoint allows Dio to pass judgement on men who were not from the same social circles, such as M. Oclatinius Adventus, the former *frumentarius* whom Macrinus appointed *praefectus urbi*.[84] In his opinion, Adventus could not read 'because of his lack of proper education' (ὑπ' ἀπαιδευσίας) (79[78].14.1). Dio's preoccupation with *paideia* influenced his portrayal of emperors, such as Nero, as Shushma Malik argues in Chapter 7. In contrast with Tacitus and Suetonius, who pay great attention to Nero's philhellenism (if only to denigrate it), Dio strips Nero of any Hellenic accomplishment at all. He is not an emperor who goes to Greece to display his talents, but to make war on the Greeks. Nero's lack of *paideia* anticipates the portrayal of Commodus in Dio's contemporary narrative, whose performances are a campaign not against the Greeks, but against the Romans themselves. Dio's emperors, therefore, are not designed to be read or interpreted in isolation: the accounts of their rise and fall, virtues and vices, and conduct good and bad are able to be compared and contrasted across the course of the *Roman History*.

IV

The biographical impulse manifests itself in the imperial books of the *Roman History* not only in the portraits of the emperors themselves, but also in the role played by the cast of characters that surrounds them, their wives and children, slaves and freedmen, senators and *equites*. These were the people who constituted the imperial court, whether they lived with the emperor or attended his *salutatio* (greeting ceremony) on a daily basis. The court was a new institution of government which developed under the monarchical *res publica* and came to sit alongside pre-existing Republican institutions such as the senate, magistrates, and the *comitia* (assemblies of the people).[85] Many aspects of court life were performed

---

[82] Note the comments of Millar 1964: 41–2.   [83] Jones 2016.

[84] *PIR*² O 9; Davenport 2012b: 197–8; Molin 2016b: 475–6.

[85] For ancient awareness of the Roman imperial court as an institution, see Wallace-Hadrill 1996: 283–4; Paterson 2007: 127–8. On the institutionalisation of the court across the first two centuries AD, see Winterling 1999.

openly, as emperors greeted their *amici* and the aristocracy at large, received embassies, hosted dinners, and embarked on journeys. But the real decisions were very often made beyond closed doors, where an emperor could consult his closest advisors. The idea that imperial government could function in this manner was not challenged by Dio or other citizens of the monarchical state, the sort of people whom Adam Kemezis characterises in Chapter 1 as the 'political public'.[86] But they did expect that an emperor should cooperate with the senate and select the right sort of men to serve as his counsellors – senators, jurists, and administrators, rather than wives, freedmen, slaves, or soldiers.[87] Indeed, the image of Dio as an imperial advisor plays a role in his own self-presentation in the contemporary narrative, the implication being that a good emperor surrounds himself with men like Dio.[88] One problem with this ideal, which Dio recognised, was that not all emperors chose to rule in a consultative fashion and kept their real thoughts and intentions secret from even those at court. This created an unstable and uncertain environment which generated rumours to make sense of or anticipate an emperor's whim, a problem explored by Caillan Davenport in Chapter 2.

Members of the court play a part in bringing structure to the *Roman History*, as imperial reigns are often divided according to the rise and fall of wives such as Messalina and Agrippina or advisors like Sejanus and Plautianus.[89] This combination of the annalistic and biographical modes is something more than a narrative device, as it reflects the real power which these individuals wielded. According to Dio, Plautianus' power was regarded as greater than that of the emperor himself, and his downfall precipitated the exile or death of his friends and clients (77[76].4.5, 5.3–6 [Xiph./*EV*]). But the importance of courtiers extended far beyond the few great men and women. In Chapter 11, Barbara Saylor Rodgers examines Dio's characterisation of the emperors and the rich cast of individuals who surround them. He was a historian always on the lookout for the *agathoi* and *kaloi*, the right sort of men who bring probity to a regime, such as the great Antonine generals Ulpius Marcellus, Aufidius Victorinus, and the future emperor Pertinax. But Dio was perhaps more interested in cataloguing the many and varied ways in which advisors could be

---

[86] Kemezis, Chapter 1, Section V.
[87] On cooperation with the senate, see Dio 53.17.2; Millar 1964: 74. For imperial advisors, see Jones 2016: 306–9 and Chapter 7 by Shushma Malik in this volume.
[88] Davenport 2012a: 799–803.
[89] Pelling 1997a: 120–1. For the Plautianus phase, see Scott 2017: 158–9.

bad than good. Rodgers draws attention to the extraordinarily rich vocabulary which Dio deploys to express disapproval of emperors and their associates. One of the features of this vocabulary of vice is that it is used to censure inadequate and deviant individuals in both the Republican and imperial narratives, ensuring continuity and coherence throughout the *Roman History*. The sort of men who were unworthy *principes* in the Republic remain unworthy assistants to the *princeps* in the monarchical state.[90] This problem becomes particularly acute when the emperor is a child or youth and depends on such men for good advice and guidance, an issue highlighted in several chapters in this book, especially those by Adam Kemezis, Shushma Malik, and Barbara Saylor Rodgers. What hope was there for Nero, if he was educated by a hypocrite such as Seneca, or Elagabalus, if he was surrounded by profligates and prostitutes? In this way, the problem of defective individuals is more serious in the imperial period than under the Republic: in a democracy, poor magistrates can be easily replaced through elections or brought to trial, but in a court-based society, they continue to exercise influence until they lose favour or their emperor is removed. The wait could be a long one – twelve years in the case of the unworthy and murderous Commodus. His demise finally brought the elderly senator Claudius Pompeianus out of hiding and back into the *curia*, where his reappearance was taken by the young Dio as an indication of the restoration of proper government after the anarchy of Commodus (74[73].3.3 [Xiph./*EV*]).[91]

For Dio, therefore, the political culture of the Roman empire was about more than the character of the emperor and his virtues and vices: it was about the networks of power and influence that radiated outward from the centre and which gave the imperial system structure and cohesion.[92] Our historian would probably have agreed with Ronald Syme's famous statement that 'Roman history, Republican or Imperial, is the history of the governing class'.[93] An emperor's appointment of senators and *equites* to suitable military and administrative posts is a major feature of the speech of Maecenas, reflecting Dio's own preoccupation with proper order in government and administration. But Dio is also interested in telling the stories of the individual members of the governing class, in a way that had not really been seen since Tacitus, who

---

[90] On Augustus as one of many *principes* competing for power, see Hillard 2011: 219–21.

[91] *PIR*² C 974; 74(73).3.3 (Xiph./*EV*).

[92] On Suetonius' lack of interest in politics, see Hägg 2012: 220–1. This is not to demean the artistry in Suetonius' writing or the originality of his prose.

[93] Syme 1939: 7.

brought them to life both in his monograph *Agricola* and in his annalistic histories. The appeal of writing political biographies of great men was born out of Rome's transformation from Republic to Principate.[94] For this was the period in which senators and *equites* embraced a new form of autobiography on a massive scale – the practice of inscribing their career in permanent format.[95] This genre allowed these men both to emphasise their collective identity as an aristocracy devoted to serving the *res publica* and to draw attention to their individual achievements.[96] Dio's portraits of individuals, much like Tacitus' famous character sketches and necrologies, are also designed to commemorate the men who served the Roman emperors, as Christopher Mallan discusses in Chapter 12. Sometimes these are senators who simply had illustrious careers, at other times they are great men who are brought down by tyrannical emperors; their commemoration performs a similar function to the genre of *exitus* literature which became particularly popular in the imperial age.[97] Dio's method of characterising emperors and their associates fits in with what David Konstan and Robyn Walsh have termed 'civic' biography. This was a genre which reaffirmed the collective values of the governing class.[98]

The prosopographical detail is particularly rich for the Severan books. This allows us to build up a picture of the sensible and right-thinking men who frequently sit in judgement on emperors in the *Roman History*, as Barbara Saylor Rodgers explores in Chapter 11. We also get a sense of Dio's rivals – not merely the obvious candidates such as the soldiers-turned-senators – but more conventional cases, such as Didius Julianus, whom Dio had proven guilty time and time again in the law courts (74[73].12.2 [Xiph.]). The rivalries within the senatorial order must have been exacerbated by the civil wars which dominated the Severan period. The speech of Cassius Clemens, arraigned before Septimius Severus for supporting his opponent Pescennius Niger, strikes a note of pathos in this regard:

> 'I,' he said, 'was acquainted with neither you nor Niger, but finding myself in the midst of his partisans, I was constrained to look to the moment, not with the purpose of fighting you, but of deposing Julianus. I therefore did nothing wrong, either in this respect, since I strove in the beginning for the same ends as you, nor later, in

---

[94] Geiger 1985: 116; Hägg 2012: 187–8, 232–8.   [95] Eck 1984.
[96] See the studies of Eck 1995; Eck 2009; Alföldy 2001; Davenport 2019: 256–9, 318–36.
[97] For this genre, see Harker 2008: 144–6; Hägg 2012: 236–8.   [98] Konstan and Walsh 2016: 27–8.

refusing to desert the master once given me by the will of Heaven and to come over to you.' (75(74).9.1–2 [Xiph.])[99]

Severus was amazed at the frankness of Clemens, and allowed him to live, with only half his property confiscated.[100] The speech encapsulates how easily a civil war could make or break senators – for other men, such as L. Fabius Cilo, it was a career-defining moment. Cilo had finally received a suffect consulship in AD 193 after a fairly undistinguished career, but his command of Severus' armies saw him become *praefectus urbi, cos. II ord.* in 204, and one of the most prominent aristocrats of the age.[101] One cannot escape the conclusion that Dio's final summation of his own career in Book 80 strikes a note of triumphalism not only on the basis of his achievements, but also because he survived the vagaries of fortune.[102]

The decisions of emperors, their advisors, and the senate had ramifications for the *res publica* at large. Dio presents the particular style of consultative monarchy established by Augustus as beneficial to the Roman people. It was one which produced 'a monarchy without terrors' and allowed people to live in 'a democracy . . . without discord', as Dio puts it in his summation of Augustus' life and career:

> So, it was both on account of these things, and because by combining monarchy with democracy he preserved their freedom for them and at the same time established order and security, so that they were free alike from the license of a democracy and from the insolence of a tyranny, living at once in a liberty of moderation and in a monarchy without terrors; they were subjects of royalty, yet not slaves, and citizens of a democracy, yet without discord. (56.43.4)[103]

This passage illustrates one of the basic principles of Dio's portrait of the citizen body at large. He discusses how political changes affected the people, and whether they endorsed these changes, but he is not interested in the mechanics of popular political participation.[104] As we discussed

---

[99] *PIR²* C 489. "ἐγώ", ἔφη, "οὔτε σὲ οὔτε Νίγρον ἠπιστάμην, καταληφθεὶς δὲ δὴ ἐν τῇ ἐκείνου μερίδι τὸ παρὸν ἀναγκαίως ἐθεράπευσα, οὐχ ὡς σοὶ πολεμήσων ἀλλ' ὡς Ἰουλιανὸν καταλύσων. οὔτ' οὖν ἐν τούτῳ τι ἠδίκησα, τὰ αὐτά σοι κατ' ἀρχὰς σπουδάσας, οὔθ' ὅτι μὴ πρὸς σὲ ὕστερον, ἐγκαταλιπὼν ὃν ἅπαξ ὑπὸ τοῦ δαιμονίου ἔλαχον, μετέστην"·
[100] For frankness of speech in Dio, see Mallan 2016.
[101] *PIR²* F 27; *CIL* VI 1408 = *ILS* 1141; *CIL* VI 1409 = *ILS* 1142.
[102] Cf. Scott 2018a: 246–7, who offers a different reading.
[103] διά τε οὖν ταῦτα, καὶ ὅτι τὴν μοναρχίαν τῇ δημοκρατίᾳ μίξας τό τε ἐλεύθερόν σφισιν ἐτήρησε καὶ τὸ κόσμιον τό τε ἀσφαλὲς προσπαρεσκεύασεν, ὥστ' ἔξω μὲν τοῦ δημοκρατικοῦ θράσους ἔξω δὲ καὶ τῶν τυραννικῶν ὕβρεων ὄντας ἔν τε ἐλευθερίᾳ σώφρονι καὶ ἐν μοναρχίᾳ ἀδεεῖ ζῆν, βασιλευομένους τε ἄνευ δουλείας καὶ δημοκρατουμένους ἄνευ διχοστασίας, δεινῶς αὐτὸν ἐπόθουν.
[104] De Blois 1997.

above, the programmatic passage of 53.19 is concerned with the flow of information from the emperor outwards, not that the *comitia* ceased to have a determining role in political decision-making. In the *Roman History*, the citizenry of Rome has a narrative role to play in endorsing the transition from Republic to monarchy, a change which brings with it peace and prosperity. Dio is not interested in creating a nuanced and complex picture of the Roman people but focuses on their role in his vision of monarchical political culture. This comes down to approving or censuring individual emperors.[105] In this way, the people constituted what might be called a 'vast and amorphous moral presence', to borrow Emma Dench's term for the appearance of Italians in the speeches of Cicero.[106] When the people turn against Macrinus and his son Diadumenianus at the horse races staged in Rome to celebrate the latter's birthday, it serves as a turning point in Dio's narrative which signals the beginning of the end for Macrinus (79 [78].20.1–3). This does not mean that Dio's portrayal of the Roman people is unsympathetic – far from it, as Monica Hellström argues in Chapter 9. Instead, they represent 'the potential, and nobility, vested in the Roman state'.[107] When they are neglected, brutalised or slaughtered by individual emperors, such as Caligula and Nero, their fate is a sad commentary on the conduct of the *princeps* and the declining health of the body public. These incidents are dramatised by verbs of seeing and hearing, which puts the reader in the category of an eyewitness, experiencing the trauma along with the people. Sometimes the list of imperial victims becomes too many to count, elevating the account into something akin to one of Rhiannon Ash's 'wonder narratives'. We, the readers, are expected to be as astonished as Dio at the catalogues of imperial brutality.[108]

If Dio's body public – the citizenry of the *res publica* – plays such an important narrative role in the *Roman History* and its conception of political culture, we ought to ask what Dio's attitude to the admission of new members was. Yet the study of citizenship in Dio has very often been overshadowed by the historian's infamous pronouncement on the *constitutio Antoniniana* (Antonine Constitution):

> on account of which [the abolition of various tax exemptions] he made all of the people in his empire Romans, ostensibly honouring them, but in reality

---

[105] For scholarly investigations of the social and political culture of the Roman people, and particularly their political roles, see Horsfall 2003; Courrier 2014; Kröss 2017.

[106] Dench 2013: 128.   [107] Chapter 9, Section I.

[108] For imperial violence as a theme in the *Roman History*, especially in the contemporary narrative, see Molin 2016b: 479–80.

to increase his revenues by this means too, since foreigners did not pay most of these [taxes]. (78[77].9.5 [*EV*])[109]

In Chapter 10, Myles Lavan takes an original approach to this passage by examining it not in the context of Dio's hostile account of Caracalla's reign, but in the conceptual framework of the *Roman History* at large. Lavan shows how two quite different views of the extension of Roman citizenship are present in the work. There is the idea that universal enfranchisement is a positive development, as it allows all men of honour to form part of the Roman community, as expressed in the speech of Maecenas in Book 52. But this is then set against the view, articulated by Augustus in Book 56, that citizenship should not be distributed widely, in order to preserve the distinction between Romans and their subjects. These different viewpoints are echoed by a range of characters in the history, but, as Lavan demonstrates, not by Dio himself. There is no firm pronouncement in Dio's authorial voice – even in the famous passage on Caracalla's edict, which is really concerned with the emperor's tax grab. This leads to the conclusion that citizenship was a topic regarded as worthy of inclusion and discussion in the *Roman History*, but not as a major theme. Although Dio recounted the life stories of emperors and their associates, the 'biography of the *populus Romanus*' was not a story Dio was interested in telling. That does not mean he did not respect the citizen body – as Hellström shows, he clearly did – but it acted as a foil for his larger argument about the rise and fall of systems of government and the great men who held positions of authority. Dio's vision of the political culture of the Roman imperial monarchy is thus an incomplete one.

V

We lose sight of Cassius Dio and his history in the mid third century, though his descendants continued to belong to the senate.[110] Herodian is the last author before the age of Justinian to engage in any meaningful way with Dio's work.[111] Unsurprisingly, given his theme, it was perhaps only

---

[109] οὗ ἕνεκα καὶ Ῥωμαίους πάντας τοὺς ἐν τῇ ἀρχῇ αὐτοῦ, λόγῳ μὲν τιμῶν, ἔργῳ δὲ ὅπως πλείω αὐτῷ καὶ ἐκ τοῦ τοιούτου προσίῃ διὰ τὸ τοὺς ξένους τὰ πολλὰ αὐτῶν μὴ συντελεῖν, ἀπέδειξεν.

[110] Cassius Dio, *cos. ord.* 291, was probably his grandson (*PLRE* I Dio); Molin 2016a: 437.

[111] Scholarly opinions on the extent of Herodian's use of Dio differ, however: compare Kolb 1972 and Sidebottom 1998. The author of the *Historia Augusta*, although he did employ Herodian as a source, does not seem to have relied on Dio (Syme 1971: 48). *Codex Vaticanus graecus* 1288 (latter part of the fifth century) is our earliest evidence for the transmission of Dio's work. The MS preserves numerous marginal annotations, in a different hand to the main scribal hand of the body text.

the final eight books that were of interest. The fate of Dio's history-writing contemporaries is little better. The imperial biographies of Marius Maximus were mined for information in the fourth century by the author of the *Historia Augusta* and probably by Ausonius for his epigrams on the emperors. Yet the production of the *Historia Augusta*, along with shorter works like Aurelius Victor's *De Caesaribus* ('On the Caesars') and the *Epitome de Caesaribus* ('Short History about the Caesars'), perhaps rendered Maximus' work redundant, and it is likely to have disappeared long before the Carolingian age, and possibly before even the age of Cassiodorus. Asinius Quadratus' history is cited in the *Historia Augusta*, but it is not until the sixth century that we find more certain references to his oeuvre in the works of Agathias and Stephanus of Byzantium.[112] Dio's Christian contemporaries fared a little better – at least in terms of their indirect legacy. The chronicler Julius Africanus was of singular importance to the newly developing Christian chronographic tradition. Yet of all these authors, it is certainly Dio who would have the most significant legacy: for unlike the works of Marius Maximus, Quadratus, and Julius Africanus, Dio's work would be preserved. Its preservation, albeit in a highly mutilated and abbreviated state, is indicative of the importance of Dio's history for generations of scholars and readers. Indeed, as argued by Alicia Simpson in Chapter 13, Dio's history came to represent the quintessential account of the Roman past for members of the Byzantine intelligentsia.

Prior to the western European Renaissance, we may single out two periods where Dio's history enjoyed the attention of historians and antiquarians. In both cases, the scene is Constantinople, the heart and head of what survived of the Roman empire. The first period was during the sixth and seventh centuries AD. One author in particular may be singled out, Peter the Patrician. Peter's *History* is dependent on Dio up until and including the reign of Elagabalus. From the surviving fragments of the work, to say that it is dependent on Dio is an understatement. Indeed, from what we can tell, the first part of Peter's work is little more than an abridged paraphrase of Dio's history. The quality of the work is debatable. A close contemporary of Peter, Menander the Guardsman, depreciated the literary merits of his works.[113] The surviving excerpts from his *History* bear out Menander's assessment. Peter's language often

---

[112] For the fragments of Asinius Quadratus, see *FRHist* II.1128–43. The fundamental study of Quadratus is Zecchini 1998.

[113] For Peter's lapses from an appropriately Attic register, note Menander Protector's censorious judgement (F 6.2, Blockley 1983 = *ES* 'Menander' F 11), with Cameron 2011: 660.

falls short of the high register of Dio's Greek, and his vocabulary is infused with Latinisms.[114]

Yet quality aside, Peter's work reveals some interesting and important features about the transmission and reception of Dio's work. First, Peter's focus is on imperial history.[115] The first fragment deals with the rogue general Labienus in the aftermath of the battle of Philippi. It is not unreasonable to suppose that the work began with the formation of the triumvirate of Lepidus, Antony, and Octavian.[116] Moreover, if Niebuhr's contention that Peter's work was organised as a series of imperial lives (or at least reign by reign) is correct, then we see the beginning of a process that would attempt to transform Dio's annalistic history into a series of imperial biographies.[117] In this respect, Peter may have been governed by pragmatism. By the age of Justinian, annalistic histories in the traditional Roman mode had long fallen into desuetude. Moreover, the biographical approach was perhaps the most obvious way to rework Dio's history, especially for someone who was intending to continue Dio's history through to the reign of Constantius II. Indeed, as we have already seen, this basic structure is found in the imperial books of the *Roman History* itself.

In some respects, Peter's history is more Dionian than Dio's. This may be observed in Peter's approach to *apophthegmata* (sayings and maxims). From what we can tell from the surviving excerpts, Peter trawled his copy of Dio for noteworthy *bons mots*, especially those which had the potential to illustrate the quality of a ruler. This in itself is unexceptional. As recognised by Plutarch long before, an offhand remark by a great man (or woman) could reveal much about their inner character.[118] However, Peter does more than simply transcribe Dio's original text. In several instances, Peter appears to have transformed statements originally in indirect speech into direct speech. In one particular case, where Dio alludes to a line from Euripides' *Phoenissae* (393), Peter presents the actual lines from Euripides in direct speech.[119]

---

[114] E.g. *ES* 'Petrus Patricius' F 4 = F 7, Banchich 2015; cf. 57.14.1. Note Peter's use of ληγᾶτα (sc. 'legacies'/'bequests').

[115] It seems likely that Peter's history commenced with the murder of Julius Caesar and terminated with the reign of Constantius II (Banchich 2015: 9).

[116] If this is so, then we may note the similarity between this approach and that of the editors of the second edition of the *Cambridge Ancient History* (vol. X). Cf. Pelling 1996: 1: 'On the 27 November 43, the *Lex Titia* initiated a period of absolute rule at Rome'.

[117] Seemingly endorsed by Banchich 2015: 5.   [118] Plut. *Alex.* 1.2. Cf. Duff 1999: 15–18.

[119] 58.24.4: ἵνα τὴν τοῦ κρατοῦντος ἀβουλίαν φέρῃ. Peter F 20 (ed. Banchich 2015): τὰς τῶν κρατούντων ἀμαθίας φέρειν χρεών.

It would be misleading to overplay the importance of Dio in this period. Dio's history was doubtless of particular importance for the antiquarians of Late Antiquity. Certainly, the *Roman History* was mined for facts by the antiquarian John Lydus, especially for Dio's comments on the origins of Roman political institutions. John of Antioch used Dio's history only as a subsidiary source.[120] Otherwise, Dio seems to have had little impression on the major historians of the period from Procopius to Theophylact Simocatta. For these authors of contemporary history, the classical historiographical antecedents were more congenial models for emulation and imitation than the authors of history under the Principate.

The second period which saw a resurgence of interest in Dio's history is that of the tenth to twelfth centuries, which is considered in Alicia Simpson's contribution. The Macedonian dynasty was in many ways a watershed in Byzantine political and intellectual history. A minor manifestation of this change may be seen in the way scholars engaged with Dio's *Roman History*. The previous centuries reveal little interaction with Dio's work, with the exception of the author of the grammatical treatise *On Syntax* (περὶ συντάξεως) and pseudo-Maximus the Confessor's *Florilegium*.[121] This was perhaps inevitable. The historical tastes of the mid seventh through the late ninth centuries were not conducive to the sort of history written by Cassius Dio. Chronicles, not classicising histories, still less imperial biographies, were the dominant mode of historical writing. Moreover, a historian like Cassius Dio could contribute nothing to the series of theological and spiritual controversies which dominated the attention of the foremost minds of seventh- to mid ninth-century Byzantium.

The shift in taste began in the later ninth century and gathered momentum in the tenth. The writing of history, and especially history in the form of a concatenation of imperial biographies, came back into vogue.[122] The works of Genesius and those attributed to Theophanes Continuatus are illustrative of this trend. There was a clear impulse to preserve the past, driven by the considerable resources of Constantine VII, that most self-consciously bookish of tenth-century emperors. It is from this period that we have some of our most important medieval Greek manuscripts of authors as diverse as Sophocles, Aristophanes, and Cassius Dio. This shift was not the result of imperial caprice, a moment in intellectual history

---

[120] Note that the so-called Salmasian Fragments (*Excerpta Salmasiana*), sometimes attributed to John of Antioch, show a greater fidelity to Dio's history than the fragments of John's world preserved in the *Excerpta Constantiniana*.

[121] For a summary of the reception of Dio in Late Antiquity, see Mallan 2019: 78–83.

[122] For this change, see the recent treatment by Neméth 2018: 145–64.

that would die with the emperor, or leading court figures such as Basil the Bastard. Rather, the change seems to reflect the ways in which the political and intellectual elites of Byzantium thought about their state.

In a well-known authorial interjection, the eleventh-century writer John Xiphilinus says that he intended to copy those parts of Dio's imperial narrative that were important to his own time. Xiphilinus constructed a political genealogy which bound the politics of the court of Michael VII (r. 1071–8) to the history of the early Roman empire.[123] For Xiphilinus this was not the history of particular institutions, the sorts of details which appealed so much to Cassius Dio. Rather for Xiphilinus, when he speaks of 'our [way of] life and *politeuma*' (ἡμᾶς βίον καὶ πολίτευμα), he means, first and foremost, a system of government headed by an emperor. The emperors of the past could be looked upon as models for emulation and authority. Michael Psellus (a contemporary of Xiphilinus, and a friend of the epitomator's scholarly uncle, the Patriarch John Xiphilinus), describes Romanus III (r. 1028–34) as wishing to model his reign on the rulers of the Antonine period, especially Marcus Aurelius, 'the philosopher ... and Augustus', and (like Marcus) to be 'skilled in letters and in war'.[124] Later, Psellus says that his one-time pupil, Michael VII, had immersed himself in the deeds of Hadrian and Trajan as part of his preparation for the performance of his military duties.[125] Occasionally, the weight of tradition could become oppressive. Michael Attaleiates was wont to compare the men of his own day unfavourably with the Romans of the past.[126] Even so, men of virtue could join the Roman exemplar-tradition: Nicephorus III (r. 1078–81), the heroic figure in Attaleiates' *History*, is presented as a descendant of the Republican Fabii as well as of Constantine I.[127]

The period between the accession of Constantine VII and the Sack of Constantinople in 1204 is particularly important for our assessment of Cassius Dio. Not only because it was in this period that the text of Dio was preserved and protected from oblivion, but also because this was perhaps the last time when Dio's history was regarded as a living text. It was reformed and refashioned by the likes of Zonaras, Xiphilinus, and even the excerptors working for Constantine VII, not because they wanted to

---

[123] The identity and career of John Xiphilinus is re-evaluated by Kruse 2019, who argues that he was a prominent court official.

[124] Psellus, *Chron.* 3.2: βουλόμενος δὲ ἐς τοὺς ἀρχαίους Ἀντωνίνους ἐκείνους, τόν τε φιλοσοφώτατον Μάρκον καὶ τὸν Σεβαστόν, ἀπεικάσαι τὴν ἑαυτοῦ βασιλείαν, δυοῖν τούτων ἀντείχετο, τῆς τε περὶ τοὺς λόγους σπουδῆς καὶ τῆς περὶ τὰ ὅπλα φροντίδος.

[125] Psellus, *Chron.* 7.   [126] Attaleiates 17.14 (ed. Kaldellis and Krallis 2012 = Bekker, pp. 114–15).

[127] Attaleiates 27.7–12 (ed. Kaldellis and Krallis 2012 = Bekker, pp. 217–20). See further Leidholm 2018.

preserve it, but because they believed the work was of immediate relevance and of use for explaining their own place in history and political institutions.

VI

It can no longer be said that Dio is an underappreciated or under-studied historian. The boom in Dio scholarship over the past twenty years, as outlined by Christopher Pelling in the Epilogue to this volume, has done much to bring the historian into the scholarly mainstream. Yet, as Pelling says, there is still more work to be done. Dio has much to offer the various sides of Classical studies: whether ancient history, language and literature, or even Classical reception, and scholars working in these fields can bring new perspectives to the study of the *Roman History*. Without doubt, the usefulness of Dio and the Dionian tradition extends beyond the realm of imperial politics. One suspects there is still much more Dio can tell the historian of ideas, religion, or gender studies.

Even so, Dio's primary value is as a work of political history, and no serious study of the Roman imperial monarchy can be written without reference to the *Roman History*. Dio's work was one which charted the political and institutional changes that transformed Rome across almost one thousand years of its history, from a monarchy, to a Republic, to a monarchy again. Dio was a participant in the imperial system and was aware of how political discourses could change, sometimes with bewildering rapidity. For Dio, the personality of the *princeps* was important – it was easier to deal with a Marcus Aurelius than a Caracalla – but this was not the only thing that mattered. Dio's *Roman History* is as much an attempt to explain a system of government, or rather a series of systems, how these systems worked, and how they broke down.

I

Imperial and Political Narratives

Vox populi, vox mea? *Information, Evaluation and Public Opinion in Dio's Account of the Principate*

Adam M. Kemezis

I Introduction

An ungrateful posterity has loaded Cassius Dio with any number of criticisms, fair and otherwise, but he cannot reasonably be accused of diffidence or ambiguity in expressing his opinions of emperors. In the twenty-four books he devotes to Augustus' successors, Dio misses few opportunities to let us know which of them and their actions he liked or disliked. Where another author might have used subtleties of shading or allowed the material to speak for itself, Dio is typically explicit and unambiguous.

Thus, we are left in no doubt that Marcus Aurelius was virtuous even before he received a good education, that Commodus was not wicked by nature and that Trajan's drunkenness and pederasty did not constitute serious failings.[1] Dio does everything but give his emperors a star rating. Even where (as with Septimius Severus and Macrinus) moderns have trouble figuring out what Dio's overall view of an emperor was, it is not because he has failed to deliver an opinion, but rather because he has delivered multiple seemingly incompatible ones.

This often comes off as a personality quirk: one imagines that Dio's everyday conversation must have been exasperatingly full of ex cathedra pronouncements. Nonetheless, his views appear self-consciously

---

I am most grateful to the editors for the invitation to appear in this volume and for their comments and those of the anonymous reader. Portions of this chapter were read at the Classical Association annual meeting of 2016 and as an invited talk in Jesper Madsen's graduate seminar at the University of Southern Denmark. Many thanks are due to the participants and organizers on both occasions and to my fellow participants in the volume who have kindly sent feedback. All translations are the author's own.

[1] Respectively, 72(71).35.2 (EV), 73(72).1.1 (EV), 68.7.4 (EV). As can be seen from these citations, our impression of Dio is conditioned by transmission, since the *Excerpta Valesiana* explicitly preserve fragments on 'virtues and vices'. That said, his more or less complete text of Books 57–60 certainly does not convey a radically different impression.

representative of his class, and as such scholars have done much to reconstruct the criteria of judgement he uses, which in turn can serve as a proxy for senatorial mentality more generally.[2] This article aims to complement such work by examining not so much the content of the opinions found in Dio's work but rather how, when, why and by whom they are formulated and expressed.

The question 'What was Dio's opinion of [emperor x]' is much more complex than is often acknowledged. In any political system that has identifiable rulers, there will naturally be opinions about those rulers on the part of whatever political public exists. But the processes by which those opinions are formed and expressed are specific to a given political culture and indeed make up a key component of that culture. Critical variables include, as noted, the criteria by which rulers are judged, but many other factors remain. What part of society is authorized to make judgements? On what knowledge are these judgements based, and how does one obtain that knowledge? In what contexts and through what media is it safe or appropriate to deliver them? What does one hope or expect to achieve by doing so? How do they relate to one's larger impression of the course of history or the current state of affairs?

Dio's history is a uniquely rich document of how all these questions played out in the political culture of the high Roman empire, for several reasons. Not only is Dio opinionated, but he is also self-reflectively so and provides much explicit and implicit commentary on how public opinion functioned under the emperors. This is all the more true because, as we will see, Dio heavily identifies with the traditional Roman political classes as a whole and presents his literary activity as an integral part of an overall process of dealing with emperors that is a defining political role for the Roman people in its various segments.

Moreover, while Dio so eagerly embraces the task of evaluating his rulers, he is also explicit about the constraints of doing such work under an authoritarian regime. In Dio's world the emperors, or the powerful men around them, place strict limits on what can be known and said about political events.[3] Dio describes, and through his history contributes to, the workings of an elite discourse that is always at least potentially at odds with the ruler. This is equally true for Tacitus, Suetonius and anyone else writing about emperors, but Dio is unique in the amount of explicit

[2] Important contributions include Millar 1964; Bering-Staschewski 1981; Edmondson 1992: 46–53; Gowing 1997; Pelling 1997a; De Blois 1998; Martini 2010; Schulz 2014; Davenport 2014; Madsen 2016; Coltelloni-Trannoy 2016; Devillers 2016a.

[3] See now Mallan 2016 for Dio's view of free speech and its limits under the emperors.

attention he gives to the issue and in how much he associates his own narrative voice with that of the Roman political community at large. As we will see, his own views are often interwoven with statements of contemporary public opinion. In his final books, Dio combines the role of contemporary observer and posterity-minded historian and presents that role as a critical part of the traditional Roman political culture that is unravelling along with (and thanks to) the Severan dynasty.

This chapter will begin with Dio's methodological statements about information and political discourse under the Principate. These will be read in terms of the concepts of the 'public transcript' and 'hidden transcript' within unequal power relationships. I will then examine Dio's narrative of the Julio-Claudian, Flavian and Antonine dynasties for how he presents his own judgements and those of the contemporary public. Lastly, I will examine what changes occur in the Severan period, when Dio's status changes as he becomes part of the contemporary public, and the nature of the emperor's performance changes as emperors become younger and less conformable to earlier norms.

II Dio's Methodological Agenda

Dio's view of how one talks about emperors needs to be understood in relation to a methodological statement of his that has received much attention but still warrants fuller explication. In his Book 53, after a long description of the political arrangements of 27 BC by which Caesar's heir became Augustus, Dio reflects on the consequences for his own narrative. He initially describes the relatively open informational circumstances of the Republic, before drawing the contrast:

> But from that time on [27 BC], things began to happen secretly and through private correspondence, and if ever anything is made public, it is discounted inasmuch as there is no way to cross-check it. People suppose that everything is said and done according to the wishes of the various rulers and their associates. Therefore, many things are rumoured to occur that never in fact do, many things that actually do take place are not known and, in sum, everything is reported quite differently from the way it happens. And what is more, the size of the Empire and the multitude of things that go on make it difficult to be precise about them. Lots of events occur in Rome, there is a lot going on in the provinces, and just about every day something happens on the enemy frontiers. Nobody can easily find out about any of these things except the people who are directly involved in them, and most people do not know that they are even going on in the first place. *For which reasons I also will narrate events from this point, or as many of them as is necessary, just as they*

were publicly reported, whether they really happened that way or some other way. To these, however, will be added where possible something of my own opinion, wherever the great amount that I have read, heard and seen allows me to bring up some further evidence over and above the general chatter (53.19.3–6, emphasis mine).[4]

Most readings of this passage concentrate on the first two-thirds, in which Dio lays out the problem. Dio's words are typically (and reasonably) taken as a more or less accurate statement of the problems faced by imperial historians in general. Less attention is paid to Dio's solution, which is very much his own. The claim of presenting facts 'just as they were publicly reported, whether they really happened that way or some other way' is truly remarkable for an ancient historian. Many authors express doubts about the knowability of the legendary distant past, and Tacitus among others is known for attributing many of his best anecdotes to rumour.[5] Dio, however, is blandly disclaiming responsibility for the factual truth of more than a thousand pages' worth of narrative of the recent history of his own community. His final qualification about his personal knowledge is a substantial one, but it remains a qualification of a wide-reaching norm.[6]

Dio is thus claiming to pass on in large part what anthropologist James C. Scott has called the 'public transcript', the version of events that it is possible for both rulers and ruled to articulate in each other's presence.[7] Much of the rest of this chapter will examine how Dio follows through on this methodological claim and what effect it has on his narrative. As any

---

[4] ἐκ δὲ δὴ τοῦ χρόνου ἐκείνου τὰ μὲν πλείω κρύφα καὶ δι' ἀπορρήτων γίγνεσθαι ἤρξατο, εἰ δέ πού τινα καὶ δημοσιευθείη, ἀλλὰ ἀνεξέλεγκτά γε ὄντα ἀπιστεῖται· καὶ γὰρ λέγεσθαι καὶ πράττεσθαι πάντα πρός τὰ τῶν ἀεὶ κρατούντων τῶν τε παραδυναστευόντων σφίσι βουλήματα ὑποπτεύεται. καὶ κατὰ τοῦτο πολλὰ μὲν οὐ γιγνόμενα θρυλεῖται, πολλὰ δὲ καὶ πάνυ συμβαίνοντα ἀγνοεῖται, πάντα δὲ ὡς εἰπεῖν ἄλλως πως ἢ ὡς πράττεται διαθροεῖται. καὶ μέντοι καὶ τὸ τῆς ἀρχῆς μέγεθος τό τε τῶν πραγμάτων πλῆθος δυσχερεστάτην τὴν ἀκρίβειαν αὐτῶν παρέχεται. ἕν τε γὰρ τῇ Ῥώμῃ συχνὰ καὶ παρὰ τῷ ὑπηκόῳ αὐτῆς πολλά, πρός τε τὸ πολέμιον ἀεὶ καὶ καθ' ἡμέραν ὡς εἰπεῖν γίγνεταί τι, περὶ ὧν τὸ μὲν σαφὲς οὐδεὶς ῥᾳδίως ἔξω τῶν πραττόντων αὐτὰ γιγνώσκει, πλεῖστοι δ'ὅσοι οὐδ' ἀκούουσι τὴν ἀρχὴν ὅτι γέγονεν. ὅθενπερ καὶ ἐγὼ πάντα τὰ ἑξῆς, ὅσα γε καὶ ἀναγκαῖον ἔσται εἰπεῖν, ὡς που καὶ δεδήμωται φράσω, εἴτ' ὄντως οὕτως εἴτε καὶ ἑτέρως πως ἔχει. προσέσται μέντοι τι αὐτοῖς καὶ τῆς ἐμῆς δοξασίας, ἐς ὅσον ἐνδέχεται, ἐν οἷς ἄλλο τι μᾶλλον ἢ τὸ θρυλούμενον ἠδυνήθην ἐκ πολλῶν ὧν ἀνέγνων ἢ καὶ ἤκουσα ἢ καὶ εἶδον τεκμήρασθαι. This passage is also considered at length by Davenport in the next essay of this volume.

[5] For the tropes of the 'mythical', see Marincola 1997: 117–27. On rumour as a component of Tacitean historiography, see e.g. Gibson 1998.

[6] See also Dio 54.15.2–3, where Dio makes a similar statement specifically about conspiracies against the ruler.

[7] Set forth in Scott 1990. The idea of 'public' and 'hidden transcripts' was employed to much profit by Bartsch 1994 and has recently proven fruitful in explorations of Tacitus; see Schulz 2015 and Spielberg 2019.

casual reader can attest, it does not cause Dio to produce an 'official history' that replicates emperors' own accounts of their own actions.[8] On the contrary, as we will see, critical voices constantly make themselves heard, delivering often hostile interpretations of emperors' actions and character. Caillan Davenport, in the essay following this one, will explore these through the modern sociological study of rumour and how it operates in low-information conditions. In Scott's terms, these stories function as a 'hidden transcript', the account of a power relationship that subordinates share with one another when the master is not listening. In imperial Rome, such accounts find literary expression only after an emperor is dead and either officially disgraced or far enough in the past that the present ruler is not ideologically beholden to his memory.

The 'public vs. hidden' distinction is naturally reminiscent of the ways ancient historians had of recognizing discrepancies between appearance and reality, most notably the Thucydidean contrast between *logos* and *ergon*, which Dio himself often uses (in the form λόγῳ and ἔργῳ). Scott's formulation is particularly well suited to Dio, however, in that his 'hidden transcript', like Dio's 'some further evidence over and above the general chatter', does not claim to be a complete alternative version of the events in the public transcript. The master's (read 'emperor's') control of public discourse in his own lifetime does not allow his subordinates to fully articulate such a narrative of events as they happen, at any rate not in a medium where it can be seen by outside observers or readers in future generations. Rather, as Scott has it, 'the hidden transcript is derivative in the sense that it consists of those offstage speeches, gestures, and practices that confirm, contradict or inflect what appears in the public transcript'.[9]

The idea that historiography under the emperors represents something like a hidden transcript is by no means unique to Dio. The circumstances that applied to him were inherent in the system and did not go otherwise uncommented on. The most prominent such comments are undoubtedly those of Tacitus in the prefaces to his *Histories* and *Annals*. These passages are indeed often cited alongside Dio's methodological comments. It is worth highlighting some key differences between the two authors' approaches.

Tacitus' prefaces contain straightforward critiques of imperial-era historiography relative to its republican ancestor. The difference is

---

[8] As emphasized by Rich (1990: 153), speaking of 'the generally accepted account ... which was not necessarily the authorities' version'.

[9] Scott 1990: 4–5.

fundamentally ethical: republican histories were written 'with a brilliance equal to their freedom' (*pari eloquentia ac libertate*) (Tac. *Hist.* 1.1.1), whereas those of the monarchic period are infected by bias, either flattery of living emperors or spiteful attacks on dead ones. In effect, Tacitus considers the hidden transcript that emerges after an emperor's death to be no less mendacious than the public transcript produced in his lifetime.[10] He means us to connect this literary decline with an ethical malaise that, as he will show, affects the Roman elite as a whole. And, crucially, it is a phenomenon from which Tacitus himself claims to be exempt, either due to his moral rectitude (*Hist.* 1.1.3) or because the events are far enough in the past (*Ann.* 1.1).

For Dio, by contrast, the problem is practical and informational. With the best will in the world, one simply cannot find things out. The problems of bias that Tacitus mentions are remarkably absent. Still, the two positions are not quite as far apart as this might suggest. Tacitus (*Hist.* 1.1.1) does mention informational problems under the monarchy, at least initially, though they are seemingly superseded by the larger ethical issues. Equally, when Dio speaks of the many voices of the Republic being reduced to one, presumably that is because the people who do know the truth first-hand fail to disclose it for self-interested reasons not dissimilar to the biases found in Tacitus. But the rhetorical consequences for Dio's subsequent narrative are completely different from those in Tacitus' case, not least because Dio emphatically does not present himself as an exception. On the contrary, Dio is in the first instance explaining his own work rather than setting inferior predecessors up as a foil. Where Tacitus diagnoses a problem and immediately claims to have solved it, Dio is faced with a fundamental condition that can be mitigated but never removed. To understand how this plays out further, we can turn to Dio's actual narrative.

III   Scepticism and Deduction

The first place to examine how Dio's limited-information historiography works is the many instances in which he effectively presents the public and hidden transcripts side by side. Throughout his Principate narrative, there are any number of places where Dio describes an emperor's action,

[10] Cf. Scott 1990: 5: 'Power relations are not, alas, so straightforward that we can call what is said in power-laden contexts false and what is said offstage true. Nor can we simplistically describe the former as a realm of necessity and the latter as a realm of freedom.'

followed by first the reason the emperor gave for it and then the genuine reason, both explicitly labelled as such.[11] These notices, and much analogous material, give an impression of Dio as a sceptical figure who takes it for granted that all emperors are economical with the truth, and many are chronic liars. The latter will tend to be 'bad' emperors in Dio's overall judgement, but even their 'good' counterparts come off only as less systematically mendacious rather than actually honest.

Such passages display a stereotyped language and structure. Caligula executed many people after Macro's death ostensibly (πρόφασιν μὲν) because they had taken part in the deaths of his father and siblings but in truth (τὸ δ' ἀληθὲς) because he wanted their money (59.10.7). Later on, the same emperor made his expedition to Gaul on the pretext (πρόφασιν μὲν) of war preparations among the Germanic peoples, but really (ἔργῳ) the motive once again was the wealth of Gaul and Spain (59.21.2). Claudius expelled one Umbonius Silo from the senate because the latter, as governor of Baetica, had sent insufficient grain to the troops in Mauretania (60.24.7). 'That was the accusation, though certainly not the real reason' (τοῦτο γὰρ κατηγορήθη, ἐπεὶ τό γε ἀληθὲς οὐχ οὕτως εἶχεν), which was that Silo had fallen afoul of Claudius' freedmen. Perhaps most famously, Caracalla is said to have made his universal grant of citizenship nominally (λόγῳ) as an honour but in reality (ἔργῳ) to increase tax liabilities (78-[77].9.3 [EV]).[12] To consider 'good' emperors, Trajan invaded Armenia supposedly (πρόφασιν μὲν) because the king was aligning himself with Parthia, but in truth (τῇ δ' ἀληθείᾳ) out of a desire for glory (68.17.1 [Xiph.]). In that case, Dio does suggest a critique of Trajan's actions, but praiseworthy actions can be described in the same way. When Nerva is faced with a conspiracy, he publicly presents the suspects with swords, ostensibly (λόγῳ) so that the latter can test their sharpness but in fact (ἔργῳ) to demonstrate his own indifference to his personal safety (68.3.2 [Xiph.]).

These examples have similarities beyond the word level, however. From an informational point of view, they work much the same way. None of the 'genuine reasons' involved requires the kind of privileged inside information or documents that one might expect from Suetonius or the level of imaginative psychological reconstruction that Tacitus often uses.[13] Rather

---

[11] For more examples, see Edmondson 1992: 34–5, 47–8, also Schulz 2019: 207–10 for Nero and Domitian.

[12] See further the detailed examination of this passage by Myles Lavan in Chapter 10.

[13] Schulz (2019: 207–8) discusses Dio's focalization through Nero after Agrippina's murder. Dio does include details that could not have been publicly known, but they are in considerably less depth than

they seem like deductive conclusions based on what Dio takes to be a core truth about the emperor or reign in question. Caligula always needs money for his excesses, and that is a default explanation for events in his reign. Claudius is manipulated by freedmen and wives, and any examples of misrule from his time can be laid at their door. Trajan's lust for glory is an ambivalent example of the same phenomenon, and Nerva's placing of public above personal interests is a wholly positive one.[14] In all these cases, the same reasoning is used to explain multiple actions, which may or may not have alternative public pretexts. Once the core characteristics of a reign have been established, they can be used as interpretive tools in constructing a hidden transcript even when no additional information is available about the specific incident in question.

IV Historians and Contemporaries

The question then remains of who it is that does the establishing and the constructing. Are the conclusions in question Dio's own, or is he reporting the impressions of contemporaries? It is not always clear. The latter is certainly possible, since the deductions in question do not require hindsight and are typically based on publicly visible phenomena. Caligula's greed must have been obvious to everyone. Any politically astute person in Claudius' time would presumably have figured out how much the freedmen's opinions mattered, though it is less certain whether Claudius himself was aware. Nerva's action is a gesture (ἐπιδεικνύμενος) that can work only if his genuine motives are implicitly clear to the conspirators and presumably also the public at large. Nonetheless, the language Dio uses, with its overtones of Thucydidean discernment, suggests that the opinions are, if not his own, then at any rate ones he strongly endorses based on a rigorous use of his critical faculties.

This implies that when Dio uses these faculties to evaluate long-dead rulers, his action is analogous to, and may replicate, how those rulers were evaluated by their contemporaries. Many of Dio's historiographical predecessors had deliberately differentiated their voices from contemporary observers, most obviously Tacitus in the prefaces quoted earlier. Even Thucydides, the original eyewitness historian, had distanced himself from contemporary political discourse when he claimed to be writing for distant posterity rather than for

the parallel Tacitean narrative and can be read as contemporary inferences rather than Dio's own dramatization.

[14] Schulz 2014 notes the heavy causal significance that Dio lends to Nero's theatrical obsession and Domitian's military pretenses.

the audiences of his own time (1.22.4). Rationales are many: contemporaries are too biased or self-interested to care about the truth, or too preoccupied with ephemeral trivia to engage in serious analysis.[15]

Dio makes remarkably little use of these tropes. On the contrary, he seems comfortable identifying his own voice with that of contemporary public opinion. This blurring of roles extends well beyond the instances of 'appearance-reality' language that I have cited so far. A notable proportion of the judgements on emperors expressed in Dio are in fact framed as contemporary opinion. Dio is frequently willing to say on his own authority that an emperor was good or bad, but just as often he will instead say that the emperor was praised or criticized.

Language about contemporaries' praise or blame is heavily interspersed in all the sections of Dio's work that contain explicit ethical evaluation of an emperor. In some cases, the opinion is expressed in a specific setting, and that expression itself becomes a historical event, as when crowds cheer Caligula's prostituting of senatorial women but protest when he fails to give adequate public notice of new tax laws, to which latter he responds with a massacre (59.10–11 [EV; John Ant.]). More often, however, Dio simply mentions that an action was praised or censured without offering any specific circumstances. In these cases, the praise or censure seems to be mentioned for its own sake, and to be offered for readers' consideration on the same discursive level with the comments Dio makes in his own voice. These remarks are as frequent as Dio's *propria persona* comments and are often used interchangeably with the latter. Other historians certainly do cite contemporary rumours and reactions, but with Dio such statements do a remarkable amount of the interpretive work by which his system of good and bad emperors is established.

Thus in many instances, Dio incorporates contemporary opinions as formal structuring devices. They can serve as a sort of subject heading allowing Dio to make a transition from a section on good deeds to one on bad, a function for which Dio also uses statements in his own voice. A catalogue of Caligula's actions in AD 38 begins by stating 'Gaius did the following things that were good and worthy of praise' (Γάιος δὲ καλὰ μὲν ἐπαίνου τε ἄξια τάδε ἔπραξε) (59.9.4). This generic praiseworthiness soon becomes more concrete, however, when we are told that a few of these acts 'pleased everyone' (πᾶσιν ἤρεσεν) (59.9.6), whereas his restoration of popular elections and some largesses 'gratified the mob but grieved the intelligent' (τῷ μὲν φαύλῳ ἐχαρίσατο, τοὺς δ' ἔμφρονας ἐλύπησε) (59.9.7). There then follows a rather

---

[15] On this tradition within the discourse of historiographical bias, see Luce 1989; Marincola 1997: 158–75.

longer list of negative actions characterized as 'things that earned censure from all alike' (ἐπαίτια δὲ δὴ πρὸς πάντων ὁμοίως) (59.10.1). Similar examples are Dio's remark that the good actions Claudius did himself 'were praised by everyone' (ὑφ' ἁπάντων ἐπηνεῖτο) (60.8.4), as opposed to the actions that can be assigned to his wives and freedmen.[16]

In most of these instances, Dio leaves us to suppose that he agrees with the contemporary verdict and assumes we will do so too. Typically, the actions in question are such that, within the implied value system of Dio's narrative, their merit or depravity is too evident to require explicit comment. There are, however, a surprising number of episodes in which the emperor is laughed at. Often the laughter comes from an ironic discrepancy of some sort: Galba coming back from Spain carries a huge sword that looks ridiculous on his aged frame (63[64].3.4 [Xiph.]); Hadrian decrees honours for Antinous that are absurd in themselves, but the more so given how slow he had been to do the same for his sister Paulina (69.11.4 [EV]). After the Scribonianus conspiracy and Arria's death have shocked public opinion, Claudius buffoonishly throws out inappropriate Greek quotations to soldiers and senators alike (60.16.7–8).[17] In all these cases, Dio gives readers the necessary information to perceive the irony or absurdity and thus to replicate the laughter of contemporaries. This practice of deliberately presenting inconsistencies is a principal technique of Dio's in his more unambiguously negative emperor portrayals. Nero's stage performances and Domitian's sham military posturing generate dissonances that are meant to evoke actions of Commodus and Caracalla that his readers witnessed and that he will narrate from personal experience.[18]

V Dio's Political Public

Dio's history of the emperors is framed as a history of how emperors were experienced by his class.[19] Their judgements and opinions are not only

---

[16] See also the transition from Tiberius' praiseworthy legislation to his sexual depravity (58.22.1) and Zonaras' list of Vitellius' few good points (64[65].6). The extended analysis of the latter in Davenport 2014 draws many conclusions relevant to Dio's imperial narrative as a whole. For the structural workings of these paired lists, see Coltelloni-Trannoy 2016b: 351.

[17] This last story is ironically juxtaposed with the various stories in 60.17 about Claudius' depriving a Lycian notable for citizenship for not knowing Latin, even as Messalina and the freedmen are selling citizenship grants cheaply and indiscriminately. Many passages of this kind are antitheses and include a behaviour for which the emperor was praised.

[18] See the important analysis of Schulz 2014.

[19] Potter (2011: 331) speaks of Dio's contemporary books as 'a memoir of the governing class', and in many ways the same could be said of the Principate narrative as a whole. See also Scott 2018a and Mallan (Chapter 12) in this volume.

rhetorical propositions for readers to endorse; they are also historical content in themselves. Watching emperors, reacting to them, trying to understand and judge them, is the defining political activity of the political world to which Dio and his implied readers belong, and Dio's history is an integral continuation of that activity.

Having examined how public opinion is expressed in (and by) Dio, it remains to look at the function of that expression. Discourse around an emperor is never simply idle chatter, innocent of political meaning. One important function of this discourse was simply to exist as such. Dio is defining himself and his readers as members of a political community whose role, as senators, *equites* or citizens, included knowing, caring and talking about the affairs of the commonwealth. In practice, for Dio, 'the affairs of the commonwealth' consist mostly of the public actions of the emperor, thus his political class is far more of an audience than an actor. They remain, however, a highly interactive audience whose responses are a crucial part of the performance. The correct (for Dio) performances of this role can be seen in such tableaux as the funerals of Augustus (56.31–4) and Pertinax (75[74].4–5 [Xiph.]). Negative versions, in which an emperor forces the public into an inappropriate audience role, include Nero's staged burlesque where nobles perform and are mocked by inhabitants of the provinces their ancestors conquered (62[61].17 [Xiph.]), Domitian's macabre banquet in black (67.9 [Xiph.]) and above all Commodus' arena performances. The men who overthrow that emperor, as with Caligula and Nero before him, are motivated in no small part by disgust at the performances and humiliation at having to take part in them.[20]

As one might expect, Dio's version of the political public is not socially homogenous or egalitarian. It does include non-elites, above all the city populace of Rome, whose role is admirably explored by Monica Hellström in Chapter 9 of this volume.[21] Dio can be snobbishly dismissive but is well attuned to their uses as a vector for hidden transcripts, not least because the relative freedom of the anonymous crowd contrasts with the servility of elites who are subject to the emperor's gaze. In the longer scale of the hidden transcript as revealed through historiography, however, social privilege remains intact even alongside the shared subordination to the emperor, and above all the role of the senate as favoured custodian of the Roman past. Dio's history aims to assert and maintain his *ordo's* control

---

[20] See 73(72).22.1 (Xiph.) on Commodus, 59.29.6–7 (Xiph.) on Caligula and 63(63).22.4–6 (Xiph.) on Nero.

[21] On the city plebs in Dio, see also De Blois 1997.

over a partially clandestine but socially sanctioned form of discourse, in part by recording how the senate's function of commenting on its rulers has from the start been inseparable from the Roman monarchical state.

There is, to be sure, more to Dio's political world than unilateral assertion of status. The forming and expressing of opinions are part of a negotiation between public and emperor that has high practical stakes on both sides. People naturally want to obtain the good things an emperor can bestow and avoid the harm he can inflict, and a necessary part of that is understanding his actions and forming a working model of his character. This must often be done in spite of the emperor's best efforts to keep his subjects off balance. Thus, Dio's opening sketch of Tiberius focusses above all on the difficulties that his unpredictable manner presented to those around him. His most common method was to pretend to emotions that were the opposite of those he really felt.[22] If he had simply been consistent in this, however, 'one could easily have been secure once one had gained experience of him' (εὐφύλακτος ἂν τοῖς ἐς πεῖραν αὐτοῦ ἐλθοῦσιν ἦν) (57.1.3) because one could deduce his genuine thoughts based on his pretence. To prevent this, Tiberius punished those who treated him in a contrary fashion. Dio's exposition on this point has been criticized for lacking the psychological acuity of Tacitus, but this is to illustrate the limits of Dio's curiosity.[23]

The emperor's character interests him less for its own sake than as the material that courtiers have to work with. Thus, good emperors, such as Trajan, are above all those with knowable characters, who allow those around them to be sure where they stand.[24] The results are not always edifying: Marcus' embrace of philosophy causes courtiers to affect similar inclinations (72[71].35.2 [EV]). Allowing for a certain cynicism on Dio's part, the atmosphere under the Antonines, in which subjects can form accurate and positive estimates of their rulers, still leads in his view to an era of idealized good government, as the most competent members of the elite take prominent roles in administration.[25]

Less tangibly but no less significantly, the public's function of evaluating rulers gives them control over an important resource in the form of the honours they can bestow on living and above all dead rulers. Dio

---

[22] See further Christopher Mallan's analysis of Tiberius in Chapter 6.
[23] For the critique, see Syme 1958: 273. Pelling (1997a: 126) incorporates it into an insightful reading of Dio's quasi-biographical technique.
[24] Thus at 68.6.2 (EV), Trajan's third chief virtue, along with justice (δικαιότης) and courage (ἀνδρεία) is 'simplicity of character' (ἁπλότης τῶν ἠθῶν).
[25] For examples, see Kemezis 2012.

comments much on how honours figure into the public transcript, through their being formally declared, and the hidden transcript, through his own posthumous characterization of them and reportage of people's 'true feelings' at the time.[26] Even the emperors themselves join in by being hypersensitive to the economy of honours. Not one but two emperors, Caligula (59.16) and Septimius Severus (76.75.8 [Xiph.]), have direct-speech orations in which they criticize the hypocrisy of the senate's honorific practices relative to their unpopular but not formally disgraced immediate predecessors (Tiberius and Commodus, respectively).[27] Caligula, in particular, stresses that the senate bestows honours on emperors regardless of how they are treated, and that any emperor who tries by his behaviour to actually earn their sincere praise will be needlessly jeopardizing his safety. Both speeches are ostensibly given in the senate, but their blunt take on the relationship of ruler to ruled is precisely the kind of speech that the senate's formal setting is designed to exclude from the public transcript. The emperors are straying far off script, and we are probably not meant to suppose that such speeches were really delivered. Rather Dio is imagining the version of the hidden transcript generated by tyrannical emperors who chafe at the forms of public opinion that Dio has been chronicling in the rest of his narrative.[28]

VI The Severan Present

The death of Marcus Aurelius in 180 brings forth what is probably the most quoted of all Dio's opinions (72[71].36.4 [EV]). In his view the transition from Marcus to his son Commodus represented 'a decline from a realm of gold to one of iron and rust, both for the affairs of the Romans at the time and for my history' (ἀπὸ χρυσῆς τε βασιλείας ἐς σιδηρᾶν καὶ κατιωμένην τῶν τε πραγμάτων τοῖς τότε Ῥωμαίοις καὶ ἡμῖν νῦν καταπεσούσης τῆς ἱστορίας). The Antonine nostalgia is evident, but questions remain. The first concerns the span of events to which the statement refers. Are we talking here simply about the coming of an individual bad emperor, not different in kind from Caligula or Nero, or does the 'iron and rust' category extend to all subsequent events, making the whole Severan era categorically bad in unprecedented ways that go beyond the vices of any single emperor?

---

[26] See e.g. 58.2 (posthumous honors for Livia); 59.25 (after Caligula's 'British expedition'); 67.4 (EV) (after Domitian's German war); 73(72).15 (Xiph.) (contrast between Marcus and Commodus).

[27] For Caligula's speech, see the commentaries of Faur 1978 and Edmondson 1992: 161–2.

[28] See Scott 1990: 10–13 for hidden transcripts generated by masters when they are no longer required to perform their role before subordinates.

How is the answer affected by the coincidence that the decline occurs just as Dio becomes a contemporary witness of events?

The former, larger, question may best be answered by way of the latter. Thus far I have put forward a static reading of Dio's imperial narrative. His methods and assumptions about the imperial role and how it is described and commented on have not changed from Augustus to Marcus, however different the actors in that role may have been.[29] I will further argue that the decades after Marcus' death, for which Dio is a contemporary narrator, mark for Dio a critical negative shift in the relationship of the monarchy to the political public. This shift is in itself a significant part of the decline that Dio diagnoses, and constitutes a threat to the privileged role that he had constructed for his peers in the earlier narrative.

To complement the passage quoted above on Marcus' death, Dio's surviving text includes a formal transition to his role as contemporary narrator. Late in Commodus' reign, after describing some of that emperor's sillier escapades in the arena, Dio adds:

> Let no-one suppose that in adding such things to my history I degrade its dignity. Ordinarily I should not have mentioned them, but since they originated with the emperor, and I saw, heard or uttered all of them in person, I have resolved to hold back none of them. Instead I will pass them to the memory of future generations just as with the greatest and most important events. And likewise for all the events of my time I will take special care and narrate in detail more than previously, because I was there when they happened and I know of no-one else who has both the ability to write a worthwhile history and an accurate knowledge of events equal to my own (73[72].18.3–4 [Xiph.]).[30]

The watershed here is less marked than its Augustan-era counterpart in Book 53. The informational conditions of the regime have not changed objectively; it is only the narrator's relationship to the events that is different. Dio is stepping into the position previously held by the past elites whose opinions he has been reporting. Earlier eras (we are to infer)

[29] On Dio's Principate narrative as a distinct 'narrative mode', see Kemezis 2014: 139–45. Further considerations about form and structure can be found in Coltelloni-Trannoy 2016a and Devillers 2016b.

[30] καὶ μή μέ τις κηλιδοῦν τὸν τῆς ἱστορίας ὄγκον, ὅτι καὶ τὰ τοιαῦτα συγγράφω, νομίσῃ. ἄλλως μὲν γὰρ οὐκ ἂν εἶπον αὐτά· ἐπειδὴ δὲ πρός τε τοῦ αὐτοκράτορος ἐγένετο καὶ παρὼν αὐτὸς ἐγὼ καὶ εἶδον ἕκαστα καὶ ἤκουσα καὶ ἐλάλησα, δίκαιον ἡγησάμην μηδὲν αὐτῶν ἀποκρύψασθαι, ἀλλὰ καὶ αὐτά, ὥσπερ τι ἄλλο τῶν μεγίστων καὶ ἀναγκαιοτάτων, τῇ μνήμῃ τῶν ἐσέπειτα ἐσομένων παραδοῦναι. καὶ μέντοι καὶ τἆλλα πάντα τὰ ἐπ' ἐμοῦ πραχθέντα καὶ λεπτουργήσω καὶ λεπτολογήσω μᾶλλον ἢ τὰ πρότερα, ὅτι τε συνεγενόμην αὐτοῖς, καὶ ὅτι μηδένα ἄλλον οἶδα τῶν τι δυναμένων ἐς συγγραφὴν ἀξίαν λόγου καταθέσθαι διηκριβωκότα αὐτὰ ὁμοίως ἐμοί.

produced contemporary histories with a scope analogous to the higher level of detail that Dio will now be employing. Dio is obliged to include within that scope some highly unedifying material about Commodus, but the same was true under previous bad emperors. Dio's final claim about his own worth as a historian is more about his social position and education than his personal experience. It suggests that political commentary remains a status prerogative of his sort of people. Taken at face value, the quoted passage suggests considerable continuity.

The subsequent narrative, however, calls into question key elements of that continuity. In particular, there are two crucial assumptions in Dio's statement that become less valid as his Severan narrative progresses. The first is seen in his justification that the actions 'originated with the emperor'. For Dio, an emperor should be an inherently significant person whose actions, for good or bad, are the stuff of history. The second assumption is found in the somewhat vague phrase συνεγενόμην αὐτοῖς, 'I was there when they happened'. Back in Book 53, Dio had acknowledged that a great deal of the action of politics takes place away from public view, but even so, there remained a generally known version of events that bore some relationship to reality, albeit a distant or even inverse one. The public transcript was not the truth, but neither was it a meaningless fabrication: contemporaries could use it to form judgements about their rulers, and Dio could make it the basis of a critical narrative. Being physically and socially present at the imperial centre in Rome gave one enough information to play one's role as a member of the political community.

These assumptions seem rather basic, but if one considers the narrative present of Dio's history, in the years after 229, it is not clear that either of them holds good any longer. The current emperor, Alexander Severus, is no longer the child who was deposited on his cousin's throne in 222, but neither, in Dio's version, is he a functioning adult emperor. Where one might expect pro forma encomia of the living emperor, Dio's surviving text contains no meaningful comment on Alexander's character or actions.[31] The 'account' of his reign (80[80].1–5 [Xiph., EV]) consists of dire comments on mayhem in the streets of Rome, the rise of Ardashir in the east

---

[31] Dio (80[80].1.2 [Xiph.]) does signal the changed nature of his narrative of Alexander, attributing it to his having been away from Rome. However, this accounts only for the brevity of the account, not for its lack of emphasis on the emperor. Dio's accounts of Elagabalus and Alexander are both characterized by affirmative compositional choices that go beyond any response to actual informational problems. Mallan (2016: 274) sees a veiled critique of Alexander through the whole later Severan narrative going back to Caracalla. For further reflections on Dio's narrative of Severus Alexander, see Chapter 12 by Christopher Mallan.

and military indiscipline everywhere. The emperor himself appears passive
and ineffectual. Only two actions are attributed to him, and both are futile.
The first is the appointment of Ulpian as praetorian prefect (80[80].1
[Xiph.]), whom Alexander is then powerless to save when the guard revolts
against him (80[80].2.2 [Xiph.]). The second replicates this pattern with Dio
himself, as Alexander is unable to support the historian as consul in the face
of praetorian discontent (80[80].5 [Xiph.]), leading to Dio's humiliation and
enforced retirement. The token gesture of support that Alexander later gives
Dio only underscores the unreality of the former's claim to rule.[32]

This is a novelty for Dio: there have previously been villainous or weak
emperors, but Alexander is simply a nonentity whose actions are without
historical significance. Even when earlier emperors did not rule directly, they
delegated power to identifiable figures, be they Nero's tutors, Commodus'
favourites or powerful prefects under Tiberius and Septimius Severus. No such
locus of power is seen under Alexander. He is clearly a puppet, but it is not clear
that anyone is holding the strings after Ulpian's death. It is possible based on
a fragment of Zonaras that Dio's original text gave more play to Julia Mamaea,
as Herodian does, but when Xiphilinus mentions her in the Ulpian narrative,
she appears just as powerless as her son.[33] And if there is no perceptible locus of
power, it follows that one cannot speak of political events coherently as before.
The practices of observing and evaluating emperors, by which the elite had
previously generated a hidden transcript, no longer have a focus. In reality,
power-political manoeuvrings must continue, involving lower-status interest
groups such as the praetorians and palace staff as well as presumably members
of the established political classes. But in Dio's version those classes can no
longer fill their traditional role as a political public. His quasi-exile to Bithynia
and silence about subsequent events are a metonymy for the end of public
discourse as he knew it.

This distressing condition is not simply a consequence of Alexander's
having come to the throne as a child. If anything, for Dio the reverse is true,
and the adolescent cipher-emperor is the natural result of processes seen

---

[32] For the botched second consulship and virtual exile to Nicaea, see Kemezis 2014: 289–92.

[33] The Zonaras fragment (12.15) describes how Alexander on taking the throne places his mother Mamaea in
a position of power, whereupon she associates the 'best men of the senate' (κὰκ τῆς γερουσίας τοὺς
ἀμείνονας) with the new regime as 'advisors' (συμβούλους). It is printed by Boissevain after his text of
Dio (3.477), and the editor considers it likely drawn from Dio based on some characteristic vocabulary. If
this event was described in Dio, it would most naturally have come in the same context as the
appointment of Ulpian preserved by Xiphilinus. At 80(80).2.2 (Xiph.) Ulpian is said to flee from his
assassins to both Alexander and Mamaea, only to be killed anyway. In the sequel the main conspirator
Epagathus is put out of the way, but Xiphilinus at any rate describes the incident with vague passives that
leave no clue as to who actually does step into the vacuum left by Ulpian.

under previous Severans. Elagabalus' reign had in its way been just as murky as Alexander's. Dio does, to be sure, describe the older cousin's character and actions in detail, but the detail is rather different from the model of earlier emperors. Instead of publicly visible actions filtered through contemporary public opinion, Dio describes outrageous actions within the palace in a satirical mode that is meant to be read as empty propaganda.[34] Dio conveys the same sense as with Alexander, that one cannot tell by whom, or even where, things are really being run. Of the two political figures from Elagabalus' reign that Dio describes in any detail, the first, Gannys, never even reaches Rome before he is murdered by Elagabalus in a highly stereotyped moment of tyrannical rage (80[79].6). The second, Comazon, is explicitly labelled as insignificant, being compared to a theatrical mask that is left on stage as a placeholder between scenes (80[79].21.2 [EV]). The emperor's grandmother Maesa is not accorded by Dio the power-behind-the-throne role that Herodian gives her. The account as a whole is not meant to be read as a coherent or accurate explanation of Elagabalus' short reign, but as the impressions of an excluded observer who has lost both his means of information and his authoritative voice.

Elements of this same exclusion can be seen with Macrinus, whose reign takes place in Syria and is known about in Rome mainly through the somewhat delusional letters he writes to the senate. Caracalla is shown systematically neglecting his public functions and ignoring the traditional governing classes in favour of the army. Septimius Severus, for all his failings, remains for Dio the last emperor who actually carried out the role as Dio understood it. The 'obituary notice' in which Dio describes Severus' daily routine (77[76].17 [Xiph.]) is an acknowledgement that the emperor was at all events a recognizable elite Roman male who could be judged by the standards of his peers, and who held power in Rome or delegated it to a prefect in much the same way as Tiberius had to Sejanus.

VII Conclusion

This mention of Sejanus allows us to conclude by once again putting Dio alongside Tacitus. The two have many evident parallels as the main surviving examples of senatorial historiography under the empire. However, they represent quite different stages in the evolving relationship

---

[34] The rest of this paragraph summarizes arguments made more fully in Kemezis 2016b. See also Osgood 2016 for the satirical aspect.

of the senatorial aristocracy to the monarchical regime.[35] Tacitus writes
from a present under Trajan and Hadrian that he himself characterizes in
explicitly positive terms, about past events that are for the most part
negative. For him the troubles of the past cast a shadow forward to darken,
or at least complicate, the presumed felicity of the present. He portrays the
senate as a ruling class with aspirations to collective and individual freedom
of action. The emperors' efforts to establish their power clash with and may
indeed negate these aspirations. If there is a single 'Tacitean question', it is
that of how much he has made his peace with the senate's place under one-
man rule.

   For Dio, writing a hundred years later, the perspective is quite different.
The present is unambiguously negative and on a downward trajectory.[36]
The past, on the other hand, has more ups and downs than Tacitus',
including largely positive moments under the Antonines.[37] And crucially,
the pre-Severan past as a whole maintains consistent norms from which the
present represents an unprecedented deviation. Without doubt, Dio consistently makes the emperor his central structuring device, more exclusively
than Tacitus. Dio's senate is much less of an independent actor in power
politics.[38] We should be cautious, however, in drawing the inference that
Dio's history is fundamentally 'biographical' in the sense of being preoccupied with the character or psychology of single individuals.[39] As
Christopher Pelling has cogently demonstrated, Dio is less interested in
rulers as interestingly different individuals than as varying interpretations
of the same basic role, who demonstrate generalizable truths about how
imperial history works.[40]

   These generalizable truths are above all about the ruler's relationship
with the elite. The emperor may be the star, but he is not in a one-man
show, and Dio views him through the eyes of the supporting cast and the
audience and rates him above all on how he makes the whole performance
come off. Rather than a ruling class with power, Dio's senate is a status elite

---

[35] For an illuminating recent comparison, see Devillers 2016a.
[36] Coltelloni-Trannoy 2016b sees a more positive outlook, with Alexander Severus' rule being held up
   as a possible hopeful development.
[37] See Caillan Davenport's analysis of the Antonine age in Chapter 8.
[38] Devillers 2016a makes several detailed comparisons of parallel passages in Dio and Tacitus,
   demonstrating the greater structural centrality of the emperor for the former author. Edmondson
   (1992: 23) considers that Dio anachronistically underrates the influence of the Julio-Claudian senate,
   based on the power relationships prevailing in his own time.
[39] The idea of Dio as 'biographical history' goes back to Questa 1957, see also De Blois 1998. Important
   modifications can be found in Pelling 1997a, while the observations of Coudry 2016b on Dio's
   treatments of Pompey and Julius Caesar apply in many ways to the emperors as well.
[40] Pelling 1997a: 135–44.

with prerogatives. These prerogatives were defined above all in relation to the emperor: being his privileged courtiers and administrators while he lived and his official judges after his death. It is this function that Dio emphasizes in the past precisely in order to point out its decline in the present.

The senate that Dio portrays under the earlier dynasties has 'solved' the Tacitean problem of adapting to monarchy. Unlike with Tacitus, there is no inherent tension between the senate's role and the emperor's power. On the contrary, the senate's role requires that there be a responsible emperor wielding actual power. Ideally, he is a good emperor who can associate the Fathers with him in enlightened rule. But even under Caligula and Nero, the senate had a defined and privileged part to play as the emperor's chief critics, clandestinely while he lived and openly thereafter. The problem of Dio's present is not that power has moved upwards, but rather that it has become diffused downwards, to the various other interest groups within the elite that are the moving forces behind the regimes of Macrinus, Elagabalus and Alexander, leaving no object for the senate's evaluating gaze. Dio portrays a monarchy that is vanishing and taking with it the senate as he knows it.

Like any prophet of doom, Dio is refuted by a world that fails to end. Child emperors were a temporary trend. The elite in the decades after Dio, including possibly his own descendants, would retain wealth and influence, and find high places in the new order.[41] And later Roman history has no shortage of confident historians sitting in judgement of their rulers, from Aurelius Victor to Ammianus, Eunapius and even the Historia Augusta. Still, Dio's character and voice remain distinctive because, paradoxically, they are not wholly his own. Idiosyncratic as Dio seems to be, he pointedly speaks for a group that is defined not in literary, intellectual or even social-class terms, but rather by its political role. That role is inseparable from the story he tells and the way he tells it, including that it ends in his own person. The class to which he belonged would survive the third century, but the political culture he chronicled and exemplified would not.

---

[41] For a possible consular descendant of Dio, see *PIR*² C 491. On the survival of the senatorial class after the Severan period, see Mennen 2011.

CHAPTER 2

News, Rumour, and the Political Culture of the Roman Imperial Monarchy in the Roman History

Caillan Davenport

I Introduction: The Statues of Plautianus

In his narrative of the reign of Septimius Severus, Cassius Dio includes a memorable anecdote concerning the rivalry between the emperor and his powerful praetorian prefect, C. Fulvius Plautianus:

> On one occasion, when a great many images of Plautianus had been made (this incident is well worth relating), Severus was displeased at their number and caused some of them to be melted down, and in consequence a rumour (θροῦς) spread to the cities that the prefect had been overthrown and had perished. So, some of them demolished his images, an act for which they were later punished. Among these was the governor of Sardinia, Raecius Constans, a very well-regarded man. (76(75).16.2 [Xiph.])[1]

Dio's description of the events which led to the downfall of Raecius Constans is practically a textbook account of how rumours develop,

This paper was originally presented at the 'Cassius Dio and the Principate' seminar in Nyborg, Denmark, in February 2018. I would like to thank very warmly Jesper Majbom Madsen and Carsten Hjort Lange for their invitation to speak at this event and for their generous hospitality in Denmark. My research has benefitted from the comments of the participants in the Nyborg seminar and from the feedback of members of the SPQR Roman History Discussion Forum at Macquarie University. I am grateful to Adam Kemezis, Christopher Mallan, Meaghan McEvoy, and Christopher Pelling for their comments on this written version. My research has been generously supported by an Australian Research Council Discovery Early Career Researcher Award (DE150101110) and by an Experienced Researcher Fellowship from the Alexander von Humboldt Foundation, held at the Goethe-Universität in Frankfurt am Main.

[1] Εἰκόνων δέ ποτε πολλῶν τῷ Πλαυτιανῷ γενομένων (ἄξιον γὰρ ἀφηγήσασθαι τὸ πραχθέν) δυσχεράνας πρὸς τὸ πλῆθος ὁ Σεουῆρός τινας αὐτῶν συνεχώνευσε, καὶ ἐς τὰς πόλεις ἐκ τούτου θροῦς διῆλθεν ὡς καὶ καθῄρηται καὶ διέφθαρται, καί τινες συνέτριψαν εἰκόνας αὐτοῦ, ἐφ' ᾧ ὕστερον ἐκολάσθησαν· ἐν οἷς ἦν καὶ ὁ τῆς Σαρδοῦς ἄρχων Ῥάκιος Κώνστας, ἀνὴρ ἐλλογιμώτατος. The translations in this chapter are from the Loeb Classical Library edition by E. Cary, with occasional modifications.

circulate, and take hold within communities.[2] Sociologists and anthropologists define rumour as unofficial and unverified information.[3] It is primarily a sense-making phenomenon: rumours emerge as attempts to explain ambiguous situations about which there is a shortage of reliable news from official sources.[4] Rumours are not inherently wild and implausible to those who spread them; indeed, they are rooted in social and cultural norms.[5] Interest in, and the circulation of, rumour is often motivated by risk management, as people attempt to understand an ambiguous situation and consider how they might best respond to it.[6]

In the anecdote about Plautianus related by Dio, the fact that people saw his statues being melted down (presumably in Rome) generated a rumour that the powerful prefect had fallen from grace.[7] Dio's narrative suggests that there was no attempt by the Roman state to communicate an official reason for the statues' removal (for example, by the publication and circulation of a senatorial decree or an imperial letter), presumably because the act was hurriedly carried out at Severus' whim. This meant that Romans had to make sense of what they were seeing for themselves.[8] Plautianus' disgrace and downfall emerged as a plausible explanation, since Romans had long been accustomed to seeing the statues of condemned individuals destroyed as the result of memory sanctions authorised by the state (a process which we commonly refer to as *damnatio memoriae*, although this is not an ancient term).[9] The subsequent spread of this rumour throughout the cities of the empire, and the destruction of Plautianus' images in these locations by individuals such as Raecius

---

[2] The *Historia Augusta* (*Sev.* 14.5–7) has a garbled version of the same events, in which Severus condemns Plautianus, has his statues removed, and then changes his mind.

[3] Kapferer 1990: 13–15; Di Fonzo and Bordia 2007: 13, 17.

[4] Allport and Postman 1947: 2, 37; Shibutani 1966: 17, 62; Di Fonzo and Bordia 2007: 13–15, 238. On the importance of oral transmission of rumour, see Scott 1990: 144–5. This phenomenon of sense-making rumour is distinct from fabricated stories which are spread deliberately rather than as an organic social response. As noted by Di Fonzo and Bordia 2007: 79: 'malicious intent in rumor birth cannot sustain rumor growth'.

[5] Allport and Postman 1947: 153; Shibutani 1966: 76–7, 128; Paillard 1990: 133–4; Gavard 1993; Fargette 2007: 314.

[6] Di Fonzo and Bordia 2007: 15, 71–2. For another case study applying these theories to the historiography of the Severan period, see Davenport 2017.

[7] The statues of Plautianus throughout the empire apparently outnumbered those of Severus, Caracalla, and Geta (76[75].14.7 [Xiph./*EV*]).

[8] When an individual's memory was condemned by the *res publica*, the official record of the decision would be contained in a senatorial decree (*senatus consultum*). See Flower 2006: 132–8 (on the *SC de Cn. Pisone patre*), 235–6 (senatorial decisions about the death of Domitian).

[9] On the destruction of images as part of memory sanctions, see Vittinghoff 1936: 13–18; Varner 2004. For the modern coinage *damnatio memoriae* and the formulations used by Romans to express the various processes now grouped under this term, see Vittinghoff 1936: 12–13, 64–74.

Constans, can be ascribed to the risk-management impulse. They had not received any official information about the prefect's downfall, yet they obviously felt a need to rid themselves of Plautianus' statues. Perhaps these individuals feared that the messengers with the official news had failed to reach them, or maybe they wished to pre-empt its arrival in order to show themselves especially loyal to the emperor. Regardless of the real reason for their decisions, Constans and others did not want to be caught with Plautianus' images still standing in their cities.[10] As Maud Gleason has memorably remarked about this incident, 'shifts in imperial favour were prudent to anticipate, but dangerous to get wrong'.[11] As it turned out, this rumour, though inherently plausible, was indeed wrong, because none of those involved in spreading it had access to accurate information as to why Plautianus' statues were being melted down, even the equestrian governor of Sardinia.[12] The real intentions of Septimius Severus remained a mystery to them.

The lack of official information about why Plautianus' statues were being destroyed, and the subsequent generation of rumours in order to compensate for this void, recalls a problem raised by Dio himself in Book 53, Chapter 19, of the *Roman History*. Following his account of the award of the name Augustus to Octavian and the first constitutional settlement of 27 BC, Dio describes how, in his view, the new monarchical regime changed the flow of political information:

> Formerly, as we know, all matters were reported to the senate and to the people, even if they happened at a distance; hence all learned of them and many recorded them, and consequently the truth regarding them, no matter to what extent fear or favour, friendship or enmity, coloured the reports of certain writers, was always to a certain extent to be found in the works of the other writers who wrote of the same events and in the public records. But after this time most things that happened began to be kept secret and concealed, and even though some things are perchance made public, they are distrusted just because they cannot be verified; for it is suspected that everything is said and done with reference to the wishes of the men in power at the time and of their associates. As a result, much that never occurs is circulated (θρυλεῖται), and much that happens beyond a doubt is unknown,

---

[10] For cities as centres of rumour, see Fargette 2007: 316–17. Such 'dread rumours', which focus on negative outcomes and consequences, always spread more swiftly than other forms of unofficial information (Di Fonzo and Bordia 2007: 75).

[11] Gleason 2011: 53.

[12] This anecdote foreshadows the eventual downfall of Plautianus in 77(76).3.1–6.3 (Xiph./*EV*). For the very thorough destruction of Plautianus' statues after his condemnation in 205, see Varner 2004: 161–4.

and in the case of nearly every event a version gains currency that is different from the way it really happened. Furthermore, the very magnitude of the empire and the multitude of things that occur render accuracy regarding them most difficult. In Rome, for example, much is going on, and much in the subject territory, while, as regards our enemies, there is something happening all the time, in fact, every day, and concerning these things no one except the participants can easily have correct information, and most people do not even hear of them at all. Hence in my own narrative of later events, so far as they need to be mentioned, everything that I shall say will be in accordance with the reports that have been given out, whether it be really the truth or otherwise. In addition to these reports, however, my own opinion will be given, as far as possible, whenever I have been able, from the abundant evidence which I have gathered from my reading, from hearsay, and from what I have seen, to form a judgement that differs from the common report. (53.19.2–6)[13]

This is a justly famous passage, which has been extensively discussed for the methodological insights it provides into Dio's use of sources and how this informed his approach to historical writing.[14] However, it is also possible to offer different, but complementary, readings of 53.19, which place the passage in the context of the wider narrative strategies of the *Roman History*.[15] In Chapter 1 of this volume, Adam Kemezis discussed how Dio's incorporation of stories about emperors, regardless of their truth, into the *Roman History* allowed him to juxtapose the emperors' own official version of events with oppositional readings.[16] This chapter will

---

[13] πρότερον μὲν γὰρ ἔς τε τὴν βουλὴν καὶ ἐς τὸν δῆμον πάντα, καὶ εἰ πόρρω που συμβαίη, ἐσεφέρετο· καὶ διὰ τοῦτο πάντες τε αὐτὰ ἐμάνθανον καὶ πολλοὶ συνέγραφον, κἀκ τούτου καὶ ἡ ἀλήθεια αὐτῶν, εἰ καὶ τὰ μάλιστα καὶ φόβῳ τινὰ καὶ χάριτι φιλίᾳ τε καὶ ἔχθρᾳ τισὶν ἐρρήθη, παρὰ γοῦν τοῖς ἄλλοις τοῖς τὰ αὐτὰ γράψασι τοῖς τε ὑπομνήμασι τοῖς δημοσίοις τρόπον τινὰ εὑρίσκετο. ἐκ δὲ δὴ τοῦ χρόνου ἐκείνου τὰ μὲν πλείω κρύφα καὶ δι' ἀπορρήτων γίγνεσθαι ἤρξατο, εἰ δέ πού τινα καὶ δημοσιευθείη, ἀλλὰ ἀνεξέλεγκτά γε ὄντα ἀπιστεῖται· καὶ γὰρ λέγεσθαι καὶ πράττεσθαι πάντα πρὸς τὰ τῶν ἀεὶ κρατούντων τῶν τε παραδυναστευόντων σφίσι βουλήματα ὑποπτεύεται. καὶ κατὰ τοῦτο πολλὰ μὲν οὐ γιγνόμενα θρυλεῖται, πολλὰ δὲ καὶ πάνυ συμβαίνοντα ἀγνοεῖται, πάντα δὲ ὡς εἰπεῖν ἄλλως πως ἢ ὡς πράττεται διαθροεῖται. καὶ μέντοι καὶ τὸ τῆς ἀρχῆς μέγεθος τό τε τῶν πραγμάτων πλῆθος δυσχερεστάτην τὴν ἀκρίβειαν αὐτῶν παρέχεται. ἔν τε γὰρ τῇ Ῥώμῃ συχνὰ καὶ παρὰ τῷ ὑπηκόῳ αὐτῆς πολλά, πρός τε τὸ πολέμιον ἀεὶ καὶ καθ' ἡμέραν ὡς εἰπεῖν γίγνεταί τι, περὶ ὧν τὸ μὲν σαφὲς οὐδεὶς ῥᾳδίως ἔξω τῶν πραττόντων αὐτὰ γιγνώσκει, πλεῖστοι δ' ὅσοι οὐδ' ἀκούουσι τὴν ἀρχὴν ὅτι γέγονεν. ὅθενπερ καὶ ἐγὼ πάντα τὰ ἑξῆς, ὅσα γε καὶ ἀναγκαῖον ἔσται εἰπεῖν, ὡς που καὶ δεδήμωται φράσω, εἴτ' ὄντως οὕτως εἴτε καὶ ἑτέρως πως ἔχει. προσέσται μέντοι τι αὐτοῖς καὶ τῆς ἐμῆς δοξασίας, ἐς ὅσον ἐνδέχεται, ἐν οἷς ἄλλο τι μᾶλλον ἢ τὸ θρυλούμενον ἠδυνήθην ἐκ πολλῶν ὧν ἀνέγνων ἢ καὶ ἤκουσα ἢ καὶ εἶδον τεκμήρασθαι.

[14] Some examples from standard works include Millar 1964: 37–8; Manuwald 1979: 94–5, 105–6; Potter 1999: 85–6; Hose 2007: 464–5. This is not a criticism of this approach, merely an observation about one key way of reading this passage. For Dio's use of documentary sources in the imperial books of the *Roman History*, see Chapter 3 by Cesare Letta in this volume.

[15] Kemezis 2014: 94–7.

[16] For similar observations about the use of rumour in Tacitus, see Feldherr 2009b, esp. 185–6.

complement Kemezis' analysis by drawing attention to another narrative strategy employed by Dio, namely the connection between rumour and the Roman imperial monarchy in the *Roman History*. Dio, as is well known, regarded monarchy as the best form of government for an empire of the size of Rome's.[17] But that does not mean that he did not recognise its problems.[18]

In 53.19, as in the Plautianus passage which opened this chapter, Dio has revealed his keen understanding of the mechanics of rumour. This can be observed not only in his connection between rumour and the lack of reliable news and information, but also in his awareness that secrecy and censorship give rise to rumour generation.[19] Similar sentiments about the restricted flow of information under a monarchy can also be found in Tacitus and Eunapius, to name just two ancient authors, which indicates it was a concern shared by historians of the Roman empire.[20] Rumours are particularly known to emerge, flourish, and be embellished in what scholars call 'high-interest contexts'.[21] In the Roman imperial monarchy, the most significant high-interest context was the emperor himself. People at all social levels, from senators to slaves, were interested in news about the emperors which had the potential to affect their lives. To take just one example, the death of an emperor without a designated successor could result in a bloody civil war, which would cost the lives of soldiers and civilians.[22]

This chapter does not attempt to analyse the historical veracity of the rumours presented by Dio, nor does it engage in an in-depth examination of the historicity of his claims that accurate information was more difficult to come by under the emperors than during the Republic. It is sufficient to note that scholars such as Ray Laurence, Peter O'Neill, and Cristina Rosillo-López have shown that political rumours did indeed circulate in the Roman Republic in response to the lack of reliable news.[23] People

---

[17] This is widely acknowledged by scholars, e.g. Rich 1989: 95–6; Reinhold and Swan 1990: 158–9, 165–6; Gowing 1992: 25–6; Hose 1994: 430–2.

[18] See especially Manuwald 1979: 8–26, highlighting the positive and negative aspects of monarchy in Dio's political thought. One key problem was the issue of the succession, explored by Davenport and Mallan 2014.

[19] Shibutani 1966: 59.

[20] On similarities between Tacitus and Dio, see Hardie 2012: 286–8, and for Tacitus' own use of rumour as a narrative technique, Shatzman 1974, esp. 555–6; Giua 1998; Gibson 1998; Feldherr 2009b. See further Chapter 1 by Adam Kemezis, who also emphasises the differences between the two writers. For Late Antiquity, see Eunapius, *History*, Fragment 50 (ed. Blockley 1983).

[21] Di Fonzo and Bordia 2007: 141.

[22] For interest in royal deaths in other monarchical societies, see Fox 1997: 613–14; Shagan 2001: 39–49.

[23] Laurence 1994; O'Neill 2003; Rosillo-López 2017.

listened to speeches and watched happenings in the *forum Romanum* in an attempt to gain insights into political decisions that would affect their lives, and their interpretation or misinterpretation of these events resulted in different accounts being spread throughout the city.[24] So there are grounds for suspecting that some aspects of Dio's contrast between the Republic and the imperial monarchy were at least 'overstated', as John Rich has pointed out.[25] This chapter, however, takes a historiographical perspective, seeking to understand why Dio chose to frame 53.19 through the lens of rumour by exploring the role and function of news and rumour within the narrative. In the *Roman History*, the incidence and frequency of sense-making rumours, generated by the lack of verifiable and reliable political information, is a feature of Dio's account of the last decades of the Roman Republic and the competition between the dynasts, before emerging as a prominent aspect of monarchical political culture in the imperial books.[26]

II   Rumour and Political Change

The first fifty-one books of the *Roman History* up to the year 29 BC, as Dio explains to his readers at the start of Book 52, told the story of Romans under kingship, the Republic, and great men (*dynasteiai*).[27] Following the defeat of Antony and the establishment of Octavian's supremacy, Rome became a monarchy once again (52.1.1). Dio's narrative of the Roman imperial monarchy properly begins in Book 53, after the interlude of the Agrippa–Maecenas debate in Book 52.[28] Adam Kemezis has plausibly argued that these phases within the *Roman History* can be understood as different 'narrative modes' of history-writing. To Dio's own division at the beginning of Book 52, he has added the 'contemporary' mode, consisting of Books 73(72)–80(80), which cover the historian's own time.[29] In particular, Kemezis has noted that a shift occurs in Dio's account in the

---

[24] See the rich discussion of public events by Morstein-Marx 2004: 68–112.   [25] Rich 1990: 152.
[26] This study is based on the concept of rumour, not individual words and their meanings. Dio uses a range of different terms, such as θροῦς, φήμη, λόγος, and cognate verbs (e.g. θρυλέω) to describe rumour.
[27] On Dio's perceptions of these different forms of government, see Millar 1964: 74–5.
[28] The bibliography on these speeches is vast: Millar 1964: 102–18 remains the best introduction. See Kemezis 2014: 129 on the speeches of Book 52 marking a separation between the different narrative modes.
[29] Kemezis 2014: 94–104. Schulz 2019a: 255–6 has identified a further later division in the *Roman History*, arguing that the period from Nerva to Marcus Aurelius constitutes a united whole within 'communicative memory'. I discuss this further in Chapter 8 of this volume, which focusses on Dio's portrayal of the Antonine emperors.

late second century BC, after which the narrative is marked by a new
emphasis on the destabilising power and influence of individual politicians
that presaged the end of the Republic.[30] This contrasted with the unity and
'collective action' of the political elite during the narrative of the middle
Republic.[31] Such a change, Kemezis proposed, represented the division
between the mid-Republican narrative mode and that of the late Republic
(*dynasteia*).[32]

The study of the role of rumour as a sense-making phenomenon
throughout the entirety of the *Roman History* and across these different
narrative modes is hampered by the often-incomplete state of the text.[33]
Only Books 36–60, covering the period from 68 BC to AD 47, of the *Roman
History*, survive complete or relatively complete. We must therefore tread
carefully when examining the other parts of the history for which we
depend primarily on fragments and the works of Byzantine historians,
especially the poorly preserved Books 1–35 which include Dio's narrative of
the Regal period and the early and middle Republic.[34] Rumour does not
play an appreciable role as an aspect of political culture in the surviving
epitomised portions and fragments of these books.[35] In contrast, rumour
does feature prominently in the late Republican narrative, the period of
rivalry between the great men, from the 60s BC onwards, with incidents of

[30] See further Coudry 2016b on the characterisation of these late Republican politicians.
[31] Kemezis 2014: 102, 110, and see F. 52, as the paradigmatic statement of this united *res publica*. This
does not mean, of course, that pre-eminent individuals did not emerge in Dio's narrative of the
middle Republic (e.g. Simons 2009: 200–40, esp. 222–40, and Coudry 2019: 131–40 on Scipio
Africanus). Moreover, we can observe distinct phases even within the mid-Republican narrative, as
shown by Simons 2009: 120–86. The key difference is that the rivalry and competition between
individual politicians did not result in the transformation of the Roman state, as it did in Dio's
account of the late Republic.
[32] Kemezis (2014: 109) has made his points very cautiously, stating that the 'use of *dynasteia* as
a technical term, like the idea of narrative modes generally, is a critical construct of my own, not
necessarily one Dio as author would have formulated in the same way'. One should bear this in mind
when reading the critique of Lindholmer 2018.
[33] In undertaking this study, I have read all the extant books, epitomised sections, and fragments of the
Roman History in search for rumours which functioned as a collective social response to ambiguous
situations.
[34] On the transmission and structure of these books, see in particular Simons 2009: 25–32; Fromentin
2013; Mallan 2019. The loss of the original text of Books 1 and 2, which covered the Regal period, is
particularly to be lamented in the context of the present study. Their survival would have allowed
more detailed comparison between the early Roman and the later imperial monarchy in the *Roman
History*, and particularly whether sense-making rumour played a role in shaping political culture
under the kings. The surviving fragments have, however, allowed Schulz 2019b to draw out some
key thematic strands shared by the two monarchical narratives.
[35] I have excluded deliberately fabricated stories, such as the rumour manufactured and spread by
Valerius Publicola (F. 13.2). As noted above, these malicious tales represent a different phenomenon
from sense-making rumour, which is the focus of Dio's methodological statement in 53.19.

rumour becoming more frequent the closer one gets to Octavian assuming sole power. This suggests that the increasing presence of rumour in the *Roman History* could be a result of a change in narrative modes between the middle and late Republic.[36] But we must be cautious. One could argue that this is a distorted pattern, manufactured by the fact that we only have Dio's original narrative for the final decades of the Republic. There is merit to this point. Even the fragmentary state of Books 22–35 makes it difficult to ascertain whether rumour played a significant role in the first part of Dio's late Republican narrative phase (featuring the rise of Tiberius Gracchus and other individuals suspected at aiming at sole rule), which marked a break from the 'collective action' of the middle Republic.[37] All we can state is that rumour as a sense-making phenomenon does not feature in the surviving fragments or epitomised sections of the *Roman History* before the 60s BC. This is suggestive, rather than conclusive, evidence for Dio's authorial intentions.

Therefore, I will not engage in further speculation about the earlier books of the *Roman History*, and instead focus on the role played by rumour in the change between Dio's late Republican and monarchical narrative modes. In the *dynasteia* mode, rumour manifests itself in two ways. First, rumours are generated by the heightened state of anxiety which results from the rivalry between the great men. Secondly, rumours emerge under Julius Caesar and the triumvirate of Lepidus, Antony, and Octavian, as a consequence of the restriction of official information by their regimes.[38] I propose that this attention to rumour represents a deliberate authorial strategy on Dio's part. It forms part of his exploration of the impact of the competition for one-man rule on the Roman world and foreshadows the change in the flow of accurate news, and the corresponding flourishing of rumour, that would form a fundamental part of the political culture of the imperial monarchy.[39]

---

[36] There are other thematic and stylistic transitions within the *Roman History* at this point, which could lend support to this argument. One is the adaptation of the annalistic framework to focus on key individuals, a narrative change which accompanies the transformation of the state itself, on which see Gowing 1992: 34–5, 60.

[37] For Tiberius Gracchus as a turning point in the narrative, especially marking the phase of *dynasteia*, see Dio F. 83.1–8. The idea of fear and uncertainty can be found in these fragmentary books, for example, in the portions dealing with Sulla's proscriptions (F.109.13–20). But there is no discussion of rumour surviving in these fragments.

[38] On Dio's negative portrayal of the triumvirate, see Gowing 1992: 35.

[39] For the themes of Dio's late Republican narrative anticipating the account of the Principate, see Rich 1989: 92–3; Gowing 1992: 35. See further Coudry (2016b: 295–6), who identifies dissimulation and secrecy as one particular theme.

We will begin with the first category outlined above: rumours being generated as a result of anxiety. This is a feature of Dio's account of the Catilinarian conspiracy of 63 BC. Elections in Rome were always subjects of rumour (as they are in almost every society), but the attempt by Catiline to seize sole power for himself took this to a new level, prompting a period of 'sustained collective tension' (to use the terminology of the sociologist Tamotsu Shibutani).[40] This type of social environment commonly leads to rumour generation as people furiously speculate about the outcome of events.[41] The Catilinarian conspiracy was thus an appropriate point for Dio to explore rumour as a consequence of political uncertainty. He writes that when Cicero appeared in the assembly wearing a breastplate, a rumour (φήμη) spread that a conspiracy had been formed against the consul, which roused the emotions of the people; up to this point Cicero had spoken of Catiline only to the senate (37.29.4–5). The inclusion of this spontaneous rumour based on the careful observation of public behaviour in the narrative reveals Dio's keen appreciation of rumour generation. As Ray Laurence has remarked, watching people and events was the main way in which rumours spread amongst the Roman people when they did not have access to accurate information about political events.[42] Dio writes that a story (λόγος) later circulated that M. Licinius Crassus had been one of the conspirators, but this rumour failed to gain traction because it was not believable (37.35.1–2). Indeed, one of the primary tenets of rumour generation is that people must regard unofficial information as plausible and trust the sources of their news in order to pass it on to others.[43]

Rumours appear frequently in Dio's narrative of the civil wars between Pompey and Caesar, the dictatorship of Caesar, and the triumviral regime, as a way of demonstrating the uncertainty engendered by competition between the great men. In his account of 48 BC, Dio states that the hopes and fears of the supporters of both Pompey and Caesar were said to fluctuate daily according to the 'generation of rumours' (λογοποιουμένων) (42.17.4). With the crucial battles in the civil war happening far away from Rome, the people of the city craved accurate and reliable news: when first informed of the defeat of Pompey at Pharsalus, they refuse to believe the report until Pompey's ring arrives in the city as proof (42.18.1–19.1). The award of Caesar's dictatorship did not

[40] Shibutani 1966: 46. On elections and rumour, see Allport and Postman 1947: 184, and for the case of Rome, Rosillo-López 2017: 82–3.
[41] On anxiety and rumour, see Di Fonzo and Bordia 2007: 50, 71–2.
[42] Laurence 1994: 62–3. For the theory behind this conclusion, see Allport and Postman 1947: 116.
[43] Shibutani 1966: 76–95; Di Fonzo and Bordia 2007: 90, 100–1.

quell the climate of fear and anxiety, according to Dio's narrative. For example, Dio describes how Antony's wearing of a sword in all his public appearances over the course of 48 BC gave rise to suspicion that violence might be forthcoming from Caesar himself (42.27.3).

There are two key rumour events worth highlighting in the triumviral narrative. The first occurs after Caesar's assassination in 44 BC. With the appearance of a comet in the skies, tensions in Rome were high.[44] Dio describes how Antony and Octavian engaged in acrimonious public one-upmanship, including an incident in which Antony had Octavian dragged from the courts by his lictors. Their rivalry sparks a 'rumour' (θροῦς) that 'something unexpected' (τι νέον) would occur (45.7.3).[45] This is a further example of rumour emerging from the observation of public happenings, as with the case of Catiline above. The second event takes place in 42 BC, when Octavian falls ill and is slow to return to Italy after the defeat of Brutus and Cassius at Philippi. The people of Rome are gripped with anxiety and, consequently, numerous 'stories' (λόγοι) begin to circulate throughout the city. Dio describes some rumours that Octavian had died and other tales that he was devising wickedness against the citizens (recalling the suspicions about Caesar's attitude to the people described above). Consequently, the residents of Rome begin to hide their property, plan their escape, or simply surrender to their fate (48.3.1–6). This account represents a manifestation of rumour as risk management, as we noted earlier: in times of crisis, when there is a lack of accurate news, rumours begin to circulate as people ponder what will happen and put contingencies in place. In this case, the rumours cease only with the arrival of accurate news, in the form of Octavian's letter to the senate (48.3.6).

We turn now to the second context of rumour generation in Dio's late Republican narrative mode: the restriction of news from official sources, which foreshadows the secrecy of a monarchy under Augustus.[46] The vision of Republican politics laid out by Dio in 53.19 assumed an idealised free flow of information between senate and people, and the accurate and public recording of events, which could accordingly be consulted by all. These information channels change throughout Dio's narrative of the declining Republic. In his account of 46 BC, the historian describes how people were uncertain as to the underlying significance and meaning of

---

[44] On the Roman understanding of comets, and as portents in particular, see Pliny, *NH* 2.89–95, esp. 92–3. For the appearance of Caesar's comet and the different narratives it generated, see Gurval 1997; Pandey 2018: 35–82.

[45] On this rivalry between Octavian and Antony as portrayed by Dio, see Manuwald 1979: 36–8.

[46] For Caesar and Octavian's role in the *dynasteia* phase of Dio's narrative, see Kemezis 2014: 115–26.

Caesar's new honours, such as the awarding of the dictatorship for ten years and the right to select magistrates, and the erection of the statue of him as a hero. This led them to suspect that terrible things would soon happen (43.14.3–15.2). Caesar therefore decides to make official announcements about his intentions to the senate and the people, in accordance with Republican custom, and this, together with his subsequent actions, successfully puts a stop to speculation (43.18.6). Dio's depiction of Caesar's practices should be contrasted with those of the triumvirs, Lepidus, Antony, and Octavian. When these men meet near Bononia in October 43 BC to establish the terms of their alliance, they agree that for five years 'they should manage public business, whether or not they made any communication about it to the people and the senate' (ὥστε τά τε ἄλλα πάντα, κἂν μηδὲν ὑπὲρ αὐτῶν μήτε τῷ δήμῳ μήτε τῇ βουλῇ κοινώσωσι, διοικεῖν) (46.55.3). Such a decision represented the withdrawal of political decision-making behind closed doors, restricting the flow of official information, which Dio identifies as a key aspect of a monarchical regime.[47]

The tension between the triumvirs Antony and Octavian represents the climax of rumour generation in the *dynasteia* narrative mode. At the beginning of Book 50, Dio observes that their government was no longer a democracy (the Republican system), but not yet a monarchy (as it would become under Augustus) (50.1.1). This collegiate – but hardly collegial – regime is marked by deliberate attempts by both parties to restrict the flow of accurate information (50.8.1). For example, Octavian suppresses news of Antony's positive achievements in the East, including the annexation of Armenia, in order to limit public support for him in Rome (49.41.5). Instead, Octavian announces to the senate Antony's other actions, including the donations of Alexandria and his proclamation that Caesarion is the son of Caesar.[48] This announcement means that the Roman people start to believe in other rumours (θρυλούμενα), namely that Antony intends to give Rome to Cleopatra, and that he wants to make Alexandria the capital of the empire (50.4.1). Dio represents Octavian as manipulating and restricting the channels of public political communication, which marks the demise

---

[47] In a telling parallel, an early fragment of the *Roman History* (F 11.5–6) shows that the restriction of information was a feature of the reign of Tarquinius Superbus. See Schulz (2019b: 325–6) on this control over political news presaging the themes of the imperial books. The original text of the *Roman History* may well have emphasised this theme more as part of the narrative of the age of the kings.

[48] On the historical background to the alliance between Antony and Cleopatra, and the attacks levelled by Antony and Octavian against each other, see Pelling 1996: 29–30, 36, 40–5.

of the openness that in his view characterised the government of the Republic.[49] The stories about Antony's ambitions that circulate as a result of Octavian's hold on power in Rome conform to the pattern of rumour generation described by Dio.

This analysis of the role of rumour in the late Republican narrative of the *Roman History* offers a different perspective on the historiographical excursus in 53.19, in which Dio presents the return of monarchy to Rome under Augustus as a turning point in the flow of political news and information. In particular, I would argue that Dio uses rumour in the late Republican books of the *Roman History* to anticipate and foreshadow this transformative moment. It may have been the case that rumour as a sense-making phenomenon did not figure significantly in Dio's account of the middle Republic, the period in which individuals worked together for the good of the state, based on the surviving fragments and epitomised sections. But we cannot press such a conclusion too far, given the lapidary state of the text. What we can say is that rumour generation does play a significant part in the final part of the late Republican narrative mode, the period of the *dynasteiai*, for two interconnected reasons. Firstly, this period of anxiety and uncertainty marked the demise of the traditional political culture of the Republic, which, according to Dio, included the open communication of decision-making to both the senate and the people. Secondly, political decisions became the domain of a few powerful men and increasingly hidden from the public eye, and hence rumours emerged to fill the demand for accurate information about political events. For Dio, this foreshadowed the state of affairs under Rome's imperial monarchy.[50]

III   Rumour and Monarchy

In the aftermath of Augustus and Agrippa's controversial revision of the senatorial roll in 18 BC, Dio states that many resentful senators were accused of plotting against the *princeps* and his colleague. He comments:

---

[49] On Dio's presentation of Octavian as the defining individual in this portion of the history, see Manuwald 1979: 27–76. In a nuanced discussion, Pelling (1997a: 121–2) has distinguished between the books dealing with the politics of the 60s–40s, in which individuals play a prominent, but not yet dominant, role in structuring the narrative, and the 'move towards biostructure', found in the triumviral books with a particular focus on Octavian.

[50] Once again, Dio's observations about rumour generation are on point with modern sociological approaches. As Shibutani (1966: 62) remarked: 'Unsatisfied demand for news – the *discrepancy* between information needed to come to terms with a changing environment and what is provided by formal news channels – constitutes the crucial condition of rumor construction.'

It is not possible, of course, for those on the outside to have certain knowledge of such matters; for whatever measures a ruler takes, either personally or through the senate, for the punishment of men for alleged plots against himself, are generally looked upon with suspicion as having been done out of spite, no matter how just such measures may be. For this reason, it is my purpose to report in all such cases simply the recorded version of the affair, without busying myself with anything beyond the published account, except in perfectly patent cases, or giving a hint as to the justice or injustice of the act or as to the truth or falsity of the report. (54.15.2–3)[51]

As with the programmatic 53.19, this passage functions as an important statement about Dio's methodology and use of sources.[52] For the purposes of this chapter, I would like to focus on the first part of the passage about the attitudes of the Roman people to imperial actions, which 'are generally looked upon with suspicion as having been done out of spite, no matter how just such measures may be'. This remark reveals considerable perspicacity on Dio's part for two reasons. Firstly, the sociologist Tamotsu Shibutani has observed that rumours not only flourish in response to situations in which people lack reliable news, but also when 'institutional channels are not completely trusted'.[53] The notion that the news from official sources could not be trusted recurs throughout the imperial narrative of the *Roman History*. For example, Dio writes that when Commodus' death was first reported, people thought the story had been circulated by the emperor to test their loyalty, with provincial governors even imprisoning the messengers who brought them the news (74[73].2.5–6 [*EV*]). Secondly, historians of monarchical regimes have often pointed out that stories about kings and queens commonly conform to cultural preconceptions about autocratic behaviour, regardless of the exact facts of any individual case.[54] Rumours therefore emerge as very simplified versions of complex political intrigue in which monarchs and their family members appear and behave as stock characters.[55]

---

[51] οὐ γὰρ ἔστιν ἀκριβῶς τὰ τοιαῦτα τοῖς ἔξω αὐτῶν οὖσιν εἰδέναι· πολλὰ γὰρ ὧν ἂν ὁ κρατῶν πρὸς τιμωρίαν, ὡς καὶ ἐπιβεβουλευμένος, ἤτοι δι' ἑαυτοῦ ἢ καὶ διὰ τῆς γερουσίας πράξῃ, ὑποπτεύεται κατ' ἐπήρειαν, κἂν ὅτι μάλιστα δικαιότατα συμβῇ, γεγονέναι. καὶ διὰ τοῦτο καὶ ἐγὼ γνώμην ἔχω περὶ πάντων τῶν τοιουτοτρόπων αὐτὰ τὰ λεγόμενα συγγράψαι, μηδὲν ὑπὲρ τὰ δεδημοσιευμένα, πλὴν τῶν πάνυ φανερῶν, μήτε πολυπραγμονῶν μήθ' ὑπολέγων, μήτ' εἰ δικαίως μήτ' εἰ ἀδίκως τι γέγονε, μήτ' εἰ ψευδῶς μήτε εἰ ἀληθῶς εἴρηται.
[52] For the connection between the two passages, see Rich 1990: 190–1.
[53] Shibutani 1966: 131, 134.   [54] Gavard 1993; Fox 1997: 615–6; Duindam 2016: 276–81.
[55] Coast 2014: 90.

The connection between the substance of rumours and assumptions about imperial behaviour emerges clearly in Dio's Augustan narrative. For example, Dio describes how in 16 BC Augustus leaves Rome for Gaul, proclaiming that his presence was needed because of military problems in the region. This official version was not trusted. The real reason for Augustus' departure, Dio says, was that the *princeps*' moral legislation had angered senators and he wished to leave their city to avoid their resentment.[56] However, Dio also reports another story that Augustus was suspected of absconding from Rome together with Maecenas' wife Terentia, with whom he was having an affair, because they wanted to conduct their relationship 'without being the subject of rumour' (ἄνευ θροῦ) (54.19.3). Here we have multiple versions of one incident: what Dio states was the real reason, Augustus' official version, and the rumour, all of which were quite different. This reflects Dio's technique of juxtaposing the 'public' and 'hidden' transcript of imperial behaviour, as explored by Adam Kemezis in Chapter 1. Here I wish to emphasise that the substance of the rumour echoes popular conceptions of imperial behaviour, including the pattern of Roman interest in imperial sex lives.[57] Similar preconceptions about the devious, jealous, and immoral behaviour of monarchs and their family members can be seen in other stories in the *Roman History*, such as the tale that Livia was involved in the death of Marcellus, the rumours about why Tiberius withdrew to Rhodes, and stories about Tiberius' later departure to Capri and reluctance to return to Rome as *princeps*.[58] Many of these rumours are not unique to Dio, of course, but their incorporation into the narrative of the *Roman History* serves a different purpose than their presence in Suetonius, for example, in which they illustrate imperial vices according to the author's rubrics.[59] For Dio, such rumours were a distinctive facet of monarchical political culture, which marked a change from the Republic.

Partway through the reign of the emperor Claudius, we lose the original full books of the *Roman History* and must instead rely on fragments from the *Excerpta Constantiniana*, the condensed version of Dio found in the *Epitome* of Xiphilinus, and the *History* of Zonaras. We are therefore

---

[56] This is not at all implausible, given the resistance to Augustus' legislation, on which see now Eck 2019.

[57] On sex and Roman emperors, see particularly Wallace-Hadrill 1983: 171–4; Vout 2007; Blanshard 2010: 65–87.

[58] These stories appear at 53.33.4, 55.9.7–9, 58.24.2.

[59] Compare, for example, Suet. *Tib.* 11–12, 59–62 on Tiberius' two retirements to Rhodes and Capri: the Suetonian account of Capri contains tales of sexual depravity not found in Dio.

dependent on the choices made by Byzantine authors for understanding Dio's text and his narrative strategies.[60] That said, Xiphilinus, our most significant source for the imperial books, usually (but not always) preserves Dio's original wording, which makes it possible to gauge the historian's views and sentiments.[61] Therefore, despite the loss of the complete original text, we can continue to trace the role played by rumour in Dio's imperial narrative through these epitomised portions and excerpts.

One key passage from Dio's account of the reign of Nero demonstrates that the secrecy and mystery which surrounded the imperial court could only be penetrated when the outcomes of political intrigues manifested themselves in the public arena. In this passage, Dio writes that the breakdown of the relationship between Nero and Agrippina had a very public result:

> He also used the same excuse in the case of his mother; for he would not allow any soldier to attend her, declaring that no one except the emperor ought to be guarded by them. This revealed even to the masses his hatred of her. Nearly everything, to be sure, that he and his mother said to each other or that they did each day was reported outside the palace, yet it did not all reach the public, and hence various conjectures were made and various stories circulated. For, in view of the depravity and lewdness of the pair, everything that could conceivably happen was circulated (διεθροεῖτο) as having actually taken place, and reports possessing any credibility were believed as true. But when the people now saw Agrippina unaccompanied for the first time by the praetorians, most of them took care not to fall in with her even by accident, and if anyone did chance to meet her, he would hastily get out of the way without saying a word. (61[61].8.4-5 [EV/Xiph.])[62]

The events which led to the circulation of rumours about Nero and Agrippina are in accord with Dio's earlier statements about this phenomenon in 53.19 and 54.15. The public interest in the relationship between Nero and Agrippina was very high, since the prominence of the young

[60] See particularly Mallan 2013b.
[61] Millar 1964: 2; Brunt 1980: 488–92; Schmidt 1997: 2605; Berbessou-Broustet 2016: 83–5. See Mallan 2013b: 621–2 on Dio's first-person statements preserved in Xiphilinus.
[62] τῇ δὲ αὐτῇ σκήψει καὶ πρὸς τὴν μητέρα ἐχρήσατο· οὐδὲ γὰρ οὐδὲ ἐκείνῃ συνεῖναι στρατιώτην τινὰ ἐπέτρεπε, λέγων μηδένα ἄλλον ὑπ' αὐτῶν πλὴν τοῦ αὐτοκράτορος φρουρεῖσθαι χρῆναι. καὶ τοῦτό γε καὶ ἐς τοὺς πολλοὺς τὴν ἔχθραν αὐτοῦ ἐξέφηνεν. τὰ μὲν γὰρ ἄλλα ὅσα καθ' ἑκάστην ὡς εἰπεῖν ἡμέραν καὶ ἔλεγον ἐς ἀλλήλους καὶ ἔπραττον, ἐξῄει μὲν ἐκ τοῦ παλατίου, οὐ μέντοι καὶ πάντα ἐδημοσιεύετο, ἀλλὰ κατείκαζον αὐτὰ καὶ ἐλογοποίουν ἄλλοι ἄλλως· πρὸς γὰρ δὴ τὴν πονηρίαν τήν τε ἀσέλγειάν σφων τά τε ἐνδεχόμενα γενέσθαι ὡς γεγονότα διεθροεῖτο καὶ τὰ πιθανότητά τινα λεχθῆναι ἔχοντα ὡς καὶ ἀληθῆ ἐπιστεύετο· τότε δὲ πρῶτον ἰδόντες αὐτὴν ἄνευ δορυφόρων οἱ μὲν πολλοὶ ἐφυλάττοντο μηδ' ἐκ συντυχίας αὐτῇ συμμῖξαι, εἰ δέ πού τις καὶ συνέτυχε, διὰ ταχέων ἄν, μηδὲν εἰπών, ἀπηλλάγη.

emperor's mother in the public image of the regime represented an unusual situation for Romans.[63] They could ascertain Agrippina's importance not only from her public image as articulated through coins, monuments, and other media, but also by observing the honours given to her, including the personal guard of praetorians.[64] These extraordinary honours demanded explanation, so rumours of a sexual relationship between mother and son began to circulate.[65] When Agrippina emerged in public without her praetorian guard, people were able to deduce that, for whatever reason, the relationship between her and Nero had soured, and that she was no longer as prominent as she had been before. This vignette is one of the best pieces of evidence that Dio possessed a good understanding of how Romans attempted to make sense of court politics.

But one might justly ask why Dio considered stories about Augustus' affair with Maecenas' wife, Livia plotting against Marcellus, Tiberius' retirement from public life, or the sexual relationship between Nero and Agrippina to be significant political news, given that they were not concerned with weighty matters such as legislation or diplomacy. The answer is that these rumours were at their core concerned with the question of the imperial succession and political stability in general, which mattered very much to Romans up and down the social spectrum. The *Roman History* includes many rumours about how emperors died, and who was suspected of killing them, as seen in the cases of Vespasian, Titus, Trajan, and Marcus Aurelius.[66] An orderly transfer of power meant peace, while a contested succession could lead to war and its many attendant ills. Dio describes how rumours flourished about Tiberius' legitimacy after Augustus' death, which the new *princeps* tried to turn to his advantage in order to limit the possibility of revolt (57.3.3–5). Even the fascination with sex at court was not merely prurient but could have genuine political explanatory force. Caroline Vout has shown how sex between emperors and their eventual heirs was used as a way of explaining the choice of successors.[67] Dio includes these rumours about intrigue and competition at the imperial court because

---

[63] On the ambiguous relationships between imperial mothers and sons, see Davenport 2017: 79–87.

[64] For Agrippina's public image, see Ginsburg 2006: 55–105.

[65] For example, 62(61).11.3–4 (Xiph.). The inclusion of these and other sexual stories about Nero in the *Roman History* emphasised the emperor's femininity (Schulz 2019a: 189–90, 221). For Dio's account of Nero, see Chapter 7 by Shushma Malik.

[66] 66(66).17.1 (Xiph.), 66(66).26.2 (Xiph.), 68.33.2 (Xiph.), 71.3.1¹ (Xiph.), 72(71).33.4² (Xiph.).

[67] Vout 2007: 3.

they tied into the wider themes of imperial suitability and succession in the monarchical books of the *Roman History*.[68]

It is in this context that we should place Dio's extraordinary account of the revolt of the governor of Syria, Avidius Cassius, against the emperor Marcus Aurelius in AD 175 (72[71].22.2–23.2 [Xiph.]). Dio presents the story as follows. When Marcus falls ill, his wife, Faustina the Younger, writes to Cassius to ask him to seize the throne to prevent her young and stupid son Commodus succeeding to the purple. Cassius is considering what course of action to take when a 'report' (ἀγγελία) comes to him that Marcus has died, and he declares himself emperor without confirming the accuracy of the information. Marcus himself tries to suppress the news of the insurrection as long as possible, until the soldiers are roused up by 'rumour' (φήμη) and the emperor is forced to act against Cassius, whom he had long considered a trustworthy and reliable general. Dio's depiction of this astonishing series of events recalls his observations in 53.19 about the size of the empire and the difficulty in obtaining good information when one is far away from the centre of power, a problem which in the end proved fatal to Avidius Cassius. The historian knew that rumours about imperial politics were never mere idle speculation, but a matter of life and death for all concerned.

IV   The Imperial Centre

The rumours that we have examined thus far are largely the product of people trying to ascertain the workings of the Roman imperial monarchy from the outside looking in, either because they were separated from the emperor by distance (as in the case of the senatorial legate Avidius Cassius) or because they did not have privileged access in the first place (the people observing Nero and Agrippina). But the *Roman History* demonstrates that the problem of accessing reliable news and information was not experienced only in these situations.[69] The world of the imperial court itself was a fertile breeding ground for rumour, which, I would argue, was largely driven by courtiers' desire for self-preservation.[70] Proximity to the emperor did not ensure that one knew his real thoughts and motivations, prompting

---

[68]   For Dio's exploration of the problems of imperial succession, see Davenport and Mallan 2014; Ando 2016; Madsen 2016.

[69]   See Gibson 1998: 125–6, quite rightly arguing that it was not only the 'politically unimportant' who engaged in rumour generation and circulation.

[70]   On tension as part of the social environment of the Roman imperial court, see Wallace-Hadrill 1996: 305–6.

the emergence of rumours to explain what he had done or to express anxiety about things he might do. It is in Dio's 'contemporary' narrative mode, covering the reigns of Commodus and the Severan emperors, that we can observe the impact of these aspects of monarchical rule on the historian and his peers.[71] Dio was himself well aware of the ramifications of misinterpreting the emperor's whim: he served on the council that condemned Raecius Constans, the governor of Sardinia who pulled down Plautianus' statues because he had misread Septimius Severus' intentions (76[75].16.3–4 [Xiph.]).[72]

Personal experience of the regimes of Commodus and the Severan emperors, and the many fault lines in the imperial succession during this period, taught Dio that the acclamation of a new emperor could lead to the reconfiguration of court circles and the creation of new lines of communication and access to information.[73] A particularly telling example of rumour generation at court occurs in his account of the reign of Commodus. Dio writes that the young emperor had killed virtually all his father's advisors, except for three men, Ti. Claudius Pompeianus, P. Helvius Pertinax, and C. Aufidius Victorinus (73[72].4.1–2 [Xiph.]).[74] Victorinus continues to serve Commodus as urban prefect, but he endures 'frequent rumours and many reports' (πολλῆς μὲν φήμης πολλῶν δὲ καὶ λόγων) that Commodus wanted him dead. This leads Victorinus to confront Commodus' chief henchman, the praetorian prefect Sex. Tigidius Perennis, to ask why his death had not yet come to pass. Perennis' answer is not on record, but we do know that Victorinus escaped the wrath of both emperor and prefect, eventually dying of natural causes, which is more than can be said for his tormentors (73[72].11.1–2 [*EV*/ Xiph.]).[75] The anecdote is important because it illustrates the way in

---

[71] For the contemporary narrative mode, see Kemezis 2014: 96–7, and on Dio's status as a privileged narrator of this period, Schulz 2019a: 181. On the anxiety of senatorial life depicted in the contemporary narrative, see Millar 1964: 18, 147–8; Hose 1994: 406–9. For the influence of Dio's experiences and encounters with emperors on the *Roman History* at large, note Gowing 1992: 32, 289–94 on the triumviral books, Reinhold and Swan 1990: 157–69 on the Augustan narrative, and Schulz 2019a: 251–4 on Dio's portrayal of early emperors. Dio often reacted against Severan rulers in his depiction of good emperors: see, for example, Martini 2010 on the contrast between Marcus Aurelius and Caracalla.

[72] Gleason 2011: 53.

[73] In Chapter 1, Adam Kemezis has argued that the senatorial order, Dio's political public, becomes increasingly excluded under the later Severan emperors. For political upheaval, alliances, and imperial friendships, see the case studies of the reigns of Caracalla and Macrinus in Davenport 2012a and Davenport 2012b.

[74] Dio's presentation of the careers of these men is examined by Kemezis 2012.

[75] For the likelihood that Dio's Greek means Victorinus died a natural death rather than committed suicide as translated by E. Cary in the Loeb Classical Library edition, see Kemezis 2012: 390, n. 11.

which rumours could be generated at court: given the execution of so many adherents of Marcus Aurelius, it would have been perfectly plausible to imagine that Commodus would soon be turning his attention to Victorinus and his colleagues. But they were spared, Dio tells us, for reasons unknown. When no one could really know the emperor's mind, rumour flourished.

In her important article on Dio's world as portrayed in the contemporary books of the *Roman History*, Maud Gleason has drawn attention to the unstable nature of identity politics under Commodus and the Severan dynasty.[76] This period was marked by civil wars and usurpations (especially between AD 193–7 and AD 217–18), memory sanctions against failed imperial rivals and treasonous citizens (like Plautianus and his unfortunate daughter Plautilla), and the assumption of new names and identities by emperors themselves (such as Septimius Severus' adoption as the son of Marcus Aurelius, and Elagabalus' claim to be Caracalla's illegitimate offspring). These circumstances, Gleason has persuasively argued, influenced the themes and contents of the contemporary narrative in Books 73(72)–80(80), as Dio drew upon stories in circulation during his own lifetime to dramatise these negotiations of personal and political identity.[77] One particular Dionian tale, foregrounded by Gleason in her article, describes how Commodus hunted down Sex. Quintilius Condianus, the consul of 180, who was said to have faked his own death after the execution of his father and uncle.[78] Dio relates that many men were executed because of their resemblance to Condianus, their heads travelling all the way to Rome to be presented to Commodus, but no one knew whether or not he had really been caught and executed. A man claiming to be Condianus subsequently appeared in Rome in the reign of Pertinax, an event which Dio himself witnessed. The imposture of the false Condianus was revealed only when he could not adequately answer the emperor's erudite questions about Greek matters.

There are two separate but related phenomena at work here. The first is the rumour that Condianus, with the help of a ram's carcass, was able to fake his death. This story, and another tale about an Emesene prince fleeing to Persia to avoid being executed by Commodus, suggests that 'people in senatorial circles harbored escape fantasies', to quote Gleason.[79] Indeed, one almost gets a sense of Dio's own relief when, at the conclusion of the

---

[76] Gleason 2011.   [77] On Dio's use of oral sources, see Millar 1964: 121; Gleason 2011: 35, 45.
[78] The full tale – Dio refers to Condianus' manner of escaping death as a λόγος – appears in 73(72).6.1–7.2 (Xiph. / EV).
[79] Gleason 2011: 49.

Roman History, he writes that he was able to retire to his homeland of Bithynia after his second consulship in AD 229 (80[80].5.2–3 [Xiph./*EV*]).

The second phenomenon is the impersonation of Condianus itself. One of the conditions that makes imposture possible is the ambiguous nature of the real person's death.[80] The pseudo-Condianus exploited this in order to lay claim to the real senator's status and estate. The tale of this pretender fits with Dio's observations in 53.19 about the circulation of unverifiable information throughout the empire and the near impossibility of obtaining certainty about rumours. But the dénouement, in which the pretender is unmasked by Pertinax, also demonstrates that this uncertainty long prevailed at the imperial court until the emperor was presented with a real, living individual whose *bona fides* he could question.[81] This is a situation in which the emperor himself is affected by rumour and must sort out fact from fiction.[82]

John Rich has observed that Dio's methodological precepts articulated in 53.19 and 54.15 'did not prevent him from freely retailing anecdotes about court politics'.[83] Dio did not deviate from this practice of emperor-centred historiography, which required the use of such anecdotes, regardless of their authenticity. These stories effectively demonstrated the harsh reality of life under the Roman imperial monarchy, in which survival and success fundamentally depended on one man: the emperor. This helps us to understand the antithesis between the circulation of news and information under the Republic and the empire articulated by Dio in 53.19. The historicity of this dichotomy is open to challenge on the grounds that, as many historians have shown, rumour was indeed a part of the political culture of the Roman Republic. But I would argue that the specific difference Dio wished to highlight in his *Roman History* was that the Republic was a system of government run by a collective of leading individuals whose decisions were subject to close examination, whereas the monarchy depended on one man, whose thoughts and motivations were ultimately inscrutable even to the courtiers who surrounded him.

V   Conclusion

Book 53, Chapter 19 is a key transitional passage in Cassius Dio's *Roman History*. It is an extremely rich chapter, capable of being read in many

---

[80] Hug 2009: 217.

[81] See also the earlier story about Tiberius questioning Clemens, who claimed to be Agrippa Postumus (57.16.3–4).

[82] A point made by Gibson (1998: 126) in relation to both Dio and Tacitus.   [83] Rich 1990: 7.

different ways, as it connects with diverse aspects of Dio's narrative and methodological strategies. In this chapter, I have endeavoured to highlight the role played by news and rumour in this passage and within the *Roman History* at large. I have focussed primarily on the phenomenon of sense-making rumours, which emerge as attempts to explain ambiguous situations about which there is insufficient information or when the news that is available is considered unreliable. Dio's depiction of the mechanics of rumour generation and circulation, as shown in the passage about Plautianus' statues, among numerous others, reveals that he, like Tacitus, possessed a keen understanding of how rumour functioned.

The theme of news and rumour connects the pre-monarchical and monarchical portions of the *Roman History*, with 53.19 acting as a fulcrum between the two. It is difficult to make a conclusive determination about the place of sense-making rumours in Dio's account of the middle Republic, given the very lacunose state of the text. What we can say is that rumour does not play a role in the surviving portions of the mid-Republican narrative mode, which is primarily characterised by the leaders of the Roman state working together. But any conclusions drawn from this should not be pressed too far. In contrast, Dio's original account of the late Roman Republic from the 60s BC onwards, encompassing the later stages of the *dynasteia* narrative, does survive. In this part of the *Roman History*, Dio shows how rumours emerge in response to political uncertainty and the anxiety engendered by competition between great men, as well as by the attempts to restrict the flow of news under the triumvirate. I have argued that these incidents of rumour function as a thematic device, one of many such narrative strategies used by the historian to mark the transition from the Republic to the imperial monarchy in his work. The presence of rumour as an aspect of late Republican and triumviral political culture anticipates and presages the establishment of the monarchy under Augustus. The new monarchical regime is characterised both by restricted channels of information and by mistrust of official news even when provided, a situation which caused rumour to flourish.

The rumours in Dio's imperial books cover a wide range of subjects from tales of imperial affairs and sexual shenanigans to stories about political misjudgements and civil wars. Although seemingly disparate on the surface, many of these rumours share a preoccupation with the stability of government and the imperial succession, topics which were of interest to individuals from all levels of society because war, revolt, and disorder had the real capacity to affect people's lives. But rumour and speculation did not only occur outside the imperial court. The impossibility of knowing the mind of the emperor – who, in a monarchical regime was the ultimate political decision-maker – created an atmosphere of acute anxiety among the court society. Dio had first-hand experience of the vicissitudes of court life, and the way in which secrecy and ambiguity, supplemented by courtiers' desire for self-preservation, caused rumour to flourish. In the *Roman History*, Dio observes that the institution of a monarchy under Augustus had brought with it peace and security after years of civil wars (56.43.4–44.2). But the price for this, as he well knew, was secrecy and speculation.

CHAPTER 3

Literary and Documentary Sources in Dio's Narrative of the Roman Emperors

Cesare Letta

I Introduction

For a long period, studies of Cassius Dio's *Roman History* focussed solely on the literary sources he might have relied on, even if this led to results which were highly contradictory and unconvincing. The only certainty seemed to be the almost universal conviction that Dio did not use any form of documents, or at least he did not consult them directly. In a series of articles published over the last thirty years, I have shown that this statement is unsustainable, at least for the narrative of Dio's lifetime. Furthermore, it is highly likely that he used documents for his narrative of the early Principate. On this ground I would like to investigate here Dio's sources, both literary and documentary, mainly to understand and appreciate his working method.

II Literary Sources

Cassius Dio's *Roman History* has strenuously resisted all efforts to identify its sources. Almost two centuries of *Quellenforschung* ('source investigation') have given elusive and contradictory results, not only for the fragmentary sections of the work, but also for the books for which the original text survives.[1] For the period of Julius Caesar to the reign of Severus Alexander, most of the results of this source investigation have been negative. We will begin with the rise of the dynasts from Caesar to Augustus. Since Eduard Schwartz's seminal entry in the *Realencyclopädie*, all scholars accept that Dio does not depend on Caesar for the Gallic nor for the civil war.[2] Nevertheless almost surely

---

I would like to thank Kevin Painter and Margherita Facella for their assistance in revising my English text. All translations of Dio's *Roman History* are my own.

[1] See especially Millar 1964.

[2] Schwartz 1899: 1706–8; Hagendahl 1944 on the mutiny of Vesontio; Van Stekelenburg 1971: 43–8 and 1976: 43–57 on Caesar's speech at Placentia; Zecchini 1978: 33 on the whole Gallic War; Berti 1988: 9–21 on the civil war.

he knew both works.[3] The use of Sallust's historical works also seems unlikely, although Dio mentions the man himself at 40.63.4.[4] There has been a range of viewpoints regarding Dio's use of Livy's *Ab Vrbe Condita* ('From the Foundation of the City'). According to Schwartz and other early scholars, Dio relied on Livy for at least parts of the period considered here,[5] but the thorough analysis of Manuwald has proved that he does not depend on Livy.[6] The prevailing view is now that Dio usually preferred other authors, but knew Livy well and occasionally used him, always together with other sources.[7]

The results for the Principate are similarly negative. Regarding the Jewish War under Nero and Vespasian, Dio does not depend on Josephus' account, although he does mention him.[8] It is difficult to appreciate Plutarch's presence in Dio, given that only the *Otho* and *Galba* survive from Plutarch's *Caesars*. What we can say is that his relationship with Plutarch seems similar to that which he had with Livy. Dio probably knew Plutarch's series of imperial biographies, but surely did not depend on them; he may have used the *Caesars* together with other sources.[9] The same is true for both Tacitus[10] and Suetonius.[11] As pointed

---

[3] Cf. Pelling 1982; Lachenaud and Coudry 2011: xli–l for a concordance; Kemezis 2016a: 243–7.

[4] Schwartz (1899: 1706), who points out in 36.14.3 a polemical attitude towards the Sallustian version of Lucullus' campaign, reflected in Plut., *Luc.* 33; Millar 1964: 34; Kuhn-Chen 2002: 136.

[5] Schwartz 1899: 1697–99 (from book 36 on), 1710–14 (an increase up to Caesar's death); Bender 1961: 13–14 (the main source for the period 69–30 BC); Van Stekelenburg 1971: 43–60, 156 (on Caesar's civil war); Van Stekelenburg 1976.

[6] See Manuwald (1979: 168–253), according to whom the disagreements prevail, despite many similarities; see also Reinhold 1988: 7–8; Kuhn-Chen 2002: 136; Sidebottom 2007: 77; Fromentin 2016: 179.

[7] Rich 1990: 7; Freyburger and Roddaz 1991: xxiii. Zecchini (2016: 119–20) speaks of an 'attitude ... rivale'. According to De Franchis (2016: 194) and François (2016: 231), Dio sought to compete with Livy as a sort of '*anti-modèle*'. Westall (2016: 53–7) recognizes in 41.61.1–5 (on the *omina* relating to Pharsalus) an example of Livy's use together with other sources for the same matter.

[8] 65(66).1.4 (Xiph.). Therefore, Brizzi (2016) thinks that 65(66).4–6 (Xiph.) depends on Justus of Tiberias.

[9] Schwartz (1899: 1714) excludes the direct use of Plutarch (cf. 1710: two quotations in the frr. 40.5 and 107.1 are excerptor's additions); Freyburger and Roddaz 1991: xxi–xxiii.

[10] Schwartz 1899: 1714–15; Manuwald 1979: 69, 115–19, 128–66; Noè 1994: 13; Gowing 1997: 2563; Devilliers (2016a: 241), according to whom 'les divergences de projet ou de sensibilité' in comparison with Tacitus explain why 'Dion ne l'a pas choisi comme source principale'; Devilliers 2016b: 327.

[11] Schwartz (1899: 1705, 1714) points out the divergences on the *omina*; Millar (1964: 85–6), on the reign of Augustus, points out some important coincidences (e.g. 56.29.4, cf. Suet., *Aug.* 97.3; 53.16.7–8, cf. Suet., *Aug.* 7.4), but also equally significant differences (56.30.3–4, cf. Suet., *Aug.* 28.5); Manuwald (1979: 258–68) comes to the same conclusion for 54.11.7 (cf. Suet., *Aug.* 42.1), 53.22.2–3 (cf. Suet., *Aug.* 52) and 54.35.3 (cf. Suet., *Aug.* 91.2); Rich 1990: 8. Freyburger and Roddaz (1991: xxiii) point out that Dio knew Suetonius, whereas Champlin (2003: 224, n. 20) and Lange (2016) postulate a common source for 62 [63].3.4–5.3 [Xiph.] and Suet., *Ner.* 13 dealing with the triumph of AD 63. As Chris Mallan kindly suggests to me, the annalistic nature of much of Dio's imperial narrative might have made Suetonius difficult to use as a source.

out by Jérôme France, Maecenas' discussion of the relationship between
security, army, and taxation (52.28.1) echoes Cerialis' words in Tacitus
(*Hist.* 4.74.1).[12] This suggests that Dio knew Tacitus well, but opted not to
utilize him straightforwardly as his source. Moreover, my own analysis of
the *senatus consulta* ('senatorial decrees') reported in Dio's *Roman History*
has confirmed that in each case where a comparison is possible Dio's text is
not based on Tacitus, nor on Suetonius.[13]

Against this background, it is immediately apparent that the many
attempts to identify Dio's sources with authors whose works are more or
less completely lost are even more uncertain. Many historians of the civil
wars and the beginnings of the Principate have been mentioned as sources,
without any conclusive proof: Asinius Pollio,[14] Cremutius Cordus,[15]
Nicolaus of Damascus,[16] L. Scribonius Libo,[17] Seneca the Elder.[18] For
the first century AD, almost all pre-Tacitean authors have been suggested,
including Aufidius Bassus,[19] Cluvius Rufus,[20] Servilius Nonianus,[21] and
Pliny the Elder.[22] Dio did use some non-historiographical literary works,
such as Cicero's *Philippics*[23] and Seneca's *De Clementia* ('On Clemency').[24]
In the presence of such limited evidence, my view is that Dio read
practically all the authors mentioned above, but his *Roman History* is not
a mere collage of excerpts, abstracts, or paraphrases from their works.

---

[12] France 2016: 782.

[13] Cf. Letta 2019a: 242: for Tacitus the passages examined are seven; for Suetonius seventeen.

[14] Gabba 1957: 323–7 (for Fufius Calenus' speech against Cicero in 46.1–28); Berti 1988: 9–21 (for the civil war between Caesar and Pompey); Freyburger and Roddaz 1991: xxiii.

[15] Millar (1964: 85) only points out the positive mention of Cordus' work in 57.24.2–3; Zecchini 1987: 33–57; Rich 1990: 7; Cresci 1998: 16–17. Westall (2016: 53–7, 74–5) proposes Cremutius Cordus as a source for the *omina* relating to Pharsalus (41.61.1–5), the *bellum Perusinum* (48.14.1–6), and the narrative of the actions taken by Cassius and Brutus in the East and other passages.

[16] Freyburger and Roddaz 1991: xxiii.   [17] Berti 1988: 9–21.

[18] Freyburger and Roddaz 1991: xxiii.

[19] See Marx 1933: 323; Gabba 1955: 313, n. 4; Townend 1961: 232, 239–40; Rich 1990: 7; Noè 1994: 14–16, 159; Cresci 1998: 16–17; but Millar 1964: 84 and Manuwald 1979: 257–8 remain sceptical.

[20] Townend 1961: 230–7, 241–8.   [21] Devilliers 2016a: 235–6; Platon 2016: 653.

[22] Townend 1961: 232–4, 237–9. Lange (2016: 21) seems implicitly to identify Pliny as the common source of 62 (63).3.4–5.3 (Xiph.) and Suet., *Ner.* 13 dealing with the triumph of AD 63.

[23] Stuart 1904: 108, n. 1; Gabba 1957: 321, 337; Millar 1964: 54; Van Stekelenburg 1971: 79–87; Manuwald 1979: 271–2; Gowing 1992: 238; Rich 1990: 8; Kemezis 2014: 112, 113, n. 53, who also points out that some arguments, drawn from the speech *De imperio Cn. Pompei* ('On the command of Gnaeus Pompeius') dealing with the command against Mithridates, are included by Dio (36.31–36) in the debate on the command against the pirates.

[24] In the narrative of Cinna's conspiracy, Dio (55.14–22) inserts a debate between Livia and Augustus on the advantages of clemency, which is clearly inspired by Sen. *Clem.* 1.9; cf. Adler 1909; Millar 1964: 78; Rich 1990: 8; Sion-Jenkis 2016: 732. According to some scholars, however, Dio's knowledge of this work must have been mediated by another source: see Van Stekelenburg 1971: 130–41; Manuwald 1979: 120–2, 125.

Rather, he chose, combined, interpreted, and re-elaborated the rich material at his disposal, according to his own conception of human history and his own literary taste, to such an extent that it is almost impossible to detect any sure trace of a single source.

We now move into the high empire, the age of the Antonines and Severans. It has sometimes been considered that Dio may have used Arrian for Rome's relationship with the Parthians,[25] and some scholars have gone as far as to assume that Dio drew on Aelius Antipater's work on the deeds of Septimius Severus[26] or on Marius Maximus' biographies.[27] Agnès Molinier-Arbo has proposed that Dio's judgements on Perennis, Pertinax, and Didius Julianus, which are dramatically different to statements of the *Historia Augusta* on the same matters, prove that Dio was engaged in a polemic against his source Marius Maximus. But the arguments she produces are quite unconvincing: it is difficult to attribute to a supporter of Septimius Severus, as Marius Maximus was, a defence of Didius Julianus and denigration of Pertinax.[28]

The reality is that the only sources explicitly mentioned by Dio are two imperial autobiographies, those of Augustus[29] and Hadrian.[30] Proposals to identify in Dio's narrative some quotations from Septimius Severus's memoirs[31] and even from Caracalla's works[32] stem from the

---

[25] Bender 1961. Arrian is mentioned in 69.15.1 (Xiph.), but not as a source; the Suda attributes to Dio, probably wrongly, also a biography of Arrian (Millar 1964: 70; Sidebottom 2007: 59–60).

[26] Millar 1964: 22. More recently Moscovich (2004: 354) assumed that Antipater, the teacher of Caracalla and Geta, was one of Dio's informants inside the Severan court.

[27] Smits 1914: 29–35, 59–68, 94–103 (for Commodus). According to Chausson (1995: 193–4), the comparison between 76(75).10.3 (Xiph.) and HA, *Sev.* 15.6, who explicitly quotes Marius Maximus on Laetus' death, demonstrates that Dio drew on the biographer.

[28] Cf. Molinier-Arbo 2009: 288–9. Her hypothesis of Marius Maximus' ties with the Salvii Iuliani is at odds with the inaccuracy of *HA, Did.* 1.1, which considers Salvius Iulianus to be the great-grandfather of the emperor rather than his great-uncle or maternal uncle (cf. Chausson 2000).

[29] 44.35.3, where the number given by *RGDA* 15.1 is wrongly considered the number given 'by others'; 'probably Dio got his notes muddled', as correctly observed by Rich (1990: 7, n. 33); cf. Schwartz 1899: 1710; Bender 1961: 14; Noè 1994: 108; Cresci 1998: 18; France 2016: 775–6.

[30] 66.17.1 (Xiph.) (on Vespasian's death) and 69.11.2 (Xiph.) (on Antinous' death); cf. Schwartz 1899: 1710; Millar 1964: 34; Bender 1961: 17; Kuhn-Chen 2002: 135. According to Cortés Copete (2016), 68.4 (Xiph.) on Trajan's origin could be drawn from Hadrian's memoirs, in the same way that they are used and cited by HA, *Hadr.* 1.1 on Hadrian's origin.

[31] 76(75).7.4–8.4 (Xiph.), with the speech Severus made before the senate after his victory at Lugdunum, would derive from his memoirs. See also Schettino 2001: 547ff and Kemezis 2014: 58–59 (Urso 2016: 13–14 is more prudent). According to Zecchini (2016: 121), Severus would also be the source for Dio's pamphlet on the civil wars, which was subsequently incorporated into the *Roman History*.

[32] 79(78).2.1, so interpreted by Kuhn-Chen 2002: 135; Sidebottom 2007: 55. According to Westall (2012) (followed by Kemezis 2014: 77, n. 148), the information on the lion fighting beside Caracalla in 79(78).1.4–5 (Xiph.) came from the *Commentarius de bello Parthico*.

misunderstanding of two passages. Although Dio presumably knew Severus' autobiography, when he disputes the emperor's version of Albinus' death, he does not refer to that work, but rather to an official letter of the emperor to the senate, illustrated unambiguously by the fact that he uses ἔγραψεν ('he wrote'), not γράφει ('he writes'), as when he is citing Augustus' or Hadrian's memoirs.[33] As regards the alleged memoirs or *Commentarius de bello Parthico* ('Commentary on the Parthian War') attributed to Caracalla, I think I have shown that the βιβλίον (*biblion*, 'book') which Dio talks about at 79(78).2.1 was a pamphlet written against the emperor, not by him.[34] This passage is an incomplete sentence at the beginning of the *Codex Vaticanus graecus* 1288, which reports the original text of Dio's work: 'but this is the truth: for I have read the book written about him' (ἀλλ'ἀλήθεια· καὶ γὰρ τῷ βιβλίῳ τῷ περὶ αὐτοῦ γραφέντι οἱ ἐνέτυχον). Dio has personally read that *biblion* and adduces it as proof of what he had said in the lost preceding lines. According to Westall, περὶ αὐτοῦ refers to the Parthian War and γραφέντι οἱ indicates Caracalla as the author of the *biblion*. As a matter of fact, on the basis of its context, the narrative in the *lacuna* surely concerned Caracalla's relationship with the senators rather than his eastern campaign; therefore, περὶ αὐτοῦ means 'about him [sc. Caracalla]', and the author of the *biblion* cannot be the emperor himself.

This overview has highlighted two fundamental aspects of Dio's working method: his use of many different sources at a time, and his tendency to use them with a great independence.[35] Having undertaken his extensive research, Dio crafted his *Roman History* as an original narrative, wherein it is almost impossible to recognize a sole or prevailing source. This leads us to disagree with those scholars who have argued that Dio used one source at a time.[36] Instead, we must take at face value Dio's words when he declares that he had read practically everything and had chosen only what he

[33] Cf. Letta 2016a: 259, n. 54. This difficulty is clearly recognized by Chausson (1995), who is forced to say: 'C'est par recoupement [regarding the more explicit quotes in the *Historia Augusta* and Herodian] qu'on peut plausiblement supposer que le verbe ἔγραψεν utilisé par Dion fait référence à l'Autobiographie'.

[34] Letta 2016a: 263–6.

[35] See already Millar 1964: 85; Reinhold 1988: 6–7; Murison 1999: 12. Cf. Rich 1990: 5–6: 'he drew on a range of sources, and in shaping and adapting them contributed much of his own … and it is precisely this greater independence of treatment that is the distinctive quality of Dio's history'. See also Freyburger and Roddaz 1991: xxiv: 'il sélectionne ou élimine sans jamais suivre la même source continuellement, mais à partir des éléments bruts qu'il a rassemblés, recrée et reconstruit pour intégrer les différents donnés dans un ensemble cohérent qui lui est propre'.

[36] See e.g. Pelling 1982: 146–8; Swan 1987: 272–9; Swan 1997: 2530, 2548. Against this view see already Letta 2003: 599–600.

regarded as most significant.[37] We must think that Dio, in collecting his material over ten years, accumulated an enormous amount of notes, whose organizing criterion was basically annalistic; then, in drafting his text, he proceeded to choose the material which he regarded as the most appropriate for his narrative.[38]

III Documentary Sources

The prevailing scholarly view has long been that Dio used only literary sources and knew of the copious material traceable to documentary records such as *acta senatus* ('records of the senate') or *acta diurna* ('records of daily events') only indirectly, thanks to the mediation of his sources.[39] However, this perspective has been subject to a number of challenges over the years.[40] In particular, I have tried on several occasions to show that Dio made extensive use of archival documents, reading them directly and incorporating the information from them into his *Roman History*.[41] Dio's interest in documentary evidence for the Principate is demonstrated by the large number of references to *senatus consulta*, edicts, and official letters of emperors. The historian often points out procedural or ceremonial aspects of the promulgation of these documents and sometimes provides direct quotations.

In his narrative of the period from Augustus to Marcus Aurelius, Dio cites a wide range of documents.[42] There are exchanges of diplomatic correspondence between Augustus and Phraates V (55.10.20–21) and between Vespasian and Vologeses I (65[66].11.3 [Xiph.]); official letters

---

[37] F. 1.2; 53.19.6 and 73(72).23.5 (Xiph.); cf. Fromentin (2016: 180), according to whom it is necessary 'qu'on le prenne au mot et au sérieux'.

[38] Cf. Rich 1990: 6: 'in the writing stage Dio worked mainly from his own notes, only occasionally consulting the original texts'. On the ten years spent by Dio in gathering his material and the twelve spent in drawing up his work, see now Letta 2019b: 174–5.

[39] Millar 1964: 37, 62 (who also speaks of 'the fund of common knowledge'); Reinhold 1988, 8 ('there is no doubt that Dio, like Livy, was a "book historian"'); Reinhold and Swan 1990: 172–3; Rich 1990: 6, 8; Noè 1994: 21–2; Murison 1999: 12; Swan 2004: 23; Ferrary 2010: 10.

[40] Andersen 1938: 13–14, 22; Bender 1961: 17; Freyburger and Roddaz 1991: xxiii–xxiv; Cresci 1998: 17–18.

[41] Letta 1979: 139–48 for the contemporary age; Letta 2003 for Caesar's and Augustus' times; Letta 2016a for any kind of document in the whole work; Letta 2016b for the *acta senatus*; Letta 2019a for the *senatus consulta*. In my opinion, Dio's intention to use archival documents is stated in his methodological passage at 53.19.3–6: sentences as ὥς που δεδήμοται φράσω or δεδημοσιευμένα refer to published official documents rather than to historiographical narratives (Letta 2016a: 247). For a different view, see Adam Kemezis in Chapter 1 of this volume.

[42] I do not share the scepticism professed in this volume by Adam Kemezis in Chapter 1 (on some quotations from Caligula's or Severus' speeches) and Monica Hellström in Chapter 9 (on the acclamations of Nero at 62[63].20.6 Xiph.).

sent to the senate by various emperors, such as Tiberius (58.4.3), Caligula
(59.28.8),[43] Hadrian (69.2.3 [Xiph.], 69.14.3 [Xiph.]; 69.17.3 [Xiph.]),
Marcus Aurelius (72 [71].30.1–2 [Xiph.]); official speeches delivered in
the *curia* by emperors, notably Caligula (59.16.1–7), Claudius (60.5.5;
11.7), and Marcus Aurelius (72 [71].33.2 [Xiph.]), or by senators, as in the
case of Vatinius in Nero's time (62 [63].15.1 [Xiph.]); there is even the text
of the dedicatory inscription voted for Poppaea's temple after her death,
which may have been no longer extant in Dio's time (63.26.3 [*EV* 257^b]).
The number of direct quotations from official documents increases dramatically during the contemporary books of the *Roman History* which
cover Dio's lifetime. He preserves verbatim extracts of letters and speeches,
read and pronounced in the senate when Dio was surely far from Rome:
therefore, he is highly likely to have only subsequently drawn their wording
from the *acta senatus*. These include four letters of Caracalla,[44] four of
Macrinus,[45] and eleven of Elagabalus.[46] Perhaps the most significant is
a quotation from a letter sent by Caracalla from Alexandria, during his
turbulent stay in that city, with reference to the execution of some
ἐργολάβοι ('contractors') alluded also in a papyrus from Hermoupolis.[47]

In many cases, Dio's history provides numerous details which do not
appear in other sources regarding individual *senatus consulta* or specific
sittings of the senate. All scholars agree that the ultimate origin of these
details is in the *acta senatus*, but generally they prefer to assume that the
information has been mediated through one or more literary sources. One
example of this is Dio's description of the honours conferred on various
occasions to Julius Caesar.[48] Whereas Suetonius (*Caes.* 76.2) and Appian
(*BC* 2.106.440–443) provide a disordered list of the various *senatus consulta*,
Dio is the only author who provides a coherent series of three decrees,
arranged in a chronological sequence from 46 to 44 BC. These decrees show
an intensification in the divine language to describe Caesar. The

[43] Cf. Letta 2016a: 254: perhaps part of a speech delivered in senate by the emperor rather than of
a letter.

[44] 78(77).18.2 (Xiph.), 78(77).20.2 (Xiph.), 78(77).22.2 (Xiph.), 78(77).23.2-2^a (Xiph./*EV*); 79(78).8.3;
1.4–5 and 2.1; cf. Letta 2016a: 262–6.

[45] 79(78).16.5; 79(78).21.1–3; 79(78).36.1 and 79(78).38.1–2; 79(78).36.5; cf. Letta 2016a: 266–7.

[46] 79(78).16.5; 79(78).21.1–3; 79(78).36.1; 79(78).36.5; 79(78).38.1–2; 80(79).1, 2–4; 80(79).2.2; 80-
(79).4.4; 80(79).8.1; 80(79).18.4 (Pet. Pat. [*ES*]); 80(79).18.5 (Pet. Pat.[*ES*]); cf. Letta 2016a: 267–8.

[47] 78(77).22.2 (*ES*); for the papyrus see Musurillo 1954: 77–9, no. XVIII; cf. Letta 2016a: 262–3; in
general on the massacre, see Letta 2016c: 268.

[48] 43.14.3–6 (46 BC); 43.44–6 (45 BC); 44.4–7 (44 BC); 47.18–19 (42 BC). According to Ferrary (2010:
10) 'il n'est pas nécessaire de supposer … qu'il aurait directement consulté les *acta senatus*'; see,
however, Letta 2019a, passages 3, 4, 6 and 8, and what is said here below for the inscription on the
restored temple of Capitoline Jupiter.

inscription on the statue of 46 BC refers to Caesar as *semideus* ('semi-divine') (43.14.6), but by 45 BC he is styled *deus invictus* ('unconquered god') (43.45.3), and in 44 BC as *Iuppiter Iulius* (44.6.4).[49]

Equally meaningful is Dio's report of the sitting of the senate just following Augustus' death, with the reading of his βιβλία τέσσερα ('four volumes').[50] These were the instructions for the obsequies, the *Res Gestae*, the *breviarium totius imperii* ('account of the entire empire') and the *mandata*/ἐντολαί ('instructions') for Tiberius and the people. There is no contradiction with Suetonius (*Aug.* 101.6), who refers to *tribus voluminibus* ('three volumes') and Tacitus (*Ann.* 1.11.3–4), who speaks about a sole *libellus* ('book'), to which Augustus 'added his advice' (*addiderat ... consilium*), for that refers to the *mandata* Dio talks about. As Swan has shown,[51] in the senatorial session preceding Augustus' funeral ceremony all four βιβλία were read (as Dio states), whereas in the sitting after the funeral, only the *breviarium* and the *mandata* were (re-)read (thus Tacitus). I have argued, *contra* Ober, that the content of Augustus' *mandata* reported by Dio is fully credible.[52] According to Ober, the 'advance for keeping the empire within limits' (*consilium coercendi intra terminos imperii*) was a fabrication of Tiberius, presented by him as an oral suggestion received from the dying Augustus. In reality, during that sitting Tiberius did not take the floor, and Augustus' communications were read by the younger Drusus. As a matter of fact, the *mandata* reported by Dio are wholly believable, as shown by all of Augustus' previous strategic decisions. In his *mandata*, the first *princeps* indicated to his successors four boundaries (*terminos*) that he advised should not be overstepped: the Euphrates, the Danube, the Rhine, and the Ocean (that is the Channel). This was consistent with the renouncement of his desire to conquer the Parthian kingdom, Dacia, Germany (from AD 9), and Britain.

In addition, I believe that two important excursuses elsewhere in the *Roman History* result from Dio's thorough reading of Augustus' *breviarium totius imperii*.[53] The first one is the list of the provinces in 27 BC (53.12.4–9),

---

[49] Cf. Letta 2019a, on the passages 3, 4, 6. For *semideus* as the Latin equivalent of the Greek ἡμίθεος see already Ovid., *Met.* 1.192. As for Dio's Δία ... Ἰούλιον, it cannot mean *divus Iulius*, as maintained by Clauss (1999: 50 and n. 58): its obvious meaning as *Iuppiter Iulius* is confirmed by Dio's comment on Antonius as a sort of *flamen Dialis* (44.6.4: ἱερέα ... τινὰ Διάλιον).

[50] 56.31–33.   [51] Swan 2004: 214–15.

[52] Cf. Letta 2016a: 270–3 (against Ober 1982). See also Chapter 10 by Myles Lavan in this volume: though refusing Ober's suggestion that Tacitus could be referring to verbal advice to Tiberius, he concludes 'Augustus did not really leave such testamentary advice'.

[53] Cf. Letta 2016a: 273–5, where I argue that knowledge of the *breviarium*, which was easier to look at in the archives of the senate, and richer in details, may explain why Dio did not use in this context the *Res Gestae divi Augusti*. Cf. Chapter 4 in this volume, in which Christina Kuhn convincingly argues that Dio did know and use the *Res Gestae* in Tiberius' funerary speech for Augustus. I have already

where the apparent anachronisms stem from Dio's expressly declared effort to present the picture of the Augustan empire with reference to the present time; furthermore, he applies to 27 BC, that is, to the beginning of Augustan Principate, the picture he really drew from a document of AD 14 (the *breviarium totius imperii*).[54] The list of the legions in 5 BC (55.23.2–7) reflects Dio's intention of mentioning only the Augustan legions which still existed in his own time. Likely he compared the list of the Augustan *breviarium* with a Severan register (κατάλογος) alluded at 55.24.5. Hence there were some errors and uncertainties which remain in the *Roman History*.

Secondly, I would argue that the detailed description of Augustus' obsequies (56.34) is based on the minutes of the senatorial session in which the fathers added further provisions for the ceremony to those made by Augustus itself, as expressly asserted by Dio. The funeral oration was pronounced by Tiberius 'in accordance with a decree' (κατὰ δόγμα) (56.34.4); the bier was carried through the *porta triumphalis* 'in accordance with the decree of the senate' (κατὰ τὰ τῇ βουλῇ δόξαντα) (56.42.1); the funeral pyre was lit by the centurions 'just as they decided in the senate' (ὥς που τῇ βουλῇ ἐδόκει) (56.42.3); the duration of the mourning was respected 'in accordance with the decree' (κατὰ ψήφισμα) (56.43.1). Therefore, it is reasonable to suppose that Dio consulted the *acta senatus* in other similar circumstances, such as the divine honours for Augustus (56.46) and the decisions of the senate at the deaths of Livia, Drusilla, and Faustina the Younger (58.2.1–3; 59.11.1–5; 72 [71].27.1 [Xiph.]). It is also likely that he conducted archival research concerning the decrees in honour of Sejanus (58.4.4 and 7.4), Macro (58.12.7–8), Tiberius (58.12.8), Caligula (59.4.4), Claudius (60.22.1–2), Trajan (68.29.2–3 [Xiph.]), and on the occasion of the dedication of the temple of *divus Augustus* in AD 37 (59.7), and Tiridates' coronation (62 [63].6.1 [Xiph.]).[55]

I find it exceedingly difficult to believe that Dio's knowledge of all the above documents was only second-hand, mediated by literary sources, especially when we consider sections of his work dealing with contemporary history. In the Severan books, the use of the *acta senatus* is evident for the quotations of official letters of emperors read in the senate on occasions

---

pointed out above a similar Dio's strategy for Cicero's and Seneca's works, not directly utilized as historical sources but clearly echoed in fictional speeches.

[54] See now also Hurlet, in Bellissime and Hurlet 2018: xliii–xliv.

[55] Hurlet in Bellissime and Hurlet 2018: li adds 53.30.3 (honours for the physician Antonius Musa in 23 BC).

when Dio was certainly absent.[56] It is not possible to regard these quotes only as 'reports sent by friends' who had been present at the sittings,[57] because at least once Dio himself claims he had performed an archival search. At the time of his first consulate, he was able to check the enormous number of complaints for adultery submitted during Severus' reign.[58] Since Dio undertook systematic searches in the archives at his disposal during his consulship, I see no reason to rule out that he also did so in the course of researching the *Roman History*.

IV Dio's Use of Documents: Some Case Studies

Dio's use of the archives is confirmed by a series of passages in which the historian reports decisions of the senate which were never carried out, but which he assumed had been implemented. The best explanation for such cases is that Dio drew his information only from the reading of a *senatus consultum* in the *acta senatus*.[59] For example, the *Roman History* refers to the alleged enlargements of the *pomerium* (the sacred boundary of Rome) carried out by Caesar[60] and Augustus.[61] It is likely that Dio found only the *senatus consulta* authorizing these enlargements, and he wrongly assumed that they had been fully implemented.

The clearest example of this practice is perhaps the passage where Dio reports, among the honours voted for Caesar by the senate in 46 BC, the decision to replace Lutatius Catulus' name with Caesar's name in the inscription on the restored *Capitolium*, the Temple of Jupiter Optimus Maximus on the Capitoline Hill.[62] The historian explicitly states he has reported only the honours accepted by Caesar: it is clear therefore that he regards these decisions as carried out, even though we have it on the authority of Tacitus (*Hist.* 3.72.3) that 'among all the works of the emperors, the name of Lutatius Catulus remained up to the time of Vitellius' (*Lutatii Catuli nomen inter tanta Caesarum opera usque ad Vitellium mansit*). Dio probably drew on the *senatus consultum* for his information, which he could neither correct on the basis of a literary

---

[56] See a list of passages in Letta 2016a: 262–8.   [57] Cf. Millar 1964: 122.

[58] 77(76).16.4 (Xiph.); cf. Letta 1979: 121; Letta 2016a: 246, where I point out that the number refers to the entire reign of Septimius Severus, not only to the year of his first consulate. For the date of this first consulate (which I think was AD 222) see now Letta 2019b: 163–71 (esp. 169). For a different view both on Dio's first consulate (ca AD 205) and on the period to which the number of complaints refers, see Christopher Mallan (Chapter 12) in this volume.

[59] Cf. Letta 2016a: 250–2.

[60] 45.50.1–2 (Letta 2019a, passage 5); cf. Letta 2016a: 250; Maccari 2015: 320–2.

[61] 55.6.6 (Letta 2019a, passage 14); cf. also Rich 1990: 224.   [62] 43.14.6 (Letta 2019a, passage 13).

source, nor through autopsy of the inscription, which was impossible after the fire of AD 69. If then Dio relied only on a *senatus consultum* for this single decision, we have to assume that the same applies to the whole section on the honours voted by the senate to Caesar after the battle of Thapsus.

There are several other cases in which it can be assumed that Dio used senatorial decrees for his information. A *senatus consultum* entrusting to Munatius Plancus and Aemilius Lepidus the foundation of Lugdunum must be the basis of Dio's statement that both founded this colony, even though it was actually founded by Plancus alone.[63] The same explanation also applies to Dio's report of the decrees of the senate in 20 BC to celebrate the return of the Parthian standards. The historian records three decisions, which were certainly blocked by Augustus's veto: a temple to Mars Ultor on the Capitol, an arch, and an *ovatio* (a minor triumph) for Augustus on the occasion of his return to the city.[64] However, as Dio himself tells us, Augustus in fact entered the city by night, without any pomp and ceremony.[65] This proves that Dio used the *senatus consultum* including these three decisions for his narrative of the events of 20 BC; he missed, however, Augustus's subsequent waiver, even though he found in another source the news of Augustus entering the city by night among the events of 19 BC. The fact that he did not subsequently revise his work will have precluded the possibility that Dio noticed and eliminated the contradiction.[66] Dio's use of the *senatus consulta* continued throughout the Julio-Claudian period. Firstly, according to Dio (56.46.2), a lictor was assigned to Livia following a decision by the senate; however, we have it on the authority of Tacitus that Tiberius forbade it.[67] Secondly, Dio (59.28.2–3) states that in AD 40 Caligula actually built (ποιήσασθαι) two temples dedicated to himself, one by vote of the senate and the other on his own initiative and at his own expense on the Palatine. Suetonius, however, refers only to the temple on the Palatine. Therefore, it is virtually certain that the other one voted for by the senate was never built.[68] Dio's data-gathering criterion seems essentially annalistic, not only for the material drawn from literary sources but also for those drawn from documents.

[63] 44.50.3–6 (Letta 2019a, passage 7); on Plancus see Suet. *Perd. libr. rel.* (p. 289 Roth); *CIL* X 6087 = *ILS* 886; cf. Letta 2016a: 251 and already Carsana 2000: 206–7.
[64] 54.8.2–3 (Letta 2019a, passage 10); cf. Letta 2016a: 251–2. See especially Rich 1998 on Augustus' decision to stop all these actions.
[65] 54.10.4. [66] On the lack of any revision in Dio's *Roman History* see Letta 2019b: 175–7.
[67] Tac. *Ann.* 1.14.2; cf. Sion-Jenkis 2016: 733–4, n. 53.
[68] Suet. *Calig.* 22.4–7; cf. Letta 2019a, passage 45.

Therefore, as we have seen, he regarded that decisions on a temple, an arch, and an *ovatio* found among the material of 20 BC had been carried out, without noticing the contradiction with the news that Augustus entered the city by night found amongst the material of 19 BC.

This working method and the use of *senatus consulta* can also explain two of Dio's apparent mistakes as regards the dating of the events. Firstly, according to Dio (54.27.2), Augustus was named *pontifex maximus* in 13 BC, even though we know that the *comitia* voted on this matter only on 6 March 12 BC. As shown by John Scheid, Dio here refers to Augustus's nomination by the senate, interpreting it very probably as in immediate operation, in accordance with the practice of his own time, when only the senate decided.[69] In any case it is clear that here Dio's only source of information was the *senatus consultum* of 13 BC. Secondly, Dio (56.46.5) reports amongst the events of AD 14 the first *ludi Palatini* ('Palatine games') put on by Livia, but these were actually celebrated 17–19 January, AD 15.[70] These *ludi* would have been authorized by the senate, probably in the *senatus consultum* of 14 AD concerning the divine honours for Augustus, to which Dio referred in the previous lines. His discussion of the *ludi Palatini* with reference to AD 14 instead of 15 can thus be explained by the fact that the *senatus consultum* of 14 was his only source.[71]

It is even possible to detect use of the *acta senatus* in some of the speeches in Dio's history. In a passage of his speech against Cicero (46.4.2–3), Calenus says that Cicero's father owned some *fullonicae* ('fulleries').[72] This information agrees with Plutarch (*Cic.* 1.1–2), according to whom he was born and brought up 'in a fuller's shop' (ἐν γναφείῳ τινὶ). Filippo Coarelli has pointed out that Calenus knew Cicero's family well (cf. *Cic. Phil.* 8.13), and this allusion to *fullonicae* is likely to have been genuinely present in his original speech. According to Coarelli, Dio drew this information from an annalistic source, perhaps Livy, who could read the original speech.[73] However, it is equally likely that Dio read this speech first-hand in the *acta senatus*.

This conclusion allows us to suppose that Dio also conducted research in the *acta urbis* ('records of the city of Rome'). There are several cases that suggest this: Caesar's refusal of the royal title (44.11.3), the envoy of the newborn Drusus to his father's house (48.44.4), the privilege of *salutatio*

[69] Scheid 2016: 790. [70] Letta 2019a, passage 20.
[71] Swan 2004: 357 speaks only about an error of Dio. [72] Cf. *supra*, note 13.
[73] Coarelli 1996: 201.

accorded to Livia (57.12.2) and to Agrippina (61[60].33.1 [*EV* 231]), the straightening of a leaning *porticus* in AD 23 (57.21.5), the divulgation of the charges against Tiberius (57.23.1–3 [Xiph.]).

Finally, contrary to the views of many scholars,[74] I would argue that Dio cited epigraphic documents directly.[75] Among the most interesting cases are the epitaphs of Verginius Rufus (68.2.4 [Xiph.]), C. Sulpicius Similis (69.19.2 [Xiph.]), and the Batavian horseman who crossed the Danube fully armed in the presence of Hadrian (69.9.6).[76] We can also suppose autopsy of the inscriptions on the Augustan arch of Ariminum (53.22.1–3),[77] on an aqueduct, the *aqua Virgo* (54.11.7),[78] on the column of Trajan (68.16.3 [Xiph.]),[79] and on Commodus' colossus (73[72].22.3 [Xiph.]).

V Conclusion

In this chapter, I have argued that Dio's account of the Principate in the *Roman History* was based on extensive and thorough reading of historical and other literary sources, but he reworked the material he found there with great independence. Moreover, it is clear that he drew much information from systematic reading of the documentary sources, above all the archives of the senate, but also the *acta urbis* and inscriptions. In doing so, Dio followed the same criteria which applied to literary sources, making use of only a small portion of the material he had gathered. We should note that he probably employed only a fraction of the material he gathered, in accordance with his methodological principle of omitting meaningless details, so as not to bore his readers with long, tedious lists. Therefore, Dio's reports are mostly only selective samples, as he himself repeatedly points out, so that his reader could rest

---

[74] Stuart 1904; Millar 1964: 37; Bender 1961: 18–19; Swan 1987: 277–8; Reinhold 1988: 8–9.

[75] Letta 2003: 607–15; Letta 2016a: 280–8. On Dio's interest in the inscriptions see now Dalla Rosa 2017.

[76] Cf. *CIL* III 3676 = *ILS* 2558.

[77] Cf. *CIL* XI 365 = *ILS* 8. Dio's comment implies that he knew well the reading of this inscription, where Augustus took the credit for financing the restoration of all of Italian roads, whereas the historian knew that many of them were financed by *viri triumphales* ('triumphant generals') as testified by Suet. *Aug.* 30.3 and *Tib.* 1.7.57–62 and confirmed by some inscriptions (*CIL* X 6895, 6897, 6899–901 = *ILS* 889; *AE* 1969–70, 89).

[78] Dio says that Agrippa in 19 BC added to its name the epithet *Augusta*, a detail he could draw only from the original inscription, since afterwards the name *Augusta* was reserved only for the *aqua Alsietina*, as testified by Frontin. *Aq.* 11 and an inscription (*CIL* XI 3772a = *ILS* 3796).

[79] Cf. *CIL* VI 960 = *ILS* 294.

assured that there was extensive and detailed evidence behind all of his statements.[80] Dio was particularly interested in the honours and festivities for emperors, as well as institutional, procedural, and ceremonial aspects of the Roman state, which he collected with the intention of comparing them with his own time. This material allowed him to trace the foundation of the Roman imperial monarchy under Augustus and its development under subsequent emperors.[81]

---

[80] See the conclusion in Letta (2019a: 241–3). For some examples of Dio's selectivity see also Christopher Mallan (Chapter 6) in this volume on Dio's silence concerning Tiberius' *imperium* after his adoption.

[81] Cf. Letta 2016a: 288–9; 2016b: 257.

CHAPTER 4

'Now Comes the Greatest Marvel of All!' (79[78].8.2)
Dio's Roman Emperors and the Incredible

Rhiannon Ash

I Introduction: Too Much Fun?

In ancient historiography, writers narrating extraordinary incidents had to strike a delicate balance in positioning themselves on the spectrum between pleasure and utility.[1] On the one hand, material which could strike audiences as alluringly marvellous or miraculous risked debasing the weighty historical narrative in which it was embedded. This danger inspires historians to use various distancing strategies to offer pre-emptive defence. For example, Tacitus, describing serpents guarding the baby Nero, edgily adds that this was 'material beyond belief which was made to resemble foreign wonders' (*fabulosa et externis miraculis assimilata*) (*Ann.* 11.11.3).[2] A sense of trivialization could all too easily be triggered if a historian inadvertently stirred associations with lowlier genres such as paradoxography or the novel, or aligned the work discreditably with other subfields within the genre perceived as déclassé, such as sensationalizing Hellenistic historiography.[3] Duris of Samos (*fl.* 340–260 BC) is perhaps most conspicuously associated with this sort of historical writing: as Walbank enticingly summarizes, his surviving fragments narrate 'wonder-tales, travellers' yarns, prodigious births, scandalous customs, love-intrigues,

---

I offer my warmest thanks to the editors of this volume, Caillan Davenport and Christopher Mallan, both for the invitation to contribute to this project and for their invaluable comments on points of detail in this article. Their observations have improved it at every turn. In this article I use Cary's translations of Dio, but sometimes with substantial modifications.

[1] Walbank 1990 is crucial on the contrast between history for instruction and history for pleasure (a running theme in Polybius' history: 1.4.11, 2.56.11, 5.75.6, 6.2.8, 7.7.8, 11.19a.1–3, 15.36.3, 31.30.1).

[2] The story is also in Suetonius, *Ner.* 6.4 and Dio 61(61).2.4 (Xiph.) (although the epitomized story preserved here is less sensational than the Latin versions). Malloch (2013: 194–5) discusses this case. Tacitus elsewhere expresses concern about narrating *incredibilia* (*Hist.* 2.50.2; *Ann.* 4.11.3). Also important is Tacitus *Ann.* 4.33.3 (with Woodman 1988: 183–5), apparently denying that his narrative will give pleasure (particularly compared with Republican historiography), although inevitably there are deeper complexities in play.

[3] An important passage is Polybius 3.47.6–48, identifying Hannibal crossing the Alps as a setting where 'paradoxology' had disrupted proper historical writing by his sources. See Feldherr 2009a: 313.

elaborate costumes . . . or almost human animals, such as the dolphin that fell in love with a boy'.[4]

Yet ancient audiences certainly enjoyed a good story. Even austere readers of history were engaged by the selective inclusion of incredible tales. As Pliny observes while discussing historical writing: 'For people are naturally inquisitive and captivated by the narration of facts, however unadorned . . .' (*sunt enim homines natura curiosi et quamlibet nuda rerum cognitione capiuntur*) (*Ep.* 5.8.4).[5] Such curiosities certainly had an established place in historical narratives, particularly those with an eastern focus, such as Ctesias of Cnidus' *Indica* and *Persica* in which he 'brought the fabulous worlds of the East before his Greek audience's eyes'.[6] Equally, keeping fantastic subject matter within clearly designated, separate ethnographical sections of narrative or locating such stories on the distant geographical margins offered reassuring ways to defuse its disruptive potential and to make it safe.[7] Inclusion of this sort of entertaining material, if done deftly and selectively, could increase the chances of a historical narrative being enjoyed and therefore ultimately enhance its longevity. Sometimes too, conspicuously labelling an incident as unbelievable or marvellous could conveniently allow a historian to include a fantastic story while simultaneously denying responsibility for its inclusion by acknowledging its implausibility. Alternatively, ostentatiously and austerely parading the omission of fantastic material in one place in a narrative can give an author greater licence to include it elsewhere. An intriguing example of this technique is Xiphilinus' epitomized version of Dio, where Xiphilinus (51.6–20), omitting Dio's list (47.40–1) of signs and portents presaging the outcome of Philippi, praises Polybius as a better historian because he leaves out such material. As Mallan observes, 'Xiphilinus' objections appear largely superficial and do not represent a statement of authorial policy. In fact, Xiphilinus shows particular relish in repeating many of Dio's descriptions of portentous events'.[8]

---

[4] Walbank 1990: 259. Fairly typical of Duris of Samos' narrative mode is the detail that some Indians habitually copulate with animals, producing human–animal hybrids as offspring (*FGrH* 76, fr.48 = Plin. *HN* 7.30; with Beagon 2005: 160).
[5] Polybius 9.1.2–5 considers different consumers of historical narratives including 'the curious and lovers of recondite material' who enjoy reading about foundations of cities and colonies. Entertainment can take different forms for different consumers.
[6] Marincola 1997: 22.
[7] See Ash (2018a) on the geographical distribution of marvels in post-Domitianic literature. One intriguing author of marvel narratives is Vespasian's supporter, Licinius Mucianus. On his *Mirabilia* see Ash 2007.
[8] Mallan 2013b: 624.

This sort of delicate balancing act between pleasure and utility confronted all writers of history in the ancient world. Yet the methodological issues connected with narrating the marvellous become especially significant when we deal with authors whose text survives wholly or partly through excerpts and epitomes. Cassius Dio is just such a writer. His *Roman History,* opening with Aeneas' arrival in Italy and (in its final form) covering events until AD 229, was originally 80 books long.[9] The narrative is extant for the period 69 BC to AD 46 (36.1.1–60.28.1), albeit with significant lacunae for the material after 6 BC. For the period AD 46–229 (60.28.2 to the end of book 80), we depend on substantial fragments preserved by two main intermediaries. Firstly, we have Joannes Xiphilinus (11th century) whose epitome of Dio was commissioned by the Byzantine emperor Michael VII Doukas (ruled 1071–8). Xiphilinus condenses Dio's Books 36–80, which covered events running from Pompey to Severus Alexander (ruled AD 222–35).[10] Xiphilinus, who was engaged by the big personalities of the Roman past, is more than capable of 'amending or correcting Dio', which is 'a feature of his conscious display of his own erudition and authorial self-representation'.[11] Many (though not all) of Dio's embedded speeches ended up on Xiphilinus' cutting-room floor, although the epitomizer is often prepared to quote his source verbatim (including some of Dio's first-person interventions in the *Roman History*); and he seems to have had a copy of Dio's text close by as he worked.[12] Secondly, there is Joannes Zonaras (twelfth century), a Byzantine writer from Constantinople whose ambitious and wide-ranging *Epitome historiarum* (running from the 'creation' to 1118 and written after his withdrawal from public life to a monastery) drew on various writers (including Dio) for Roman history.[13] As Mallan reminds us, Zonaras 'should

---

[9] Dio's working practices and publication date involve some complex issues. There is no clear scholarly consensus. Swan (2004: 35) suggests that Dio in c. AD 223 published books 1–76, covering events until Septimius Severus' death (AD 211), but then circulated a second edition comprising books 1–80 and covering events until Dio's retirement in AD 229. Barnes (1984: 252) argues that Dio composed most of the work between AD 220 and 231 (or perhaps even later). Kemezis (2014: 282–93) summarizes the many different scholarly views about the date of composition and mode of publication, arguing (283) that Dio 'retained and exercised substantial editorial control until the entire history was circulated in the early 230s'.

[10] Swan 2004: 36. Dio became consul for a second time in AD 229 under Severus Alexander as the emperor's colleague. See further Davenport 2011. Mallan 2013b offers a balanced account of Xiphilinus' techniques in assembling his *Epitome*. See too Millar 1964: 195–203, Brunt 1980: 489–92, and Simpson in Chapter 13 in this volume.

[11] Mallan 2013b: 640.

[12] In Chapter 10, Lavan notes 'the extreme rarity of extended direct speech in the imperial books', probably reflecting Xiphilinus' interventions. Simpson in Chapter 13 discusses which speeches appealed to Xiphilinus.

[13] Swan 2004: 37. As Gowing (1997: 2561) clarifies, Xiphilinus' epitome is particularly important for the imperial period, while Zonaras 'although particularly useful for the reconstruction of books 1–21, is less important for the imperial books, since his work was both distinctly less ambitious than

be thought more as a serious historian rather than an epitomator'.[14] Certainly, he draws on an impressive range of Classical sources (including Herodotus, Plutarch, Xenophon, Josephus, Philostratus, and Cassius Dio) and he includes a preface, accentuating amongst other things the didactic purpose of his work.

Essentially, in a heavyweight genre such as historiography and within a long, detailed narrative such as Dio's *Roman History*, sensational episodes were especially likely to catch an epitomizer's eye and to offer attractive material for someone taking excerpts from a continuous narrative.[15] What this may mean is that in the *Roman History*'s excerpted and epitomized sections, there is potentially some warping in play: episodes about marvels may be disproportionately represented, potentially reflecting the individual interests of those mining the narrative more than the original balance of Dio's own account. Although we may have enough unmediated sections of the *Roman History* to be reasonably confident about Dio's broad working methods and historiographical priorities, nonetheless we must still be sensitive towards the superimposed agendas of Zonaras and Xiphilinus and how these might mediate our sense of Dio's priorities and his representation of particular emperors. So, as Gowing sensibly warns us, 'we cannot be certain … that Xiphilinus' account of the Neronian period transmits any of Dio's exact words'.[16] Similarly, Kaldellis cogently observes: 'We are the heirs and captives of the Byzantines' choices about what to copy and what not. Most of the extant historians survived not because of their style but their subject-matter, which reflected a distinctively Byzantine view of the past'.[17] Likewise, writers excerpting from continuous narratives are quite capable of omitting material which they found uninteresting or irrelevant. So, at one point, Xiphilinus candidly clarifies that he is omitting the names of those killed unjustly by the emperor Caracalla because, although Dio and his contemporaries knew

---

Xiphilinus' and, in parts, derived from Xiphilinus rather than from Dio directly'. See too Malik in Chapter 7 for Xiphilinus' treatment of Nero.

[14] Mallan 2018: 366. Zonaras himself seems to have used Xiphilinus for the period from Nerva to Elagabalus (Mallan 2018: 359, n. 34). On Zonaras and his sources see further Büttner-Wobst 1890: 121–70 and more generally Simpson (Chapter 13).

[15] A memorable example of this practice is Pliny the Younger excerpting passages from Livy's history after his uncle had left to inspect Vesuvius' eruption (*Ep.* 6.20.5). Perhaps the budding orator was extracting speeches, or even strange natural phenomena? Chew (2011: 233) notes the appeal and entertainment value of selecting discrete self-contained episodes from longer narratives: 'just like the Homeric bards, a travelling storyteller might not repeat an entire epic but select interesting episodes: Achilles hosts Priam, Odysseus fights the Cyclops, Penelope fools the suitors, or even Damayantī chooses Nala'.

[16] Gowing 1997: 2561. For Dio's account of Nero's reign, see Chapter 7 by Malik.

[17] Kaldellis 2012: 85.

and cared about these people, such victims were just names in his own day (78[77].6.1 [Xiph.]).[18]

Even given the *Roman History*'s fragmented state, it is still clear that Cassius Dio is intrigued by strange and marvellous phenomena of various sorts. The inclusion of such material does not just reflect the tastes of the epitomizers but forms an essential and distinctive part of Dio's historiographical toolkit. One facet of this is the deployment of striking dreams, including the ending of the whole *Roman History* where Dio focuses on his own dream telling him to finish by quoting Homer *Iliad* 11.163–4 about Zeus removing Hector from the dangers of the battlefield (80[80].5.3 [*EV/* Xiph.]). This ending is even more striking because Dio could so easily have included the Homeric quote without embedding it in a dream. Moreover, even before embarking on his ambitious historical narrative, Dio produced a much shorter work (not extant) about the signs and dreams forecasting Septimius Severus' principate (AD 193–211) – and he even sent this work to the emperor (73[72].23.1–2 [Xiph.]).[19] Dio's professed literary debut reveals (amongst other things) his interest in the predictive powers of extraordinary phenomena.[20] So too does his claim that he was inspired by *to daimonion* in a dream to write a monograph on the great wars and civil conflicts triggered by Commodus' overthrow (73[72].23.1–2 [Xiph.]).[21] Dreams are just one facet of Dio's broad interest in strange phenomena. Frequently in the *Roman History*'s surviving sections, Dio explicitly highlights the marvellous and the paradoxical and exploits such material in various creative ways, particularly when portraying emperors and their entourage, as we will see. Equally expressive is the issue of who does and does not receive such attention: for example, when Antoninus (Caracalla),

---

[18] Brunt 1980: 488–92; Mallan 2013b: 622–3.

[19] Dio's complicated attitude towards Septimius Severus has understandably attracted scholars' attention. Rubin (1980: 41–84) usefully analyses the various shifts and inconsistencies in Dio's position (essentially 'positive despite his severe criticism of some aspects of the Emperor's personality and of his reign', Rubin 1980: 51). Birley (1999: 103) notes how Dio accentuates the positive in presenting Severus' accession and 'fails to give an objective impression' of the event. Rantala (2016: 161) acknowledges that Dio eulogizes the emperor (77[76].16–17 [Xiph./*EV*] but also stresses that he is prepared to criticize him (particularly his relationship with the senate). Madsen (2016: 154) pinpoints in Severus 'a deceptive leader who did and said all the right things at the beginning of his reign, when he needed the senate's support in civil wars against Niger and Albinus; yet the moment he had freed himself from that opposition, he too turned on the senate in the effort to pave the way for his sons' succession'.

[20] Embedding omens and prodigies in historical accounts is a distinctive aspect of Roman historiography (Levene 1993; Davies 2004).

[21] Dio's account of this dream (normally dated between February and December AD 211) and surrounding events, preserved by Xiphilinus, is also important in analysing when he wrote the *Roman History* (Swan 1997: 2549–55). See Pelling 1997b on dreams in Roman historians more widely.

Dio's *bête noire*, falls physically and mentally sick, he is not given any divine response despite his copious and prolonged prayers and offerings to the most prominent gods (78[77].15.2–7 [*EV*/Xiph.]). Not everyone was ignored in this way, not least of all Dio himself, who emphasizes supernatural forces and the divine as crucial elements in influencing and guiding him. So, the goddess Tyche was the 'overseer of his life's course' (73[72].23.3–4 [Xiph.]). Both Dio's initial call to history and his decision to end the narrative by quoting Homer *Iliad* 11.163–4 (80[80].5.3 [*EV*/Xiph.]) were motivated (he explains) by divinely inspired dreams.[22] Dio's interest in such matters also generates some particularly vivid and memorable visual snapshots, such as the eerie detail that in AD 69 'many giant footprints' were seen on the Capitoline hill in Rome, 'presumably of some spirits that had descended from it' (64[65].8.2 [Xiph.]). Gods were traditionally perceived as bigger than humans and so naturally, the massive footprints imply that Jupiter (the biggest god of them all) has left his temple, disgusted at the destruction unleashed by the civil wars.[23]

Keeping these initial points in mind, let us first consider (as far as is possible) Dio's language of wonder and his patterns in identifying particular items as extraordinary, particularly in relation to the Roman emperors. Secondly, we will then turn to two case-studies of (epitomized) wonder-narratives to see what they reveal more broadly about Dio's exploitation of the marvellous in the *Roman History*.

II   A Lexicon of Wonder

What sort of language within the *Roman History* opens up the register of wonder? In the imperial books 53–80 the lexicon of wonder most frequently clusters around cognates of θαυμάζω (*thaumazo*, 'I wonder, marvel at'), namely ἐθαύμαζον (53.11.1, 53.31.1), θαυμαστόν (55.1.3, 56.4.2, 58.19.4), θαυμάσας (55.11.2, 67.18.1 [Xiph.], 76[75].4.7 [Xiph.]), ὃ καὶ θαυμάσειεν ἄν τις (56.25.7), θαυμασθῆναι (57.19.8), τῇ θαυματοποιίᾳ (57.21.5), σωτηρία θαυμασιωτέρᾳ (59.19.1), θαυμάζειν (59.19.4), θαῦμά (60.28.3), πῶς οὐκ ἄν

---

[22] See Marincola 1997: 48–51 on Dio's divine call to history.

[23] Cf. Ajax's belated realization that 'Calchas' was actually a god (Poseidon) because of his huge footprints (Homer, *Iliad* 13.68–75, with Janko 1992: 52 and Turkeltaub 2007: 57, n. 17). Heliodorus, *Aithiopika* 3.12.2 has a priest thoughtfully cite this very passage to explain how to recognize divine visitors. Hekster 2010 usefully discusses the phenomenon of 'reversed epiphanies' where gods appear solely in order to announce their departure. He highlights an incident before Commodus' death, when footprints of the gods were seen departing from the Forum (*HA Comm.* 16.2), and cites other important passages where tutelary gods abandon cities (Aesch. *Sept.* 217–18; Livy 5.21–2; Horace, *Odes* 2.1.25–8; Virgil, *Aen.* 2.351–2; Tac. *Hist.* 5.13.1).

τις ... θαυμάσειε; (68.13.2 [Xiph.]), and θαυμάσαι (76[75].16.1 [Xiph.], 79[78].7.1). A smaller but nonetheless significant 'family' uses forms such as παράδοξον ('incredible') (56.4.3), παράδοξος (72[71].8.1 [Xiph.]), παραδοξότατα (72[71].8.1 [Xiph.]), and παράδοξα (77[76].8.1 [Xiph.]). Finally, there are also expressions such as ἐν τοῖς παραλόγοις ('in extraordinary situations') (56.44.2), ἔξω τοῦ νενομισμένου ('out of the ordinary') (57.12.4), and καταπλαγῆναι ('to be amazed') (62[63].7.1 [Xiph.]). Naturally, as the *Roman History* is increasingly articulated through epitomizers, it is difficult to distinguish clearly between Dio's own language and that of third parties, but generally this is the kind of terminology which signals wonder and crosses the boundary between the epitomized and non-epitomized parts of the work.[24]

Greek and Roman authors can use a range of devices to signal that the narrative is entering the realm of wonders. Sometimes incidents can be pointedly offset from the main narrative and formally labelled as marvellous even before an author showcases them. This technique deploys an enticing narrative 'hook' to draw audiences into the anecdote. By preemptively categorizing something as amazing, an author can raise our expectations (whatever the reality).[25] Such episodes are often presented as distinct narrative units with a clear beginning, middle, and end, while the narrative's forward momentum is temporarily suspended and the author's powers of description are put on display. In these cases, the authorial intervention (whether Dio's or his epitomizers') is partly a *captatio beneuolentiae* at an episode's start either to entice readers or to signal unease about something odd which might demean the grandeur of historiography (of course, the intervention could serve both purposes). So, when Dio describes Aelius Gallus' soldiers invading Arabia (24 BC), he signals that they will suffer 'a disease unlike any of those commonly encountered' (τὸ δὲ δὴ νόσημα οὐδενὶ τῶν συνήθων ὅμοιον) (53.29.5). As Rich observes, 'Dio is only really interested in the disease, a congenial topic for a historian who took Thucydides as his model'.[26] Dio is more restrained when describing ambassadors from India ('the first Roman diplomatic contacts with India'),[27] who brought tigers as a gift (allegedly then seen in Rome for

---

[24] Broadly speaking, Books 53 to 60.28.1 are preserved in Dio's words (albeit with some lacunae) and Books 60.28.2–80 are relayed by epitomizers and in *excerpta*.

[25] Conversely, Dio sometimes signals that we should *not* be surprised: when Nero marries Sporus, Dio says that we should not be amazed, given Nero's sexual abuse of young boys and girls tied to stakes in the arena (62[63].13.2 [Xiph.]). Or when discussing the Nile's source and mount Atlas, Dio urges that 'nobody should be surprised if we have discovered things unknown to the ancient Greeks' (θαυμάσῃ μηδεὶς εἰ τὰ τοῖς ἀρχαίοις Ἕλλησιν ἄγνωστα ἐξηυρήκαμεν) (76[75].13.5 [Xiph.]).

[26] Rich 1990: 165.   [27] Rich 1990: 185.

the first time). Included in their entourage was a boy without arms resembling one of the Hermae who used his feet like hands, whether to fire a bow or even to play a trumpet. There was surely some authorial scope here for accentuating amazement, but Dio's tone is conspicuously sober, even tetchy: 'I do not know how he did this: for I just write what is told' (οὐκ οἶδ' ὅπως· γράφω γὰρ τὰ λεγόμενα) (54.9.9). Perhaps the boy is so obviously strange that highlighting this was unnecessary; or Dio may have wanted to be economical with candid expressions of amazement to prevent them from becoming hackneyed.[28] In historiographical terms, it pointedly shaped the relationship between a historian and his readers to tone down the register of the marvellous when relaying material about India – a geographical region associated *par excellence* with the paradoxical. Less is more.

Elsewhere, some marvels are insistently defined as such and presented structurally in ways which draw attention to them. So Dio first gives a cluster of extraordinary material which presaged Domitian's end (67.16 [Xiph.]) and then pre-emptively flags up one more 'most astonishing fact' (τι . . . παραδοξότατον) (67.17.1 [Xiph.]). However, he then plays with his readers by announcing that he will only relay this extraordinary story after narrating Domitian's death. After whetting our appetites with this advance notice, he then narrates the murder and enticingly emphasizes for a second time (again, before giving any details) 'the matter which I said surprised me above everything else' (ὃ δ' εἶπον ὅτι ὑπὲρ πάντα τἆλλα θαυμάσας ἔχω) (67.18.1 [Xiph.]). The marvel in question turns out to be the strange incident when Apollonius of Tyana, having climbed a rock in Ephesus at just the moment when Domitian was being murdered, began to utter the exact words of those murdering the emperor in Rome.[29] Dio, anticipating a cynical response, then insists that this happened, although one might doubt it 'ten thousand times over' (μυριάκις) (67.18.2 [Xiph.]). This pointed offsetting of one story from the rest could suggest that Dio thought that it might test an audience's credibility; or perhaps more likely, the arrangement implies that he regarded it as particularly vivid and strange, more worthy of attention than all the other stories. Either way,

---

[28] Rich (1990: 185) suggests that Dio's account 'may derive ultimately from the eyewitness report of . . . Nicolaus of Damascus, the source of Strabo's similar account'. On Nicolaus' biography, see Toher 2009.

[29] Cf. Phil. *VA* 8.26, who has more emphasis on Apollonius' gestures and physical movements. Mallan (2018: 362–3) comments perceptively on the differences between the versions of this story in Zonaras (apparently citing Philostratus' account, but actually giving details which appear to derive from Dio) and Xiphilinus (preserving Dio's account).

the epitomizers appear to have preserved a deliberative narrative trajectory put together by Dio who (like Suetonius before him) saw the rich potential of assassination narratives for displaying his artistry and creativity.[30]

Dio's postponed but climactic presentation of the strange incident involving Apollonius of Tyana is an elaborate example of his narrative technique of highlighting wonder insistently at a pivotal point in his account, the end of the Flavian dynasty. Yet Dio also triggers amazement in more straightforward ways by pre-emptive labels elsewhere in his text. So he dubs 'worthy of amazement' (θαύματος ἄξιον) (65[66].3.1 [Xiph.]) the fact that in AD 70 the Lingonian leader Julius Sabinus assembled a military force and called himself Caesar; and he insists that the besieged people of Byzantium in AD 194 carry out a 'most terrible act' (δεινότατον ἔργον) by resorting to cannibalism (75[74].12.6 [Xiph.]). Another intriguing example of this technique of pre-emptive labelling is Dio's account of Julius Calvaster, whose life was saved 'in a most extraordinary way' (παραδοξότατα) when Domitian almost condemned him for participating in a revolt (67.11.4 [Xiph.]). So, when Calvaster was accused of having met suspiciously often with Antonius Saturninus (the governor of Germany who had revolted from Domitian), he saved himself by claiming that their assignations had been sexual, not revolutionary. A fringe benefit of this narrative gambit of explicitly labelling the incident as extraordinary before relaying it is that Dio also signals his awareness that the upcoming material was perhaps discordant with the dignity of historiography. In structural terms, this narrative technique has much in common with the fabulists' device of the *promythium*, the brief summarizing overview before the fable which prompts readers to decode the story in a certain way.[31] This in itself may hint at Dio's historiography suspending 'business as usual' and entering a different narrative realm associated with a different genre. Finally, the extraordinary salvation of one man, Calvaster, makes him stand out from the dismal anonymous crowd of unnamed victims punished by Domitian, whose total number (Dio clarifies) would be impossible to discover (67.11.3 [*EV*]).[32] The narrated incident signals the power of

---

[30] See Ash 2016 for Suetonius' narrative techniques in presenting assassinations of emperors.
[31] Libby (2010: 549, n. 11) considers the device in Phaedrus. The parallel technique is the *epimythium* concluding a fable. As Henderson (2001: 174) observes, 'compilers of literary fables vary their *pro-* and *epimythia* so far as is possible, but the staple fare is still bald declaration of a stark proposition', but he also acknowledeges the potential for such reassuring messages to get destabilized by fabulists.
[32] Dio's *aporia* recalls various epic devices for conveying the impossibility of expressing huge numbers. See further Gowers 2005: 171–2.

historiography to save individuals from obscurity and to confront tyrannical conduct with posterity's disapproval.

Elsewhere, Dio signals wonder and grabs attention by deploying rhetorical questions. When describing Trajan's stone bridge across the river Danube, he asks questions which presuppose that the answers are already clear:

> How could one not wonder at the expenditure lavished on the [abutments]? How could one not wonder at the way in which each of them was placed in a river so expansive, in water so swirling, and on such a muddy bed? (68.13.2 [Xiph.]).[33]

This presentation highlights what we might call 'oblique wonder', emphasizing not so much the object itself, but the mechanisms behind its creation as the marvellous element.[34] The stone bridge is the tangible legacy of Trajan's impressive command over resources (in this case, money) and of his engineers' practical scientific skills in completing the project in this challenging fluvial location. Yet for Dio the most extraordinary element is the less tangible reality of the imperial infrastructure which made the construction project possible in the first place. That assessment may reflect Dio's own experience as a senator all too aware of the practical challenges which can impede progress and bringing projects to fruition. As a narrative device, it may also involve a degree of *para prosdokian*, whereby the focal point of Dio's surprise (namely, the background circumstances rather than the bridge itself) is itself surprising for readers well versed in wonders.

Of course, Dio is certainly capable of embedding in his narrative mechanical devices which are extraordinary in and of themselves. A memorable example is (Zonaras' paraphrase of) Archimedes' various contraptions which allowed the besieged people of Syracuse to prolong their resistance to the Roman consul Marcellus and his army in 212 BC:

> Archimedes by means of his mechanisms suspended stones and hoplites in the air, suddenly letting them down and then drawing them up again. And he would lift up ships, even ones equipped with towers, by means of other devices which he dropped on them; and raising them aloft, would let them drop suddenly, so that when they fell into the water they were sunk by the impact. At last, in an incredible manner he burned up the whole Roman fleet. For by tilting a kind of mirror toward the sun he concentrated the sun's beam upon it; and owing to the thickness and smoothness of the mirror he

---

[33] πῶς οὐκ ἄν τις τὸ ἀνάλωμα τὸ ἐς αὐτὰς δαπανηθὲν θαυμάσειε; πῶς δ᾽ οὐκ ἄν τὸν τρόπον ὃν ἕκαστα αὐτῶν ἔν τε ποταμῷ πολλῷ καὶ ἐν ὕδατι δινώδει δαπέδῳ τε ἰλυώδει ἐγένετο;

[34] See Davenport in Chapter 8 of this volume on Trajan's bridge.

ignited the air from this beam and kindled a great flame, the whole of which he directed upon the ships that lay at anchor in the path of the fire, until he consumed them all. (Zonaras 9.4, extracting material from *Roman History* Book 15)[35]

Unfortunately, there is no way of telling in narrative terms how Dio originally presented this material, although it could have taken the form of a minicatalogue of clustered examples showcasing Archimedes' technical skills. The circumstances leading up to Archimedes' death when Syracuse was eventually sacked had become notorious, since they had already been narrated by many authors before Dio. Polybius' version (*Hist.* 8.3–7) describes Archimedes' devices in great detail and celebrates his skills: 'Such a great and marvellous thing does the genius of one man show itself to be when properly applied to certain matters' (8.7.7).[36] Yet since Dio's contemporary readers may have had jaded palates when it came to reading about Archimedes' spectacular contraptions at Syracuse, it may have required particular ingenuity to stir wonder. Certainly, this is an instance of a layered clustering of fantastic elements, where later authors variously exaggerate their descriptions to outdo their predecessors or import entirely new elements (such as the parabolic burning mirror) which do not feature in the earlier versions.[37]

One other important narrative device exploited by Dio involves the 'mediated wonder' where astonished characters *within* the text respond to events by demonstrating amazement. These internal viewers offer chronologically anchored astonishment, which external readers may or may not straightforwardly share.[38] For example, people are amazed (ἐθαύμαζον)

[35] καὶ λίθους γὰρ καὶ ὁπλίτας μηχανήμασιν ἀπαρτῶν καθίει τε ἐξαπιναίως αὐτοὺς καὶ ἀνέσπα ἀνέσπα δι' ὀλίγου. ταῖς τε ναυσὶ καὶ ταῖς πυργοφόροις ἑτέρας ἐπιρρίπτων ἀνεῖλκέ τε αὐτὰς καὶ μετεωρίζων ἀθρόως ἠφίει, ὥστε ἐμπιπτούσας εἰς τὸ ὕδωρ ῥύμῃ βαπτίζεσθαι. καὶ τέλος σύμπαν τὸ ναυτικὸν τῶν Ῥωμαίων παραδόξως κατέπρησε. κάτοπτρον γάρ τι πρὸς τὸν ἥλιον ἀνατείνας τήν τε ἀκτῖνα αὐτοῦ ἐς αὐτὸ εἰσεδέξατο καὶ τὸν ἀέρα ἀπ' αὐτῆς τῇ πυκνότητι καὶ τῇ λειότητι τοῦ κατόπτρου πυρώσας φλόγα τε μεγάλην ἐξέκαυσε καὶ πᾶσαν αὐτὴν ἐς τὰς ναῦς ὑπὸ τὴν τοῦ πυρὸς ὁδὸν ὁρμούσας ἐνέβαλε καὶ πάσας κατέκαυσεν.

[36] οὕτως εἷς ἀνὴρ καὶ μία ψυχὴ δεόντως ἡρμοσμένη πρὸς ἔνια τῶν πραγμάτων μέγα τι χρῆμα φαίνεται γίνεσθαι καὶ θαυμάσιον.

[37] Archimedes' devices (which 'caught the imagination of antiquity and are widely described', Walbank 1967: 71) also feature at Livy 24.34,1–16; Plut. *Marc.* 14–17 (*Marc.* 15: θέαμα φρικῶδες, 'a dreadful spectacle'); Silius Italicus 14.300–52. Cicero (*Fin.* 5.50) suggests that Archimedes was so absorbed in studying geometry that he even failed to notice that the Romans had taken the city. Valerius Maximus (9.8.7 ext. 7) gives a version of his last words. Pliny the Elder (*HN* 7.125) suggests that Archimedes was killed despite Marcellus' orders that he should be spared (cf. Cic. *Verr.* II.4.131 for Marcellus lamenting his death). On Archimedes' afterlife, see further Jaeger 2008 and Gowers 2010.

[38] In Chapter 10 of this volume, Lavan highlights the polyphony of embedded voices in Dio's text, which lends an intriguing 'interpretative openness' to his history. This reading can be extended to Dio's internal viewers.

(53.31.2) that Augustus, dangerously ill, did not name Marcellus his successor despite obviously favouring him. Or there is Tiridates' astonishment at viewing cities in Asia (AD 66) after visiting Rome: 'this only increased his amazement at the Roman empire's strength and beauty' (ὥστε καὶ ἐξ ἐκείνων τὴν τῶν Ῥωμαίων ἀρχὴν καταπλαγῆναι καὶ ἰσχύος ἕνεκα καὶ κάλλους) (62[63].7.1 [Xiph.]).³⁹ These examples involve particular reactions to specific events or experiences. Elsewhere, Dio embeds contemporaries' amazement in his narrative in a sustained and overarching way, generating an atmosphere reflecting a general ethos of wonder. So, in narrating Tiberius' principate, Dio pinpoints an important turning point:

> Tiberius changed so much after the death of Germanicus that although previously he had been greatly praised, at that point indeed he became much more a source of amazement. (57.19.8 [Xiph./*EV*])⁴⁰

What this conveys to Dio's readership is that after AD 19 Tiberius' contemporaries are in a constant state of considerable wonder at their strange emperor over a period of years, rather than being amazed by a single event or spectacle. Sometimes as the narrative approaches Dio's own era, he himself becomes one of the astonished internal viewers in his own text. In AD 200, so many athletes participated in a gymnastic contest 'that we were amazed how the course could contain them' (ὥσθ᾽ ἡμᾶς θαυμάσαι πῶς αὐτοὺς τὸ στάδιον ἐχώρησε) (76[75].16.1 [Xiph.]). Dio thus inscribes himself as eyewitness within his own text highlighting 'autoptic wonder'.⁴¹ Or in AD 196, Dio explains how he saw a curious fine rain resembling silver which fell from a clear sky in Augustus' forum and miraculously enabled him to coat bronze coins in silver (ὃ δὲ δὴ μάλιστα θαυμάσας ἔχω) (76[75].4.7 [Xiph.]). Here, he engagingly inscribes himself into his text as a kind of natural scientist. One of the most conspicuous places where Dio focalizes wonder through himself is his catalogue of the many astonishing portents which unfolded before the death of Caracalla in AD 217: 'At this point in my account, all manner of wonders come to my mind' (καί μοι καὶ ἐνταῦθα τοῦ λόγου θαυμάσαι πάμπολλα ἐπέρχεται) (79[78].7.1).

---

³⁹ The simple 'marvelling barbarian' awestruck at Rome's wonders is something of a stock character (e.g. Tacitus *Ann.* 13.54.3, with Ash 2018b: 153–4).

⁴⁰ οὕτω μετὰ τὸν τοῦ Γερμανικοῦ θάνατον μετεβάλετο ὥστε αὐτὸν μεγάλως καὶ πρότερον ἐπαινούμενον πολλῷ δὴ τότε μᾶλλον θαυμασθῆναι. On this passage, see Mallan in Chapter 6, although I interpret Dio's emphasis on wonder here as potentially more ambivalent for Tiberius' characterization after Germanicus' death.

⁴¹ See in this volume Davenport in Chapter 8 for Dio adopting the 'authorial persona of an eyewitness' and Mallan in Chapter 12 for how 'Dio weaves himself and his experiences into his narrative to a degree which is striking'.

These include the 'greatest' marvel (τὸ δὲ δὴ μέγιστον) (79[78].8.2) after
a chariot race when the crowd turned towards a cawing jackdaw and greeted
the bird (prophetically) as Martialis (the emperor's future killer). The finale
of this catalogue of prophetic wonders is his account of the emperor's
prophetic quotation from Euripides, which was addressed to Dio himself
at the Saturnalia in Nicomedia. Thus, Dio compellingly inscribes himself
into the text as a witness to validate this particular portent.

Finally, another potentially expressive narrative technique concerning
the marvellous is the question of where such episodes appear within
individual books. We have already seen one important example concluding
Book 67, involving Apollonius of Tyana in Ephesus and Domitian's
assassination in Rome. Binding together the ends of the book and emperor
like this illustrates wider patterns in Dio which Pelling has called 'bio-
structuring'.[42] Given the epitomized state of much of Dio's imperial
narrative (and consequently the floating and unanchored status of some
narrative units), we cannot always engage confidently with this presentational technique.[43] Even so, we have one powerful example opening Book
55 (and 9 BC, 'the year with which Livy's history ceases').[44] In a cluster of
portents foreshadowing the elder Drusus' death, Dio describes the general's unsuccessful attempt to cross the river Elbe during his final campaign
in Germany before setting up trophies and withdrawing:

> This was because a woman of more than human stature met him and said
> 'To where, I ask you, do you hurry now, insatiable Drusus? It is not your fate
> to see all these things. Go away. For the end of your labours and your life is
> now at hand'. It is astonishing that a pronouncement like this should be sent
> to anyone from the divine sphere, but I cannot disbelieve it, for what it
> foretold straightaway came to pass: Drusus hurried back and on the way,
> before reaching the Rhine, died from some disease. (55.1.3–4)[45]

Various aspects of this story are striking. It would be intriguing to know
Dio's source for this episode (also narrated much more succinctly at

---

[42] Pelling 1997a: 117–18. See too Devillers 2016b.

[43] Some surviving epitomized and excerpted material simply lacks book numbers. Swan 2004: 383,
n. 44: his appendix 15 (383–5) usefully summarizes the differences between the book numbers of
Boissevain's edition and Cary's Loeb edition. We do have some indexes (surviving for books 37–57,
59, 79), not by Dio and added later, which give a table of contents and list consuls.

[44] Swan 2004: 39.

[45] γυνὴ γάρ τις μείζων ἢ κατὰ ἀνθρώπου φύσιν ἀπαντήσασα αὐτῷ ἔφη "ποῖ δῆτα ἐπείγῃ, Δροῦσε
ἀκόρεστε; οὐ πάντα σοι ταῦτα ἰδεῖν πέπρωται. Ἀλλ' ἄπιθι· καὶ γάρ σοι καὶ τῶν ἔργων καὶ τοῦ βίου
τελευτὴ ἤδη πάρεστι". Θαυμαστὸν μὲν οὖν τό τινα φωνὴν παρὰ τοῦ δαιμονίου τοιαύτην τῳ
γενέσθαι, οὐ μέντοι καὶ ἀπιστεῖν ἔχω· παραχρῆμα γὰρ ἀπέβη, σπουδῇ τε ὑποστρέψαντος αὐτοῦ
καὶ ἐν τῇ ὁδῷ νόσῳ τινί, πρὶν ἐπὶ τὸν Ῥῆνον ἐλθεῖν, τελευτήσαντος.

Suetonius, *Claud.* 1.3), which seems to glorify (or reflect a positive tradition of) Drusus' generalship. So, this giant woman with a divine aura magisterially ordering Drusus to turn back at the Elbe conveniently justifies his suspension of campaigning.[46] This detail looks like a face-saving fiction with a panegyrical dimension, invented or embellished subsequently to please Tiberius, whose lightning dash to his dying brother constituted a famous *exemplum* of fraternal loyalty.[47] The story also aggrandizes Drusus by aligning him with Alexander the Great, who reached the Ocean only to hear a mysterious voice commanding him to turn back.[48] In this vignette, Drusus also emerges positively in comparison with Julius Caesar encountering the doleful apparition of the *patria* at the river Rubicon:[49] whereas Caesar transgressed and disobeyed, Drusus commendably listens and turns back.[50] Lucan's version of the apparition's short dissuasive speech at the Rubicon, with its anaphora of *quo* and appeal to citizenship,[51] evokes (amongst other texts) the emotive opening of Horace *Epode* 7.1 with its distinctive anadiplosis as the poet desperately tries to stop his fellow citizens from plunging into civil war.[52] The opening question of Dio's mysterious apparition – 'To where, I ask you, do you hurry now, insatiable Drusus?' (ποῖ δῆτα ἐπείγῃ, Δροῦσε ἀκόρεστε;) – seems to allude to both these texts, except that civil war is replaced with foreign campaigns, and Dio's Drusus trumps both Lucan's Caesar and Horace's reckless fellow Romans by nobly resisting the impulse for further warfare. It is also striking that Dio only says broadly that Drusus died from illness. He thereby withholds the rather degrading details in Livy that Drusus had a terrible accident and suffered a grisly decline for thirty days after a horse fell on him

---

[46] Cf. Hellström in Chapter 9 of this volume on hints that the 'grim maiden' who entered the arena and started to abuse Cleander was actually the goddess Roma.

[47] Dio also includes some negative material about the elder Drusus at the opening of Book 55. Timpe (1967) thinks that Dio used a Tiberian source which had some reservations about Drusus' impetuous generalship.

[48] Sen. *Contr.* 7.7.19. Tacitus similarly aligns the elder Drusus and Alexander confronted by *Oceanus* (*Germ* 34.2). Malloch (2013: 309–10) assembles examples of similar apparitions. Mallan 2017b considers the Alexander-motif in Dio.

[49] Luc. 1.185–94; Suet. *Iul.* 32; cf. Plut. *Caes.* 32. See Pelling 1997b: 200–1; Roche 2009: 206–10; and Beneker 2011 (74: 'It is only in the literature of the Neronian period and later that we find fully developed "Rubicon narratives"').

[50] Strikingly, Dio himself (41.4) narrates the civil war's opening without mentioning the Rubicon (Beneker 2011: 75).

[51] Luc. 1.190–2: 'To where do you march further on? To where do you carry my standards, men? If you come lawfully, if you are citizens, only this far is it permissible to come' (*quo tenditis ultra? | quo fertis mea signa, uiri? si iure uenitis,| si ciues, huc usque licet*).

[52] Hor. *Epod.* 7.1: 'To where to where do you wicked men rush?' (*quo quo scelesti ruitis?*).

and broke his leg.[53] By prominently placing this marvel of the female apparition at the book's opening, Dio both aggrandizes a member of the imperial household and sets up enveloping structural connection between his death in 9 BC and Augustus' death which ends Book 56. By opening Book 55 with Drusus' death, Dio may also be thoughtfully considering those (bilingual) readers coming to his *Roman History* from Livy's *Ab Vrbe Condita* where Drusus' death is (perhaps unintentionally) the last event narrated in Book 142.[54] Such readers of Livy, looking for a subsequent historical narrative as a continuation, might find it easier to begin with a new book, and they might appreciate starting with a striking story. Hence, Dio opens Book 55 with a convenient dovetail joint between *Ab Vrbe Condita* and the *Roman History* – and a marvellous and spectacular incident at the river Elbe.[55]

III   Case Study One: The Miraculous Rainstorm

Perhaps the most memorable marvels in the *Roman History* are when Dio presents dramatically developed and complex wonder-stories which stand out from the surviving main narrative. Two examples are particularly conspicuous. The first happens during what turns out to be an extraordinary battle between the Romans and the Quadi on the Danube under the leadership of Marcus Aurelius (AD 172).[56] The backdrop to this battle was a period of intense crisis after legions from the Rhine and Danube were transferred to confront a serious threat from the Parthians early in Marcus Aurelius' principate. This hole in the Roman defences proved too tempting for the northern tribes, who opportunistically invaded late in AD 166 or early in AD 167. The Romans' ability to respond effectively to this second emergency was then seriously compromised by a devastating outbreak of plague which crossed the empire with the soldiers who had been its first unlucky victims as they returned from the east.[57]

---

[53] Livy *Per.* 142.
[54] See Letta in Chapter 3 of this volume for the consensus that Dio knew Livy well and occasionally used him and Malik in Chapter 7 for his fluency in Latin.
[55] Even if this was not Dio's main concern, the person who later compiled the synopsis of Book 55 emphasizes that Drusus' death opens the book.
[56] Dio dates the battle to AD 174, but scholars propose that AD 172 is correct (Birley 1987: 171; Salomies 1990: 107; Israelowich 2008: 85, n. 7).
[57] Birley (1987: 149–50) describes the plague's route and impact, which may have been long-lasting, particularly in Egypt, as van Minnen (2001) suggests from analysing *P.Oxy.* LXVI 4527. Galen observed it first-hand. See further Littman and Littman 1973.

It was during the subsequent campaigns to confront the northern invaders that this battle against the Quadi took place.[58] The wonder itself resulted in an 'unexpected victory' (νίκη παράδοξος), which Dio explicitly attributes to divine intervention (παρὰ θεοῦ) (72[71].8.1 [Xiph.]). The point about divine provenance is further underscored by emphatic repetition even before the narrative proper begins – 'the divine power saved the Romans in a most unexpected way' (τοὺς Ῥωμαίους παραδοξότατα τὸ θεῖον ἐξέσωσε) (72[71].8.1 [Xiph.]) – through using a proleptic and pro-mythic narrative device like the one introduced during Domitian's assassination. Dio then (finally) explains what happened. While the battle is in full swing, the Romans are surrounded by the (numerically superior) Quadi, who, in a curious twist, abruptly stop fighting, hoping that the stifling conditions will force the trapped and thirsty Romans to surrender, and effectively do their work for them:

> So, while the Romans, in terrible trouble from fatigue, wounds, the heat of the sun, and thirst, were able neither to fight nor retreat, but stood in the battle line and at their posts, being scorched by the heat, suddenly many clouds gathered and a mighty rain, not without divine inspiration, burst upon them. Indeed, there is a story that Arnuphis, an Egyptian magician who was a companion of Marcus, had invoked by means of enchantments various deities and in particular Hermes, the god of the air, and by this means attracted the rain. (72[71].8.3-4 [Xiph.])[59]

This intriguing sequence illuminates Dio's historiographical concerns in various ways. The serendipitous rainstorm is immediately identified (in litotes) as heaven-sent and as indicating divine favour towards the Romans.[60] It is triggered by the Egyptian *magus* Arnuphis' successful intervention to win help from Hermes Aerios – Mercury (or so the story goes).[61] Dio's tentative

---

[58] See Birley (1987: 159–83) on the northern wars (esp. 172–4 on this battle).

[59] τῶν οὖν Ῥωμαίων ἐν παντὶ κακοῦ καὶ ἐκ τοῦ καμάτου καὶ ἐκ τῶν τραυμάτων τοῦ τε ἡλίου καὶ τοῦ δίψους γενομένων, καὶ μήτε μάχεσθαι διὰ ταῦτα μήτε χωρῆσαί πη δυναμένων, ἀλλ᾽ ἔν τε τῇ τάξει καὶ τοῖς τόποις ἐστηκότων καὶ κατακαιομένων, νέφη πολλὰ ἐξαίφνης συνέδραμε καὶ ὑετὸς πολὺς οὐκ ἀθεεὶ κατερράγη· καὶ γάρ τοι λόγος ἔχει Ἀρνοῦφίν τινα μάγον Αἰγύπτιον συνόντα τῷ Μάρκῳ ἄλλους τέ τινας δαίμονας καὶ τὸν Ἑρμῆν τὸν ἀέριον ὅτι μάλιστα μαγγανείαις τισὶν ἐπικαλέσασθαι καὶ δι᾽ αὐτῶν τὸν ὄμβρον ἐπισπάσασθαι.

[60] Israelowich (2008) crucially discusses the political and historiographical conflicts surrounding the marvel, which has understandably attracted scholarly interest, including the substantial monograph by Kovács 2009. This current article cannot address all the significant issues of interpretation associated with the timely rainstorm but aims primarily to consider its coherence with wider narrative patterns about marvels within Dio's *Roman History*.

[61] 'The coins that were struck to commemorate the event bore the legend RELIG(io) AVG(usti) with a depiction of a Graeco-Roman Hermes-Mercury and an Egyptian temple, hinting that some connection to the Egyptian priest was acknowledged' (Israelowich 2008: 88).

introduction of this detail is a classic case of a historian distancing himself
from potentially controversial material by attributing it to an anonymous
third party. Yet why is Dio so cautious about this explanation that the
Egyptian Arnuphis prompted the miraculous rainstorm? After all, Dio is
clearly completely untroubled by the basic notion that the rainstorm was
heaven-sent. That is not the problem. Perhaps the real discomfort for him is
the idea that the *princeps* Marcus Aurelius habitually travelled with an
Egyptian *magus*. This is an exotic detail which some Roman readers might
have regarded as controversial or demeaning to the reputation of an emperor
whom Dio generally favoured. Like many ancient historians, Dio paid attention to which emperors had the right sort of advisors and which did not: so,
his hostile comments on Sempronius Rufus, the eunuch, juggler, and magi-
cian from Spain who advised Caracalla, show this phenomenon at work
(78[77].17.2 [*EV*/Xiph.]).[62] Dio's discomfort about Arnuphis was probably
further intensified by his particular prejudices against the Egyptians as
a people.[63] In the short term, there were also powerful political reasons why
Marcus Aurelius might have wanted to play up links between an Egyptian
magus and the rain miracle. For in spring AD 175, he faced another crisis when
a challenger, Avidius Cassius (born in Egypt, c. AD 130), had declared himself
emperor, actually ruled for three months, and controlled much of the Roman
east. As Israelowich suggests, Marcus Aurelius' allocation of the pivotal role to
the Egyptian *magus* in the rain-miracle 'was useful in Egypt in order to
demonstrate to the local population and legions that a local deity favoured
his reign, protected his army on the battlefield, and actively intervened to
guarantee its victory'.[64] A short-term crisis therefore crucially underpinned
one important detail of the story.[65]

   Yet in the longer term, historiographical concerns exerted a significant
influence. Dio's most compelling reason for his cautious presentation must
be that in the years after AD 172, this marvel's provenance became significantly
contested, as different groups (pagan and Christian) tussled with each other in

---

[62] See in this volume Saylor Rodgers (Chapter 11) on the damage done to emperors' reputations
   through unsuitable companions and advisors, and Mallan (Chapter 12) for some memorable
   examples of how Dio *could* have responded to Arnuphis if he had been attached to a less respected
   emperor.
[63] Throughout the *Roman History* 'Dio's anti-Alexandrian, anti-Egyptian prejudices abound'
   (Reinhold 1988: 141), although since he was a high-ranking senator, he had never been to Egypt
   himself (Meyer 1988: 227–8).
[64] Israelowich 2008: 97.
[65] Caillan Davenport points out to me that the rain miracle is also a convenient way to justify Marcus
   Aurelius accepting the acclamation as *imperator* by the soldiers without first seeking the senate's
   approval.

trying to allocate their own respective gods as the miracle workers.[66] On the one hand, coins minted in AD 173–5 by Marcus Aurelius bearing the legend RELIG(io) AVG(usti) and depicting Mercury seem to give credit to this god for some kind of helpful intervention, and some scholars have connected this with the rain miracle.[67] More certainly, one panel (Scene XVI) on the Aurelian column (voted by the senate in AD 175 but not finished until AD 193) ascribed the miracle and victory to an unidentifiable but vividly depicted deity with long, flowing hair (Figure 4.1).[68] On the other hand, the bishop and Christian apologist Apollinaris of Hierapolis (preserved at Eusebius, *HE* 5.5.1–2) wrote a treatise addressed to Marcus Aurelius (AD 176) stridently claiming that the *Christian* god had intervened in the battle after responding to the (Christian) legionaries, thereby allowing further Christian writers to appropriate the marvel over the coming centuries.[69] Millar suggests that the detail about Arnuphis the rain-conjuror's intervention reflects the 'official version' of the strange events on the Danube.[70] If Marcus Aurelius was indeed 'one of Dio's favourite emperors',[71] Dio's distancing formulation could be intended to preserve at least some veneer of historiographical independence, or at least to signal his awareness that the divine originator of this marvel is contested.[72]

---

[66] Kovács (2009: 23–93) assembles and discusses thirty-nine written sources about the rain miracle, running from the earliest surviving reference by Tertullian (*Apol.* 5.25, a brief mention in c. AD 197 of the 'rain obtained by the prayers of the Christians who happened to be soldiers' [*Christianorum forte militum precationibus impetrato imbri*]) through to the poetic chronicle of the monk Ephraim written in Greek in c. 1313. Amongst the earliest sources, Dio's version is the most extensive and ambitious.

[67] *BMCRE* IV (Marcus Aurelius) 1441, 1442, 1443. The coins depict a temple with four columns, viewed from the front, on a podium of four steps, with a statue of Mercury wearing a *petasus* and a short robe, holding a purse in his right hand and a caduceus in his left hand. The columns have heads at the top. The semicircular pediment contains a tortoise, cock, head, ram, head *petasus*, winged caduceus, and purse. On these coins see Kovács (2009: 107–11), who remains cautious about whether they are conclusively associated with this rain miracle.

[68] Moore (2012) confirms the column's completion date through an inscription (*CIL* VI 1585a-b) about the imperial freedman Adrastus, appointed as watchman (itself a significant detail), who requested land near the column and materials for building a house (suggesting a need for long-term vigilance). Pirson (1996: 174) comments on the column's 'reassuring images of constantly superior Romans and defenceless, beaten and humiliated barbarians' as reflecting contemporaries' 'need for self-affirmation in insecure times'. Interestingly Kovács (2009: 109) notes that the contentious figure of Arnuphis does not seem to be depicted on the Aurelian column.

[69] Israelowich (2008: 86–91) traces the various tussles between the sources, noting (90) that Apollinaris' report is 'historically inaccurate' because the twelfth legion from Melitene in Cappadocia could not have been active on the Danube or manned by Christians. That detail certainly did not stop Apollinaris from trying to lay claim to the miracle.

[70] Millar 1964: 179.

[71] Madsen 2016: 152. See too in this volume Kemezis (Chapter 1) on the 'virtuous' Marcus Aurelius, Davenport (Chapter 8) and Rodgers (Chapter 11) on his positive characterization.

[72] Even so, he appears to have failed. Marincola (1997: 200) highlights his 'loss of formal objectivity' particularly when it came to emperors.

Figure 4.1 Scene XVI from the Column of Marcus Aurelius in Rome, depicting the rain miracle

One reader who reacted particularly badly to Dio allocating a pivotal role to Arnuphis was the epitomizer Xiphilinus, who dramatically suspends the narrative at this point to intervene stridently in the first person and to challenge Dio's explanation for the rainstorm. In a long digression covering a whole chapter (72[71].9 [Xiph.]), Xiphilinus indignantly claims that Dio was deliberately misrepresenting the facts: instead, he claims, a legion of Christians from Melitene had prayed to their god to save the army by the rainstorm. This remarkable intervention apparently won them from Marcus Aurelius the honorific title 'Thundering legion' (72[71].9.6 [Xiph.]). As the nephew of Patriarch John VIII of Constantinople, Xiphilinus apparently felt aggrieved that Dio had removed credit for triggering the miracle from the Christian soldiers and attributed it instead (however cautiously) to the Egyptian Arnuphis.[73] Xiphilinus prefers to endorse the Christian tradition which attributed the rainstorm to the Christian god.[74]

---

[73] See Mallan (2013b: 613, n. 8) on the family relationship between nephew and uncle.

[74] Mallan (2013b: 642) suggests another reading of the rain miracle in Xiphilinus as 'not so much a case of Christian polemic one thousand years too late, but rather as a vehicle for describing an emperor in

The scale and *indignatio* of Xiphilinus' intervention are striking, particularly since the story is not yet even finished. After dramatically undermining the credibility of the narrative which underpins his own account, Xiphilinus then hands back the narrative to Dio for the story's final part (72[71].10 [Xiph.]). Initially, the focus is on the Romans guzzling down water and even their own blood:

> And when the barbarians now charged upon them, they drank and fought at the same time; and some, becoming wounded, actually gulped down the blood that flowed into their helmets, along with the water.[75]

This strange, disturbing image of thirsty Romans drinking their own blood certainly vividly expresses their desperation. Given the divine backdrop (and Xiphilinus' emphasis on Christianity) and the blood's apparently restorative power, the detail may even allow scope for comparing transubstantiation, except that here the soldiers drink their own blood rather than symbolically imbibing Christ's blood. However that may be, in broad terms the brave soldiers drinking their own blood invite readings of the battle which allow Christianized readings of the episode (whether positively or negatively).[76] This sort of detail can also be compared with battle scenes from epic. For example, Virgil describes the Trojan fighter Dryops' death: 'so Dryops struck the ground with his forehead and vomited up thick gore' (*at ille | fronte ferit terram et crassum uomit ore cruorem*) (*Aen.* 10.348–9). Whereas the dying Dryops vomits out his own blood, Dio's soldiers by drinking their own blood are restored to life.[77] We can also compare Juvenal's account of a clash (AD 127) between the inhabitants of two Egyptian towns, Ombi and Tentyra, which culminates in an act of cannibalism during the fighting (15.33–92) – Juvenal pointedly calls this incident *mirandum* (15.27). One man even draws his fingers over the ground to taste the blood when the cadaver has been eaten (15.93) – a chilling detail.[78]

Yet Dio's story of the battle on the Danube is not quite finished. While the Romans are busy drinking down water and blood, they almost succumb once again to the barbarian attack, until a miraculous storm erupts and pelts the barbarians with thunderbolts:

---

terms that were recognizable for an eleventh-century audience, this is, as an appropriately pious monarch'.

[75] καὶ τῶν βαρβάρων σφίσιν ἐπιδραμόντων ἔπινόν τε ὁμοῦ καὶ ἐμάχοντο, καὶ ἤδη γέ τινες τιτρωσκόμενοι τό τε αἷμα περιχεόμενον ἐς τὰ κράνη καὶ τὸ ὕδωρ ἅμα ἀνερρόφουν.

[76] See Wagemakers (2010) on imputations of cannibalism against early Christians.

[77] As Harrison (1991: 163) notes, '*cruor* is generally used like Homeric βρότος for fresh-spilt blood'.

[78] On this incident, see Ash 2018: 140–4.

Thus, it was possible to see in one and the same place water and fire simultaneously descending from the sky: while those on the one side were being drenched and drinking, the others were being consumed by fire and dying. The fire did not touch the Romans and, if it fell anywhere among them, it was immediately extinguished, but the shower did the barbarians no good, but, like so much oil, actually fed the flames that were consuming them, and they had to search for water even while being drenched with rain. Some wounded themselves in order to quench the fire with their blood, and others rushed over to the side of the Romans, convinced that they alone had the saving water. (72[71].10.3 [Xiph.])[79]

What started out as a battle narrative on the human plane now spills over and extends vertically into the sky, becoming a massive elemental conflict between hostile fire (attacking the Quadi) and benign water or liquid (supporting the Romans).[80] What are we to make of this? One could compare Stoic theories of cyclical *ekpurosis* or conflagration, where the world is periodically and cathartically destroyed by cleansing fire. Yet in this battle-scene, the damage inflicted by the fire is highly partisan, targeting only the 'barbarians' (as the Quadi are called). This precise delivery of punitive thunderbolts suggests (reassuring) divine justice and depicts a controlling force which counteracts, for example, Lucretius' argument (*DRN* 6.387–422) that it is wrong to assume that Jupiter unleashes thunderbolts because they fail to strike the guilty.[81] At the very least, the spectacular display of violence descending from the sky seems to endorse the reading of this battle on the Danube as expressing divine intervention and interest in human affairs, as the gods unleash weapons to aid the Romans and punish the Quadi in a spectacular theomachy. The Quadi stand no chance, as divine support for the Romans is underscored. A suggestive linguistic detail confirms this broad dynamic. At the end of this passage, we can see a curious mirroring (with *uariatio*) of an earlier moment in the battle: where the wounded Romans (τινες τιτρωσκόμενοι) had initially drunk their own blood to survive, now the desperate Quadi even wound themselves (ἑαυτοὺς ἐτίτρωσκον) to try to extinguish the

---

[79] ἦν οὖν ὁρᾶν ἐν τῷ αὐτῷ χωρίῳ ὕδωρ τε ἅμα καὶ πῦρ ἐκ τοῦ οὐρανοῦ φερόμενα· καὶ οἱ μὲν ὑγραίνοντό τε καὶ ἔπινον, οἱ δὲ ἐπυροῦντο καὶ ἔθνησκον· καὶ οὔτε τῶν Ῥωμαίων τὸ πῦρ ἥπτετο, ἀλλ᾽ εἴ που καὶ προσέμιξέ σφισιν, εὐθὺς ἐσβέννυτο, οὔτε τοὺς βαρβάρους ὁ ὑετὸς ὠφέλει, ἀλλὰ καὶ ἐπὶ μᾶλλον τὴν φλόγα αὐτῶν ὥσπερ ἔλαιον ἤγειρεν, ὕδωρ τε ὑόμενοι ἐζήτουν. καὶ οἱ μὲν ἑαυτοὺς ἐτίτρωσκον ὡς καὶ τῷ αἵματι τὸ πῦρ κατασβέσοντες, οἱ δὲ καὶ πρὸς τοὺς Ῥωμαίους προσέτρεχον ὡς καὶ μόνους σωτήριον ὕδωρ ἔχοντας·

[80] For another instance of the effects of thirst on an army, see Dio 75(75).2.2 [Xiph.] (with Mallan 2017b: 132–3) on Severus and his army after crossing the Euphrates during his conquest of Mesopotamia.

[81] Virgil plays with this Lucretian passage in Iarbas' belligerent speech to Jupiter (*Aen.* 4.206–18).

flames.[82] The miraculous rainstorm must be the most visually spectacular and reassuringly partisan marvel narrative which survives from the entire *Roman History*.

IV   Case Study Two: The Bald Senator

A second wonder narrative unfolds in Rome during the principate of Septimius Severus. It is arguably less spectacular than the rain miracle, but nonetheless intriguing and billed in advance as an 'extraordinary affair even in the hearing' (παράδοξα ὄντα καὶ ἀκουσθῆναι) (77[76].8.1 [Xiph.]). This is the case of Popilius Pedo Apronianus, accused (AD 205) on apparently flimsy grounds of aspiring to become emperor. The details, preserved by Xiphilinus, blend together farcical elements and a chilling finale. Dio explains what happened. After Apronianus' nurse (not even Apronianus himself) had dreamed that he would become emperor and rumours subsequently circulated that he had resorted to magic to achieve this goal, Apronianus was condemned in his absence while governing Asia.[83] Dio reports this gloomy outcome before revealing that when the evidence was presented to the senate, collective panic was triggered by the evidence of one witness being read out. This person had claimed that a certain 'bald-headed senator' had eavesdropped and heard about the nurse's dream about Apronianus' illustrious imperial future.[84] Yet the bald senator had shrewdly decided to keep quiet, although that now meant that the eaves-dropper risked charges of collusion. What happens next is partly comical, but also unsettling:

> And although nobody was confident, except those who had unusually thick hair, yet we all looked round at the men with less hair and a murmur ran about: 'It's so-and-so', 'No it's so-and-so'. I will not conceal what happened to me then, ridiculous as it is. I was so disconcerted that I actually felt with my hand to see whether I had any hair on my head. Many others likewise had the same experience. And we very carefully turned to look at those who were more or less bald, as if we should thereby divert the danger threatening ourselves towards these men. We continued to do this until the statement was read that the bald man in question had

[82] See Wills (1996: 194–201) on such 'battle polyptoton'.
[83] Liebs (2012: 14–23) assembles and discusses Roman trials involving accusations of black magic, including this one (p. 22). Rives (2003) discusses technical aspects of the illegality of magic, arguing that the Roman law on magic grounded in the *lex Cornelia* gradually shifted from a focus on harmful and uncanny actions to a concern with religious deviance.
[84] One could compare here Tacitus' account of the eavesdropping senators in the ceiling (*Ann.* 4.69), although Dio's senator seems much less malicious.

worn a purple-bordered toga. When this detail came out, we turned to look at Baebius Marcellinus; for he was aedile at the time and he was extremely bald. (77[76].8.4–6 [Xiph.])[85]

Xiphilinus, as is his normal practice, has preserved Dio's first-person singular verbs (οὐκ ἀποκρύψομαι, 'I will not conceal'; συνεσχέθην, 'I was disconcerted') immortalizing his own shameful and irrational conduct, even in spontaneously feeling his own head to check whether he has hair and is therefore safe.[86] Other senators too had the same reflex reaction.[87] Yet collective guilt comes across particularly sharply with the switch to the first-person plural verb (ἀφεωρῶμεν, 'we turned to look') as the senators by their collective gaze seek to deflect the danger from themselves and turn it onto their bald colleagues.[88] What happens next is grim. After the witness is brought into the senate and then identifies Baebius Marcellinus (thanks to somebody's 'almost imperceptible nod', νεύματί τινος ἀφανεῖ), he was taken from the senate house and having briefly addressed his four children, he had his (bald) head cut off, apparently with the emperor completely unaware.[89] Here farce turns deadly. The main defendant in this case, Pedo Apronianus, proconsul of Asia, has totally disappeared from the story as Dio instead puts the spotlight on a seemingly innocent bystander and victim, Baebius Marcellinus, who happens to be bald. Here a dark marvel narrative accentuates collective shame and the senators' crippling inability to act appropriately, as they eagerly deflect danger from themselves and direct it at an alternative party.[90] Elements of the story may be ridiculous,

---

[85] καὶ ἐθάρσει μὲν οὐδεὶς πλὴν τῶν πάνυ κομώντων, πάντες δὲ τοὺς τοιούτους περιεβλέπομεν, καὶ ἦν θροῦς 'ὁ δεῖνά ἐστιν' 'οὔκ, ἀλλ᾽ ὁ δεῖνα'. οὐκ ἀποκρύψομαι τὸ τότε μοι συμβάν, εἰ καὶ γελοιότατόν ἐστιν· τοσαύτη γὰρ ἀμηχανίᾳ συνεσχέθην ὥστε καὶ τῆς κεφαλῆς τὰς τρίχας τῇ χειρὶ ζητῆσαι. τὸ δ᾽ αὐτὸ τοῦτο καὶ ἕτεροι πολλοὶ ἔπαθον. καὶ πάνυ γε ἐς τοὺς φαλακροειδεῖς ἀφεωρῶμεν ὡς καὶ ⟨ἐς⟩ ἐκείνους τὸν ἑαυτῶν κίνδυνον ἀπωθούμενοι, πρὶν δὴ προσανεγνώσθη ὅτι ἄρα περιπόρφυρον ἱμάτιον ὁ φαλακρὸς ἐκεῖνος εἶχε. λεχθέντος γὰρ τούτου πρὸς Βαίβιον Μαρκελλῖνον ἀπείδομεν· ἠγορανομήκει γὰρ τότε καὶ ἦν φαλακρότατος.

[86] Mallan (2013b: 621) considers Xiphilinus' practice of preserving Dio's first-person interventions. 'Dio exceeds any previous historian in number and scale of preserved autobiographical participatory remarks' (Marincola 1997: 199).

[87] See Kemezis in this volume (Chapter 1) on Dio's own political class as 'a highly interactive audience whose responses are an integral part of the performance'.

[88] This is a particularly disturbing instance of Dio's use of the first-person plural where we see him 'frequently using the first-person plural in the contemporary narrative to express the views and experiences of the *amplissimus ordo*' (Davenport and Mallan in the Introduction). Gleason (2011: 55) offers an illuminating discussion of Dio's use of first-person pronouns in this passage.

[89] A fragmentary inscription from Ephesus (*CIL* III 427 = *ILS* 430; written in Latin and followed by a Greek version) celebrating Severus' *prouidentia* has been taken as referring to the successful suppression of Pedo Apronianus' bid for power (Noreña 2011: 94, n. 207).

[90] The technique of deflecting guilt is deployed in forensic oratory (e.g. Cicero's *Pro Roscio Amerino* where Chrysogonus is cast as the real criminal).

but the undignified scramble of the senators to save themselves by finding a convenient bald scapegoat recalls earlier powerful narratives immortalizing collective senatorial shame under an oppressive emperor, such as Tacitus' despairing accusation of senatorial collusion in the tyranny of Domitian:

> [S]oon it was our hands which dragged Helvidius to prison; the looks which Mauricius and Rusticus gave us put us to shame, Senecio drenched us in his innocent blood. (*Agricola* 45.1)[91]

Tacitus' retroactive accusation of himself and his fellow senators is a relevant point of comparison because of his use of the visual element as a means to accentuate focus on the sense of collective shame. Dio may well be self-consciously reprising Tacitus' painful denunciation of the senators' collective conduct under Domitian. Yet the comparison with this passage of Tacitus also brings out an important difference. In Dio's passage, it is clear that (unlike Tacitus' oppressive Domitian) the emperor Septimius Severus is completely unaware of these events: the senators themselves take the lead in this corrosive and self-destructive behaviour, whether because of dubious patterns of conduct learned over many decades or because their desire for self-preservation is so strong they are prepared to sacrifice anyone to save their own lives.[92] Indeed, if we consider story patterns involving tyrannical emperors, such as Nero mocking the severed head of Cornelius Sulla for being prematurely grey (Tac. *Ann.* 14.57.4) or the severed head of Rubellius Plautus for having such a big nose (Tac. *Ann.* 14.59.3; Dio 62[62].14.1 [*EV*]), then the expected ending involving a cruel imperial joke is conspicuous by its absence.[93] Ultimately, what is most intriguing about this narrative segment is which elements Dio has in mind when he pre-emptively describes the episode as extraordinary: is it the impact of the nurse's dream on Apronianus' future? The speed of his condemnation? The presence of an eavesdropping bald-headed senator? The scale of the panic amongst the senators when this is revealed? The scramble to convict Baebius Marcellinus? The fact that he is beheaded even before Septimius Severus learns anything about the case? Or all these factors together? Dio uses a very inclusive and all-encompassing formula for introducing and

---

[91] *mox nostrae duxere Helvidium in carcerem manus; nos Maurici Rusticique uisus adflixit, nos innocenti sanguine Senecio perfudit.*

[92] Another example of senators condemning other senators features in Macrinus' principate, the case of Priscilianus, where Dio is less disturbed because he is a supporter of Caracalla (79[78].21).

[93] Nero's quips exemplify 'talking dog' jokes, where the obviously extraordinary element is ignored in favour of correcting the dog's pronunciation (Plass 1985: 208).

identifying the incredible elements, namely the τὰ περὶ τὸν Ἀπρωνιανόν, 'events surrounding Apronianus'. On this basis it is all the kaleidoscopic strange parts of the story together which are incredible.

V Conclusion

We have seen that Dio and his epitomizers are all alive to the impact of categorizing particular episodes as extraordinary and associating certain emperors with the incredible (whether in positive or negative ways). Arresting presentational techniques include pointedly offsetting marvels from the main narrative (including promythic labels), mediating wonders through characters within the text, highlighting autopsy, presenting something as an 'oblique wonder' which emphasizes not so much the object itself, but the mechanisms behind it as the marvellous element, exploiting a book's structure to position marvels prominently, and even (paradoxically) not calling something a marvel when it clearly seems to be one. Some marvels, such as Marcus Aurelius and the miraculous rainstorm, attract an ongoing agonistic focus for 'ownership', both before and after Dio wrote. Other incredible events are much darker, such as the humiliating circumstances leading to the execution of the bald-headed senator – an incident which reflects collective senatorial guilt and which most of Dio's contemporaries would surely rather have consigned to oblivion. From a Roman perspective, Dio's wonders operate on a broad spectrum, running from the uplifting and positive to the humiliating and negative, thus evoking the broad dynamics of exemplarity in Roman historiography. This raises another point. Many of Dio's marvels are not totally unanchored or frivolous but usually have a political or moralising point. Generally, although excessive reliance on such narrative modes of wonder can potentially be problematic for historiography, Dio happily embeds the marvellous in his history of the Principate in illuminating ways which are expressive about his own perceptions of the nature of imperial power. Particularly as the narrative approaches Dio's own era, he seems increasingly willing to open up the register of the marvellous and to suggest that the boundary between the human and divine spheres is permeable. He himself seems to inhabit a world where marvels become increasingly normal, not always in a positive way, but they are clearly a hugely important thread in the fabric of his particular brand of historiography.

Emperors and Biographies

CHAPTER 5

Cassius Dio's Funeral Speech for Augustus
Sources, Rhetoric, Messages

Christina T. Kuhn

I Introduction

Composed in grand style and put in the mouths of various historical protagonists at key historical moments, the speeches in Cassius Dio's *Roman History* have long attracted interest as a worthwhile subject for investigation.[1] The scholarly debate shows that their interpretation is complex and challenging: to what extent are they rhetorical set pieces shaped by the culture of the Second Sophistic of Dio's own time; how far are they the places 'where the original thought of Dio is to be found'?[2] Especially in recent years there has been a renewed interest in the analysis of these speeches.[3] Scholars have explored more carefully their relationship to each other, their concrete historical and narrative contexts and the skilful way with which Dio creates different levels of interpretation. A more nuanced view of Dio the historian has doubtless emerged.

Within the Augustan narrative of Dio's *Roman History*, particular attention must be paid to the *oratio funebris* ('funeral oration') in honour of the deceased Augustus, given by the future emperor Tiberius before the people in the Forum Romanum in 14 AD (56.35–41).[4] It is embedded in Dio's detailed report of the emperor's death and funeral ceremony towards

---

I would like to thank Caillan Davenport, Christopher Mallan and Emily Patterson for their helpful comments and suggestions. All English translations of the passages quoted from Cassius Dio's *Roman History* have been taken from vol. 7 of the Loeb Classical Library edition, translated by Earnest Cary, based on the version of Herbert B. Foster.

[1] For a list of the speeches in Dio's *Roman History*, see Schwartz 1899: 1718–19, to which must be added Antony's funeral speech (44.36–49) and Hadrian's adoption speech (69.20.2–5). For a study of the speeches in Dio see above all Millar 1961; Millar 1964: 78–83.

[2] Gabba 1984: 70–1.

[3] See, for example, the studies by Kemezis 2007; Adler 2011; Davenport and Mallan 2014; Burden-Strevens 2015a; 2016.

[4] The fact that Tiberius gave a speech as part of the funerary celebrations for Augustus is also attested by Suetonius (*Aug.* 100.3). Remarkably, it is not mentioned by Tacitus in his Augustan narrative in Book 1 of the *Annals*.

the end of Book 56. It not only forms the apex of Dio's account of Augustus' rise to power and his establishment of the Principate in the preceding twelve books (45–56) but also presents the first of two retrospect-ive commemorations of Augustus in Dio. It thus sets the tone for the overall final assessment of the first emperor of Rome in Book 56. Given the special importance of this speech, it is indeed surprising that it has received little in-depth analysis by modern scholars.[5] Those interested in Dio's assessment of Augustus in Book 56 have predominantly focussed on the second retrospect at 56.43–6 due to its striking parallels with Tacitus' famous account (*Ann.* 1.9–10). Just as the scholarly discourse became mesmerized by the question of whether Tacitus and Dio were drawing on a common literary source (and, if so, which of the two was closer to it),[6] so, too, scholarly attention shifted away from Tiberius' speech as a composition in its own right.

It is the purpose of the following analysis to refocus attention on Tiberius' funeral speech in order to shed light on some under-researched aspects and illuminate Dio's working method as a historian. I shall argue that the composition of the oration (56.35–41) offered Dio the ideal opportunity of presenting the perspective of the imperial *domus* at a turning point in Roman history. I will pay particular attention to the rhetoric, sources and messages of the speech. We are in the fortunate position of having the *Res Gestae Divi Augusti*, which provides us with Augustus' own assessment of his principate and the best-preserved mani-festation of the imperial version of events.[7] By means of comparison of the *Res Gestae* and Tiberius' speech, this article not only explores Dio's poten-tial use of this document but also examines how close Dio's reconstruction of the imperial perspective came to the original. The analysis of similarities and differences between the texts is a most revealing guide to Dio's working method, preoccupations and preconceptions as a historian. Finally, I shall explore how the composition of the speech, together with the paragraphs following the speech (56.43–6), allowed Dio to communi-cate more precisely his own place as a historian in his work.

---

[5] The most detailed studies of Tiberius' funeral speech are Manuwald 1979: 133–40; Kierdorf 1980: 154–8; Giua 1983; Swan 2004: 325–39.

[6] For this debate about the common source, see esp. Schwartz 1899: 1716–17; Klinger 1953: 635–42; Tränkle 1969: 115–18; Flach 1973: 126–36; Manuwald 1980: 140–67; Rich 1989: 104–8. See also Swan 2004: 345–6 for a useful summary of the different positions. Syme (1958: 272) remained sceptical of this common source and warns us that 'the theory is seductive, but not convincing' since 'it explains too much'. In the same vein, see Urban 1979: 73.

[7] For the text and commentary, see esp. Brunt and Moore 1973; Cooley 2009.

II (Re)constructing the 'Imperial Perspective': Sources and Influences

At the beginning of our analysis, it is worth remembering that speeches in Roman historiography were not intended to provide the reader with a verbatim record of the actual speech.[8] There is general consensus among scholars that the speeches in Dio's *Roman History* are compositions by their author and that the funeral speech in Book 56 was no exception to this practice.[9] Unfortunately, we cannot be certain as to whether Dio drew on an existing rhetorical model when composing the speech,[10] or whether he completely invented it from scratch. In any case, his aim will have been to produce an oration which was 'a rhetorically possible version'.[11] In practice, this meant that he had to write a speech that was appropriate for both the solemn occasion of a state funeral and for its presenter, Tiberius, the adoptive son of Augustus, and later successor. Put in the mouth of a member of the imperial *domus*, the function of the speech was meant to be a manifestation of the 'imperial perspective' – a perspective which, as we shall see, was not necessarily in line with that of the senate or the people and which should not be equated *a priori* with Dio's own views.[12] Whatever sources Dio may have consulted during his research for the speech, we must be aware that he felt free to recreate, reshape and interpret his material. This was common practice in Roman historiography. Thus, as a working hypothesis for the following analysis, we can with good reason assume that Tiberius' funeral speech, like so many other speeches in Roman historiography, is characterized by 'a mixture of what was actually known and what could be surmised'.[13]

Before we reflect upon Dio's sources, the content and tone of the speech warrant closer examination. The speech exclusively deals with the public deeds of Augustus and is, at first glance, entirely encomiastic: Tiberius praises Augustus as the glorious avenger of his father, a wise lawgiver and, above all, the saviour of the *res publica*, who, from his youth until his death,

---

[8] On speeches in Greek and Roman historiography, see esp. Marincola 2007.

[9] See e.g. Millar 1964: 101; Swan 2004: 26, 325; Manuwald 1979: 133.

[10] As suggested by Manuwald 1979: 135. What we can say with certainty, however, is that no rhetorical blueprint of the speech has come down to us. This is not to say that Dio did not use any other historical sources when composing it. However, Marincola (2007: 129) has argued that 'a historian generally avoided including a speech in his history that was already published in literary form and available to the public'.

[11] Pelling 1983: 225.

[12] See Giua 1983, who argues that the speech presents Dio's own views. Against this argument, see Swan 2004: 28; Rich 1989: 104, n. 105; Pelling 1983: 224.

[13] Marincola 2007: 121.

excelled all others in his extraordinary achievements on behalf of the state. Augustus was not driven by personal ambition but by the circumstances of his time. The well-being of the *res publica* had always been his prime concern. Once Augustus had come to power, everybody benefitted from his leadership, since he made the state happier and more powerful. Even his greatest enemies were treated with unprecedented clemency. Peace, order and security were restored by him after the turmoil of the civil wars, and the Romans could henceforth enjoy a wide range of amenities due to Augustus' extraordinary generosity: magnificent public buildings, food and money gifts, games and spectacles. Moreover, he established a well-functioning system of laws, honours and rewards. The emperor surpassed all previous statesmen in the virtues of clemency and modesty and exhibited utmost humility in his dealings with both the elite and the people: senators gained new prestige and could fully exercise their right to vote and free speech, while the people continued to hold elections in the assemblies. In addition, there had been a remarkable improvement in the situation of the provincials and allies since maladministration and exploitation had become obsolete under Augustus.

Though the tone of the speech is predominantly encomiastic; it is noteworthy that there are occasional hints of vindication discernible throughout the text.[14] As oblique references, they appear in the form of two rhetorical strategies, which deserve further consideration at this point. There is, first, the emphasis on the constitutionality and legality of Augustus' rise to power and his deeds. When summarizing the key stages of Augustus' career, Tiberius reminds his audience that it was they who had elevated Augustus to the extraordinary position he held in the *res publica*. Each major section of the speech culminates in a statement which stresses the responsibility of the people:

- 'you chose him praetor and appointed him consul at an age when some are unwilling to serve even as common soldiers' (56.36.5);[15]
- 'you constrained him for a time at least to be your leader' (56.39.5);[16]
- 'you compelled him for a second, a third, a fourth, and a fifth time to continue in the management of affairs' (56.39.6);[17]

---

[14] On this aspect, see also Swan 2004: 326.
[15] στρατηγὸν αὐτὸν εἵλεσθε καὶ ὕπατον ἀπεδείξατε ἐκεῖνο τῆς ἡλικίας ἔχοντα ἐν ᾧ μηδὲ στρατεύεσθαί τινες ἐθέλουσιν.
[16] προκρίναντες ἠναγκάσατε χρόνον γέ τινα ὑμῶν προστῆναι.
[17] καὶ δεύτερον αὖθις καὶ τρίτον τέταρτόν τε καὶ πέμπτον ἐξεβιάσασθε αὐτὸν ἐν τῇ τῶν κοινῶν διαχειρίσει ἐμμεῖναι.

– 'you, with good reason, made him your leader and a father of the people, that you honoured him with many marks of esteem and with ever so many consulships, and that you finally made him a demigod and declared him to be immortal' (56.41.9).[18]

The message is unambiguous: Augustus did not usurp power but was chosen and appointed emperor in a legal way. By highlighting the people's share in the making of the *princeps*, the speech stresses the political legitimacy of Augustus' position. Dio's choice of words is revealing here: 'you constrained' (ἠναγκάσατε) and 'you compelled' (ἐξεβιάσασθε) suggest that the initiative came from the people and that considerable pressure was exerted on Augustus to take on power. The *recusatio imperii* of Augustus in 27 BC, so vividly described by Dio at the start of Book 53, immediately comes to mind: Augustus only assumed power because the senators had urged him to do so (53.2–12).[19] The first emperor had demonstrated due modesty and moderation and had set the paradigmatic standard for all later emperors. Any form of criticism concerning the legality of his position would, therefore, be unfounded.

The second strategy employed in the speech is the use of the concessive rhetorical structure 'it is true ... but ... '. Remarkably, some negative aspects of Augustus' rule are broached in the speech, but they are immediately refuted with an explanation of why the emperor had no choice but to act as he did. Tiberius, for instance, refers to Augustus' alliance with Antony and Lepidus during the triumviral period in order to oppose Brutus and Cassius, but emphasizes that he only did so because he could not fight them all simultaneously (56.37.3). Tiberius further admits that the civil wars should never have been waged by Augustus, but, in the same breath, underlines that all the other wars had brought about extraordinary benefits for Rome (56.37.4). The strategic device of admitting and refuting is likewise employed when Tiberius comes to speak about the rights of the people: he acknowledges that it is certainly true that legal cases were taken away from the people and transferred to the courts; these were, however, as he explains, only the cases that were difficult to judge (56.40.4).[20] These examples demonstrate how the speech takes up allegations that critics of Augustus may have levelled against the emperor. By tackling and

---

[18] εἰκότως καὶ προστάτην αὐτὸν καὶ πατέρα δημόσιον ἐποιήσασθε, καὶ ἄλλοις τε πολλοῖς καὶ ὑπατείαις πλείσταις ἐπεγαυρώσατε, καὶ τὸ τελευταῖον καὶ ἥρωα ἀπεδείξατε καὶ ἀθάνατον ἀπεφήνατε.

[19] On the 'ritual' of *recusatio imperii*, see Huttner 2004.

[20] On Dio's view of the 'people', see Swan 2004: 334, and Chapter 9 of this volume by Monica Hellström.

countering them, Tiberius gets across the point that, whatever Augustus did, he had good reason to do so, because he always acted in the interest of the *res publica*.

Besides the rhetoric of vindication, there is another striking feature that requires consideration: Tiberius' blatant use of half-truths. The speech includes several euphemistic statements, which highlight the positive effects of measures taken by Augustus, whilst omitting their strongly negative implications. Tiberius, for instance, stresses that Augustus had an excellent relationship with the senators and had increased their esteem by removing from their community 'the scum that had come to the surface from the factions' (τὸ φαῦλον τὸ ἐκ τῶν στάσεων ἐπιπολάσαν) (56.41.3). However, he does not say a single word about the controversial nature of these purges of the senate, which ruined the careers of many senators.[21] Consider, too, Augustus' legislation on marriage: Tiberius praises the rewards that the emperor established to encourage marriage and increase childbirth (56.41.6). What he leaves unmentioned, however, are the harsh penalties that were introduced for those who did not comply with the new social norms and the public protests that broke out.[22] Moreover, Augustus is portrayed as a statesman who was exclusively driven by his filial loyalty towards Caesar and his goodwill for the *res publica* during the triumviral period. His personal ambitions are entirely glossed over by Tiberius.[23]

It thus becomes evident that Tiberius' speech is characterized by a mixture of praise, justification and half-truths. It is this feature which is reminiscent of one key text from the Augustan period: the *Res Gestae Divi Augusti* (henceforth *RGDA*). Even though earlier scholarship has shed important light on Dio's (potential) sources, hardly any attention has been devoted to the question of whether Dio has drawn on the *RGDA* for the composition of his *Roman History*.[24] This neglect is striking insofar as Dio himself attests to the fact that he was aware of the existence of this important epigraphic document:[25] in the passages preceding the funeral

---

[21] See Suet. *Aug.* 35. According to Suetonius, Augustus needed the protection of ten senatorial friends and even had to wear armour when enforcing these measures. See also Swan 2004: 336–7.

[22] See 56.1–10 and Suet. *Aug.* 34, with Swan 2004: 338.

[23] See Swan 2004: 328. Compare with Tac. *Ann.* 1.10.

[24] On Dio's use of sources, see esp. Kuhn-Chen 2002: 135–42. On the (potential) sources used for the Augustan narrative, see Millar 1964: 83–92; Swan 2004: 21ff.; Reinhold and Swan 1990: 171–3. No discussion of the *RGDA* is offered by these scholars. Note, however, the brief mention of the *RGDA* by Pelling 1983: 225; cf. also Cesare Letta's views on Dio's use of the *RGDA* expressed in Chapter 3 of this volume. Until the study of Urban 1979, the same neglect is evident as to the question of whether Tacitus used the *Res Gestae*.

[25] For Dio's use of documents and inscriptions, see Chapter 3 by Cesare Letta.

eulogy, Dio explicitly refers to it, when he mentions that the *RGDA* was one of the four documents attached to Augustus' testament (56.33.1). The *RGDA* was inscribed on bronze tablets, which were set up in front of Augustus' Mausoleum on the Field of Mars after Augustus' death. It is certainly possible that Dio had come across the text in Rome or in Asia Minor, where copies of the *RGDA* were inscribed in some places.[26] This becomes even more likely when we consider what he reveals about his working method:

> I spent ten years in collecting all the achievements of the Romans from the beginning down to the death of Severus, and twelve years more in composing my work. (73[72].23.5 [Xiph.])[27]

According to this statement, Dio had read widely for his work, and we must surmise that he will not have ignored such an important state document as the *RGDA*. Certainly, the author of the *RGDA*, Augustus, was not identical with Tiberius, into whose mouth Dio had put the speech. However, Tiberius was Augustus' adopted son and colleague in the final years of government. For Dio, Tiberius was a representative of the imperial *domus*, whose members (despite the personal tensions that existed between them) shared an active interest in representing imperial rule in a particular way to the public.

If we assume that it was Dio's intention to produce a speech appropriate for a member of the imperial *domus*, the important question arises of how successful he was in realizing this goal. In the following, it will be instructive to compare the *RGDA*, which is the most authoritative document of Augustus' self-perception and assessment of his own achievements, with Dio's speech put in Tiberius' mouth. Parallels between the texts can suggest Dio's potential use of the *RGDA*. But more importantly, they may help us to determine how far Dio's version deviates from Augustus' own assessment and thus trace disparities in the speech generated by his own concerns and preconceptions.

First, it is noteworthy that, like the *RGDA*, Tiberius' speech exclusively focuses on the public deeds of Augustus. Dio reports that two speeches were given at the funeral (56.34.4–35.1).[28] The first was delivered by

---

[26] On the display of the *RGDA* in Rome and the provinces, see esp. Cooley 2009: 3–22. On Dio's personal background and the stages of his career, see esp. Millar 1964: 5–27; Barnes 1984; Rich 1989: 87–9; Molin 2016a; Letta 2019.

[27] συνέλεξα δὲ πάντα τὰ ἀπ' ἀρχῆς τοῖς Ῥωμαίοις μέχρι τῆς Σεουήρου μεταλλαγῆς πραχθέντα ἐν ἔτεσι δέκα, καὶ συνέγραψα ἐν ἄλλοις δώδεκα. On Dio's working method, see further Rich 1989: 89–92.

[28] As Kierdorf (1980: 158) has aptly noted, the speech must be understood 'als Teil einer Doppelrede'.

Tiberius' son, Drusus; it dealt with what had to be said about the deceased Augustus 'in a private capacity by relatives' (ἰδίᾳ καὶ παρὰ τῶν συγγενῶν) (56.35.1). With only a brief mention, Dio skips over this speech to make Tiberius' public address the focal point of his account. As to the structure of the speech, Tiberius' oration resembles the *RGDA* in so far as it starts chronologically with Octavian's rise to power, then adopts a thematic structure, which covers topics such as Augustus' benefactions to the people, his building activities, his relationship with the senate and the provinces, and his sponsorship of games.[29] Like the *RGDA*, it then culminates in a section on the award of the title *pater patriae*.[30] The beginning of the speech at 56.37, which centres on Octavian's rise to power, is of particular interest. Just as in *RGDA* 1–2, Augustus is praised for taking the initiative for avenging his father at an incredibly young age and for rescuing the *res publica* by restoring liberty. It is for these services that the people made him head of state. A juxtaposition of the two passages (56.37 and *RGDA* 1–2) suggests that Tiberius' speech follows the core account of the *RGDA* but is embellished by Dio with further information and details. Note, in particular, the effective comparison between Augustus and Hercules: whereas Augustus acted on his own initiative to save the state, Hercules had only acted at the behest of others. It may be no coincidence that Dio here creatively plays with the idea of Augustus' personal initiative to turn it into the *tertium comparationis* of his historical comparison.

Furthermore, the rhetoric of justification, which we have described as a distinct feature of the speech, finds clear parallels in the *RGDA*. Here, Augustus places great emphasis on the legitimacy of his position: he stresses that positions were conferred on him in accordance with tradition and/or by decree of the senate and the people; that he had a colleague in office several times; that he declined excessive powers; that the people acted unanimously and voluntarily in support of him.[31] Particularly noteworthy is his claim in *RGDA* 34.1 to have returned all power from his control to that of the senate and the people in 28/7 BC.[32] Likewise, Tiberius praises Augustus' decision to return all power into the hands of the senate and the people after putting an end to the civil wars: 'he had no one to fear or suspect, but might have ruled alone with the approval of all; yet he saw fit

---

[29] On the structure of the speech, see Kierdorf 1980: 155; remarkably, however, he does not note the similarity with the *Res Gestae*.

[30] Compare 56.41.9 with *RGDA* 35.1.   [31] Cf. *RGDA* 5, 6, 8, 9, 10, 22.

[32] Compare with *RGDA* 34.1: 'I transferred the republic from my power to the dominion of the senate and people of Rome' (*rem publicam ex mea potestate in senatus populique Romani arbitrium transtuli*) (trans. Brunt and Moore 1973: 35).

not to do this, but laid the arms, the provinces, and the money at your feet' (56.39.4).[33]

Some finer details deserve mention, too. In *RGDA* 10.2, Augustus stresses that he did not remove his enemy Lepidus from the office of *pontifex maximus*, but waited until his death before he took on the position. Remarkably, the same point is singled out for praise by Dio when Tiberius speaks of the *clementia* shown by Augustus towards his rival Lepidus (56.38.2).[34] Moreover, just like the *RGDA*, the speech stresses that public buildings were restored by Augustus without removing the names of the original builders.[35] Other aspects of Augustus' rule praised in the *RGDA* (the revision of the senatorial roll, the restoration of the public treasury, the money gifts made to the people and soldiers, the protection of the provinces and allies, the many sponsored games and building works) also find explicit mention in Tiberius' speech.[36]

Even though we cannot trace any direct quotations from the *RGDA*, the *Res Gestae* still appears to resonate throughout Tiberius' speech. Hence it can hardly be dismissed that Dio may have drawn on this important document to develop a perspective that would approach that of the imperial *domus*. This is not to say that the *RGDA* may have been the only source he consulted. We know that Dio worked with a wide range of sources in producing his *Roman History*, possibly including Suetonius' *Life of Augustus*.[37] It is indeed noteworthy that, content-wise, Tiberius' speech shows several close parallels to Suetonius' account of Augustus.[38] Nonetheless, the *RGDA* will have offered the historian a particularly helpful means of deciding which key achievements should be singled out for praise – more so, indeed, than Suetonius' work. After all, given the manifold services of Augustus for the *res publica* during his long rule, the selection of material was certainly a difficult challenge.[39]

---

[33] καὶ μήτε φοβούμενός τινα μήθ' ὑποπτεύων, ἀλλ' ἐξὸν αὐτῷ πάντων συνεπαινούντων μόνῳ ἄρχειν, οὐκ ἠξίωσεν, ἀλλὰ καὶ τὰ ὅπλα καὶ τὰ ἔθνη καὶ τὰ χρήματα ἐς τὸ μέσον ὑμῖν κατέθηκεν.

[34] This is also mentioned in 49.15.3; 54.15.8; Suet. *Aug.* 31.

[35] Compare *RGDA* 19–20 with 56.40.5. The same point is made in Suet. *Aug.* 29.

[36] Senatorial purges: *RGDA* 8.2; 56.41.2; public treasury: *RGDA* 17; 56.40.4; gifts to the People: *RGDA* 15; 56.41.4; rewards to soldiers: *RGDA* 16.2, 17.2; 56.41.6; provinces/allies: *RGDA* 26.2–3; 56.40.2; 41.4; games: *RGDA* 22–3; 56.41.4; building works: *RGDA* 19–21; 56.41.4.

[37] On Dio's use of Suetonius as a source, see Millar 1984: 85–6. Note, however, Power (2014: 218–19), who has argued that Dio neglected Suetonius. See further Cesare Letta's examination of Dio's literary sources in Chapter 3.

[38] See e.g. Suet. *Aug.* 21, 29, 31.

[39] Accordingly, we should not be surprised that reference is made to this matter of selecting material in Tiberius' speech (56.37.5–7).

But let us return to the question of how authentic Dio's reconstruction of the imperial version of events was. There is a striking difference between Augustus' own presentation of his achievements in the *RGDA* and Tiberius' funeral oration, which must not be neglected at this point: whereas the *RGDA* provides the reader with long, detailed sections on the wars waged by the emperor against foreign kings and peoples, and glorifies the expansion of the boundaries of the Empire,[40] Dio ignores this issue in Tiberius' speech. No mention is made of Augustus' conquest of Egypt or his military campaigns in Germany, Spain, Gaul or the Alps. In an attempt to explain this striking omission of Augustus' military achievements, Kierdorf has drawn attention to the fact that Augustus was not deemed the best general and that he had engaged in the evils of civil war.[41] In his view, Dio deliberately glossed over the topic of warfare in order to present the emperor in a more positive light. However, this explanation is not entirely convincing since the negative sides of Augustus' warfare are not totally omitted but alluded to in the speech elsewhere at 56.37.4. Moreover, if it were Dio's goal to compose a speech suitable for a member of the imperial *domus*, he will have known that military achievements played a key role in Augustus' self-representation and that a member of the imperial *domus* will not have passed over them. Against this background, it seems more plausible to explain this omission with Dio's own views on expansion and imperialism:[42] he firmly believed that uncontrolled expansion for the mere sake of expanding the boundaries of the empire was undesirable. This attitude is made explicit in his criticism of the Eastern military exploits of the emperors of his own time.[43] Against this background, it may not be surprising to find that Dio presents Augustus as a figure driven only by necessity[44] and as a military leader who showed due moderation as regards the expansion of the boundaries of the empire and further territorial conquest:

'Or, again, shall I not tell how satisfied he was with our possessions acquired once for all under the compulsion of necessity, but refused to subjugate any additional territory, the acquisition of which might, while seeming to give us a wider sway, have entailed the loss of even what we had?' (56.41.7)[45]

[40] See *RGDA* 26–33.
[41] See Kierdorf 1980: 155–6, with Suet. *Aug.* 10. On Dio's rather critical presentation of Augustus as a military general, see also Reinhold and Swan 1990: 160–1.
[42] For Dio's attitude towards war and expansion, see esp. Ober 1982: 320–1; Reinhold and Swan 1990: 162–4; Kuhn-Chen 2002: 202–4. See further Chapter 8 by Caillan Davenport in this volume.
[43] See especially 75(75).3.3 (Xiph.), with Millar 1964: 82 and Swan 2004: 338.
[44] On the force of 'necessity' in Dio's work, see Gabba 1984: 72.
[45] τί δέ; τὸ τοῖς ἅπαξ ἀναγκαίως κτηθεῖσιν ἀρκεσθῆναι αὐτὸν καὶ μηδὲν ἕτερον προσκατεργάσασθαι ἐθελῆσαι, ἐξ οὗ πλειόνων ἂν δόξαντες ἄρχειν καὶ τὰ ὄντα ἀπωλέσαμεν. Dio's words are reminiscent

This is, of course, a distorted anachronistic picture of Augustus' foreign policy; there is no doubt that in reality Augustus showed clear signs of pursuing an aggressive imperialism.[46] However, we should be wary of assuming that Dio entirely 'invented' the notion of Augustan moderation in foreign policy. We must also take into account the possibility that the passage reflects Dio's interpretation of Augustus' claim that he waged only 'just wars',[47] which obviously fitted well with Dio's agenda of a defensive foreign policy. Put into the mouth of Tiberius, who was well-known for his non-expansionistic policy during his reign, the message gains special authenticity.

Dio's careful selection of those aspects which suit his own agenda, whilst ignoring those which do not, also becomes evident when we turn to the theme of imperial virtues. We know from *RGDA* 34 that Augustus was proud of being honoured by the senate with the *clipeus virtutis* for his valour (*virtus*), mercy (*clementia*), justice (*iustitia*) and piety (*pietas*). Tiberius' speech, too, praises Augustus as an emperor who excelled in *clementia* (ἐπιείκεια).[48] However, the remaining virtues for which he was honoured by the senate in 27 BC are not mentioned. Instead, Augustus is made the embodiment of those imperial virtues which later became relevant for the concept of the *civilis princeps* during the High Empire.[49] Besides his *clementia*, he is lauded for his prudence, generosity and civility. We must note that these are the cardinal virtues which, in Dio's political thought, characterized the ideal emperor.[50]

Once we start searching for Dio's own imprint on Tiberius' speech, further examples can be found. Dio's literary fingerprints likewise become visible when we consider the historical *exempla* adduced by Tiberius to underline Augustus' extraordinariness. At the beginning of the speech Tiberius refers to Romulus and Alexander the Great, arguing that if he compared the young Augustus to these kings, he would be at risk of belittling Augustus' achievements (56.36.3).[51] Certainly, we know that

---

of an earlier passage at 56.33.5, where he reports a fourth document which was allegedly attached to Augustus' testament and *inter alia* advised Tiberius to keep the empire within its limits. Ober 1982 regards this document as a forgery by Dio, based on an invention of Tiberius, who had presumably received this piece of advice only orally from Augustus. However, the authenticity of this document is defended by Cesare Letta in Chapter 3 of this volume and Letta 2016a: 270–3.

[46] Reinhold and Swan 1990: 162–3. On Augustus' foreign policy and its nature, see esp. Meyer 1961; Brunt 1963; Ober 1982: 317–19; Gruen 1996; Gruen 1990.

[47] See *RGDA* 26.3. This notion is also found in Suet. *Aug.* 21.

[48] On the theme of *clementia* in Dio, see Giua 1981; Rich 1989: 107–8; Kuhn-Chen: 2002: 160–3; Davenport 2014: 104–5, 113–14.

[49] See Wallace-Hadrill 1981; Wallace-Hadrill 1982.

[50] On these virtues in Dio's work, see Kuhn-Chen 2002: 143–81.

[51] On Augustus' relationship to Alexander the Great: Kühnen 2008: 121–61; on the reference to Alexander the Great in Tiberius' speech: Swan 2004: 329; Carlsen 2016: 319–21. For the complex use of the Alexander motif in Dio's *Roman History*, cf. Carlsen 2016; Mallan 2017.

Augustus showed special interest in these two historical figures and cautiously alluded to them in his public representation.[52] However, given the Romans' dislike of monarchy during the age of Augustus, it is doubtful whether the historical Tiberius would have used these figures as *comparanda* in a funeral speech. After all, having learnt a lesson from the assassination of Caesar, Augustus carefully avoided any direct references to kingship during his lifetime: he chose the honorific title of *Augustus* over that of *Romulus* and deprecated all those offices which could have reminded people of a monarchical position.[53] In his succession policy, too, Augustus had exercised due caution to avoid the impression of dynasty-building. The ideology of the Principate was incompatible with explicit allusions to kingship. It is, therefore, plausible to suggest that the selection of these two kings as historical *comparanda* reflects Dio's own preferences and must be understood in the context of the Severan period, during which there was great enthusiasm for Alexander.[54] The same holds true for his choice of Hercules, who is referred to soon after, in order to demonstrate that Augustus surpassed the divine hero through his initiative (56.36.4). Once again, the impact of Dio's third-century perspective becomes visible here: while Hercules did not play any role in the representation of the Julio-Claudian emperors and would certainly not have been mentioned by the historical Tiberius, the Severan emperors (under whom Dio wrote) frequently alluded to Hercules on coins and statuary.[55] A third-century readership was familiar with Hercules in the context of imperial representation and, as has been rightly pointed out, will not have failed to notice the indirect comparison between Caracalla and Augustus that Dio is suggesting here.[56]

The anachronisms outlined above must have been of special contemporary relevance for Dio's third-century audience. Dio insinuated comparisons between Augustus and the emperors of his own time and the attentive reader could draw his own conclusions from the implied parallels.[57] Dio's own third-century imprint on the speech should not,

---

[52] See e.g. Augustus' visit to Alexander's tomb and his seal with the image of Alexander the Great (51.16.5; Suet. *Aug.* 18, 50); it is also noteworthy that Augustus' house on the Palatine was built near the hut of Romulus (53.16.5).

[53] See 53.16.7; 54.1–2; Suet. *Aug.* 7.2; *RGDA* 5.

[54] On the *imitatio Alexandri* during the Severan age, see Kühnen 2008: 175–94.

[55] On Commodus and Hercules: Swan 2004: 329, with 73(72).7.2 (Xiph./*EV*), 15–16 (Xiph.), 20.2 (Xiph./*EV*), 22.3 (Xiph.). For Hercules' role in the representation of Severan emperors, see Lichtenberger 2011 and Rowan 2012.

[56] Cf. Swan 2004: 329.

[57] For another example of a contemporary reference in the speech, see Giua 1983: 447–9, who points out that Dio draws a comparison between Augustus and Septimius Severus in 56.38.

however, distract us from the fact that, with its distinct mixture of praise, vindication and half-truths, he had composed a speech which effectively captured the imperial tone and vision of events and which could have been given by a member of the imperial household of the early Principate.

III Motivations and Messages

Dio makes sparing use of speeches as a literary device in his work. It is, therefore, illuminating to explore his motivation for inserting a speech into the narrative at a particular point, as he did with Tiberius' funeral speech. First and foremost, there can be no denying the fact that the composition of a speech provided the senatorial historiographer with an ideal opportunity of displaying his erudition and rhetorical skills. Dio was a prominent representative of an educated elite that was well trained in rhetoric, familiar with the conventions taught in the rhetorical schools of the Second Sophistic and keen to display his *paideia*.[58] This becomes most obvious in the rhetorical commonplaces employed by Dio in the opening of Tiberius' speech.[59] However, we would underestimate Dio as a historian if we simply regarded the speech as another oratorical showpiece to impress his readers. Manuwald has rightly pointed out that there are striking discrepancies between Dio's depiction of Augustus in Tiberius' speech and his earlier narrative of Augustus in Books 45–56.[60] He has, therefore, suggested that Dio inserted the speech in order to show, by means of irony ('bewußte Ironisierung'), that Tiberius was distorting the truth.[61] However, this interpretation must be viewed with caution, since it makes Dio, as Pelling has aptly noted, 'too subtle'.[62] This is not to say that Dio was not able to employ this rhetorical device but that it is doubtful that irony was his prime motive for composing the speech.

Instead, we should perhaps place more emphasis on the assumption that Dio had a keen interest in exploring the imperial perspective at the end of Augustus' reign. After all, as he had shown in Book 56, the last decade of Augustus' reign had seen major disasters and setbacks, be they in domestic politics or foreign affairs. Dio reports in detail about the public

---

[58] See Swan 2004: 4; Fomin 2016.
[59] See Fomin 2016: 233. The same rhetorical cliché can be found in Antony's funeral speech for Caesar (44.36–49) and thus attests to Dio's familiarity with the genre of the *oratio funebris*.
[60] For a list of these differences, see Manuwald 1979: 136–9.   [61] Manuwald 1979: 133–4.
[62] Pelling 1983: 224. Cf. also Swan 2004: 326: 'one end that Dio wanted to achieve through it . . . was to transport his readers to a living theatre of Roman and world history at a moment of epochal transition in a way that was beyond the possibilities of mere narrative'.

dissatisfaction with the emperor's marriage legislation (56.1–10) and taxation (56.28), the upheavals in Dalmatia and Pannonia (56.11–17) and the Roman military disaster in the Teutoburg Forest (56.18–24). How did the imperial *domus* present Augustus and his achievements in view of such setbacks? What did they regard as his key accomplishments, for which he was to be praised publicly after his death? Did the imperial *domus* have good arguments to justify the emperor's course of action? And did Augustus really deserve deification for his services? However pro-Augustan Dio was, these must have been crucial questions in the mind of the historian, and it is for this reason that he must have been eager to present the viewpoint of the imperial *domus*. I have argued above that much in the speech suggests that Dio could have used the *RGDA* when composing Tiberius' speech. This text represented the imperial perspective *par excellence* and, as its publication dates to around the same time in which the speech is set, it must have been most tempting for Dio to draw on it to reconstruct the imperial view.

In addition, we should note that the insertion of Tiberius' speech as evidence for the imperial view provided Dio with the opportunity of making an important statement about the role of the senatorial elite. It will not have escaped the attentive reader of his *Roman History* that Dio had produced an account of Augustus in Books 45–56 with its own tone, emphasis and interpretation. The Augustus that here emerges from Dio's narrative also captures the ruthless, manipulative and hypocritical sides of the emperor's character and is thus a far more nuanced portrayal of a ruler than the Augustus eulogized by Tiberius in the funeral speech.[63] By creating this tension between the main narrative and Tiberius' speech,[64] Dio was able to communicate to his readers the important message that he was not in any way slavishly following the imperial view in his own account of the events.[65] In this way, he was able to underline the role of the senatorial elite as an 'intermediary' between the emperor and the people.[66] Despite being loyal to the emperor and pro-monarchic in his stance, the senatorial historian proved capable of independent, critical thought, as reflected in his own nuanced way of looking at the events.[67]

---

[63] On Dio's nuanced portrayal of Augustus, see esp. Manuwald 1979: 27–70; Reinhold and Swan 1990; Rich 1989.

[64] See n. 60.   [65] This aspect is only briefly hinted at by Manuwald 1979: 139.

[66] On Dio's view of the senatorial order, see Gabba 1984: 73–4, who highlights the notion of the senators as 'intermediaries'.

[67] On Dio's self-fashioning as a historian in his *Roman History*, see Mallan 2016: 274 and Mallan (Chapter 12) in this volume.

Moreover, the speech is used by Dio as a platform to develop the themes of good government and the emperor's virtues. We must remember that these are the topics that Dio keenly explored throughout his *Roman History*.[68] As we have seen, Augustus is described by Tiberius as an emperor who excelled through prudence, generosity, civility and, above all, clemency – in short: the embodiment of an ideal *princeps*.[69] Tiberius' message is clear: if the Principate is to function well, it needs an emperor of Augustus' merit and distinction. Or to put it in Tiberius' words, the speech provides 'most excellent instruction in the character and constitution of our government' (διδασκαλίαν ἀκριβῆ τοῦ τε τρόπου καὶ τῆς καταστάσεως τῆς πολιτείας) (56.37.7). It thus was to serve an educative purpose. By making a member of the imperial *domus*, the mouthpiece of the key principles of good governance and leadership, Dio was able to convey an important message to his readers: namely, that this canon of virtues and precepts of good government was not the product of the wishful thinking of the third-century senatorial elite, which Dio represented. On the contrary, it was acknowledged and cherished by the imperial *domus* itself right from the beginning of the Principate. Moreover, by inserting the speech shortly before the beginning of Book 57, which deals with Tiberius' reign, Dio invites his readers to compare Augustus to his successor, Tiberius, and to all the emperors who followed him, including those of Dio's own time.[70] Can Tiberius live up to the high standards of imperial rule, which the imperial *domus* itself had established and praised at the end of the Augustan principate?

Remarkably, Dio comments on this question in the paragraphs following close upon the speech (56.43–5). Much ink has been spilled on these final paragraphs of Book 56, particularly with a view towards their relationship with Tacitus' account (*Ann.* 1.9–10). There is no point in reiterating the old debate about the sources.[71] For our purpose, it may suffice to stress that these paragraphs can be read as reflections on the effectiveness of Tiberius' rhetoric. We have seen that Dio had Tiberius stress the educative role of his speech. As Dio suggests, however, its immediate educative effect

---

[68] See Millar 1964: 79–82. The theme is, for instance, covered in the debate between Agrippa and Maecenas (52.2–40), in Caesar's speech before the senate in 46 BC (43.15.2–18) and Hadrian's adoption speech (69.20.1–5). For a close analysis of the topic of the best leader in Hadrian's speech, see Mallan and Davenport 2014: esp. 640–50.

[69] For Tiberius' speech as a guide to imperial virtues, see Carlsen 2016: 320–1; Swan 2004: 332.

[70] Swan (2004: 14–15) argues that Dio makes Augustus 'his exemplar' and a role model for his own time. Swan stresses that, in the light of the Antonine emperors (esp. Marcus Aurelius), this choice was not a matter of course.

[71] On this debate, cf. n. 6.

was modest. Tiberius' excessive praise of Augustus did not motivate the people to respond and express their gratitude and grief on the emperor's death instantly. As we learn from Dio, it took indeed some time before many citizens started mourning properly: 'Real grief was not in the hearts of many at the time, but later was felt by all' (τὸ δ' ἀληθὲς ἐν μὲν τῷ παραχρῆμα οὐ πολλοὶ ὕστερον δὲ πάντες ἔσχον) (56.43.1). It was only after a while that they realized Augustus' exceptional qualities as an emperor. And only in hindsight did they understand that Augustus had established a government that was the perfect blend of monarchy and democracy, since it had brought about freedom, order and security for the citizens (56.43.4). In Dio's view, it is human nature that accounts for their failure: 'for human nature is so constituted that in good fortune it does not so fully perceive its happiness as it misses it when misfortune has come' (καὶ γὰρ φιλεῖ πως τὸ ἀνθρώπειον οὐχ οὕτω τι εὐπαθοῦν τῆς εὐδαιμονίας αἰσθάνεσθαι ὡς δυστυχῆσαν ποθεῖν αὐτήν) (56.45.1). According to Dio, it was Tiberius who personified this misfortune. It was only through the negative contrast with his reign that the people eventually came to realize the loss that they had experienced in AD 14 (56.45).[72] What Dio is suggesting here is that the speech 'educated' neither Tiberius (who deviated as an emperor from the standards praised by himself) nor the contemporary audience (who did not immediately understand the exceptionality of Augustus' achievements). As Dio sees it, contemporaries are unable to properly assess and appreciate the achievements of a ruler, since they are in the midst of the historical process, unaware of any later permutations of the Principate. With this observation on an essential trait of the people's mentality, Dio is finally able to extol his own insight and prudence as a historian. It is the historian who, in hindsight, is best able to judge the historical events due to his comprehensive knowledge of the further developments of the Principate. It is a judgement which, in his view, is superior to that of contemporary witnesses. The final assessment of Augustus' achievements, which Dio presents in 56.43–4, is positive and in line with his own pro-monarchic tendencies:[73]

---

[72] Dio (56.45.3) also relates the rumour that 'some suspected that Augustus, with full knowledge of Tiberius' character, had purposely appointed him his successor that his own glory might be enhanced thereby' (τινὰς καὶ ἐς τὸν Αὔγουστον ὑποπτεῦσαι ὅτι ἐξεπίτηδες τὸν Τιβέριον, καίπερ εὖ εἰδὼς ὁποῖος ἦν, διάδοχον ἀπέδειξεν, ἵνα αὐτὸς εὐδοξήσῃ). He seems to realize that this argument is not without risk if he wishes to present Augustus as the paradigm of the good emperor; he thus tries to scotch the rumour by stating that it came into existence only later. Interestingly, the same rumour is reported in Tac. Ann. 1.10 and Suet. Tib. 21.2–3.

[73] For Dio's assessment of Augustus in 56.43–5, cf. also Giua 1983: 451–4; Swan 2004: 345–50.

Not alone for these reasons did the Romans greatly miss him, but also because by combining monarchy with democracy he preserved their freedom for them and at the same time established order and security, so that they were free alike from the license of a democracy and from the insolence of a tyranny, living at once in a liberty of moderation and in a monarchy without terrors; they were subjects of royalty, yet not slaves, and citizens of a democracy, yet without discord (...) but summing them all up briefly, I may state that he put an end to all the factional discord, transferred the government in a way to give it the greatest power, and vastly strengthened it. (56.43.4–44.2)[74]

With his special focus on the constitutional features of the new Augustan order and praise of its ideal combination of democracy and monarchy,[75] Dio goes beyond the Tiberian assessment in the funerary speech and thus raises the analysis of the Augustan principate to a higher level, as was possible for a third-century historian writing with the benefit of hindsight.

IV Conclusion

Our analysis of Tiberius' funeral speech for Augustus has revealed that Dio showed a keen interest in examining the perspective of the imperial *domus* at a turning point in Roman history and exploring its relationship to his own judgement of Augustus, which he had offered in the main narrative of Books 45–56. I have argued that Dio may have drawn on the *RGDA* as a model when composing Tiberius' speech, since it echoes the distinct mixture of praise, justification and half-truths of this significant document of Augustan propaganda. We have also seen that Dio's reconstruction of the perspective of the imperial *domus* was not entirely accurate. Leaving his own imprint on the text by broaching concerns related to his own time, Dio established the contemporary relevance of the speech for his third-century audience. The modern reader must be careful not to be too quick to read into such anachronisms a 'failure of historical imagination' on the part of Dio. For Dio and his readers, these anachronisms were no more

---

[74] διά τε οὖν ταῦτα, καὶ ὅτι τὴν μοναρχίαν τῇ δημοκρατίᾳ μίξας τό τε ἐλεύθερόν σφισιν ἐτήρησε καὶ τὸ κόσμιον τό τε ἀσφαλὲς προσπαρεσκεύασεν, ἀδεεῖ ζῆν, βασιλευομένους τε ἄνευ δουλείας καὶ δημοκρατουμένους ἄνευ διχοστασίας, δεινῶς αὐτὸν ἐπόθουν [...] κεφάλαιον δὲ ἐφ' ἅπασιν αὐτοῖς γράφω ὅτι τό τε στασιάζον πᾶν ἔπαυσε καὶ τὸ πολίτευμα πρός τε τὸ κράτιστον μετεκόσμησε καὶ ἰσχυρῶς ἐκράτυνεν [...].
[75] On Dio's constitutional views, cf. esp. Millar 1964: 74–7; Kuhn-Chen 2002: 182–201.

than 'timeless truths' that linked the present with the past.[76] By presenting Augustus as a paradigm of civic virtues and good government, the speech provided Dio's readers with basic criteria for assessing later emperors, including those of their own time. Moreover, the attentive reader of the speech and the context in which it is embedded will not have failed to understand another important message that Dio intended to convey: the self-presentation of the third-century senatorial historian as an independent observer and reliable judge of historical events.

[76] Quotations from Marincola 2007: 132.

CHAPTER 6

'... But He Possessed a Most Singular Nature'
Cassius Dio on Tiberius

Christopher Mallan

I Introduction

One of the effects of the dynastically influenced imperial portraiture of the second and early third centuries AD is that emperors start to look alike. Hadrian's visage dissolves into that of Antoninus Pius, Antoninus' into that of Marcus Aurelius, Marcus' into that of Commodus. Even the boy Caracalla, properly M. Aurelius Antoninus, scion of a Romanised North African and an Emesine Syrian, is represented in portraiture as the spitting image of a generic Antonine youth. Features that were once distinct are softened by the sculptor, fashioned, as it were, into the serene blandness that was representative of Antonine piety. The same observation may be applied to those portraits of emperors that appear in rhetoric of the age. Much has been written as to whether the anodyne *Eis Basilea* oration, a speech in praise of an emperor, was a composition addressed to Antoninus Pius, Philip the Arab, Septimius Severus, or alternatively a rhetorical exercise variously dated between the second and the ninth centuries.[1] Yet genuine or not, the point is that the contents of the oration are so general, so stereotypical, that it could be legitimately seen to apply to any number of emperors, or no emperor in particular.

Superficially, there may seem something of imperial Antonine or Severan statuary about the emperors that appear in Dio's history. They are, in most cases, variations on a common theme. Bad emperors tend to persecute (virtuous) members of the elite, while leading lewd or luxurious

---

I am grateful to Rhiannon Ash, Caillan Davenport, Helen Tanner, Chris Pelling, and John Rich who have offered advice and criticism of this chapter at various stages. An earlier version of this chapter appeared in my (2015) Oxford DPhil thesis, *A Historical and Historiographical Commentary on Cassius Dio's Roman History 57.1.1–17.8*. Translations are the author's own unless otherwise stated.

[1] [Aristid.] *Or.* 35. To get a sense of the debate, see Jones 1972; Stertz 1979; De Blois 1986; cf. Barker 1957: 220–5. Whenever the oration was composed, Barker's suggestion that it was written in the ninth century has been roundly (but not always cogently) rejected. Here it is taken to be of either second or third century date.

lifestyles themselves. Good emperors, conversely, typically behave in just the opposite manner. Such an approach was conventional. It had long been a staple of Greek historiography to judge the quality of a regime (or period of history) by the ethical quality of its ruler. This was, certainly, in part a result of the influence of rhetoric that drew upon the dominant ethical commonplaces of the age. The rhetorical handbooks provided models from which encomiastic speeches could be structured. It was the job of the rhetor to select from the categories those which most pertained to the virtues (real or imagined) possessed by the emperor. These models were essentially late Classical in origin, and a path may be detected linking the encomiastic productions of Isocrates and Xenophon with the panegyrics delivered to the various late Roman warlords and dynasts represented in eleven of the twelve so-called *Panegyrici Latini*.[2] Not only was the form stereotyped, but so too was the language. When the late second-century grammarian Julius Pollux came to write about the language used to describe kings in the first book of his *Onomasticon* ('Directory of Vocabulary'), he produced an extensive list of adjectives of desirable virtues and qualities.[3] Immediately following this list was a list of antonyms, used to describe tyrants: a reminder, if ever one was needed, of how easy it was to switch from encomium to vituperation.[4]

Yet mention of these rhetorical works should give us reason to pause. Dio was a historian who took his task seriously and was writing an extensive annalistic history of considerable sophistication. He was not writing a historical handbook *de Caesaribus* ('On the Caesars'). Although Dio was influenced undoubtedly by rhetoric and contemporary discourses on kingship, Dio's emperors are, on closer inspection, not a series of cardboard cut-outs of good and bad emperors. As a historian he was interested in the personal and external factors that motivated his protagonists to act in the way they did. Moreover, he tried to make clear distinctions between appearances and realities, between what was professed and what was actually done. Furthermore, it is notable that Dio is often more interested in how the men who became emperors performed their duties, rather than just documenting and judging them based on their abstract

---

[2] For the development of this sort of praise literature (*encomia, laudationes*, panegyrics), see in general Nixon and Rodgers 1994: 1–3, 10–14, 23–4. For the stereotypical aspects of encomiastic speeches, with an emphasis on characterisation (specifically Isocrates' *Evagoras*), see Halliwell 1990: 42–3, 56–7.

[3] Poll. 1.40–2 (Bethe 1900: I, 12–13).

[4] E.g. Arist. *Rhet.* 1368a.33–7; [Arist.] *Rhet.* AD *Alex.* 1425b.36–40. For an excellent discussion of how historians 're-coded' once positive images of emperors, see Schulz 2019a: 30–1, 83, 97–8.

qualities – their virtues and their vices.[5] Dio's portrayal of Tiberius provides an illustration of these features.

It is an indisputable fact that Dio's history becomes more biographical from Book 51 onwards, at least to the extent that his material is arranged tightly around the person of the reigning emperor. Dio's treatment of Tiberius is a useful case study for investigating how this method works. Perhaps uniquely of the emperors covered in the work, Tiberius enjoyed an illustrious career before his accession to the purple in middle age.[6] Indeed, Dio pays significant attention to tracking Tiberius' political career prior to his accession. But the question of how exactly Dio conceived of Tiberius' position in August AD 14 is one that has not received appropriate consideration, although it is of importance when considering the opening of Book 57. There are also questions of a more literary-historiographical nature. Whether Dio's comments on Tiberius' early career have a bearing on the characterisation of Tiberius presented in Books 57 and 58 has been doubted. According to Pelling, '[u]nder Augustus, Tiberius has not yet passed the "threshold of biography" – that is, he has not yet become important enough to excite any real personal interest'.[7] The sentence raises two important questions. First, if 57.1 does indeed mark the 'threshold of biography' we may legitimately wonder how Dio approached the figure of Tiberius before he crossed this threshold – that is, in the pre-accession narrative. Second, we need to determine what the possible functions of the biographical elements actually are in the overarching narrative concerning Tiberius and his reign. By approaching Dio's portrayal of Tiberius from both literary-historiographical and historical perspectives, this chapter will address these questions.

II   Dio and the Pre-imperial Career of Tiberius

Although supplying one of the fullest accounts of Tiberius' pre-accession career, Dio's account appears insubstantial and unsatisfying as history. Whether through ignorance or design, Dio pays little attention to describing the constitutional position of Tiberius or the extent of his *imperium* in either AD 4 or 13.[8] This apparent defect is not peculiar to Dio. The general absence of reliable or conclusive evidence for Tiberius' constitutional

---

[5] See the stimulating treatment of Kemezis 2014, especially 139–40.

[6] It is impossible to draw concrete conclusions on this issue, owning to the fragmentary nature of Dio's imperial narrative and Xiphilinus' more tightly controlled biographical focus. For which see Mallan 2013b: especially 630–44, and the contribution of Simpson in this volume (Chapter 13).

[7] Pelling 1997a: 127.   [8] Cf. Swan 2004: 85.

position following his adoption by Augustus has resulted in many ingenious explanations by scholars to define his position at the time of and immediately following Augustus' death. It has been reasoned that Tiberius possessed *imperium maius* ('greater power of command') equal to that of Augustus, which did not require renewal upon Augustus' death, along with the crucial *tribunicia potestas* ('tribunician power').[9] Much of this interpretation hinges on the interpretation of Velleius' statement (2.121.1): 'at the request of his father that he should have in all the provinces and armies a power equal to his own, the senate and Roman people so decreed' (*senatus populusque Romanus postulante patre eius, ut aequum ei ius in omnibus provinciis exercitibusque esset, quam erat ipsi, decreto complexus est*).[10] Suetonius too knew of a law, presumably the same as that mentioned by Velleius, which gave Tiberius joint authority over the provinces (*Tib.* 21.1). Tacitus' comment that Tiberius was *collega imperii* ('partner in command') with Augustus (*Ann.* 1.3) sheds little light on the matter: Tacitus' description seems like an informal formulation, which does not seem to indicate Tiberius' official title or position. The date of this law is not given by either Suetonius or Velleius, but from the context of the narrative it seems likely that it was granted to Tiberius either in late (September?) AD 12 or early 13.[11]

Less clear is the extent of the powers enjoyed by Tiberius. We should not expect precise constitutional formulations from either Velleius or Suetonius, but even if we take that into account, their versions leave the exact extent of the powers Tiberius received in AD 12/13 poorly defined. Particularly important for the events following Augustus' death is the question of whether Tiberius' *imperium* in AD 13/14 extended to Italy and Rome. It has been argued that Augustus' statement concerning the census of AD 13/14 indicates Tiberius' possession of *imperium* in Italy in AD 14.[12] Yet the wording of the document only describes Augustus' own powers at the time of the census and is not explicit as to whether

[9] Brunt 1974a: 171–4, 179–80; Levick 1976: 75, 79–81.
[10] Trans. F. W. Shipley, Loeb Classical Library edition.
[11] Brunt 1974a: 171–3; Woodman 1977: 210–11; Swan 2004: 294; Ferrary 2009: 125–6 with n. 129; cf. Goodyear 1972: 112.
[12] *RGDA* 8.4: 'And for a third time I conducted a census with consular power with Tiberius Caesar my son as colleague in the consulship of Sextus Pompeius and Sextus Appuleius') (*[et te]rtium consulari cum imperio lustrum conlega Tib(erio) Cae[sare filio] m[eo feci], Sex(to) Pompeio et Sex(to) Appuleio co(n)s(ulibus)*) (trans. Cooley 2009: 66). Brunt 1962: 72; Brunt and Moore 1973: 51–2; Levick 1976: 63; *contra* Jones 1951: 118 = Jones 1960: 16. Cooley (2009: 143) does not address this issue, noting simply the connection between the passage in the *RGDA* and the law enacted in 14 to allow Tiberius to be Augustus' colleague in the census (Suet. *Tib.* 21).

Tiberius' (implied) *censoria potestas* ('censorial power') derived from his possession of the same consular *imperium* held by Augustus, as argued by Hardy and assumed by Brunt and Moore.[13] Moreover, while Suetonius (*Tib.* 21.1) groups the extension of Tiberius' powers over the provinces and the authorisation of the census under the one law, he does not connect Tiberius' censorial authority with his new extended command.

Given the importance attributed to these powers by historians, these omissions by Dio are surprising. On the whole, Dio was interested in the constitutional developments and the granting of novel political powers during the Augustan period.[14] Moreover, it is not as if Dio failed to appreciate the importance of the *imperium* granted to Augustus over the imperial provinces in 27 BC: Dio quite rightly saw this as one of the foundations of Augustus' power (53.16.1).[15] Yet, there is no trace in Dio's narrative of the laws that supposedly elevated Tiberius to the same position as Augustus (with respect to his *imperium maius*) prior to Augustus' death, as indicated by Suetonius. It is, of course, possible that such material once existed in Dio's account: Books 55 and 56, where we should expect to find such details, are lacunose. Particularly unfortunate is the loss of the end of Dio's account of AD 13, where it is possible that Dio referred to this extension of Tiberius' *imperium*, should it have occurred in that year.[16] However, this seems unlikely. Had Dio included such details, we should expect them to have been grouped together with his brief account of the renewal of Tiberius' *tribunicia potestas* and the advancement of Drusus (56.28.1). More tellingly, Dio's silence on such matters is found elsewhere: since the publication of *P. Colon.* 4701, it is almost certain that Agrippa possessed *imperium maius* over the provinces at the time of his death, and thus must have been granted to him with the award of *tribunicia potestas* in either 18 or 13 BC.[17]

These are not the only instances where Dio is extremely selective in reporting specific grants of power. When describing the punitive expedition by Tiberius and Germanicus mounted in AD 11 in the wake of the

---

[13] Hardy 1919: 48–9.

[14] Syme (1978: 56): 'That being so, the historian [sc. Dio], whose interest in constitutional matters is patent, and sometimes excessive, ought not to have missed the grant of an imperium over provinces and armies equal and equipollent to that of Caesar Augustus.'

[15] Cf. Brunt 1977: 96; Cotton and Yakobson 2002: 193–4. For the settlements of 28 and 27 BC, see Rich and Williams 1999: especially 188–213; Ferrary 2009: 92–9.

[16] For the lacuna at 56.28.6, see Boissevain II.540–1.

[17] The *editio princeps* of the so-called *laudatio funebris* (*P. Colon.* 4701) is that of Koenen 1970. For discussion of Agrippa's ἐξουσία (as termed in the *laudatio*), see Koenen 1970: 269–83; Gray 1970; Gruen 2005: 44. For Agrippa's *provincia*, see Lacey 1996: 117–31.

Varian disaster, Dio comments on Germanicus' proconsular authority (56.25.2),[18] but not on that possessed by Tiberius. Similar silences occur with respect to the precise nature of Tiberius' authority in his campaigns in Illyricum and Dalmatia between AD 6 and 9 (55.30.1; cf. 56.12.1), or those in Germany between AD 4 and 6 (55.28.5). Of course, Dio would have recognised that these campaigns entailed Tiberius' possession of some form of proconsular *imperium*: by the time of his adoption in AD 4, Tiberius had already been consul twice (in 13 BC and 7 BC) and so was eligible for the command of armies in the provinces. Hence, Dio's silence concerning the details of Tiberius' *imperium* following his adoption could have been due to Dio's belief that Tiberius' authority in these campaigns was not in any way extraordinary or surprising, at least insofar as it was not beyond the usual *imperium* possessed by proconsular or propraetorian military commanders. Indeed, in his description of the German campaigns of AD 4, Tiberius is identified as only one of several commanders (55.28.5), and the nature or extent of his *imperium* is left undisclosed.

It remains to be discussed in what terms Dio interpreted Tiberius' position in AD 14. Two features characterise Dio's understanding of Tiberius' position prior to Augustus' death: his possession of the *tribunicia potestas* and his designation as Augustus' 'successor' (διάδοχος). These two things are obviously connected. Dio is careful to record the conferral of the *tribunicia potestas* upon Tiberius in 6 BC (55.9.4), AD 4 (55.13.2 [Xiph.]) and its renewal in AD 13 (56.28.1). Why he should have placed such emphasis on this is not difficult to understand: Dio recognised the importance of these powers for Augustus and subsequent emperors.[19] Moreover, Dio connected Augustus' conferral of the *tribunicia potestas* to select individuals as being indicative of his nomination of a successor,[20] in a way that grants of *imperium* were not. Hence, Dio records Augustus' grant of the tribunician powers to Agrippa in 18 BC (54.12.4) in such a way as to indicate he was the chosen successor, should Augustus predecease him (53.31.2–5). Similarly, Velleius regarded the initial grant of tribunician powers to Tiberius in 6 BC and AD 4 as elevating him to a position of (near) equality with Augustus, and in the case of the latter, designating him as Augustus' successor.[21]

The imperial succession plans of Augustus were of as much interest to Dio as they have been to latter-day historians.[22] Dio introduced the theme

---

[18] Brunt 1974: 185; Syme 1978: 57; Swan 2004: 278. [19] 53.17.10, 53.32.6; cf. Tac. *Ann.* 3.56.
[20] Brunt and Moore 1973: 47; Lacey 1979; Rich 1990: 169. [21] Vell. Pat. 2.99.1; 2.103.1–3.
[22] For the modern bibliography and summary, see Rowe 2002: 1–22; Gruen 2005; Lott 2012: 4–24; Stevenson 2013. For Dio's treatment of the imperial succession throughout the *Roman History*, see Davenport and Mallan 2014; cf. Ando 2016.

of succession, appropriately, in his account of Augustus' illness in 23 BC. At this point, Dio says that Augustus did not (overtly) appoint a successor (διάδοχον μὲν οὐδένα ἀπέδειξε), but gave his ring to Agrippa,[23] and a book containing the public revenues and military forces to the consul (*suffectus*) Cn. Calpurnius Piso (53.30.1–2).[24] Under the events of 17 BC Dio (54.18.1) describes how Augustus adopted Gaius and Lucius as 'successors to the empire' (διαδόχους τῆς ἀρχῆς). Tiberius' role in the Augustan narrative is defined largely by his part in Augustus' succession plans. Hence, under 6 BC, Dio (55.9.7) notes that one of the explanations given for Tiberius' retirement to Rhodes was his anger at not being designated 'Caesar' (ὅτι μὴ καὶ Καῖσαρ ἀπεδείχθη) by Augustus.[25]

The adoptions of AD 4 (55.13.2–3) are presented as Augustus securing Tiberius, Agrippa Postumus, and Germanicus as his successors (sc. διάδοχοι).[26] The same language appears at the beginning of Tiberius' funeral oration for Augustus, where Tiberius describes himself as 'the child and successor of Augustus' (τοῦ καὶ παιδὸς αὐτοῦ καὶ διαδόχου) (56.35.2). The appropriateness of such a statement to the historical context of Augustus' funeral has been rightly questioned.[27] But the language itself is not anachronistic, at least for Greek writers of the Augustan age: Strabo describes Tiberius in almost identical terms,[28] just as Nicolaus of Damascus styled the young Octavian, Julius Caesar's 'child   and   appointed   successor'   (τὸν   παῖδα   καὶ   διάδοχον

---

[23] Dio's account recalls the 'vulgate' tradition of Alexander's death, whereby Alexander gave his ring to Perdiccas, but did not nominate a successor (Diod. Sic. 17.117.3; Curt. 10.5.4; Justin. 12.15.12). Cf. Rich 1990: 165–6.

[24] For Piso: *PIR²* C 286; Syme 1986: 368.

[25] It has been thought that Dio's vocabulary here (sc. Καῖσαρ) is anachronistic (cf. 53.18.2), reflecting the later usage of the name Caesar to denote a successor (Rich 1990: 229, followed by Pelling 1997a: 142 n. 81), based on the assumption that the title 'Caesar' (to denote an heir) did not become standard practice until the reign of Hadrian and the adoption of L. Ceionius Commodus in AD 136 (cf. Mommsen 1887 2.2: 1139–40; Hammond 1957: 28–31). However, the extent to which Dio's comment is an anachronism may not be as great as it first appears. It was not unknown in the first century AD to think of a successor as a Caesar, at least in an informal sense: for Plutarch (writing probably in the reign of Domitian) describes Piso as being 'designated Caesar' by Galba as a result of his adoption (*Galba* 23.2; cf. 64(63).5.1 [Xiph.]). For the Flavian date of Plutarch's *Galba*, see Hardy 1906: 309–11; Jones 1966: 71. Note now Stadter (2015: 65–9), who argues for a Vespasianic date.

[26] The surviving text of 55.13.2 does not mention the adoption of Agrippa. However, it is likely that his omission is due to Xiphilinus rather than Dio: see Swan 2004: 141–2; *pace* Levick 1966: 229–30.

[27] Cf. Millar 1964: 101.

[28] Strabo 6.4.2: 'Augustus Caesar, from the time he assumed the absolute authority, and is now being afforded them by his son and successor, Tiberius' (Καῖσάρ τε ὁ Σεβαστὸς παρέσχεν ἀφ᾽ οὗ παρέλαβε τὴν ἐξουσίαν αὐτοτελῆ καὶ νῦν ὁ διαδεξάμενος υἱὸς ἐκεῖνον παρέχει Τιβέριος) (trans. H. L. Jones, Loeb Classical Library edition). Cf. 3.3.8.

ἀποδειχθέντα).²⁹ Moreover, Tiberius' comments are consistent with his portrayal up to that point in the narrative.³⁰ Furthermore, Tiberius' comments add to the thematic unity of Book 56, which opens with Augustus' speech to the *equites*, where he expresses the importance of children (as successors) for the future of individual families and the Roman state.

Dio had certainly stressed some of the steps Augustus made to groom Tiberius as his successor. With the exception of the grant of the *tribunicia potestas*, these appear predominantly as gestures designed to augment Tiberius' position by association, an imperial colleague in deeds, if not in a formal constitutional sense.³¹ Hence, Dio tells us that when Augustus had augmented the *aerarium militare* ('military treasury') with his own funds, he had advertised that the donation had been made jointly with Tiberius (55.25.2).³² Similarly, Dio notes the instances where Augustus and Tiberius shared joint salutations as *imperator*.³³ In his description of AD 13, Dio emphasises the importance of Augustus' and Tiberius' joint role in the reformed *consilium* ('imperial council'), which had been created in response to Augustus' declining health.³⁴ We may assume that Dio duly recorded, in a now lost passage, the performance of the *lustrum* ('purification ceremony') by Tiberius and Augustus in AD 14.³⁵

In summary, the following points may be noted with respect to Dio's representation of Tiberius' position at the point of Augustus' death. The first is the inevitability of Tiberius' succession. It is this that gives Tiberius' behaviour at 57.2–7 so much of its force. Dio invites the reader to ask why the man who has been designated successor should take so long to accept

---

²⁹ Nic. Dam. *Caes.* 115 (= *FGrH* 90 F 130.xxix); cf. 118 (= *FGrH* 90 F 130.xxix), 120 (*FGrH* 90 F 130.xxx). For the notion of the 'succession' to Caesar, note also, 45.41.3 (speech of Cicero); Plut. *Ant.* 16.3 (sc. τὴν Καίσαρος διαδοχήν) with Pelling 1988: 157.

³⁰ Swan 2004: 327. How Tiberius' frankness at this point accords with his subsequent characterisation (especially 57.1) is less easily reconciled.

³¹ The augmentation and consolidation of Tiberius' position through his association with Augustus is a feature of the coinage produced late in Augustus' reign at Lugdunum featuring Augustus on the obverse and Tiberius on the reverse. e.g. *RIC* I² (Augustus) nos. 220, 221, 222, 223, 224, 225, 226. For discussion on the degree to which coinage was used to promote Tiberius following his adoption, see Sutherland 1951: 73–8.

³² Dio is apparently referring to the same donation mentioned by Augustus in the *Res Gestae* (*RGDA* 17), yet without, unsurprisingly, mention of Tiberius. See further, Swan 2004: 175.

³³ 55.6.4, 55.28.6, 56.17.1. For the dating of these salutations, see Barnes 1974: 23–36; Syme 1979: 315–17; Swan 2004: 264–5; Cooley 2009: 122.

³⁴ 56.28.2–3; cf. Crook 1955: 14–18; Swan 2004: 294–6.

³⁵ Cf. *RGDA* 8; Suet. *Tib.* 21.1. This is preferable to the suggestion of Jones (1960: 23) that Dio simply omitted it altogether. Cf. Astin 1963: 230.

the Principate when it was finally his. The second is the absence of any attempt to explore the full legal basis for Tiberius' power. Such information must have been available to him, for as we have seen, Dio notes the granting of special commands to Gaius Caesar and Germanicus, but only when such a grant was unusual. Not so for Tiberius. The thing that matters most for Dio with respect to Tiberius' career was his designation as Augustus' successor. By avoiding discussion of these constitutional points Dio emphasises the monarchic nature of the Augustan regime and what was the essentially extra-constitutional position of the emperor and the organisation of the succession.

III   Characterising Tiberius

The framework within which Dio describes Tiberius' pre-accession career provides little opportunity to develop his characterisation of the man who would be Augustus' successor. As we have just seen, Tiberius' function in the narrative leading up to Book 57 is largely, but not exclusively, as a passive participant in events, either as Augustus' general or Augustus' successor. Dio's discussion of Tiberius' nature, which comes at 57.1, appears to have been deliberately delayed, so that it could function as a way of introducing the new reign and the succession debate of AD 14. Indeed, we get the impression that for Dio it only became necessary to understand Tiberius' nature when he became an active political player, that is, as 'emperor'.[36] But if Tiberius' native dissimulation, ostensibly the topic of 57.1, was (seemingly) not important to Dio's characterisation of Tiberius before he became emperor, we may wonder if there are other aspects of his characterisation that are developed in these early books, and if so, whether these are carried over into Dio's portrayal of Tiberius the emperor.

In several important respects Dio largely eschews the temptation to foreshadow his characterisation of Tiberius in his pre-accession narrative. In this respect Dio's portrayal of Augustus' successor is distinct from the likes of Suetonius or, indeed, Velleius. This may be seen in several presentational choices Dio makes. Although on many occasions a keen

---

[36] From what we can make of Dio's truncated imperial narrative, this seems to be his general approach. For example, of those emperors who had distinguished pre-imperial careers, Dio (in most cases represented by Xiphilinus) does not appear to reveal to the reader much about their character prior to their accession. Occasionally, we are afforded clues to the quality of the successor, such as to Marcus' excellence (69.21.1–2 [Xiph.]), Commodus' inadequacy (72[71].22.3 [Xiph.]), or Caracalla's general viciousness (77[76].7.1–2 [Xiph., EV]; 77[76].14.1 [Xiph.]), etc.

prosopographer,[37] Dio makes little of Tiberius' familial connections. To be sure, Tiberius' parentage is duly recorded at his introduction into the narrative (48.15.3–4).[38] But unlike Tacitus or Suetonius, Dio makes virtually nothing of the anti-Claudian tradition of Roman historiography in his portrayal of the emperor. The salient feature was that Tiberius was of noble birth, and that he was the stepson of Augustus.

Similar observations may be made about Dio's attitude towards Tiberius' education. We know that by the time Dio came to write his history there were numerous stories concerning Tiberius' intellectual pursuits and his rhetorical accomplishments.[39] However, Dio provides little information regarding Tiberius' education beyond the ostensibly offhand comment at 57.1.1 where he is styled a *pepaideumenos*. There are minor exceptions to this general rule. At 55.9.5, Dio says that Tiberius' sojourn on Rhodes in 6 BC was made on the *pretext* of acquiring further education, and two later anecdotes from his reign reveal Tiberius' somewhat pedantic streak in his desire to use pure Latin in legal contexts (57.15.2, 57.17.1–3; cf. Suet. *Tib.* 71). Dio attributes to Tiberius an apophthegm, with the emperor quoting lines from Attic tragedy (58.23.4).[40] However, such quotations are hardly authentic evidence for Tiberius' Greek literary leanings.[41] Nor should we regard them as evidence of a subtle authorial agenda which attempted to portray Tiberius as an educated emperor. Indeed, there is a tendency for emperors in Dio to quote the classical canon. Even those whom Dio portrays as having had few (if any) meaningful educative experiences are adept at producing an apt (and often ironic) tag.[42]

Perhaps more significantly, the pre-accession narrative contains virtually nothing that might indicate Tiberius' virtues or vices that would become evident during his reign. Only towards the end of Book 56 do we get a hint of his quality, yet this is only the report of rumour that Augustus appreciated his stepson's character and that he had chosen him as his successor so as to enhance his own posthumous reputation

---

[37] See the succinct judgment of Millar 1964: 164: '[Dio] is a born prosopographer'; Graham 1974: especially 142–3. For an example of Dio's awareness of such details even in his Republican narrative, note his comments concerning the grandfather of the conspirator P. Cornelius Lentulus at 46.20.5.

[38] Dio was clearly attracted to the twist of fate that saw the scion of a one-time follower of Antony become Caesar's (sc. Augustus') ultimate successor.

[39] E.g. Suet. *Tib.* 70–1; Tac. *Ann.* 13.3; Fronto, AD *Verum Imp.* 2.1.10 (Van den Hout 1988: 123.7–8).

[40] Cf. Kannicht and Snell *TrGF* 2.145 (Adesp.) no. 513.

[41] Cf. Horsfall 1979: 87; *pace* Rutledge 2008: 462–4.

[42] E.g. Caligula: 59.19.2; Caracalla: 79(78).8.4; cf. Horsfall 1979: 87. See also Power 2011, who notes the ironic use of quotations in Suetonius' *Divus Claudius*. For Tiberius' education and literary tastes, see Levick 1976: 15–18; Kaimio 1979: 132–3; Syme 1986: 349–52, 360–2; Rutledge 2008: 453–67.

(56.45.3).[43] The vocabulary Dio employs for Tiberius in his pre-accession phase is conspicuous for the absence of any of the typical ethical vocabulary so tied to discourses of kingship. This is particularly evident throughout Dio's narratives of Tiberius' military campaigns in the last two decades of Augustus' rule. Dio could have created a different picture. The material was available to Dio to present a strongly positive impression of Tiberius and his qualities. Tacitus, although never speaking of Tiberius' military exploits directly or in any detail, clearly knew them and was prepared to regard them positively. For the Latin annalist, the admirable qualities displayed by Tiberius *sub Augusto* gradually disappeared after his accession (Tac. *Ann.* 6.51). More explicitly, the enthusiastic Velleius was keen to demonstrate how the successes of the campaigns were clear proof of Tiberius' virtues.[44] Yet in Dio's version the future emperor's actions are narrated without the adornment of praise.[45] Even Tiberius' desperate flight to his brother's side during the latter's critical illness is described dispassionately, and there is little hint of Tiberius' well-reputed fraternal *pietas* (55.2.1).[46] Indeed, if we are expecting a straightforward ethical profile of Tiberius as an emperor-in-waiting, we are disappointed. We are given few clear indications whether or not Tiberius would prove *capax imperii*.[47]

Of all the possible vices that Dio could choose to discuss during the narrative of Tiberus' reign, it was his bloodthirstiness (μιαιφονία) and cruelty (ὠμότης) that receive the greatest attention. These were, after all, the characteristics that Dio thought were at the heart of Tiberius' encouragement of treason trials.[48] In Dio's mind, the emperor's zealousness in pursuing these investigations was one of the great disasters of his reign.[49] In

---

[43] This is a theme that Dio plays with in his accounts of the succession from Tiberius to Caligula, where each emperor chooses a successor that is worse than himself (58.24.3–4). Cf. Edmondson 1992: 49–50; Swan 2004: 350; Davenport and Mallan 2014: 648–9. On rumour in the *Roman History*, see Chapter 2 in this volume by Caillan Davenport.

[44] Note especially Vell. Pat. 2.104.3–4, where Velleius claims to be a witness to Tiberius' qualities and great deeds during the campaigns of AD 4.

[45] Syme (1978: 52) notes that more space is given to Drusus' actions, at the expense of Tiberius' achievements.

[46] Note the exemplary version of Tiberius' actions preserved in Val. Max. 5.5.3; [Ov.] *Consol. ad Liv.* 83–94; Plin. *HN* 7.84. See further, Wardle 2002; Woodman 2006: 308–9; Champlin 2011: 76–7.

[47] By no means an idle question: whether an imperial candidate was worthy of the position was a topic of interest to Dio, just as it was to his historiographical predecessors and successors. For this idea in Dio's work, note, especially the speech Dio gives to the emperor Hadrian concerning the adoption of Antoninus Pius (69.20 [Xiph.]). For discussion of which see Davenport and Mallan 2014.

[48] 58.22.4–5; 58.24.4; cf. 57.19.1 (Xiph./Zonar.); cf. Saylor Rodgers' discussion of Dio's ethical vocabulary in Chapter 11.

[49] That an emperor should not pursue such charges is part of the advice given by Maecenas (52.31.7–8) and is echoed in the speech of Livia (55.19.6). Cf. Edmondson 1992: 51.

this respect Dio was working firmly within the established historiograph-
ical/biographical tradition concerning Augustus' successor. Suetonius
devotes several chapters to the various manifestations of Tiberius' cruelty
(*Tib.* 57–62).[50] Yet, whereas the biographer was keen to illustrate how
cruelty was evident in Tiberius' character from an early age (*Tib.* 57), this is
not the case for Dio's portrayal. Such foreshadowing is simply not necessary for Dio's method of portraying Tiberius. For Dio, the sort of cruelty or
'bloodthirstiness' exhibited by Tiberius is a vice that becomes relevant only
once an individual becomes emperor or the most powerful individual in
the state. This may be taken further. 'Bloodthirstiness' or μιαιφονία is
a strong word in Dio's vocabulary. If we are to think in terms of Pelling's
'trans-regnal themes', we may note that is a common characteristic in Dio's
mind of those individuals who pursued proscriptions and judicial
murders.[51] Dio's comment about Tiberius' behaviour, therefore, situates
the emperor in a line of murderous autocrats, recalling the likes of Sulla
and anticipating the behaviour of emperors to come.

The absence of these stock Suetonian or, indeed, Plutarchan elements
and biographical techniques in Dio's sketch of Tiberius may not be
especially surprising, and it conforms to our impression of the circum-
scribed nature of Dio's portrayal of Tiberius in the Augustan books.
Nevertheless, as we shall see, Dio's skeletal portrayal of the pre-accession
Tiberius does contain one important element that feeds directly into his
characterisation in Books 57 and 58. For this point of continuity, we need
to look beyond Tiberius' virtues and vices, to his ascribed motivations.

Dio's narrative of Tiberius' retirement to Rhodes provides a clue to what
these motivations might be. It occurs in one of the few instances where Dio
attempts to interpret Tiberius' motivation prior to the death of Augustus.
Dio begins by describing Augustus' decision to chastise Gaius and Lucius
by granting the *tribunicia potestas* to Tiberius (55.9.4–7):

> Wishing to chasten them [sc. Gaius and Lucius] more strictly in some way,
> he bestowed upon Tiberius the tribunician power for five years and the
> command of Armenia (which was becoming hostile following the death of
> Tigranes). (5) But it came to pass that he gave offence to them as well as to
> Tiberius: on the one hand, the former because they thought they had been

[50] For Tiberius' 'bloodthirsty' nature, note also Tacitus' vivid statement (*Ann.* 6.39) concerning
Tiberius' decision to move closer to the city of Rome.
[51] The list of individuals Dio identified as 'bloodthirsty' is ominous: Sulla F 109.12 (*EV*), cf. 43.50.2;
59.4.1, Caligula 59.10.2; Domitian 67.18.1 (Xiph.); Commodus 73(72).1.1 (Xiph./*EV*); Caracalla
79(78).9.3 (Xiph.); Elagabalus 80(79).3.3. For μιαιφονία as a trait of tyrants generally, note Plut.
Mor. 457A [*de cohibenda ira*].

overlooked, to Tiberius, on the other hand, because he feared their anger. Anyway, Tiberius set off for Rhodes on the pretext of needing some further study, without taking with him other companions, nor indeed entire retinue, so that his presence and actions would be of no concern to them. (6) And he made the journey in the manner of a private individual, [. . .] and having arrived on the island neither did nor said anything arrogant. (7) So, although this is the truest reason for his exile, there is also a story that he did this because of his wife Julia, as he was no longer able to put up with her – at any rate he left her in Rome [. . .].[52]

Dio's explanations seem weak; or so it has been suggested.[53] More worryingly, the tone is odd. The historian's sudden adoption of a quasi-Thucydidean register (sc. ἡ … ἀληθεστάτη αἰτία, 'the truest reason') almost lapses into literary burlesque.[54] Rarely, if ever, is Dio so clumsy. Why he should choose to evoke Thucydides at this point is obscure – was Tiberius' retirement to Rhodes really sufficient to warrant such an allusion?[55] Yet the very inappropriateness of Dio's attention-seeking phraseology may just be the point.[56] It is jarring because it is seemingly so inappropriate to the content of the passage. As such, it draws the reader's attention to Tiberius' motivating fear of Gaius and Lucius as rivals in the imperial succession.

To appreciate the force of the passage, it is perhaps necessary to go back further, to the earliest comments Dio makes concerning the adult Tiberius. In 20 BC, the young Tiberius was sent to Armenia at the head of an embassy to reinstall the puppet-king Tigranes.[57] The mission was a success,

---

[52] βουληθεὶς δὲ δὴ τρόπον <τινὰ> μᾶλλον αὐτοὺς σωφρονίσαι, τῷ Τιβερίῳ τήν τε ἐξουσίαν τὴν δημαρχικὴν ἐς πέντε ἔτη ἔνειμε καὶ τὴν Ἀρμενίαν ἀλλοτριουμένην μετὰ τὸν τοῦ Τιγράνου θάνατον προσέταξε. [5] συνέβη δ' αὐτῷ καὶ ἐκείνοις καὶ τῷ Τιβερίῳ μάτην προσκροῦσαι, τοῖς μὲν ὅτι παρεωρᾶσθαι ἔδοξαν, τῷ δὲ ὅτι τὴν ὀργὴν αὐτῶν ἐφοβήθη. ἀμέλει καὶ ἐς Ῥόδον ὡς καὶ παιδεύσεώς τινος δεόμενος ἐστάλη, μήτ' ἄλλους τινὰς μήτε τὴν θεραπείαν πᾶσαν ἐπαγόμενος, ἵν' ἐκποδὼν σφισι καὶ τῇ ὄψει καὶ τοῖς ἔργοις γένηται. [6] καὶ τήν τε ὁδὸν ἰδιωτικῶς ἐποιήσατο, [. . .] καὶ ἐς τὴν νῆσον ἐλθὼν οὐδὲν ὀγκηρὸν οὔτε ἔπραττεν οὔτε ἔλεγεν. [7] ἡ μὲν οὖν ἀληθεστάτη αἰτία τῆς ἐκδημίας αὐτοῦ τοιαύτη ἐστί, λόγου δέ τινα ἔχει καὶ διὰ τὴν γυναῖκα τὴν Ἰουλίαν, ὅτι μηκέτ' αὐτὴν φέρειν ἐδύνατο, τοῦτο ποιῆσαι· κατέλιπε γοῦν αὐτὴν ἐν τῇ Ῥώμῃ [. . .]. The passage is an amalgam of Xiphilinus' and the EV, for which, see Boissevain II.487–8. The similarity of Xiphilinus and the EV indicates that the reconstructed text is close, if not identical to Dio's original.

[53] Pelling 1997a: 142. Seager (1972: 31) follows a line of explanation which is close to Dio's. Note also Levick 1972 who sees Tiberius' pride as a major motivating facet in his Rhodian exile, and his fear of Gaius for the period after 1 BC.

[54] Cf. Thucydides 1.23. Thucydides' ἀληθεστάτη πρόφασις was often glossed as ἀληθεστάτη αἰτία; see e.g. Dion. Hal. Epist. ad Amm. 6; Schol. in Thuc. (ed. Hude 1927: 26).

[55] Dio is perhaps not alone in affecting a Thucydidean register at this historical juncture. Cf. Syme (1986: 84): 'The truest explanation is declared in the pretext put out later on'. The superiority of Dio's effort is patent.

[56] For another less extreme example of this, see 57.6.2.

[57] For the mission, see Anderson 1934: 260, 263–4; Magie 1950: 476; Levick 1976: 26–7; Sherwin-White 1984: 325.

due predominantly to the actions of the Armenians themselves who deposed Artaxias.[58] Nevertheless, Dio reports that Tiberius began to adopt a majestic bearing (sc. ἐσεμνύνετο),[59] chiefly because sacrifices were voted to commemorate his accomplishments (54.9.5).[60] Dio then goes on to add that after the occurrence of a series of omens just as Tiberius and his retinue approached the field of Philippi, Tiberius 'began thinking about the monarchy' (καὶ περὶ τῆς μοναρχίας ἐνενόει) (54.9.6).[61] Tiberius' imperial aspirations are thus signalled early.[62] Dio does this, in part, as a way of foreshadowing Tiberius' later assumption of power, just as he does for other future emperors. Yet, on closer inspection, what Dio does here is actually more interesting than it first appears. Elsewhere, Dio would have noted the *omina imperii* and stopped at that. However, by focalising these comments through the character of Tiberius, Dio is able to graft onto the future emperor what we may term an imperial mindset,[63] of which fear of other imperial aspirants was a part.[64]

Fear of rivals, borne out by his desire for power, therefore, becomes Tiberius' motivating factor at these nascent stages of his characterisation in the *Roman History*.[65] More than this, it is also a constant (perhaps *the* constant) feature of Dio's characterisation of Tiberius in both his pre- and post-accession narratives. At 57.3.1–2, Dio explains Tiberius' delay in accepting the Principate as being partly due to his nature, but partly due to his fear of the soldiery in Pannonia and Germany, Germanicus, and the possibility of a coup within Italy.[66] Moreover in AD 14, as in 6 BC, Tiberius

---

[58] Artaxias II, who ruled between c. 33 and 20 BC, was the son of Artavazd II, and the brother of his successor Tigranes III. Dio notes that he had overseen the execution of Romans in Armenia, sometime before 30 BC (51.16.2). For the stemma of the family of Artaxias II, see Lang 1983: 513.

[59] Or the sort of bearing appropriate for a king? Cf. Xen. *Cyr.* 8.3.1.

[60] Levick (1976: 26) indicates that this remark concerning this behaviour is derived from a hostile source. However, Dio's comment is perfectly consonant with his own conception of the effect excessive honours have on individuals, and his comment on Tiberius' behaviour need not have been derived from his source.

[61] Cf. Suet. *Tib.* 14.3 (omen at Philippi).

[62] We may note that Velleius 2.94 uses Tiberius' embassy to Armenia in a similar way as Dio, insofar as it marks the point at which Tiberius appears as an appropriately kingly successor to Augustus.

[63] Cf. Caesar's desire for 'great power' after receiving a dream while a quaestor in Spain (37.52.2).

[64] E.g. 55.13.1. More generally, fear (especially of the bold or conspicuously virtuous) is a basic characteristic feature of tyrants: Xen. *Hiero* 5.1–2; 6.4, 6.15, 7.10; Plut. *Dion* 9.7; Cic. *Tusc. Disp.* 5.20–1[57–62]; App. *BC* 5.79.334. Note too Augustus' comments in the Livia–Augustus dialogue: 55.15.1–2.

[65] Pelling 1997a: 141. For fear as a motivating force in the Roman historians, see the comments and discussion of Levene 1997. For the importance of fear as a driving factor in human actions in Dio, see Kuhn-Chen 2002: 174–6 (with abundant examples); cf. Hose 2007: 464. Fear is recognised as an important catalyst for individual motivation and historical causation in the Greek historians as well – and especially in Thucydides, for which see Desmond 2006.

[66] Tiberius' fear of Germanicus is reiterated at 57.4.1.

hoped to save himself by appearing as a private individual (57.3.2). Following the suppression of the mutinies, Tiberius remains fearful of Germanicus, and additionally of the elder Agrippina (57.6.2), and it was perhaps this fear of a rival that brought about the best years of Tiberius as ruler in Dio's mind (57.7.1, 13.6). Dio maintains this characteristic into Book 58, where Tiberius becomes fearful of the inordinate power of Sejanus (58.4.1). Although Tacitus too notes Tiberius' fear of Sejanus, for Tacitus this was just another feature that kept Tiberius' vices in check,[67] whereas for Dio this fear is an emotion that prompts Tiberius to action, allowing him to plan and execute the downfall of his once trusted lieutenant.[68]

As noted by Levene, '[f]ear is frequently attributed to characters in what seem like quite neutral contexts, without any obvious indication that it is a defect'.[69] Indeed, such an idea clearly applies to Dio's presentation of Tiberius' fear. It is simply another complementary facet of Dio's overarching characterisation of the emperor. The result of this is not a picture of Tiberius as a particularly timorous emperor, at least not in the way that Dio would portray the emperor Claudius.[70] Nor is it the same as Suetonius' image of a fretful Tiberius that emerges towards the end of the *Life* (*Tib.* 63–6). Rather, Dio's characterisation of Tiberius' fear feeds into what we may regard as an overarching portrayal of Tiberius as a quintessentially cautious or safe emperor. Indeed, the contrast with Claudius is important. Whereas Claudius' fearfulness allows his wives and freedmen to gain control over him (and the organs of state),[71] in the case of Tiberius, his fear either augments his control of events or drives him to make well-considered decisions.[72]

There is another observation to make here. Contrary to what has generally been supposed, Dio has succeeded in making what may be loosely termed a psychologically consistent portrait of Tiberius that continues from his earliest years as a politically active player through to his death. It is true that this portrait works only on the most superficial of readings. This is not, however, to deprecate what Dio has achieved. On the one hand, his Tiberius may be responding to the sorts of typical fears that

---

[67] Cf. Tac. *Ann.* 6.51.
[68] Dio also says that Tiberius had even prepared to flee Capri, lest Sejanus sail against him (58.13.1).
[69] Levene 1997: 129.
[70] Or indeed in the way Marañón (1956: 50–1) would do in his (now pseudo-) psychoanalytical study of the emperor.
[71] E.g. 60.2.4–7, 61(60).31.5 (Xiph.).
[72] Even in the case of Germanicus, whose intentions Tiberius misinterpreted, we can still appreciate that Tiberius acted in an appropriate manner, e.g. 57.6.3.

any imperial aspirant or emperor might feel. But we should note that Dio does not ascribe such motivations to every emperor or imperial claimant. Moreover, while fear may be almost ubiquitous as a driving emotion in Dio, not every historical character reacts to it in the same way. The case of Macrinus may serve as an appropriate illustration. Macrinus, like Tiberius, desired to become emperor after a soothsayer had foretold his accession (79[78].4.1, 11.4). Fear then compelled him to engineer the murder of Caracalla, lest the emperor hear of the prophecy (79[78].4.4).[73]

IV Thinking with Tiberius: The Emperor's Nature

As we would expect, the narrative of Tiberius' reign does see a change in terms of Dio's willingness to engage in more direct characterisation. Yet how this characterisation should be read is less clear-cut. Nowhere is this more explicit than in Dio's elaborate opening sketch of the emperor's nature. The passage, positioned at the narrative 'threshold' of Tiberius' reign, requires comment, not least because it is the longest passage of direct characterisation Dio devotes to the emperor. Let us confine ourselves to the opening two sections of Dio's outline:

> [1] Such things came to pass concerning Augustus, but as for Tiberius, he was a patrician and had been well-educated, but he possessed a most singular nature. For as he pretended things which he did not desire, and of the things he said, nothing (so to speak) was what he wanted. But making his words the opposite of his actual design, he denied everything which he longed for, and advocated everything which he hated. He would show signs of being angry at those with whom he was not in the least bit vexed but would appear to be mild with those whom he was especially angry. [2] He would make a show of[74] pitying those whom he punished severely but would maintain a grudge against those whom he pardoned. Occasionally, he would approach an enemy as if a boon companion, and a close friend as if a complete stranger. On the whole he thought it not advantageous for an emperor to be open about what he was thinking, for, he said, many great mistakes arise from this sort of behaviour, whereas in many cases the opposite behaviour bought about both more frequent and more significant successes. (57.1.1–2)[75]

---

[73] That fear of a king/tyrant was regarded as a common cause of usurpation, note Arist. *Pol.* 1311b.-36–40; cf. 55.19.5.

[74] Or 'pretended to'. For the range of translations or possible implications of Dio's use of the ironic particle δῆθεν, see Denniston 1954: 264–6 and Rich 1990: 15.

[75] [1] ταῦτα μὲν κατὰ Αὔγουστον ἐγένετο, Τιβέριος δὲ εὐπατρίδης μὲν ἦν καὶ ἐπεπαίδευτο, φύσει δὲ ἰδιωτάτῃ ἐκέχρητο. οὔτε γὰρ ὧν ἐπεθύμει προσεποιεῖτό τι, καὶ ὧν ἔλεγεν οὐδὲν ὡς εἰπεῖν ἐβούλετο, ἀλλ' ἐναντιωτάτους τῇ προαιρέσει τοὺς λόγους ποιούμενος πᾶν τε ὃ ἐπόθει ἠρνεῖτο καὶ πᾶν ὃ

Dio thus draws the reader's attention to three aspects of Tiberius' character –
his birth, education, and nature, but expands on only one of them: his
natural inclination for dissimulation (εἰρωνεία/*dissimulatio*). Yet how particular this sort of dissimulation was to Tiberius (sc. φύσει δὲ ἰδιωτάτῃ
ἐκέχρητο, 'he possessed a most singular nature') in the context of the
Roman History seems at first dubious. As Christopher Pelling noted, Dio's
Augustus was a master at dissimulation, just as Caligula was decidedly
not, and that Tiberius' dissimulation merely highlights (again) one of the
work's 'trans-regnal themes'.[76] The same observation may be made of
other figures of Dio's Republican narrative, with the likes of Caesar and
Pompey as good examples.[77] All this is true, but perhaps Dio's point is
that Tiberius' peculiarity was that such behaviour came naturally to him,
whereas for the others it is a deliberate strategy (which, of course, it was
for Tiberius as well). This is what perhaps made Tiberius' nature so
singular in Dio's mind.

Dio's elaborate sketch at 57.1 has all the hallmarks of a programmatic
statement. By priming the reader in the way that he does, it would seem
that the text is asking the reader to double guess Tiberius' motivations and
his actions throughout the subsequent narrative as well. Yet we may
wonder how important knowledge of Tiberius' *dissimulatio* is for interpreting the ensuing narrative of Tiberius' reign.[78] Certainly Tiberius'
dissimulation sets the tone for Dio's account of Tiberius' *cunctatio*
('delay') during September AD 14. Yet even here it is not given as the sole
reason for the emperor's delay: Tiberius' behaviour following the death of
Augustus is ascribed to both his natural disposition and his response to
external factors (57.3.1, 57.3.5). Perhaps, therefore, we need to think about
57.1 not just in terms of the role of Tiberius' dissimulation in explaining his
conduct throughout the ensuing narrative. The important feature of 57.1 is
the emphasis on social interaction and behaviour. Dio's focus emphasises
how difficult it was for those individuals who came into contact with
Tiberius to deal with the cryptic emperor (57.1.3–6).[79] In an important
way it is this feature that neatly anticipates the tenor of much of the
following narrative, which contains many anecdotes of Tiberius'

ἐμίσει προετείνετο· ὠργίζετό τε ἐν οἷς ἥκιστα ἐθυμοῦτο, καὶ ἐπιεικὴς ἐν οἷς μάλιστα ἠγανάκτει
ἐδόκει εἶναι· [2] ἠλέει τε δῆθεν οὓς σφόδρα ἐκόλαζε, καὶ ἐχαλέπαινεν οἷς συνεγίγνωσκε· τόν τε
ἔχθιστον ὡς οἰκειότατον ἔστιν ὅτε ἑώρα, καὶ τῷ φιλτάτῳ ὡς ἀλλοτριωτάτῳ προσεφέρετο. τό τε
σύμπαν οὐκ ἠξίου τὸν αὐταρχοῦντα κατάδηλον ὧν φρονεῖ εἶναι· ἔκ τε γὰρ τούτου πολλὰ καὶ
μεγάλα πταίεσθαι καὶ ἐκ τοῦ ἐναντίου πολλῷ πλείω καὶ μείζω κατορθοῦσθαι ἔλεγε.

[76] Pelling 1997a: 128–9.
[77] E.g. 36.24.5–6 (Pompey); 38.1.1–2 (Caesar); 37.58.1 (Caesar, Pompey, Crassus).
[78] Cf. Pelling 1997a: 126, n. 36.   [79] Edmondson 1992: 51.

interactions with individuals from all strata of Roman society: from men of consular rank to assorted political nonentities.[80]

Dio's portrayal of Tiberius' handling of these various individuals and the groups within Roman society provided him with the opportunity to develop the most striking feature of his characterisation of the emperor. Although so difficult for others to read, Dio's Tiberius is something of a master interpreter of human nature and motivation. Hence, Tiberius grooms Caligula, knowing full well the latter's viciousness (58.23.1–4).[81] He remains one step ahead of his opponents, real or imagined. Tiberius outmanoeuvres the popular Germanicus at the start of his reign. Later, with respect to Sejanus – again a man whose nature, we are told, Tiberius understood thoroughly – Tiberius removed the praetorian prefect before he became a more serious threat to his position. The same is seen in Tiberius' handling of the senate. Dio portrays Tiberius' treatment of the senate as characterised by an unsettling mixture of deference and menace.[82] Perhaps the most vivid episode comes in Book 58 following the fall of Sejanus. Dio notes how the senate attempted to instigate measures that would enable them to assassinate the emperor with ease (58.17.1). Tiberius, however, sidesteps this possible threat by showing honour to the senate while augmenting the loyalty of the praetorians.[83]

In a comparison between Tiberius and his successor, Dio observes that whereas Tiberius concentrated power in his own hands and used agents to carry out his wishes,[84] Caligula was the slave of charioteers and other (socially and ethically) unsavoury types (59.5.2). The idea responds directly to Tiberius' own precept quoted at 57.1.2, that an emperor should avoid disclosing his own thoughts. The revelation of these *arcana imperii* ('imperial secrets') effectively bookend the Tiberian narrative and provide another level of interpretative framework which the reader may use for understanding Dio's account of the emperor's reign.

---

[80] For the latter, note the exchange between Tiberius and the inventor of unbreakable glass: 57.21.5–7 (Xiph.). The story, of course, provides a neat illustration of Tiberius' jealousy (φθόνος) – a characteristic that Dio leaves otherwise undeveloped.

[81] Cf. Dio's comments regarding Severus and Caracalla (77(76).14.1 [Xiph.], 77(76).14.7 [Xiph.]). Interestingly, in the case of Augustus' adoption of Tiberius, Dio neither endorses nor refutes the view that Augustus appreciated Tiberius' nature (56.45.3; cf. Tac. *Ann.* 1.10.7; Swan 2004: 350). This is consonant with Dio's characterisation of Tiberius' generally inscrutable nature.

[82] Xiphilinus juxtaposes two anecdotes that illustrate these two methods: 57.24.5 (Xiph.), 57.24.8 (Xiph.).

[83] The issue of the proposed senatorial bodyguard for Tiberius (and related measures) is described at length: 58.17.3–18.6. Dio's emphasis is markedly different from the parallel account of Tacitus (*Ann.* 6.2–3).

[84] Such as Sejanus, or the senate itself (58.16.3–5).

It is also possible to think about 57.1 not solely in terms of the narrative of his reign but retrospectively in terms of the pre-accession narrative. Pelling is certainly right when he notes that virtually nothing in the pre-accession narrative suggests Tiberius' possession of such a nature.[85] Nevertheless, Dio's account of Tiberius' nature answers one question that Dio must have had in his mind when confronted with the history of Tiberius' early career. How was it that Tiberius, although desiring the imperial power for over thirty years, did not make any attempt to seize the purple from Augustus?[86] This fact must have struck Dio as exceptional. After all, this would have been the natural response according to what we may regard as Dio's standard reading of imperial psychology. Certainly, this is how a range of emperors and pretenders such as Severus, Avidius Cassius, or indeed a Caligula, would have behaved.[87] Tiberius instead bided his time.

V Thinking with Tiberius: Virtues and Vices

Tiberius' virtues and vices, which, as we saw, were so underdeveloped in the pre-accession narrative, receive greater attention over the course of Books 57 and 58. Yet even here there are problems of interpretation. Although Dio describes Tiberius by using a more conventional ethical vocabulary during the course of Books 57 and 58, the results are somewhat lacklustre. Nowhere is this truer than at the close to Dio's narrative of Tiberius' reign. Dio's judgement is surprisingly bland:

> Tiberius had a great many virtues indeed, but also a great many vices, and had used one or the other as if he possessed those <qualities> alone. (58.28.5)[88]

It is a low-key close to Dio's two-book account of Tiberius' reign. The passage invites comparison with Tacitus' more elaborate close to Book 6 of the *Annals*. Indeed, comparison is instructive. Tacitus says:

---

[85] Pelling 1997a: 126–7, although noting 54.9.5–7, 55.11.2 as possible examples.
[86] Cf. 54.9.5 discussed above.
[87] Cf. 74(73).14.3–4 (Xiph.) (Septimius Severus, Pescennius Niger, Clodius Albinus); Avidius Cassius 72(71).22.2–23.2 (Xiph.); 58.28.2–3 (Caligula). We need not confine this observation to the imperial period, for it applies equally to Dio's late Republican dynasts. For this mindset in the Republican narrative, see Rich 1989: 92–3.
[88] Τιβέριος μὲν δὴ πλείστας μὲν ἀρετὰς πλείστας δὲ καὶ κακίας ἔχων, καὶ ἑκατέραις αὐταῖς ὡς καὶ μόναις κεχρημένος [...].

His character, again, has its separate epochs. There was a noble season in his life and fame while he lived a private citizen or a great official under Augustus; an inscrutable and disingenuous period of hypocritical virtues while Germanicus and Drusus remained: with his mother alive, he was still an amalgam of good and evil; so long as he loved, or feared, Sejanus, he was loathed for his cruelty, but his lust was veiled; finally, when the restraints of shame and fear were gone, and nothing remained but to follow his own bent, he plunged impartially into crime and into ignominy. (*Ann.* 6.51.3)[89]

On the face of it, Tacitus says exactly what Dio does not.[90] The descent into all-consuming vice that is a feature of the Tacitean account is absent from Dio's brusque summation. This is surprising, and the reader perhaps expects more from the historian. Like Tacitus, Dio uses the death of Germanicus to signal a change in Tiberius' behaviour and leads us to expect such a negative change in Tiberius' conduct (57.13.6). Certainly, there are profound negative trends in Tiberius' conduct following the death of Germanicus, but Dio does not appear to be claiming simply that the death of Germanicus brought out Tiberius' vices.[91] Nor does Dio claim that Tiberius' conduct was unimpeachable in the period before Germanicus' death. Hence, the change brought about by the death of Germanicus is not one of total moral disintegration. Tiberius may appear less like the good emperor than he did in the narrative prior to Germanicus' death, but Germanicus' death does not trigger a change into a Caligula-like monster.[92] Indeed, a passage preserved in the *Excerpta de virtutibus et vitiis* ('Excerpts of virtues and vices') suggests that Tiberius was still about to act in a praiseworthy manner, despite the loss of his rival:

Thus was the general change in Tiberius after Germanicus' death that just as he was previously the object of great praise for many things, after this point he was the cause of even more amazement. (57.19.8 [*EV*])[93]

---

[89] *morum quoque tempora illi diuersa: egregium uita famaque, quoad priuatus uel in imperiis sub Augusto fuit; occultum ac subdolum fingendis uirtutibus, donec Germanicus ac Drusus superfuere; idem inter bona malaque mixtus incolumi matre; intestabilis saeuitia, sed obtectis libidinibus, dum Seianum dilexit timuitue: postremo in scelera simul ac dedecora prorupit, postquam remoto pudore et metu suo tantum ingenio utebatur* (trans. J. Jackson, Loeb Classical Library edition).

[90] For Tacitus' summation (the interpretation of which is by no means straightforward), note Martin 2001: 192–6, 199–202; cf. Woodman 1989 = 1998: 155–67; Pelling 1997a: 122, n. 25.

[91] Note 57.13.6.

[92] Sulla would perhaps be a better example of such a change, at least in terms of Dio's narrative: F 109.1–3 (*EV*).

[93] τὸ μὲν οὖν σύμπαν οὕτω μετὰ τὸν τοῦ Γερμανικοῦ θάνατον μετεβάλετο ὥστε αὐτὸν μεγάλως καὶ πρότερον ἐπαινούμενον πολλῷ δὲ τότε μᾶλλον θαυμασθῆναι.

We may suspect the *Excerpta* has here preserved Dio's wording closely if not exactly. At any rate, the punchline is appropriately Dionian and does not seem to be a gloss made by one of the compilers of the *Excerpta*.[94] Moreover, the comment at 57.19.8 is consonant with Dio's summation at 58.28.5 and is entirely appropriate to his intervening narrative.

The ambivalent tone of 58.28.5 is indicative of the tenor of Dio's account of Tiberius' reign in Books 57 and 58, where praise and censure are interspersed.[95] The annalistic sections following Dio's sketch of the general manner of Tiberius' conduct (57.7–13), but before the death of Germanicus, contain a mixture of anecdotes that do not always reflect well on Tiberius. For example, Dio highlights instances of Tiberius' inconsistency, both in terms of his behaviour when confronted with similar circumstances, and inconsistency when it came to any deviations from his general pattern of behaviour outlined in 57.7–13.[96] Zonaras perhaps captures the sense of this best when he summarises the period before Germanicus' death by stating simply that 'up to this point Tiberius did many good things and erred in only a few matters' (μέχρι μὲν οὖν τοῦ χρόνου τούτου πλεῖστα χρηστὰ ὁ Τιβέριος ἔπραξε καὶ βραχέα ἐξήμαρτεν) (57.19.1 [Zonar.]).[97]

The change between the pre- and post-Germanicus Tiberius is therefore by no means stark. It is true that Tiberius begins to display some of the more characteristic behaviour of a tyrant following the death of his adopted son. He becomes harsh (χαλεπός), he becomes less accessible on account of his withdrawal to Capri, and he begins to rule by attempting to instil fear in his subjects.[98] Even so, right up to the end of his reign, Dio makes a point of recording Tiberius' actions for which he was praised, not only those which illustrated his vices. Hence, Dio notes Tiberius' generosity to the victims of fires and floods that hit Rome in AD 36 (58.26.5), a feature of Tiberius' demonstrative euergetism carried over from his early reign (57.16.2; 57.17.7–8). There is also praise for Tiberius' continuing refusal of honours, as well as sundry acts of beneficence (58.21.5–22.1). Even

---

[94] It should be noted, though, that the excerptors were more likely to alter the beginnings and endings of the text: Roberto 2009: 79. However, changes to the beginnings of excerpted text are more common.
[95] Cf. Baar 1990: 228.
[96] E.g. the anecdotes collected at 57.15. Note also Tiberius' execution of the wag who was dispatched to 'carry his own message to Augustus' (57.14.1), an anecdote used by Suetonius to illustrate Tiberius' cruelty.
[97] For the attempted reconstruction of this passage, see Boissevain II.579.
[98] Or more precisely in the senate: 57.24.5 (Xiph.).

Tiberius' acts of clemency are not omitted,[99] which given the centrality of *clementia*/ἐπιείκεια in Dio's thought world is significant.[100]

The same applies to the reports of Tiberius' vices. Dio was more comfortable condemning the vices in rulers and statesmen than in extolling their virtues.[101] Yet, Dio is notably (and surprisingly) sparing when it came to reporting Tiberius' reputed personal vices. The hostile historiographical tradition gave him ample material to work with. However, the salacious tales reported by Suetonius and to a lesser degree by Tacitus are largely eschewed by Dio.[102] To be sure, there are references to Tiberius' sexual excesses and his reputation for licentiousness (ἀσέλγεια).[103] But Dio does little to embroider upon these stories.[104] Why this should be the case is not easy to pinpoint. It cannot be due to the fragmentary state of the text. Neither Dio nor his epitomators were prudish when it came to engaging with so called 'discourses of depravity'.[105] After all, such anecdotes were of fundamental importance to illustrating an individual's vices, and Dio, with his keen sense of a good anecdote, knew this more than most. Perhaps the most likely explanation for this omission is that Dio did not regard these encounters as having a major influence on the character of his rule: unlike the likes of Caligula, Nero, or Elagabalus, Tiberius never became a slave to any particular paramour, whore, or catamite.

At 57.13.6, when noting the change Germanicus' death brought upon Tiberius' general conduct, Dio professes ignorance as to whether Tiberius was in fact by nature good or was simply affecting virtue and leaves the issue there without further discussion. The question of character change was an important one for the more ethically minded writers of antiquity.[106] Elsewhere, Dio seems to admit the possibility: Commodus, according to Dio, was not naturally wicked but weak willed, and was led astray to the

---

[99] E.g. Tiberius' dismissal of the charges against Cornelius Lentulus (57.24.8 [Xiph.]). Tacitus (*Ann.* 4.29) places the event under the year AD 24. Note also the examples of the praetor (and later consul) L. Apronius Caesianus (*PIR²* A 972) and the *eques* M. Terentius (*PIR²* T 64) (58.19.1–5).

[100] As noted well by Rich (1989: 97, 103; 1990: 16–17), clemency was perhaps the most important imperial virtue for an emperor to possess in Dio's mind. See also Kuhn-Chen 2002: 160–3. For the importance of *clementia* generally for authors of the second century, see Schettino 1998.

[101] For Dio's *kakoetheia*, see the still insightful comments of Niebuhr 1875: 62–3. See now Chapter 11 by Barbara Saylor Rodgers in this volume.

[102] E.g. Suet. *Tib.* 42–5; Tac. *Ann.* 6.1.

[103] 58.22.1, 3–4; cf. 59.4.1. Here the intention is to contrast it with Tiberius' previously most chaste or self-restrained (sc. σωφρονέστατα) existence (57.13.3).

[104] 58.22.3–4 illustrates this charge with the story of Tiberius' intention to seduce the daughter of Sex. Marius (*PIR²* M 295). Cf. Tac. *Ann.* 6.19.1.

[105] For this term, see Langlands 2006: 319.

[106] For the standard discussions, note Gill 1983; Swain 1989; and Gill 2006: 416–61.

extent that his new habits became a second nature to him (73(72)1.1 [Xiph./ *EV*]).[107] In the case of Tiberius, however, Dio remains evasive.

Dio's deliberate agnosticism may be read in different ways. On the one hand, it feeds into the historian's characterisation of Tiberius. It emphasises the fundamental, enigmatic nature of the emperor: to such an extent that even the (usually omniscient) historian cannot penetrate Tiberius' inner nature.[108] On the other, it presents the reader with an important question. Does it matter whether an emperor was by nature good or bad, so long as he behaved in an appropriate manner? Here we appreciate another important departure from the Tacitean and Suetonian Tiberius. So much of their generally pejorative portrayals of Tiberius hinges on charges of hypocrisy, and by extension, uncovering the real Tiberius. Although Dio is an author who made much of identifying the distinction between word and deed, appearance and reality, this seems far less central to his treatment of Tiberius – at least in terms of his overall assessment of the emperor's conduct.

Yet for Dio, appearances mattered as much as realities.[109] After all, the sort of shamming exhibited by Tiberius was at the very heart of Dio's (and indeed other authors') conception of what may be termed the *civilis princeps*.[110] Fundamentally, this idea was not peculiar to the Roman imperial period. It is implicit in Aristotle's *Politics*, where Aristotle discusses how a tyrant might reduce the likelihood of being overthrown by affecting kingly behaviour.[111] Although we cannot say whether or not Dio knew his Aristotle, the comparison between book five of the *Politics* and the imperial books of Dio is, nevertheless, instructive. When Aristotle discusses the two ways in which tyrannies might be preserved he has nothing to say about the inner character of the tyrant. Rather he reduces it to a matter of behaviour – a tyrant might use the traditional methods of oppression or he could affect kingly behaviour. In a way, this is exactly what is played out over the course of Books 57 and 58. Tiberius maintains his power by both appearing as a good king, while at other times employing the tactics of oppression.

[107] Similarly, Dio notes that Tiberius Gracchus' nature underwent a change (F 83.1 [*EV*]).
[108] Cf. Pelling 2010a: 382–3 on this sort of mimetic quality of Tacitus' narrative when dealing with Tiberius.
[109] Cf. Rich 1989: 100–1. See Kemezis 2014: 136–9 on the symbolic importance the Republican magistracies represented in Dio's conception of the Principate.
[110] Or as is perhaps more appropriate for Dio, the ἀγαθὸς αὐτοκράτωρ or δημοτικὸς αὐτοκράτωρ.
[111] Arist. *Pol.* 1313a.34-1315b.10; but most explicitly, note 1315a41-1315b1. The importance for a tyrant to appear (sc. φαίνεσθαι) to act appropriately is key to Aristotle's discussion on the preservation of tyrannies: cf. Newman 1902: 4.466–7.

Here we are left with a final problem of interpretation. Dio couched his characterisation of Tiberius in what we may describe as moralising terms. Yet the purpose or function of this moralising is not entirely clear. It has been suggested that Dio intended the moralising elements in his characterisations of individuals within the *Roman History* to fulfil a didactic function, providing his readers with models of good and bad behaviour that they should follow or avoid.[112] That Dio's Tiberius is part of a protreptic exercise in morality appears unlikely. Rather, it seems that Dio uses Tiberius as a way of exploring various facets of Roman autocracy, as well as a way of exploring historical questions pertaining to the reign of Tiberius. Certainly, Dio's characterisation of Tiberius provides and encourages judgements on the emperor's character and conduct. But if anything, Dio's method is geared to describing and appraising Tiberius' conduct in individual episodes rather than producing what we might think of as a uniform ethical portrait of the emperor.[113] The language may often be ethically loaded, but it seems to serve no other function than to evaluate, or occasionally to explain Tiberius' actions at any given point. What makes Dio's portrayal of Tiberius so interesting in this regard is that he should construct Tiberius as an *exemplum* of these two modes of kingship. Thus, Dio's account of Tiberius' reign functions best when understood not in terms of Tiberius' individual character but of the character of his rule. Around the figure of Tiberius, Dio is able to raise questions about and explore the ways in which an emperor could go about exercising and maintaining his power.

VI　Conclusion

It has become conventional to think about the reign of Tiberius in terms of failure. The phrase 'the tragedy of Tiberius' has become stereotypical. The character of the emperor is central in such appraisals. Yet although the figure of Tiberius is central to Dio's treatment of the years AD 14 to 37, such a conclusion is not the picture that emerges from his narrative. For this reason, Dio's account of the reign of Tiberius and the emperor himself, although lacking the 'bite', 'intensity', 'colour', or psychological nuance critics tend to ascribe to the Tacitean counterpart, nevertheless deserves consideration in its own right.[114]

---

[112] Edmondson 1992: 48–9.　　[113] Cf. Kemezis 2014: 102.
[114] For this judgement, see Syme 1958: 273.

The foregoing discussion has examined the ways in which Dio approached his characterisation of Tiberius. The result, as I have argued, is not without sophistication. Dio's presentation of Tiberius in the pre-accession narrative is faintly, yet consistently drawn – perhaps more than has been hitherto recognised. The figure of Tiberius in this part of the *Roman History* is structured around the question of the succession to Augustus. When it came to the narrative of his reign, the overarching historical problem for Dio, as perhaps it was for Tacitus, was how it was that Tiberius managed to survive as long as he did.[115] As the history of the emperors from Augustus down to Dio's own day had shown, out-and-out tyrants or imperial incompetents did not usually last the twenty-three years Tiberius endured in power. Dio's characterisation of the emperor and his style of rule goes some way to explaining how this was achieved. Dio focuses on Tiberius' actions – his interest in Tiberius is as a political operator, which is best understood in the broader narrative context of the *Roman History*. Tiberius' personal character was of importance to this agenda, but it was not the only aspect that mattered.

[115] Syme 1958: 429.

CHAPTER 7

An Emperor's War on Greece
Cassius Dio's Nero

Shushma Malik

I Introduction

Cassius Dio's account of Nero's reign is relentless. The historian barrages his readers with tales of murder, debauchery, subversion, and perversion to create an uncompromising image of an out-and-out despot. Even Commodus is allowed a brief early moment to be 'guiltless' (ἄκακος) (73[72].1.1 [*EV*]);[1] whereas from the instant of Nero's birth the future emperor is destined to kill his mother and rule as a tyrant (61[61].1.1–2 [Xiph.]).[2] That being said, Nero was not exactly praised by other ancient historians and biographers either, at least those authors whose works survive. Nor did the emperor necessarily fare any better when he later became the subject of a satire, or the topic of fictitious philosophical discussions by leading thinkers of his day.[3] In fact, so firmly was Nero's reputation established and entrenched in antiquity that, by the Renaissance, the emperor's name had literally become the dictionary definition of a tyrant.[4]

What is particularly distinctive about Cassius Dio's portrayal of Nero, however, is the way in which the historian characterises the emperor's relationship with Greece during his tour of the province in AD 66–8. Nero has long had a reputation as a lover of Greek world, a point on which our ancient authors largely agree.[5] In contrast, Dio's Nero waged war (literally

---

[1] All translations from Dio's *Roman History* in this chapter are from Cary's Loeb Classical Library edition, unless otherwise indicated. My sincere thanks to the editors of this volume for their comments on drafts of this chapter.
[2] Schulz 2019a: 259.
[3] Such as ps.-Lucian's *Nero: Or the Digging of the Isthmus*, Juv. *Sat.* 8, and Philostr. *VA* 4.36–5.41.
[4] For example, Francis Holyoke (1627), *Dictionarium Etymologicum Latinum Antiquis*: '[Nero] was so cruell and inhumaine, that every Tyrant after him was called Nero.' This example and many others are discussed in Gwyn 1991: 433–40.
[5] This extends beyond Achaea to Asia, Alexandria, and the eastern Roman empire. For example, see Suet. *Ner.* 20.3 for Nero's alleged preference for Alexandrian clappers and 19.1 for Nero's plan to visit

and metaphorically) on the Greeks, subjecting them to endless inept
theatrical performances on the one hand but, on the other, massacring
leading families for their money, robbing temples of their treasures, abolishing the oracle at Delphi, and causing the very ground at the Isthmus at
Corinth to rupture and bleed (62[63].8.2–16.2 [Xiph.; *EV*]). In building
this picture, Dio breaks away from his Greek-speaking predecessors who,
despite readily enumerating and accepting Nero's many faults, see the
emperor's liberation of Achaea from taxes in AD 67 as a redeeming feature
of his relationship with the province. In Greece itself, inscriptions were still
visible that honoured Nero for his actions and described him as 'a lover of
the Greeks' (φιλέλλην),[6] albeit with Nero's name posthumously erased.[7]
Dio devotes less than a sentence to the event (62[63].11.1 [Xiph.])[8] and
appears to contradict the idea of freedom almost immediately when he
describes the entire empire as 'under the control' (ἐδούλευσε) of Nero and
his freedman Helios (62[63].12.2 [Xiph.]).[9] In his systematic condemnation of every aspect of Nero's reign, Dio departs not only from Greek
sources, but from Latin historiography too.[10] Nero's characterisation, in
the decades following his death, was not straightforwardly negative. As
Josephus (*AJ* 20.154) famously writes, positive accounts of Nero's reign
were produced in the first century AD, and it is possible to pick through the
accounts of Tacitus and Suetonius to find complimentary passages.[11] For
Dio, this would not do.

Alexandria. All three of the Nero pretenders also came from the east: Tac. *Hist.* 2.8.1; 66(66).19.3b
(Zonar.); Suet. *Ner.* 57.2. Further, the Judaeo-Christian Sibylline Oracles make clear references to
Nero's (somewhat destructive) return from the East, *Sib. Or.* 5:14–219, 365–74; 8:155–7.

[6] Mratschek (2013: 46) discusses how this adjective is unique to Nero – it is not part of the title of
Hellenistic kings, nor is it applied to any other emperors.

[7] For example, the Acraephia inscription (*ILS* 8794 = Sherk, *Hadrian* 71) and the Parthenon
inscription (*IG* II² 3277 = Sherk, *Hadrian* 78A; Carroll 1982: 59–74; Spawforth 1994: 234–7). For
an up-to-date discussion of the epigraphic evidence of Nero's liberation of Greece, see Manders and
Slootjes 2015: 991–7.

[8] While Suetonius also pays the freedom of Greece little heed (*Ner.* 24.2) and it comes after the *divisio*
of *Ner.* 19.3, Greek writers give the event more attention, e.g. Paus. 7.17.3–4; Plut. *Flam.* 12.8, *Mor.*
567F; Philostr. *VA* 5.41.

[9] While ἐδούλευσε comes from Xiphilinus' work, if Dio did use it, it is a pointed contradiction of the
language used on the Acraephia inscription. There Nero proclaims the 'freedom' (ἐλευθερίαν) of
Greece from being subject (ἐδουλεύσατε) to others. See also Lavan (2013: 235–6) for more on the
language of Greece's 'enslavement' to Rome, and its peculiarity to Nero.

[10] On Dio's sources (and his independence from Tacitus and Suetonius), see Letta in this volume
(Chapter 3).

[11] For example, the first section of Suetonius' biography: *Ner.* 6–18; Tac. *Ann.* 13.26 (law concerning
freedmen), 14.42–5 (siding with the senate against the People), 14.40–1 (law against false prosecutions), 13.5 (the sustained freedom of the senate).

II Cassius Dio and His Text

Why this would not do for Dio has to do partly with his own context as a senator under Commodus, and partly with his obligations as a *pepaideumenos* (an educated, cultured man) writing history. But, before we explore these reasons in more detail, a note on the state of Dio's text. As things currently stand, it is extremely difficult to know what of our text is the product of Dio and what the product of an epitomator. Very little of Dio's original account of Nero survives, and none survives in direct manuscript tradition of the *Roman History*. U. P. Boissevain (1895–1931) was the last in a series of editors to put together various epitomes and excerpts to create an edition of Dio's history, but for the section on Nero (Books 61–3), editors mainly had to rely on the epitome of the eleventh-century Byzantine author Xiphilinus.[12] Only on rare occasions does the tenth-century *Excerpta Constantiniana*, a collection cut from larger historical works and rearranged according to topic, provide supplementary or complementary passages for comparison.[13]

Some of the most alarming features of Xiphilinus' method as an epitomator are his selections and omissions. Indeed, without the *Excerpta*, we would not have Dio's version of Corbulo's campaigns in Armenia, nor Nero's response to Vindex's revolt.[14] Moreover, as Mallan has demonstrated, Xiphilinus reshaped Dio's narrative from annalistic history into a series of biographies, which meant leaving out historical elements that did not directly speak to an emperor's character.[15] That being said, very few episodes in Dio's account speak to Nero's character more than his tour of Greece. For the authors whose texts partly comprise the literary movement now known as the Second Sophistic (Plutarch, Dio Chrysostom, Pausanias, Philostratus),[16] the tour, in particular Nero's liberation of Greece, makes frequent appearances. Nero's attitude to the Greeks is seen as a defining feature of his reign – he was the first emperor to visit Achaea since Augustus, and numismatic evidence shows that Achaean

---

[12] On Xiphilinus and his method, see Mallan 2013b: 610–44; Brunt 1980: 488–92; Millar 1964: 2. For a summary of the sources available from which we can reconstruct Dio's Julio-Claudians, see Edmondson 1992: 28–9. On Nero specifically, see Gowing 1997: 2560–4.

[13] On the organisation of the *Excerpta Constantiniana*, see Németh 2016: 253–65. Note also the contribution of Alicia Simpson (Chapter 13).

[14] As noted by Gowing 1997: 2561.

[15] Mallan 2013b: 617–25; Brunt 1980: 489. Pelling (1997a: 117–18) also discusses how Dio's own style facilitated a biographical structure, describing (if reluctantly) Dio's writing as 'biostructure'.

[16] Whitmarsh (2005) offers a valuable introduction to the Second Sophistic. Philostratus 'coined' the term (*VS* 481), although he saw the second sophistic starting not in the early imperial period, but in the fourth century BC with Aeschines.

provincial mints produced more coins of Nero than of any other Julio-Claudian emperor, including Augustus.[17] While, owing to the textual tradition, we cannot necessarily conduct an in-depth study of Dio's precise language,[18] we can carry out a broader analysis of the modes of behaviour attributed to Nero during his time in Greece, and how they relate to other accounts from both the Greek- and Latin-speaking worlds. Thus, an approach based upon broader themes can help us overcome some of the problems with Dio's text.[19]

Back now to Dio's methodology. As Gowing has argued, Dio's characterisation of Nero must have been impacted by Commodus, the theatrical, Neronian-style tyrant, during whose principate Dio served as a senator.[20] Commodus and Nero were of a similar age; Commodus was eighteen when he became emperor and thirty-one upon his death, Nero sixteen and thirty. Moreover, they appear to have shared a passion for performative violence aimed at the Roman senatorial elite. For example, the Julius Montanus episode from accounts on Nero compares, in terms of its performativity, with Dio's own lived experience as a senatorial witness to one of Commodus' gladiatorial spectacles. Both episodes are highly theatrical, with the emperors dressed up in either a costume and wig or the garb of a gladiator, and both emperors performed on their respective 'stage', the arena for Commodus and the city of Rome for Nero.[21] Nero, roaming the city in disguise one night, was beaten by the senator Julius Montanus whose wife the emperor had manhandled. Nero was not angry while he thought his performance had been effective – Montanus could not possibly have known that he was striking the emperor. However, once Montanus made the mistake of sending Nero an apology letter, revealing that he knew it was the emperor all along, the senator was forced to commit suicide (61[61].9.3–4 [Xiph.]).[22] While Nero's audience believed his performance, they were safe. Once the façade cracked, the consequences were deadly.[23]

Dio's Commodus instilled a similar fear in elite, educated men. Commodus' theatre was the gladiatorial arena, where senators were often

---

[17] See Hekster et al. 2014: 25; Manders and Slootjes 2015: 998.   [18] Gowing 1997: 2561.

[19] Such an approach has recently been employed by Schulz 2014: 405–34, esp. 406–7; 2016: 276–96. See also Gowing 1997: 2567–86.

[20] Gowing 1997: 2558–90. Pelling (1997a: 136–7), too, has noted that Dio's account of Nero stands out among the Julio-Claudians for the interesting and colourful details it includes.

[21] Bartsch 1994: 10–31, Edwards 1994: 91–3, and Gowing 1997: 2570–1 all explore the concept of Nero turning the city into his own theatre. See also Kemezis in this volume (Chapter 1).

[22] Cf. Tac. *Ann.* 13.25.1; Suet. *Ner.* 26.2.

[23] A comparison could be made here to Thrasea Paetus, who is forced to commit suicide largely because he refuses to engage with Nero's performances: 62(62).26.3–4 (Xiph.).

'invited' to watch his shows. Dio recounts being in the audience when Commodus cut off an ostrich's head and, with a grin on his face, exhibited it to the rows of senators. As with Nero, the response of the senators is key. Had they laughed, in other words not taken Commodus' performed threat seriously, they would have been in danger. The fact that they managed to suppress their laughter by chewing laurel leaves, Dio says, spared their lives (73[72].21.1–2 [Xiph.]). Living under such performative constraints must have coloured Dio's interpretation of Nero. He could not let an emperor so seemingly close to Commodus in character and nature be understood by anyone as a man worthy of the title, which those who found some value in Nero's philhellenism may have been able to do. While Dio was constrained by the likelihood that Commodus remained in his audience's living memory,[24] he had no such problem with Nero. Thus, his portrayal of the first century's 'Commodus' could be shaped with relative, if not complete, freedom.

If Commodus loomed over Nero's characterisation specifically, guiding the criteria by which all emperors were judged was Dio's role as a *pepaideumenos*, a man of culture, educated in the classical Greek canon.[25] Even though he was fluent in Latin, Dio followed other writers of the Second Sophistic by imitating Thucydidean Greek in his history.[26] Further, as Jones has pointed out, the dual yardsticks against which emperors' success were measured in his history represent the primary concerns of a senatorial *pepaideumenos*: (1) the types of men in an emperor's *consilium principis* (his group of advisers) and whether their advice was heeded, and (2) the emperor's understanding and demonstration of *paideia*.[27] In fact, part of being a senator by Dio's time was to be a *pepaideumenos*; as Asirvatham neatly summarises, 'the truest way of viewing the act of *paideia* [Dio's history] represents is as "senatorial" rather than "Greek" or "Roman".'[28] As a senator and historian, then, Dio had the responsibility to ensure his Nero fell short of the mark in these categories of success.

For Dio, Nero's principal advisors, Seneca and Burrus, were the 'most sensible men' (φρονιμώτατοί) in the court (61[61].3.3[*EV*]); however, this was

---

[24] As Barnes (1984: 240–55) has argued, Dio probably composed his history between c. AD 222 and 234, although there is still no consensus on this point.

[25] Recently, Jones (2016: 298–302) has presented the range of quotations in Dio's *History* of Greek literary staples, including Plato and Homer. See in particular F 30.2; 80(80).5.3 (Xiph.).

[26] Asirvatham 2017: 485–6; Potter 2011: 331–4. On Dio's debt to Thucydides, see Hose 2007: 464–5. On Dio as 'politically Roman but culturally Greek', see Millar 1964: 191; Aalders 1986: 284; Swain 1996: 402–8; de Blois 1998: 3406–7; Burden-Strevens 2015: 289–90, 296–7.

[27] Jones 2016: 306–11.   [28] Asirvatham 2017: 485. See also Kemezis in this volume (Chapter 1).

not a compliment considering that Nero's other advisers were people like the power-hungry Agrippina and the 'vulgar' (φορτικός) Pallas (61[61].3.2 [Xiph./ *ELg*]). Moreover, the *princeps* consistently ignored any good advice offered to him (61[61].4.5 [*EV*]). This caused Burrus a great deal of frustration and, after speaking out about his treatment of Octavia, Nero had the praetorian prefect poisoned (61[62].13.1–3 [Xiph.]). Seneca lasted longer but was not a man of the same moral compass as his colleague. In fact, Dio's Seneca was an immoral hypocrite: 'while denouncing tyranny, he was making himself the teacher of a tyrant' (καὶ γὰρ τυραννίδος κατηγορῶν τυραννοδιδάσκαλος ἐγίνετο) (61[61].10.1–6 [Xiph./*EV*]).[29] The impressionable Nero outright fails the *consilium* test.[30] This is a point on which Dio and the Latin sources largely agree.[31]

Nero's demonstration of *paideia* is a more complex category, particularly because Nero's education in Greek and the classics is a point with contention between Dio and our other historians. Before Dio, writers held that Nero could compose poetry and deliver speeches and arguments in the Greek language. Indeed, Suetonius (*Ner.* 49.3) has the emperor at the moment of his death recite a line from the *Iliad* (10.535): 'The thunder of swift-footed horses echoes around my ears' (ἵππων μ' ὠκυπόδων ἀμφὶ κτύπος οὔατα βάλλει).[32] However, this part of Nero's biography is never alluded to by Dio. The omission underpins Dio's treatment of Nero's philhellenism; as both appreciation and demonstration of *paideia* necessitate a meaningful understanding of Greek culture,[33] Nero cannot be seen to be well-versed in the classics. The historian's own status as *pepaideumenos* means he cannot allow such an emperor as Nero (i.e. Commodus) to be associated with a cultured, senatorial attribute. This attitude reaches its climax at the point of Nero's trip to Greece, when Nero's entire lack of culture and refinement translates into the wanton destruction of the land which any *pepaideumenos* would revere as second only to Rome.[34]

---

[29] Cf. 62(61).12.1 (Xiph.). However, when Seneca had earlier appeared as tutor of Gaius, Dio was more complimentary, see 59.19.7–8.

[30] See Jones (2016: 307) for examples of good imperial *consilia*.

[31] Although Seneca is not vilified by Tacitus or Suetonius and the influence of Seneca and Burrus lasted a lot longer with Tacitus' Nero than with Dio's: Suet. *Ner.* 15.1; Tac. *Ann.* 14.1.

[32] Trans. Edwards 2000: 225. Cf. Nero changing an unknown Greek quotation at *Ner.* 38.1. Dio puts the unchanged version in the mouth of Tiberius (58.23.4).

[33] Jones (2016: 309–10) gives several examples of 'good' emperors showing appreciation for *paideia*, among them Nero's predecessors Augustus, who practised Greek oratory, and Claudius, who wrote histories (45.2.8 and 60.2.1).

[34] On the central role of Greece, and Athens in particular, in the continuation of *paideia* during the Second Sophistic, see Bowie 2015: 239–53.

III   A Philhellene Stripped of Hellenism

In recent years, Verena Schulz has contended that Nero's war (πόλεμος) on
Greece as described by Dio should be seen as an extension of Nero's artistic
theatricality – while pretending to be peaceful, Nero ransacks the
province.[35] While theatricality is certainly a leading motif, I will argue
that Dio's inclusion of the emperor's dissimulation in relation to Greece is
part of a larger point: that Nero was no philhellene at all. Where Tacitus
and Suetonius take great pains to stress philhellenism as a (usually negative)
Neronian trait, the same episodes either do not appear in Dio's history or
have the 'Greekness' removed from them. Indeed, even other Greek
authors' main criticism of Vespasian, that he revoked Greece's freedom,
does not appear in Dio's account.[36] To include it would have drawn
further attention to Nero's accomplishment, and to criticise Vespasian
would have been an implicit endorsement of Nero's action. As we will see,
this would not have fit with Dio's illustration of a dangerous tyrant – one
incapable of a genuine appreciation for anything, including Greece.

There are episodes recounted by Tacitus and Suetonius that point to
Nero's philhellenism before his trip to Greece. As a child, Tacitus (*Ann.*
13.3.3) tells us, Nero was proficient in traditionally Greek skills: he enjoyed
'engraving, painting, practicing songs or his control of horses; and sometimes in the composing of poems he showed that he had elements of
learning'.[37] The passage recalls Virgil's famous lines in the sixth book of
the *Aeneid* (6.847–53) in which the spirit of Anchises tells his son Aeneas to
conquer and govern the people of the world rather than beating bronze or
carving marble; in other words, outlining Roman versus Greek
activities.[38] Suetonius conveys the same message in a slightly different
way. His Nero was foremost an accomplished poet, with a concerted
interest in painting and sculpture (Suet. *Ner.* 52.1).[39] Cassius Dio, on the
other hand, avoids the subject of Nero's artistic and literary skill as a child

---

[35] Schulz 2014: 412–13.
[36] The narrative structure of the epitome at book 65(66) does not seem to suggest omission of this
episode. Dio (65[66].11.2–3 [Xiph.]) does mention that Vespasian went with Nero on his tour of
Greece, but the wider discussion is of Vespasian's ability not to hold a grudge. There is no suggestion
that his revocation would have been a part of this section, and there is no logical place for it
elsewhere as the majority of Dio's narrative focuses on Rome.
[37] *caelare pingere, cantus aut regimen equorum exercere; et aliquando carminibus pangendis inesse sibi
elementa doctrinae ostendebat* (trans. Woodman 2004: 246).
[38] Cf. Hor. *Ep.* 2.1.
[39] Fantham (2013: 25) describes poetry, unlike singing, as an 'acceptable diversion'. In chapter 54,
Suetonius describes Nero as wanting to dance the part of Virgil's Turnus – an enemy of the Romans,
but certainly not a Greek. This is one of the only instances of Nero wanting to perform a non-Greek
part.

altogether. All he says on the subject of education is that Nero was in training under his mother Agrippina to become emperor, and that his education was delegated to Seneca, of whom, as we have seen, Dio thought very little.[40] This is key to Dio's rejection of Nero's grasp of *paideia*, and lays the foundation for depicting an emperor who would continually misinterpret the true meaning of Greek culture.

As Nero progressed from childhood into adolescence, his practice of the Greek arts continued. Tacitus and Suetonius tell us that, just before Nero became emperor, one of his most successful speeches in the senate argued for the freedom of the Rhodians.[41] Moreover, the speech was delivered in Greek. Also during that same year, AD 53, Nero secured (again speaking in Greek) exemption for Ilium from public taxation and remission for Apamea in Asia Minor of taxes for five years.[42] Tacitus and Suetonius are clear that Nero gave these speeches in the same year as he married Octavia. When the marriage to Octavia is mentioned by Dio, however, Nero has not just delivered persuasive addresses for the benefit of Greeks but pledged a horse race on the occasion that Claudius should recover from his illness (61[60].33.9–10 [Zonar.]). The episode is used by Dio to demonstrate Agrippina's machinations to ensure Nero's succession – it was she who ordered Nero to deliver the speech in order to win favour with the people. A defining moment of philhellenism in the life of Nero as told by both Tacitus and Suetonius is disregarded by Dio.

Similar omissions and manipulations occur when Nero takes up the role of *princeps*, and the variety of ways in which he could show his affinity with the Greek world increased. In both public and private spheres, the Latin sources stress Nero's 'Greekness' – his style of dress, the games he instituted, and his relationships with both men and women are all couched in Greek terms.[43] Needless to say, Tacitus and Suetonius used Nero's love of Greece and Greek things to undermine his success as a Roman emperor; however, that Nero's love was sincere was not questioned. While Suetonius on the whole ramps up Nero's 'Greekness' to a greater extent than Tacitus, both refer to innovations made or actions taken by the emperor as Hellenic in nature. The main example that crosses both Latin authors is the Greek style of Nero's games, particularly the Juvenalia (AD 59) and the quinquennial

---

[40] 61(60).32.3 (*EV*). Notably, Dio does not even mention the dancer and the barber of Suet. *Ner.* 6.3 as Nero's tutors. As noted by Schulz (2019a: 183–4), Dio's tyrannical Domitian is also the enemy of learned men.

[41] Tac. *Ann.* 12.58.2; Suet. *Ner.* 7.2, *Claud.* 25.3.   [42] Tac. *Ann.* 12.58.2; Suet. *Ner.* 7.2.

[43] For example, Tac. *Ann.* 14.15, 20–1, 47, 15.33; Suet. *Ner.* 12.3–4, 20.1, 22.3, 25.1, 28.2, 51.1, 53.1.

Neronia (AD 60 and 64/5).[44] In addition, Suetonius fleshes out his biography with a number of examples of Nero speaking in Greek to friends, occasionally dressing in a Greek fashion, and lamenting that only the Greeks could properly appreciate his arts. Indirectly, arguably any reference to Nero's performances on stage or racing in the stadium would remind an elite reader of his foreignness, but particularly of his 'Greekness'.[45] For Tacitus and Suetonius, the criticism is that Nero was un-Roman; the implication is that he favoured Greece. In contrast, no favour is shown by Dio's Nero towards Hellas, especially when the emperor eventually reaches Achaea itself.

According to Suetonius (*Ner.* 12.4), at the Juvenalia (thrown to celebrate Nero shaving off his first beard) Nero imitated a custom from Olympia by allowing the Vestal Virgins to watch athletic contests.[46] At the *ludi Maximi* ('games for Jupiter') he awarded Roman citizenship to Greek youths performing pyrrhic dances (Suet. *Ner.* 12.1). When established, the Neronia was split into three parts (music, gymnastics, riding) after the Greek fashion and Nero gifted all senators and equestrians with oil to mark the dedication of his baths and gymnasium (Suet. *Ner.* 12.3). All of these details appear in Suetonius' collection of the better parts of Nero's reign.[47] Tacitus did not see the events in such a favourable light. For the senator, such extravagance as that displayed at the Greek quinquennial Neronia would never have been possible during the Republic, when the money would have come out of the public purse (Tac. *Ann.* 14.20–1). Moreover, the Juvenalia promoted vices amongst the elite so extreme that 'outrages and infamy swelled, and nothing made a greater contribution of lust to the long-standing corruption of behavior than did that cesspit' (Tac. *Ann.* 14.15.3).[48] Similarly, the Neronia signals for Tacitus (*Ann.* 14.20) the 'overthrow of ancestral morality' (*patrios mores ... everti*). Men, women, and youths of all ranks were, either willingly or through coercion,

---

[44] Suetonius describes the second Neronia as taking place before the proper time (Suet. *Ner.* 21.1).

[45] The Roman inherited both chariot racing and drama performances from the Greeks. This contrasts to gladiatorial fights, which are most likely of Etruscan origin. However, Fantham (2013: 19) points out that Suetonius only dedicates a small section of his narrative to Nero's chariot racing as it was not really that scandalous. This contrasts with the scandal caused by his singing.

[46] The custom in Olympia was to allow the priestesses of Ceres to watch the contests.

[47] While not beyond reproach in this section, particularly when Nero forced 400 senators and 600 equestrians to fight in the arena (Suet. *Ner.* 12.1), Nero did provide excellent entertainment for Rome.

[48] *inde gliscere flagitia et infamia, nec ulla moribus olim corruptis plus libidinum circumdedit quam illa conluvies* (trans. Woodman 2004: 282). Tacitus goes on to say that never, since the annexation of Asia and Achaea and the games thrown by Lucius Mummius, has someone of respectable rank behaved in such a way as to perform on the stage.

performing (or, being polluted – *polluantur*) on stage at Nero's festival. A vital part of the Neronia passage is Tacitus' emphasis that the games were conducted in the Greek style – Nero the philhellene followed Greek custom, but Greek custom perverts Roman values.[49]

In Dio's narrative, the games are not identified as noticeably Greek. In fact, his account of the Juvenalia is introduced with a particularly Roman episode, Nero offering his first beard to Jupiter Capitolinus. Dio then depicts senators and an octogenarian woman being forced to perform on stage while wishing that they had been killed instead (62[61].19.1–4 [Xiph.]). Dio continues with a diatribe against Nero's own performances, describing how soldiers were stationed in the audience to 'prompt' clapping and cheering (62[61].20.3–4 [Xiph.]). The audience, including senators, proclaimed Nero 'Glorious Caesar', 'Augustus', and 'Pythian', much as they would when Nero was proclaimed Victor for his lyre-playing again at the Neronia a year later (62[61].20.5, 21.1–2 [Xiph.]). Both the soldiers' participation and the honorific titles foreshadow Nero's visit to Greece, where the same titles were used by soldiers leading an audience under similar duress.[50] Where Greece features in the Juvenalia and Neronia, then, is not in their sponsorship by a philhellene, but rather in their role as prototypes for the kind of suffering Nero would later inflict upon audiences in Achaea.

Suetonius, given his particular focus on character and the rhetorical slant of his biographies,[51] stresses Nero's 'Greekness' as an attribute far more than Tacitus. Nero's ability to speak Greek is mentioned several times, often in relation to his desire to perform on the stage. The emperor recited a Greek proverb when professing his intention to act and sing in public and declared that only the Greeks could fully appreciate his musical talent (Suet. *Ner.* 20.1, 22.3). In a sinister twist on the same theme, after Claudius' death by poisoned mushrooms, Suetonius (*Ner.* 33.1) has it that Nero took to using a Greek phrase in public: mushrooms are the 'food of the gods' (*deorum cibum*).[52] Tacitus does not mention the episode at all, but it speaks too much to Nero's character for Dio to leave it out.[53] In his version,

[49] This is an old argument dating back at least as far as the Punic and Macedonian wars, and not one which Suetonius takes up on this occasion. When Nero 'triumphs' in Rome over his victories in competitions in Greece, however, Suetonius is more derisive (Suet. *Ner.* 25).

[50] My thanks to Caillan Davenport for drawing this point to my attention. Nero's visit to Greece is discussed in the following section.

[51] Barton 1994: 50–2.   [52] Trans. Edwards 2000: 212.

[53] See Pelling (1997a: 138–9) on Dio's regular use of anecdotes. Moreover, there is the famous methodological statement of Dio's at 53.19.6, in which he reveals reports and hearsay as amongst his sources. On this passage, see now Chapter 1 by Kemezis and Chapter 2 by Davenport.

however, the proverb is Nero's own invention and has no connection whatsoever to the Greeks (61[60].35.4 [Xiph.]). Where Suetonius stresses Nero's use (even if somewhat theatrical, superficial, and limited) of the Greek language, this is another aspect of Nero's 'Greekness' rejected by Dio. Moreover, the significance of the episode is escalated – the sinister proverb became the emperor's own.[54]

For the Romans, Greek art and culture should be reserved for time dedicated to leisure, for instance during retirement.[55] To take an interest in Greek pursuits such as singing, reciting poetry, chariot racing, and playing the lyre whilst also (or rather, instead of) running the empire was the preserve of bad emperors such as Gaius (and later Commodus). As we have seen, Tacitus regards the Juvenalia as encouraging 'debauchery and infamy' (*flagitia et infamia*), and the Neronia as the final straw in the obliteration of national morality. These themes are accelerated by Tacitus when Nero decides to visit Naples, because it is a Greek city, to perform in public for the first time in AD 64. A mob of people from surrounding areas hear of the emperor's visit and flock to the amphitheatre. Following his performance, Tacitus (*Ann.* 15.33–4) reports that the theatre collapsed – an event seen as 'miserable' (*tristis*) by most but regarded by Nero as providential and numinous. Suetonius' version is once again slightly different but contains a similar message about the success of Nero's performance. When the theatre collapses, it is due to an earthquake and not tied to the emperor's opprobrium (Suet. *Ner.* 20.3). However, Nero does not deal with the situation well: the earthquake took place during his performance and the emperor simply refused to stop singing. In both accounts, there follows around Nero an atmosphere of corruption, destroying people and architecture alike. The core of this corruption lies in Nero's choice to be a better singer, performer, and follower of the Greek arts than he was an emperor.

For Dio, when it came to Nero's stage performances, the emperor's lack of professionalism was not the main story. Instead, they showed the abuse Nero continuously inflicted upon the Greek arts. Dio's Nero was not a good performer; in fact, he was woefully inadequate. During the Juvenalia, his singing voice was so weak that he made an audience laugh and cry at the same time (62[61].20.2 *EV*/Xiph.).[56] Moreover, performing

---

[54] This builds upon a theme we already see in reference to the emperor Gaius, who was known across a variety of writers for having shouted the Homeric line (*Il.* 23.724): ἤ μ' ἀνάειρ' ἤ ἐγὼ σέ ('either lift me, or I will lift you'), see 59.28.6–7 (*EV*); Suet. *Calig.* 22.4; Sen. *Dial.* 3.20.8. Dio's Nero does not borrow as Gaius does.

[55] In relation to Nero, see Mratschek 2013: 46–7.

[56] *EV*: character of singing voice; Xiph: audience response. In Suetonius' account, the fact that Nero is a good singer is used in a barb against him (see *Ner.* 39.3), although he also admits that Nero's voice, when he began his lessons, was weak and husky (*Ner.* 20.1).

in such a way did not convince Dio of Nero's Hellenism, but rather of his femininity. In a speech supposedly given by Boudicca, Nero's cultural pursuits serve to show that he is like a woman, not like a Greek (62[62].6.3 [Xiph.]). As Dio's narrative reaches the year AD 64, he does not mention Naples, but remarks that Nero had the audacity to drive chariots in public (he does not mention where). This is followed by a description of opulent dinner parties, before moving to the account of the fire of Rome (62[62].15 [Xiph.]). Xiphilinus certainly condensed Dio's work and perhaps left out the trip, given it was just a precursor to his performances in Greece. However, it is also consistent with Dio's rejection of Nero's philhellenism to leave out the trip to Naples altogether. Ignoring Naples allows Dio out of a thorny situation – he neither needs to profess explicitly Nero's preference for Greek cities, nor does he need to account for the support of the audience there. Ignoring this episode makes the climax of blood and gore in Achaea more potent.

IV Nero the Anti-Hellene

Having set the tone of Nero's character, Dio enters full flow into a diatribe against the emperor by describing his trip to Achaea. Here Nero graduates to a tyrant who wages bloody war on an unsuspecting and undeserving province. While we do not know what Tacitus said on the subject, other writers including Dio's fellow Hellenes generally agreed that Nero was a lover of Greece, even if his actions were often overzealous. Yet, Dio rewrites the history books in order to bring to its apex Nero's characterisation as an emperor entirely unable to demonstrate *paideia* in any meaningful fashion. Nero, unequipped with the education afforded him by other writers, encountered a Greece he could not understand. His subsequent actions caused terror, and not pleasure, among the Greeks.

Dio's account of Nero's trip begins with a comparison between Nero and those other notable Romans who had made the same crossing before him – Flamininus, Mummius, Agrippa, and Augustus. Unlike the heroes of the Macedonian and Achaean wars and his ancestors in the imperial family, Nero did not go forth to conquer but to sing, dance, act, and drive chariots. It was not because he felt any special affection for the province and its people that he chose Greece, but because he 'desired also a foreign campaign' (ἐδεήθη καὶ ἐκστρατείας τινός): he wanted to be Victor not in battle, but of the *periodos* (the Pythian, Isthmian, Nemean, and Olympic games) (62[63].8.1–3 [*EV*]).[57] The military metaphor is extended: Nero took with him enough people for support as would have 'subdued both Parthians and all other nations' (καὶ Πάρθους ἂν καὶ τὰ ἄλλα ἔθνη ἐχειρώσατο) (62[63].8.2–3 [Xiph.]).[58] To add insult to injury, by naming the traditional institutions the emperor failed to uphold, Dio insists that Nero's actions tarnished all Roman tradition: 'a Roman, a senator, a patrician, a high priest, a Caesar, an emperor, an Augustus, named on the programme among the contestants' (ἄνδρα Ῥωμαῖον βουλευτὴν εὐπατρίδην ἀρχιερέα Καίσαρα αὐτοκράτορα Αὔγουστον ἔς τε τὸ λεύκωμα ἐν τοῖς ἀγωνισταῖς ἐγγραφόμενον) (62[63].9.1 [*EV*]).[59] Both Nero's motives and deeds were perverted, and the effects were felt in Greece and Rome. This man was no philhellene.

Moreover, Nero's audience were not entirely enamoured of the emperor. Dio contends that the general crowd 'endured' (ἔφερον) and 'approved' (ἐπῄνουν) of his performances, but the soldiers, those who under Augustus would have been fighting battles, were the most enthusiastic, hailing him not Imperator but Victor at the games (62[63].10.1 [Xiph.]).[60] This recalls Dio's account of the Juvenalia and Neronia where, as we have seen, Nero was given honorific titles by an audience also containing soldiers. Nero's audience in Rome, then, anticipates Nero's audience in Greece, where those with any sense of decency and respect for tradition and hierarchy acted purely out of self-preservation; they 'endured'. The same can be said for Nero's Greek audience – the soldiers led the way in approval, but the majority were coerced into a forced appreciation.

When Suetonius (*Ner.* 22.3–24) describes the tour, he focusses on Nero's shows in the theatre and how seriously the emperor took them, with only brief reference to the freedom of Achaea and the granting of Roman citizenship to judges at the end. Suetonius (*Ner.* 53.1) stresses how Nero acted (if perversely) like a judge at gymnastic contests and compared himself to Apollo and Hercules when he performed.[61] For Dio, however,

---

[57] See also Kennell 1988: 239–51.
[58] Instead of 'all other nations', the passage in the *EV* names the Caspians and the Ethiopians in addition to the Parthians. As Schulz (2019a: 233) has noted, Nero's trip to Greece is a markedly military episode in Dio's narrative.
[59] Dio (*EV*) continues in this vein through chapter 9.
[60] The text of the *EV* also preserves most of this passage, although only the soldiers, and not the crowd, are mentioned: οἱ δὲ στρατιῶται ταῦτα ὁρῶντες ἔφερον ἐπῄνουν. This episode recalls the senators in Commodus' arena audience proclaiming him Victor at 73(72).20.2[Xiph.]. On Nero's relationship with the people in Dio's text, see Hellström in this volume (Chapter 9).
[61] See also the inscription from the Temple of Apollo in Acraephia, Boeotia cited in n. 8. The association between Nero and Apollo and Nero and Hercules can also be seen in artistic evidence. For example, Nero appeared regularly as Apollo Citharoedus on the reverse imperial coins of AD

Nero's theatrics on stage were just the beginning. The scenario quickly turns from black comedy to out-and-out tragedy as the effects of Nero's visit are divulged:

> Now if this had been all that he did, the affair, while being a source of shame and of ridicule, would still have been thought harmless. But, as it was, he devastated the whole of Greece precisely as if he had been sent out to wage war, notwithstanding that he had left the country free; and he slew great numbers of men, women and children. At first, he commanded the children and freedmen of those who were executed to leave him half their property at their death; he allowed the victims themselves to make wills, in order that he might not appear to be killing them for their money. He invariably took all that was bequeathed to him, or at least the greater part, and in case anyone left to him or to Tigellinus less than they were expecting, his will was of no avail. Later he took away the entire property of those who were executed and banished all their children at one time by a single decree. Nor was he content with even this, but he also destroyed not a few of those who were living in exile. ... Nero, it seems, had taken away many of the foremost men to Greece, under the pretence of needing some assistance from them, merely in order that they might perish there. (62[63].11.1–12.1 [Xiph.])[62]

This dramatic overview of Nero's anti-Hellenism is extended by specific episodes – Nero's mock marriage to 'Sabina' (Sporus) was celebrated by the Greeks, a reaction hardly meant to be understood as genuine after we have heard about the 'war' waged by the emperor; his extravagant gift to the Pythia at Delphi of 400,000 sesterces shortly before abolishing the Oracle by blocking up the fissure with the bodies of people he had killed; his transfer of the territory of Cirrha in Phocis (sacred to Apollo) to the

---

62–8 (*RIC* I² Nero 73–82, 121–3, 205–12, 380–1, 384–5, 414–17, 451–5), and Apollo or Hercules appeared on the reverse of Achaean provincial coins (e.g. *RPC* I Achaea 1278, 1444/1). Moreover, Robert Weir (1999: 397–404) has argued that the frieze depicting nine of the labours of Hercules at Delphi was either produced in preparation for Nero's visit, or in preparation for a visit Nero intended to make for the Olympics in AD 71 (Suet. *Ner.* 53.1).

[62] ἀλλ' εἰ μὲν ταῦτα μόνα οὕτως ἐγεγόνει, αἰσχύνη τε ἂν καὶ χλευασία τὸ πρᾶγμα ἀκίνδυνος ἐνενόμιστο· νῦν δ' ὡς ἀληθῶς, ὥσπερ ἐπὶ πολέμῳ σταλείς, πᾶσαν μὲν τὴν Ἑλλάδα ἐλεηλάτησε, καίπερ ἐλευθέραν ἀφείς, παμπληθεῖς δὲ ἐφόνευσεν ἄνδρας γυναῖκας παῖδας. καὶ πρότερον μὲν τὴν ἡμίσειαν τῆς οὐσίας ἐκέλευσέν οἱ καὶ τὰ τέκνα καὶ τοὺς ἀπελευθέρους τῶν θανατουμένων ἀποθνήσκοντας καταλείπειν, αὐτοῖς τε ἐκείνοις διαθήκας γράφειν ἐπέτρεπεν, ὅπως μὴ τῶν χρημάτων ἕνεκα αὐτοὺς ἀποκτείνειν δοκῇ (πάντως δὲ πάντα ἢ τά γε πλείω αὐτῶν ἐλάμβανεν· εἰ γοῦν τις ἔλαττόν τι αὐτῷ ἢ τῷ Τιγελλίνῳ ὧν ἤλπιζον κατέλειπεν, οὐδὲ τῶν διαθηκῶν ὠνίνατο)· ὕστερον δὲ καὶ ὅλας τὰς οὐσίας ἀφηρεῖτο, τούς τε παῖδάς σφων πάντας ἅμα δι' ἑνὸς δόγματος ἐξήλασεν. οὐδὲ τοῦτο αὐτῷ ἐξήρκεσεν, ἀλλὰ καὶ συχνοὺς τῶν φευγόντων ἔφθειρεν. [...] συχνοὺς γὰρ ἐς τὴν Ἑλλάδα τῶν πρώτων ἐξήγαγεν ὥς τι αὐτῶν δεόμενος, ἵν' ἐκεῖ ἀποθάνωσιν. The text of the *EV* is largely the same as this passage, except at the beginning. It starts with the deaths of great numbers of men, women, and children, and does not preserve that Nero 'waged war' on or freed Greece.

soldiers; his attempt to cut through the Isthmus at Corinth which caused the ground to spurt blood and phantoms to appear; and his murder of all those foremost men whose possessions he wanted to seize (62[63].13.1–18.1 [Xiph./EV]). The passages produce a relentless read – no-one, Greek or otherwise, could possibly have supported or approved of such a tour.

So much of what Cassius Dio writes about this episode is, as far as we know, unique to him. Suetonius says little about Nero's visit to Greece, but Dio also diverges from other Greeks who mention Nero in non-historiographical texts. For example, it is highly unlikely that Nero really abolished the oracle at Delphi; as Levin points out, Plutarch, a priest at Delphi, would not have saved Nero from rebirth as a viper had he done so.[63]

Greek authors other than Dio used Nero's philhellenism to the same effect as Tacitus and Suetonius, to undermine his credibility as an emperor. However, the fact that he loved Greek things was neither denied nor necessarily a problem *per se*; rather his love (with the exception of the liberation of Greece) was so excessive that he perverted Greek customs without necessarily realising it. Thus, when Dio Chrysostom (*Or.* 31.150) condemns in no uncertain terms Nero's robbing of Greek cities and sanctuaries of their statues (Nero is 'the most immoderate of emperors', ὁ τῶν βασιλέων σφοδρότατος), he characterises his motivations as 'desire' (ἐπιθυμία) and 'hasty enthusiasm' (σπουδή), not malice (*Or.* 31.148).[64] This occurs in Chrysostom's speech to the Rhodians, in which he attempts to persuade them to stop brazenly recycling pre-existing statues to show 'honour' to a new dedicatee. Rhodes was a city whose treasures Nero left untouched – even this emperor, says Chrysostom (*Or.* 31.148), showed the city's statues more respect than its current inhabitants. As Rhodes was a city favoured by Nero, perhaps he could not reproach the emperor in stronger terms without causing offence; however, this explanation would at the same time speak to some affection for Nero felt in parts of Greece that Cassius Dio goes to great lengths to refute.

Similarly to Chrysostom, when ps.-Lucian's (likely one of the Philostrati) Menecrates asks whether Nero's digging of the Isthmus at Corinth demonstrated a Greek spirit on the part of the emperor, the

---

[63] Levin 1989: 1605–6; Plut. *Mor.* 567F–568A. That said, while not condemning him to an afterlife as a viper, Plutarch is extremely critical of Nero's other actions as *princeps*, accusing him of bringing Rome to the brink of destruction. See Plut. *Ant.* 87.4.

[64] Trans. J. W. Cohoon and H. Lamar Crosby, Loeb Classical Library edition. Susan Alcock (1994: 100–1) has very convincingly argued that Nero acted according to precedent here, particularly that of Sulla and Augustus.

philosopher Musonius Rufus replies, 'I can assure you, Menecrates, that Nero's intentions were even better than Greek' ("Ἴσθι, ὦ Μενέκρατες, καὶ βελτίω ἐντεθυμῆσθαι Νέρωνα) (Ps.-Luc. *Nero* 1).[65] As noted by Tim Whitmarsh, Musonius did not mean the emperor succeeded in being Greek; in fact, he could *never* be Greek given that his philhellenism 'springs from a traditionally Roman notion of largesse'.[66] However, there is no question he was motivated by a desire to be praised by the Greeks.[67] Nero's spirit was willing, but his rushed and haphazard planning meant that his actions usually fell short of the mark.

The same Musonius also appears as a character in Philostratus' *Life of Apollonius*, a text in which Nero is subject to criticism from the mouths of several first-century philosophers.[68] Apollonius himself severely rebukes Nero for his treatment of the Greeks, describing families evicted from their houses (but not killed) to furnish Nero with supplies for his performances (Philostr. *VA* 5.7.3–4). Nevertheless, there is hope for the emperor, if only by way of comparison. Nero may have 'disgraced his reign by making it too flat and too sharp' (τὴν δὲ ἀρχὴν ᾔσχυνεν ἀνέσει καὶ ἐπιτάσει) but at least he 'freed the Greeks in play' (παίζων ἠλευθέρωσε) while Vespasian 'enslaved them in earnest' (αὐτοὺς σπουδάζων ἐδουλώσω) (Philostr. *VA* 5.28.1, 41.4).[69] As Myles Lavan has argued, it is not extraordinary to see

[65] Trans. M. D. MacLeod, Loeb Classical Library edition.   [66] Whitmarsh 1999: 145–6.

[67] On the one hand, Musonius says that 'by breaking through two and a half miles of the Isthmus he proposed to save seafarers the voyage around the Peloponnese past Cape Malea. This would have benefitted not only commerce but also the coastal and inland cities' (τὰς γὰρ περιβολὰς τῆς Πελοποννήσου τὰς ὑπὲρ Μαλέαν ξυνῄρει τοῖς θαλαττουμένοις εἴκοσι σταδίων τοῦ Ἰσθμοῦ ῥήγματι. οὗτο δ' ἂν καὶ τὰς ἐμπορίας ὤνησε καὶ τὰς ἐπὶ θαλάττῃ πόλεις καὶ τὰς ἐν τῇ μεσογείᾳ·) (*Nero* 1). On the other, Musonius qualifies his statement with a comment on Nero's motivations and hasty planning: 'But the Isthmus had no part in the plans which he had formed from far away; it was only when he had seen what the place was like that he fell in love with a grandiose scheme, when the thought of the king who once led the Achaeans against Troy and how he severed Euboea from Boeotia by digging the Euripus at Chalcis ... For tyrannical natures, though intoxicated, yet somehow thirst to hear praises of this sort' (ὁ δὲ Ἰσθμὸς οὐ τῶν ἄποθεν αὐτῷ βεβουλευμένων, ἀλλ' ἐντυχὼν τῇ φύσει τοῦ τόπου μεγαλουργίας ἡράσθη, τόν τε βασιλέα τῶν ἐπὶ τὴν Τροίαν ποτὲ Ἀχαιῶν ἐνθυμηθείς, ὡς τὴν Εὔβοιαν τῆς Βοιωτίας ἀπέτεμεν Εὐρίπῳ τῷ περὶ τὴν Χαλκίδα ... αἱ γὰρ τύραννοι φύσεις μεθύουσι μέν, διψῶσι δέ πη καὶ ἀκοῦσαι τοῦτο φθέγμα) (*Nero* 2) (trans. M. D. MacLeod, Loeb Classical Library edition).

[68] Whitmarsh (2001: 269–305) discusses the philosopher Musonius Rufus (alongside Favorinus and Dio Chrysostom). See Kemezis (2014: 181–94) on Nero, Vespasian, and Domitian in Philostratus' *VA*; esp. 193, where Kemezis describes Vespasian's character in the *VA* as at odds with historical tradition – something that is not the case for Nero and Domitian. Bowie (1978: 1652–99) explores the ideas of tradition and reality more broadly in the *VA*, esp. 1655–7 on Musonius.

[69] Trans. C. P. Jones, Loeb Classical Library edition. These words are contained in a letter sent by Apollonius to Vespasian – the letter also survives separately to Philostratus' *VA*, although Swain (1996: 395) recommends understanding Apollonius' letters as a collection of 'fictitious epistolography', the liking of which was particularly strong in the Second Sophistic.

such language of slavery being used to describe the status of a Roman province by a non-Roman speaker, here Apollonius.[70] However, for Nero to return the Greeks to their natural, ancient state of freedom from one of enforced slavery was no mean feat. Akin to ps.-Lucian's assessment of the emperor, Apollonius believed Nero's intent to be weak and unconvincing, but his action vital and correct. Thus, we can see some congruence between our Greek writers so far. Nero is not liked, and he is not a Greek, but he is a philhellene.

Pausanias' response to Nero is harder to characterise, despite the fact that he spent more time talking about Nero than any other Julio-Claudian emperor after Augustus. Karim Arafat suggests that this is precisely *because* Nero was a philhellene, something that Pausanias made clear when he discussed Nero's liberation of Greece:

> When I consider this act of Nero it struck me how true is the remark of Plato, son of Ariston, who says that the greatest and most daring crimes are committed not by ordinary men, but by a noble soul ruined by a perverted education. (Paus. 7.17.3)[71]

That being said, Pausanias (10.7.1, 10.19.2, 9.27.3–4) censured Nero in almost as strong terms as Dio Chrysostom when describing the stolen ancient treasures of Delphi and Thespiae. To complicate matters further, when Pausanias (5.25.8, 5.26.3) discussed thefts at Olympia and Mikythos, he dealt with them quickly and dispassionately, on both occasions using a reported verb (λέγουσι, 'they say') and reserving comment on Nero's character.[72] Moreover, these passages are preceded a few chapters before by a reminder of the dedications made by Nero in Olympia: four crowns at the Temple of Zeus (Paus. 5.12.8).[73] While the emperor's dedications do not cancel out his thefts, Pausanias is more balanced in his assessment of Nero than one might expect given the number of cultural and artistic treasures taken, and given strong terms other Greeks, particularly Dio Chrysostom, had used to talk about the

---

[70] Lavan 2013: 107–9. Cassius Dio is the exception, who puts the language of slavery into Roman mouths, e.g. 38.38.4, in which Caesar describes the Romans as the masters (δεσπόζομεν) of a catalogue of peoples in the east.

[71] ἀπιδόντι οὖν ἐς τοῦτό μοι τοῦ Νέρωνος τὸ ἔργον ὀρθότατα εἰρηκέναι Πλάτων ἐφαίνετο ὁ Ἀρίστωνος, ὁπόσα ἀδικήματα μεγέθει καὶ τολμήματί ἐστιν ὑπερηρηκότα, οὐ τῶν ἐπιτυχόντων εἶναι ταῦτα ἀνθρώπων, ψυχῆς δὲ γενναίας ὑπὸ ἀτόπου παιδείας διεφθαρμένης (trans. W. H. S. Jones, Loeb Classical Library edition). See Arafat 1996: 139. The only emperor to whom he devotes as much space is Hadrian, another famously philhellenic emperor.

[72] Arafat 1996: 146–8.   [73] See Paus. 2.17.6 for offerings made by Nero at the Argive Heraion.

same events.[74] Perhaps this is because Pausanias ultimately thought that, when it came to his relationship with the Greeks, the battle between Nero's 'noble soul' and his 'perverted education' was at its most fierce.

To conclude, let us go back for a moment to the first Roman to 'free' Greece, Titus Quinctius Flamininus. Flamininus was the general responsible for liberating several Greek *poleis* from Macedonian rule in 196 BC, while not (yet) claiming the territory for the Roman empire. Nero mirrored his forbear by also making his declaration at the Isthmian Games at Corinth.[75] Like Nero's action, Flamininus' proclamation of freedom was soon reversed, when the Achaean League was defeated by the Romans at Corinth in 146 BC. If Nero's liberation was seen by those other than Dio as the emperor's one abiding feature, the same cannot be said for Flamininus. All Flamininus' Greek commentators, including Cassius Dio, seem more or less to agree that his motivations were political and not borne out of genuine regard for the Greeks. Pausanias does not mention Flamininus' liberation at all in its proper section (we might expect it at 7.8) but mentions it three books later when discussing the proposed restoration of Eleteia's ancient constitution (Paus. 10.34.4). For Pausanias, the matter of Hellenic freedom is one of endless and repeated disappointment, for which he largely blames the Achaean League (Paus. 7.8.2–17.2).[76] Siding with Flamininus was the League's first mistake: Pausanias (7.8.2) writes that the 'Romans were coming to impose their domination both on Achaeans and on the rest of Greece' ('Ρωμαῖοι σφίσι τε ἥκοιεν καὶ τῷ Ἑλληνικῷ δεσπόται προστάττειν), but the Achaeans joined them regardless.[77] Pausanias makes no suggestion of a 'noble soul' amongst Flamininus' army.

Unlike Pausanias, Plutarch does not doubt that Flamininus' intentions were honest.[78] However, the result of Greek 'freedom' was the formerly proud nation's overreliance on the military might of Rome; no longer did the Greeks fight their own battles.[79] Dio's assessment aligns with both Pausanias' and Plutarch's. Before Flamininus' defeat of Philip, the former was willing to make a truce with the Macedonian king through 'fear that if Philip were out of the way, the Greeks might recover their ancient spirit and no longer pay court to the Romans' (ὅτι ἐφοβήθη μὴ οἵ τε Ἕλληνες

---

[74] Arafat (1996: 147–8) describes Pausanias' assessment of Nero as 'quietly condemnatory' while never reaching the levels of outrage of his contemporaries. However, he disagrees with Miriam Griffin's argument that the offerings outweigh the robberies. Cf. Griffin 1984: 211.

[75] *ILS* 8794 = Sherk, *Hadrian* 71, line 6; Plut. *Flam.* 10.3.   [76] Swain 1996: 336–7.

[77] Trans. W. H. S. Jones, Loeb Classical Library edition.

[78] His depiction of Flamininus is mostly flattering, see Plut. *Flam.* 1, 9.

[79] Plut. *Flam.* 11, in which the Greeks reflect on the fate of their nation.

ὑπεξαιρεθέντος αὐτοῦ τό τε φρόνημα τὸ παλαιὸν ἀναλάβωσι καὶ σφᾶς οὐκέτι θεραπεύσωσι) (F 60.1 [*ELg*]). When Flamininus does declare Greece free, he reminds its inhabitants of the benefits a close friendship with Rome would bring, urging them to maintain the sort of intimate ties Plutarch's Greeks saw as destructive (Zonar. 9.18). All three writers treat this episode in history with some reticence. In the case of Greece's first liberator, Dio follows a rough *communis opinio*. He does not for its second. Nero is altogether too dangerous an emperor for Dio to allow ambiguity into his account. With the spectre of Commodus looming large, the idea that Nero could demonstrate aspects of senatorial *paideia* through his appreciation of Greek culture was not viable. As such, the philhellenism borne of Nero's education and acknowledged by Tacitus and Suetonius is nowhere to be found in Dio's work. When Nero manages finally to visit and tour the province, Dio's emperor misunderstands, misappropriates, and molests the people and the place at every turn. The emperor who professed himself Greece's greatest champion became through Dio its greatest enemy.

CHAPTER 8

War and Peace
Imperial Leadership in Dio's Second-Century Narrative
Caillan Davenport

I Introduction

Cassius Dio's account of the Roman empire during the second century AD has not received significant scholarly attention when compared to the centuries that precede and follow it.[1] This is at least partially due to its very fragmentary nature. In contrast with the near-complete original text of the *Roman History* that survives for the reign of Augustus and the early Julio-Claudian period, Dio's narrative of the second century must be reconstructed from Xiphilinus and the *Excerpta Constantiniana*.[2] This is compounded by the fact that Dio's account of Antoninus Pius and the joint reign of Marcus Aurelius and Lucius Verus was lost by the time Xiphilinus came to compose his *Epitome* in the eleventh century, and may indeed have already vanished before the sixth.[3] It is probably also the case that Dio's account of the period from Trajan to Marcus Aurelius has seemed less enticing as a subject for scholarly study when compared with his description of the age of Commodus and the Severans.[4] Books 73(72)–80(80), which cover the period of Dio's own political career and encounters with Roman emperors, have a distinct and memorable tone which

I would like to thank Christopher Mallan, Meaghan McEvoy, and audience members at the 2016 Classical Association Conference in Edinburgh for their thoughtful comments on my arguments. Nicola Linton provided helpful research assistance, which was funded by a University of Queensland Summer Research Scholarship. The translations in this chapter are taken from E. Cary's Loeb Classical Library edition, with some tacit modifications.
[1] Migliorati 2003 examines the period from Nerva to Antoninus Pius, offering both a historical and a historiographical study of Dio's text and other sources of evidence, such as inscriptions. Other key scholarly contributions include Millar 1964: 60–72 (Hadrian), Martini 2010, Possienke 2011, and Scott 2015 (Marcus Aurelius), Kemezis 2012 (the Antonine elite), Juntunen 2013 (the lost Antonine books), Davenport and Mallan 2014 (Hadrian's adoption speech), and Madsen 2016 (reviewing Dio's attitude to dynastic rule).
[2] On the transmission of Dio's work and its impact on the text as we have it, see Chapter 13 by Alicia Simpson in this volume.
[3] Schmidt 1989; Juntunen 2013; Mallan 2013b: 633–5.
[4] The division between the two periods is clearly signalled by Dio's famous passage on the transition from the kingdom of gold to iron and rust (Dio 72(71).36.4 [Xiph./*EV*]).

sets them apart from the rest of the *Roman History*.[5] But Books 68–72(71) deserve greater attention than they have hitherto received because of their importance to the larger structure and themes of the work.

Verena Schulz has recently argued that these books function as a coherent narrative unit within the *Roman History*. Nuancing previous discussions of Dio's thematic structure, she has identified three key phases to Dio's account of the Principate: (i) the early empire, from Augustus to Domitian; (ii) the Antonine emperors (broadly construed), from Nerva to Marcus Aurelius; and (iii) the contemporary mode, from Commodus to Severus Alexander.[6] Phases (ii) and (iii) are linked, however, by the fact that they both lie within the time span of what Schulz, following the terminology of Jan Assmann, has identified as the period of Dio's 'communicative memory', roughly eighty years from the end of Trajan's reign onwards. This is a period in which Dio and his peers could not only share memories of their own experiences but also draw on the memories of individuals from previous generations with whom they had direct contact.[7] Dio explicitly talks about his father, the senator Cassius Apronianus, as both a contemporary with whom he shared experiences, such as their visit to the Oracle of Amphilochus in Cilicia in the early 180s, as well as an elder who imparted knowledge to him, like the story of Hadrian's adoption, which took place decades earlier in AD 117.[8] The fact that the reigns of Trajan, Hadrian, Antoninus Pius, and Marcus Aurelius remained within the 'communicative memory' of Dio and his readership meant that they had special significance as a point of comparison with contemporary rulers. Indeed, Adam Kemezis has argued that Dio's account of the early Antonine emperors is designed to function as a nostalgic counterpoint to the upheavals under Commodus and the Severan dynasty.[9]

In this chapter, I will examine Dio's portrayal of five second-century emperors who ruled within the period of 'communicative memory': Trajan, Hadrian, Marcus Aurelius, Commodus, and Pertinax (unfortunately, only very brief comments about Antoninus Pius are possible given the loss of Book 70). I will focus in particular on the military abilities of

[5] For the contemporary books as a distinct portion of Dio's narrative, see Kemezis 2014: 141–5, Scott 2018a, and Chapter 12 by Christopher Mallan in this volume. For specific studies in this vein, see Gleason 2011 on identity politics under Commodus and the Severans, and Osgood 2016 on Elagabalus.
[6] Schulz 2019a: 254–7. [7] Schulz 2019a: 254, drawing on Assmann 2011: 36–44.
[8] Oracle: 73(72).7.2 (Xiph.), with Molin 2016a: 435 on the date. Adoption of Hadrian: 69.1.1–4 (Xiph.). See further Kemezis 2012: 387 on Apronianus as a communicator of past memories to Dio.
[9] Kemezis 2012; 2014: 18.

these emperors. The second century witnessed significant military campaigns of expansion (Trajan's wars in Dacia and Parthia), bloody internal revolt (the Bar Kokhba insurrection under Hadrian), and extended and brutal defensive warfare (the Parthian and Marcomannic campaigns of Lucius Verus and Marcus Aurelius). The Marcomannic Wars, waged between AD 166/7–175 and 177–80, were especially traumatic, given that the barbarian invasions threatened the security of Italy itself.[10] The Equestrian Statue, Arch, and Column of Marcus Aurelius in Rome were erected as tributes to the leader who successfully protected the empire against the odds.[11] These second-century conflicts, especially Marcus' wars, made heroes out of the senatorial and equestrian commanders who fought in them, many of whom were commemorated with public statues in Rome.[12] The most successful Antonine generals were widely regarded as *capaces imperii* ('capable of becoming emperor') and they therefore posed a challenge to the authority of Commodus after Marcus Aurelius' death. One of these marshals, P. Helvius Pertinax, even became emperor following Commodus' murder.[13]

Given the different types of wars during the second century and the recognition that military leadership represented a possible qualification for the purple, it is worth asking what role martial abilities played in Dio's idea of a good emperor. The military virtues of Dio's rulers have not been frequently discussed by scholars, but it is clear that they were an important yardstick for assessing an emperor's character.[14] To take just a few examples, Trajan and Pertinax are praised for their bravery and Galba is commended for his experience in warfare, whereas Commodus, Caracalla, and Macrinus are all said to have suffered from cowardice.[15] Military leadership thus constitutes one of Dio's 'trans-regnal themes' (to use the terminology of Christopher Pelling), ideas and concepts that transcend the biographical emphasis of the imperial books and contribute to a broader

---

[10] The 'Marcomannic Wars' is an all-encompassing term of convenience (though it is attested in Roman sources) for the conflicts between Rome and the northern tribes under Marcus Aurelius (Kovács 2009: 201–3). For the commemoration of these wars in epigraphic sources, see Varga and Pázsint 2019: 51–2.

[11] On the Arch of Marcus Aurelius focussing specifically on the emperor's virtues, see Hölscher 2003: 15. The original placement of the gilt-bronze equestrian statue, now on the Capitoline hill, is unknown (Stewart 2012: 267–8).

[12] 72(71).3.5 (Xiph.); *HA M. Ant.* 22.7. Chenault 2012: 118–22 and Kemezis 2012: 391 discuss the epigraphic evidence.

[13] On these *capaces imperii*, see Champlin 1979; Kemezis 2012: 388–402.

[14] Kuhn-Chen 2002: 157.

[15] Trajan: 68.6.3 (*EV*), 68.14.1 (Xiph.). Pertinax: 75(74).5.6 (*EV*). Galba: 63.23.1 (Xiph.). Commodus: 73(72).1.1 (*EV*). Caracalla: 78(77).18.3 (*EV*). Macrinus: 79(78).27.1.

understanding of the positive and negative aspects of the imperial office and its holders.[16]

The advice provided by Maecenas to Octavian in his speech in Book 52 of the *Roman History* points the way forward to understanding the potential military skills expected of a Roman emperor:

> Now you should be wholly inclined to peace, so far as your purpose is concerned and your desire for nothing more than you now possess, but as regards your military preparations you should be distinctly warlike (πολεμικώτατον), in order that, if possible, no one may either wish or attempt to wrong you, but if he should, that he may be punished easily and instantly. (52.37.1)[17]

In Maecenas' view, Octavian (and by implication, his eventual imperial successors) should not deliberately start conflicts and seek to extend the boundaries of the empire through military campaigns, but nevertheless must be 'distinctly warlike' in order to protect Rome's territories and peoples. This required a well-trained standing army, Maecenas observes (52.27.1–5).[18] Dio's own comments on military matters in the *Roman History* suggest that he regarded it as necessary for emperors to maintain discipline and order among the troops.[19] The theme of military control is also emphasised in a later speech, Tiberius' funeral oration for Augustus in Book 56. This looks back at the monarchical system Augustus established, and thus forms an effective counterpart to the prospective speeches of Agrippa and Maecenas in Book 52. Tiberius praises Augustus for his policy of protection, rather than of expansion, and for safeguarding the provinces and the Roman citizens (56.40.1–2, 41.7), as Christina Kuhn has highlighted in Chapter 5 of this volume.[20] There is a strong thematic thread running through both the main narrative of the *Roman History* and the

---

[16] Pelling 1997a: 124. For the theme of military leadership in Dio's account of the kings, see Schulz 2019b: 320–1.

[17] Τῇ μὲν οὖν γνώμῃ καὶ τῷ μηδενὸς πλείονος τῶν ὑπαρχόντων ἐπιθυμεῖν εἰρηνικώτατον εἶναί σε χρή, ταῖς δὲ παρασκευαῖς πολεμικώτατον, ὅπως μάλιστα μὲν μήτε ἐθελήσῃ μήτε ἐπιχειρήσῃ τις ἀδικῆσαί σε, εἰ δὲ μή, ῥᾳδίως καὶ παραχρῆμα κολασθῇ.

[18] I acknowledge here the views of many scholars who have pointed out that Maecenas is not simply a mouthpiece for Dio himself (e.g. Rich 1989: 99; Myles Lavan's discussion in Chapter 10 of this volume). This passage from the speech is worth highlighting, however, as it establishes a key theme explored by Dio himself in the *Roman History*. In this case, I believe that there is a strong correlation between the ideas of Maecenas the character and Dio the historical narrator.

[19] Harrington 1977: 161–2; Migliorati 2003: 35. Dio's Octavian was certainly not blessed with martial talent (Reinhold and Swan 1990: 160).

[20] Reinhold and Swan (1990: 162) note that this statement sits uncomfortably with the expansion that did occur under Augustus. Giua (1983) argues this speech reflects the concerns of Dio as a senator of the Severan period, but see now Chapter 5 by Christina Kuhn.

speeches given by Maecenas and Tiberius, that the ideal Roman emperor was a ruler who possessed military ability, but who did not employ this in pursuit of expansion and glory. In what follows, I shall explore how the emperors of the second century measured up to this ideal.

II Trajan

Book 68 opens with a somewhat troubled reign, as Nerva faced challenges from the praetorian guard and its prefect; his solution was to adopt Trajan to stabilise his rule (68.3.3–4 [Xiph.]). Trajan proved to be an ambitious military campaigner, leading the army in person in two Dacian Wars and on the Parthian expedition.[21] Dio begins his biographical character sketch of Trajan by noting that the emperor 'was most conspicuous for his justice, for his bravery, and for the simplicity of his habits' (πλεῖστον γὰρ ἐπί τε δικαιότητι καὶ ἐπ' ἀνδρείᾳ τῇ τε ἁπλότητι τῶν ἠθῶν διέπρεπε) (68.6.3 [EV]).[22] This opening statement leads into an account of the emperor's character, his building works, and his relationship with the senate. Trajan's vices – boys and wine – are clearly highlighted, but they are not harmful to the government of the state (68.7.4 [EV]). At the end of this assessment of the emperor, Dio, as quoted in the Constantinian *Excerpta*, returns to Trajan's military qualities:

> And even if he did delight in war (φιλοπόλεμος), nevertheless he was satisfied when success had been achieved, a most bitter foe overthrown and his countrymen exalted. Nor did the result which usually occurs in such circumstances – conceit and arrogance on the part of the soldiers – ever manifest itself during his reign; with such a firm hand did he rule them. (68.7.5 [EV])[23]

The adjective φιλοπόλεμος (*philopolemos*, 'fond of war, warlike') was not usually a flattering one; indeed, in the *Roman History* it is one of several abusive terms levelled by Lucullus against Pompey (36.46.2).[24] Nor is the love of war endorsed as a positive quality in this passage. Unlike other leaders who were *philopolemos*, Trajan's military campaigns and focus on

---

[21] The Suda (D 1239 s.v. Δίων) states that Dio wrote a separate account of Trajan's reign, but this is not usually accepted as accurate.

[22] For the character sketch as a structural element of Dio's imperial narrative, see Questa 1957 and Millar 1964: 40, developed further by Pelling 1997a: 117–18.

[23] εἰ δὲ καὶ φιλοπόλεμος ἦν, ἀλλὰ τῇ τε κατορθώσει καὶ τοῦ ἐχθίστου μὲν καθαιρέσει τοῦ οἰκείου δὲ αὐξήσει ἠρκεῖτο. οὐδὲ γὰρ οὐδ' ὅπερ εἴωθεν ἐν τοῖς τοιούτοις γίγνεσθαι, τὸ τοὺς στρατιώτας ἐξογκοῦσθαί τε καὶ ὑπερφρονεῖν, συνέβη ποτὲ ἐπ' αὐτοῦ· οὕτως ἐγκρατῶς αὐτῶν ἦρχε.

[24] *LSJ* s.v. φιλοπόλεμος· 'freq. in bad sense'. Dio himself uses φιλοπόλεμος to characterise Pyrrhus (9.40.5 [EV]) and Viriathus (22.73.4 [EV]), neither of whom are positive *exempla* as leaders.

discipline did not lead to an arrogant soldiery.[25] In Dio's account of the
Second Dacian War, Trajan is praised for his brave conduct and for setting
a good example for his troops (68.14.1 [Xiph.]). There is a causal link
expressed here between the character of an emperor and the behaviour of
his army.

The surviving portions of Dio's original work preserved in the
Constantinian *Excerpta* and in the *Epitome* of Xiphilinus indicate that his
account of Trajan's military campaigns originally occupied more than half
of Book 68. After the initial character sketch of Trajan, the narrative is
dominated by the First and Second Dacian Wars (68.8.1–14.5) – campaigns
which are separated only by a brief reference to Trajan's time in Rome –
and then the Parthian War (68.17.1–33.3).[26] Between the Second Dacian
War and the Parthian campaign, there is a short discussion of Trajan's
behaviour at Rome, including his treatment of his friends, especially
L. Licinius Sura, and his building projects (68.15.1–16.3 [Xiph., supplemented by *ELg*, *EV*]).[27] The Rome-based portion probably suffered from
some abridgement at the hands of Xiphilinus, but it is likely that Dio's
military narrative was condensed as well, since the epitomator was usually
less interested in wars and battles.[28] Despite the fact that Dio's original text
of Book 68 devoted significant space to Trajan's campaigns, one cannot
escape the impression that the historian still valued the emperor's conduct
as an administrator above his military achievements. For example, after
Trajan returns to Rome in triumph after the First Dacian War, Dio writes:
'he did not, however, as might have been expected of a man skilled in war,
pay any less attention to the civil administration, nor did he dispense
justice any the less' (οὐ μέντοι, οἷα πολεμικὸς ἀνήρ, τἆλλα ἧττον διῆγεν
ἢ καὶ ἧττον ἐδίκαζεν) (68.10.2 [*EV*]). The adjective πολεμικός (*polemikos*,
'skilled in war, warlike') emphasises Trajan's natural talents as a military
leader.[29] But again, Dio is sparing with his praise – the emperor succeeds

---

[25] Migliorati 2003: 59, 64–6.

[26] The chapters dealing with the wars, 68.8.1–15.1 and 17.1–33.3, derive from both Xiphilinus and the
Byzantine excerpta, as well as other sources (*EV*, *ELg*, *ELr*, John Ant.). Xiphilinus' *Epitome* retains
the basic structure of Dio's narrative, and we are fortunate that the *Excerpta de legationibus gentium
ad Romanos* (*ELg*) ('Excerpts of embassies from foreign peoples to Romans') and *Excerpta de
legationibus Romanorum ad gentes* (*ELr*) ('Excerpts of embassies from Romans to foreign peoples')
preserve accounts of embassies which can supplement the epitome (Bennett 2001: 214).

[27] Trajan was in Rome from mid-107 until late 113, with Sura dying c. 108 (Bennett 2001: 149).

[28] Mallan 2013b: 632.

[29] *LSJ*⁹ s.v. πολεμικός II. Dio's Pompey uses πολεμικός to describe himself in his speech to the People
(36.26.4), and Dio gives Vindex the same quality (63.22.1² [*EV*]).

almost despite his martial abilities, because he does not let them interfere with the other civilian duties expected of an emperor.

Indeed, even in the sections of Book 68 dealing with his military campaigns, Trajan the general and tactician rarely emerges from Dio's prose, except in historiographical clichés.[30] Instead, it is Trajan the diplomat and negotiator who dominates the surviving narrative of the Dacian and Parthian wars. This impression is at least partially shaped by the fact that many key passages, such as the negotiations with the Parthian king Osroes I (68.17.2–3 [*ELg*]), are preserved only in the *Excerpta de legationibus*. But it nevertheless correlates with Dio's own comments on Trajan's abilities, and the emphasis he places on the emperor as administrator and organiser, rather than as a military man. For example, Dio marvels at the construction of the bridge over the River Danube, which was designed by the architect Apollodorus of Damascus. He regards this bridge as the greatest of Trajan's accomplishments (68.13.1–6 [Xiph.]). As Rhiannon Ash argues in Chapter 4 of this volume, the bridge is described in a narrative of 'oblique wonder', as Dio shows his amazement at the emperor's control of the resources and scientific expertise necessary to construct such a monument. The balance tips firmly once again in the favour of Trajan the administrator rather than the general.

The account of how Trajan came to acquire the title of *Optimus*, as described by Xiphilinus, is pertinent to this point. The senate is said to have granted Trajan this honorific after he had annexed Armenia and received homage from several local kings (68.18.3b-23.1 [Xiph.]).[31] Trajan had been described as *Optimus Princeps* on the reverse of coins issued as early as 103.[32] But the *agnomen* was not formally bestowed by the senate and integrated into his official titulature until the summer of AD 114.[33] For the subsequent conquest of Parthian territory in northern Mesopotamia, Trajan was given the title of *Parthicus* by the senate in February AD 116, as recorded by the *Fasti Ostienses*.[34] Xiphilinus relates these events as follows:

> After he had captured Nisibis and Batnae he was given the name of *Parthicus*; but he took much greater pride in the title of *Optimus* than in all the rest, inasmuch as it referred rather to his character than to his arms. (68.23.2 [Xiph.])[35]

---

[30] See, for example, 68.23.1–2 (Xiph.) on Trajan marching on foot with his soldiers.
[31] For these events, see Bennett 2001: 191–5. [32] Bennett 2001: 105–6. [33] Griffin 2000: 123–4.
[34] *CIL* XIV 244 = *ILS* 6126.
[35] καὶ ὠνομάσθη μέν, ἐπειδὴ καὶ τὴν Νίσιβιν εἷλε καὶ τὰς Βάτνας, Παρθικός, πολλῷ δὲ μᾶλλον ἐπὶ τῇ τοῦ ὀπτίμου προσηγορίᾳ ἢ ταῖς ἄλλαις συμπάσαις, ἅτε καὶ τῶν τρόπων αὐτοῦ μᾶλλον ἢ τῶν

The account is rather contradictory: the senate bestows *Optimus* on Trajan after his accomplishments in Armenia, but the emperor himself takes pride in the title precisely because it did not refer to his military achievements. It is hard not to see Dio's own opinion behind Xiphilinus' account here, as it fits with the historian's view that an emperor's personal qualities were more important than being *polemikos*. In fact, it is probable that the senate awarded the title of *Optimus* as a way of recognising Trajan's achievements in both war and peace.

There is a strong note of criticism in Xiphilinus' explanation as to why Trajan decided to embark on the Parthian War:

> Next, he made a campaign against the Armenians and Parthians on the pretext that the Armenian king had obtained his diadem, not at his hands, but from the Parthian king, though his real reason was a desire to win renown. (68.17.1 [Xiph.])[36]

The belief that Trajan was motivated to invade Parthia by ambition rather than by sound strategic reasons may well owe its origins to contemporary criticism of the emperor, as Miriam Griffin has argued.[37] This was certainly the view expressed a little later in the second century by the orator M. Cornelius Fronto in his *Principia Historiae* (a letter to the emperor Marcus Aurelius which was intended as a sample of a projected larger history of the Parthian War of Lucius Verus).[38] Fronto and Dio both agree that Trajan dismissed the Parthian ambassadors too swiftly, which they regarded as a sign that he was determined to make war.[39] Trajan, as so many leaders before him, was driven to emulate Alexander the Great and is said to have boasted that he had advanced even further than Alexander himself (68.29.1 [Xiph.]).[40] Dio was opposed to the expansion of the empire simply to glorify a *princeps*; he levelled similar criticisms of Septimius Severus' eastern campaigns in the contemporary books of the *Roman History* (75[75].2–3 [Xiph.]). Moreover, he intensely disliked Caracalla's own attempts to model himself on Alexander (78[77].7.1–9.1 [Xiph./*EV*]). The impact of Trajan's Parthian War, and the swift

---

ὅπλων οὔσῃ, ἐσεμνύνετο. There are problems with the chronology of Xiphilinus here (Bennett 2001: 195–6; Griffin 2000: 124–5).

[36] μετὰ δὲ ταῦτα ἐστράτευσεν ἐπ' Ἀρμενίους καὶ Πάρθους, πρόφασιν μὲν ὅτι μὴ τὸ διάδημα ὑπ' αὐτοῦ εἰλήφει, ἀλλὰ παρὰ τοῦ Πάρθων βασιλέως, ὁ τῶν Ἀρμενίων βασιλεύς, τῇ δ' ἀληθείᾳ δόξης ἐπιθυμίᾳ.

[37] Griffin 2000: 126. Cf. the more sceptical Migliorati 2003: 174.

[38] Fronto, *Principia Historiae* 17–20 (van den Hout 1988: 212–14).

[39] 68.17.2–18.1 (*ELg*); Fronto, *Principia Historiae* 17 (van den Hout 1988: 212); Davenport and Manley 2014: 188.

[40] For Alexander as an *exemplum* in Dio, see Mallan 2017b. On Dio's disapproval of personal glory as a motivation for warfare, see Bertrand 2016b: 694–5.

abandonment of his conquered territory, would probably still have been remembered in Dio's day, as it lay at the furthermost reaches of communicative memory.

I would therefore suggest that in Dio's portrait of the emperor in the original text of Book 68, Trajan was praised for devoting attention to civilian government, despite his natural inclination to warfare.[41] In characterising Trajan as an emperor who succeeded despite his *philopolemos* and *polemikos* nature, Dio glosses over the fact that Trajan was selected by Nerva, a weak *princeps* at the mercy of the praetorians, precisely because of his reputation as a military man.[42] The structure of Xiphilinus' epitome, supplemented by the *Excerpta*, indicates that there was a development in Trajan's warlike tendencies as Dio's account of his reign progressed. Initially, he is praised for disciplining the soldiers, as a good emperor was supposed to do. But then Trajan is driven to invade Parthia by his desire for renown and intention to outstrip the achievements of Alexander. The *Roman History* successfully juxtaposes Trajan's undoubted ambition against his inability to retain his conquests (68.29.4 [Xiph.]).[43] The way in which this narrative unfolds might well leave the reader contemplating the deficiencies of a *polemikos* emperor.

III   Hadrian

We are fortunate that much of Dio's introductory character sketch of the emperor Hadrian which formed the beginning of Book 69 is preserved in the Constantinian *Excerpta*. This allows us to construct a picture of the historian's assessment of the emperor with a fair degree of certainty.[44] Dio commends Hadrian because 'he did not stir up any war, and he terminated those already in progress' (μήτε τινὰ πόλεμον ταράξαι καὶ τοὺς ὄντας παῦσαι) (69.5.1 [*EV*]). This is a clear reference to Trajan's Parthian campaign, which the historian regarded as fundamentally pointless, as shown by his comments on the loss of all the territory which Trajan had

[41] It is worth noting that similar praise of Trajan's civilian government can be found in Dio Chrysostom, *Orations* 2 and 4 (cf. Mallan 2017b: 142) and in Fronto, *Principia Historiae* 20 (van den Hout 1988: 213–14), with commentary in Davenport and Manley 2014: 189–91.
[42] Davenport and Mallan 2014: 650.
[43] Mallan (2017b: 141) notes that Dio's Trajan lacks a 'decisive battle' comparable to Gaugamela that would enable him to truly rival Alexander.
[44] Millar (1964: 66) notes that the biographical portion is much more detailed than the annalistic narrative.

gained (68.33.1–2 [Xiph.]).[45] Hadrian is further praised for controlling the army with a strong hand (as Trajan also had done):[46]

> He subjected the legions to the strictest discipline, so that, though strong, they were neither insubordinate nor insolent. (69.5.2 [EV])[47]

This statement in the biographical sketch is supported by the account of Hadrian's actions in the annalistic narrative of his reign (69.9.1–6 [Xiph.]). He is said to have inspected the troops and their fortifications, investigating the conduct of the soldiers and the officers, as well as the munitions, weaponry, and defences. There are typical *topoi* of the good general present here, such as the statement that Hadrian marched with his head uncovered regardless of the weather (69.9.4 [Xiph.]).[48] But evidence for Hadrian's genuine interest in the army and its discipline can be found in other sources, such as the inscribed record of his speeches to the *legio III Augusta* and several auxiliary units in Numidia.[49]

In Dio's view, Hadrian's attention to the soldiers, their training, and their conditions had a positive impact on the defence of the empire. He concludes his account of the emperor's military activities as follows:

> In sum, both by his example and by his precepts he so trained and disciplined the whole military force throughout the entire empire that even today the methods then introduced by him are the soldiers' law of campaigning. This best explains why he lived for the most part at peace with foreign nations; for as they saw his state of preparation and were themselves not only free from aggression but received money besides, they made no uprising. (69.9.4–5 [Xiph.])[50]

The impact of Hadrian's reputation within the context of Dio's narrative is shown by the actions of the Jews. He writes that the Jews did not dare to stage a revolt when the emperor was in Egypt and Syria, and only began their insurrection after he had departed for

---

[45] On Dio's preference for retaining territory rather than expanding the empire, see Bertrand 2016b: 690.

[46] Migliorati 2003: 270.

[47] καὶ τά τε στρατιωτικὰ ἀκριβέστατα ἤσκησεν, ὥστ' ἰσχύοντα μήτ' ἀπειθεῖν μήτε ὑβρίζειν.

[48] For example, Fronto, *Principia Historiae* 14 (van den Hout 1988: 210–11) makes the same statement about Lucius Verus.

[49] Birley 1997: 117–20 (general accounts of Hadrian's military interests), 210–13 (speeches to the troops); Migliorati 2003: 281–5.

[50] συνελόντι τε εἰπεῖν, οὕτω καὶ τῷ ἔργῳ καὶ τοῖς παραγγέλμασι πᾶν τὸ στρατιωτικὸν δι' ὅλης τῆς ἀρχῆς ἤσκησε καὶ κατεκόσμησεν ὥστε καὶ νῦν τὰ τότε ὑπ' αὐτοῦ ταχθέντα νόμον σφίσι τῆς στρατείας εἶναι. καὶ διὰ τοῦτο καὶ μάλιστα ἐν εἰρήνῃ τὸ πλεῖστον πρὸς τοὺς ἀλλοφύλους διεγένετο· τήν τε γὰρ παρασκευὴν αὐτοῦ ὁρῶντες, καὶ μήτε τι ἀδικούμενοι καὶ προσέτι καὶ χρήματα λαμβάνοντες, οὐδὲν ἐνεόχμωσαν.

Greece (69.12.1–2 [*EV*]).[51] We know that Hadrian did travel to the front in Judaea during the Bar Kokhba War, but the exact length of his stay is uncertain, and he preferred to wage the campaign through his legates.[52] The narrative of these events as epitomised by Xiphilinus gives only a passing indication that Hadrian was present during the campaign, and offers no description of his actions, instead referring to a letter he sent to the senate (69.12.1–14.3 [Xiph.]).[53] The overriding impression of Hadrian is that he is the very model of the military emperor envisioned by Maecenas in his speech in Book 52. He is a leader who does not start wars but sets a good example for the soldiers and keeps the troops prepared and disciplined, ready to defend the empire when necessary.[54]

The portraits of Trajan and Hadrian in Books 68 and 69 were, I would argue, designed to be read side by side to encourage Dio's contemporary readers to think about different models of imperial leadership. Trajan was clearly an excellent emperor, adept in civilian administration and a talented general, but his martial nature led him to seek glory and renown in an unnecessary war in Parthia. In contrast, Hadrian successfully maintained a state of military readiness without resorting to gratuitous expansionistic campaigns. The Jewish revolt is portrayed by Dio as a successful test of the discipline Hadrian has fostered in his troops. It is true that Hadrian himself is a somewhat ambiguous figure in the *Roman History*; he certainly suffers from character flaws which are duly highlighted (69.5.1 [Xiph.]) and his execution of senators does him no credit (69.2.5 [Xiph.], 69.23.2 [*EV*]).[55] Yet the overall impression is that Hadrian's reign was a good one, despite the complaints of the people (69.23.2–3 [*EV*]).[56] Dio rates the emperor highly for his ability to balance his administrative duties with the effective defence of the empire. His readers could not fail to notice that emperors like Septimius Severus, who wished to expand the empire in the East, and Caracalla, devoted to emulating Alexander the Great, did not live up to Hadrian's example.

---

[51] Millar (1964: 68) suggests that this passage shows Dio had good information about Hadrian's travels but did not always deploy it in a detailed fashion in the *Roman History*.

[52] Birley 1997: 272–3.   [53] Millar 1964: 69.

[54] It cannot escape one's notice that the expectations of a good emperor are met in Dio's own description of himself as a provincial governor and stern military disciplinarian (80(80).4.2 [Xiph.]). For further exploration of this idea, see Chapter 12 by Christopher Mallan.

[55] Madsen 2016: 152.   [56] Millar 1964: 66, 71; Schulz 2019a: 255–6.

IV   Marcus Aurelius

Dio's original account of Antoninus Pius and the first years of Marcus Aurelius' reign up to the death of Lucius Verus in AD 169 (Books 70–1) has been almost entirely lost. Some indication of the many qualities which recommended Pius for the purple can be found in Hadrian's adoption speech (69.20.2–5 [Xiph.]). Pius is praised for his nobility, mildness, compassion, prudence, and his ability to discharge the functions of the imperial office according to the laws. There is, however, no mention of any military ability or training as a general.[57] We can only speculate as to how this characterisation of Pius would have been developed by Dio in Book 70. Given that the wars during his reign were largely campaigns of consolidation or defence, he may have received a portrayal which focussed on his efforts to maintain the integrity of the empire and its relationship with foreign kings.[58] For example, a fragment of the *Excerpta de legationibus gentium ad Romanos* offers a brief account of the successful visit of Pharasmanes III, king of Iberia, to Rome in Pius' reign (*ELg* 56). It is possible to arrive at a more detailed treatment of Pius' successor, Marcus Aurelius, mainly thanks to Xiphilinus' epitome of Book 72(71) and the Constantinian *Excerpta*. That said, it is necessary to disregard Xiphilinus' simplistic characterisation of Marcus Aurelius as the philosopher and his co-emperor Lucius Verus as the warrior (71[71].1².1–3 [Xiph.]). This is clearly not the writing of Dio himself, whose assessment of Marcus as a campaigner is much more nuanced.[59]

In some ways, Dio's account of Marcus' reign reads like a tragedy. He is a good emperor blessed with an abundance of virtues, but he is also a man prone to ill health and destined to spend much of his reign on campaign.[60] Marcus nevertheless does his duty, defending and maintaining the frontiers, which echoes the ideals expressed in the speech of Maecenas.[61] He is supported in these campaigns by a number of loyal senatorial and equestrian commanders.[62] Rather than being a man who is naturally gifted in the arts of war, Marcus possesses the necessary qualities to lead and persevere in

---

[57] Davenport and Mallan 2014: 646–7.

[58] On the campaigns conducted under his auspices, see Speidel 2017; Michels 2018: 223–58, 285–92. For Pius and foreign kings, see Michels 2018: 258–81.

[59] Mallan (2013b: 635–40) discusses the problems of the reconstructed Book 71.

[60] For this aspect of Dio's narrative, see 72(71).3.1² (Xiph.) (warfare occupies most of his life); 72(71).6.3–4 (Xiph.) (ill health); 72(71).24.1 (Xiph.) (Marcus refers to his own misfortune in the context of the revolt of Avidius Cassius); 72(71).24.4 (Xiph.) (Marcus cites his own ill health).

[61] Possienke (2011: 54–61) shows how Dio's portrait of Marcus coheres with the principles of the speech of Maecenas.

[62] 72(71).3.2 (Xiph.), 72(71).3.5 (Xiph.); see further Kemezis 2012 on their depiction in Dio.

difficult times while triumphing over his bodily infirmities (72[71].36.2–3 [Xiph.]). Like his adoptive grandfather Hadrian, Marcus is portrayed as a firm disciplinarian of the soldiers, even declining to distribute a donative to them after a battle early in the Marcomannic Wars (72[71].3.4 [Xiph.]).[63] The *Epitome* of Xiphilinus continues:

> So temperately and so firmly did he rule them [sc. the soldiers], that even when involved in so many and so great wars, he did naught that was unseemly either by way of flattery or as the result of fear (72[71].3.4 [Xiph.]).[64]

Marcus' wars, both foreign and domestic, are defensive campaigns rather than wars of expansion, which places him in the same category as Hadrian. Indeed, Marcus is the opposite of the glory-seeking emperor that Trajan became in his later years. When Marcus is hailed *imperator* by his troops after the 'rain miracle', Dio says he only accepted this honorific title before it had been officially approved by the senate because it had been bestowed by the gods (72[71].10.5 [Xiph.]).[65]

Marcus' address to the troops after he receives news of the revolt of Avidius Cassius demonstrates his suitability for the purple. This is one of the speeches which Xiphilinus quotes from the original text of the *Roman History*; it therefore provides us with insights into Dio's own characterisation of Marcus.[66] After bemoaning the state of the empire, which is plagued by both foreign conflicts and civil wars, Marcus characterises Cassius' revolt as a failure of friendship:

> And are not both these evils surpassed in dreadfulness and horror by the discovery that there is no such thing as loyalty among men? For a plot has been formed against me by my dearest friend and I have been forced into a conflict against my will, though I have done nothing wrong or amiss. What virtue (ἀρετή), what friendship (φιλία) shall henceforth be deemed secure after this experience of mine? (72[71].24.2 [Xiph.])[67]

---

[63] See Possienke (2011: 55–6) on Dio's positive portrayal of Marcus as a leader of the soldiers, in comparison with many of his successors.

[64] οὕτω καὶ σωφρόνως καὶ ἐγκρατῶς αὐτῶν ἦρχεν, ὥστε καίπερ ἐν τοσούτοις καὶ τηλικούτοις πολέμοις ὢν μηδὲν ἔξω τοῦ προσήκοντος μήτ' ἐκ κολακείας μήτ' ἐκ φόβου ποιῆσαι. It should be noted that Dio also uses ἐγκρατῶς to describe his own disciplining of the troops in Pannonia (80[80].4.2 [Xiph.]). This is a further sign of his approval of Marcus, and the connection between the historian's own self-presentation and the ideal of a good emperor.

[65] This passage comes from Xiphilinus, but he states at the beginning of the chapter that he is quoting directly from Dio (72[71].10.1 [Xiph.]). For a detailed examination of Dio's 'rain miracle' narrative, see Rhiannon Ash's contribution (Chapter 4) in this volume.

[66] Mallan 2013b: 619.

[67] πῶς οὐκ ἀμφότερα καὶ δεινότητι καὶ ἀτοπίᾳ νικᾷ τὸ μηδὲν πιστὸν ἐν ἀνθρώποις εἶναι, ἀλλ' ἐπιβεβουλεῦσθαί τέ με ὑπὸ τοῦ φιλτάτου καὶ ἐς ἀγῶνα ἀκούσιον καθίστασθαι μήτε τι

By espousing these sentiments, Marcus transforms the civil war from a military conflict into a contest of ἀρετή (*arete*, 'personal excellence, virtue'). He characterises Cassius as a talented general (στρατηγικός), but this does not serve as proof of his personal integrity or his fitness to wear the purple (72[71].25.2 [Xiph.]). For Cassius has betrayed his emperor and his friend, revealing himself to be disloyal and lacking virtue; nevertheless, Marcus would prefer to talk to him one on one and forgive the usurper rather than risk open war (72[71].26.1–4 [Xiph.]). This is one of a series of speeches dealing with the theme of *clementia* in the imperial books of the *Roman History*, alongside Livia's dialogue with Augustus regarding the punishment of Cinna Magnus (55.14.1–22.1) and Cassius Clemens' plea to Septimius Severus (75[74].9.1–4 [Xiph.]).[68] In all three cases, the central issue of the speech is the attitude of the emperor towards fellow Romans who sought to force him from power. The message of this particular speech, and indeed Dio's entire narrative of Marcus' reign, is that a virtuous man, who is led by his character to conduct himself appropriately, is a better ruler than one with raw military talent (like Avidius Cassius). Marcus succeeds – or survives – against the odds because of his *arete* (72[71].34.4 [Xiph.]). If any *princeps* has a claim to being Dio's ideal – or idealised – emperor, it is surely Marcus.[69]

V Commodus

As was the case with Trajan and Hadrian, it is probable that Dio's portraits of Marcus Aurelius and Commodus were designed to form a contrasting pair.[70] Marcus is the virtuous emperor who faces invasions and civil wars with equanimity, while Commodus is the heir born to the purple who retreats from the frontier to spend his life in Rome engaging in simulacra of real combat in the arena.[71] Such a dichotomy is at least partially misleading, as it passes over the fact that the empire was not as severely threatened by invasion during the 180s as in

ἠδικηκότα μήτε τι πεπλημμεληκότα; τίς μὲν γὰρ ἀρετὴ ἀσφαλής, τίς δὲ φιλία ἔτι νομισθήσεται ἐμοῦ ταῦτα πεπονθότος;

[68] For clemency in Dio, see Giua 1981; Kuhn-Chen 2002: 160–3. On the speech of Livia, see Manuwald 1979: 120–7 and Adler 2011, and for connections between this theme and the actions of emperors towards defeated enemies, see Davenport 2014: 104–6. I am grateful to Christopher Mallan for his observations on this point.
[69] Martini 2010. On the idealisation of Marcus Aurelius, see further Kemezis 2014: 47, 148; Scott 2015: 160–1; Schulz 2019b: 320–2.
[70] For points of contrast between the portrayal of Marcus and Commodus, see Possienke 2011: 54–5.
[71] Dio discusses Commodus' retreat in 73(72).1.1–2 (Xiph.), 73(72).2.2 (*ELg*).

Marcus' reign.[72] Indeed, Commodus' senatorial legates competently carried out wars on his behalf when the need arose.[73] In Dio's narrative, however, Commodus is presented as jealous and paranoid of generals whose careers had flourished under his father. Illustrious senators such as P. Salvius Julianus and the Quintilii brothers, Sex. Quintilius Condianus and Sex. Quintilius Valerius Maximus, possessed military talent and the loyalty of the soldiers, which made them *capaces imperii* and a threat to Commodus (73[72].5.1–2 [*EV*], 3–4 [Xiph.]). Dio writes that Julianus, despite the large army at his disposal, refuses to stage a revolt against Commodus, both because of his loyalty to Marcus and because of his ἐπιείκεια – best translated here as 'sense of fairness' or 'virtuousness' (73[72].5.2 [*EV*]). As an honourable general who declines to rebel against a dissolute emperor, Julianus emerges as the opposite of Avidius Cassius, the commander who betrayed the friendship of a good *princeps*.

At the beginning of Book 73(72), Dio states that Commodus suffered from cowardice (δειλία), one of the qualities that kept him in the thrall of his companions (73[72].1.1 [*EV*]).[74] In AD 190, during a famine caused by a problem with the grain supply, Commodus faces the wrath of a hungry mob, which marches to his suburban villa. The emperor, 'being entirely and completely cowardly' (ἄλλως τε καὶ δειλότατος ὤν), blames his *a pugione* Cleander and then executes Cleander and his son to satisfy the people's demands (73[72].13.6 [Xiph.]). This characterisation of Commodus as a coward is one of the many ways in which Dio undermines the emperor's displays of martial ability in the arena.[75] The historian pursues a similar strategy in his portrayal of Caracalla, whose campaigns in Germany only serve to expose his extreme cowardice (78[77].13.3 [*EV*]).[76] The contrast between Marcus Aurelius and his son Commodus as military leaders comes down to a matter of *arete*. Marcus has no natural inclination for warfare, but he succeeds because of his innate excellence, which Commodus patently lacks.

---

[72] Kemezis 2014: 50. Hekster (2002: 47–9) emphasises the effectiveness of Commodus' peace with the Quadi and Marcomanni, which actually continued the policies of his father.

[73] For example, the governor Ulpius Marcellus in Britain (Birley 2005: 162–70).

[74] Claudius suffered from the same affliction, which was likewise exploited by his household (60.2.6). For emperors and their companions in Cassius Dio, see Chapter 11 by Barbara Saylor Rodgers.

[75] Dio's personal account of a senatorial audience laughing at Commodus brandishing an ostrich head in the arena captures the ridiculousness of the emperor's martial performances (73[72].21.1–2 [Xiph.]).

[76] For similarities in Commodus' and Caracalla's self-presentation as a conqueror, see Kemezis 2014: 75–6.

VI Pertinax

We conclude with the emperor Pertinax, who was not a member of the Antonine dynasty by birth or adoption, but whose career flourished under their rule. He was, like Trajan and Hadrian, a successful military officer prior to becoming emperor. The son of a freedman, he rose through the officer ranks as both an equestrian and senatorial commander under Marcus Aurelius, fighting in the Marcomannic Wars.[77] As governor of Britain under Commodus, Pertinax earned a reputation as a stern disciplinarian, suppressing a mutiny of the troops (73[72].9.2² [Xiph.]; 74[73].4.1 [Xiph.]).[78] Such a record made him a promising candidate for the purple, in accordance with the ideals of the speech of Maecenas and the qualities of his Antonine predecessors. Indeed, Dio's final judgement on Pertinax, placed after the account of his funeral in AD 193, praises him for being the right sort of leader:

> Although a warlike nature usually ends up by being harsh and a peaceful one cowardly, Pertinax excelled equally in both respects, being formidable in war and shrewd in peace. He showed boldness, of which bravery is an ingredient, toward foreigners and rebels, but clemency, into which justice enters, toward his countrymen and the orderly element. (75[74].5.6 [EV])[79]

This is the description of a perfectly balanced *princeps*, a commander who does not let his martial talents overpower his other qualities or lead him astray into expansionistic wars. One cannot help but recall Dio's portrait of the emperor Trajan, whom the historian praises for similar attention to matters of war and peace, although he is eventually overtaken by his yearning for glory. In his necrology of Pertinax, Dio goes on to ascribe a host of virtues to the emperor, describing him as σεμνός ('stately, majestic'), πρᾶος ('gentle, mild'), φρόνιμος ('prudent'), δίκαιος ('just'), οἰκονομικός ('frugal'), and μεγαλόνους ('great-minded') (75[74].5.7 [EV]). This catalogue of imperial virtues reads like a panegyric. One cannot help but recall the extravagant tributes in Tiberius' laudatory funeral oration for Augustus (56.35.1–41.9), which Christina Kuhn has discussed in Chapter 5.

---

[77] For Pertinax's career, see Lippold 1983, and for his portrayal in Dio, Kemezis 2012: 397–402.
[78] See further Birley 2005: 172–4.
[79] Ὅτι ὁ Περτίναξ, τὸ μὲν εὐπόλεμον ἄγροικον τὸ δὲ εἰρηναῖον δειλὸν ὡς τὸ πολὺ ἐκβαῖνον, ἀμφότερα κράτιστος ὁμοίως ἐγένετο, φοβερὸς μὲν πολεμῆσαι σοφὸς δὲ εἰρηνεῦσαι ὤν· καὶ τὸ μὲν θρασύ, οὗ τὸ ἀνδρεῖον μετέχει, πρός τε τὸ ἀλλόφυλον καὶ πρὸς τὸ στασιάζον, τὸ δὲ ἐπιεικές, οὗ τὸ δίκαιον μεταλαμβάνει, πρός τε τὸ οἰκεῖον καὶ πρὸς τὸ σῶφρον ἐνεδείκνυτο.

Yet there are complications with both catalogues of praise. Tiberius' generous encomium of Augustus sits uneasily with many problematic elements of the *princeps'* reign in the *Roman History*.[80] The endorsement of Augustus' policy of protecting the frontiers (mentioned at the beginning of this chapter) is at odds with the fact that his reign did see wars of expansion.[81] In her chapter, Christina Kuhn argued that Tiberius' arguments in the oration reflect the official viewpoint of the imperial *domus* at the end of Augustus' reign. The juxtaposition of these arguments with the preceding narrative would, I propose, prompt the reader to consider the appropriateness and accuracy of the official imperial view.[82] The same point can be made about Dio's own extravagant, virtue-laden praise of Pertinax. This *princeps*, a successful general, blessed with military talent, not to mention a host of other positive personal qualities, ruled for only three months before being murdered by the soldiers. His swift demise came about because the praetorian guard resented the diminution of the privileges they had enjoyed under Commodus (74[73].1.3 [Xiph.]). Encouraged by their prefect Q. Aemilius Laetus, they decide to remove Pertinax, march to the palace and – after some initial reluctance – cut the emperor down (74[73].9.1–10.2 [Xiph./*EV/ES*]).

How, then, does Dio explain Pertinax's short reign if he appeared to be such a promising *princeps* and a man whom the historian greatly admired? Dio offers the following coda to the account of the emperor's murder:

> Thus did Pertinax, who undertook to restore everything in a moment, come to his end. He failed to comprehend, though a man of wide practical experience, that one cannot with safety reform everything at once, and that the restoration of a state, in particular, requires both time and wisdom. (74[73].10.3 [Xiph.])[83]

This comment is revealing both for what Dio does and does not say. Pertinax had tried to restrain the licence of the soldiers as a good emperor should, but unlike Trajan, Hadrian, and Marcus, his attempts failed. In this case, the troops did not respond to having discipline imposed on them, nor did they follow the example set by their emperor. Dio's positive

[80] Millar 1964: 101–2. See the full discussion of Manuwald 1979: 133–40.
[81] Reinhold and Swan 1990: 161–4; Swan 2004: 338.
[82] For discussion of the 'official' and 'hidden' transcripts in the *Roman History*, see Chapter 1 by Adam Kemezis. Dio's ability to undermine the official messaging of the imperial regime is a central concern of both Kemezis 2014 and Schulz 2019a.
[83] οὕτω μὲν ὁ Περτίναξ ἐπιχειρήσας ἐν ὀλίγῳ πάντα ἀνακαλέσασθαι ἐτελεύτησεν, οὐδὲ ἔγνω καίπερ ἐμπειρότατος πραγμάτων ὤν, ὅτι ἀδύνατόν ἐστιν ἀθρόα τινὰ ἀσφαλῶς ἐπανορθοῦσθαι, ἀλλ' εἴπερ τι ἄλλο, καὶ πολιτικὴ κατάστασις καὶ χρόνου καὶ σοφίας χρῄζει.

estimation of Pertinax on both a personal and political level may well have made him reluctant to draw a direct parallel between the character of the emperor and the behaviour of soldiers on this occasion. But the passage still has a critical tone. The reforms to which Dio refers must be Pertinax's treatment of the soldiers in contrast to the laxity of Commodus, rather than his conduct in civilian administration, which is praised elsewhere (74[73].5.1–3 [Xiph.]). I would suggest, therefore, that Dio is implying – without saying so explicitly, given his admiration for the emperor – that Pertinax should have behaved more diplomatically towards Laetus and the praetorian guard in order to guarantee their long-term loyalty and ensure the longevity of his regime. Although he possessed numerous outstanding qualities, on this measure of imperial success, Pertinax fell short of the mark.

VII Conclusion

Military leadership formed an integral part of the public image of a Roman emperor, as expressed in statues, coinage, inscriptions, panegyrics, and other written and visual media. Even Antoninus Pius, who never left Italy during his reign of more than twenty years, was portrayed as a triumphant general.[84] The military image of the emperor encompassed both the material talent necessary to expand the *imperium Romanum* through conquest as well as the ability to protect Rome's territory and maintain the *pax* secured through warfare.[85] Two key speeches at the beginning of Dio's imperial narrative, the speech of Maecenas and Tiberius' funeral oration for Augustus, suggest that the second of these aspects – protection and security – was more important than the first. This viewpoint, I would argue, is echoed in the historical narrative of the *Roman History* itself, especially the books covering the second century AD, a period within the 'communicative memory' of Dio and his peers. The disastrous Parthian campaigns of Trajan, whose hard-won gains had to be swiftly abandoned, lay at the very edge of this memory. The shock of the Marcomannic Wars and the desperate fight to protect Italy and the northern provinces was a more recent and more vivid experience, and the elderly survivors of this conflict still populated the senate in Dio's age. It was thus probably no coincidence that Dio's second-century narrative

---

[84] See the discussion of Pius' public image by Boschung 2017, and the comments of Michels 2018: 293–5 on Pius as a military leader in the tradition of previous emperors.

[85] On the connection between *pax* and military conquest, see Cornwell 2017.

positively highlighted the conduct of emperors such as Hadrian and Marcus Aurelius, who maintained a vigilant frontier policy in the face of foreign threats and kept the troops disciplined and ready for defence at all times. On the other hand, it was evidently Dio's view that emperors with warlike inclinations were not necessarily the best overall leaders. They had to be able to balance these innate martial desires with attention to civilian government and the stability of the empire at large. The ideal emperor, like the ideal senator, was able to excel *domi militiaeque* ('at home and on campaign').[86] Trajan almost managed to achieve this but was ultimately undone by his relentless pursuit of glory and desire to emulate Alexander. Cowardice and neglect, as we would expect, were always the mark of a poor ruler: one of the many reasons for Commodus' failure was his preference for playing the general rather than actually being an effective leader.

Pertinax's fate offered an intriguing paradox for Dio and his readers. Pertinax was an excellent general who had won his spurs in the wars of Marcus Aurelius, earning a reputation as one of the great heroes of that age. His military abilities were complemented by a host of other virtues, which made him, on paper, an ideal emperor. Pertinax, however, was brought down by his inability to impose discipline on the soldiers, a downfall that shows that even the most distinguished military leaders could make mistakes if their innate skills did not translate into effective actions. Pertinax's fate has parallels in the *Roman History*: the equally short-lived emperor Galba also possessed military experience (63[63].23.1 [Xiph.]) but was murdered by the soldiers who were unhappy with his rule (64[63].5.1–5 [Xiph.]). Pertinax's failure can be ascribed to the fact that he moved too quickly and inappropriately in his attempt to curtail the soldiers. A repository of virtues did not mean that an emperor, regardless of the age in which he lived, was above making mistakes. In Dio's view, virtues served as a promising foundation for a reign – but they were not usually enough in and of themselves. As a historian, he often drew a distinction between an emperor's innate qualities and his conduct in office.[87] It was a rare emperor who lived up entirely to the promise of his character.

---

[86] See Dio's comments in F 18.2 (*ES*) on the difficulty of actually achieving this excellence in both fields. The ability to succeed *domi militiaeque* is a central theme of imperial praise discourse, as seen in Pliny's *Panegyricus* to Trajan; one notes, however, that Dio's Trajan is flawed in the way that a subject of a panegyric cannot be. The ideal of service *domi militiaeque* is discussed further by Christopher Mallan in Chapter 12.

[87] This is the central argument of Davenport 2014, which, while dealing with the reign of Vitellius, can be applied to the *Roman History* more generally. Dio's Vitellius had many vices, but he did sometimes act appropriately in a manner befitting the imperial office. Of course, as noted in the Introduction to this volume, there are some emperors, such as Nero, Commodus, and Caracalla,

This was a promise fulfilled only by the great Marcus Aurelius, whose *arete* gave him the strength to prevail during a reign plagued by revolts and invasions. He enforced army discipline, accepted imperatorial honours only when appropriate, and survived the insurrection of a naturally talented general like Avidius Cassius, to protect and preserve the borders of the Roman empire and its people. This was the model of Roman emperorship that Dio wished to communicate to his contemporary audience and to all his future readers. The achievements of Marcus would live long in the memory of the Romans, his successes being commemorated in a range of monuments: a gilt-bronze equestrian statue, a triumphal arch, a forty-metre-high column, and the *Roman History* of Cassius Dio.

who have no redeeming features, and their vice-laden character bears fruit in their conduct as emperor.

Political Groups and Political Culture

CHAPTER 9

'The People' and Cassius Dio

Monica Hellström

I Introduction

The subject of this chapter is to examine how, in a handful of key scenes, Cassius Dio uses depictions of the Roman people to serve his broader historiographical agenda. I argue that Dio uses his portrayal of 'the people' to highlight the significance of events and guide the reader's interpretation of them. Furthermore, I shall show how Dio uses the people to characterise individuals throughout the *Roman History*, as an element of what Marianne Coudry has described as 'stylised portraits'.[1] Many features of Dio's treatment of the Roman community appear to be unique to his narrative, and like embedded speeches, 'people scenes' should count as among those most marked by Dio's own pen.

Similar to the 'hidden transcript' treated by Adam Kemezis in Chapter 1 of this volume, Dio employs the people to paint the character of rulers and regimes. Against the common scholarly opinion that Dio regarded the people with a degree of hostility, or at best, ambivalence, I contend that Dio treats the people with sympathy, making it symbolise the potential, and nobility, vested in the Roman state. Furthermore, I aim to show how Dio's portrayal of the people reveals something about his views of politics and society, if not necessarily about the people itself. After discussing the range of terms Dio uses to denote 'the people' (II), I shall examine the types of scenes in which the people appear (III), then focus on some of their recurring roles: as victims (IV) and as commentators on political events (V, VI, VII).

I wish to express my gratitude to Caillan Davenport and Christopher Mallan for including my paper in this volume, as well as for their astute and helpful comments. Furthermore, I would like to thank the Leverhulme Trust for their generous support.
[1] Coudry 2016b: 289–91, 295, 297–9.

II Who Are 'the People'?

Dio uses a range of terms to denote the group that may be translated into English as 'the people' without any straightforward overlap with formal categories. For example, Dio does not consistently use one term to denote the *populus Romanus* as it was legally defined. Moreover, many words have overlapping, even opposing, meanings.[2] In Dio, the word δῆμος (*demos*) most often signifies the totality of Roman citizens – including elites[3] – but it can also refer to the popular assembly, the educated elite or even the 'state' (as with Agrippa at 52.13.1). He uses πλῆθος (*plethos*) to refer to the *comitium plebis*,[4] the *plebs* or the (senatorial) *populares*, but for the most part it simply denotes a plurality, whether of humans, Romans or senators.[5] Similarly ambiguous in Dio are the terms ὅμιλος (*homilos*), πολῖται (*politai*), ἄνθρωποι (*anthropoi*) or οἱ πολλοί (*hoi polloi*).[6] Dio's main concern is with the political elite, and these terms often designate some segment of it rather than the Roman masses; 'those in Rome' and 'the Romans' usually signify 'senators in Rome' (as opposed to elsewhere).[7]

Therefore, the exact meaning has to be determined in each case through careful scrutiny of the paragraph as a whole.[8] To add to the difficulty, Dio tends to select his vocabulary based on style, and sometimes allusion (ὄχλος [*ochlos*], ὅμιλος, and ἄνθρωποι can have a military streak), opting for terms with literary pedigree while consciously avoiding terms in current usage (with which he was well familiar).[9] That a contemporary reader would have confused them with actual phenomena (or was meant to do so) is unlikely. At times Dio is deliberately vague, mixing or separating social categories

---

[2] See Freyburger-Galland (1997: 47, 84–9) on the terms δῆμος, πλῆθος and ὅμιλος, which all can have general and specific, identical and opposed meanings. δῆμος most often implies 'all citizens', including the political elite.

[3] For example, at 62(63).4.2 (Xiph.), where (prior to Tiridates' entry into Rome) the *demos* is arranged according to rank.

[4] Only in Maecenas' speech and its immediate aftermath, e.g. 53.21.6–7; once also in 55.34.2.

[5] See 48.8.1: 'senators and other landowners'; 56.24–7: the senate's love for Germanicus on account of his defence of individuals before Augustus, with reference to a quaestor.

[6] Ancus Marcius aggression against οἱ πολλοί (F 8.1 [ES]) is against foreign, not internal threats. Ἄνθρωποι are most often soldiers (e.g. 64.8.3 [Xiph.]), but the term can also denote the totality of men (62[63].20.5 [Xiph.], οἱ ἄνθρωποι, καὶ αὐτῶν βολευτῶν).

[7] E.g. 'All those in Rome' (οἱ ἐν Ῥώμη ὄντες) were unwilling to change garb but forced to by the δῆμος (48.16.1); the jealous Ῥωμαῖοι cannot recall Scipio due to his popularity with the πλῆθος (F 57.62 [*EV*]). In Augustus' speech to the *equites*, these are 'the Romans' in contrast to the 'bulk' (ὄγκος) of the city: no one of lower rank should be automatically assumed to qualify as 'Roman' in Dio's work.

[8] To distinguish between the collective of Romans and that of sub-elite Romans is not always possible, and I have decided to allow for some slippage, so long as their function in the narrative is the same.

[9] Freyburger-Galland 1997: 88 (ὄχλος as martial), 89, 102. Christopher Mallan in Chapter 6 of this volume notes the lack of concern in Dio's work with legal bases for Tiberius' authority.

(such as soldiers and citizens) anachronistically as it suits his purposes.[10] Another complication is his tendency to universalise: where parallel narratives based on the same sources concern elites only, Dio often lines up all classes as participants, creating a community scene. An episode limited to a particular social context can be followed by a clause that involves the community (or humankind, in general), giving it a wider significance.

As de Blois has argued, these imprecisions and anomalies suggest that Dio's interest is not in the 'real' people of Rome, its institutions, and the fate of the *demos/populus*.[11] This may be taken further: the people is not itself the object of Dio's gaze but serves to accentuate the actions and characters of those who are – namely, emperors and senators. Not infrequently, Dio endows the people with a nobility that tends to be lost in translations; for instance, δῆμος is sometimes rendered as 'rabble' when a pejorative term is not warranted by the text, and the third-person plural is often resolved as 'the masses' when, on closer inspection, Dio refers to specific persons or subsets of society.[12] Of the terms that Dio uses to denote the people, δῆμος is almost exclusively used in a positive sense, but even his most clearly pejorative collective term – ὄχλος – cannot be straightforwardly equated with the 'mob'.[13] In fact, there are many more 'mobs' in scholarship on Dio than are present in his text.

The notion that Dio was hostile to the Roman people is in large part owed to Fergus Millar; however, the passages he cites as examples refer to senators,[14] or are *sententiae* on human behaviour,[15] in one case specifically on the college of consular tribunes (which is hardly identifiable with 'the masses'). Dio's work is replete with *sententiae*, and many that concern human nature, but these do not clearly concern the 'people'. They are

---

[10] de Blois (1997: 2668, 2673) notes the retrojection of a distinct soldiery to the kingdom.

[11] As noted by de Blois 1997: 2656–8, 2675.

[12] For instance, at 45.11.3, Cary resolved a third-person plural verb as 'citizens', ἄνθρωποι as 'the masses', but the next paragraph (the subjects carry over) reveals the former as 'Antony and Octavian', the latter as 'soldiers': the generals woo foreign troops at Brundisium with money and promises, veterans at Capua with memories of Caesar. At 44.35.1 those happy to be rid of Caesar are senators and soldiers (as per 44.34); the δῆμος is only introduced at 45.2 and is alone in protesting.

[13] During Marius' proscriptions it encompasses the elite, as part of the society as a body. It is here thrown in confusion by the violence to it, which makes for its characterisation as ὄχλος, but it is certainly not some ignoble rabble; on the contrary, it has Dio's sympathy.

[14] 53.24.1 (the fickleness of the πολλοί), shown in 53.23.6–7 to explicitly refer to senators; 58.12.4 (Sejanus' fall), describing in mounting order the righteous anger of the people, the suspect anger of the soldiers (notoriously mercenary) and the faithlessness of self-serving senators.

[15] F 5.12 (Bekker, *Anecd.*): 'whatever is human shall not submit to be ruled by that which is like it and familiar to it, partly through jealousy, partly through contempt of it'; F 24.1 (*ES*): 'human nature is for some reason accustomed in trouble to scorn what is familiar, even though it be divine, and to admire the untried'.

usually elicited by elite behaviour, and their themes – envy of peers, obstructionism, greed, quarrelsomeness – tend to be elite vices.[16] These themes appear most frequently in Dio's narrative of the period of the *dynasteiai* but disappear with the Principate.[17] In other words, Dio's pejorative judgements on human behaviour belong in the context of jostling elites.[18] This is no less clear in the imperial books, in which Dio's focus is on the relations between senators and emperors. Senators should in theory have an active role in government but repeatedly fail to live up to Dio's ideal: while 'good' emperors are few in his work, one scarcely finds a single positive action of the senate, whose members, as Rhiannon Ash notes in Chapter 4, take the lead in their self-destructive behaviour.[19]

III   'People Scenes'

(a)   Set Pieces

Although Dio's terminology for the 'people' is vague, his literary employment of it follows recognisable patterns. He uses it to construct set pieces, 'people scenes', which are regularly associated with civil wars, proscriptions (and other political crises), state ceremonies and spectacles. Dio's focus in these scenes is on individuals in power, and his representation of the people serves primarily as an illustration of their aims and character. Only rarely does the people play an active role in shaping history. A significant exception is the earliest scene that portrays collective action, the rush of the Sabine women (F 5.5–7 [*ES*]): though not featuring the Roman citizenry *per se*, it sparks its formation, resulting symbolically in the creation of the *comitium*. Dio applies the same rhetorical tools as for civil wars (see below), emphasising the sameness of the warring parties and their mixed blood.[20] In another key scene he describes, with a distinction retrojected from the empire, 'the multitude and the soldiers' (later addressed together as the

---

[16] E.g. the popular tribunes (F 17.14–15 [*ES*]), Cicero personally (38.11.1). Reinhold (1988: 217) observes that Dio's *sententiae* almost exclusively concern elites. Kemezis (2014: 102, 110–16) places these themes squarely within the elite; see also Kuhn-Chen (2002: 143–6, 165–8, 170, 179), with examples concerning senators, soldiers and emperors.

[17] Kuhn-Chen 2002: 170.

[18] Dio's antidote, *moderatio*/ἐγκράτεια or σωφροσύνη, makes no sense for those without power and resources, such as the Roman people.

[19] Cf. Chapter 11 in this volume, in which Barbara Saylor Rodgers discusses the small number of elite men who pass muster in Dio's work.

[20] Livy 1.13.1–3 mentions no *similitudo*. Appian (*Kings* 4c [*EL*]) describes the event as a petition handed to the parents.

Quirites and understood as the Roman community) searching for the deceased Romulus but persuaded by an equestrian that he had become a deity (John Ant. F 32 Müller).[21] So far Dio follows the Livian tradition, but the message from the deified king is very different: Livy has Romulus tell the Romans that their city is destined to rule the world, Dio that they should opt to always be ruled by monarchs.

Passages which emphasise the participation of the whole community often relate to monarchs, or would-be monarchs. Dio extends the cruelty of the last king, Tarquin the Proud, to reach not only senators (as by Livy) but 'other citizens', stressing that the tyrant was at odds with 'the senate, the *equites* . . . and the entire δῆμος' (F 11.4 [*EV*], cf. Zonar. 7.10).[22] 'People' passages are absent from the narrative for the early or middle Republic. Granted, this absence may have resulted from the loss of Dio's original narrative for these periods. Yet it cannot be simply a product of the caprice of Dio's epitomators and excerptors, as we do have such scenes from the Regal period, which also does not survive in Dio's original. Another potential explanation is tied to Dio's tendency to use 'people' scenes in relation to powerful individuals: as Adam Kemezis points out, these did not gather lasting clout during the Republic.[23] Significantly, the Roman community re-emerges as a protagonist with Marius and Sulla and appears at critical points of the narrative of the *dynasteiai*. As the Principate approaches, the stains from the class conflicts of the Republic have been washed away, fitting the 'people' for more symbolic roles.

(b)   Civil Wars

These symbolic roles are tied to duty and governance, functioning as a litmus test for the state of affairs. Dio's portrayal of the people takes an interesting turn in his narratives of civil wars, which allow us to catch glimpses of Dio's attitudes towards the people and their role in politics. In this light, Caesar's oration to the African troops (43.17.5–6) may be regarded as programmatic, setting out the relation between ruler and ruled as between father and child. It is characterised by πρόνοια ('foresight') and κηδεμονία ('care, solicitude') on the one hand, and trust and

---

[21] Cf. Zonar. 7.9 on the rush at the death of Tarquinius Priscus, also involving trickery. There are parallel narratives in Livy 1.16 and 1.41.

[22] Cf. Livy 1.49.1–6, not elected by the people (*qua* assembly); 1.50.6, with no hope for the citizens' love, he opted for their fear. Though describing Tarquin as unpopular, Livy does not universalise to the extent Dio does.

[23] Kemezis 2014: 105–6.

obedience on the other, in ways that are clearly meant to be understood as a generalisation of monarchy.[24] Dio lets the soldiers involved in civil war represent Roman society, long after citizen armies had become a thing of the past, at Pharsalus as well as Cremona.[25]

The civil war between Caesar and the Pompeians contains a narrative arc which articulates the effect of leadership on the population. It begins with Pompey's departure from Rome in 49 BC, described as an exodus that cleaves the minds, prayers, hopes, bodies and souls of the Romans in two (41.7.6), amid much pain and emotion, beyond the ties of kinship (41.7.2–3, 8.3). Dio describes those remaining with a trio of words beginning with πάν: 'all ... with all their wives and all their children' (πάντες ... παμπαιδὶ καὶ παγγυναικί) trailing after the leavers, calling out for them, praying to be taken with them, causing delays with their embraces (41.9.3–5). The battle itself is introduced with a trio of verbs with the prefix δία-: 'what nature had bound together by mixing their blood, they [Pompey and Caesar] then ... broke up and broke apart and broke asunder' (ὅσα γὰρ φύσις τὸ αἷμα αὐτῶν μίξασα συνέδησε, τότε ταῦτα ... διέλυον καὶ διέσπων καὶ διερρήγυσαν) (41.57.4). This is echoed by unnatural things occurring simultaneously elsewhere (41.61.1–5). The one-ness of the armies is underscored by their almost identical gear and formation (41.58.1) and mutual recognition (41.59.1–3).

Some of this belongs to the rhetorical toolbox for civil wars. However, we may note that Appian's treatment of the armies at Pharsalus and Philippi is entirely different from Dio's and starkly negative towards the people (as is his view overall).[26] The 'exodus', moreover, is unique to Dio, and so is the ensuing 'reunion'.[27] Dio elaborates the treaty between Sextus Pompey, Mark Antony and Octavian at Misenum in 39 BC into a remarkable manifestation of the people writ large, reconstituting itself like a split amoeba. 'Many soldiers and many civilians' (πολλοὶ μὲν γὰρ στρατιῶται πολλοὶ δὲ καὶ ἰδιῶται) emitted a communal shout at the sight of the commanders embracing, which made even the mountains resound (συνηχῆσαι) (48.37.1–2). Not only does Dio insert enormous audiences at an event that, far as we know, involved no spectators, he adds a natural phenomenon acting in sympathy with the sentiments of the humans, giving voice, as it were, to the very bones of Italy.[28] At the strike of this

---

[24] Note Kuhn-Chen 2002: 226.
[25] Otherwise, Dio is critical of the soldiery, and especially veterans; see e.g. de Blois 1997 *passim*, Kemezis 2014: 143–5.
[26] See Kuhn-Chen 2002: 115–22.   [27] On the 'exodus' as Dio's creation, Gowing 2016: 130.
[28] Cf. Chapter 7 by Shushma Malik in this volume on the canal enterprise of Nero, 'causing the very ground at the Isthmus at Corinth to rupture and bleed'.

terrific sound, people jumped into the sea to embrace, unable to resist the urge to merge (48.37.3). Being one, they suffered the same emotions (48.37.8–9).

The reaction underscores that the Roman community should not be toyed with: it has immense latent power. This is often manifest through a shout. A great roar (θορύβου δ᾽ οὖν πολλοῦ) erupted at Caesar's murder, which sent the city spinning in confusion (44.20.1–3). The 'shouting' (κραυγῇ) emitted by the spectating Romans when Tiridates did obeisance to Nero struck (ἐξεπλάγη) the king speechless, thinking he was about to be killed (62[63].5.1 [Xiph.]). Similar to the scene at Misenum is the cry raised in unison by the whole δῆμος when Didius Julianus was about to sacrifice to Janus: fatigued by civil war, those gathered at the ceremonies emitted a shout that so reverberated against the surrounding buildings that it would cause one to shudder (74[73].13.4 [Xiph.]). The buildings in question are those of the *forum Romanum*, the political heart of the city itself, which thus added its support to the protesting Romans. The other side of the civil war was Septimius Severus, approaching Rome with his Pannonian armies. This is not made explicit by Dio, but surely a reader would have made the connection. As Alicia Simpson argues in Chapter 13, Dio's hints that past and present civil wars were linked is in part what made his history relevant in the Byzantine period, similarly plagued by such conflicts.

Elevating a scene by universalising it is typical of Dio's narrative of the *dynasteiai*. He asserts that, although Pompey's path to power was irregular, the 'whole body of the citizenry' needed such a man as he (i.e. not him personally). The 'exodus' is emphatically universalised: although the framing narrative only concerns senators and magistrates, those leaving comprise 'virtually all of the foremost men both of the senate and the equestrian order, and in particular of the people' (ἦσαν δὲ πάντες ὡς εἰπεῖν οἱ πρῶτοι καὶ τῆς βουλῆς καὶ τῆς ἱππάδος καὶ προσέτι καὶ τοῦ ὁμίλου) (41.7.1–2).[29] All orders listen to the funeral oration for Caesar (44.45.1), and Dio describes the πλῆθος that fell at Actium as including members of the ὅμιλος, *equites*, and senators (46.33.5),[30] while parallel narratives only bothered with the senatorial dead. Strikingly, the delegation that received Octavian at Brundisium included the entire senate, 'the majority of the equestrians, and the people, as well as many others' (καὶ ἡ ἱππὰς τοῦ τε δήμου τὸ πλεῖον καὶ ἕτεροι), some because 'they wanted to' (οἱ δὲ

---

[29] Dio selects the vaguer ὅμιλος over δῆμος, which might be understood as the assembly. Those ordered to leave, as in 41.6, 41.9.7, were all senators.

[30] Listed in reverse order, allowing Dio to continue at 46.33.6 with the senators, the best of whom were murdered. That this was their own fault is clear at 46.34.1.

ἐθελονταί), all walking together (συνῆλθον) (51.4.4).[31] The emphasis on free will, universality and community is significant, as is the trio of negations that follows: 'not anything from anyone anymore' (οὐκέτ' οὐδὲν ὑπ' οὐδενός) stirred rebellion (51.4.5). The community constituted itself of its own accord as it (literally) ushered in the budding autocrat.

(c)   Spectacles and Ceremonies

Far from Cato's weak and pitiable *plebs*, the Roman community emerges as a force. This is often demonstrated by Dio through public ceremonies, where all orders are present. Their role as manifestations of society is exploited by Dio when he likens Nero's stage performances to state ceremonies (no doubt to elicit the disgust of the reader), underscoring that the whole δῆμος was forced to watch and acclaim them (62[61].20.1–5 [Xiph.]).[32] The 'most prominent' among the δῆμος (here clearly the whole community) were the most prone so to express openly their delight, hiding their grief. Here Dio expresses sympathy with their dilemma, but he often uses community scenes to accuse senators of servile flattery, beyond the demands of political oppression. They were the most enthusiastic in greeting Nero at his *adventus*, ascending with him, his soldiers and the *equites* onto the Capitol (note the absence of 'the people' in this negative context) and acclaiming him. To expose their hypocrisy in eulogising an emperor known to be an abomination Dio discloses their chants, which he in a rare address to the reader (62[63].20.6 [Xiph]) claims to be quoted verbatim (but which are no doubt his own). No chants, and no *bons mots*, are mentioned by Tacitus.

An event described in remarkably similar terms is the *adventus* of Septimius Severus, suggesting that this scene should be interpreted as a covert critique of the emperor. As at Nero's arrival, all orders were explicitly present to see the new emperor.[33] Proximity between ruler and population is otherwise a good thing, but here they approach the emperor in order to learn how the sudden change of fortune affected him. Severus is framed as a foreigner and a creature of luck, not merit. It is surely no

---

[31] 51.4.4: Cf. Appian's description (*Mith.* 24.116) of Pompey's arrival at the same port, for which no one walked the distance, and the senate progressed the least.

[32] On this scene, see Adam Kemezis (Chapter 1) and Shushma Malik (Chapter 7) in this volume, as well as Barbara Saylor Rodgers (Chapter 11) on Nero as Dio's arch-villain.

[33] 75(74).4–5 (Xiph.): οἱ ἄνθρωποι (men/citizens?), οἱ στρατιῶται (the soliders), ἡμεῖς (i.e. the senate), and ὅμιλος (the remainder) drew near.

coincidence that the vocabulary is almost identical to (and arranged in the same order as) that used for Nero's glittering pageants.

Frequent representations of the people in Dio are as audiences at games. The function of these scenes, as Newbold points out, is to highlight the virtues or (more often) vices of the emperor who gives them, not least through audience reactions.[34] Dio scrutinises in particular the elite, whose relation to monarchs underlie the many references to expenses and instances of class reversals (in which their social opposite is not 'the people' but the performers). The abuses by the ὄχλος against the deceased Commodus, Dio observes with disgust, were inversions of 'their' own former praise, often interpreted as the *plebs*.[35] The subject of 'they', however (introduced at 74[73].2.2 [Xiph.]), is universal: the senate and the people.

Newbold underscores that games scenes (including contemporary ones) are fictional and characteristic of Dio. Significantly, these scenes first occur with the proto-monarchs Pompey and Caesar,[36] and henceforth become the foremost symbol for the relation between Rome and its leaders. Dio sometimes stretches this nexus to the breaking point, as in using spectacles to criticise Tiberius even though he banned them, in two creative (and rather tenuous) ways. The ominous note at the end of Book 56 that the empire was now in the hands of Tiberius and Livia is immediately followed by a multitude causing disruption (στάσις) over the pay of actors – public behaviour, we are to understand, was to go downhill under the new regime, indicating that the regime itself was flawed. The second passage exploits Tiberius' ban on *venationes*, which John of Antioch (following Dio) claims prompted the arrangement of such elsewhere, in jerry-built wooden structures, one of which collapsed and killed several spectators (58.1.1ᵃ [John Ant.]). Tacitus paints this calamity with vivid colours, but neither blames the emperor for it nor makes it symbolise the state of affairs.[37] John of Antioch (and we may be sure, Dio) places the guilt emphatically with Tiberius, making this episode his prime piece of evidence that he harmed the Romans, 'squandering people both in public and private' (κοινῇ τε καὶ ἰδίᾳ προσαναλίσκων τοὺς ἄνδρας).[38] It sits at the very opening of book 58, which reveals his decline following the death of Germanicus.[39]

---

[34] Newbold 1975: 593–6, 600–1.   [35] 74(73).2–4 (Xiph.). Cf. Kuhn-Chen 2002: 223–4.

[36] Pompey's theatre (37.38) and complaint over Caesar's extravagances (43.24.1–2).

[37] Tac. *Ann.* 4.62–3. A freedman raised it, fudging on quality due to greed.

[38] Cf. Shushma Malik's treatment in Chapter 7 of a theatre collapse at Naples under Nero, for which the roles are reversed: Tacitus and Suetonius tie it to the emperor's character, while Dio passes over it.

[39] On this change in Tiberius, see the discussion in Chapter 6 by Christopher Mallan.

IV Harming the People

That the people come to harm is one of the hallmarks of dysfunctional regimes. The prime example is, obviously, civil war, the explicit inspiration for the *Roman History* and no doubt the reason for the elaboration of the exodus and the reunion: the body of the people is the first victim of the tremendous forces released by their sparring leaders. Citizens drown as they embrace in the Misene water, some are trampled to death, while others die from the very shock of their own shout (48.37.2–3). Didius Julianus, in reaction to the shout at his sacrifice, had those standing nearest killed, in a random, non-specific manner typical of tyrants (and also conveniently allowing for invention on Dio's part) (74[73].13.4 [Xiph.]). The pattern is established with Sulla, who also happened to kill some (unspecified) Romans (F 109.5 [*EV*]) when executing the Samnites. Marius executed at whim, by hand gesture – as though Romans were gladiators to be killed or saved by imperial caprice – and without distinction (F 102.8–11 [*EV*]), while unspecified 'others' die in the general commotion.[40] Sulla's proscriptions were an unstoppable whirlwind of death that explicitly emanated from his character, as the killers emulated his lust for slaughter in order to please him (F 109.9–10 [*EV*]). It was inescapable, as names were added by mistake (F 109.14, 17 [*EV*]), touching all and sundry and not just political opponents, as in parallel accounts.[41]

The triumviral proscriptions are described as similarly haphazard and global, with an added layer of malicious intent that points forward to the Principate. The blame is concentrated on Mark Antony (while Octavian and Lepidus are more or less exonerated) and an equally murderous Fulvia, inserted by Dio to form a proto-imperial couple who do as they please with the citizenry (47.8.2–5). It has been suggested that Dio's history, and particularly the narrative on the *dynasteiai*, is a commentary on his own time.[42] Although not the subject here, Dio does plant many cues that the ruthless, goal-oriented Severus (who also avenged himself on the supporters of his opponents) resembles Sulla, while his son has traits in common with Mark Antony (not least his name), who does evil for its own sake.[43] The cruelty escalates from widespread 'but not premeditated'

---

[40] Livy, *Per.* 80.6 makes no attempt to globalise and describes no confusion.
[41] Livy, *Per.* 86.5 limits the deaths to the senatorial elite. The narrative is agreed to be Dio's own. Millar 1964: 43 thought it 'near to being a piece of great writing'.
[42] E.g., de Blois 1997: 2669, Kemezis 2014: 103, 146.
[43] On Sulla in Dio, see Urso 2016b and Coudry 2016b: 296, who contrasts Severus' endorsement of Sulla's cruelty (as per 'his' speech) with the imperial virtue of clemency. In Chapter 7 of this volume, Shushma Malik suggests a similar parallel between Nero and Commodus.

(οὐκ ἐκ προνοίας) (47.4.1) under Sulla to a deliberate will to harm, as painfully as possible (47.4.3). πρόνοια ('foresight') is hardly an idle choice of word: it is the arch-virtue of emperors (broadcast not least under the Severans), expressing the emperor's fatherly care for the realm. Harming by accident is bad; to do so with πρόνοια is positively perverse.

Caligula and Nero, Dio asserts, nurtured a conscious desire to destroy the Roman people. Famously, Caligula exclaimed to 'the whole people together' (παντὶ τῷ δήμῳ ἅμα) that he wished it had one neck so he could chop it off, a statement that, seeing the insistence on 'all' and 'together' should be seen as referring to the entire community, as the setting also suggests (59.13.6).[44] Dio imputes a level of intent to the (no doubt fictional) deaths caused by the party favours with which Caligula showered the δῆμος at games, mixing pieces of iron with the silver and gold (59.25.5). Titus, by contrast, used wooden tokens which also represented useful gifts rather than the generous but deadly indulgences of Caligula (65[66].25.5 [Xiph.]). Dio also creates an emotional 'people' scene (and manages to associate Caligula with proscriptions) by having him slaughter the πολλοί who had, on an instant, rushed into the circus and heaved up a collective shout. The immediacy (as well as the rush, the shout and perhaps the violence) may be questioned: the cause was failure to comply with a tax law of which they were ignorant because the 'white tablet' that announced it was deliberately posted so as to be illegible, in order to create more forfeitures (59.28.10–11 [Xiph./*EV*/John Ant.]).[45]

Nero's extravagant parties also resulted in deaths (62.15 [Xiph.]). Dio styles them as including wanton abuse of citizen women by a mixed throng (συρφετώδης) of gladiators and slaves – not, significantly, Roman citizens – before the eyes of their hapless husbands and fathers, an upturning of social order that results in violence among participants and deaths and seizures of the women.[46] Tacitus (*Ann.* 15.37) mentions neither brutality nor brutes (complaining rather about using public spaces for private feasts); these are Dio's own remarks. Similarly, he makes much of the fire as conscious harm to the people, asserting that Nero 'set his heart on destroying the city and realm, which had always no doubt been his desire' (ἐπεθύμησεν ὅπερ που ἀεὶ ηὔχετο, τήν τε πόλιν ὅλην καὶ τὴν βασιλείαν ζῶν ἀναλῶσαι) (62.16.1

---

[44] It is thrown back at the emperor at his murder (59.30.1c [Xiph.]) for which an ex-consul volunteers to take the blame. This underscores that the antagonised δῆμος is not the populace.
[45] Presumably, the outrage was directed at the tax law and not the way it was posted, but this is not how the sentence is structured.
[46] What really gets Dio's goat is the upsetting of social order: the guests are συρφετώδης, a mixed crowd, and therefore unrestrained.

[Xiph.]). He underscores that it encompassed all elements of society, in vocabulary that much resembles that used for Misenum (especially at 62.16.7 [Xiph.]). Admittedly, some of these themes can be found with Tacitus as well, but he dissociates Nero from the fire, stating that the rumours that he was present were false, and he also recounts Nero's measures to alleviate its effects (*Ann.* 15.38–9).[47] Dio, by contrast, turns the fire into a manifestation of the emperor's desire to harm the Roman people, watching and relishing in the disaster.

The assertion that Romans fell ill and died due to Domitian's *faux*-stoic refusal to leave his (over-elaborate) *navalia* when the weather turned bad is also Dio's own (67.8.2–4 [Xiph.]). Suetonius and Martial relate the story but mention neither disease nor the command that the audience remain in their seats.[48] A public banquet the next day is described as a token of remorse rather than generosity and is followed by the sinister 'black dinner' (also only mentioned by Dio), where the senatorial guests are made to fear for their lives. The juxtaposition is meaningful: we are to understand that not only the lives of the wealthy are at risk when bad emperors put on shows, but everyone, including the combatants (of whom almost everyone is supposed to have died). Among many instances of Caracalla's viciousness, one episode that shows similarities with the proscriptions narrates his deliberate aim to destroy Alexandria (78[77].22–3[Xiph.]), here used as a foil for Rome (and perhaps exploiting the recent extension of Roman citizenship).[49] Here, too, violence is directed not only at the elite but at the population at large. Dio applies the trope of tricking elites to a banquet only to murder them, but he also has Caracalla – personally – kill innocent Alexandrians at random in the ensuing citywide bloodbath. Should these fail to register with his readers as properly Roman, Dio asserts that 'Roman' Romans were also killed, by accident, in the melee.

V   The People (Re)act

Motion is key to many 'people scenes', framed around a dichotomy of an ideal 'stillness' (ἡσυχία) and 'turmoil' or 'confusion' (ταραχή; θόρυβος). Rather than an instigator, the 'people' is an amplifier, making manifest the

---

[47] Tacitus describes them as to no avail since the rumours against Nero had taken root already, referring to the consequences for his *reputation* (and not the effectiveness of the measures).

[48] Schulz 2016: 283–6; Mart. *Epig.* 4.3 and Suet. *Dom.* 4.2.

[49] Cf. Shushma Malik in Chapter 7 of this volume on Dio's narrative of Nero's actions in Greece. This departs from parallel narratives in asserting that Nero wantonly destroyed the population (62[63].11.1–12.1 [Xiph.]). For citizenship in Cassius Dio, see Chapter 10 by Myles Lavan.

nature of events. The people as an entity lacks direction but is set in motion by external stimuli. The shout upon Caesar's murder made the ὅμιλος rush about frantically, setting off a chain reaction (44.20.1–4).⁵⁰ The fire under Nero released aimless and destructive movements: 'they' rush about as if struck, some into, some out of houses, caught in the contradictory state of being denied both movement and stillness (62.16.4–5 [Xiph.]). Ironically, popular action is often non-action, as in refusing to take arms.⁵¹ At Pharsalus, the citizens/soldiers responded to the battle call with silence and lack of motion, as though 'deprived of souls' (ὥσπερ ἄψυχοι) (41.58.2), and the generals feared that if allowed to last, their armies would merge.⁵² The behaviour of the people/soldiers displays their inherent nobility, in contrast to the iniquity of the situation and the ignoble motives of those who placed them in it. They were only dragged into battle by the momentum of their (less noble) allies. As Caillan Davenport points out in Chapter 8 of this volume, Dio often lets the behaviour of the armies reflect the character of their leaders, but it can also serve as a protest against them.

Even popular action is a reaction, the catalyst for which is either an individual, an external event or even a god. This largely exonerates the people, and to brand it fickle is to miss the point: it cannot but reflect current leadership. It is powerful but will-less, excitable and movable but, to Dio, innocent. Even for the complex, factious strife of the *dynasteiai* he tones down violence perpetrated by the people and by extension their guilt: the killing of Helvius Cinna after Caesar's murder is an accident due to confusion (while the people in Appian tear him, deliberately, limb from limb) (44.50.3); the partisans of Catiline are made into a citizen corps fighting valiantly and dying in droves, the guilt falling on their leader and his opponents (37.40.1–2).⁵³ Clodius' followers explicitly do *not* behave as an ὄχλος upon his murder (40.49.3), but with an eerie sense of ceremony (even when burning down the senate house) and a vigil (both Dio's additions). Action is often contemplated but not effected, as when during a famine the entire ὅμιλος rushed into the theatre (which did not yet exist) and *threatened* to kill senators and burn temples (but, significantly, did not), a scene recorded by neither Appian nor Plutarch (39.9.2).⁵⁴ Similarly

⁵⁰ The root cause, fear of being accused of complicity, only implicates the political elite.
⁵¹ See Zonar. 7.13.
⁵² Appian (*B.Civ.* 2.66–7) describes the troops on both sides as zealous for battle, greedy and arrogant, pushing their commanders towards the battle.
⁵³ Compare the parallel narrative in Appian, *B.Civ.* 2.7, which mentions the bravery only of nobles.
⁵⁴ Even though Appian, *B.Civ.* 2.18 follows the same account.

(and also exclusively with Dio), the 'people' rushed on Octavian and Mark Antony *as if* to kill them, but only as a last resort after attempting every means to display their exasperation with civil war (48.31.6). Such fictional near-violence demonstrates the potency of the (ideally passive) community if pushed to the extreme by those who should care for it. If bad leadership forces the people into action, truly bad leadership forces the people into violent action.

Popular action, thus, is used not to narrate the nobility of the people but the baseness of others, as the attack on Sejanus' statues (58.11.3) and the executions by the δῆμος of his foremost advisers and 'those who had permitted outrages to please him' (δι᾽ αὐτὸν ὑβρισάντων τι εἶδεν) (58.12.1). Though harsh, the actions are consistent and just, contrasting against the behaviour of senators who had raised Sejanus to the skies only to kill him when the tide turned. All but a few had informed against others, cowering in fear lest they be brought to justice, too (58.12.3).[55] Meanwhile the (always mercenary) praetorians raged and plundered from petty jealousy of the night watch who had been preferred over them. Dio has the δῆμος speak out against Didius Julianus while senators dissimulate (74[73].13.2–3 [Xiph.]), and it is the people that cries out against Macrinus while *equites* and senators fawn (79[78].20.1–2 [Xiph.]). Hawkins makes a case for the elite being silenced under the Principate (in contrast to popular license);[56] be that as it may, Dio places considerable guilt on the members of his class for supporting, even creating, unworthy regimes. The people receives no such censure.

The agent in these episodes glides between assembly, *plebs*, and a purely literary 'people', while other instances are more clearly universalised, such as the shout raised by the δῆμος and the urban soldiery against Caracalla's treatment of Fabius Cilo (78[77].4.2–5 [Xiph.]), putting all social categories on one side against the emperor, or the emotional scene in which the δῆμος, after protesting against Didius Julianus, took arms and ran together in the circus where they called for Pescennius Niger (74[73].13.5 [Xiph.]). Significantly, they resorted to non-action through a fasting vigil, after which they quietly dispersed. The grandest scene of popular action is also made to resemble a ceremony: the fall of Cleander, who was blamed for aggravating a famine (73[72].13.1–6 [Xiph./*EV*]). During the last bout

---

[55] Tacitus, *Ann.* 5.4–5 posits strong popular opposition to Sejanus. To Dio his support (58.4.2–3) comprised praetorians, senators and the friends of Tiberius, but not the people. 'The rest', confused by Tiberius' messages from Capri (58.6.6), are not the people but 'all but Sejanus', subject of the previous passage. Those who snub him in company (58.9.1) must also be elites.
[56] Hawkins 2017.

of races, a 'a tall and grim maiden' (παρθένος τις μεγάλη καὶ βλοσυρά) entered the arena and began abusing him. Dio hints that she was a deity, likely Roma as she has children in tow.[57] The δῆμος in unison takes up her shouts, and, *as one*, begins marching to Commodus to demand action. Dio signposts the marchers as loyal, uttering prayers for the emperor on the way to the suburban villa where he dwelled (itself a mark of his unsuitability for rule).[58] It remains controlled: the violence is attributed to Cleander, who has some (randomly) killed, and the emperor, who overreacts and kills both Cleander and his son. Only then do οἱ Ῥωμαῖοι (however we understand that body) take to violence, abusing the corpse of the executed man and passing sentences on his accomplices. Dio does not express judgement on these actions (which follow legal procedure and long-standing custom); their aim is to show what fate awaits arrogant men. There can be no doubt that the marchers have Dio's sympathy.

VI   Sense, Sensibility and Structure

Barbara Kuhn-Chen claims that Dio's people lack political understanding.[59] This is only partially true. In fact, Dio may be seen to use the actions of the people as a manner of running commentary. Occasionally this commentary is a rational, vocal one, as when, although inflamed with violent passions, the people reproach the senators for their fickle treatment of Caesar (44.50.1), or when those left behind by the exodus of 49 BC, in the midst of heightened emotions, 'reasoned' (λογιζόμενοι) that those who had left would not have wished to flee had not so many calamities befallen the state (41.8.5). Lukas De Blois observes that Dio 'cannot hide' that the people often made pronouncements on politics (as though it were Dio's intention to silence them), but it is Dio who ascribes to them these sentiments; the people 'speak out' in Dio's history because he chooses to give them a collective voice.[60] Indeed, Dio's people are surprisingly historically minded and contemplative. In the midst of Nero's fire, the people stop to reflect that a great portion of the city had been destroyed by the Gauls (62.17.3 [Xiph.]). Again, during Marius' proscription the population recalled how Romans of yore displayed ships' beaks on the rostra, not the heads of Romans (F 102.9 [*EV*]).

---

[57] Cf. the unusually tall woman/goddess who appears in the narrative at 55.1.3–4, as treated by Shushma Malik in Chapter 7 of this volume. See also Chapter 4 by Rhiannon Ash on divine inspiration.

[58] Manifest also by Commodus' ignorance of affairs until informed by the wife of Quadratus.

[59] Kuhn-Chen 2002: 222.   [60] De Blois 1997: 2659.

The soldiers who engaged in battle at Pharsalus stopped to chat (λαλεῖν) with one another across the lines and send messages with their enemies to people at home (41.59.2). The people, in short, have a mind.

In addition to a mind, Dio's people possesses sensory perception. Verbs of seeing and hearing are very frequent, often with συν- or ἅμα to mark their collectivity. During Sulla's proscriptions, much emphasis is placed on *seeing* lists and severed heads, and on those seeing them *being seen and judged* by their reactions (F 109.14–17, 21 [*EV*]). During the triumviral proscriptions the murderers knew their trade because they had *seen* and *heard* (οἱ δὲ ἰδόντες, οἱ δ' ἀκουῇ) under Sulla (47.4.1–3). The Misenum episode was a *varied sight and sound* (ποικίλην μὲν αὐτῶν θέαν ποικίλην δὲ καὶ ἀκουήν), the *sight* of relatives *defied belief* (παρὰ δόξαν θεωροῦντες ἄποροι τε ἅμα τῇ ὄψει), debilitating many who did not recognise them until they *heard* their voices (48.8.4). The technique invites the reader to share the experiences of the protagonists and accords with what Sophie Gotteland identifies as 'narrative ekphrasis', common for battle scenes and natural disasters but used more widely in Dio's work. Its role is not simply to embellish: It paints a larger truth.[61] As Gotteland observes, Dio uses the device pointedly, applying it to scenes with ideological potential.[62]

Dio's emphasis on the senses is tied to cognition (ἐπιστήμη, εἰδεῖν or λογίζεσθαι). Abnormal experiences (ἄτοπα) such as the reunion at Misenum put reason out of play, resulting in illogical movements and actions. A major cause of alarm at Pharsalus was the failure to understand speech, and only when driven 'outside their minds' (ἔκφρονες) did the soldiers attack their countrymen (41.58.3).[63] During Nero's fire people behaved as though 'distracted' (ἔμπληκτοι) (62.16.4 [Xiph.]), seeing and hearing many 'strange things' (ἄτοπα) (62.16.2 [Xiph.]), which one might find surprising seeing that, according to the next line, nothing could be seen except the fires, and nothing could be heard due to the confused shouts. A few lines down, Dio again states that nothing could be seen or understood because of the smoke and noise, for which reason some stood debilitated as though dumb, while others went mad and jumped into the fire (μήτε συνιδεῖν μήτε συνεῖναί τι ὑπὸ τοῦ καπνοῦ [which can also mean 'nonsense'] καὶ τῆς κραυγῆς) (62.16.5 [Xiph.]).

---

[61] Gotteland 2016: 382.

[62] As Rhiannon Ash notes in Chapter 4 of this volume, the amazement at the paradoxical and miraculous is often employed to similar effects in Dio's work.

[63] App. *Mith.* 14.93 describes the war against the pirates as causing perplexity by having 'nothing tangible or visible about it', but while this seems a fair description of war against an amorphous enemy, Dio's use of the theme is less relatable to actual events.

VII   The Rational People

Dio's people are a thinking, sensing body, who not only respond to their leaders as they might to natural phenomena such as fire, but also affect them. This symbiosis lies at the very heart of Dio's treatment of the Roman community and allows him to use it to illustrate leadership: ignoring or maltreating the people will backfire, as they and their leaders are part of the same organism. The key to rule lies in organising this body in ways that harness its virtues without triggering its vices, as per the advice in Maecenas' speech (52.29.1–2). This is achieved by giving each order of society its own, clearly delineated tasks, which gives them dignity and purpose. Dio's focus is again primarily on elites for whom monarchy is good: it helps them be moral in spite of themselves. One of the few views shared by Maecenas and Agrippa is that ordinary people should be kept away from politics: even the 'democratic' Agrippa shudders at the thought of allowing political agency to the low-born and uneducated, who by default can produce nothing good or noble (ἀγαθόν) (52.8–9).[64] Dio's respect for the 'people' does not translate into democratic leanings, as noted also by Myles Lavan in Chapter 10 of this volume in relation to the universal franchise. In a symbolic illustration of what constitutes sound government, Dio states that the rule of the 'servants' (οἰκέται) at Volsinii who had ousted their masters (Zonar. 8.7.1), and who in his own estimate managed the matters of state very well (and not much different from their masters), was by default unnatural and had to be overturned. He expresses no sympathy for their cause. Caesar in the African oration (41.33.1–5) describes hierarchy as instituted by nature (φύσει) and a matter of intelligence and reason. Obedience is the prerequisite for anything to exist, and under benign leadership (marked by foresight, πρόνοια) it produces stability, health and safety (κόσμος, ὑγίεια and ἀσφάλεια).

In an emotional scene Dio has the enraged Capuans (Zonar. 9.2) almost kill their senators but deliberate themselves out of this plan, persuaded by one of their number that a people without a head is helpless. This incongruous deliberation by the 'headless' is typical for Dio and accords the population ability, reason and morality – but not political agency. Several scenes have the people spontaneously instil order into itself as a response to an instinctive foreknowledge of good governance to come, or to release itself from poor leadership. The reaction to Actium is pointedly void of the excessive, destructive behaviour that marked the 'pact of

[64] For Maecenas' verdict on an ὀχλοκρατία: 52.14, Augustus': 53.8.4, Dio's own: 44.2–3.

Misenum'⁶⁵: in this case, enthusiasm engenders orderly behaviour, not deadly chaos (51.21.1–6). Similarly, we are made to understand that Galba's rule was to be sound from how the people behave at his accession, sacrificing and wearing liberty caps (63.29.1 [Xiph.]). The 'good' people engage in religious practice, as at the fasting vigil in the arena under Didius Julianus, infused with prayers against war (74[73].13.5 [Xiph.]), or even at Clodius' pyre. At the exodus in 49 BC, the people unite at the temples and spend the night in prayer and sacrifices, invoking the gods (41.7.3).

The people also triangulate the relation between leaders and gods, lending it an oracular quality that turns Nero's attempts at manipulating audience responses into more than just vanity (62[61].20.3 [Xiph.]). Divine truth, however, will out: the verses uttered against Nero, and which Dio suggests came from the Sibylline oracle, miraculously came true (62[63].18.3–4 [Xiph.]).⁶⁶ In Chapter 4, Rhiannon Ash treats a similar 'prophetic wonder', in which the crowd at the races turned to greet a jackdaw by the name of Caracalla's future killer. Those who shouted at Didius' sacrifice to Janus – note the religious setting – did so as though upon 'some command' (συγκειμένου τινός) and infused their shout with prayers for the gods (74[73].13.3–4 [Xiph.]). The protest against Cleander (73[72].13 [Xiph./EV]) was led and inspired by a deity, and those marching were engaged in prayers and blessings for the emperor and the realm.

It is against this background that the chants that amazed Dio with their regularity should be understood (76[75].4 [Xiph.]): he hints, not so subtly, that they were directed by divine inspiration. The (unspecified) 'untold multitude' (ἀμύθετοι) arrived *together* (συνῆλθον), underscoring the unity of classes. In the arena they exercised restraint – they stayed silent through the whole event until the sixth and last race (with explicit reference to the Cleander episode), at which point the chants were uttered, only to immediately cease. The spectators first prayed for the 'good fortune' (εὐτυχία) and 'safety' (σωτηρία) of the δῆμος, then hailed Roma, then complained about civil war. Dio's claim to autopsy reveals the presence of elite Romans like himself but is also a device to capture the reader's special attention.⁶⁷ That it is a faithful rendering of events is unlikely; Dio also claims autopsy to the (obviously fictional) omens with which the scene is compounded as

⁶⁵ As pointed out by Rees 2011: 38.
⁶⁶ Cf. Nero's transgression against the Delphic oracle as treated by Shushma Malik in Chapter 7: he blocked the fissure with the bodies of his victims.
⁶⁷ Also at 62(63).20 (Xiph.), the chants greeting Nero. Insistence on veracity should raise suspicion to the contrary.

though one: the chants are an exponent of divine will, expressed through the entire Roman community.[68]

VIII   Conclusion

There is more to Dio's portrayal of the people than may first meet the eye: Treating it as an organic whole, he accords it a pronounced and far more sympathetic role than either Plutarch or Appian. Granted, the primary function of the people in the *Roman History* is as a commentary on the actions and character of others (emperors, senators, soldiers), but this role gives it an almost sacred dignity. The Roman people functions both as the ultimate judge of the character of their leaders and as the canvas on which said character is projected.

Dio's 'people' is a literary construct and should not be confused with any 'real' social body. He assigns it stereotypical roles, drawing on well-established rhetorical figures that his readers would have been well pre-pared to recognise and appreciate.[69] As scholars, we must be wary of taking 'people scenes' as evidence for, say, the actual nature of the exodus of Pompey or popular opinion on Commodus. Fergus Millar interpreted the chants against Niger as historical and testifying to actual popular power, but this was not what Dio was using the scene to convey, nor did he shy away from embellishing and manipulating the account of his own time.[70] This does not mean that Dio disregarded historical accuracy. Rather, he exploited what Marion Bellissime terms 'blank spaces' in history to elabor-ate what he deemed pivotal events. Among such 'blank spaces' are the sensations, thoughts and actions of the Roman community.[71]

---

[68] Including a silver rain limited to the Forum of Augustus. Dio claims to have plated bronze coins with it, whose patina regrettably disappeared in four days. The scene appears to be a metaphor for what seemed good leadership but soon revealed its true metal (76[75].4.7 [Xiph.]) and may contain a reference to Severus' debasement of silver coinage, of which his mid third-century readers would have been painfully aware.

[69] So e.g. Fomin 2016: 219, Kemezis 2014: 103.   [70] Millar 1964: 137.   [71] Bellissime 2016a: 365.

CHAPTER 10

Citizenship, Enfranchisement and Honour in Cassius Dio

Myles Lavan

I Introduction

This was the reason why he made all the people in his empire Romans. He said he was honouring them, but his real purpose was to increase his revenues by this means too, since aliens did not pay most of these [taxes].

(78[77].9.5 [*EV*])[1]

Dio's passing reference to Caracalla's universal grant of citizenship is paradoxically one of the most widely known passages in his massive *Roman History*. His remark is obviously scathing in its assessment of Caracalla's motives. It is often read as if it were also dismissive of the *constitutio Antoniniana* itself, contributing to a still widespread belief that the grant was of little significance to contemporaries.[2] But Dio's opinion of the intrinsic merits of Caracalla's grant becomes more difficult to assess when the passage is read in the context of the *Roman History* as a whole. It has long been noted (though it is sometimes denied) that the speech of Maecenas in Book 52 advocates a universal grant of citizenship, anticipating Caracalla's edict (52.19.6). It is surely also significant that Maecenas' proposal is grounded in a proposition that the exclusion of provincials from citizenship distorts the economy of honour in the empire. This gives point to the ostensible motive of giving or showing honour (τιμῶν) to the inhabitants of the empire – a motive that might otherwise seem trivial.

This paper emerged from research on the history of Roman citizenship as I began to wonder about how our understanding of citizenship in the imperial period might have been shaped by Dio's conception of its place in Roman history. Thanks to Graham Andrews, Mirko Canevaro, Caillan Davenport, Adam Kemezis, Jesper Majbom Madsen, Christopher Mallan and especially John Rich for comments and suggestions.

[1] οὗ ἕνεκα καὶ Ῥωμαίους πάντας τοὺς ἐν τῇ ἀρχῇ αὐτοῦ, λόγῳ μὲν τιμῶν, ἔργῳ δὲ ὅπως πλείω αὐτῷ καὶ ἐκ τοῦ τοιούτου προσίῃ διὰ τὸ τοὺς ξένους τὰ πολλὰ αὐτῶν μὴ συντελεῖν, ἀπέδειξεν.

[2] Buraselis 2007: 94–120, esp. 119–20 provides an important corrective by collating the evidence of a positive contemporary response. Lavan 2016 attempts to quantify the scale of Caracalla's grant.

Why then does the narrator dismiss the universalisation of citizenship so brusquely when he comes to the grant itself?

This paper takes Dio's handling of the *constitutio Antoniniana* as a case study in the interpretive openness of his text. It aims to bring out the complexity of Dio's treatment of the diffusion of citizenship that culminated in Caracalla's grant. It is not a matter of determining which of the two passages reflects Dio's true opinion. (Fergus Millar, for one, suggested that the earlier passage was written to flatter Caracalla, while the later revealed the historian's 'own attitude'.[3]) The most salient fact is that the authorial voice nowhere expresses a clear opinion on the significance of Caracalla's grant. But that does not mean that Dio thought it unimportant. Besides the implicit endorsement in the speech of Maecenas, there are several other passages that give voice to a quite different perspective which insists on the value of a sharp distinction between Roman citizens and subjects, the most notable example being Augustus' 'political testament'. Consistency of theme and language – particularly a focus on honour and worth – makes it hard to explain away the tensions between these two visions of the role of citizenship in structuring the imperial order as merely tralaticious – that is, as Dio reproducing what he found in his sources without great concern for the overall coherence of the resulting text. It seems rather that Dio associated citizenship with a nexus of questions about subjection, worth, and honour to which he repeatedly returned.

Like much recent work on Dio, this paper assumes that his text demands interpretive work of the reader.[4] In particular, it insists on the need to distinguish between the narrative voice and other embedded voices (including that of Maecenas) and on the interpretive openness that this polyphony introduces into Dio's work – as in all works of ancient historiography.[5] It also aims to illustrate the importance of honour in Dio's text.[6] By 'honour' I mean a complex of ideas about the public recognition of individual worth evoked by τιμή, its cognates and related lexemes denoting worth and esteem. In Dio's history, I will argue, the most

---

[3] Millar 1964: 104–5.   [4] Kemezis 2014 is exemplary.

[5] See further Rich 2019; Fromentin et al. 2016: 14; Bellissime 2016a, esp. 366–7; Bellissime 2016b; Lachenaud 2016; Davenport and Mallan 2014; Hose 1994: 364. The interpretation of speeches is discussed further in this volume by Caillan Davenport and Christopher Mallan in the Introduction and Christina Kuhn in Chapter 5. The question of the relationship between narrative and embedded voices recurs in the discussion of moral judgements by Davenport and Mallan and in Chapter 11 by Barbara Saylor Rodgers. On polyphony, see also the epilogue by Christopher Pelling.

[6] On the importance of honour for Dio, see also Lendon 1997: 113–20 and Chapter 1 by Adam Kemezis and Chapter 12 by Christopher Mallan in this volume.

important implications of the spread of citizenship are its effects on the empire's economy of honour.

II   Dio on the Spread of Citizenship

It needs to be said at the outset that the spread of Roman citizenship does not seem to have been central to the macro-narrative of the *Roman History*. Despite some uncertainty about the chronology of composition, it is clear that at least half of the work, and conceivably all of it, was written after Caracalla's grant.[7] Dio was thus the first historian of Rome to see the spread of Roman citizenship as we do – as a process that culminated in universal citizenship. Yet there is no evidence that Dio saw this progressive expansion as one of the principal threads in Roman history.

It is possible that this is due to the vagaries of survival, since none of the three most obvious horizons in the expansion of Roman citizenship fall in the portion of Dio's work that has been transmitted intact.[8] The first is the reorganisation of most of the Latin, Hernician, Volscian and Campanian communities as *municipia* of Roman citizens (in many cases with the new status of *civitas sine suffragio*) in the aftermath of the Latin Revolt of 341–338 BC. Here we are almost entirely reliant on the twelfth-century epitome of Zonaras. There is independent evidence that Dio (like earlier historians) represented citizenship as playing a role in the outbreak of the revolt and its aftermath, but that aspect of his narrative was ignored by Zonaras and hence is all but lost to us.[9] The enfranchisement of peninsular Italy after the Social War is another obvious watershed. But it falls in the void between Book 21 (the last book used by Zonaras for the history of the Republic) and Book 36 (where the first manuscript of Dio begins). We thus

---

[7] Dio states that he spent ten years researching and twelve years writing his history (or at least the books to the death of Septimius Severus) (73[72].23.5 [Xiph.]) but does not mention when he began or ended. Various hypotheses have been proposed. Gabba 1955: 295–30 and Millar 1964 assumed he started work soon after Severus came to power and had him writing AD 206/7–218/19. In the 1970s and 80s several scholars proposed a much later chronology, with Dio not beginning work until after the death of Septimius Severus and hence writing in the 220s and early 230s (Barnes 1984 presents the most compelling case). More recently, Rich 1990: 3–4; Swan 2004: 28–36; and Millar 2005: 29–31 have proposed a revised early chronology that has Dio writing 210/1–222/23. Others have suggested early composition followed by revision in the 220s (most recently Kemezis 2014: 282–93 who places the start of the twelve years of writing somewhere between 204 and 207). See Kemezis 2014: 282–93 for the most recent overview of the problem.

[8] For a short history of the spread of Roman citizenship, see Lavan 2018.

[9] Zonaras makes no mention of citizenship in his brief account of the revolt and its aftermath (7.26.1–9). Yet, a short verbatim extract in the *Excerpta Constantiniana* (F 35.10 [*ES*]) demonstrates that Dio's original had, in fact, represented the revolt as having been precipitated by a frustrated desire for Roman citizenship. See Urso 2013: 74 and Section IV of this chapter.

have no idea how Dio presented the role of citizenship in the outbreak of the revolt or the series of laws that granted citizenship to the Italians in 90 and 89 BC.[10] The next great discontinuity in the history of enfranchisement was the *constitutio Antoniniana* itself, but it falls in the final quarter of the work, for which we are almost entirely reliant on Xiphilinus' epitome. The famous remark quoted in the epigraph survives only by the slimmest of threads. Xiphilinus himself does not even mention the grant in his summary, so Dio's reference to it survives only thanks to an opportune verbatim extract in the *Excerpta Constantiniana* (a corpus of excerpts from classical historians, arranged by theme, commissioned by Constantine Porphyrogenitus in the tenth century).[11] It follows that we cannot quite be certain that Dio did not say more about the grant elsewhere in his narrative.[12]

Nevertheless, the minimalism of the notices that we do have is revealing. Besides the passing reference to the *constitutio Antoniniana*, there is the enfranchisement of Cisalpine Gaul by Julius Caesar, which falls in the extant books. Dio records it without any comment on its merits or effects: 'He granted citizenship to the Gauls who lived between the Alps and the Po, because he had been their governor' (τοῖς Γαλάταις τοῖς ἐντὸς τῶν Ἄλπεων ὑπὲρ τὸν Ἠριδανὸν οἰκοῦσι τὴν πολιτείαν, ἅτε καὶ ἄρξας αὐτῶν, ἀπέδωκε) (41.36.4). It receives no more elaboration than his grant of citizenship to Gades earlier that year (41.24.1). In both cases, the only comment is an observation about a personal connection to Caesar, by way of explanation. The handful of notices of later grants by triumvirs and emperors are similarly bare.[13] Despite these unpromisingly bare records of citizenship grants, however, there are suggestions that Dio saw larger issues at stake in the extension of citizenship. The key lies not in the narrative but in speeches and other embedded voices.

[10] All that survives is an excerpt concerning failed negotiations with the Samnites in Nola (who held out long after the other rebels surrendered) in which the Samnites demand citizenship not just for themselves but for deserters (F 102.7 [*ELr*]; for the context, see Salmon 1967: 374).

[11] Xiphilinus compresses 78(77).9.2–6 (*EV*) into just five words before repeating 9.6–7 essentially verbatim. See Boissevain III.381–3. I am grateful to Graham Andrews for pointing this out to me.

[12] Speculation as to where another reference may have fallen is complicated by uncertainty both about the structure of Dio's narrative of his reign and about the date and context of the *constitutio Antoniniana* itself. A date between February and July 212 seems most likely given the order of the three edicts on *P. Giss.* 40 I, but a date as late as 213 remains possible. See especially Wolff 1976: 13–20 and Buraselis 2007: 1 n. 1.

[13] 43.39.5 (Caesar in Spain), 44.53.3 (Antony), 48.45.3 (Tingis), 54.25.1 (Augustus in Spain and Gaul), 60.7.2 (Claudius), 72(71).19.1 (*ELg*) (Marcus Aurelius).

III   Maecenas on Universal Citizenship

The most important text is in the speech of Maecenas in Book 52. Among
the many concrete proposals in the second half of his speech, Maecenas
advises Augustus to replenish the senatorial and equestrian orders from the
best men in the provinces, on grounds that lead him to further suggest that
all subjects should 'be given a share of the πολιτεία (*politeia*)':

> (4) The more honourable men are connected to you, the more easily you
> will be able to administer everything in times of crisis (5) and the more easily
> you will persuade the subjects (οἱ ἀρχόμενοι) that you are not treating them
> like slaves or as in any way inferior to us, but rather are sharing all our
> advantages with them, including rulership (ἡγεμονία). (6) I won't retract
> that as a slip of the tongue. On the contrary I will go further and say that
> they must all be given a share of the πολιτεία. Having an equal share of this
> too, they will be our loyal allies, as if we were all living in a single city and
> reckoning it to be the true city and their own (cities) to be fields and villages.
> But we will return to this matter later to examine more carefully what must
> be done in order to avoid granting them everything at once. (52.19.4–6)[14]

Most scholars have construed 'they must all be given a share of the
πολιτεία' as a proposal for a universal grant of Roman citizenship, such
as Caracalla eventually effected with the *constitutio Antoniniana*.[15] But
several dissenters have denied that it has anything to do with citizenship.
Indeed, two of the three modern translators of the *Roman History* (Earnest
Cary and Alessandro Stroppa) construe πολιτεία as 'government',

[14] (4) ὅσῳ γὰρ ἂν πλείους εὐδόκιμοι ἄνδρες συνῶσί σοι, τοσούτῳ ῥᾷον αὐτός τε ἐν δέοντι πάντα
διοικήσεις, (5) καὶ τοὺς ἀρχομένους πείσεις ὅτι οὔτε ὡς δούλοις σφίσιν οὔθ' ὡς χείροσί πῃ ἡμῶν οὖσι
χρῇ, ἀλλὰ τά τε ἄλλα ἀγαθὰ πάντα τὰ ὑπάρχοντα ἡμῖν καὶ τὴν ἡγεμονίαν αὐτοῖς κοινοῖ, ὅπως ὡς
οἰκείαν αὐτὴν σπουδάζωσι. (6) καὶ τοσοῦτόν γε δέω τοῦθ' ὡς οὐκ ὀρθῶς εἰρημένον ἀναθέσθαι,
ὥστε καὶ τῆς πολιτείας πᾶσί σφισι μεταδοθῆναί φημι δεῖν, ἵνα καὶ ταύτης ἰσομοιροῦντες πιστοὶ
σύμμαχοι ἡμῖν ὦσιν, ὥσπερ τινὰ μίαν τὴν ἡμετέραν πόλιν οἰκοῦντες, καὶ ταύτην μὲν ὄντως πόλιν τὰ
δὲ δὴ σφέτερα ἀγροὺς καὶ κώμας νομίζοντες εἶναι. ἀλλὰ περὶ μὲν τούτου αὖθις ἀκριβέστερον
σκεψόμεθα ἃ χρὴ πρᾶξαι, ἵνα μὴ καὶ πάντα ἀθρόα αὐτοῖς χαρισώμεθα·
[15] The interpretation can be traced back to Wilhelm Xylander's seminal Latin translation (*ut hoc
insuper addam, omnibus iis esse ciuitatem donandam*, Xylander 1558). Xylander's interpretation was
endorsed by Dio's most important early modern editors in their revised versions of his translation –
H. Stephanus 1591 (*omnibus iis esse ciuitatem donandam*), Leunclavius 1606 (*omnibus iis ciuitatem esse
donandam*) and Reimarus 1750–2 (*omnibus iis civitatem esse dandam*) – and followed by all the
vernacular translations of the eighteenth and nineteenth centuries: Wagner 1783–96 ('man müsse
allen römischen Unterthanen das römische Bürgerrecht verleihen'), Penzel 1786–99 ('das ich
vielmehr ihnen allen das Bürgerrecht zu ertheilen rathe'), Viviani 1790–2 ('Anzi sono di parere
che si debba concedere la nostra cittadinanza a tutti loro'), Tafel 1831–44 ('Ich spreche sogar für Alle
das römisches Bürgerrecht an') and Gros and Boissée 1845–70 ('je prétends qu'il faut leur accorder à
tous le droit de cité'). The interpretation has been taken for granted by almost all modern scholars of
Dio. See, for example, Meyer 1891: 5; Millar 1964: 104–5; Hammond 1932: 92; Manuwald 1979: 22;
Steidle 1988: 204, 208; Hose 1994: 428; and Kemezis 2014: 127 n. 88.

interpreting the proposal as a matter of access to political office rather than citizenship.[16] Estelle Bertrand has recently suggested that πολιτεία just denotes a particular style of civic life.[17] Meanwhile, Valerio Marotta, while accepting the reference to citizenship, has wondered whether the intended beneficiaries were just the propertied elites rather than the population as a whole.[18] The decidedly abstract character of Dio's language here (notably the words ἀρχόμενοι, ἡγεμονία and πολιτεία) certainly introduces a potential for ambiguity and the near-unanimity of earlier scholarship is no guarantee against error. The *communis opinio* thus demands a reasoned defence against these dissenting readings.

The crux of the matter is the meaning of πολιτεία here. It is certainly a vague and capacious word in Dio, as elsewhere.[19] In Dio's usage, it can bear a range of related but distinct meanings including citizenship, the state (as a community of citizens), the constitution of the state and public life.[20] In many instances, the meaning is not easily disambiguated. In conjunction with verbs of giving, removing and possessing, however, πολιτεία always denotes citizenship. This is a particularly frequent usage, accounting for eighteen of sixty-six instances of πολιτεία in Dio (excluding the passage under discussion).[21] The citizenship in question is always Roman, even though it is almost never labelled as such.[22]

---

[16] 'I declare that the citizens ought every one actually to be given a share in the government' (Cary 1914–27). 'Dichiaro che tutti devono essere chiamati a prendere parte al governo' (Cresci Marrone et al. 1998). Earlier translators had followed Xylander in understanding πολιτεία as 'citizenship' (see above). The error (for so I will argue it is) seems to have originated with Herbert Foster, the first English translator of Dio and the model for Cary's Loeb translation: 'I say they ought all to be given a share in the government' (Foster 1874–1906: iv 19). Stroppa in turn seems to have followed Cary. The third modern translation, by Otto Veh, retains the conventional interpretation: 'ich vielmehr es als Notwendigkeit betrachte, sämtlichen sogar am Bürgerrecht Anteil zu geben' (Veh and Wirth 1985–92: iv 66). The only modern commentary, Reinhold 1988, inexplicably leaves this sentence without comment.

[17] Bertrand 2016: 720 n. 108 ('le mode de vie civique en vigueur à Rome').

[18] Marotta 2009: 105–6.

[19] Schofield 2006: 31–5; Harte and Lane 2013; Coltelloni-Trannoy 2016.

[20] Citizenship (see below), state (e.g. 41.57.1), constitution (e.g. 52.20.2), public life (e.g. 46.2.1). See further Freyburger-Galland 1997: 43–7.

[21] F 35.10 (*ES*) (οἱ Ῥωμαῖοι τὴν πολιτείαν αὐτοῖς ἔδωκαν), F 102.7 (*ELr*) (πολιτείαν … ἑαυτοῖς … δοθῆναι), 41.24.1 (τοῖς γε Γαδειρεῦσι πολιτείαν ἅπασιν ἔδωκεν), 41.63.3 (Γαλάταις τοῖς ἐντὸς τῶν Ἄλπεων ὑπὲρ τὸν Ἠριδανὸν οἰκοῦσι τὴν πολιτείαν … ἀπέδωκε), 43.39.5 (ἔδωκε … πολιτείαν τέ τισι), 44.53.3 (ἄλλοις πολιτείαν, ἄλλοις ἀτέλειαν πωλῶν), 45.23.6 (πολιτείας … τούς τε ἔχοντας ἀφῄρηται … καὶ τοῖς μὴ λαβοῦσι δέδωκε), 45.25.2 (τὰς πολιτείας καὶ τὰς ἀτελείας πωλεῖν), 48.45.3 (τοῖς τε Τιγγιτανοῖς πολιτεία ἐδόθη), 54.25.1 (τὴν πολιτείαν τοῖς μὲν δοὺς τοὺς δ' ἀφελόμενος), 57.17.2 (ἀνθρώποις … πολιτείαν Ῥωμαίων … δοῦναι), 60.7.2 (πολιτείᾳ τιμηθέντες), 60.17.4 (ἀναξίους τῆς πολιτείας ἀπήλασε), 60.17.7 (τοῖς τῆς πολιτείας παρ' αὐτοῦ τυχοῦσιν), 60.17.8 (τὴν πολιτείαν … ἐπώλουν), 63[64].8.2,2 (*EV*) (τοῖς τε ξένοις πολιτείαν ἐδίδου), 72[71].19.1 (*ELg*) (πολιτείαν … ἔχειν ἄξιοι).

[22] The single exception in which πολιτεία is explicitly qualified as Ῥωμαίων is 57.17.2.

Nevertheless, the construction used here – 'give a share of (μεταδίδωμι) the πολιτεία' – may appear vaguer than the more frequent 'give (δίδωμι) the πολιτεία'. But proof that it has the same meaning can be found four books later when Dio uses exactly the same phrase in a speech in which Augustus reproaches Roman citizens for failing to produce enough children to reproduce the citizen body:

> Do we not free our slaves chiefly for the express purpose of making out of them as many citizens as possible? And do we not give our allies a share of the citizenship in order that our numbers may increase? (56.7.6)[23]

Σύμμαχοι ('allies') is one of Dio's three regular terms for non-citizens, the others being ὑπήκοοι and ξένοι.[24] Augustus pairs the manumission of slaves and the enfranchisement of aliens in two grammatically parallel sentences, his point being that both practices illustrate the value placed on expanding the citizen body. Hence 'give a share of the πολιτεία' must denote enfranchisement here. It thus takes its place alongside 'bring into the πολιτεία' (ἐς τὴν πολιτείαν ... ἐσάγειν, 37.9.3) and 'inscribe in the πολιτεία' (ἐς τὴν πολιτείαν ἐσγράφειν, F 28.2 [EV] and 56.33.3) as variants on the usual 'give the πολιτεία' (τὴν πολιτείαν δοῦναι) in Dio's lexicon of enfranchisement.[25]

Who are the intended beneficiaries? The indirect object of the verb μεταδοθῆναί is πᾶσί σφισι ('all of them'), which refers back to οἱ ἀρχόμενοι in the preceding sentence. Ἀρχόμενοι (archomenoi) is Dio's most generic term for subjects. It usually denotes a population subject to a single figure – a king, emperor, governor, commander or generic ruler. When juxtaposed with the emperor, the ἀρχόμενοι are normally the whole population of the empire.[26] The category recurs twice more in Maecenas' speech, both times juxtaposed with the emperor alone.[27] The structure of this sentence, which balances the ἀρχόμενοι against 'you' (αὐτός τε ... διοικήσεις, καὶ τοὺς

[23] ἢ τοὺς μὲν δούλους δι' αὐτὸ τοῦτο μάλιστα ἐλευθεροῦμεν, ὅπως ὡς πλείστους ἐξ αὐτῶν πολίτας ποιώμεθα, τοῖς τε συμμάχοις τῆς πολιτείας μεταδίδομεν ὅπως πληθύωμεν (trans. E. Cary, Loeb Classical Library edition, adapted). Again Foster 1874–1906 ('give a share in the government') appears to have misled Cary 1914–27 ('give our allies a share in the government') and hence Cresci Marrone et al. 1998 ('rendendo partecipi del nostro governo'). But Veh and Wirth 1985–92 ('geben ... Anteil am Bürgerrecht') and all earlier translators back to Xylander 1558 (ciuitatem communicabimus) recognise the more precise meaning here.
[24] For the binary σύμμαχοι ~πολῖται, see 39.33.2, 56.7.6 and 56.23.1. This parallels the usage of Latin socii (see Lavan 2013, ch. 1).
[25] For the eleven instances of τὴν πολιτείαν δοῦναι, see n. 21 above.
[26] See, for example, 53.18.3, where Dio includes 'us' among the emperor's ἀρχόμενοι in an excursus on the title pater patriae.
[27] 52.25.4, 52.34.1.

ἀρχομένους πείσεις [sections 4–5 in the passage]), initially favours the same interpretation here. It therefore comes as a surprise to find 'them' (σφίσιν) opposed to 'us' (ἡμῶν) in the clause that follows. Where is the line between 'us' and 'them' to be drawn? Meyer Reinhold, in his commentary on this passage, glosses ἀρχόμενοι as 'all free persons below the rank of Dio's aristocratic elites, the senators and *equites*'.[28] This makes some sense in this context as Maecenas has just been discussing the recruitment of these orders. But Maecenas has also repeatedly foregrounded a spatial distinction between Italians and provincials, first by enjoining Augustus to recruit senators not just from Italy but also from among the 'allies and subjects' (καὶ παρὰ τῶν συμμάχων τῶν τε ὑπηκόων, 52.19.2), secondly by suggesting that this is the best way to ensure the loyalty of the provinces (ἔθνη, 52.19.3), and thirdly by recommending the equestrian order be recruited from the best men 'in each place' (ἑκασταχόθι, 19.4). In this context, it is more natural to understand ἀρχόμενοι as denoting specifically the inhabitants of the provinces, functioning as a synonym for ὑπήκοοι and σύμμαχοι, the two terms that Dio normally uses together or individually to refer to the provincial and/or non-citizen population (a distinction that Dio often blurs).[29] The variation is appropriate because Dio has just used both other terms a few sentences earlier. In any case there is nothing that can restrict its meaning to some subset of non-citizen provincials, such as the propertied elite, as Marotta suggested.

The natural reading of Dio's language is reinforced by the reader's contextual knowledge. On all plausible chronologies, the speech of Maecenas was written after the *constitutio Antoniniana*.[30] Given knowledge of that grant, it would be hard to interpret a proposal to give all the *archomenoi* a share of the *politeia* as anything other than an anticipation of the universal enfranchisement that Caracalla had, in fact, effected. Indeed, the anachronism of the proposal seems to be signposted by Maecenas' own move – unique in the body of the speech – to postpone further discussion: 'We will return to this matter again to examine more carefully what must be done in order to avoid granting them everything at once' (52.19.6).[31] The deferral and the warning

---

[28] Reinhold 1988: 189.

[29] The phrases ὑπήκοοι, τὸ ὑπήκοον and ἡ ὑπήκοος are frequently used to denote both provincials as opposed to Italians (36.36.4, 37.25.4, 41.59.4, 42.20.4, 52.21.8, 57.2.5, 65[66].8.4 [*EV*]) and peregrines in contradistinction to citizens (57.6.2, 60.2.5). For σύμμαχοι see n. 24 above. In other contexts, Dio deploys ὑπήκοοι and σύμμαχοι as mutually exclusive categories in a triad whose third component is either the population of Italy (52.19.2) or the citizen body (41.57.3, 52.27.1, 59.21.3). See also Freyburger-Galland 1997: 41–2.

[30] See n. 7 above.

[31] Reinhold (1988: 190) suggests that Maecenas delivers on his promise to return to the matter later in the speech, with the discussion of 'the curtailment of the rights and expenditures of cities' at

against premature action mark this proposal in particular, as something to be realised in the future. This is an explicit concession to the reader's knowledge that this is an action that was not taken until Dio's own time.

IV Citizenship in the Speech of Maecenas

What is this proposal doing in Maecenas' speech?[32] The long second half of the speech with its detailed recommendations about how the empire should be administered – quite different from the more abstract discussion of monarchy and *demokratia* in its first half and the preceding speech of Agrippa – is a highly idiosyncratic text. Some obvious anachronisms have led many scholars to the conclusion that the second half of the speech originated as a 'political pamphlet' laying out a programme of reform for his own troubled times and was inserted later – and somewhat incongruously – into the debate on monarchy.[33] Dissenting voices have insisted that the speech is, in fact, integrated into the narrative in which it is embedded and well fitted to its dramatic context of 29 BC.[34] The best readings acknowledge that neither of these positions can account for the speech in its entirety. It is a complex text that performs multiple functions simultaneously: helping to frame the transition from the republican to the imperial narratives, exploring the key challenges that faced Augustus and his successors and setting out an idealised vision of how the empire should function (an ideal with implications for Dio's own time).[35] A better understanding of the function of speeches in historiography has also undermined the notion of Maecenas as a 'mouthpiece' for Dio. Embedded speeches are a distinctive feature of the genre. The many functions they perform require a sharp distinction between their speakers and the narrative voice.[36] For all the parallels between the speech and statements by the narrator, the conventions of the genre of historiography leave an unbridgeable divide between embedded speech and narrative. 'Maecenas is not Dio.'[37]

52.30.2–10. But there is no mention of citizenship there. Rather, Maecenas' deferral takes us outside the compass of his speech to an undetermined point in the future.

[32] See Kemezis 2018 for a slightly different perspective. Where he is interested in the possibility of distinguishing the grant imagined by Maecenas from the historical *constitutio Antoniniana*, I focus on the close parallels between them. It is striking that Maecenas is made to imagine universal rather than selective enfranchisement as the best way to realise an aristocratic order.

[33] Most influentially Meyer 1891; Bleicken 1962; and Millar 1964: 106–18 esp. 107 ('political pamphlet').

[34] Hammond 1932; Schmidt 1999.

[35] See especially Rich 1989: 98–100; Rich 1990: 14–15; Kemezis 2014: 127–35.

[36] See Marincola 2007 for a survey of speech in historiography, focussing on the Greek tradition.

[37] Rich 1989: 99. Kemezis 2014: 132–3 notes the speech's uncompromising commitment to 'centralization and uniformity' as a potentially vulnerable idiosyncrasy of Maecenas' vision.

The anachronisms in the speech cannot all be explained as a programme for Dio's present. Maecenas' proposals collapse the history of the Principate, ranging from institutions that can be attributed to Augustus (e.g. the standing army, 52.27), through various later developments that were established practice by the Severan period (e.g. the judicial responsibilities of the *praefectus urbi*, 52.21.2) to ideas that would be innovations in Dio's own time (e.g. the office of 'sub-censor', 52.21.3–7). Dio implicitly acknowledges the collapse of chronology in his description of Augustus' response to Maecenas' speech:

> He did not, however, immediately put into effect all his suggestions, fearing to meet with failure at some point if he purposed to change the ways of all mankind at a stroke; but he introduced some reforms at the moment and some at a later time, leaving still others for those to effect who should subsequently hold the Principate, in the belief that as time passed a better opportunity would be found to put these last into operation. (52.41.1–2)[38]

This comment frames Maecenas' proposals as a blueprint for the organisation of the empire whose realisation was initiated by Augustus and developed by his successors, with some work still to be done.

Universal citizenship clearly falls into the category of reforms that were at best inchoate under Augustus but had been realised by the time of writing. As Adam Kemezis has observed, Maecenas' proposal works to represent the recent *constitutio Antoniniana* as the natural conclusion of the piecemeal diffusion of citizenship that was in its early stages under Augustus and had produced the Antonine aristocracy into which Dio himself was born.[39] The proposal has a rationale that is well integrated with the rest of the speech. Commentary has tended to focus on the metaphor that follows it – the empire as a polis in which Rome is the urban centre and Italy and the provinces the *chora*.[40] But it is the sentence that precedes it that provides the motivation for the proposal:

> The more honourable men are connected to you, the more easily you will be able to administer everything in times of crisis and the more easily you will

---

[38] οὐ μέντοι καὶ πάντα εὐθὺς ὥσπερ ὑπετέθειτο ἔπραξε, φοβηθεὶς μὴ καὶ σφαλῇ τι, ἀθρόως μεταρρυθμίσαι τοὺς ἀνθρώπους ἐθελήσας· ἀλλὰ τὰ μὲν παραχρῆμα μετεκόσμησε τὰ δ' ὕστερον, καί τινα καὶ τοῖς μετὰ ταῦτα ἄρξουσι ποιῆσαι κατέλιπεν ὡς καὶ κατὰ καιρὸν μᾶλλον ἐν τῷ χρόνῳ γενησόμενα (trans. E. Cary, Loeb Classical Library edition).

[39] See Kemezis 2018: 101: 'Dio is looking at the present of imperially decreed universal citizenship, but he is trying to integrate it into the historical processes that created the Antonine aristocracy from which he sprang, and which he still idealizes in its various forms and sees as the rightful organic continuation of the monarchical state that Augustus created.'

[40] Reinhold 1988 *ad loc.*

persuade the *archomenoi* that you are not treating them like slaves (ὡς δούλοις) or as in any way inferior (χείρους) to us, but rather are sharing all our advantages (τὰ ὑπάρχοντα) with them, including rulership. (52.19.4–5)[41]

This is what prompts the proposal of universal citizenship.

The reference to advantages evokes the material privileges of citizenship. But the idea of being treated like slaves and the language of inferiority also foreground questions of honour and worth. Maecenas is certainly not proposing a great levelling. His speech is profoundly aristocratic in its values. It assumes a natural hierarchy in which those with wealth and ancestry also excel in virtue, ability and judgement. The regime he proposes is one in which Augustus rules in collaboration with 'the best men' (οἱ ἄριστοι, 52.14.3, οἱ ἄριστοι ἄνδρες, 52.15.1), his 'equals in honour' (ὁμότιμοι, 15.1). The 'best men' is a familiar aristocratic trope that equates social status with moral worth. A cluster of related tropes pervades the speech: 'the prudent class' (τὸ σῶφρον, 52.14.5), 'the best class' (τὸ βέλτιστον, 52.14.5), 'men of good repute' (εὐδόκιμοι ἄνδρες, 52.19.4). Maecenas gives a more precise definition of an aristocracy of birth, virtue and wealth in his advice that the senatorial order be recruited from all 'the noblest, best and wealthiest men' (τούς τε γενναιοτάτους καὶ τοὺς ἀρίστους τούς τε πλουσιωτάτους, 52.19.2). The triad is echoed three sentences later in his specification of the criteria for admission to the equestrian order ('such men as hold second place in their several districts as regards birth, excellence and wealth', τὰ δευτερεῖα ἑκασταχόθι καὶ γένει καὶ ἀρετῇ καὶ πλούτῳ φερομένους, 52.19.4), and again when he insists on the need for these distinctions (πλοῦτον ... εὐγένειαν ... ἄλλο τι ἀρετῆς, 52.26.4) to be combined with a suitable education. The underlying hierarchy of worth is to be made manifest in the hierarchy of honour. True democracy, he insists, 'prefers for honour the prudent class everywhere' (τό τε σῶφρον πανταχοῦ προτιμῶσα, 52.14.5) and 'accords all men equality according to their worth' (τὸ ἴσον ἅπασι κατὰ τὴν ἀξίαν ἀπονέμουσα, 52.14.5). It would thus be nonsensical to construe Maecenas' recommendation that Augustus 'persuade the subjects ... that they are not being treated as in any way inferior to us' as a proposal for an egalitarian social order. Rather, what he is envisaging is a social order in which men of birth, wealth

---

[41] ὅσῳ γὰρ ἂν πλείους εὐδόκιμοι ἄνδρες συνῶσί σοι, τοσούτῳ ῥᾷον αὐτός τε ἐν δέοντι πάντα διοικήσεις, (5) καὶ τοὺς ἀρχομένους πείσεις ὅτι οὔτε ὡς δούλοις σφίσιν οὔθ' ὡς χείροσί πῃ ἡμῶν οὖσι χρῇ, ἀλλὰ τά τε ἄλλα ἀγαθὰ πάντα τὰ ὑπάρχοντα ἡμῖν καὶ τὴν ἡγεμονίαν αὐτοῖς κοινοῖ, ὅπως ὡς οἰκείαν αὐτὴν σπουδάζωσι.

and ability are not despised merely because they lack Roman citizenship. His objective is not to collapse the hierarchy of honour, but rather to remove a source of distortion within it. As such, the proposal to make citizenship universal in order to erase the distinction between citizens and non-citizens is consonant with his later proposals to provincialise Italy (52.22) and make tribute universal (52.28.6), both of which would remove privileges that elevated Italy over the provinces. Together these measures would eliminate the two distinctions that could be seen as constituting a class of subjects (ὑπήκooι) that cuts across the hierarchy of worth. Eliminating these distortions would allow men to be evaluated by their personal merits alone.[42]

V Discrepant Voices

Maecenas' speech invites the reader to conceive of Caracalla's edict as the realisation of a project conceived by Maecenas and Augustus but deliberately postponed until a more opportune moment. This makes it all the more remarkable that the *constitutio Antoniniana* itself is then dismissed so brusquely in the narrative of Caracalla's reign. The tension between Maecenas' implicit endorsement and the narrator's dismissive notice is not an isolated phenomenon. There are other jarring notes that suggest that Dio's handling of the topic of enfranchisement is more complex than it may at first appear. The most striking example is the contradiction between Maecenas' proposal of universal enfranchisement and the entirely opposite advice in Augustus' own instructions to his successors a few books later. Dio records that Augustus left a book containing directions on several matters to be read after his death. The first instruction concerned enfranchisement:

> The fourth [book contained] various instructions and commands for Tiberius and the public, among them that they should not free many slaves, lest they fill the city with a heterogeneous rabble, and that they should not enrol many people as citizens, to ensure that the distinction between themselves and the subjects remained clear. (56.33.3 [Xiph.])[43]

---

[42] On the two distinctions underlying Dio's use of ὑπήκooι and cognates, see n. 29 above.

[43] τὸ τέταρτον ἐντολὰς καὶ ἐπισκήψεις τῷ Τιβερίῳ καὶ τῷ κοινῷ, ἄλλας τε καὶ ὅπως μήτ’ ἀπελευθερῶσι πολλούς, ἵνα μὴ παντοδαποῦ ὄχλου τὴν πόλιν πληρώσωσι, μήτ’ αὖ ἐς τὴν πολιτείαν συχνοὺς ἐσγράφωσιν, ἵνα πολὺ τὸ διάφορον αὐτοῖς πρὸς τοὺς ὑπηκόους ᾖ.

The passage fell in one of the missing folios of the *Codex Marcianus*, but Xiphilinus seems to have reproduced the missing text largely intact (though there may have been some abbreviation).[44]

Whereas Maecenas sought to convince Augustus of the desirability of enfranchising the whole population of the empire, Augustus enjoins Tiberius to grant citizenship sparingly. He views both the manumission of slaves (the other source of new citizens) and the enfranchisement of aliens as potentially problematic. Whereas Augustus' anxiety about slaves relates to their heterogeneity and low character, his anxiety about aliens concerns hierarchy within the empire. He insists on the desirability of a sharp distinction between 'themselves' (i.e. the Roman people) and their subjects (ὑπήκοοι, Dio's usual term for non-citizens and/or provincials as a subject population).[45] He sees an exclusive citizenship as the key to maintaining that divide. Augustus' instructions are doubly opposed to Maecenas' earlier advice. Not only does Augustus dismiss the idea of mass enfranchisement, but he also rejects the premise on which Maecenas' proposal of universal enfranchisement was based. Maecenas' vision of a hierarchy of honour based solely on birth, wealth and excellence is implicitly rejected by Augustus when he insists on the need to maintain a distinction between a ruling people and its ὑπήκοοι.

Like the description of the will and other texts that precedes it, this is a record of a historical document rather than a speech. The conventions of the genre would not normally allow the same degree of freedom as in the composition of a speech. But the historicity of this particular document is highly controversial. Dio records that Augustus left four books with his will: (i) instructions for his funeral, (ii) his *Res Gestae*, (iii) an overview of military, fiscal and administrative matters (Suetonius' *breviarium totius imperii*) and (iv) instructions and advice on various topics, of which Dio specifies three: restricting the enfranchisement of slaves and peregrines, avoiding the concentration of power in the hands of one person and ending imperial expansion. But Suetonius says that Augustus only left three documents – the first three listed by Dio; he makes no mention of any testamentary advice or instructions.[46] Tacitus confirms the existence of the *breviarium* and notes that Augustus had also advised against further expansion, without indicating whether that advice was in the *breviarium* or a separate document.[47] It has been suggested that the fourth document

---

[44] Boissevain II.544.   [45] See n. 29, above.   [46] Suet. *Aug.* 101.6.

[47] Tac. *Ann.* 1.11.3-4. Letta 2016b: 252 is rightly critical of Ober's suggestion that Tacitus could be referring to verbal advice to Tiberius (Ober 1982: 312). The natural reading is that this is a text. See further Chapter 3 by Cesare Letta in this volume.

has been invented by Dio to provide a speech-like opportunity to further explore ideas about the governance of the empire.[48] If it is an invention, it develops ideas that were already associated with Augustus. Tacitus records his advice against expanding the empire, and Suetonius notes elsewhere that Augustus was reluctant to enfranchise too many peregrines because he did not want the Roman people to be polluted by foreign blood or the distinction of Roman citizenship to be cheapened.[49] But it remains possible that it is Suetonius who is mistaken in the list of documents: It is clear that Augustus left advice in some form, yet Suetonius omits to mention it. No certainty is possible on the limited evidence available.[50] If the invention hypothesis is right, then Dio has constructed a striking contradiction with the earlier advice of Maecenas by making citizenship one of its three subjects. Even if he is just following an earlier tradition, he may have given greater emphasis to the topic of citizenship (he implies that the three topics he mentions are just a selection). In any case, he has expressed Augustus' vision in his own language of social distinction.[51]

Other voices in the text extend the implicit tension between Maecenas and Augustus earlier and later in Dio's history. Maecenas probably echoed the language of proponents of enfranchisement at the time of the Latin Revolt (around Book 7) and the Social War (somewhere in Books 30 to 35). Even though Dio's narratives of both these pivotal moments in the history of the citizenship have been lost, one hint of the role that considerations of honour played in them can be found in Zonaras' synopsis of his account of the Latin Revolt.

As mentioned earlier, citizenship is entirely absent from Zonaras' narrative of the revolt. He attributes the revolt to the growing pride of the Latins:

> Now the Latins, although under treaty with the Romans, revolted and began war. They were filled with pride (φρόνημα) for the reason that they had an abundance of youthful warriors and had become thoroughly expert

---

[48] Ober 1982, building on Hohl 1937.

[49] *sincerum atque ab omni colluvione peregrini ac servilis sanguinis incorruptum servare populum . . . civitatis Romanae vulgari honorem* (Suet. *Aug.* 40.3).

[50] Rich 1990: 17 is agnostic; Swan 1997 is inclined to disbelieve Dio; Letta 2016b: 25-2 defends Dio, suggesting that he was relying on the *acta senatus* from the senate meeting in which the texts were read.

[51] In the context of social relations, Dio uses διαφέρειν and its cognates to denote superiority and inferiority, not mere difference. See διάφορον ('inferior') at 50.19.1, διαφέρειν ('be superior') at 41.31.2 and διαφερόντως at 38.39.3 ('rising above', again with reference to the superiority of the Roman people and in close proximity to ἀξίωμα, discussed further below).

in warfare as a result of their constant campaigning with the Romans. (Zonar. 7.26.1)[52]

Zonaras makes no mention of the massive extension of citizenship that followed the revolt, merely noting that the Latins were defeated.[53] But a verbatim extract from the end of Dio's original indicates that he attributed the revolt at least in part to Latin demands for citizenship that were rejected by the Romans:

> The Romans, by way of bringing the Latins in turn to a condition of friendliness, granted them citizenship, so that they secured equal privileges with themselves. Those rights which they would not share with that nation when it threatened war and for which they underwent so many dangers they voluntarily voted to it now that it had been conquered. Thus they rewarded some for their alliance and others because they had made no move to rebel. (F 35.10 [ES])[54]

The implicit narrative of demands for citizenship rejected, revolt against Rome and then citizenship granted after Roman victory is clearly anachronistic, reimagining the Latin Revolt as an earlier iteration of the Social War.[55] A similar conflation is implicit in some aspects of Livy's parallel account, notably the speeches attributed to the Latin leader and in his representation of the grants of citizenship that followed as a form of reward.[56] But Dio evokes the parallel more boldly here. He may well be responsible for the emphasis.[57]

---

[52] Λατῖνοι δὲ καίπερ ἔνσπονδοι τοῖς Ῥωμαίοις ὄντες ἀπέστησαν καὶ πόλεμον ἤραντο, ἐν φρονήματι γεγονότες ὅτι τε νεότητι ἤκμαζον καὶ τὰ πολεμικὰ ἐκ τῆς ἀεὶ σὺν αὐτοῖς στρατείας ἀκριβῶς ἤσκηντο. (trans. E. Cary, Loeb Classical Library edition)

[53] Zonar. 7.26.5: οἱ μὲν οὖν Λατῖνοι οὕτως ἥττηντο.

[54] Ὅτι ἀνθυπαγόμενοι τοὺς Λατίνους ἐς εὔνοιαν οἱ Ῥωμαῖοι τὴν πολιτείαν αὐτοῖς ἔδωκαν, ὥστε καὶ τῶν ὁμοίων σφίσι μεταλαμβάνειν· ὧν γὰρ ἀπειλοῦσι τὸν πόλεμον οὐ μετέδοσαν καὶ δι' ἃ τοσούτους κινδύνους ὑπέστησαν, ταῦτα τότε κρατήσαντες αὐτῶν αὐτεπάγγελτοι τούτοις ἐψηφίσαντο, τοὺς μὲν τῆς συμμαχίας, τοὺς δὲ ὅτι μηδὲν ἐνεόχμωσαν ἀμειβόμενοι. (trans. E. Cary, Loeb Classical Library edition)

[55] Urso 2013.   [56] Oakley 1997–2005: 2.409–10 and 538; Urso 2013: 78–9.

[57] Urso 2013: 77–8 argues that F 35.10 (ES) implies a perspective hostile to the enfranchisement of the Italians and must date back to a historian of the early first century BC. But the observation that the Romans granting what they initially refused can equally well be understood as critical of the initial refusal to share citizenship as of the later decision to grant it, so there is no need to assume a near-contemporary critic as the source. Urso also assumes that the parallel was only invoked at the end of Dio's narrative, but the sentence that survives in F 35.10 (ES) would be odd if there had been no discussion of citizenship at the start of the narrative. It is more likely that demands for citizenship figured in his account of the outbreak of the revolt, but were omitted by Zonaras, as with this remark about the aftermath of the revolt.

The conflict over citizenship has disappeared in Zonaras' version, but Zonaras does, however, preserve one indication that Dio described it in terms that anticipated Maecenas' language in Book 52. While recounting the single combat between Titus Manlius and a Latin commander that resulted in Manlius' execution for disobedience, Zonaras includes a brief passage of direct speech, probably taken verbatim from Dio, in which the Latin challenges Manlius to single combat:[58]

> Are you not the son of Torquatus? Do you not give yourself airs because of your father's torc? Or are you Romans strong and courageous against those vicious Gauls, but fear us Latins? Why, then, do you presume [ἀξιοῦτε] to rule over us? Why do you issue commands as if we were inferior to you [ὡς χείροσιν ὑμῶν]? (Zonar. 7.26.4)[59]

The speech hints at Latin grievances that have otherwise been elided by Zonaras. The accusation that the Romans treat the Latins 'as if we were inferior to you' anticipates precisely the language in which Maecenas couches his proposal of a universal grant of citizenship – as a means of persuading the subjects that they are not being treated 'as in any way inferior to us' (ὡς χείροσί πῃ ἡμῶν, 52.19.5). The focus on questions of worth and honour can also be seen in the use of the verb ἀξιόω (literally, 'deem worthy of'). It may also survive in Zonaras' attribution of the revolt to Latin φρόνημα at the beginning of his narrative, since Dio often uses that noun to express the internal dimension of honour – what Julian Pitt-Rivers called the 'claim to pride'.[60] The focus on worth is unparalleled in Livy's version of the exchange.[61] In short, it seems likely that Dio

[58] On Zonaras' fidelity to Dio's original when he does reproduce direct speech, see Bellissime and Berbessou-Brouset 2016: 107.

[59] οὐ σὺ μέντοι Τουρκουάτου υἱὸς εἶ; οὐ σεμνύνει τῷ στρεπτῷ τοῦ πατρός; ἢ πρὸς μὲν Γαλάτας ἀνθρώπους φθόρους ἔρρωσθε καὶ ἀνδρίζεσθε, τοὺς δὲ δὴ Λατίνους ἡμᾶς φοβεῖσθε; τί οὖν ἄρχειν ἡμῶν ἀξιοῦτε; τί δ' ὡς χείροσιν ὑμῶν ἐπιτάσσετε; (trans. E. Cary, Loeb Classical Library edition, adapted)

[60] For the use of φρόνημα and its cognates with regard to the hierarchy of honour, see especially 5.21.1 (οἱ Φάβιοι ἐπί τε τῷ γένει καὶ τῷ πλούτῳ ὅμοια τοῖς ἀρίστοις φρονοῦντες), 20.68.1 (οἱ Ῥόδιοι φρόνημα πολὺ πρότερον σχόντες), 50.28.3 (τοῦ τὸ ἀξίωμα τὸ τῶν προγόνων διασῶσαι, τοῦ τὸ φρόνημα τὸ οἰκεῖον φυλάξαι) and 52.8.2–5 (esp. οὐ γὰρ ἔστιν οὔτ' ἄνευ φρονήματος ἀξιόλογον ἄνδρα φῦναι). On the internal and external aspects of honour, see Julian Pitt-Rivers' seminal definition: 'Honor is the value of a person in his own eyes but also in the eyes of his society. It is his estimation of his own worth, his *claim* to pride, but it is also the acknowledgement of that claim, his excellence recognised by society, his *right* to pride' (Pitt-Rivers 1977: 1).

[61] Livy 8.7.3–8, where the Latin commander merely asserts his greater prowess: *cernatur quantum eques Latinus Romano praestet.*

represented the Latins' desire for Roman citizenship as growing out of a sense that their exclusion from the citizen body made them seem contemptible to the Romans.

Conceiving the desirability of citizenship in terms of worth, honour and contempt is certainly not original to Dio. It is already present in the early imperial historiography of the Social War.[62] What is clear, however, is that Dio followed that tradition and perhaps accentuated the focus on honour in his account of the Latin Revolt. One can only assume that he presented the origins of the Social War in similar terms, though that account has been lost entirely. Most importantly, he returned to the same ideas and language in making Maecenas' case for universal citizenship. In so doing, he made an important leap – one that would probably have been unimaginable for most early imperial historians – from the familiar case for granting citizenship to all Latins or Italians to the more novel case for extending it to all provincials.

But the proponents of mass enfranchisement do not stand unchallenged in Dio's work. We can assume that figures opposed to the extension of citizenship to the Latins and Italians were allowed to voice arguments for maintaining the distinction between the Roman people and its subjects, arguments that probably found some echoes in Augustus' warning against extending citizenship too widely. Similar sentiments continue to be expressed by Roman speakers in the imperial books, most notably in the speech of Suetonius Paulinus in Book 62. Dio's account of Boudicca's revolt under Nero included an extensive *hortatio* by the Roman commander. The speech takes on particular importance because of the extreme rarity of extended direct speech in the imperial books.[63] The text is transmitted largely or wholly intact in Xiphilinus' epitome (62[61].9–11 [Xiph.]).[64]

Paulinus cites several reasons to be confident of victory, the last of which is the inherent superiority of the Romans over their subjects:

> For my part, I hope, above all, that victory will be ours; first, because the gods are our allies . . . ; second, because of the courage that is our heritage, since we are Romans and have triumphed over all mankind by our valour;

[62] See, for example, Velleius 2.15.2 on the grievances of the Italians: They had not been admitted into citizenship of a state that through their efforts had reached the exalted position (*fastigium*) from which it was able to despise (*fastidire*) men of the same race and blood as foreigners and aliens. See also 2.20.5 on concern to preserve the *dignitas* of the old citizens after the grants.

[63] It is one of just three certain examples in Books 61–80 (the others being the paired speech of Boudicca and Marcus Aurelius' speech at 71.24–6). See Rich 2019.

[64] On Xiphilinus' reproduction of speeches in Dio, see Mallan 2013b and Berbessou-Broustet 2016.

next, because of our experience ... ; and lastly, because of our honour [ἀξίωμα], for those with whom we are about to engage are not rivals, but our slaves, whom we conquered even when they were free and independent. (62[62].11.3 [Xiph.])[65]

Paulinus assures his men that they can be confident of victory because the provincial rebels are inferior by virtue of their status as conquered subjects. His claim centres on the concept of ἀξίωμα. A cognate of ἀξιόω ('deem worthy'), it serves to denote social distinction of various kinds (rank, status, reputation), clothing them in the language of worth.[66] It expresses a vision of the social order in which the hierarchy of honour and rank reflects an underlying, natural hierarchy of character and ability. The interweaving of social and natural inferiority implicit in the use of ἀξίωμα is repeated in the slave metaphor that follows. This simultaneously disparages the Britons as contemptible and equates this with a real inferiority that will be revealed on the battlefield. Paulinus' insistence that the British provincials are slaves (δούλοις ἡμετέροις) because they are subjects is precisely what Maecenas seeks to deny when he advises Augustus to persuade the subjects that you are not treating them 'like slaves' (ὡς δούλοις). Suetonius thus takes his place alongside Augustus in implicitly rejecting Maecenas' view that an exclusive citizenship distorts the economy of honour, instead insisting on the superiority of the ruling people over its subjects.

VI   The Narrative Voice

The attentive reader of the *Roman History* is confronted with two sharply divergent visions of the proper function of Roman citizenship, visions that seem to have come into conflict in at least three contexts – with regard to the Latins in the fourth century BC, the Italians in the late Republic and the provincials in the imperial period. The visions are articulated in a shared language of honour. The thematisation of honour has precedent in the historiographical tradition on the Latin Revolt and the Social War, but Dio seems to have accentuated the focus and to have extended the theme into the imperial period, implicitly constructing a parallel between the provincials of the Principate and the Latins and Italians of the Republic. The

---

[65] μάλιστα μὲν οὖν ἔγωγε νικήσειν ἡμᾶς ἐλπίζω καὶ τῇ παρὰ τῶν θεῶν συμμαχίᾳ ... καὶ τῇ πατρῴᾳ ἡμῶν ἀνδρίᾳ, Ῥωμαίους τε ὄντας καὶ ταῖς ἀρεταῖς ἁπάντων ἀνθρώπων κεκρατηκότας, καὶ ταῖς ἐμπειρίαις ... τῷ τε ἀξιώματι (οὐ γὰρ ἀντιπάλοις τισὶν ἀλλὰ δούλοις ἡμετέροις συμβαλοῦμεν, οὓς καὶ ἐλευθέρους καὶ αὐτονόμους ὄντας ἐνικήσαμεν)· (trans. E. Cary, Loeb Classical Library edition, adapted)

[66] On the place of ἀξίωμα in the Greek lexicon of honour, see Lendon 1997: 277.

recurring connections between citizenship and honour are too consistent to be discounted as the fossils of earlier writing.

Yet it is striking that the two visions are always attributed to historical figures within the text, usually in embedded speeches, and that the narrator provides no commentary on the contradiction between them. One might suspect that Dio, himself the progeny of a propertied Bithynian family that probably acquired citizenship in the early principate, would be more likely to identify with the vision articulated by Maecenas than that attributed to Augustus and implicitly espoused by Suetonius Paulinus. Yet the narrator remains silent – even when he comes to the *constitutio Antoniniana* itself.

The closest the narrator comes to pronouncing on the theme of citizenship and honour is in the narrative of the reign of Claudius. His reign is unique in eliciting a synoptic discussion of issues related to citizenship (60.17.4–8). Dio records that Claudius stripped Roman citizenship from some who did not deserve of it, but also granted it without restraint to many others. For some reason, Dio sees fit to explain why Roman citizenship was considered so desirable:

> Since Romans were held in higher esteem (προετετίμηντο) than non-citizens (ξένων) in almost every respect, many petitioned for it from himself personally and purchased it from Messalina and the Caesariani [imperial freedmen and slaves]. (60.17.5)[67]

The verb προτιμάω is a significant choice to express the privileges of citizenship. It emphasises not so much the material benefits that arise from preferential treatment as the evaluation of worth that underlies it. This is the same language in which Maecenas articulates his vision of an aristocratic order which 'prefers for honour the prudent class everywhere' (τό τε σῶφρον πανταχοῦ προτιμῶσα) (52.14.5). Thus, we seem to see the narrator thinking in the same terms he attributes to Maecenas. Yet the narrator still provides no explicit comment on the merits or failings of an imperial order in which the first determinant of a free man's worth was whether or not he was a Roman citizen. A reader convinced by Maecenas would see this as a distortion of the natural social order. But one who aligns with Augustus and Suetonius Paulinus would see it as entirely appropriate – albeit jeopardised by Claudius' indiscriminate use of enfranchisement. One may well suspect that Dio's sympathies put him in the former camp, but they remain elusive here.

---

[67] ἐπειδὴ γὰρ ἐν πᾶσιν ὡς εἰπεῖν οἱ Ῥωμαῖοι τῶν ξένων προετετίμηντο, πολλοὶ αὐτὴν παρά τε αὐτοῦ ἐκείνου ᾐτοῦντο καὶ παρὰ τῆς Μεσσαλίνης τῶν τε Καισαρείων ὠνοῦντο.

The famous reference to the *constitutio Antoniniana* is similarly ambivalent:

> This was the reason why he made all the people in his empire Romans. He said he was giving/showing them honour, but his real purpose was to increase his revenues by this means, since aliens did not pay most of these [taxes]. (78(77).9.5 [*EV*])[68]

This passage falls far outside the extant books of Dio. Xiphilinus' summary does not even mention the grant. But the sentence is preserved in a long extract in the tenth-century *Excerpta Constantiniana*. Since editorial interventions in the *Excerpta* tend to be concentrated at the beginning and end of excerpts and this particular sentence is deep in the body of a relatively lengthy excerpt, it almost certainly preserves Dio verbatim.[69] We can be confident that he did not say any more about the grant here, though it remains possible that there was another notice elsewhere that was similarly ignored by Xiphilinus.

The remark clearly disparages Caracalla by impugning his motives, but it makes no explicit comment about the intrinsic merits of the grant itself. The placement certainly raises questions about its importance. The issue is not just its brevity but the way it is nested deep inside an account of Caracalla's fiscal exactions. The reference to the citizenship grant is a parenthetical remark appended to a description of an increase in the manumission and inheritance taxes (both levied exclusively on citizens), which is itself just the last of four forms of exaction that impoverished the empire as a whole (the others being the crown tax, contributions of provisions and 'gifts') – all of which are listed just by way of preamble (78[77].9.2–5 [*EV*]) to Dio's real focus: the extraordinary exactions that fell specifically on senators (78[77].9.6–7 [*EV*]).

Yet, it is notable that even this brief remark revisits the familiar nexus of citizenship and honour. Dio writes that the ostensible purpose of the grant was to give or show honour (τιμῶν) to the non-citizen population. A casual reader might assume that the criticism of Caracalla is compounded by the fact that even his professed motive was trivial. In the context of the whole work, however, the goal of honouring peregrines is far from insignificant. This was essentially the rationale for Maecenas' proposal of universal enfranchisement and is the key point of contention in the scattered discussion of the merits of enfranchisement. Whatever imperial

---

[68] οὗ ἕνεκα καὶ Ῥωμαίους πάντας τοὺς ἐν τῇ ἀρχῇ αὐτοῦ, λόγῳ μὲν τιμῶν, ἔργῳ δὲ ὅπως πλείω αὐτῷ καὶ ἐκ τοῦ τοιούτου προσίῃ διὰ τὸ τοὺς ξένους τὰ πολλὰ αὐτῶν μὴ συντελεῖν, ἀπέδειξεν.

[69] Boissevain III.771–2; Roberto 2009; and Rich 2016: 272–4.

pronouncements Dio may be alluding to here, he seems to have para-phrased them in his own language. Does this mean that the grant itself and its declared purpose should be seen as meritorious, even if the real motive is not? Again, the narrator remains silent.

Fergus Millar (for whom the connection between Maecenas' proposal and Caracalla's grant was self-evident) explained the discrepancy by sug-gesting that the two texts were written for different audiences. The speech of Maecenas, he suggested, was originally written for Caracalla while he and Dio were both in Nicomedia, whereas the later remark reflects Dio's 'own attitude'.[70] His explanation depends on unprovable speculation about the precise date of composition. It is also hard to reconcile with the fact that the proposal is so well integrated into Maecenas' speech as a whole (not to mention the fact that it was not excised during later revisions). It is surely at least as plausible that Dio did see the grant as having intrinsic merit, and that this emerges in Book 52, but that his overarching conception of Caracalla's reign as disastrous precluded him from dwelling on its beneficial aspects when he came to write his final books. Instead, he chose to frame it in the context of Caracalla's fiscal policy, as providing yet more proof of his rapacity – which allowed him to avoid expressing a judgement about the effects of the grant itself. Yet, it is remarkable that the historian's own assessment is left unspoken.

VII   Conclusion

Should Roman citizenship be the privilege and distinguishing mark of a ruling people? Or does an exclusive citizenship distort the economy of honour in ways that might weaken the empire? These are questions that recur across the vast sweep of the *Roman History*. Dio's interest in them can be seen most clearly in his decision to embed a clearly anachronistic proposal of universal enfranchisement in Maecenas' vision of an ideal monarchy, but also in his inclusion of a contradictory perspective in Augustus' political testament (particularly if it is an invention) and the *hortatio* of Suetonius Paulinus (one of relatively few extended speeches in the imperial books), not to mention his own passing remarks about the relationship between citizenship and honour under Claudius and about Caracalla's grant. These passages were probably anticipated in his narra-tives of the Latin Revolt and the Social War. One can only suspect that Dio's treatment of the whole subject of enfranchisement originally stood in

---

[70] Millar 1964: 104–5.

dialogue with a wider contemporary discussion, otherwise lost to us, of Caracalla's edict and the merits of universal citizenship.

The consistency of focus and language across such a large canvas is striking. Yet, so is the indirectness with which Dio handles the topic. Not only is discussion essentially limited to the speeches, but even there it is widely dispersed. There is no sign that the merits of expanding the citizen body were made the object of explicit debate in paired speeches in the imperial books – though they may have been in the narrative of the Latin Revolt and or the Social War. This obliquity is not uncharacteristic of the *Roman History* as a whole. Even on questions that are central to the narrative – such as the development of the Roman state or the proper relationship between the monarch and the aristocracy – much of the conceptual work is done in speeches. As Valérie Fromentin and her collaborators neatly put it, analysis is 'diffracted' through multiple speakers; the resulting diversity of points of view reveals the ambiguities inherent in politics, allowing readers to come to their own conclusions.[71] What is true for central preoccupations applies even more to second-order concerns such as the spread of Roman citizenship. The issue clearly interested Dio, not least in the ways that it impinged on the economy of honour in the empire. But it seems relatively peripheral to his conception of the sweep of Roman history. In this respect, the question of the merits of universal enfranchisement is perhaps similar to that of the ethics of Roman imperialism, a topic explored in a similarly dispersed fashion in the speech of Caesar at Vesontio (38.36–46) and, much earlier in the work, in the debate about war with Carthage after the capture of Saguntum, which survives only as a few small excerpts (F 55.1–8 [*ES*]). The relationship between the arguments of 'Caesar' and the authorial perspective has given rise to similar problems of interpretation.[72] The 'diffraction' of analysis is particularly obvious with these ancillary themes.

Given Dio's background, we may well suspect that his sympathies lay with 'Maecenas' rather than 'Augustus' and 'Suetonius Paulinus' on this point. But our desire to close this gap does violence to the genre of historiography. To reduce 'Maecenas' to a 'mouthpiece' for the author is to collapse a polyphony that is characteristic of the *Roman History* and of ancient historiography, in general. Both work and genre are willing to pose questions without giving clear answers.

---

[71] Fromentin et al. 2016b: 14.   [72] See most recently Kemezis 2016a.

CHAPTER 11

The Company They Keep
Emperors and Their Associates

Barbara Saylor Rodgers

I Introduction

Direct description of a man's (or a woman's) behavior, especially in the case of vicious behavior, is the very stuff of exemplary history.[1] For the historian operating in this genre, the rhetorical practice of definition by opposites[2] can be applied to character as well as to abstract concepts. Cassius Dio knew this well. His history often shows how a ruler or anyone in a position of authority ought not to behave, and thus what actions are preferable.[3] This knowledge enables both reader and author to anticipate what is coming (cf. Thuc. 1.22.4), choose what is best (cf. Livy, *Praef.* 10), and be a good man under a bad prince (cf. Tac. *Agr.* 42.4 and Christopher Pelling in the Epilogue), as if the historian's voice served the function of the Socratic *daimonion*.

In this chapter, I examine the moral vocabulary Dio employs most frequently to describe emperors and their associates.[4] Although the text as we have it is an imperfect representation of the author's work, Dio's vocabulary of praise and blame appears to be diachronically consistent through the years of Republic and empire and vicissitudes of manuscript and excerpt. His positive assessments are often general, whereas his negative vocabulary is wide and fairly specific.[5] His views of empire are in many

---

[1] Cf. Hor. *Sat.* 1.4.105–26. A good example from an earlier era is Polybius' comparison of Hannibal and Flaminius, which leads directly to a brief discussion of generalship (Polyb. 3.80–1); Dio's narrative of Trasimene (F 57.7 [*ES*] cf. Zonar. 8.25) reflects the judgment. Livy, *Praef.* 10 is the best summation of his own overall purpose and informs our understanding of others'. All translations are the author's own unless noted.

[2] Arist. *Top.* 153a25ff.; Cic. *Top.* 48.   [3] 'The mechanics of kingship': see Mallan 2013b: 643–4.

[4] The specific vocabulary items chosen for study here do not cover every sort of imperial vice or virtue, and ignore at least one important activity of most rulers, commissioning and building various structures, some of value and others characterized as waste. Edwards 1993: 137–72 offers many examples. Cf. Schulz 2019a: 64–9, 236–9.

[5] Cf. Molin 2006: 442, 'les défauts et les vices des empereurs sont clairement mentionnés', and Mallan in Chapter 12, 'vitriol came easily to Dio'.

respects unexceptional – he regarded a good monarchy as the best form of government (if only the monarch be worthy) – and explicit in cases where the narrative does not make his judgment clear.[6] The best men are readily identified but few; when he wrote that Marcus Aurelius was a truly good man, he asserted and reasserted that this emperor was not a fake:

> It is clear that he did all things not in pretense (οὐ προσποιητῶς) but from excellence (ἐξ ἀρετῆς). For having lived fifty-eight years, ten months, and twenty-two days, and within that time having ruled with Antoninus a considerable time and on his own for nineteen years and eleven days, he remained the same person throughout and was changed in no respect (ὅμοιος διὰ πάντων ἐγένετο καὶ ἐν οὐδενὶ ἠλλοιώθη). Thus, he was truly a good man (ἀγαθὸς ἀνήρ) and had nothing of pretense (οὐδὲν προσποιητὸν) in him. (72[71].34.4–5 [Xiph./*EV*])[7]

Denial of negative attributes is prominent in this assessment. Pertinax offers a similar example when the historian enumerates his good qualities after his belated funeral (75[74].5.6–7 [*EV*]). Here is praise of a stable personality and consistent balance in both the emperor's character and the historian's description of it: unchanged by events, he displayed a half-dozen virtues and lacked each virtue's opposite vice.[8]

Lack of pretense denotes the good, but its presence often characterizes the powerless or the evil.[9] The adjective προσποιητός ('put on, feigned') and related verb (προσποιέω)[10] characterize the history of the Republic and especially the period of the civil wars leading to the ascendancy of

---

[6] See, for example, Aalders 1986; Reinhold 1986: 214; Swain 1996: 403; De Blois 1998: 3406–14; Kemezis 2014: 94–149.

[7] καὶ ὅτι οὐ προσποιητῶς ἀλλ᾽ ἐξ ἀρετῆς πάντα ἔπραττε, πρόδηλον· ἔτη γὰρ ὀκτὼ καὶ πεντήκοντα καὶ μῆνας δέκα ἡμέρας τε εἴκοσι καὶ δύο ζήσας, κἂν τούτοις τῷ τε πρὶν Ἀντωνίνῳ συχνὸν χρόνον ὑπάρξας καὶ αὐτὸς ἐννέα καὶ δεκα ἔτη καὶ ἕνδεκα ἡμέρας αὐταρχήσας, ὅμοιος διὰ πάντων ἐγένετο καὶ ἐν οὐδενὶ ἠλλοιώθη. οὕτως ὡς ἀληθῶς ἀγαθὸς ἀνὴρ ἦν καὶ οὐδὲν προσποιητὸν εἶχε.

[8] Reinhold (1988: 137) observed of Dio's assessment of Antony at 51.15.2, five virtues were 'nullified in him by their opposites as vices'.

[9] Pretense might save one from various dangers: Domitius Afer pretending to be overcome by Gaius' oratory (59.19.7), senators praying for Gaius' recovery as if they cared (59.24.6), Claudius feigning simple-mindedness (59.23.5, 60.2.4), the senate reacting to the news of Agrippina's demise (62-[61].15.1 [Xiph.]), Nero's audience members pretending to collapse and die (62[63].15.3 [Xiph.]). Gleason (2011: 47) contrasts Dio's version of the audience's behavior (nightmare) to Suetonius' (farce). Shushma Malik describes in Chapter 7 the peril of lacking such pretense. For a discussion of Tiberius' dissimulation, see Christopher Mallan's Chapter 5 in this volume, especially section IV.

[10] The verb has other meanings but only the sense of feign, that is, *simulo* or *dissimulo*, is discussed here. There are other ways to express the same notion, approximately, for example, priding oneself on little to nothing, as Tiberius does at 54.9.4. I have not looked at the usage of πρόφασις because there is no equivalent adjective, it is particular rather than descriptive, and relates not to an individual's character but to what a person employs in a given situation.

Octavian as much as the time of later emperors,[11] and the verb figures prominently in the speech attributed to Maecenas in book 52.[12] In the imperial period, those who disguise their natures or motives include Tiberius, Gaius, Nero and Agrippina, Otho, Domitian, Didius Julianus, Severus, and Caracalla: these are the predecessors and successors whom Marcus Aurelius did not resemble.[13]

II   What Traits Make a Good Man?

Dio describes his model emperor in the passage cited above but tells of few similar men in the extant history. He found models of Roman probity in the Republic: C. Fabricius, as impoverished as he was incorruptible, appears in conversation with Pyrrhus in an early set piece from the history. Not only did he parry Pyrrhus' compliments regarding his worth and reputation (καὶ ἀγαθὸν καὶ ἐλλόγιμον ἄνδρα), proffered gifts, and request to accompany him back to Greece, but he lectured Pyrrhus on the paradoxical poverty that comes about from always wanting more than one has, the quality of ἀπληστία (aplestia, literally 'not-enough-ness', F 40.33–6 [ES]).[14] P. Rutilius Rufus, railroaded on a charge of repetundae because he had defended provincials against tax collectors, was another worthy

---

[11] False friendship in a context relating to Pyrrhus (F 40.15 [ES]); Syphax's abandoning feigned friendship for the Romans (F 57.67 [P]; termed φιλίας ἡ δόκησις at Zon. 9.12); Viriathus' pretending to knowledge of secrets (F 73.4 [EV]; cf. Caesar 44.38.7); Fimbria's feigned fiscal honesty (F 108.2 [EV]); pretended enmities of Sulla's adherents (F 109.9 [EV]); Pompey's attempts to disguise his desires (36.24.6; cf. Caelius in Cicero Fam. 8.1.3); Caesar's disguised enmity for Cicero (38.14.7); Pompey's and Crassus' dissimulation about the consulship (39.27.2); Caesar mourning Pompey's death (42.8.2); Caesar describing his genuine nature to the senate (43.15.5), after denying (43.15.3) that Marius and Cinna and Sulla won power in civil strife and behaved badly; Antony thrice in praise of Caesar (44.37.2, 44.38.7, 44.47.1); Octavian's and Antony's pretense of goodwill (45.8.3). At the beginning of the triumviral period, Antony, Lepidus, and Octavian entered into a pretense of an accord, despite a terrible hatred for each other (46.54.4). At 49.18.7, Dio uses the verb 'fabricated' (ἐπλάττετο) of the appearance of friendship Octavian still professed after the death of Sex. Pompeius; Reinhold (1988: 45) notes the irony in this passage.

[12] See de Blois (1994: 166–8) for discussion and enumeration of the necessary virtues. Cf. de Blois 1998: 3406 and de Blois 1998–99: 271–2. Ando's analysis (2016: 570–2) embraces the disjunction between outward forms of acceptable monarchy and the realities of power, especially in the role now expected of senators, and the consequences. Reinhold (1986: 219–21) discusses the relevance of Maecenas' advice to Dio's own time and contemporary problems, and the remarkable passage on the ruler-cult. Fishwick (1990) notes the details of the advice pertinent to the ruler-cult and date of composition of book 52. Piatkowski (1984: 601) has shown that Dio's sympathies were with limited and appropriate reverence for official purposes, for example, the honor due Pertinax for his efforts on behalf of the empire.

[13] Tiberius (57.1 at length, 57.3.2, 58.4.9, 58.19.6, 58.24.4), Gaius (59.23.1, 59.28.7 [Xiph./EV]), Nero and his mother (61[60].35.2 [Xiph.]); Otho (65[64].7.3 [Xiph.]); Domitian (67[66].9.3 [Xiph.], 67.2.6 and 7 [EV / Xiph.], 67.4.2 [Xiph. / EV]), Julianus (74[73].13.3 [Xiph.]), Severus (77[76].2.3 Xiph. / EV), and Caracalla (78[77].1.4 [Xiph.], 78[77].11.5 [EV], 78[77].12.2a [EV], 78[77].22.1 [Xiph.]).

[14] This is one of Dio's favorite terms of disapproval; see below.

individual (ἀνὴρ ἀγαθός); Dio notes that C. Marius had a hand in his condemnation because he perceived a man of such excellence (ἄριστος) and good reputation (εὐδοκιμώτατος) as a nuisance (F 97.3 [*EV*]). In both cases, the outstanding Roman was not only good but widely regarded as such, thus truly *nobilis*. Other examples from the late Republic, however, are problematical: Gabinius' calling Pompey (36.27.2) a good man for not wishing to hold the command against the pirates, the very command, Dio had written, that Pompey desired very much; people's belief that Crassus and Pompey were good men (38.5.5); Cato on the duty of a good man (himself) (40.58.4);[15] Cicero on the duty of a good man (himself) (45.18.3); Calenus on the duty of a good man (not Cicero) (46.22.1).

The phrases ἀγαθὸς ἀνήρ ('good man') or καλοὶ κἀγαθοί ('excellent people') recur through the transition to imperial rule and up to Dio's time, but rarely in the historian's own voice;[16] ἀρετή ('virtue, excellence') and ἄριστος ('best') also describe a small number of those he believed to be well-regarded individuals: Agrippa (54.29.2 and 54.31.1); Maecenas (55.7.4); M. Junius Silanus (59.8.4); Corbulo (61[60].30.4,5 [Xiph.]);[17] L. Junius Silanus (61[60].31.7 [*EV*] and 8 [Zonar.]); Thrasea Paetus and Barea Soranus (62.26.1 [Xiph.]); Bassaeus Rufus, except that he was not well educated (72[71].5.2 [Xiph.]); Avidius Cassius, save for one little mistake (72[71].22.2 [Xiph.]); Ulpius Marcellus (73[72].8.6 [Xiph./*EV*]); C. Aufidius Victorinus (73[72].11.2 [*EV*/Xiph.]; Pertinax (74[73].1.1 [Xiph.]);[18] and Eclectus when he alone did not desert Pertinax (74[73].10.2 [Xiph./*EV*]).[19]

---

[15] Dio does not himself call Cato or Catulus, another late Republican figure, a good man, but notes that both were consistently favorable to the common good (Catulus at 36.30.5 and 37.46.3, Cato at 37.22.2–3, 43.11.6); Cato shows up less admirably in other passages, e.g., 38.7.6, 39.22. These were Cicero's judgments, stated both publicly and in letters; for those and other references, see Gruen (1974: 13, 50–1) for Catulus and (54) for Cato.

[16] Maecenas spoke of anyone worthy of remaining a senator 52.19.2, of people worth treating well 52.26.5, and of honorable philosophers such as Areius and Athenodorus 52.36.4; Augustus described good men, in general (e.g., himself) 55.15.7. Suetonius Paulinus urged his soldiers to fight well (62.10.1 [Xiph.]); Trajan swore not to kill nor deprive of rights any good man (68.5.1 [Xiph.]); Caracalla hated them all (78(77).16.4 [*EV*]).

[17] Yet Tiridates' unique description of Corbulo as a good slave (ἀγαθὸν ἀνδράποδον) (62[63].6.5 [Xiph.]) is an ironic twist on the complimentary phrase.

[18] Kemezis (2012: 399) regards the inclusion of Pertinax among the καλοὶ κἀγαθοί a marker of social standing. Cf. Christopher Mallan in Chapter 12.

[19] Cf. Sempronius Densus (63[64].4.4–5 [Xiph., Zonar.]), Galba's only defender, 'most worthy to be remembered'. A third category of excellence is those who might have ruled but did not, often suffering as a result of their loyalty, upright actors who rejected rebellion. These include Germanicus, Corbulo, Avidius Cassius, Salvius Julianus, Tarrutenius Paternus and Perennis (57.18.8, 62.19.3–4 [Xiph.], 72[71].22.2 [Xiph.], 73[72].51–2 [*EV*], 73[72].10.1 [Xiph.]). The theme

Thus, from the time of Augustus, Dio specifically notes a baker's dozen of good men. On the other side of the scale was one who was conspicuously *not* a good man, and that by birth:

> Yet Domitius, the father of Nero, foresaw clearly enough his son's future depravity and licentiousness, and this not as the result of any oracle but by his knowledge of his own and Agrippina's character; for he declared: 'It is impossible for any good man to be sprung from me and this woman.' (61[61].2.3 [Xiph.])[20]

Nero is the worst of emperors,[21] whose vices covered the whole range of Dio's vocabulary of deficit, the negative role model who can be used to gauge the limitations of all others, the paradigm of what a person ought not to be. If there is a way not to behave, he does it; if there is a character trait that no decent person should have, he has it. If there is a negative epithet in the extant corpus that the historian does not attribute to Nero, one may blame the omission on a lacuna.

III Dio's Ethical Vocabulary

Although the historian expresses disapproval in many ways, he employs a special vocabulary for certain imperial people, their associates and family members, many of whom can be grouped together because they display specific unwholesome traits and behave similarly.[22] Some seem merely to be cruel and bloodthirsty, with a side of pretense. The most unworthy, however, are defined especially by what they lack: the term most often employed, with or without other undesirable attributes, is the noun ἀσέλγεια (*aselgeia*, 'licentiousness') and the related adjective and verb,

---

also occurs in panegyric, e.g. Drepanius Pacatus (*Pan. Lat.* 12[2].6.2). Verginius Rufus is a special case; see Levick 1985.

[20] καίτοι καὶ τὴν πονηρίαν καὶ τὴν ἀσέλγειαν τὴν τοῦ Νέρωνος καὶ ὁ Δομίτιος ὁ πατὴρ ἱκανῶς, οὐκ ἐκ μαντείας ἀλλ' ἐκ τῶν τρόπων τῶν τε ἑαυτοῦ καὶ τῶν τῆς Ἀγριππίνης. προείδετο, καὶ εἶπεν ὅτι 'ἀδύνατόν ἐστιν ἄνδρα τινὰ ἀγαθὸν ἔκ τε ἐμοῦ καὶ ἐκ ταύτης γεννηθῆναι' (trans. E. Cary, Loeb Classical Library edition). Suetonius describes several Domitii Ahenobarbi, most of them marked by egregious faults including arrogance, cowardice and cruelty; Nero's father seems the worst of the lot (*Nero* 5). Suetonius (*Nero* 6.1) reports a more specific negative appraisal than Dio's general statement: *praesagio fuit etiam Domiti patris vox, ... negantis quicquam ex se et Agrippina nisi detestabile et malo publico nasci potuisse* ('the statement of his father Domitius was like a prediction, when he denied that anything could be born from himself and Agrippina other than an abomination and public calamity').

[21] This is judging by variety of negative epithets. Elagabalus is presented as worse in many respects, noted most recently by Schulz 2019a: 252. For Dio's portrait of Nero, see Chapter 7 by Shushma Malik in this volume.

[22] Cf. Kemezis 2014: 144; Schulz 2019a: 249–54.

upon which the extensive catalogue of negative epithets depends. This notion used absolutely indicates sexual impropriety or profligacy; at best it denotes excess, greed, or filth. Dio's disapproval further encompasses one alpha privative after another, often in combination with ὠμότης ('savagery, cruelty') or other lamentable qualities and behaviors:[23] ἀκάθαρτος ('unclean'), ἀκόλαστος ('undisciplined'), ἀναίσχυντος ('shameless'), ἄνομος ('lawless'), ἀνόσιος ('unholy'), ἄπληστος ('insatiate'), ἀσεβής ('impious'), ἀσελγής ('licentious, profligate'), ἀσχήμων ('disgraceful'), ἄσωτος ('profligate').[24] In this company, ἄφρων ('senseless') seems neutral.

To return to ἀσέλγεια, Maecenas worried about this aspect of character in his advice to Augustus (52.26.6, 52.31.8, 52.34.8). When Nero's father Cn. Domitius Ahenobarbus offered his judgment of the character of his offspring, he acknowledged both his own shortcomings and his wife's (61.2.3 [Xiph.]); the father's reported judgment corresponded to a point somewhat earlier in the text, where Dio had stated that there was nothing that could satisfy Agrippina.[25]

Little remains of Dio's history of the early Republic, yet the available narratives are consistent with accounts of later events. Prior to summoning aid from Pyrrhus, the Tarentines, feeling unjustifiably secure in their hostility, indulged in an excess of misbehavior (ἀσέλγεια) and suffered for it (F 39.3 [ES]).[26] Like the Tarentines, Ariovistus, according to Dio's Caesar, combined ὕβρις with ἀσέλγεια (38.42.3), and like the Tarentines, paid for his excesses. Extreme lack of control, often accompanied by hubris, greed, filth, a lack of shame – all ways of expressing an emptiness where morality and control should be – are terms used to denigrate one's enemies or persons to be wary of, for example, Cicero speaking against Antony and Calenus responding to Cicero, Maecenas warning Augustus of ignorant and incontinent people who are so easily led on to misbehavior (52.26.6), Augustus berating unmarried men (56.5.7), Tiberius noting those to be removed from the senate (57.10.4).[27] When Dio's Calenus

---

[23] Either a general term such as πονηρία (wickedness) or ὕβρις (wanton violence) or something more specific: μιαιφονία (bloodguiltiness), μιαρία (coarseness), παρανομία (lawlessness), πλεονεξία (greed), τρυφή (love of luxury). Sommer (2004: 97–8) lists various characteristics of bad emperors, with multiple examples for each, save Vitellius' particular faults.

[24] Some of the notions, listed here as adjectives, appear as nouns and verbs.

[25] 61(60).33.12 [Zonar.]: οὐδὲν δὲ ἀρκοῦν τῇ Ἀγριππίνῃ ἐδόκει.

[26] Cf. their rudeness at F 39.8 [ELr]).

[27] Cicero's speech achieves several of the usual combinations – ἀσέλγεια with πλεονεξία ('greed') (45.26.1) and ἀναισχυντία ('shamelessness') (45.26.3) – and accuses Antony of ἀσελγῶς βεβιωκότα ('having lived wantonly') with ἐπὶ πᾶν ὕβρεως χωρήσειν ('about to reach the utmost extent of wanton violence') (45.35.4) and behaving κακῶς καὶ ἀσελγῶς ('evilly and licentiously') (45.37.2).

accused Cicero of pimping out his wife and having sex with his daughter
(46.18.6), he raised other issues that will recur in the history of the empire:
sexual profligacy, prostitution of oneself or enforced prostitution of others,
and incest.[28]

It was commonly held that a Roman man's worst character flaws
rendered him unmanly. These flaws were the sort of vices that one would
find in a barbarian, an easterner, or a woman.[29] Women and others of weak
psychic constitution are readily identified with lack of restraint; this very
characteristic made Cleopatra appealing to Antony (48.28.3; cf. 51.15.4)[30]
and sent Augustus' daughter into exile (55.10.12), whence Tiberius did not
recall her (57.18.1a). But what of our emperors, and those who advised,
influenced, or controlled them? One of the worst manifestations of a bad
ruler was the combination of imperial misbehavior with the multiplication
of tyrants under his regime when he failed to restrain family members and
other close associates.

Dio's representation of later emperors may be influenced by the record
of earlier ones and Republican predecessors; his narrative often echoes
something already seen, such as Commodus' similarity to aspects of Gaius,
Nero, or Domitian.[31] Dio's method of characterization can best be demonstrated by following the chronological order of the narrative, beginning
with the Republican players.

IV Republican Civil Wars

The struggles involving the Social War and aftermath, to Sulla's death, are
not well preserved in Dio's account. Even so, the fragmentary narrative
preserves Dio's comments regarding Marius' insatiable desire (ἀπληστία)
for killing (F 102.10 [EV]), Sulla's sudden revelation of his terrible true
nature (F 109. 2 [EV]) and desire and accomplishment of surpassing his
predecessors in outrages committed (F 109.3 [EV]) and bloodthirstiness
(μιαιφονία) (F 109.12 [EV]), the pretense of Sulla's imitators (F 109.9 [EV]).
During the interim until the second round, remembrance was vivid
(37.20.6, 41.5.1 & 8.5, 41.16.2–3). Sulla's ὠμότης was hated by the people,

---

Calenus says that Cicero also called Antony ἀσελγῆ καὶ μιαρόν ('wanton and corrupt') (46.16.3).
Maecenas to Augustus 52.26.6; Tiberius and the senate 57.10.4.

[28] Williams (2010: 160) observes that a man considered effeminate, as Cicero in Calenus' rejoinder, is
associated with 'inappropriate sexual practices with women'.

[29] Edwards 1993: 78–84; Schulz 2019a: 188–90.

[30] Reinhold 1988: 137, commentary on 51.15.2–4.

[31] Cf. Schulz 2019a: 251, and 254–7, the section on 'hot memory'.

who were afraid to have Pompey as dictator (40.45.5). Caesar gained some credit for his treatment of opponents' families, in contrast to Sulla's bloodthirstiness (μιαιφονία) (43.50.2).[32]

Although Dio gives Lepidus and Octavian credit for a certain humane restraint during their proscriptions, he says Antony's killings were savage and pitiless (ὠμῶς καὶ ἀνηλεῶς ... ἔκτεινε) (47.8.1).[33] Despite the horrors of the period, the triumviri were determined to be praised for their restraint in not having more people killed, as they were intent upon emulating neither Marius' and Sulla's ὠμότης so as to be hated nor Caesar's clemency (ἐπιείκεια) so as to be despised and plotted against (47.13.3–4).

V The Julio-Claudians

Augustus, often regarded as one of Dio's models of a good ruler,[34] suffers little negative description. Harsh, indeed, he was when young and faced with a civil war and rivals, not at all genuine at times.[35] But overall, his reign was a boon for the Roman state. He lived long, saw an end to civil strife, and indulged in the use of force only when necessary (56.44). And of personal sexual misbehavior, such as Suetonius relates,[36] there is but the merest hint in Dio's narrative, and only then as part of Dio's report of Livia's careful lack of attention to Augustus' sexual playthings (58.6.5). There seems to be in operation a particular sort of double standard, not just between what men and women may do, but between the actions of an emperor despised after his death and what a well-regarded ruler allowed himself in taking advantage of weaker persons. We may note what Dio says of Trajan at 68.7.4 (Xiph./*EV*):

> I know that he was passionate about wine and boys, but if anything shameful or base had come from these passions, he would have been blamed

[32] Urso 2016b discusses Dio's unfavorable moral judgment of Sulla while arguing that it was Caesar, not Sulla, who was first, in Dio's opinion, to use the office of dictator to establish a δυναστεία.

[33] Cf. Monica Hellström's phrase in Chapter 9, 'evil for its own sake'.

[34] See Chapter 5 by Christina Kuhn in this volume for Dio's clear awareness of his own agenda in constructing the funeral oration attributed to Tiberius: this 'official' version differs from the historian's summing-up of Augustus, and the concessive apologia and half-truths in the oration are noteworthy.

[35] For example, 56.47.1 for the pretense involved in relations with the senate.

[36] Suet. *Aug.* 68–71, where, to be sure, the biographer excuses some of Augustus' activities as means of spying and offers most of the information in defense of the emperor's heterosexuality. Robert Graves' translation 'disproved the accusation of prostituting his body to men (*infamiam impudicitiae*) by the decent normality of his sex life (*castitate*)' is unforgettable.

for it, yet he could drink a quantity of wine while remaining sober and he hurt no one in his relations with boys.[37]

No complaint, no foul.

Tiberius loses nothing of his reputation for harsh cruelty in Dio's remaining account, nor does his assistant Sejanus. Yet beyond the mention of Tiberius' love affairs with both men and women of good families, and one unfortunate case cited of a man who tried to shield his daughter from the emperor (58.22.1–3), Dio's history says nothing of the allegations that one can read in Suetonius (*Tib.* 43–5), and it may be that nothing would be found if we had the entire text. On the contrary, Dio cites Tiberius' dislike and attempted repression of those who indulged themselves excessively, including his son Drusus (57.13.1, 3; 57.23.4), whose cruelty also angered him. Perhaps the most one may expect from Dio is the notice that Tiberius behaved very well for some time,[38] until he did not, and he prevented others from behaving licentiously (ἀσελγαίνειν) (57.13.3). Dio's notice that Sejanus had been the παιδικά ('favorite') of M. Gavius Apicius arouses suspicions regarding his relationship with Tiberius, but the historian does not make the same connection that he does when introducing Vitellius, once Tiberius' παιδικά (64[63].4.2 [Xiph.]). Self-indulgence (ἀσωτία), however, is expensive; Apicius ended his life when he feared that his few remaining millions condemned him to die a poor man and perish from starvation (57.19.5). Tiberius' precaution in appointing a guardian for a senator who was living profligately (ἀσελγῶς) (57.23.4) may have been prompted by a reasonable concern that the man retain financial resources enough to stay in the senate. One might conclude from Dio's final assessment that Tiberius was two different men (58.28.5). Yet, Tiberius' penchant for licentiousness was noted when Gaius became emperor and Dio says that he was even worse than his predecessor, for both are marked by ἀσέλγεια and μιαιφονία (59.4.1). This is Dio's second notice of a downward trend in the person of the ruler, a development both pleasing to and deliberately brought about by the dying emperor: Tiberius believed that his successor would behave so badly that his own misdeeds would be forgotten (58.23.3–4). Augustus had considered Tiberius a suitable successor for a similar reason (56.45.3). Dio makes this point explicitly at 59.5.1.

---

[37] καὶ οἶδα μὲν ὅτι καὶ περὶ μειράκια καὶ περὶ οἶνον ἐσπουδάκει. ἀλλ' εἰ μέν τι ἐκ τούτων ἢ αἰσχρὸν ἢ κακὸν ἢ ἐδεδράκει ἢ ἐπεπόνθει, ἐπηγορίαν ἂν εἶχε, νῦν δὲ τοῦ τε οἴνου διακόρως ἔπινε καὶ νήφων ἦν, ἔν τε τοῖς παιδικοῖς οὐδένα ἐλύπησεν.

[38] In Chapter 6, Christopher Mallan aptly denotes the historian's attitude as 'ambivalence' or 'agnosticism' about an emperor who understood and manipulated others all too well.

Although Dio does not specifically note this similarity, Gaius, like Tiberius, was very fond of illicit sexual relationships (μοιχικώτατος) (59.3.3), but he had his own particular vices as well, especially the joy he felt in others' deaths and his insatiable desire for the sight of bloodshed (59.10.2);[39] his ὠμότης extended to sending random spectators from the crowd to the beasts when criminals were in short supply (59.10.3). His thirst for spending money on spectacles (races, gladiators, and other sorts) was unquenchable (59.2.5). Like a small child, Gaius wanted to play, to be entertained by whatever could hold his fascinated attention, and to be observed by everyone in so doing (59.7.5). In his desire to be amused after his own fashion, Gaius found himself constantly in financial embarrassment: nothing sufficed to meet his expenses (οὐδὲν αὐτῷ ἐξήρκει) (59.10.7).[40] Gaius attracted censure for the banishments of numerous people, including his sisters,[41] and for prosecutions, which began immediately after his spectacular bridge-building and -crossing and triumphal show at the Bay of Baiae (59.17).[42] Yet this extravagance may not have been without serious purpose.[43] The banishments and trials eliminated potential familial or senatorial rivals.[44] Most Romans believed that his savagery and wantonness would increase (59.24.1; cf. 59.25.7 [Zonar.]), although one segment of the city's population, the mob, rejoiced in the enforced prostitution of the wives and children of leading citizens (59.28.8–10 [Xiph./*EV*]). There was method in his licentiousness, for by this shameful and terrible means, among others, he continued to raise money to pay for his indulgences. There is no pity in this narrative for the young man who wanted to be anything other than a human being or an emperor (59.26.8 [Xiph./*EV*]), who masqueraded as one god after another, and Dio's scorn embraces Gaius' pretense of deity and links it specifically to these practices (59.28.8 [Xiph./*EV*]). In death, he learned that he really was not divine (59.30.1 [Zonar./John Ant.]). In Dio's telling, Gaius was bloodthirsty, licentious, incapable of being satisfied in any respect,

---

[39] The quality of ἀπληστία that Fabricius had found in Pyrrhus.

[40] The combination of a negative with the verb ἀρκέω or ἐξαρκέω (be sufficient) is an alternative means of indicating profligacy: cf. Agrippina (61[60].33.12 [Zonar.]). Fabricius, the upright Republican opponent of Pyrrhus described above, praised a tolerable sufficiency (F 40.35 [*ES*]: 'my possessions are enough for me') and even Otho could be brought in for comparison in one situation, if not most, because Dio writes that he thought there had been enough war already and did not even care if he might win the next battle, so unwilling was he to have it fought (63[64].13.1 [Xiph./Zonar.]).

[41] The reason Dio gives is their many unholy and licentious acts (59.22.8).

[42] Icks 2017: 323–5 (on Dio's puncturing of Gaius' performance).   [43] Winterling 2011: 126–31.

[44] Kleijwegt 1994; Winterling 2011: 107–23; Lange 2016: 106–7.

unhappy with his very identity, and feigning alternate realities to the extent
that in addition to playing a god he invented stories to dramatize or
exaggerate himself (59.23.1, 59.28.7 [Xiph./*EV*]).

Despite his discomfort with Livia's influence[45] and the emphasis on how
great Sejanus had grown in Tiberius' reign, and despite Sejanus' attempts
to remove potential rivals, Tiberius never lost control (59.5.2), as Dio
makes clear.[46] The next three Julio-Claudians are not so capable. Dio
states that Gaius brought a new weakness to the imperial power, one to
be repeated by several later emperors, a lack of control: ruled by chariot
drivers and gladiators, he was a slave to dancers and other theatrical figures
(59.5.2). Gaius is portrayed as a child, controlled by others. The narrative of
later books shows that Claudius, kept infantilized by his maintenance
within the imperial household among the women and pretense of mental
incompetence, is shown to be like a child to be managed by women and
freedmen (or slaves 60.2.4), holding the title of ruler while manipulated by
others (60.2.5), and that Nero, made emperor at age 17, is the third child in
a row, again controlled by a series of women and underlings.

Claudius' reign began when soldiers discovered him hiding fearfully in
the Palace (60.1.2–3 [Xiph.]). Early in the narration of the reign, Dio
distinguishes Claudius the tool of wives and others from Claudius the
sensible administrator and begins with details of the many enactments and
practices that meet with the historian's approval. The emperor's deeds are
separated specifically from those that were quite different and whose
impetus came not from Claudius but from his freedmen and from
Messalina (60.8.4). Claudius' cowardice clouded his reason (60.2.6), left
him prey to manifold fears, and offered an easy path to manipulation,
especially for Messalina and three prominent freedmen (Narcissus, Pallas,
Callistus). Dio leaves little specific information about the freedmen other
than their amassing of power and wealth, and that Narcissus had to be sent
out of town before Claudius could be killed, so there was some loyalty (or
self-preservation) involved in that relationship.[47] Messalina was the most
licentious imperial woman in the history, whose only passion was apparently sex: ἀσελγεστάτη, πορνικωτάτη ('most licentious', 'most whorish')

---

[45] See recent discussion in Adler 2011: 139–41, 152–4.
[46] 57.22.1 (Xiph.), 58.2.7 (Xiph.), 58.4.1 (Xiph.), 58.5.1 (Xiph.); Sejanus seems to have imitated
Augustus' use of adultery as a means to gain information, if the report at 58.3.8 (Xiph.) is true.
See also Mallan in Chapter 6 on Tiberius' retention of control.
[47] There is only the briefest notice of Polybius, whom Messalina has killed despite her relationship
with him (61[60].31.2 [*EV* / Xiph. / Zonar.]), and whose death puts the other freedmen on notice of
their precarious position as her allies.

(60.14.3). Her excesses were directed to adulterous affairs, behavior as a prostitute from within the Palace, and forcing other women to behave similarly (60.18.1, 61[60].31.1 [*EV*/Xiph./Zonar.]). Finally, unable to be satisfied by these forms of misbehavior (61[60].31.1 [*EV*/ Xiph./Zonar.]) she resolved to embark upon a series of actual marriages, but the first such outrageous celebration was followed swiftly by her death.

Claudius himself was a model of moderation (60.12.5) except when he was not: his insatiable interest in alcohol and in sex could not be fulfilled (60.2.5–6). He also took excessive pleasure in watching gladiators fight and in having malefactors killed in public (60.13.3); other more reprehensible murders followed these, but at the instigation of his handlers (60.14.1) rather than from his own volition: the image employed in these sections is a kind of gluttony communicated by compounds of the verb πίμπλημι ('to fill').[48] He shared the trait for unwholesome fulfilment with Nero, Vitellius, and Didius Julianus.[49] Dio's Claudius is a coward, given to overindulgence in consumption of alcohol, sexual activity, and forms of bloodshed, and not really in control of very much other than what his wives or freedmen allowed him to do.

One may find detailed assessments of Dio's Nero elsewhere,[50] so my task is again to focus on how Dio chooses to record the characteristics of his reign. If it is fair to attribute to the ruler the unchecked tendencies of his advisors, associates, friends, and lovers, the list grows longer through Nero's regime. Early on, when admonished by Seneca,[51] Burrus, or his mother, he was sure to say that he would reform but then went right back to what he was doing, led on by his immoral companions, who reminded him that he could, in fact, do as he wished (61.4.4–5 [Xiph./*EV*]).[52] He was like a scolded child, always agreeing to do better but without real intent. Emulating and surpassing the excesses of Gaius became a goal (61.5.1 [Xiph./*EV*]).[53] There were many

---

[48] During the early years of the triumvirate, Antony is said to have filled himself with the sight of his opponents' severed heads, even while he was eating (47.8.2). In several passages, the exact nature of what a person fills up on is not specified other than with the word desire (ἐπιθυμία), singular or plural, with ἀναπίμπλημι: 48.39.1, 52.7.4, 55.14.5.

[49] Nero after the death of Britannicus (61.7.5 [*EV*/ Xiph.] πάντων ὧν ἤθελεν ἐπ᾽ ἀδείας ἐνεπίμπλατο); Vitellius (64[65].1.3 [*EV*]) at the sight of the dead at Cremona, although in the arena; Julianus (74[73].13.1 [Xiph.]) eating his fill of expensive food while Pertinax's body remained in the Palace.

[50] See Chapter 7 in this volume, and Gowing 1997.

[51] No paragon himself to Dio, especially in his preference for grown-up men (61.10.4 [Xiph. / *EV*], 62.6.4); cf. Williams 2010: 89; Shushma Malik in Chapter 7 calls Dio's Seneca 'an immoral hypocrite'.

[52] And, as Osgood (2016: 189) observes, not really hindered by the adults in charge.

[53] Noted by Madsen (2016: 148–9) in discussion of Dio's belief that dynastic succession had failed the Julio-Claudians and would fail again.

influences and enablers: Agrippina his mother, Lucusta the purveyor of poisons, the mistresses Acte and then Poppaea, Otho's wife and later Nero's. The more notorious advisors or henchmen include Helios, a freedman to whom the Romans were as enslaved as they were to Nero, the difference between the emperor and former slave neatly described as a role reversal (62[63].12.2 [Xiph.]): 'they differed in this respect, that Augustus' descendant emulated lyre players and tragic actors,[54] and Claudius' freedman emulated Caesar'.[55] One outcome of the role playing was that Subrius Flavius (62.24.2 [Xiph.]) entered into a conspiracy specifically not to be enslaved to a charioteer and lyre player. Here is a reversal of right order, as those who practiced what Nero does were likely to be slaves of free people, not vice versa. Nero killed both his wives, Octavia (after divorce) by execution and Poppaea by a kick, but found spouses of a different sort in the freedmen Pythagoras and Sporus, the latter castrated at Nero's order.[56] Compared to the power exercised by Helios, Dio apparently finds Tigellinus almost negligible because he was always with Nero and did not act on his own (62[63].12.3 [Xiph.]), although Tigellinus had been an excellent choice to replace Burrus because he excelled all other men in ἀσέλγεια and μιαιφονία (62[62].13.3 [Xiph.]).

With Nero or his companions come all the terms of opprobrium, generally being a scoundrel (πονηρία) along with his mother (61.8.5 [EV/Xiph.]). Indeed, Nero possesses a full suite of vices: He perpetrates violence upon others (ὑβρίζειν), he is savage and bloodthirsty (ὠμότης, μιαιφονία), he is never satisfied (62[63].8.3 [Xiph./EV], 62[63].11.3 [Xiph./EV], adding gratuitous murder to confiscation of property), he is generally wanton (ἀπληστία, ἀκολασία: 62[62].15.1 [Xiph.]),[57] and displays the sort of bad form rather being like a woman (ἀσχημοσύνη).[58] To round this off, he is also 'unholy' (ἀνόσιος). Such behavior was too much for his advisors: Seneca, Faenius

---

[54] Williams (2010: 285) notes that in Vindex's speech (63.22.4 [Xiph.]) Nero's appearances on stage were the culmination of his unmanly behavior.

[55] ἐν ἑνὶ δὲ τούτῳ διήλλασσον, ὅτι ὁ μὲν τοῦ Αὐγούστου ἀπόγονος κιθαρῳδοὺς καὶ τραγῳδούς, ὁ δὲ τοῦ Κλαυδίου ἀπελεύθερος Καίσαρας ἐζήλου. Molin (2006: 447) notes that Commodus and Caracalla also promoted the grossly unworthy.

[56] Dio describes their threesome at 62(63).13.1–2 (Xiph.).

[57] Nero and but a few others display ἀκολασία (a lack of having been punished and thus a lack of restraint), but all are either women or like women or undisciplined children: Nero, Agrippina, Messalina, Caracalla, and the wife of Pertinax.

[58] Certain rare traits belong to a limited group, in which Nero is prominent, but ἀσχημοσύνη is his alone although via the related verb or adjective Dio shows a few others embodying the essence of the noun. The meaning, literally formless, is to be shameful, unseemly, weak and womanlike, an image generalized from any or all of the soldiers defeated by Cleopatra or her Egyptians, Nero's victims if they were also his flatterers, a eunuch, Elagabalus.

Rufus, and others plotted against him when he hit the trifecta of vices.[59] These conspiracies came to nothing. In Nero's case, who was the slave and who the enslaved? And if so many of this emperor's actions were stage-managed performances,[60] Dio has instructions for how to receive the show: proper-thinking people (62[61].18.1 [Xiph.], οἱ νοῦν ἔχοντες), who mourned the actual stage appearances of Nero and those that he forced to perform in public, stand in for the sensible members of the Roman senate and people as a whole. Eventually, Nero's behavior proved too much for the noble-spirited Vindex,[61] whose revolt against Nero set off the chain reaction of events that led to the emperor's downfall.

VI   The Civil Wars of 69

The period of civil strife after Nero's death revealed any number of actors, individual and collective, behaving badly.[62] The soldiers in the Germanies wanted rewards, but neither Galba nor their commander Verginius Rufus would fulfil (ἀποπληρῶσαι) their desires (63[64].4.1 [Xiph./Zonar.]), so they proposed Vitellius as one who would do, and this was the beginning of the end for Galba, especially after he adopted Piso, not Otho, as his heir. Otho, who was expected to be more profligate than Nero (63[64].8.2[1] [Xiph.]),[63] behaved in a way that did not come naturally, attempting (63[64].7.3 [Xiph.]) and failing to conciliate the opposition (63[64].8.3–9.3 [Xiph./EV]), for he had kept with him many who had been close to Nero[64] and, worse, taught the soldiers the most dreadful lessons of all. And yet, the historian allows that his voluntary death overshadowed his impious and base behavior (63[64].15.2 [Xiph./Zonar.] ἀσέβεια and πονηρία): Not wanting to be like Marius, Cinna, or Sulla, he had had enough (63[64].13.2 [Xiph./Zonar.]). When the soldiers chose Vitellius, they either ignored his history as Tiberius' παιδικά and his licentious lifestyle (ἀσέλγεια), or perhaps liked him the better for it.[65]

---

[59] 62.24.1: οὔτε γὰρ τὴν ἀσχημοσύνην οὔτε τὴν ἀσέλγειαν οὔτε τὴν ὠμότητα αὐτοῦ ἔτι φέρειν ἐδύναντο ('they could no longer endure his disgracefulness nor his licentiousness nor his bloodthirstiness').

[60] E.g., Baldwin 1979; Champlin 2003.

[61] 63(62).22 (Xiph.) (speech of Vindex). Cf. Schulz 2019a: 213 on Vindex as focalizer and narrator of dissatisfaction with Nero.

[62] Cf. combatants in the period of civil strife following Caesar's assassination: 47.17.6, 49.13.1.

[63] Cf. Murison (1999: 51–2, 56–7) on Otho's adoption of, or acquiescence in, Nero's name. Charles and Anagnostou-Laoutides (2013–14) have made a case that Otho's reputation as a passively effeminate man grew from his assimilation to Nero and generic descriptions of a type of tyrant.

[64] Including Sporus (63[64].8.3 [Xiph./EV]); Murison (1999: 57) observes, 'Dio seems to have a slightly morbid interest in the eunuch Sporus'.

[65] 63(64).4.2 (Xiph.); licentiousness combined with love of luxury at 64(65).2.1 (Xiph./EV).

As emperor, Vitellius was a model of hubris, the grossest sort of gluttony ('he feasted insatiably, ingesting and constantly vomiting up everything'),[66] reckless spending, and an inability to be satisfied by any existing standard of luxury, including Nero's Golden House (64[65].2.2 [Xiph./*EV*], 64[65].4.1 [Xiph./*EV*]). Perhaps worst, Vitellius wanted to imitate Nero: Proper-thinking people (οἱ νοῦν ἔχοντες) (64[65].7.3 *EV*)) could not approve of this any more than they had approved of Nero in performance. During his final public appearance, people noted Nero's extravagant spending (ἀσωτία) (64[65].20.3 [Xiph.]). Inconstant in adversity (64[65].16 [Xiph.]), Dio's Vitellius was not entirely bad;[67] the historian also gives him the same last words as Tacitus reports (*Hist.* 3.85.1) and has created a suitably purple description of the former ruler's final progress through the city (64[65].20.2–3 [Xiph.]).

VII   The Flavians

Vespasian's accession offers over a decade of relief, despite the removal of Helvidius Priscus, whose words and actions Dio describes as hubristic (65[66].12.2–3 [*EV*], cf. Suet. *Vesp.* 15). Titus, like his father, became better when emperor than he had been previously: here (66[66].18.1–2 [Xiph.]) the historian offers a reason for what reads as an explanation of Tacitus on Vespasian (*Hist.* 1.50), that a deputy might abuse power but a person responsible for the whole cares about his reputation.[68]

Domitian, however, resentful and jealous of both his father and his brother,[69] seems a throwback to Gaius in some ways: He demanded a new mode of address, δεσπότης καὶ θεός ('master and god', *dominus et deus* in Latin).[70] When on a military campaign against the Dacians, he sent the army on to do the work and stayed behind in Moesia indulging himself as usual (67.6.3 [Xiph./*EV*]). Physically indolent (ἄπονος), without daring (ἄτολμος), insatiably licentious, he preferred to spend his time with

---

[66] See the interesting note on the physiological effects of the practice in Murison 1999: 78.

[67] See Davenport 2014.

[68] Madsen (2016: 157) notes that Dio judged Titus weak because he did not remove his brother in consequence of Domitian's plans, ultimately successful, to eliminate him (66.26.3–4 [Xiph.]), and links this failing with that of Severus. In both cases the emperor protected and suffered from an heir rather than sacrifice the heir for the benefit of the state.

[69] Murison (1999: 204) suggests that Dio's apparently personal dislike of Domitian may have been based both upon the sources and his experiences under Commodus and Caracalla. Cf. Schulz 2019a: 252.

[70] 67.4.7 (Zonar.) spoken and written, 67.13.4 (Xiph./Zonar.); cf. 59.28 (Xiph./*EV*) and 59.30.1 (Zonar./John Ant.). For the Latin expression *dominus et deus*, note Suet. *Dom.* 13.2.

women and boys (καὶ ἀσώτατος καὶ ἀσελγέστατος). The list of four alpha privatives, two absolutes and two superlatives displays Domitian's nature as one thing lacking after another. He revealed his hypocrisy when punishing others for sexual misbehavior of which he was guilty himself, sometimes in company with the very persons being punished.[71] Faithless (ἄπιστος, another alpha privative), he fabricated (ἐπλάττετο) affection for those whom he would soon destroy (67.1.3 [Xiph./*EV*]).[72] Love of spectacles and games (67[67].7.4 [*ELr*], 67[67].8.1 [Xiph.]), constant need of funds to pay for these, numerous deaths related to fundraising as well as to suspicions of conspiracy (e.g., 67.11.3 [*EV*]; cf. Gaius in 59.21), or to very old and trivial offenses,[73] put him into the company of the worst Julio-Claudians, or the last of the Antonines. As Domitian was being killed, Apollonius of Tyana is said to have shouted his approval of the death of the murderer (μιαιφόνος) (67[67].18.1 [Xiph.]).

VIII Five Good Emperors and Commodus

The next five rulers have a record not of unmitigated excellence, but fairly close, with Hadrian the outlier but overall, in Dio's appraisal, a good ruler (69.5–7 [Xiph.]).[74] For many later generations, Trajan was the most often cited role model, an emperor who played his part well. Dio's praise encompasses many excellent qualities and a number of positive statements about Trajan's bravery, justice, simplicity of his disposition, strength of body and mind, generosity, affability, dignity – one could add more (68[68].6–8 [Xiph./*EV*]).[75] Yet even here, there is evidence of assertion by denial of the opposite: neither hating nor fearing nor envying anyone, he was least of all a slave to anger, refrained from taking the property of others, and did not support enormous expenses related to defense and infrastructure by killing anyone. Trajan regarded the senate's award of the honorific *Optimus* as his greatest honor (68[68].23.1–2 [Xiph.]).[76] But

---

[71] 67.12.1 (Xiph./Zonar.); cf. 59.22.8. Charles and Anagnostou-Laoutides (2010) discuss Suetonius' subtler delineation of this hypocrisy.

[72] Schulz 2019a: 26, 28.

[73] Cf. Schulz 2019a: 220. Kragelund (2012: 500) assembles a list of eight such victims other than Maternus.

[74] On Dio and the Antonines, see Chapter 8 by Caillan Davenport.

[75] See the catalogue of desirable imperial behaviors in Wallace-Hadrill (1982: 44) and the discussion of Dio's choice of δημοτικός to translate *civilis*. Yet despite the praise, in Chapter 8 Caillan Davenport observes that Dio seems unimpressed by Trajan's military exploits, listed with the functionally negative annotation that the military campaigns did not interfere with his attention to civil affairs.

[76] Dio transliterates the word and gives the equivalent as ἄριστος.

Marcus Aurelius, with whom this essay began, was the emperor most highly esteemed by the historian, καθαρός, χρηστός, εὐσεβής ('pure, good, pious') (72[71].30.2 [Xiph./*EV*]) in his pardon of all who had taken part in the rebellion of Avidius Cassius, despite their ἀνοσιουργία ('lack of holiness'). What Dio found especially admirable was that, endowed with a frail physical nature and a preference for thought and study over action, and allotted by fate countless troubles throughout his reign, Marcus Aurelius nevertheless did his duty and did it well: 'he survived, and saved the empire' (αὐτός τε διεγένετο καὶ τὴν ἀρχὴν διεσώσατο) (72[71].36.3 [Xiph./*EV*]).

Marcus Aurelius was succeeded by his own child, a teenager at his father's death, and another case of arrested imperial development. Dio presents him (73[72].1.1 [Xiph./*EV*]) as having acquired a nature licentious and bloodthirsty (ἀσελγῆ καὶ μιαιφόνον), despite being essentially without evil (ἄκακος) but a slave to his companions because of cowardice and great simplicity (ἁπλότης).[77] Commodus was an emptiness waiting to be filled. For a person not born with an evil nature, he quickly displayed many of the qualities of an unsuitable ruler, including a demand to be addressed as a god (73[72].16.1 [Xiph./*EV*]) like another Gaius or Domitian,[78] passionate about chariot racing (73[72].9.1 [Xiph./*EV*]) like Gaius and Nero,[79] a sponsor of expensive entertainments (73[72].16 [Xiph./*EV*])who acquired the necessary funds by the well-tried method of accusations, confiscations, executions. The parallels with his predecessors, especially Gaius, become clear with the details Dio gives of the exits of their predecessors: both Tiberius and Marcus advise bystanders to look to the rising, not the setting, sun, and both are helped on their way by adherents of the young men who will inherit the empire.[80] It is hard to know what to make of this equivalence of Marcus Aurelius to Tiberius, but the phrase was originally attributed to Sulla who saw that Pompey would soon supplant him (Plut. *Pomp.* 14.4). In the amphitheater (73[72].17–20 [Xiph./*EV*]) he killed countless animals and eventually humans as well. These entertainments in Dio's account became nearly constant and escalated beyond child's play – however, that word (παιδιαί) may be understood for amusements of more normal times – into one long, murderous tantrum. He destroyed most of

---

[77] The latter trait had figured as one of Trajan's positive elements. Clearly there is a difference between simplicity (shallowness?) and simplicity of manners.

[78] Millar (1964: 132) notes the parallel between Commodus' and Gaius' divine pretensions.

[79] In Chapter 7, Shushma Malik notes the performative similarities between Commodus and Nero, albeit in different theatres, and that Dio's hostile treatment of Nero is due in part to this similarity.

[80] Hose 2011: 119.

those who had held honor or influence under his father (73[72].4 [Xiph.] and 5 [*EV*/Xiph.]), just as Domitian had resented and removed anyone esteemed by Vespasian or Titus (67.2 [Xiph./*EV*]).[81]

Those who held most influence were the freedmen, led by Cleander, who had free rein – 'putting everything up for sale, behaving violently and licentiously' (πωλοῦντες πάντα, ὑβρίζοντες, ἀσελγαίνοντες) – after the death of Perennis (73[72].10.2 [*EV*/Xiph.]). Dio does not even name all of those who found favor with Commodus; there were, for example, 'some filthy and ridiculous men' (κοπρίας τινὰς καὶ γελωτοποιούς) whom he enriched 'because of their hubris and licentiousness' (διὰ τὴν ὕβριν τήν τε ἀσέλγειαν) (74[73].6.2 [Xiph./*EV*]). Pertinax published their names with the amounts of their awards but did not otherwise harm them. Cleander, having become *cubicularius* after killing Saoterus and many other people, met his fate in turn as the result of another's plotting, and not without some cause (73[72].12–13 [Xiph./*EV*]); his son and various satellites perished as well.[82] Coward that he was, Commodus readily surrendered his chamberlain to the people (73[72].13.6 [Xiph./*EV*]). The freedwoman Marcia, married to Eclectus and sexual partner of Commodus, reported the riots that preceded Cleander's death (73[72].13.5 [Xiph./*EV*]). She later conspired with Eclectus and Laetus to eliminate Commodus himself, aiming to pre-empt his turning on them (73[72].22 [Xiph.]). So fraught were the times that once again, unless the detail is a doublet, there was a rash of murders by poisoned needles, just as had occurred in Domitian's reign (73[72].14.4 [Xiph./*EV*]; 67.11.6 [Xiph./Zonar.]).[83]

IX   The Civil Wars of 193–7

The choice of Pertinax brings to mind elements of the elevation of Galba or Nerva,[84] and is worth discussion in a different context.[85] For the purposes of this chapter, Pertinax is one of the models described near the beginning,[86] whose unaffected behavior, simple tastes, and decency to the senate were among his best qualities, and a contrast to the people of Rome (74[73].2.4

---

[81] Cf. nn. 69 and 79 above.

[82] Pertinax, likely one of those who had not scrupled to work with Cleander upon various occasions, was not implicated; Strobel 2004: 521–2.

[83] See Murison (1999: 23, 26, 204) for parallels; Schulz 2019a: 252.

[84] Murison 1999: 23–4; Davenport 2014: 99; Davenport and Mallan 2014: 647; Kemezis 2014: 55.

[85] The narrative of Pasek 2013 is extremely detailed on the end of Commodus and the reign and assassination of Pertinax; it is enhanced by the prosopographical section (Dramatis Personae) appended.

[86] But see Strobel 2004: 532.

[Xiph.]) as well as to his immediate successor, marked as χρηματιστής τε ἄπληστος καὶ ἀναλωτὴς ἀσελγής ('insatiable seeker of money and profligate spender') (74[73].11.2 [Xiph.]). During his brief reign, Pertinax tried to right all imperial systems at once,[87] recognized his wife's imperfection,[88] took measures to prevent the praetorians from theft, and upset the imperial freedmen who had been used to doing as they pleased (sc. ἀσελγαίνειν) (74[73].8.1 [Xiph./EV]). The praetorian prefect Laetus fomented the rebellion, and in Julianus, the soldiers found an emperor more to their taste.[89] The contrast between Pertinax and Didius Julianus could not have been more stark, nor Dio's grief and distaste more evident.[90] It may have been true that Julianus was, as he said himself, most worthy (ἀξιώτατος) to rule (74[73].12.4 [Xiph.]), but Dio disagrees, using the same term: 'speaking most worthily of himself' (ἀξίως ἑαυτοῦ λέγοντος).[91] There followed a few months of mutual pretense on the part of Julianus and a number of senators (74[73].12–13 [Xiph.]) and the unpleasant spectacle of Julianus' slavish flattery of the senate.[92] Dio avers that no one was taken in by his act. The armies elsewhere put up three imperial candidates, and Severus was the first to reach Rome, whereupon Julianus was killed, despite his questioning the reason for his death (74[73].17.5 [Xiph.]).

X The Severans

Dio offers a few hints of hostility to Severus. First, his statement that Commodus was the last of the true Aurelii (73[72].22.6 [Xiph.]) undermines the pretention of the dynasty that they were the legitimate successors of Commodus. Furthermore, Severus' praise for Marius, Sulla, and Augustus combined with deprecation of Pompey's and Caesar's ἐπιείκεια is by no means intended to be positive.[93] Entering Rome at the beginning of his

---

[87] Dio attributes the downfall of Pertinax to the haste with which he embarked upon reforms (74[73.] 10.3 [Xiph./EV]). Other factors contributed; see, for example, Champlin 1979, Schöpe 2011.

[88] Specifically, her ἀκολασία (74[73].7.2 [Xiph.]).

[89] For detailed narrative of the assassination following mostly Dio and HA, see Birley 1999: 93–6. Appelbaum (2007) argues that there was no auction of the empire by the Praetorians after the death of Pertinax, but that the killing had to do with Laetus' and the Praetorians' desire not to have his or their power diminished. He believes also that Julianus may have had knowledge of the planned assassination; Pasek (2013: 280–4) disagrees, and distances Laetus from the mutiny as well.

[90] Kemezis 2012: 400–2.   [91] Leaning (1989: 555) agrees with Julianus' assessment.

[92] 74(73).14.1–2 (Xiph.): ἀνελευθέρως ... ἀκράτῳ ... τὸ ἔξωθεν τοῦ εἰκότος ('like a slave, weak, untoward').

[93] 76(75).8.1 (Xiph.); he might have added Pertinax (75[74].5.6 [EV]). Dio's allusion to the civil wars of the first century BC stands as a warning, whereas Herodian's (3.7.8) magnified Severus' achievement. See Schettino 2001: 543–7, and Urso 2016b: 13–22.

reign, Severus made a series of promises welcome to the senate, only to break them (75[74].2.1–2 [Xiph./*EV*]). In Dio's eyes, Severus revealed himself as anything but ἀγαθὸς αὐτοκράτωρ ('a good emperor') (76[75].7.4 [Xiph.])[94] when he celebrated the destruction of Albinus, his erstwhile Caesar, and mistreated his body, then adopted himself retroactively as the son of Marcus Aurelius and brother to Commodus.[95] Dio makes a show of correcting the official line, when he asserts that he is giving an accurate account of Albinus' suicide, or perhaps the aftermath, against what Severus had written about the same event (76[75].7.3 [Xiph.]).[96]

For a long time after establishing himself as Augustus, Severus allowed Plautianus, possibly his relative, possibly a person once condemned by Pertinax for gross misbehavior,[97] to exercise more power as praetorian prefect than even Sejanus (58.14.1) and failed to raise either of his sons to be a decent human being. Plautianus had many followers of his own, one of his flatterers being Caecilius Agricola, who had more πονηρία and ἀσέλγεια than anyone else (77[76].5.6 [Xiph./*EV*]). According to Dio, Plautianus killed a number of people, especially potential rivals in the praetorian guard, and took, stole, or demanded more than Severus did. Before relating that he had a hundred well-born Roman men castrated, some of them married adult men, to provide the best attendants for his daughter (76[75].14.2–5 [Xiph./*EV*]), Dio says that he believes Plautianus' outrageous behavior and inability to be satisfied (ἀπληστία) are demonstrated by his having sent centurions to find and bring back special striped horses from islands in the Persian gulf (76[75].14.3 [Xiph./*EV*]). The blame, Dio adds, belonged to Severus (76[75].15.1 [Xiph.]). Plautianus had become so profligate (ἀσωτότατος) (76[75].15.7 [Xiph./*EV*]) that he spent almost all his time feeding his appetite for food and wine, maidens and boys.[98] It was Caracalla who finally engineered the accusation that destroyed Plautianus and managed to pull it off (77 [76].3–4 [Xiph./*EV*]).[99] Dio recounts the accusations that followed,

---

[94] Unlike Pertinax, who was exactly that, with specific details: 74(73).5.2 (Xiph.). See Molin 2006: 442.

[95] Discussions of Dio's overall assessment of Severus, positive with negative, include Millar 1964: 138–41; Birley 1989: 198–200; Madsen 2016; Rantala 2016.

[96] Cf. Rantala 2016: 166–8, Cesare Letta in Chapter 2 and cf. Chapter 1, where Adam Kemezis discusses Dio's various approaches to imperial narratives.

[97] 74(73).15.4 (*EV*): ἐπὶ πονηρίᾳ καὶ ἀπληστίᾳ ἀσελγείᾳ τε.

[98] His feasting involved almost simultaneous vomiting of whatever he had ingested; Vitellius (64-[65].2.2 [Xiph., *EV*]) behaved similarly, although Dio says that he was nourished (somehow) by the passage of food but that Plautianus could not derive any sustenance from what he ate, so quickly did he lose it.

[99] Bingham and Imrie (2015) make a case against Dio's version, and argue that the plan to kill Severus and Caracalla was genuine.

including the remarkable session in the senate on the topic of the fateful dream, the bald senator who heard it described, and Dio's own feeling of helplessness as he stood witness (77[76].8.4 [Xiph.]).[100]

Severus had proved incapable of managing his sons, and now with Plautianus dead both Geta and Caracalla knew no limit to their enjoyment of doing whatever they wished, including violating women and boys (77[76].7.1 [EV/ Xiph.]). Evidently not content to wait for his father to die, Caracalla tried to kill both his brother and father (77-[76].14 [Xiph.]), yet Severus for whatever motive did not remove him.[101] Dio finds Severus' paternal affection misplaced in view of the fates of his other son and of the empire. Geta's fate was quickly sealed, although his brother improperly honored his Manes as a means of insult (78[77].12.6 [EV]). Like Gaius, Nero, and Commodus, Caracalla devoted his attention to chariot racing (and driving), and like Commodus he killed countless animals in the amphitheatre (78[77].10.1–2 [Xiph.]). Like Domitian, he loathed his brother. He resembled his father in one telling respect, his esteem for Sulla, whose grave he found and had restored because he emulated his cruelty (ὠμότης 78[77].13.7 [EV]). He committed an excessive number of murders (78[77].16.1 [EV/Xiph.]), including the deaths of four Vestals, one of whom he had dishonored himself. But that was his pattern: An adulterer himself, like Domitian he inflicted capital punishment on others for the same thing (78[77].16.4 [EV]).[102]

On his eastern expedition, Caracalla spent the winter at Nicomedia, where he entertained himself driving chariots, killing beasts, fighting as a gladiator, drinking and feasting with soldiers, the latter in front of senators whom he would neither admit nor allow to satisfy thirst or hunger (78[77].17.4 [Xiph./EV]). Not entirely idle, he squeezed in some preparations for attacks on Armenia and Parthia while continuing his usual practices: ἐμιαιφόνει καὶ παρηνόμει καὶ τὰ χρήματα κατανήλισκεν ('shedding blood, breaking laws, squandering money') (78[77].18.1 [Xiph/EV]).

---

[100] The scene of senators looking to see which of their fellows were most bald, and Dio feeling his own head of hair to make sure of its existence, has been frequently noted and commented upon. Gleason (2011: 54–6) is especially valuable. Note also Rhiannon Ash's discussion of this scene in Chapter 4 in this volume, and the telling measure of shared shame among the senators.

[101] 77(76).14.7 (Xiph.): ὑπεξαιρεῖν, the verb Dio says Severus used of what Marcus Aurelius ought to have done to Commodus. Davenport and Mallan (2014: 657–61), in the context of the adoption speech given by Dio to Hadrian, note the similarities between the historian's accounts of the two natural heirs.

[102] At 78(77).24.2 (EV) Dio describes Caracalla as a self-styled σώφρων (moderate) who punished others' ἀσέλγεια. See also Schulz 2019a: 252 for concise collection of some parallels.

His assistants were several: The eunuch Sempronius Rufus attained great authority[103] – Dio avers that this was the most disgraceful and unworthy situation (ἀσχημονέστατον καὶ ἀναξιώτατον) (78[77].17.2 [Xiph./*EV*]) – and the freedmen Epagathus and Theocritus, one worse than the other, more powerful than the prefects, although only the latter was specifically charged with wide-scale fraud and murder (78[77].21.2–4 [Xiph.]). Although he had granted his mother considerable authority, he had no use for the good advice she offered him (78[77].18.2 [Xiph./*EV*]).[104] Dio's description of the powers that Julia Domna acquired does tend to emasculate,[105] or perhaps infantilize, the emperor. At any rate, the son suffers by comparison.[106] During his stay at Antioch (78[77].20 [Xiph.]) Caracalla resembled more than one predecessor at a time, indulging in luxury like Vitellius and complaining of his toils and dangers like Gaius (cf. 59.23.1). The last atrocity of the outgoing regime was the slaughter of the Alexandrians. He began his visit with a pretense of affection (78[77].22.1 [Xiph.]), and, not neglecting to steal or squander as much wealth as could be found, including from some holy places, he directed his soldiers to commit constant and indiscriminate murders (μιαιφονίαι) through the city, whose remaining inhabitants were left with physical barriers, guards, and loss of public entertainment or nourishment (78[77].22–23.1 [Xiph.], 23.2 [*EV*], and 23.3–4 [Xiph./*EV*]).[107] In the course of the expedition against the Parthians, when the opposition's gathering of a large army frightened the cowardly emperor (79[78].3.1), a delayed message prevented Caracalla from learning of a potential danger closer to himself, and thus he perished ignobly when Macrinus sought safety in action (79[78].4.4–5.5). Not reluctant to reveal his loathing,[108] from this point in the narrative Dio employs terms other than Antoninus to describe the deceased ruler: Bassianus or Caracallus or Tarautas (after a gladiator who was ugly and exceptionally bloodthirsty) (79[78].9.3).[109] Part of the post-mortem dishonor involved enumeration back at Rome of all Caracalla's μιαιφονίαι.

---

[103] Davenport (2012a: 812) believes that by 'us' Dio may indicate the court rather than the senate and people of Rome.

[104] Mallan 2013a: 746.   [105] Langford 2013: 119 with n. 20.

[106] See Mallan (2013a: 756–7) for discussion of the link between Marcus Aurelius and Julia Domna and their unsatisfactory sons.

[107] Monica Hellström offers more details of this rampage in Chapter 9.

[108] Cf. Millar 1964: 150; Meckler (1999: 40) uses the word bias; Davenport (2012a: 797–803) discusses Dio's alienation from the courts of Severus and Caracalla. Scott (2015: 161) argues that Dio described Caracalla as he believed him to be rather than a created figure typical of tyrants; the contempt becomes open during the narrative of the abortive Parthian campaign (see Scott 2018b: 32).

[109] See Schulz 2019a: 261–3 on Dio's erasure of memory employing nicknames and denying official imperial genealogies.

Macrinus was possessed of a good character but inadequate background for the position in which he found himself,[110] being the first equestrian to become emperor without having been senator (79[78].11), a coward by virtue of being a Moor (79[78].27.1),[111] and at a loss to manage civil affairs in an appropriate manner or to prosecute the war against the Parthian Artabanus, although he did manage to make peace with both the Parthians and Armenians (79[78].27). Eventually felled in civil war, he gained a disquisition from Dio on sensible behavior and not desiring things above one's station (79[78].41),[112] and leaves the pages of the history.

The penultimate ruler counted as Severan, Elagabalus the alleged son of Caracalla, also called Pseudantoninus (79[78].32.3), Avitus, the Assyrian, or Sardanapallos (80[79].1.1) and Tiberinus after death (80[79].1.1, 80[79].21.3 [Xiph./*EV*]), was never anything but young, nor, in Dio's telling, anything but disgusting.[113] The activities in which he immersed himself were the most shameful, lawless, and bloodstained (80[79].3.3); what he both did and allowed others to do to him were ἀσελγέστατα (80[79].5.5). The purge that marked the beginning of his reign included his supporter Gannys, who had a few faults but in particular wanted Elagabalus to behave in a manner fitting his position (σωφρόνως τε καὶ ἐμφρόνως ζῆν) (80[79] 6.3).[114] Thanks to the overturning of all propriety, men of no standing whatever attempted usurpation (80[79].7.2).[115]

Unable even to be a man (ἀνήρ),[116] he somehow managed to dishonor the Vestal Aquilia Severa in a most unholy manner (ἀσεβέστατα)

---

[110]   Dio's portrait is at odds with itself but can be reduced to 'good man, wrong man for the job' (Scott 2012: 20–1).

[111]   See discussion in Scott 2018b: 79–80.

[112]   Swain (1996: 405 n. 20) notes that Dio attributes the failure to the lack of senatorial standing. Cf. Gleason 2011: 66–9; Davenport and Mallan 2014: 647; Scott 2018b: 100–1.

[113]   Millar (1964: 170) observes, 'A fiercely hostile and fantastic conception of an Emperor's conduct can easily be the accurate reflection of contemporary rumour and belief.' Icks (2008: 482–6) demonstrates the tropes that allowed the sources, especially Dio and Herodian, to emphasize the aspects of Elagabalus' behavior and policies that typified effete oriental despots, while not ignoring the religious innovation. Kemezis (2016: 359) states that contemporaries seem to have preferred 'stories about sex to stories about religion' to explain his death. Sommer (2004) and Osgood (2016) detail how the image is, after all, an image that, as Sommer (2004: 96) writes, reveals more about the image's creator than about its subject. Scott (2018b: 109–10) cautions that the narrative followed the ruler's death. Schulz (2019a: 252–4) collects Dio's accounts of Elagabalus' transgressive religious and sexual activities.

[114]   Scott (2018b: 122) notes the parallel with Burrus and Seneca as Nero's sober advisors.

[115]   A senator whose last position had been centurion, and the son of a medical doctor. See Molin (2016: 473–6) for an assemblage of examples.

[116]   80(79).9.1 (Xiph.). There is also the notice, preserved in Zonaras, that Elagabalus wanted to have a vagina created in his body (80[79].16.7 [Zonar.]); Icks (2012: 100) argues that the tale was probably genuinely from Dio. This is not to say the story is true. Yet it may well have been believable if the

(80[79].9.3). The adverb appears redundant, but perhaps not. In telling of this relatively brief but memorable reign, Dio repeats all of the words relating both to violation of what is sacred and to sexual misbehavior and excess, including terms for prostitutes and prostitution.[117] Introduction of a new god and practice of new cult rituals were manifestations of the same un-Roman, eastern decadence; Maecenas' advice to ensure one's immortality was to observe traditional religious practices strictly and exclusively.[118] His companions and favorites were equally unwholesome but not equally adorned with opprobrium, although Aurelius Eubulus was so notorious for both licentiousness and filth that the people had wanted to remove him long before they actually did (80[79].21.1 [Xiph./*EV*]). With his favorite Hierocles, as well as others, Elagabalus played the role of a Roman *matrona* who often cheated on her spouse (80[79].15.3 [Xiph./*EV*]). There is scarcely room in the catalogue to enumerate the non-sexual misdemeanors such as promoting unsuitable men to office (Comazon as praetorian prefect, consul, and prefect of the city, 80[79].4.1), squandering wealth, confiscations, and murders, but these occurred as well (such as deaths of some of Macrinus' followers and a great many others) (80[79] 6.3). His ultimate reward was well deserved, 'a most suitable recompense for his filth' (ἀξιώτατον τῆς μιαρίας τῆς ἑαυτοῦ μισθὸν) (80[79].17.1 [Xiph.]).[119]

XI   Conclusion

Dio's practice of placing a summation of an emperor's qualities early in the narrative of each reign[120] gives the reader the appropriate lenses through which to read, advance warning of what to look out for so as not to miss anything. Although he seems to have regarded Marcus Aurelius as the best of imperial role models, his introduction of Trajan offers the best general outline of what sort of person makes an effective ruler if there is no

---

emperor displayed as many feminine traits as historians have asserted; cf. Bittarello 2011: 96–100. See, too, Molin 2016: 481.

[117] For example, 80(79).13.2–3 (Xiph./*EV*); adultery: 80(79).15.3 (Xiph./*EV*); filth (μιαρία): 80(79).17.1 (Xiph.), 80(79).21.1 (Xiph./*EV*) and uncleanliness (ἀκαθαρσία): 80(79).13.4 (Xiph./*EV*), sexual licentiousness (verb, noun, adverb): 79.5.5, 80(79).13.1 and 3 (Xiph./*EV*), 80(79).15.3 (Xiph./*EV*), 80[79].19.3 (Xiph.).

[118] 52.36.1–2; Scott 2018b: 7. Piatkowski (1984: 600–4) compares the practices of Gaius, Commodus, Caracalla, and Elagabalus.

[119] Kemezis 2016, after careful scrutiny of available evidence, concludes that the coup occurred in political circumstances typical of the era, circumstances that would reappear later in the century.

[120] Cf. Mallan 2013b: 636.

philosopher available. Moral qualities aside – and as noted above Trajan possessed the best of these – he was the right age physically and mentally, neither adolescent nor dotard.[121]

But to make a child or virtual child an emperor risks more than the misfortune of getting whatever person genetics serves up, a system that Dio did not favor. An adolescent emperor may engage in playing games without caring about consequences, in being seen and performing for applause, imitating the actions of others who claim the attention of an audience: charioteers, gladiators, stage performers. He may cease to distinguish between role playing and reality.[122] A child who does not realize that he is mortal or fears that he is all too human may assume a divine persona (Gaius, Nero, Commodus), another may try to overcome weakness in assumed strength and act the thug and would-be commander of men (Domitian, Caracalla).[123] A good ruler chooses his subordinates carefully and monitors them well; a bad one attracts the worst influencers who lead him to do their will.

An immature ruler is likely to be impulsive, self-centered, and, without the capacity for serious thought, rejoicing in pushing at boundaries and learning that there are none, other than the termini of life itself. Proper-thinking people (οἱ νοῦν ἔχοντες) can only mourn, do their best, offer warnings perhaps, and wait for something better. Dio and others like himself, who surely knew how to think properly and preferred excellence to profligacy (74[73].3.4 [Xiph.]), often had to gauge themselves as well as others by what they were not.[124]

---

[121] 68.6.3 (Xiph./*EV*): τῷ τε γὰρ σώματι ἔρρωτο (δεύτερον γὰρ καὶ τεσσαρακοστὸν ἄγων ἔτος ἦρξεν) ὡς ἐξ ἴσου πάντα τοῖς ἄλλοις τρόπον τινὰ πονεῖσθαι, καὶ τῆς ψυχῆς ἤκμαζεν ὡς μήθ᾿ ὑπὸ νεότητος θρασύνεσθαι μήθ᾿ ὑπὸ γήρως ἀμβλύνεσθαι. ('He was physically vigorous (for he began to rule in his forty-second year) so as to partake in all tasks equally with the others and had maturity of spirit to the extent that he was neither audacious because of youth nor slowed down by age.')

[122] Gowing 1997: 2587.

[123] As de Blois (1998: 3413–14) observed, Dio had no opinion whatever of 'Commodus' self-worship, Caracalla's Alexander mania and Elagabalus' religious experiments'.

[124] I do not have words adequate to express my gratitude for the encouragement and guidance of the editors Caillan Davenport and Christopher Mallan. Their patience, generosity, and hard work have extended over almost four years at the time of this writing.

CHAPTER 12

Dio and His Friends
Autobiography and Biography in Cassius Dio's Contemporary Narrative

Christopher Mallan

I Introduction

In the age of the Severans, Cassius Dio was a senator whose views of himself and of his world made him something of a living anachronism. Dio believed in a form of republican monarchy more attuned to the age of Pliny than to the age of Philostratus or indeed, of pseudo-Oppian.[1] He believed in the fundamental necessity of traditional Roman institutions.[2] He believed that the imperial office should pass to the most qualified man rather than be determined by accident of birth.[3] Above all, he believed in the importance and primacy of his social class and political caste. During his lifetime in politics Dio would see these beliefs challenged, abused, and discarded by the men of the ruling dynasty.

As we may expect from such a man, Dio's contemporary history is coloured with disappointment and resentment. He treats the emperors of his own day with a degree of 'parrhesiastic' vigour and venom that is generally absent from his earlier imperial narrative, and which, more importantly, he was not willing (or able) to exercise during his long political career.[4] His account of the emperor known to us as Elagabalus, for example, is a model of sustained vituperative discourse, and as such has been the subject of much recent analysis.[5] As a contemporary witness and

---

I would like to thank Caillan Davenport and Helen Tanner for their feedback on this chapter. All dates in this chapter are AD, unless otherwise noted, and translations are the author's own except where stated.

[1] E.g. Dio uses the adjective δημοτικός as a term of praise for emperors who consulted the senate: e.g. 57.9.1 (referring to the conduct described in 57.7.2–9.3); 74(73).3.4 (Xiph./*EV*). For δημοτικός as loosely cognate with the Latin *civilis*, see Wallace-Hadrill 1982: 44.

[2] Thus Kemezis 2014:126–39.

[3] For Dio's attitude to the question of imperial succession, see Davenport and Mallan 2014.

[4] As I have argued elsewhere: Mallan 2016. For *parrhesia* as an ideal quality for a historian, see Lucian, *Hist. conscrib.* 41.

[5] Most recently, see Icks 2008, Osgood 2016; Kemezis 2016b; Scott 2018b.

occasional participant of events, Dio's account of the period from the murder of Commodus through to the liquidation of Elagabalus is perhaps one of the most interesting parts of his *Roman History* – even when viewed through the narrowing lens of the imperfect textual tradition of his work. Racy, piquant, sometimes prurient; without doubt, Dio's is the most vivid account of the Severan age to have survived from antiquity.[6]

Yet there is more to the 'Severan Narrative' than the Severans. Any reader of the text will see that Dio's account of the period is highly personal and, one might add, highly personalised.[7] Dio weaves himself and his experiences into his narrative to a degree which is striking. Of his historiographical precursors, who wrote in a similar mode to Dio, only Polybius, Josephus, and perhaps Nicolaus of Damascus include a similarly high degree of autobiographical content.[8] Even in its truncated and abbreviated form, the character of the historian emerges, clear and unmistakable. Indeed, by the time Dio reached the reign of Severus Alexander, this history has, in fact, turned into an autobiography. Like most autobiographical endeavours, ancient and modern, it is an attempt of positive self-fashioning. Here Dio's comments about his contemporaries matter too. Dio is, to borrow from the vernacular of the twenty-first century, a dedicated 'virtue signaller'. Indeed, what Dio chooses to say about his contemporaries tells us much about Dio's construction of his persona as the senatorial historian.

As an historian of contemporary events and an observer of those men around him, Cassius Dio was the Edward Hyde of his generation.[9] Like the Earl of Clarendon, Dio was a master of the character sketch. Dio's history, more than any other literary source for the high politics of the Severan era, allows us to put flesh on the bones of the men who made up the non-imperial aristocracy. Yet we may ask, what can these portraits tell us about Dio's personal attitudes and opinions? We may go further and ask how these fit into the broader commemorative culture of the late-Antonine and

---

[6] In Millar's judgment (1964: 173): 'He [Dio] makes no attempt to step away from the standpoint which personal circumstance had given him, to avoid *studium et ira*, or to impose a pattern on his experience. Such limitations perhaps raise rather than lower the historical value of these books.'

[7] E.g., see Millar 1964: 119–73; Molin 2016b: 469–82; Scott 2018a.

[8] We may be tempted to add Appian to this list, if we were to go on the basis of the surviving fragment from his twenty-fourth (and final) book, the *Arabian History*. For comments on this aspect of Dio's later books, and specifically their position between 'memoir and history', Hidber 2004 and Scott 2018a.

[9] Edward Hyde, First Earl of Clarendon, wrote the *History of the Rebellion and Civil Wars in England*. Clarendon was also High Chancellor of England under Charles II, and Chancellor of the University of Oxford.

Severan periods and the so-called economy of honour?[10] This chapter is an attempt to answer these questions. It is, in essence, about the processes of literary commemoration and self-fashioning in Dio's contemporary narrative, and what this tells us about his representation of contemporary senatorial culture.

This chapter falls into two parts. We shall begin by considering how Dio presents himself to the reader, and the purpose of this authorial persona.[11] As we shall see, his autobiographical statements contain three conspicuous leitmotifs: his senatorial ethic, his proximity to the powerful, and his divine favour. From here we shall move to some of Dio's character sketches of his contemporaries, and about the ideals (or vices) his coevals are made to represent, and how these feed into Dio's representation of political culture under the Severans and his place within that culture.

II The Historian on Himself

By tradition, Roman senators were expected to serve the state *domi militiaeque* – at home and on military campaign.[12] The advent of the Principate of Augustus reduced the opportunity for senators to win military glory for themselves: any military victory was counted to be that of the supreme commander, the emperor himself. Military virtue was an imperial monopoly.[13] Yet the senatorial ideal continued until well into the third century. The so-called 'career inscriptions' of prominent members of the senatorial and equestrian aristocracies showed how these men wished to be remembered.[14] Archaeologists have found no such inscription for Dio. But our historian did leave a career inscription of sorts – not in stone, but in his *Roman History*.

In early 193, Cassius Dio conceived a desire to write history. It was a year of considerable anxiety for Dio, then a man in his early thirties. The omens at the end of 192 had been alarming. Eagles had circled the Capitol and an owl, hooting ominously, was observed on that very hill as well. A great fire,

[10] The most insightful discussion on the concept of honour in Roman political culture remains that of Lendon 1997.
[11] Scott (2018a: 233) is quite right in differentiating between Dio the character and occasional participant in the narrative *Roman History* and Dio the persona of the historian, or in the language of narratology, the primary focaliser. For the purpose of this chapter, my chief concern is how the former contributes to the latter. When I speak of Dio, I am referring to man and his authorial persona.
[12] Cf. Campbell 1984: 317–62.   [13] Tac. *Agr.* 39.
[14] On the genre of the 'career inscription', see Alföldy 2001; Eck 1995; Eck 1999; Eck 2009; Davenport 2019: 256–60.

which had started in the Temple of Peace, had swept through Rome, even damaging the imperial residence on the Palatine Hill. It was in this conflagration that the great medical writer, Galen, lost many of his books and medical collections.[15] The written records of the city were also badly damaged or lost outright: a reminder of the fragility of the written record of the past which must have impressed itself on the mind of the budding historian. On New Year's Eve 192, the emperor Commodus was assassinated in a palace organised putsch. His replacement, a grave, experienced military man,[16] P. Helvius Pertinax, showed Dio favour, nominating him one of the praetors for the following year. Yet by 28 March, Pertinax too lay dead, murdered by the disgruntled praetorian guard, and was replaced by the odious plutocrat Didius Julianus, a senator who had notoriously outbid his rival to the leadership of the state. Worryingly for Dio, Julianus had been a one-time opponent of his in the courtroom, and the praetor designate was concerned for his future (74[73].12.2 [Xiph.]).

The accession of Julianus failed to win consensus among his senatorial peers, and three provincial governors revolted: Pescennius Niger in Syria, Septimius Severus in Pannonia, and Clodius Albinus in Britain. All men had command of military resources and made a bid for power. Severus reached Rome before the others and seized the empire.

Without question, 193 was Dio's crisis year. What Dio would do for the rest of his life was settled during those turbulent months, where five imperial aspirants would claim the throne. It was the year Dio's career began in a meaningful way, and the year he set himself on his course to write history. Pertinax designated Dio as one of the praetors for the following year (194) (74[73].12.2 [Xiph.]). The fact that Dio adds this detail, the first specific detail he offers of his career, is intended to show the esteem in which he was held, for to be nominated by the emperor was a mark of honour.[17] As we shall see, this sort of comment is a feature of the subsequent narrative.

It was at this point that Dio had received the first of his dreams. The year, so it appears, was 193. Dio says:

---

[15] Galen, *Peri alupias* 12b-37. For a translation and discussion of this text (*On Avoiding Distress*), see Nutton 2013.

[16] See Chapter 8 by Caillan Davenport for Dio's take on Pertinax's military credentials.

[17] Birley 1981: 15; cf. Duncan-Jones 2016: 24–5. For Dio's comments on the development of this practice under Tiberius, note 58.20.3–4.

(1) But after this [sc. the death of Commodus] there occurred wars and great civil strife, and I put together a narrative of these events arising from this particular cause. I had written and circulated a pamphlet about the dreams and signs through which Severus expected to gain the imperial power; (2) and Severus, after reading a copy I sent him, wrote me a long and complimentary acknowledgement. This letter I received about nightfall, and soon after fell asleep; and in my dreams the Divine Power (τὸ δαιμόνιον) commanded me to write history. [...] (3) And inasmuch as it won the high approval, not only of others, but in particular, of Severus himself, I then conceived a desire to compile a record of everything else that concerned the Romans. Therefore, I decided to leave this first composition no longer as a separate composition, but to incorporate it into the present history, in order that in a single work I might write down and leave behind me a record of everything from the beginning down to the point that shall seem best to Tyche. (4) This goddess gives me strength to continue my history when I become timid and disposed to shrink from it; when I grow weary and would resign the task, she wins me back by sending dreams, and with fair hopes that future times will permit my history to survive and never dim its lustre; she, it seems, has fallen to my lot as guardian of the course of my life, and therefore, I have dedicated myself to her (73[72].23.1–5 [Xiph.]).[18]

The passage reveals much about Dio the man, his world, and the nature of his history. We see Dio's self-representation as a man who was the recipient of both imperial favour as well as divine favour. As noted by Hidber, this is an unusual combination in ancient historiography, incorporating tropes more familiar to panegyric (political favour) and poetry (divine inspiration) than to history.[19] The passage also introduces an individual who, along with his dysfunctional family, would play a major role in Dio's life and dreams, Lucius Septimius Severus.

[18] (1) πόλεμοι δὲ μετὰ τοῦτο καὶ στάσεις μέγισται συνέβησαν, συνέθηκα δ᾽ ἐγὼ τούτων τὴν συγγραφὴν ἐξ αἰτίας τοιᾶσδε. βιβλίον τι περὶ τῶν ὀνειράτων καὶ τῶν σημείων δι᾽ ὧν ὁ Σεουῆρος τὴν αὐτοκράτορα ἀρχὴν ἤλπισε, γράψας ἐδημοσίευσα· (2) καὶ αὐτῷ καὶ ἐκεῖνος πεμφθέντι παρ᾽ ἐμοῦ ἐντυχὼν πολλά μοι καὶ καλὰ ἀντεπέστειλε. ταῦτ᾽ οὖν ἐγὼ τὰ γράμματα πρὸς ἑσπέραν ἤδη λαβὼν κατέδαρθον, καί μοι καθεύδοντι προσέταξε τὸ δαιμόνιον ἱστορίαν γράφειν. [...] (3) καὶ ἐπειδή γε τοῖς τε ἄλλοις καὶ αὐτῷ τῷ Σεουήρῳ μάλιστα ἤρεσε, τότε δὴ καὶ τἆλλα πάντα τὰ τοῖς Ῥωμαίοις προσήκοντα συνθεῖναι ἐπεθύμησα· καὶ διὰ τοῦτο οὐκέτι ἰδίᾳ ἐκεῖνο ὑπολιπεῖν ἀλλ᾽ ἐς τήνδε τὴν συγγραφὴν ἐμβαλεῖν ἔδοξέ μοι, ἵν᾽ ἐν μιᾷ πραγματείᾳ ἀπ᾽ ἀρχῆς πάντα, μέχρις ἂν καὶ τῇ Τύχῃ δόξῃ, γράψας καταλίπω. (4) τὴν δὲ δὴ θεὸν ταύτην ἐπιρρωννύουσάν με πρὸς τὴν ἱστορίαν εὐλαβῶς πρὸς αὐτὴν καὶ ὀκνηρῶς διακείμενον, καὶ πονούμενον ἀπαγορεύοντά τε ἀνακτωμένην δι᾽ ὀνειράτων, καὶ καλὰς ἐλπίδας περὶ τοῦ μέλλοντος χρόνου διδοῦσάν μοι ὡς ὑπολειψομένου τὴν ἱστορίαν καὶ οὐδαμῶς ἀμαυρώσοντος, ἐπίσκοπον τῆς τοῦ βίου διαγωγῆς, ὡς ἔοικε, εἴληχα, καὶ διὰ τοῦτο αὐτῇ ἀνάκειμαι. (trans. E. Cary, Loeb Classical Library edition, adapted)
[19] Hidber 2004: 188–9; cf. Marincola 1997: 48–9.

The figure of Severus appears in the second of Dio's autobiographical dreams. In that dream, Dio tells the reader how he knew that he would continue writing history of events after the death of Caracalla.[20] The dream features Dio in the presence of Severus, surveying the extent of the Roman empire. The emperor says to the dreaming senatorial historian: 'Come [. . .] here, Dio, stand close by, in order that you may learn accurately and write down all the things spoken and done' (δεῦρο [. . .] Δίων, ἐνταῦθα πλησίον πρόσελθε, ἵνα πάντα καὶ τὰ λεγόμενα καὶ τὰ γιγνόμενα καὶ μάθῃς ἀκριβῶς καὶ συγγράψῃς) (79[78]10.2 [Xiph.]). *Prima facie*, the dream serves as an appeal for the accuracy of his post-Severus narrative, one in which he would be an eyewitness.[21] From a narrative perspective, one important thing about these two passages is that Dio chose to incorporate this information at their (almost) correct chronological positions in history, not, as we might otherwise expect in the case of the first dream, at the beginning of his work, which me may expect to be its obvious narrative position within the *Roman History*. Yet these autobiographical details are significant for another reason. Throughout the *Roman History*, Dio was alert to including only 'those details worthy of memory'.[22] Patently for our historian, his personal experiences passed this test, and he viewed his experiences as being part of the Roman story.

The symbolism of the second dream is particularly striking and worth noting. Severus appears here as a symbol of imperial power.[23] His interaction with Dio encapsulates the ideal of the *civilis princeps*: the dream-emperor is accessible and affable towards his senatorial colleague. In this context, it is easy to play the Freudian and to interpret such a dream as wish fulfilment on the part of the dreamer. But there may be more to it than this. Dio was clearly interested in the interpretation of dreams, as were many of his contemporaries, and they would have been alert to the symbolism of the dream. From the evidence of Artemidorus (4.31.1–2), dreams featuring emperors seem to have been regarded as auspicious. Hence, we may read it in a similar way to his first dream, where Dio is encouraged, and thus favoured, by the goddess Tyche. In both dreams

---

[20] Although the dream seemingly occurred in 211, after the death of Severus and before that of Geta.
[21] Note 73(72).23.5 (Xiph.), where Dio suggests that his narrative up to the death of Severus had been compiled from what had been written. Cf. F 1.2 (*ES*).
[22] E.g. 57.14.1: λέξω . . . ὅσα γε καὶ μνήμης ἄξιά ἐστιν; cf. F 1.2 (*ES*): συνέγραψα δὲ οὐ πάντα ἀλλ' ὅσα ἐξέκρινα.
[23] As discussed already by Adam Kemezis in Chapter 1, Dio's overall attitude towards Severus the man was complex and is not easily discerned from the text of the *Roman History*.

Dio's literary endeavour is supported ultimately by the heavenly power (τὸ δαιμόνιον, *to daimonion*).

Writing and politics were two sides of the same coin for Dio. The overtures he made to Severus, specifically the book on the omens and portents, apparently secured his nomination for the praetorship in 194. However, Dio does not appeared to have enjoyed any particular favour during the reign of Severus, despite the fact he likes to give the impression that he was an insider. On several occasions Dio was certainly part of a larger group of senatorial advisors to the emperor (*consilium principis*). One such occasion was the trial of Raecius Constans, a one-time governor of Sardinia, who was accused of having destroyed images of the praetorian prefect, Plautianus, in early 206 (76[75].16.3–4 [Xiph.]).[24] But it would be wrong to construe such bodies as being a fixed or official 'court of justice', or that Dio was a confidant to the emperor: as we know, emperors often chose their advisors on an ad hoc basis.[25]

Even so, Dio was not entirely in the cold during Severus' reign. In the imperial economy of honour, political advancement was not entirely dependent on intimacy with the emperor, and it was most likely under Severus that Dio first held the consulship. The year of his suffect consulship is generally assumed to be 205, the year before the trial of Raecius Constans.[26] Dio adds that in the year that he was consul, he found the names of three thousand men and women who had been indicted for adultery under the legislation which had been enacted by the emperor to crack down on the morals of members of the Roman élites (77[76].16.4 [Xiph.]). For much of this period, Dio appears to have remained in Italy. He had a house in Capua, where he spent his free time researching and writing his history (77[76].2.1 [Xiph.]). Indeed, contrary to his relationship with Severus implied in his second dream, it seems fairly clear from the evidence of Dio's career that he was not on any terms of great intimacy with Severus.

Dio reappears in the narrative of the reign of Caracalla. The location is the Bithynian city of Nicomedia, where Dio was part of the imperial entourage (78[77].17–18 [Xiph.]).[27] The experience appears to have

---

[24] For discussion of this passage, see Davenport 2012a: 799–80. The incident of Raecius Constans is discussed further in Chapter 2 by Caillan Davenport.

[25] Cf. Dio's comments about appointments to the imperial *consilium* under Tiberius: 57.17.9 (Xiph.).

[26] Dio's suffect consulship almost certainly occurred in the reign of Severus, and it is usually given as ca. 205: e.g. *PIR²* C 492; Millar 1964: 204–7; Syme 1971: 145; Davenport 2011: 282. Molin (2016a: 440) opts for a slightly later date, ca. 207. Cesare Letta (Chapter 3 [n. 58]) puts forward a date in the 220s; cf. Letta 2019b: 163–71.

[27] This was either in 214/215 or, as argued by Letta 1994 and others, 213/214. For a summary of the scholarship on the dating of this event, see Scott 2018b: 1 n. 3.

solidified Dio's opinion on the surviving son of Severus. A violent fratri-
cide, the youthful emperor, with his ill-conceived desire to emulate
Alexander the Great, was, in Dio's view, manifestly ill-equipped to
rule.[28] The experience was doubtless one of conflicting emotions for the
historian. On the one hand it afforded the semblance of honour and
imperial favour. On the other hand, it meant that Dio had to endure the
sort of behaviour from Caracalla which Dio found most disrespectful.
What remains of Dio's narrative of this event conforms to the usual pattern
of Dio's first-hand narratives: exemplary behaviour on his own part, often
dubious behaviour on the part of the emperor.

From what we can tell, Dio's relationship with Caracalla was no closer
than that with Severus.[29] Formal provincial appointments proved elusive
under both emperors, and we hear of no receipt of emoluments or
preferment.[30] It was not until the accession of the low-born Macrinus
that we know for certain that Dio saw service in the provinces. He was
appointed curator of the Asian cities of Pergamum and Smyrna. Before the
fourth century, *curatores* were appointed directly by the emperor, from
candidates of usually senatorial or equestrian rank.[31] It might have been the
case that the Bithynian Dio was appointed as *curator* of these Asian cities
for a specific reason, but, alas, Dio provides no context for this appointment. At any rate, Dio remained in this post for an uncertain period of
time, although seemingly this appointment continued into the reign of
Elagabalus. Certainly, it is clear that Dio was absent from Rome for much
if not all of the period between 218 and 222.[32]

We now have arrived at the final phase of Dio's career, the part on which
Dio furnishes the most information. It is in some ways the most problematic. The following details are supplied immediately after his narration of
the death of Elagabalus (which occurred in 222). Dio says with almost
lapidary brevity:

> (2) From Asia I went straight to Bithynia as I had fallen ill, and from there
> I went to take up my governorship of Africa; (3) no sooner had I returned to
> Italy I was then sent almost immediately to Dalmatia then on to Pannonia

---

[28] Cf. Gleason 2011: 62–5; Mallan 2017b: 134–6 for Dio's portrayal of Caracalla as a 'pseudo-
Alexander'.
[29] Davenport 2012a; cf. Scott 2015.
[30] Or at least none that Dio tells us about. It has been conjectured that Dio had some governorship in
a minor province during the reign of Severus, on the basis of an imperial rescript to 'Dio', preserved
in the *Digest* (50.12.7, citing the jurist Paulus).
[31] For *curatores*, see Burton 1979.
[32] Which, of course, compromises (or explains?) his claims for autopsy for the post-Caracalla narrative
implicit in his narrative of his second dream.

to govern over those people, and after this I returned to Rome and to Campania from where I made preparations to return home. (80[80].1.2–3 [Xiph.])[33]

These postings cover the reigns of three emperors: Macrinus, Elagabalus, and Severus Alexander. The dating or length of each appointment evades precise identification.[34] This vagueness is clearly intentional. Syme suggested that Dio wanted to suppress knowledge of his advancement under the odious Elagabalus,[35] yet such a conclusion must not be regarded as inevitable. If, indeed, Dio were the recipient of favour from Elagabalus there is no trace in Dio's career record. Neither the continuation of Dio's curatorship of Pergamum and Smyrna during the early years of Elagabalus' reign, nor his governorship of North Africa in either 221 or 222 can be construed as the product of imperial favouritism.[36] After all, the proconsulship of Africa was determined by the lot rather than direct imperial appointment. The governorships in Dalmatia and Pannonia fell between the years 223 and 228, but their duration is unknown.[37] For Dio's narrative purposes, it was not the dating of these appointments that was important, but the very fact that that he had held them.

The brevity of this passage is reminiscent of the so-called *cursus* inscriptions mentioned above, which typically list the (major) posts held by the honorand.[38] The similarity between Dio's account of his career and the

---

[33] (2) ἔκ τε γὰρ τῆς Ἀσίας ἐς τὴν Βιθυνίαν ἐλθὼν ἠρρώστησα, κἀκεῖθεν πρὸς τὴν Ἀφρικῇ ἡγεμονίαν ἠπείχθην, (3) ἐπανελθών τε ἐς τὴν Ἰταλίαν εὐθέως ὡς εἰπεῖν ἔς τε τὴν Δελματίαν κἀντεῦθεν ἐς τὴν Παννονίαν τὴν ἄνω ἄρξων ἐπέμφθην, καὶ μετὰ τοῦτ' ἐς τὴν Ῥώμην καὶ ἐς τὴν Καμπανίαν ἀφικόμενος παραχρῆμα οἴκαδε ἐξωρμήθην.

[34] For attempted reconstructions of the chronology of Dio's career, see Syme 1971: 144–5; Barnes 1984: 240–55, 243–5; Leunissen 1989: 162 with nn. 147, 219, 240–1; Schmidt 1997: 2636–8; Molin 2016a; Scott 2018a: 232; Scott 2018b: 1.

[35] Syme 1971: 144.

[36] Syme (1971: 145) dates Dio's appointment to the governorship of Africa to 221/222, which gained some general acceptance: cf. Leunissen (1989: 219), who opts for a general date around 222; Thomasson (1996: 87) suggests 221. Note, however, Molin (2016a: 446), who places the governorship of Africa in 222/3 or 224/5, Dalmatia in 224 or 225, and Pannonia beginning in 225 or 226. Scott (2018a: 1) opts for the later dating of each of these appointments, with Dio's proconsulship of Africa dated to 223/4.

[37] Dalmatia: Leunissen 1989: 240; Pannonia Superior: Leunissen 1989: 259.

[38] E.g. *CIL* VIII 597 = *AE* 2003, 1975, an inscription commemorating Dio's (likely) coeval, C. Junius Faustinus Postumianus. In this inscription, we are presented first with Postumianus' status as a senator, consul, and *comes* of the emperors (Severus and Caracalla). These details are followed by his propraetorian legateships of Lower Moesia, Belgica, and Lusitania, before noting less exalted offices. For the dating of this inscription, see Birley 2005: 193. Note too, *CIL* X 6764 = *AE* 2014, 1455, an honorific inscription for another contemporary of Dio's, L. Marius Maximus Perpetuus Aurelianus, which highlights the most important of Maximus' offices: that of urban prefect, his proconsulships of Africa and Asia, his curatorship, and his second consulship (the year in which the inscription was set up). For a sample of the standard scholarship on the genre of career inscriptions, see footnote 14 (above).

body of inscriptional evidence is not, I would argue, superficial, but rather broadly indicative of the way that members of the senatorial elite conceptualised and commemorated their careers. In this context, Dio's list of postings was a way for him to express his prestige and his fulfilment of the traditional senatorial ideal of service *domi militiaeque*.[39] We may draw this parallel even further, if we consider what Dio does and does not reveal about his career the contemporary narrative. Dio mentions some of his offices (*praetor, curator, proconsul Africae, legatus Augusti pro praetore, consul ordinarius*), while seemingly omitting others.[40] This pattern of inclusion and omission is consistent with the findings of a recent statistical study by Richard Duncan-Jones of senatorial *cursus* inscriptions, where it is revealed that it was not uncommon for career inscriptions of senior members of the *ordo* to omit sub-praetorian offices in the *cursus*, praetorian proconsulships, and minor priesthoods.[41]

As Lendon has demonstrated, it was the accumulation of honours that mattered greatly to members of the governing class, as it denoted the esteem with which the individual was held.[42] Dio's own view was slightly more sophisticated than this: Dio was a man who recognised the importance of birth as well as the accumulation of offices.[43] Nevertheless, by grouping the provincial appointments together in the way that he does, and linking them with verbs of motion signifying his progression from one command to the next, Dio is able to amplify the sense of movement – a praiseworthy sense of senatorial *industria* – which builds upon the sense of movement already present in Dio's account of his career.

Dio fought in no wars. Even so, he prided himself on his ability to keep his soldiers in check. When Dio came to describe his own administration in Pannonia, he says that he governed strictly (ἐγκρατῶς) (80[80].4.2 [Xiph.]).[44] Dio considered that his disciplined style of command was the reason for his unpopularity among the (disorderly) praetorians at Rome,[45] as they (according to Dio) feared that someone with such an approach would attempt to instil a similar level discipline in them (80[80].4.2 [Xiph.]).[46] Dio saw this

---

[39] Cf. Eck (1999: 52), on the role of career inscriptions in communicating senatorial self-representation.
[40] For these offices, see Millar 1964: 15–17; Molin 2016: 438–40.   [41] Duncan-Jones 2016: 81–6.
[42] Lendon 1997: 181.   [43] As noted by Graham 1974: 142–4.
[44] Here we may note Dio goes beyond the typical accounts of senatorial careers, as found on inscriptions, where, as Campbell notes (1984: 329): 'A career inscription by itself can tell us only what posts a man held; it cannot explain why he held them, how he performed, or exactly what he did in them, [. . .].'
[45] Or as Cleve (1988: 123) suggests, the 'Pannonians'.
[46] Dio is, perhaps, insinuating that he was a candidate for the office of urban prefect, which along with an iterated consulship were the two great honours that an emperor could bestow.

ideal manifest in his imperial *exemplum*, Marcus Aurelius, whom he praised for refusing to accede to the demands of the soldiery for further monetary incentives. Indeed, Dio describes Marcus ruling the soldiers 'in a disciplined manner and strictly' (σωφρόνως καὶ ἐγκρατῶς) (72[71].3.4 [Xiph.]).[47] As Dio would lament later in his history, Caracalla's decision to limit the right to discipline the army to himself alone only resulted in the soldiers 'acting as tyrants over us' (ἐτυράννησαν ἡμῶν) (78[77].17.3 [Xiph.]).

That an ill-disciplined, 'tyrannical' army should react violently to Dio's style of command was a natural response in Dio's thought world. It was the way tyrants reacted to those who attempted to instil virtuous behaviour.[48] Therefore, by describing the nature of his command in Pannonia, Dio conveys far more than the notion that he fancied himself as some sort of martinet.[49] When Dio says he ruled 'strictly' he is communicating to the reader his ethical position in opposition to that possessed by the soldiery. He was a man of self-restraint.[50]

Furthermore, self-restraint was important to Dio's conception of a good governor. Dio's praise of C. Julius Severus, an imperial legate sent by Hadrian to Bithynia,[51] personified the orderly conduct expected of a provincial administrator (69.14.4 [Xiph./*EV*]).[52] Roman governors were not all so well behaved. In a well-known anecdote, Dio has a Dalmatian embassy assign the blame for unrest in the province to the rapacity of Roman governors (56.16.3). In another, he includes the Tiberian *bon mot* that he preferred his 'sheep shorn but not flayed' (κείρεσθαί μου τὰ πρόβατα, ἀλλ' οὐκ ἀποξύρεσθαι βούλομαι) (57.10.5).[53] It has been suggested that Dio's Bithynian origins meant that he had a keen interest in the execution of proper forms of provincial administration.[54] Indeed, the time Dio spent in Bithynia and Asia during the 210s might have provided him with first-hand experience of the effects the militarisation of Asia Minor had on the local populations during the Severan period.[55] However, on this issue, neither Dio's provincial origins nor his experiences should be

---

[47] See further Chapter 8 by Caillan Davenport.

[48] Such was the reaction of the tyrannical Elagabalus when Gannys had 'compelled him to live temperately and prudently' (σωφρόνως τε καὶ ἐμφρόνως ζῆν ὑπ' αὐτοῦ [i.e. Gannys] ἠναγκάζετο) (80[79].6.3).

[49] As has often been assumed: e.g. Millar 1961: 13; van Stekelenburg 1976: 57; Eisman 1977: 664.

[50] For the importance of self-restraint in Greco-Roman thought, see the classic study of North 1966. For self-restraint (*sophrosyne*) in Cassius Dio, see Mallan 2014: 765–7.

[51] For the career of C. Iulius Severus in Bithynia, see Magie 1950: 1.626, 2.1486–8.

[52] Cf. Kemezis 2012: 393.   [53] Cf. Suet. *Tib.* 32.2.   [54] Ameling 1984: 133–5.

[55] For the effects of the militarisation of Asia and Bithynia on the provincial communities, see Mitchell 1995: 1.228–34.

overstated, as it was expected that a governor should refrain from corrupt practice and, in the case of those provinces with a military presence, protect the provincial communities from being maltreated by the army.[56] Hence, we should focus on how Dio positions himself within the narrative, not only as a governor who clashed with the Pannonian legions, but also as an individual senator performing his duties according to the senatorial ideal.

The apogee of Dio's career came at the end of 228 when he was appointed consul *ordinarius* for the year 229. What is more, he would share the consulship with the emperor himself. The appointment was controversial and the praetorians at Rome objected. But Dio says that Severus Alexander ignored their complaints and showed him great honour – even defraying the costs usually associated with high office (80[80].5.1 [Xiph.]). Stories of kings and emperors turning deaf ears to (false) allegations are a familiar enough motif in ancient historiography and apologetic.[57] Certainly, such stories are intended to reveal something about the nature of the ruler, but in some instances they are intended to amplify the moral worth of the recipient of trust and favour from the king.[58] For an individual senator to be trusted by an emperor was a mark of distinction. Hence, we see yet again that Dio's focus is on cataloguing his own honours rather than describing the reigning emperor. The fact that he had received an iterated consulship (with all expenses paid) was sufficient to convey to his readers a clear picture of the esteem in which Dio was held: the quality of the emperor was immaterial.[59]

Severus Alexander ordered Dio to avoid Rome during the period of Dio's consulship, fearing lest the soldiers should kill the consul on sight (80[80].5.1 [Xiph.]). Dio obeyed his emperor. Dio goes on to reveal that when he was in the company of Alexander both at Rome and in Campania, the soldiers saw him without offering him any violence (80[80].5.2

---

[56] E.g. *Digest* 1.18.6.5–7. For a general discussion of the relationship between the army, provincials, and the Roman provincial administration, see Campbell 1984: 244–63.

[57] The various versions of the story told about Alexander and his doctor, Philip, are perhaps best indicative of this *topos*. E.g. Curtius. 3.6.1–17; Val. Max. 3.8. ext. 6; Plut. *Alex.* 19.2–5; Arrian *Anab.* 2.4.7–11. Moreover, in the Livia–Augustus dialogue, Dio has 'Livia' expound on the commonplace that a (good) ruler should pay no heed to false accusations and rumours (55.18.3–19.3).

[58] E.g. Joseph. *Vita* 423; 424–5; 428. Dio's story (68.15.3² – 16.1 [*EV*/Xiph.]) of how Trajan honoured Licinius Sura despite the calumnies spoken against Sura is an example of how such a story could be designed to reflect well upon both an emperor and his subject. For Dio's portrayal of Alexander as a nonentity, see Chapter 1 by Adam Kemezis.

[59] Iterated consulships tended to be awarded to those senators who were close to the emperor or whom the emperor sought to confer particular honour on at the end of their careers: Davenport 2011 (for comments on iterated consulships under the Severans, and especially Severus Alexander); cf. Syme 1956: 267 = *RP* 1.294–5; Lendon 1997: 150–1.

[Xiph.]). This one sentence reveals two key features about Dio's self-portrayal. Firstly, as he had done in the cases of Septimius Severus and Caracalla, Dio presents himself as the associate of the reigning emperor: in this case a member of the *consilium*, whose personal safety is a concern for the emperor.[60] For Dio, the honour of being in the emperor's *consilium* was more important than his personal regard for the emperor. Secondly, the fact that the soldiers did not harm Dio (despite his lack of protection) perhaps emphasised in his eyes the efficacy of his guardian spirit.[61] However, Dio evidently did not wish to tempt his divine protector(s): His decision to retire from the public life on account of 'an affliction of the feet' may be construed as a diplomatic illness.

III   Friends and Foes of Cassius Dio

There is depth to Dio's picture of himself. We can calibrate this description further by turning from what he says about himself to what he says about others. Here Dio's biting comments do not always reflect well on the historian. Indeed, it was Niebuhr who noted Dio's reputation for κακοήθεια ('malignity').[62] Dio did not suffer fools, and his wit, when it emerged, was often sarcastic and bitter.

From the evidence of the surviving text, it cannot be said that Dio (unlike the aforementioned Clarendon) had any particular genius for friendship. Indeed, Dio's contemporary narrative (or what survives of it) provides more evidence of the men he despised than those whom he liked. Only once in the surviving narrative does Dio identify someone as a friend. The man, at least in Xiphilinus' *Epitome*, is unnamed, but the historian does say that he was one of the suffect consuls for the last months of 196 (76[75].4.2–3 [Xiph.]). From this scrap of evidence, we may deduce that the historian's friend was probably some years his senior, but beyond this we can say nothing more. Dio's original text may have included the consul's name, but in some respects the man's personal identity is irrelevant. The epitomator knew that Dio's friend's consular status, rather than his name, was the most important feature of the man's identity.

---

[60] That Dio was a 'close companion' of Septimius and Caracalla, as maintained by Crook (1955: 82), is unlikely.

[61] Dio, as a devotee of *Tyche*, believed that this divinity protected his life (73(72).23.4 [Xiph.]). For a discussion of the role of *Tyche* and dreams in Dio's work, see Schmidt 1999: 98–102; cf. Marincola 1997: 48–51. For an overview of the concepts of *daimones* and *to daimonion*, see Dodds 1965: 37–68; Alt 2006.

[62] Niebuhr 1875: 62.

Adam Kemezis has argued elsewhere that Dio idolised the men of his father's generation.[63] This is certainly true. Dio certainly admired the great senatorial figures of the 170s and 180s, those men who could and did serve *domi militiaeque* under the philosopher-emperor Marcus Aurelius. But it would be wrong to assume that Dio despised all his contemporaries, or that he felt that it was impossible to enjoy a good career; as we have seen, Dio's presentation of his own career was one that conformed to the traditional ideal.

Dio was, in Fergus Millar's words 'a born prosopographer'.[64] Even in its highly truncated and lacunose form, the contemporary books are rich with details concerning his contemporaries, some of whom are known only from Dio's narrative. The accounts of the men Dio despised attract us first. Vitriol came easily to Dio, and the judgments he offers on some of the men who attained high office are intensely pejorative. In particular, Dio was clearly distressed by the flashy parvenus he saw infiltrating the senate and infesting the imperial courts of the later Severan emperors. This rogues' gallery makes for entertaining reading. A few examples illustrate a pattern of the types of men Dio despised. Notorious in Dio's eyes was Aurelius Zoticus, a one-time cook, who rose to become keeper of the bedchamber under the unmanly Elagabalus, his only recommendation being the prodigious size of his *membrum virile* (80[79].16.1–6 [Xiph./*EV*]). Then there was Theocritus, a freedman and a dancer by profession, until advanced by Caracalla to a position of great authority (78[77].21.2–4 [*EV*/Xiph.]). P. Valerius Comazon, a favourite of Elagabalus (and perhaps more importantly of Elagabalus' grandmother, Julia Maesa), was hinted to have begun his career on the stage before rising to prefect of the praetorian guard and then being adlected into the senate by Elagabalus. To Dio's disbelief and chagrin, Comazon was given consular honours and even went on to hold the consulship (*cos.* II in 220)[65] and advanced to being Prefect of the City of Rome an unprecedented three times between the years 219 and 222 (80-[79].4.1–2; 80[79].21.1–2 [Xiph.]).[66]

Another man promoted by both Caracalla and Macrinus was Marcius Claudius Agrippa (79[78].13.2–4).[67] The son of slaves (so we are told), Agrippa had a career which was nothing short of startling. Starting life as a woman's hairdresser, Agrippa became a functionary in the imperial treasury. Later he was banished under Severus, then recalled by Caracalla

[63] Kemezis 2012.   [64] Millar 1964: 164.
[65] Comazon's first consulship was an ornamental one: 80(79).4.2 cf. *PIR*² V 59.
[66] 80(79).4.1–2; 80(79).21.1–2 (Xiph.).   [67] *PIR*² M 224.

and adlected into the senate with the rank of ex-praetor. This man was then dispatched as propraetorian governor of Pannonia in late 217.[68] If we appreciate such a career as remarkable, for Dio it was nothing short of scandalous. It had long been the case that political influence had been dependent on an individual's proximity to the emperor. Yet it is easy to understand Dio's resentment at the promotion of these grotesque upstarts: men recruited from the cookhouse, the bedchamber, and the chorus line. They were all nonentities who had been catapulted into the senate, thanks to the favour of capricious emperors, without having to work their way up the *cursus honorum* in the manner Dio had to do. Their elevation debased the very currency of the economy of honour.[69] Moreover, by condemning these men and the emperors who enabled their careers, Dio was able to signal to his readers his own virtue and adherence to the idealised ethical code of his order.

Discrimination on grounds of education as well as birth was perfectly legitimate in Dio's world. This is most readily seen in what the historian says about M. Oclatinius Adventus, a man advanced by the emperor Macrinus.[70] Like Macrinus himself, Adventus was of undistinguished parentage. Under Caracalla, Adventus had held minor military positions before becoming *princeps peregrinorum*, then an imperial procurator in Britain, then co-praefect of the praetorian guard with Macrinus (79[78].14.1–4).[71] After Caracalla's death, Adventus' career accelerated: He was adlected into the senate with the rank of consul and was granted the exulted position of prefect of the city of Rome. Such a meteoric career was unusual; yet what made Adventus all the more notorious in the eyes of Dio was that the man could (evidently) neither read nor write. According to Dio, Adventus 'could not carry on a respectable conversation when consul with anyone in the senate' (οὐδὲ διαλεχθῆναί τινι ἐν τῷ συνεδρίῳ καλῶς ὑπατεύων ἠδυνήθη) (79[78].14.2). His advancement was suspected to be a ruse to distract people from Macrinus' equestrian origins. Dio's comments follow the maxim (coined in a later age) that first-rate people choose first-rate candidates. Second-rate people choose third-rate candidates.

To understand the scorn Dio had for men like Adventus, we need to remember that the world of the Greco-Roman élite in which Dio moved was one where literary accomplishments were highly prized. Indeed, men

---

[68] Date of governorship: Leunissen 1989: 257.　[69] See further Davenport 2012a: 808–11.
[70] *PIR*² O 9.
[71] Davenport 2012b: 197–8. For Adventus' procuratorship in Britain, see *RIB* 1.1234; *RIB* 1.1462.

could be appointed to high office on the favour gained by their literary output. It was a literary culture that was not only bilingual but one where a man might be judged by his mastery of the Classical (usually Attic) Greek idiom.[72] It is why in an earlier generation Marcus Aurelius and his former tutor, Marcus Cornelius Fronto, exchanged some letters in a high-register Greek, or why Claudius Aelianus, an Italian contemporary of Dio's, chose to write not in his native Latin but in Greek, redolent of the fifth and fourth centuries BC. Yet if Dio's attitude was unashamedly snobbish by the (self-consciously) egalitarian standards of the twenty-first century, then we should note to his credit that Dio's opinions on class and birth right were not entirely inflexible. The exemplary Pertinax, according to Dio, was of undistinguished birth (74[73].1.1 [Xiph.]). On this particular point, Dio may even be understating the truth of his origins. According to a later fourth-century biography, Pertinax's father was of freedman status (*HA Pert.* 1.1). Pertinax had, however, enjoyed advancement under Marcus Aurelius and risen through the senate. He was convenient proof that first-rate people chose first-rate candidates.

It was a conventional belief that 'bad emperors' or tyrants persecuted men and women who were conspicuous for their virtue.[73] 'Good emperors' by contrast did not feel threatened by men (and women) of excellence. It was important for those who were persecuted to die well. Dio (and his epitomators) include many accounts of women and men who were martyred under tyrannical rulers. These notices serve as commemoration of their exemplary lives.

History was (and perhaps still is) about commemoration as much as condemnation. Then as now, it was felt that victims of tyrants or tyrannical regimes deserved to be commemorated. Just as the twentieth century had Sophie and Hans Scholl, so the late second century had the brothers Quintilii – Sex. Quintilius Valerius Maximus and Sex. Quintilius Condianus – *consules ordinarii* in 151, who lived and died together, were the very model of fraternal concord.[74] Both were men of virtue, military accomplishment, and erudition (73[72].5.3–4 [Xiph.]). In other words, they were men who excelled *domi militiaeque* and in the realm of *paideia*. Yet, despite glittering careers under Antoninus Pius and Marcus Aurelius, both fell foul of Commodus and perished early in his reign. The son of Quintilius Valerius Maximus, who shared his uncle's name Sex. Quintilius

---

[72] For views on the importance of the mastery of higher-register Greek to the elite culture of the second and third centuries, see, *inter alios*, Swain 1996: 17–42; Whitmarsh 2005: 41–56.

[73] E.g. Hdt. 5.92; Arist. Pol. 1311a15-23. For this idea in Dio, see Mallan 2014: 763.

[74] Sextus Quintilius Condianus: *PIR*² Q 21; Sextus Quintilius Valerius Maximus: *PIR*² Q 27.

Condianus, was sentenced to death by Commodus along with his father and his uncle. The younger Quintilius Condianus had been one of the ordinary consuls in the year Commodus had succeeded to the sole rule (180). He was, according to Dio, a man 'by nature superior to all others on account of his learning' (φύσει τε καὶ παιδείᾳ τῶν ἄλλων διαφέρων) (73[72].6.1 [Xiph.]).

By the time Dio came around to writing his history, his memory of these men must have been imperfect – if he had contact with them, Dio would only have been an impressionable young man, barely out of his teens. Yet the younger Quintilius clearly became a cult hero of sorts, at least among members of Dio's political caste, and was at the centre of conspiratorial speculation and rumour. Dio tells us how the younger Quintilius had faked his own death and substituted the carcass of a ram for that of himself in his coffin (73[72].6.1–5 [Xiph.]). After that, Quintilius vanished and was apparently never apprehended. Quintilius was patently a master of disguise. Dio adds a strange coda to this story, comprising an event at which he himself was present (73[72].6.4–7.1 [Xiph.]). Approximately ten years after the disappearance of the younger Quintilius, in early 193, a man claiming to be Quintilius appeared in Rome before Pertinax. Yet when Pertinax quizzed him about Hellenic culture, the man was at a loss and could not answer (let alone, understand) the question. The imposture was exposed, the pseudo-Quintilius killed, and the mystery of the real Quintilius continued.[75]

Not all the men commemorated by Dio were wrapped in such beguiling mythologies. A brief fragment of what was once perhaps a longer obituary notice concerns a certain Thrasea Priscus – or to give his full name, L. Valerius Publicola Messala Helvidius Thrasea Priscus Minicius Natalis. In what survives of Dio's original text, Thrasea Priscus is described as a man 'second to none in either nobility of birth or intelligence' (ἄνδρα οὐδενὸς οὔτε γένει οὔτε φρονήσει δεύτερον) (78[77].5.5 [*EV*]). Thankfully, we know more about this man from epigraphic evidence, not least an inscribed statue base once supporting a statue of Thrasea Priscus from the Latin town of Lavinium, where Priscus was a civic patron and *curator*.[76] Priscus enjoyed a distinguished career of service. As a young man he was a *IIIvir monetalis*, then military tribune, probably in Pannonia, under the joint rule of Marcus and Commodus. He then reached the consulship

---

[75] See Gleason 2011 for this and other cases of masquerades in Dio, and Chapter 2 by Caillan Davenport in this volume on rumours about the younger Quintilius.
[76] *AE* 1998, 280.

(*ordinarius* with Gaius Domitius Dexter, *cos. II ord.*) in the year 196 – the same year, we may remember, as Dio's consular friend was suffect consul. Priscus perished in early 212 or late 211, an apparent victim of Caracalla's purge following the execution of his brother, Geta, in December 211. Old Thrasea Priscus was just the sort of man Dio admired. He was well educated and had risen through the *cursus* in a manner perhaps not dissimilar to Dio himself.

Yet some men, good men, survived the regimes of tyrants, and Dio's commemorative notices are not confined to senatorial martyrs. Dio knew, as did Tacitus and Pliny before him, that good men could exist under bad emperors. Occasionally we catch glimpses of such individuals. Dio's sketch of Pollienus Auspex (the elder) reveals a man who was a kindred spirit. What we know of the career of Pollienus Auspex is derived primarily from an inscription which was erected in the Lycian town of Xanthus (south-western Turkey) in honour of his great-granddaughter, a woman named Polliena Honorata.[77] Some years senior to Dio, Auspex enjoyed a career similar to that of the historian. Auspex reached the suffect consulship under the joint rule of Marcus and Commodus before going on to the governorship of Dalmatia (under Marcus and Commodus), a post which Cassius Apronianus and Dio were to hold under later emperors. As Dio would do in the 220s, Auspex went on to hold the proconsulship of Africa, either late in the reign of Commodus or early in the reign of Severus.[78] The Xanthus inscription also tells us that Auspex served as a 'judge deputising for the emperors' (ἐν χώρᾳ Σεβαστοῦ δικά|σαντος). The use of the plural 'emperors' can only mean that Auspex had this position either under Marcus Aurelius and Commodus (176–80) or under Severus and Caracalla (198–211). Auspex had a son and grandson, who also enjoyed distinguished careers.[79] About these men, who were closer in age to Dio, our text of Dio is silent.

What we do not get a sense of in the Xanthus inscription is Auspex's humanity. What apparently attracted Dio to the elder Auspex was his sense of humour and frankness of speech. Dio records one particular witticism whereby Auspex, after Severus had adopted himself into the family of Marcus Aurelius, congratulated the emperor, 'that you have found a father' (ὅτι πατέρα εὗρες) (77[76].9.4 [Xiph.]). To Severus' credit, Auspex suffered no harm for his barbed comment. Dio's commemoration

---

[77] *IGRR* 3.618 = *ILS* 8841. For discussion, see Birley 2005: 348–50; Mennen 2011: 116–18.
[78] Leunissen 1989: 214 n. 7; *PIR²* P 537.
[79] Pollienus Auspex (the younger): *PIR²* P 538; Tiberius Julius Pollienus Auspex: *PIR²* P 539.

of Auspex is personal and sincere, and Dio might well have been a friend of the older consular. Dio says that Auspex 'was the most clever man imaginable for jokes and light conversation, for despising all mankind, gratifying his friends, and taking vengeance on his enemy' (77[76].9.3 [Xiph.]).[80] This is not the usual bland language of commemoration. Dio's text, as we have, it makes no mention of Auspex' family, birth, or career achievements, the sort of thing one might expect to find.

One might say Auspex was a man after Dio's own heart. Dio was a historian who took a generally grim view of human nature, closer to Hobbes in *Leviathan* than to Thucydides. The majority of mankind were governed by greed and self-interest. Exceptions were rare. Auspex represented the sort of independence of mind and action which Dio himself would come to display in writing the history of his own times. Dio's sense of humour, when it emerges, shows a fondness for sarcasm and waspishness.[81] We may note, with some degree of surprise, that on one occasion Dio provides a humorous exchange, whereby an illiterate centurion cannot tell the difference between Greek and Latin (72[71].5.3 [Pet. Pat.]), which finds a modern parallel in the 1980s BBC television series *Yes Minister*.[82]

It was not only the good, the bad, or the egregious who attracted Dio's attention. Dio's comments offer a glimpse into the lives of senators who might have otherwise disappeared entirely from the historical record. One such man was Domitius Florus, who, after his quaestorship under Severus, had served as keeper of the *acta senatus* (79[78].22.2). Florus had fallen foul of Plautianus and as a result had failed to achieve the rank of aedile. Some eleven years after the death of Plautianus, Florus finally secured election as tribune in 217, thanks to the active support of his allies in the senate. We may wonder if Dio was one of Florus' senatorial friends who had helped him restart his career. At any rate, it seems unlikely that Dio should supply details of this obscure individual, had he not some personal interest in Florus' career.

Let us consider one final individual for whom Dio's narrative provides the only evidence for his existence. During Severus' conflict with Clodius

---

[80] οὗτος δεινότατος ἀνθρώπων ἐγένετο σκῶψαι, στωμύλασθαι, πάντων ἀνθρώπων καταφρονῆσαι, φίλοις χαρίσασθαι, ἐχθρὸν ἀμύνασθαι.
[81] E.g. Dio's comment on the suffect consul for 16, Vibius Rufus, a man who had married Cicero's widow and who habitually sat in a chair occupied by Julius Caesar. Dio says (57.15.6): 'For he thought that he would become an orator on account of his wife, and a Caesar on account of his chair' (ὥσπερ ἢ διὰ τὴν γυναῖκα ῥήτωρ ἢ διὰ τὸν δίφρον Καῖσαρ ἐσόμενος).
[82] The minister Jim Hacker incorrectly identifies the Virgilian line *timeo Danaos et dona ferentes* as being a 'Greek tag'.

Albinus (196–7), Dio tells us that Severus' cause was aided by an obscure individual, an elementary school teacher (*ludimagister*) by profession, named Numerianus (76[75].5.1–3 [Xiph.]).[83] This one-time teacher impersonated a senator in order to gain support and inflicted a military defeat upon the forces of Albinus and raised a large sum of money for Severus. In thanks for his support, Severus offered him honours (including senatorial rank when it emerged that he was not a member of that order); but Numerianus refused, preferring instead to live a quiet life on a modest stipend provided by the emperor. There is no indication that Dio ever met this man. Yet what seemed to have struck Dio as the most remarkable thing about his career was the fact that, despite his imposture, he still knew his place in Roman society and did not attempt to usurp honours which were above his station. The fact that he was the very antithesis of men like Comazon or Aurelius Zoticus made him worthy of commemoration. Numerianus, the educator, knew how much his status entitled him to draw from the economy of honour.

IV   Conclusion

Dio was a man with a keen sense of the intolerable. Yet the martyr's crown was not for our historian, for Dio was a survivor. As a result, his contemporary history is one of pent-up resentment. He had seen good men die or be passed over in favour of flashy popinjays or semi-literates. The rapid promotion of such men represented a challenge to the hierarchical world view Dio possessed. History offered Dio an avenue of release from this resentment; an opportunity to say the things he could never have said in public.[84] It was also a place where he could commemorate his own career and those of the men around him.

For Dio, a man could (and should) be judged by his class, rank, and learning. Dio's self-portrayal is that of a senator, first and foremost.[85] Whether by condemning the vices in others or highlighting his own exemplary conduct, Dio presents the reader with a rounded ethical self-portrait. He saw himself as a senator who fulfilled his duty in a manner that

---

[83] *PIR*² N 198. For the generally low social standing of these men, see Laes 2007. Cf. Kemezis' comments regarding *grammatici* (2012: 399): 'Literary professionals such as *grammatici* tended to complicate this picture greatly, in that their skills gave them a cultural prestige and even power independent of whatever other kinds of social standing they might or might not possess.'

[84] For this point in full, see Mallan 2016: 272–5.

[85] As noted correctly by Scott (2018a: 233): 'While the cast of characters changes [. . .] the one constant reference point is Dio, the senate, and his membership therein.'

was consistent with the traditional ideal of his order, service to the state (*domi militiaeque*). In this respect, his account of his own career functions in much the same way as career inscriptions do. Yet Dio's order was one which placed particular importance on Greek learning, *paideia*. In this context, it would be wrong to assert that some sort of 'Greekness' played a role in Dio's view of himself. "For, in the third century, attainments in the field of paideia may be seen as a senatorial ideal, at least for some'.[86] Dio was also keen to emphasise the honour in which he was held, whether by emperors (irrespective of their own qualities) or the favour he was shown by the heavenly power, who assisted his endeavours through dreams.

Unsurprisingly, it was to men much like himself that Dio was attracted. Interestingly, there does not appear to be any geographical bias to Dio's judgements: The men whom he admired were not necessarily from the Greek east, but they were men who possessed (in the main) some degree of learning, and who came from the same social group. It has been argued that Dio believed that the ambitions of senators of his generation were hamstrung by the rulers which they served, unlike the great generation of the age of Marcus Aurelius.[87] This is only partly true. The men whom Dio celebrates in his contemporary narrative are men who did enjoy traditional careers, who excelled *domi militiaeque*. This is not to say that such a career was easy, especially when the economy of honour was controlled by a Caracalla or an Elagabalus. Yet it was possible all the same, albeit (as it would have appeared to Dio) with a little help from the *daimonion*.

[86] On *paideia*, see Chapter 7 by Shushma Malik in this volume. For Dio as *pepaideumenos*, see Burden-Strevens 2015b.
[87] Cf. Kemezis 2012: 402.

IV

Reception and Reflection

CHAPTER 13

The Reception of Cassius Dio's Imperial Narrative in Byzantium (Tenth–Twelfth Centuries)

Alicia Simpson

I Introduction

The term 'Roman antiquarianism' has come to describe a revived interest in the Roman past in tenth–twelfth-century Byzantium. The roots of the phenomenon have been traced to the imperial court of Constantine VII Porphyrogenitus (945–59), and even earlier, to the intellectual pursuits of the patriarch Photius in the ninth century, and largely explained on the basis of a conscious revival of the Roman political heritage.[1] In this context, the *Roman History* of Cassius Dio, the most comprehensive account of ancient Rome from mythical times to the reign of Alexander Severus, played a leading role in familiarizing Byzantine audiences with Rome, attaining the status of a canonical text on Roman history. Classical scholars have long studied the excerpts from Dio's history contained in the *Excerpta Constantiniana*, the massive historical compendium commissioned by Constantine VII, as well as the important epitomes of the history made by John Xiphilinus and John Zonaras in the eleventh and twelfth centuries respectively. Since Dio's lengthy text has not been preserved in its entirety (of the original eighty books, 36–60 covering the years 68 BC to AD 47 have survived almost complete), the Byzantine excerpts and epitomes have generally been treated as sources for the reconstruction of its lost parts. More recently, however, there have been attempts to consider the excerpts and epitomes on their own, as this approach can reveal much about

I would like to express my gratitude to Athanasios Markopoulos and to the editors of the volume, Christopher Mallan and Caillan Davenport, for their careful reading of the text and for their valuable corrections, comments, and suggestions. Needless to say, any shortcomings are my own. References to Xiphilinus are taken from Boissevain's edition which is appended to the third volume of his edition of Cassius Dio, and which follows the pagination of Dindorf/Stephanus. References to the *Excerpta* follow the critical edition of de Boor et al. (1903–10). The text of Zonaras is that of Pinder and Büttner-Wobst (1841–97) in the *Corpus Scriptorum Historiae Byzantinae* (*CSHB*) series.
[1] Markopoulos 2006: 277–97.

Byzantine attitudes to and uses of the Roman past through the reception of Dio's *Roman History*.

Though this study will focus on the tenth to twelfth centuries, it is best that we begin with the patriarch Photius (c. 810 – after 893) and his summaries and evaluations of ancient and early Byzantine historians in the *Bibliotheca*, as this can provide us with valuable insights into how these authors and their histories were perceived in ninth-century Byzantium.[2]

II   From Photius to Constantine VII

Photius, a classical scholar and avid reader of Greek and Roman historians, had read, among others, Herodotus (60), Theopompus (176), Flavius Josephus (48), Diodorus Siculus (70 and 244), Dionysius of Halicarnassus (83), Appian (57), Arrian (91), and Cassius Dio (71). As gleaned from the selection and varying lengths of his entries, the patriarch's interests primarily lay in Eastern Roman/early Byzantine history, that is, the period from Constantine I, the first Christian emperor, to the ninth century. At the same time he devotes special attention to ancient Near Eastern and Macedonian history (e.g. Ktesias, *Persica* 72; Arrian, *Anabasis of Alexander* 91), shows some interest in the early and Republican history of Rome (see the entry for Appian 57 and the extended epitomes of Diodorus Siculus 244 and Memnon of Heraclea 224)[3] but seems somewhat indifferent to the imperial period (i.e. from Augustus to Constantine). In his brief notice for Dio's *Roman History*, Photius merely notes the lengthy time covered by the history – 'from the arrival of Aeneas in Italy ... to the murder of Antoninus' – and comments the following on style rather than substance (Phot. *Bib. cod.* 71):

> His style is grandiose and bombastic, reflecting the consciousness of mighty events. His language is full of antiquated constructions, and of words in keeping with the importance of the events described. His periods are full of protracted parentheses and ill-timed inversions. The rhythm and the abrupt interruptions, being carefully employed, owing to the general clearness, escape the notice of the casual reader. The speeches, after the style of those in Thucydides, but clearer, are excellent. In almost everything else also Thucydides is his model.[4]

---

[2] The standard edition is that of Henri 1951–91. For studies, see Mendels 1986: 196–206; Croke 2006: 59–70; Markopoulos 2006: 283–5; Kaldellis 2012: 79.
[3] On Photius' epitomes (codd. 234–80), see Treadgold 1980: 37–5; on the patriarch's interest in Diodorus of Sicily, who is given the longest set of excerpts, see Pfuntner 2015: 256–72.
[4] Ἔστι δὲ τὴν φράσιν μεγαλοπρεπῶς τε καὶ εἰς ὄγκον διεσκευασμένος, ὅτι καὶ μεγάλων ἔργων ἐννοίας ἀπαγγέλλει. Ἀρχαϊκῶν τε αὐτῷ συντάξεων ὁ λόγος μεστὸς καὶ λέξεων πρεπουσῶν μεγέθει, περίοδοί τε μετὰ παρενθέσεων παρατεταμέναι καὶ ὑπερβατῶν εὔκαιρος χρῆσις. Ῥυθμός τε καὶ ἀναπαύσεις εἰς ἐπιμέλειαν ἠσκημένα διὰ τὸ σαφὲς οὐκ ἔστι τοῖς ἁπλῶς ἀναγινώσκουσιν ἐμφανῆ. Ἐν

Although Photius' readings and literary criticisms appear to have been a personal endeavour,[5] they nevertheless reflect the political and cultural climate of the times, indicating that the Byzantine historical outlook was very much focused on the history of the Eastern Roman/Byzantine world and the empires of the ancient Near East.[6] Interest in Roman history was stimulated in the tenth century probably as a result of the systematic efforts undertaken in the imperial palace involving grandiose collecting and excerpting projects with the aim of systematizing the knowledge of the past, especially the Roman/Byzantine imperial past. The leading figures were the emperors Leo VI (886–912, a one-time student of Photius who came to be known as 'Leo the Wise') and his scholar son Constantine VII. The projects they commissioned included legal, hagiographical, military, historical compilations, and anthologies, all steeped in ancient knowledge.[7] In the realm of history, Constantine VII commissioned the so-called *Excerpta Constantiniana*, a voluminous assemblage of excerpts from historians ranging from the fifth century BC to the ninth century AD. The collection was arranged in thematic categories – from the monarchy to warfare, diplomacy, political affairs, geography, ethnography, and morality – and aimed to function as a repository of historical writings on various subjects.[8] The majority of historians excerpted early Byzantine history, the ancient history of the Near East, Greek mythical history, and the historical background of the Bible, thus reflecting the preferences and priorities of the imperial court, and more generally the intellectual trends of the times. However, the inclusion of historians such as Dio, Dionysius of Halicarnassus, Appian, and Polybius points to an increased interest in Roman history.[9] For our purposes, excerpts from Dio appear in the following sections:

(i)   *Excerpta de Legationibus 'ELg' (On embassies)* 1.81–9, 410–35
(ii) *Excerpta de Virtutibus et Vitiis 'EV' (On virtues and vices)* 2².235–407
(iii) *Excerpta de Sententiis 'ES' (On gnomic statements)* 4.408–52

δέ γε ταῖς δημηγορίαις, ἄριστος καὶ μιμητὴς Θουκυδίδου, πλὴν εἴ τι πρὸς τὸ σαφέστερον ἀφορᾷ. Σχεδὸν δὲ κἂν τοῖς ἄλλοις Θουκυδίδης ἐστὶν αὐτῷ ὁ κανών (trans. J. H. Freese, Translations of Christian Literature edition).
[5] Though an intellectual and cultural revival was already under way: Lemerle 1971. An English translation was published by H. Lindsay and A. Moffatt in 1986.
[6] For the lack of interest in the history of the Greek-city states and ancient Rome, see Jeffreys 1979: 215–28, 230.
[7] Magdalino 2013a: 219–31; Magdalino 2013b: 187–209.
[8] Of the original fifty-three categories only a few have survived in whole or partially. On the *Excerpta*, see Flusin 2002: 537–59; Németh 2016: 253–74; Németh 2018; Roberto 2009: 71–84; and the useful discussions in Treadgold 2013: 153–65 and Kaldellis 2015a: 35–47. For Dio, see Molin 2004: 209–13 and Mallan 2019.
[9] For a complete list of works contained in the *Excerpta*, see Németh 2018: 4–11.

Though the excerptors were missing certain sections of Dio, they
nevertheless managed to cover almost the whole range of the *Roman
History*.[10] With some minor alterations, largely consisting of grammatical changes and the omission of clauses or sentences, they generally
preserve Dio's words and thus are of considerable value in those cases
where the original has been lost.[11] Looking at the surviving sections of
the *Excerpta* we can immediately observe that Dio was used extensively in the *Excerpta de Virtutibus et Vitiis*, meaning that his narrative
offered the excerptors a wealth of materials with which to illustrate
virtue and vice.[12] Examining the relevant section, we notice that the
majority of excerpts deal with personalities of the imperial period.[13]
And while some figures are given cursory treatment (e.g. the emperors
of the Flavian dynasty), others receive extensive attention.
Conspicuous are the personalities of Mark Antony (*EV* 136–66) and
Nero (*EV* 228–58), no doubt because they represented well-known
paradigms of vice. If we take a look at the selection process and
methodology of the excerptors, we will find that they preserve, for
example, a dozen fragments – some extremely condensed – on Julius
Caesar (*EV* 124–35), corresponding to Dio 42–4, from the ascension to
Caesar to his assassination (though the event is not included in this
selection).[14]

Through the excerptors follow the order of Dio's narrative, their selection of certain passages and the omission of others necessarily means the
loss of narrative continuum. What is more, their cut-and-paste method, in

---

[10] See in detail, Juntunen 2013: 459–86.

[11] For the methodology and alterations of the excerptors, see Flusin 2002 and Roberto 2009.

[12] In fact, the excerpts from Dio are the longest of any other author in the relevant section, extending to
127 pages in the printed edition. The only other authors that come close are Josephus (124 pages) and
Polybius (109 pages).

[13] Extracts 1–166 early Roman and Republican period; extracts 167–405 imperial period.

[14] *EV* 124 = 42.8 pertains to Caesar's feigned clemency towards his murdered rival Pompey; *EV* 125 =
42.34.3–35 recounts how Cleopatra charmed Caesar into backing her cause; *EV* 126 = 43.1–2 tells of
how Publius Sittius unexpectedly rendered assistance to Caesar; *EV* 127 = 43.2–3 on the corrupt
Sallust; *EV* 128 = 43.20.1–3 the soldiers admire but also jeer at Caesar on account of his love for
Cleopatra and his sojourn at the court of Nikomedes; *EV* 129 = 20 Caesar is not displeased but
delighted by their honesty; *EV* 130 = 43.24.4 under Caesar two men are executed as a sort of ritual
observance; *EV* 131 = 43.27.3 Caesar incurs censure because of his passion for Cleopatra, who is
brought to Rome and settled in his house; *EV* 132 = 43.50.2 Caesar promotes men to office not only
on account of their courage but also of their usefulness; *EV* 133 = 44.9.3 certain men take down
Caesar's statue, claiming that he did not want anything of the sort; *EV* 134 = 44.10.1–3 Caesar
removes tribunes from their office for having brought a case against a certain man who had called
him king; *EV* 135 = Dio 44.38–48 extracts from the speech-encomium delivered to the populace by
Mark Antony over Caesar's bloodied corpse.

conjunction with their often-severe condensation of passages, makes it difficult to see how anyone could have followed the excerpts without prior knowledge of Dio's text. I will return to this later, but for now it suffices to say that one principle of the selection process stands out. This is the focalization on character rather than events, which is not only appropriate for illustrating virtue and vice, but was already present in Dio, whose annalistic method became more biographical, both in terms of presentation and interpretation, beginning with the late Republican period.[15]

The culmination of this in the relevant section of the *Excerpta* is the lengthy extract from Mark Antony's speech-encomium, where the virtues and deeds of Caesar are extolled: his shrewd and discerning intellect, his affection for his friends and relatives, his clemency towards his enemies, his victorious campaigns and conquests, his acts of legislation and reconstruction, et cetera. Though Caesar's faults are not passed over in silence (e.g. his passion for Cleopatra), the truncated texts of the excerptors offer a more palliative portrait of Caesar than the one given in Dio.[16] This is the case for the brief extracts 130, 132, 133 whose condensed form and lack of context distort the original text. For example, *EV* 130 simply states that under Caesar two men were slaughtered in some sort of ritual act. There are no details given and no blame on Caesar rendered. As Dio (43.24) explains, the soldiers had rioted because Caesar had not lavished wealth on them. They did not cease their rioting until Caesar came upon them, and seizing one man, delivered him over to execution. Dio then adds that two others were slain as some sort of ritual observance in the Campus Martius though he is unable to state the cause. There is an unmistakable hint of Caesar's wrongdoing here, but the excerptors omit the statement (and, in general, leave out Dio's comments). Similarly, extract *EV* 134 states that Caesar became angry when certain officials brought suit against the first man who had called him king. When these same men issued a proclamation that they could no longer speak freely, Caesar brought them before the senate. He did not execute them, though some were calling for this punishment, but rather removed them from office. Dio's comment (44.10.4) that Caesar's reputation was damaged by this affair inasmuch as he should have punished those who called him king and not his officials who objected to the title was once again omitted by the excerptors.

In the case of Nero (*EV* 228–58; Dio, Books 61–3) the excerptors' task was made easier by the fact that Dio's presentation of the emperor was

[15] Pelling 1997a: 117–44.   [16] For Dio's portrait of Caesar, see Pitcher 2009: 267–76.

overwhelmingly negative.[17] Nero, of course, was a paradigm of vice, and this was, after all, the explicit purpose of the *Excerpta de Virtutibus et Vitiis*.[18] Looking at the excerpted passages, we can observe that they are focused on character depiction, aiming to illustrate Nero's cruelty and depravity in different situations: Nero's licentious deeds and other outrages (*EV* 238); his nocturnal revels in Rome (*EV* 239); his singing and lyre-playing (*EV* 242, 243); his 'marriage' to Sporus (*EV* 250); or the various crimes he committed in Greece (*EV* 251, 252, 253). The excerpts regarding Nero's character are supplemented by those focusing on other notorious personalities, notably his mother Agrippina (*EV* 228, 229, 230, 235). Yet, even in the selected passages, certain things are left out, as for example, in *EV* 233 (61.3.3–5.4) where Nero's character develops from that of an indulgent youth to a depraved tyrant. The excerptors follow Dio in stating that Nero's advisers, Seneca and Burrus, took over the government and allowed Nero to indulge himself in pleasures, expecting that he would not

[17] One must exercise caution in this case because Dio's narrative of the reign only survives in later epitomes, as Shushma Malik discusses in Chapter 7 in this volume. *EV* 228 = 60.32.1–2 Agrippina comes to live in the palace and gains complete control over Claudius; she makes her son Nero the son-in-law of Claudius and brings about his adoption; *EV* 229 = 60.32.3–4 Agrippina trains her son for the throne and murders many out of jealousy; *EV* 230 = 60.32.5–6 Agrippina sidelines Claudius' son Brittanicus, killing those devoted to him; *EV* 231 = 60.33.1 no one attempts to check Agrippina's power; *EV* 232 = 60.33.6 Narcissus is blamed for the caving in of the Fucine Lake; *EV* 233 = 61.3.3–5.4 Nero indulges in pleasures and commits acts of violence and outrage; *EV* 234 = 61.5–6 Nero exhausts the funds in the imperial treasury and imposes new taxes; *EV* 235 = 61.6.4 Agrippina murders Marcus Junius Silanus, using the same poison with which she had killed her husband; *EV* 236 = 61.6.5 Agrippina murdered Silanus because she did not wish him to be preferred to Nero; *EV* 237 = 61.6.6 the greedy Laelianus is sent to Armenia; *EV* 238 = 61.7.5–8.4 Nero's licentious deeds and other outrages; *EV* 239 = 61.9.2–4 Nero's nocturnal revels in Rome; *EV* 239 = 61.10.1–6 the vices of Seneca; *EV* 240 = 61.11.1 Nero comes to believe that everything he does is right and listens only to flatterers; *EV* 241 = 61.17.1–2 Nero poisons his aunt Domitia; *EV* 242 = 61.20.2 Nero's slight and indistinct voice; *EV* 243 = 61.21.2 Nero wins the lyre-playing crown without a contest; *EV* 244 = 62.13.3 Nero appoints the licentious and bloodthirsty Tigellinus as one of the commanders of the Praetorian guard; *EV* 245 = 62.14.1 Nero laughs at the misfortunes of his relatives; *EV* 246 = 62.15.7 when those assembled at Antium perish, Nero orders a festival; *EV* 247 = 62.19.2–4 the praiseworthy Corbulo, whom people hope to see emperor, keeps faith with Nero; *EV* 248 = 62.23.5–6 Corbulo conducts himself prudently before Nero; *EV* 249 = 62.27.2 Nero brings a false charge against Junius Torquarus; *EV* 250 = 68.22.2–4 Nero 'marries' Sporus; *EV* 251 = 63.8–10 Nero goes to Greece in order to drive chariots, play the lyre, make proclamations, and act in tragedies; *EV* 252 = 63.11.1–3 Nero kills a great number of Greek men, women, and children; *EV* 253; 63.11.3–12.1 Nero confiscates properties, steals votive offerings from temples, and leaves the People of Rome and Italy at the mercy of Helius; *EV* 255 = 63.14.2 Nero abolishes the oracle of Apollo; *EV* 255 = 63.17.2 those accused by Nero either kill themselves or are slain by others; *EV* 256 = 63.22.1 Vindex leads the Gauls in rebellion; *EV* 257 = 63.26.1–5 Nero is informed about the rebellion of the Gauls but does nothing; *EV* 258 = 63.27.2 Nero plans to kill the senators, burn down Rome, and escape to Alexandria.

[18] It is worth noting that Nero was an antichrist figure in the Byzantine apocalyptic tradition. The legends concerning Nero – who would return at the end of time to persecute God's people – were recorded in the *Sibylline Oracles* (a compilation variously dating from the second century BC to the seventh century AD) and borrowed in Byzantine apocalyptic prophecies (Alexander 1985: 92–4).

cause great harm to the public interest. They then proceed to describe how Nero's character changed, omitting the preceding commentary from Dio:

> they (Seneca and Brutus) did not realize that a young and self-willed spirit, when reared in unrebuked licence and absolute authority, so far from becoming sated by the indulgence of its passions, is ruined more and more by these very agencies. (61.4.2–3)[19]

We can surmise that as far as the excerptors were concerned, this comment added nothing to the negative portrait of Nero. In other cases, their extracts consist of brief statements bearing no context whatsoever (e.g. Nero's slight and indistinct singing voice (*EV* 242)), or lengthier extracts that leave out vital information (e.g. Nero's grief over the death of Sabina (*EV* 250)), which fails to mention that the emperor himself had killed her. There is no distortion here, but one would certainly need to be familiar with the original text to get the full story.

All this indicates that the excerpts were not meant to replace Dio's text (or probably any other) but rather to serve as reference guides for different subjects contained therein. This can only mean that learned Byzantine audiences (at least those who were expected to make use of the *Excerpta*) were familiar with Dio's text and knew the historical circumstances and personalities of which he wrote.[20] In this context, it is worth noting that the tenth-century manuscripts of Dio's history – *Marcianus Graecus* 395 and *Laurentianus Plut.* 70.8 – were most probably copied in Constantinople during the reign of Constantine VII.[21] What is more, not many years after the emperor's death (959), Theodosius the Deacon, who in all likelihood belonged to the clergy of Hagia Sophia or of the imperial court, wrote a panegyrical poem on the conquest of Crete in 961–2, in which he addressed the ancient authors Demosthenes, Plutarch, Dio, and Xenophon, telling them that the great figures they wrote about (respectively Phillip II, Julius Caesar, Sulla, and 'the unconquerable men') were nothing compared to the Byzantine hero Nikephoros Phokas.[22] All this means that Dio's *Roman History* was painstakingly copied, read, and excerpted in tenth-century Constantinople.[23]

---

[19] ὥσπερ οὐκ εἰδότες ὅτι ψυχὴ νέα τε καὶ αὐθάδης ἔν τε τρυφῇ ἀνεπιπλήκτῳ καὶ ἐν ἐξουσίᾳ αὐτολεῖ τραφεῖσα οὐχ ὅσος οὐ κόρον αὐτῶν ἴσχει, ἀλλὰ καὶ ἐξ αὐτῶν τούτων προσδιαφθείρεται.

[20] On this, see Mallan 2019.

[21] Cf. Mallan 2019. On the manuscripts, see Mazzucchi 1979: 125–31.

[22] *De Creta Capta* 257 (ed. U. Criscuolo). In the case of Dio, Theodosius boasts that 'Sulla was in a vain a *demokrator*.' See Urso 2016b: 29–30.

[23] The *Excerpta*, in turn, provided source material for the *Suda*, the vast literary encyclopaedia compiled in the late tenth/early eleventh century that draws on earlier collections (*lexica*, *scholia*,

III   The Eleventh Century

Interest in the Roman past continued, even becoming 'one of the distinguishing features of eleventh-century Byzantium'.[24] For Paul Magdalino,
this increased interest may have been partly spurred by the revival of legal
education under Constantine IX Monomachus (1042–55) though it was
almost certainly connected to Byzantium's need to assert its claim to the
Roman imperial heritage in the face of Western expansionism.[25] For
Markopoulos the increased interest represented the culmination of
a trend that had begun earlier and was not restricted to practical
considerations.[26] The popularity of Roman history and Roman political
and legal culture at the court of Michael VII Doukas (1071–8) is a case in
point. Michael Attaleiates' introduction to his legal synopsis (*Ponema
Nomikon*), written for Michael VII and based on the *Basilika* (the Greek
translation and adaptation of the Justinianic corpus), emphasizes the
Republican origins of Roman law, thus complementing the same
author's digressions on the Roman Republic in his *History*.[27] The
Concise History (*Historia Syntomos*), most probably composed by
Michael Psellus for his student Michael VII, begins with the reign of
Romulus and ends with that of Basil II (976–1025), utilizing the chronicle
of Symeon the Logothete and the *Roman Antiquities* of Dionysius of
Halicarnassus as its main sources.[28] The work is divided into two equal
parts with regards to Roman and Byzantine history ('Ancient Rome' and
'New Rome'), with almost every chapter dedicated to the reign of a king,
consul, or emperor.[29] This arrangement reflects the biographical trend
current in Byzantine historical writing, and in this sense, Psellus' history
can be considered as a history of Roman rulers presented in continuum
from the foundation of Rome to the eleventh century, with an emphasis
on the lives and characters of the rulers (as in Psellus' better-known

---

excerpta) and was employed specifically in those entries providing definitions of special words and
sketching the biographies of biblical and historical figures. For the abundant use of materials from
Dio, see Adler's index of authors (1928–38: 5.91–2), the entry on Dio Δ 1239, and the searchable
English translation 'Suda On-Line' (www.stoa.org/sol/). On the use of the *Excerpta* in the *Suda*, see
Németh 2018: 238–55.
[24] Markopoulos 2006: 290.   [25] Magdalino 1983: 343, and n. 108.   [26] Markopoulos 2006: 290.
[27] Krallis 2012: 192–9.
[28] Aerts 1990: xxiii–xxiv, where the editor finds only indirect use of Cassius Dio for the Roman period
(cf. *index locorum*, 217) though it is not clear whether Psellus himself had read Dio's history or was
utilizing sources that had made use of Dio's history.
[29] For Psellus' authorship and purpose, see Duffy and Papaioannou 2003: 219–29 and Neville 2018:
144–5.

Chronographia) and the didactic aim of offering paradigms of virtue and vice to the young emperor.[30]

It was also at the court of Michael VII that John Xiphilinus (nephew of the patriarch John VIII Xiphilinus) prepared an epitome of Dio's *Roman History* arranged in a series of twenty-five biographies from Pompey to Alexander Severus (Books 36–80 in Dio).[31] The biographical structure is similar to that of the *Concise History*, and given that both works were written during Michael's reign, it has been suggested that they formed part of the 'educational program' of the young emperor.[32] If this was the case, then Xiphilinus chose the most comprehensive account of Roman history and quite understandably focused his epitome on the imperial period. His task as an epitomator was made easier by Dio's own structure, which, as we have seen, was not exclusively annalistic but rather presented a focus on individual emperors and dynasties.[33] Xiphilinus' epitome of the imperial period is three times as long as that of the Republican period, and about one quarter of Dio's length.[34] Though the reduction of the material is considerable, Xiphilinus' abridgment follows Dio's narrative almost verbatim – including the ancient author's first-person remarks – even if he interjects his own views at different points in the narrative and makes occasional use of other sources (such as Plutarch's *Lives* and Eusebius' *Ecclesiastical History*).[35] With regards to the selection and omission of material, it was once thought that Xiphilinus' choices were random, thus resulting in 'a spasmodic and often barely intelligible narrative'.[36] However, careful study of the Byzantine epitomator's agenda and methods has shown that he abridged Dio's account in such a way as to highlight and simplify its biographical elements.[37]

---

[30] In this context, it is no coincidence that Psellus tells the story of the first six consuls of Rome, but then skips the rest of Republican history (on account of the lack of continuity in leadership) to pick up the thread with Julius Caesar so that the good deeds of emperors may be imitated and the bad ones criticized: Psellos, *Historia Syntomos*, 11. For the biographical trend, see Markopoulos 2010: 697–715. For Psellus' interest in Roman history, see Dželebdžić 2005: 23–33; Markopoulos 2006: 293–6.

[31] The text is in Boissevain 3.479–730. The *Epitome* is of crucial importance for the period from the reign of Claudius to that of Alexander Severus, since Dio's original of these sections is lost. See Brunt 1980: 488–92; Mallan 2013b: 610–44. On the identity of Xiphilinus, see Kruse 2019: 257–74, who suggests that the epitomator was not a monk but a member of the imperial administration. On Xiphilinus' working method: Millar 1964: 195–203 and Schmidt 1989: 55–9.

[32] Juntunen 2015: 144: Xiphilinus identifies himself as a nephew of the homonymous patriarch and tells us that he is writing under Michael VII Doukas (Xiph. 87.5–11).

[33] Cf. Pelling 1997a.   [34] Treadgold 2013: 311.

[35] Brunt 1980: 489. Xiphilinus' interjections are noted by Boissevain in the margin and listed in Treadgold 2013: 311 n. 11.

[36] Millar 1964: 2.   [37] Mallan 2013b: 617–43.

Let us take a closer look. First a comment on Xiphilinus' choice to begin with Book 36 – and we can safely assume that it was a choice rather than a necessity since the later author John Zonaras had the earlier books of Dio at his disposal (with the exception of 23–35).[38] For C. M. Mazzuchi it is not coincidental that the Byzantine text begins with the piratical campaign, and then moves on to Pompey's eastern campaigns, of which the capture of Jerusalem in 56 BC (Book 37) was a part. He argues that this was a central event in the Byzantine chronicle tradition, conceptualized almost as the beginning of a new historical era in which the Roman conquerors would embrace Christianity and become the new chosen peoples.[39] This is plausible, but there is a more suitable explanation. Pompey was a central figure in the transformation of Rome from Republic to the imperial monarchy; and before he captured Jerusalem, he had annexed the Pontus (including the city of Byzantion that was later to become Constantinople), Bithynia, Phoenicia, and Syria. He then reorganized and extended the empire's eastern provinces (i.e. those lands that constituted the heart of the Byzantine Empire). Pompey was, therefore, of special interest to Byzantine audiences.[40] Having said that, it is important to note that Xiphilinus' presentation of the period 69 BC– 27 BC is a preliminary to that of the imperial period,[41] which he prefaces with a personal comment when reaching the 'constitutional settlement' marking the beginning of the Principate in 27 BC:

> I will now relate each event to the degree that it is necessary, and especially from this point on, because our own lives and system of government depend fully on what happened at the time. (Xiph. 87.2–5)[42]

The system of government that Xiphilinus refers to is, of course, the monarchy, and it is telling that he was not the only Byzantine author of the time to show interest in the transformation of Rome from Republic to empire.[43] As such, Xiphilinus includes lengthy excerpts of the 'constitutional settlement' and of the institutions of the Principate.[44]

---

[38] Xiphilinus himself informs us that he did not have Dio's narrative of the reign of Antoninus Pius and the first half of Marcus Aurelius (Xiph. 256.6–11, 28–32), corresponding to Dio's books 70–1. Cf. Juntunen 2013: 460.

[39] Mazzuchi 1979: 135.

[40] Note also that the biographical trend in Dio begins with the dominant figures of the late Republic, i.e. Pompey, Caesar, and Cicero. Cf. Pelling 1997a: 121.

[41] Brunt 1980: 489: Xiphilinus' abridgment of Books 36–52 averages two and a half pages per book in Boissevan's edition, while for the rest (the imperial period) the average is eight pages per book.

[42] λέξω δὲ καὶ καθ' ἕκαστον ὅσα ἀναγκαῖόν ἐστι καὶ νῦν μάλιστα, διὰ τὸ πάμπλου ἀπηρτῆσθαι τῶν καιρῶν ἐκείνων τὸν καθ' ἡμᾶς βίον καὶ τὸ πολίτευμα μνημονεύσθαι. Trans. Kaldellis 2012: 75.

[43] Kaldellis 2015b: 29–31.   [44] Brunt 1980: 490.

As gleaned from the length of his biographies, Xiphilinus is interested in certain emperors more than others, and this certainly played a role in his selection of material to be included in the *Epitome*.[45] As in Dio's narrative (Books 45–56, covering the period 44 BC – AD 14), Octavian/Augustus looms large as the central figure of Rome's passage from Republic to monarchy.[46] He is followed by Nero (Books 61–3, AD 54–68), the paradigm of evil, Dio's contemporary and former benefactor Septimius Severus (Books 74–7, AD 193–211), and Tiberius (Books 57–8, AD 14–37), whose reign coincided with the ministry and death of Christ as known from the Gospels.[47] Dio's abundant and elaborate speeches – considered excellent by Photius – are targets of omission by Xiphilinus, and this is especially true for Dio's account of the Republican period (e.g. the lengthy debate between Agrippa and Maecenas on the merits of democratic and monarchic government in Book 52).[48] However, the epitomator does retain certain speeches from Dio's narrative of the imperial period, thus marking out his own preferences: the speech of Marcus Aurelius to his troops before the war against the usurper Avidius Cassius outlining the evils of civil strife and emphasizing the clemency that the victor should show the defeated (Xiph. 263.1–264.21);[49] the speeches of the Briton leader Boudica and Suetonius Paulinus, the Roman governor of Britannia, the former rousing her compatriots to rebellion against the Roman oppressors, the latter encouraging the Roman troops to put down the barbarian revolt (Xiph. 159.21–161.28; 163.16–164.5); Hadrian's speech on imperial succession and the advantages of an elected or adopted emperor (Xiph. 253.28–254.12); the speech of the Gaul Vindex on the eve of the revolt against the tyrant Nero (Xiph. 182.17–183.4); Otho's speech before the battle of Cremona emphasizing the importance of avoiding civil wars (Xiph. 192.6–30); the dialogue between Octavian and Cleopatra on the theme of imperial clemency (Xiph. 77.19–78.10); and the lengthy dialogue between Livia and Augustus culminating in her admonitions on the value of clemency to an emperor (Xiph. 104.51–112.26). Christopher Mallan has shown that these speeches are not only concerned with imperial themes but also have particular relevance to the turbulent politics of eleventh-century Byzantium inasmuch as

---

[45] Mallan 2013b: 618.

[46] Augustus: Xiph. pp. 498–547. For Dio's account of Augustus, see Millar 1964: 83–102; Rich 1989; Reinhold and Swan 1990: 155–73; Swan 2004: 13–17.

[47] Nero: Xiph. pp. 583–611; Severus: pp. 685–709; Tiberius: 547–65. For Dio's critical treatment of Severus, see Madsen 2016: 136–58 and Rantala 2016: 159–76.

[48] For what follows, see Mallan 2013b: 618–21. For speeches in Dio, see Millar 1961: 11–22; Millar 1964: 78–81; and the more recent (but opposing) views of Burden-Strevens 2016: 193–216 and Fomin 2016: 217–37.

[49] On this speech, see Chapter 8 by Caillan Davenport.

they deal with rebellions and civil wars and highlight the value of imperial clemency.[50]

In addition to this kind of selection process, it has been observed that Xiphilinus modifies and/or adds to Dio's text from other materials. In the cases that have been identified, the example of Plutarch is conspicuous. Looking at Xiphilinus' account of the civil war between Pompey and Julius Caesar, we find that he omits Dio's lengthy discussion of the circumstances that led to the civil war (40.59–6) and offers instead a brief passage that singles out the negative qualities of the protagonists – especially their *philarchia* – as the main cause of the war (Xiph. 15.26–16.7). This was almost certainly taken from Plutarch, who in his *Life of Pompey* assigns this quality to both leaders.[51] It is indicative of Xiphilinus' interest in character rather than circumstances and also explains the epitomator's recourse to the biographer Plutarch, an ancient author who was widely read and admired in Byzantium.[52] What is more, through subtle changes in the narrative, Xiphilinus highlights the fratricidal nature and cruelty of the Roman civil war, thus once again indicating his preoccupation with the circumstances of his times.[53]

Recourse to Plutarch can also be observed in the account of the assassination plot against Julius Caesar by Brutus and Cassius, where Xiphilinus pointedly rejects Dio's negative judgment of the conspirators (who had gone mad through jealousy of Caesar), preferring instead Plutarch's positive assessment of Brutus as a noble and freedom-loving man (Xiph. 3.1–11; cf. 44.1). In this instance, Xiphilinus also omits Dio's commentary on the advantages of the monarchy, since his interest is on the individual rather than the means of government.[54] As a final example, Plutarchan influence has been detected in Xiphilinus' portrait of Cleopatra – beautiful, wise, and passionate – who is not at all like Dio's seductive and treacherous queen but accords well with Plutarch's admiration of Cleopatra's qualities (notably her intelligence) and also with her overall positive image in Byzantium.[55] Thus

---

[50] Mallan 2013b. Michael VII's reign began with the civil war against Romanus IV Diogenes (d. 1072) and continued with a series of devastating rebellions: Constantine Bodin in Bulgaria, Philaretos Brachamios (a former partisan of Romanos), the Caesar John Doukas and the Norman mercenary leader Russell de Baillieul, and finally Nikephoros Bryennios and Nikephoros Botaneiates.
[51] Bialy 2017: 442.
[52] On Plutarch in Byzantium, see Humble 2013: 219–25; Humble forthcoming.
[53] Bialy 2017: 443–5.
[54] The passage in question is translated and discussed in detail by Mallan 2013b: 624–5.
[55] Juntunen 2013: 136, n. 28. I am less convinced, however, by the author's argument that the portrait of Cleopatra is meant to reflect that of the Byzantine empress Eudokia Makrembolitissa (Juntunen 2013: 144–8).

we can see how Xiphilinus slightly alters Dio's narrative to fit his biograph-ical agenda and the preoccupations of Byzantine society. And where he disagrees with Dio, he offers a different reading from alternative sources. Thus, Dio may have provided the most comprehensive account of Roman history, but that does not mean that the Byzantines slavishly followed his every word.[56]

Xiphilinus (though his epitome was most likely an imperial commission) was not the only reader of the *Roman History* in the eleventh century. His contemporary, Kekaumenos, twice mentions Dio by name in his *Advice and Anecdotes* (or *Strategikon*) a text in the tradition of advisory literature that the author wrote under Michael VII Doukas and addressed to his sons. The text contains advice on the conduct of public and domestic affairs, drawing on the author's personal experiences as well as historical examples.[57] The first passage referencing Dio comes in the part 'On Holding Public Office' and is other-wise unknown: 'And I remember what Dio the Roman said: "Even the most trustworthy men are enslaved by well-chosen words and money"' (72.13–14). Though Charlotte Roueché assigns this to a *florilegium*,[58] the second passage, which cites Dio for the tale of Regulus and the dragon, suggests that Kekaumenos was familiar with the ancient text: 'Dio the Roman, who wrote about the empire and the Republic of Rome, and told about the famous Carthaginian war, says that ... ' (82.9–18). What is more, Kekaumenos probably used Dio as a source for his description of the Vlachs (74.12–15), since he states that the Vlachs are the same as the Daci and Bessi known from Roman history, and then goes on to relate the conquest of Dacia by Trajan and the death of the Dacian king Decebalus, an account that seems in part to have been taken from Dio (68.6–15).[59]

IV   Dio under the Komneni

In the twelfth century, the age of the Komnenian *renovatio imperii* that increasingly emphasized the Byzantine Empire's Roman past,[60] the high government official and canonist John Zonaras wrote an *Epitome of Histories*, a lengthy chronicle beginning with the Creation and ending with the death of the emperor Alexios I Komnenos in 1118.[61] Indicative

---

[56] On this point, see also the examples discussed by Rhiannon Ash in Chapter 4 of this volume.
[57] For an edition and translation of Kekaumenos' *Advice and Anecdotes*, see Roueché 2013.
[58] See Roueché 2002: 124.   [59] Roueché 2002: 124–5.
[60] See Magdalino 1983 and Magdalino and Macrides 1992: 117–56.
[61] On Zonaras' *Epitome*, see Ziegler 1972: 718–23; Treadgold 2013: 388–99; Mallan 2018: 359–72; Fromentin 2013: 23–39.

of the author's historical outlook is the original division of the epitome into two parts: Books 1–9 (Creation to the Roman conquest of Corinth in 146 BC) covering Jewish and early Roman history; and Books 10–18 (Pompey to Alexios Komnenos), telling the story of imperial Rome – which, like Xiphilinus' epitome, begins slightly earlier, with Pompey – up to his own times.[62] Though Zonaras wrote in monastic retirement (on the island of St Glykeria on the Sea of Marmara), he was able to make use of a range of sources, including Josephus, Plutarch, Xenophon, Dio, Herodian, Eusebius, Malalas, George the Monk, Skylitzes, and Psellus.[63] With regards to Roman history, Zonaras deals extensively with Republican Rome, rewriting Dio from the period of the arrival of Aeneas in Italy to 146 BC (Books 7–9), though he also interweaves material from Plutarch. After an acknowledged gap owing to a lack of sources (9.31), he returns to Dio with the death of Julius Caesar (44 BC, Book 10.12) and follows him up to the reign of Nerva (AD 96–8, book 11.20), from which point on he supplements Dio's account with large sections from Plutarch, Josephus, Appian, Eusebius, and Xiphilinus' epitome. For Book 12, Antoninus Pius to Maximianus (AD 138–311), Zonaras uses Xiphilinus' epitome (rather than the original) and Eusebius and presumably another source for the non-Christian material.[64] Since the Byzantine author makes extensive use of Dio's original narrative, it is thought that he employs Xiphilinus' epitome largely as an aid, though the fact that he relies on him exclusively from the reign of Trajan onwards (AD 98) suggests that he did not have access to this part of Dio's text.[65]

For classicists, Zonaras' importance lies in his detailed and sophisticated treatment of the Roman Republic, which is derived from books of Cassius Dio that are no longer extant, and also his account of Roman history from the reign of Alexander Severus to Theodosius I, which similarly depends on sources now lost.[66] Ruth Macrides demonstrated the uniqueness of Zonaras in the Byzantine chronicle tradition: Whereas other authors were satisfied with skipping over large chunks of Roman history (from the end of the regal period to Julius Caesar), Zonaras' coverage of the Republic is lengthy and purposeful. He himself states that he will set out to show how the city of Rome was first ruled by kings and tyrants, how it was then converted into an aristocracy or democracy with consuls and dictators, and finally how it passed

---

[62] Zonaras, 1.1; 10.1.   [63] Zonaras' sources are discussed in Karpozilos 2009: 473–84.
[64] Millar 1964: 3.   [65] Bossevain III.187.
[66] For Zonaras' treatment of the Roman period, see Magdalino and Macrides 1992: 126–30 and more recently, Banchich and Lane 2009; Bellissime and Berbessou-Broustet 2016: 95–108; Kampianaki 2017a: 69–80.

to autocracy (9.31).[67] With regards to methodology it has been noted that Zonaras condenses Dio's narrative by either paraphrasing or summarizing and, in general, omits numerous sections of Dio's text, notably speeches, philosophical material, and authorial commentary.[68] If we take a look at Zonaras' abridgment of Dio's narrative of the imperial period (from the death of Julius Caesar to Nerva where he follows Dio almost exclusively), we will find that he devotes Book 10.12–38 (2.371–457, ed. Pinder) to the period from the death of Julius Caesar to that of Augustus (44 BC–AD 14). By contrast, the reign of Augustus' successors up to Nerva (AD 14–96) is related in Book 11.1–20 (3.1–64, ed. Büttner-Wobst), with the elision of material reflecting the priorities and interests of Dio (as well as his own) in Rome's transformation from Republic to an empire (Books 45–56; successors 57–67).

If we take the example of Augustus, we will find that Zonaras follows Dio closely, providing a comparatively lengthy and detailed abridgment, and occasionally preferring the more sensational material from Plutarch's *Life of Antony*, such as the romantic account of Cleopatra and Antony's flight from the battle of Actium (Zon. 10.29; Plut. *Ant.* 66–8) or their dramatic suicides (Zon. 10.30; Plut. *Ant.* 76–8), though in the case of the Egyptian queen's death he also provides Dio's version (51.14: 'Dio says that … ') because of the conflicting stories on her manner of suicide.[69] Elsewhere Zonaras makes use of the more tragic elements of Plutarch's *Life of Brutus* in relating that on the night before the battle of Philippi (42 BC), Brutus was visited by a dreadful apparition, an evil demon (a scene later made famous in Shakespeare's *Julius Caesar*); that Lucillus, pretending to be Brutus, surrendered himself and was brought before Antony so that the real Brutus could flee; and that when Brutus realized he could not escape, he cried out, 'O Zeus, do not forget the author of these ills' (Zon. 10.20; Plut. *Brut.* 48–53). At this point, Zonaras provides Dio's alternative quote ('Dio says that … '), equally poignant, whereby Brutus castigates his valour for being Fortune's slave (Zon. 10.20; Dio 49.2). What is more, having finished his account of the reign of Augustus, Zonaras adds the following information, clearly of interest to his Byzantine audiences. He says that, according to Eusebius of Caesarea, Christ was born on the forty-second year of the reign of Augustus (Eus. *Eccl. Hist.* 5.2). He then explains that Eusebius, unlike others (meaning Dio), did not count the reign of Augustus from the battle of Actium (31 BC), which would mean that Christ

[67] Magdalino and Macrides 1992: 127–31.
[68] Simons 2009: 29–32; Kampianaki 2017a: 73–4; Millar 1964: 2–3, 195–207.
[69] On Zonaras' use of Plutarch, see Kampianaki 2017b: 15–29.

was born on the twenty-ninth year of Augustus' reign. He concludes that since the Evangelist Luke dates the baptism of Christ to the fifteenth year of the reign of Tiberius (Luke 3.1) the Savior was indeed born on the twenty-ninth year of Augustus' reign (Zon. 10.39).

Given the Byzantine proclivity for civil war,[70] it is not surprising that Zonaras' coverage of the civil wars that followed the death of Caesar is rather extensive (Zon. 10.14–32), or that before proceeding to the following section he quotes Dio verbatim:

> Such were the achievements of the Romans and such their suffering under the kingship, under the Republic, and under the dominion of a few, during a period of seven hundred and twenty-five years. After this they reverted to what was, strictly speaking, a monarchy, although Caesar planned to lay down his arms and to entrust the management of the state to the senate and the people. (Dio 52.1.1)[71]

Zonaras then gives a highly condensed and simplified version of the 'constitutional settlement' of 27 BC (Dio 53.2–19). This version, however, retains the most pertinent elements: how it was made to appear that Augustus was forced into accepting autocratic powers; how his supremacy was ratified by the senate and the People; the apportionment of provinces between Augustus and the senate; how Augustus' ten-year mandate was gradually extended for life; and how he was given the title of Augustus (Zon. 10.32). Thereafter, Zonaras' main focus is on Augustus, his gradual consolidation of power and his succession. He omits military campaigns or makes vague references to them (e.g. 'Drusus and Lucius Piso subjugated many foreign nations' [Zon. 10.34]), though he does render an account of the disastrous defeat of Quintilius Varus by the Germans in AD 9 (Zon. 10.37; 56.18–24). Likewise, we read nothing of Augustus' building projects in Rome and little on his administration and laws. Augustus' character is illustrated through his relations with his close associates (Agrippa, Maecenas, Drusus, Tiberius) and more rarely through various anecdotes, such as his handling of a certain Pollio (Zon.10.34; 54.23), his advocacy of his friends in the courts (Zon.10.35; 55.4); or how his temper was moderated by Maecenas (Zon. 10.35; 55.7).

---

[70] Kaldellis 2012: 75.

[71] Ταῦτα μὲν ἔν τε τῇ βασιλείᾳ καὶ ἐν τῇ δημοκρατίᾳ ταῖς τε δυναστείαις, πέντε τε καὶ εἴκοσι καὶ ἑπτακοσίοις ἔτεσι, καὶ ἔπραξαν οἱ Ῥωμαῖοι καὶ ἔπαθον· ἐκ δὲ τούτου μοναρχεῖσθαι αὖθις ἀκριβῶς ἤρξαντο, καίτοι τοῦ Καίσαρος βουλευσαμένου τά τε ὅπλα καταθέσθαι καὶ τὰ πράγματα τῇ τε γερουσίᾳ καὶ τῷ δήμῳ ἐπιτρέψαι. (Trans. E. Cary, Loeb Classical Library edition)

It is unsurprising that Zonaras tends to summarize Dio's speeches, such as the lengthy harangue of Cicero against Mark Antony and Calenus' response in defense of Antony before the senate in 43 BC (Zon. 10.24; 45.18–45, 46.1–28). Likewise, he provides a summary of the Agrippa–Maecenas debate (Zon. 10.32; 52.2–41), the speech of Augustus before the senate (Zon. 10.32; 53.3–10) and the Livia–Augustus dialogue (Zon. 10.36; 55.14–22), often retaining the most pertinent quotes. It is curious, however, that Zonaras simply mentions the eulogy delivered at Augustus' funeral by Tiberius (Zon. 10.38; 56. 35–41) and omits Dio's assessment of Augustus (56.43–5), whereas he includes the portents presaging Augustus' death (Zon. 10.37; 56.29.2–5), the anecdote regarding his exemplary treatment of a certain Athenodorus (Zon. 10.38; 56.42.2–3), and Augustus' own words on his deathbed: 'I found Rome of clay; I leave it to you of marble' (Zon. 10.38; 56.30.3). From the above, we can conclude that Zonaras' interest is largely political: first the civil wars, then Augustus' rise and consolidation of power, and lastly his succession. In this scheme, wars of conquest, grandiose building projects, and lengthy speeches, comments and appraisals were deemed superfluous.[72]

To conclude our chapter, brief mention should be made of the twelfth-century classical scholar John Tzetzes (c. 1110 – after 1160), who produced, among other works, two books of allegories *On the Iliad* and *On the Odyssey*, scholia on Hesiod's *Work and Days*, on the plays of Aristophanes, and on Lycophron's *Alexandra*, and the *Chiliades* or more properly *Histories*, a miscellany of historical or mythological narratives and anecdotes arranged in different subject categories and written in verse.[73] In the latter work, Dio is referenced and used as a source in narratives mainly concerned with Rome: e.g. 'Hannibal' (27); 'Trajan and the Bridging of the Danube' (34); 'Gaius Julius Caesar' (68); 'Marcus Manlius and about geese, a story also complete by itself' (102–11); 'Cato the Roman' (347); 'What Cocceianus writes about Coriolanus' (60).[74] Tzetzes takes particular delight in showing off his knowledge of the ancient historian. He says, for example, that 'Dio Cassius has written this story' (34 concerning Trajan's

---

[72] Note, after this lengthy abridgment of the reign of Augustus, Zonaras records only the main events in the reign of each emperor, something which alerts us to the importance given by the chronicler to Augustus as the first Roman emperor.

[73] On Tzetzes' scholarship, see Budelmann 2002: 141–69; Pontani 2015: 378–85. On the *Histories*, see Pizzone 2017: 182–207. The narratives (660 in number) were meant to elucidate passages and explain obscure literary references in Tzetzes' letter collection.

[74] For a text of Tzetzes, see Leone 1968. For a translation, see that of Untila et al. published online at www.theoi.com/Text/TzetzesChiliades1.html.

bridging of the Danube); or that 'the Diodoruses and the Dios and others in addition say these things' (68 concerning Caesar).

The Byzantine author also makes use of and acknowledges Dio on numerous occasions in his commentary to Lycophron's *Alexandra*, which tells the story of the heroes of the Trojan war along with other mythological and historical events through the Trojan princess and prophetess Cassandra.[75] For instance, in explaining Lycophron's description of the 'narrow straits of the Ausonian Sea', Tzetzes says that 'the name Ausonia, according to Dio Cocceianus, is properly applied only to the land of the Aurunsci, situated on the coast between the Campanians and the Volsci' (Tzetzes, *Lyc.* 44). Similarly, in identifying Lycophron's 'landing-place of the Bebryces,' he states that 'Dio Cocceianus calls the Narbonenses Bebryces, writing thus: "To those who were of old Bebryces, but now Narbonenses, belongs the Pyrenees range. This range is the boundary between Spain and Gaul"' (Tzetzes, *Lyc.* 536).[76] Finally, we should also mention that Tzetzes draws upon Dio's narrative in his letters. Notable is the case of epistle 107, addressed to Manuel I Komnenos (1143–80) and containing a description of a triumphal procession that the author recommends to the emperor. The description, as Tzetzes himself acknowledges, is derived from Dio's (now lost) excursus on Roman triumphal celebrations and was really meant to put the emperor to shame.[77]

It may be tentatively noted that Tzetzes shows a preference for the early books of Dio's history rather than the later 'imperial books'. This is not surprising considering that he was a product of an age that witnessed the emergence of a class of professional literati and a classical scholar and exegete with a penchant for mythological narratives. Xiphilinus, as we have seen, simply ignores the early and Republican history of Rome. But his epitome was meant to present imperial biographies and was most probably an imperial commission. Likewise, the *Excerpta Constantiniana* – or rather the section we looked at here – shows a preference for Dio's narrative of the imperial period. Yet it too was an imperial commission. The case of Zonaras is more complicated, since he follows Dio closely for the regal and Republican periods and also for the early imperial period, but thereafter

---

[75] John Tzetzes, *On Lycophron*, see the edition of Müller 1811; the translations of Tzetzes quoted are from E. Cary's Loeb Classical Library edition.
[76] Cf. also Tzetzes, *Lyc.* 516, 602, 633 for similar explications derived from Dio. The story of Aeneas and his descendants (Tzetzes, *Lyc.* 1232), given as a testimonial of Dio's lost text in Book 1, relies more on Dionysius of Halicarnassus.
[77] John Tzetzes, *Epistulae* (ed. Leone) 141–2, 173. On the final point, see Magdalino and Macrides 1992: 119–20. On Tzetzes' letters, see Grigoriadis 2001, with a translation and commentary.

increasingly turns to alternative sources and finally switches to Xiphilinus' epitome. It should be remembered, however, that Zonaras was writing a world chronicle from the Creation to his own times and not contemporary (imperial) history in the biographical mode. Whatever the aim or preference of these authors, the fact that they read, excerpted, abridged, or otherwise made use of Dio's *Roman History* is itself significant.

V Conclusion

It has been noted that in earlier periods, from the seventh to the tenth century, Dio was mainly referenced by grammarians and moralists, who were not particularly interested in the historical content of his work.[78] Beginning in the tenth century, the revived interest in the Roman past led to a revived interest in ancient historical narratives, with Dio's *Roman History* assuming a position of prime importance. Two reasons can be suggested for this. One, from the Greek narratives of Roman history, Dio certainly offered the most comprehensive account. Dionysius of Halicarnassus stopped with the outbreak of the First Punic War in 264 BC; Polybius ended with the destruction of Carthage and Corinth in 146 BC; Diodorus of Sicily went to 60 BC; Appian continued into the second century AD but was mostly concerned with Rome's wars; and Herodian only covered the period AD 180–238. Second, Dio's combination of the annalistic and biographical modes of history and his classicizing style of prose were perfectly suited to the literary trends of the time. Perhaps we should here recall Photius' comments on Dio's grandiose literary style, reflecting, according to the patriarch, the consciousness of mighty events. For these reasons then, Dio's lengthy history was copied, excerpted for Constantine VII's grand historical complication, abridged, most likely, for the education and edification of a young emperor, summarized for Zonaras' sophisticated chronicle, and referenced and utilized by poets such as Theodosios the Deacon, classical scholars such as John Tzetzes, and educated laymen like Kekaumenos. All this reflects a familiarity with and respect for Dio's *Roman History* not only in court circles but also among the educated reading public. For the Byzantines of the period, Dio was, in the words of Tzetzes: 'Dio, writer of Roman History.'

---

[78] Mallan 2019.

And Now ... ?

Christopher Pelling

For Philip Larkin, 1963 was the year when things changed, 'between the end of the "Chatterley" ban | And the Beatles' first LP'.[1] Cassius Dio had to wait for his transformation until the following year, with the publication of Fergus Millar's *A Study of Cassius Dio*.[2] Its impact on later research has been vast, and the present volume is one of several collected works that prompt reflection on how the Dionian landscape has changed over half a century. The two volumes of *Cassius Dion: nouvelles lectures* were the product of a four-and-a-half-year research project explicitly titled *cinquante ans après Fergus Millar*,[3] and in the same year appeared *Cassius Dio: Greek Intellectual and Politician*;[4] *Cassius Dio's Forgotten History of Early Rome* and *Cassius Dio and the Late Republic* followed three years later;[5] a Brill *Companion to Cassius Dio* is promised following an Odense conference in December 2018; and now there is this collection too. Further important additions to the mix are the brilliant chapter on Dio in Kemezis' *Greek Narratives of the Roman Empire under the Severans* and Scott's historical commentary on Dio's final books;[6] as I write, Madsen's *Cassius Dio* has just appeared in Bloomsbury's *Ancients in Action* series,[7] and Burden-Strevens' book on the Republican speeches is also expected shortly.[8] It is a tribute to Dio's multifaceted achievement that the overlap across these volumes is less than might have been expected, though several of the usual suspects have contributed to more than one. It is difficult, but it may be timely, to draw breath and to consider not just where we have come but also the directions that research might take in the future.[9]

---

[1] 'Annus Mirabilis' in Larkin 1974: 34.   [2] Millar 1964.   [3] Fromentin et al. 2016a.
[4] Lange and Madsen 2016.   [5] Burden-Strevens and Lindholmer 2019; Osgood and Baron 2019.
[6] Kemezis 2014; Scott 2018b.   [7] Madsen 2020.   [8] Burden-Strevens 2020.
[9] There will be no attempt here to give a full sketch of fifty years of scholarship. Further bibliographical guidance can be found in the papers cited, together with the many other excellent contributions in those collections that there is no room to mention here.

One of the most distinctive features of Millar's book was his dismissal of traditional *Quellenforschung*. He highlighted this in his preface, anticipating that some readers would regard such a treatment as '*Hamlet* without the Prince', and reviewers were not slow to emphasise this change of scholarly direction.[10] (His bark, though, was fiercer than his bite; he was often ready to explain features of Dio's narrative in terms of their sources.) That cannot be said to have stemmed the tide of *Quellenforschung* – nor should it have done, as the questions remain important and speculation is not always pointless – and many chapters in these volumes are concerned with this (e.g. Letta in this volume). But certainly, those questions now tend to be framed differently, with a more cautious approach to identifying the works that Dio used and a greater emphasis on what he did with them. There is also much less readiness to use source criticism to explain away difficulties: there is no longer such an assumption that apparently discordant strands are to be explained in terms of one interest or bias coming from source A and the other from source B – as if it were only our surviving texts that ever showed such discordances, and lost sources must always have been thoroughly unequivocal in their slants.[11] We are now much more ready to accept such polyphony as an interesting feature of a writer, an alertness to the multiple perspectives that history has to offer, and not as a sign of inattention to the implications of his own writing.

At the same time some of the focus has shifted from writer to audience. If Dio knew his Livy, say, might some at least of his hearers and readers have known Livy too, at least in terms of a vague knowledge of how Livy had set about his task? Would they be comparing Dio against such a great predecessor and gauging how he matched up and how he was different? Is he writing *against* Livy, not just from him? Is this a 'rewriting of Roman Republican history', a 'programmatic striving to go beyond' the great work that so dominated the field?[12] The title of one paper in Fromentin et al., 'Tite-Live modèle de Cassius Dion ou contre-modèle?',[13] asks a very good question, parallel to the sort of issue that is now raised about Livy's own relation to Polybius.[14] Kuhn's contribution to the present volume suggests a similar point: if Dio is echoing Augustus' own *Res Gestae*, might that be

---

[10] Millar 1964: viii. For reviews, see Bowersock 1965: 474; Morris 1965: 184; Townend 1965: 307; McDonald 1966: 319.

[11] Millar 1964: 84: 'It is doing Dio less than justice to assume that an equivocal judgement in his work will simply be the result of using sources with opposing views.'

[12] Urso 2019: 71, cf. 69: 'Un lavoro di riscrittura della storia romana repubblicana ... suo sfôrzo programmatic per andare "al di là" di Livio.'

[13] de Franchis 2016. [14] Levene 2010.

a matter not merely of his source but also of his own critical stance, one that a knowledgeable audience might recognise? Is *RG* echoed only to be critiqued, as arguably in the speech given to Augustus' praisers at *Annals* 1.9? If so, Tacitus may certainly be the more barbed, with 1.10 immediately giving a counterblast to such echoes of Augustan propaganda; but is Dio's point that, even if the warlike slant of the propaganda was misplaced (Kuhn), some at least of what Augustus claimed was no more than the truth? Or at least the truth as Tiberius wished it to be seen as he set out the stall for his own reign?

One main reason for Millar's impatience with traditional *Quellenforschung* was again stated clearly in his preface: 'In plain terms, we do not know enough about how ancient historians worked'.[15] Millar went on to set out what we do know, and that discussion remains one of the most thorough and illuminating.[16] This has been less followed up than one might have hoped, though Gowing's treatment of the triumviral period was exemplary:[17] the working methods of other authors – Plutarch, for instance, and Livy[18] – have been more explored, even though those authors tell us much less about them than Dio does. It is doubtless right to insist that Dio often combined multiple sources (as Millar himself assumed),[19] but *how*? Did he proceed as a modern historian might, weaving together an account deriving equally and evenly from all those sources? Or did he have only one open before his eyes, and add or correct material as he went? The pure physical difficulties of handling papyrus rolls should not here be forgotten – or perhaps he was not looking at original texts at all as he wrote or dictated, but using those notes he had taken, presumably on a *codex*, during those ten years he spent in preliminary reading (72.23.5, cf. Letta in Chapter 3 of this volume)? It is admittedly much harder to analyse Dio's technique than it is with Plutarch or Livy, where we can start from detailed comparison in cases where we have what is clearly a, or the, main source; but it is hard to think that there is nothing left to be done. Dionysius of Halicarnassus, another author who is unusually explicit about his methods, might here provide an important avenue for comparison.

The most obvious change over fifty years is the readiness to explore Dio's own historical thinking and to find ideas that are interesting. Not everyone, perhaps, would agree that 'Dio is very, very smart',[20] but fewer still

---

[15] Millar 1964: viii.   [16] Millar 1964: 28-46.   [17] Gowing 1992: esp. 39–50.
[18] Plutarch: e.g. Pelling 1979 and 2002: ch. 3, van der Stockt 1999, and Stadter 2015: 119–29; Livy: Luce 1977.
[19] E.g. Millar 1964: 85.
[20] Pelling 2006: 262. One who would agree is Carsana, praising Dio's nuanced application of political theory to Roman realities: 'Anche in questo è uno storico "di razza", di altissima statura' (2016: 557).

would now follow Millar in some of his formulations of 1964: 'large-scale interpretations are clearly absent' (p. 46); 'there was no time to explain the forces at work [in Cicero's career], even if Dio understood them' (p. 55); 'the long years of working through the whole of Roman history brought Dio to formulate no general historical views whatsoever' (p. 118). Millar himself came to strike a different note: in his preface to Fromentin et al. he talked of Dio's 'impressive analyses of, for instance, the transition from republic to monarchy or the governmental structure of the Empire'.[21] Even in 1964 he clearly intended 'general historical views' to be taken in a particular way, for he allowed plenty of scope for Dio's political convictions to emerge, for instance his stress on the value from Augustus onwards of a broad senatorial involvement in government. But much more scholarly focus now falls on, for example, Dio's views of historical change and all the possibilities here that his vast chronological canvas offered to explore.

How much, after all, really did alter with the move from Republic to Principate? Clearly there was a new difficulty in finding out the truth about what was going on, with an imperial cloak of secrecy or deceit: Dio is explicit about that in one of his most famous passages (53.19), setting out the difference between what Kemezis in this volume terms the 'public transcript' and the 'hidden transcript'. Davenport brings out how important that contrast is to understand how people talked and acted in their nervous uncertainty (ch. 2 in this volume). But how much of the pattern for the later emperors is already being laid down by the big men of the late Republic, and perhaps indeed prefigured even earlier, by the massive figures of the middle Republic or even by the early kings?[22] The sense of a strong new start under Augustus is noticeably clear: the lengthy Agrippa and Maecenas debate of Book 52 provides a strong marker of a break from the past, exploring what form the new dispensation is to take. But will everything in fact be so new? Or has that pattern already been set by those Republican grandees, with their taste for power and reluctance to give it up?[23] Should we see the deceptiveness that so many of them practised as prefiguring the imperial pretences (Davenport ch. 2), where there was, at least at first, something of a republican façade – shades of Agrippa's enthusiasm for democracy – to temper the realities that are more in line with Maecenas? Or should we follow Kemezis in seeing a much stronger break, with deceptiveness no longer needed, and Octavian's own initial disingenuousness in Book 53 felt as already out

---

[21] Millar 2016: 10.   [22] Coudry 2019; Schulz 2019b.   [23] Burden-Strevens 2016.

of date?[24] And, whatever we say about the break at the end of the
Republic, how deep are the changes that happened within the
Principate itself? Marcus Aurelius' demise ended an age of gold and
ushered in an age of iron and rust (72.36.4): but how and why? Is it just
a matter of the individual deficiencies of the emperors, or is this just
revealing a potential flaw in the system that has already been there? Had
Caligula and Nero been offering just as real a template for the future as
Augustus, even if those prefigurings were only now emerging in
retrospect?

Nor are these the only issues of continuity and change. Are there other
strands that thread continuously from beginning to end? Citizenship,
perhaps (Lavan in this volume)? Dionysius of Halicarnassus saw Roman
generosity with the citizenship as a strength from the earliest days,[25] and it
is easy to sense that for his readers the theme would have an Augustan
resonance still: does Dio see it similarly? Lavan is inclined to doubt it
(Chapter 10 in this volume). Or, more broadly, take values – honour, say,
and virtue (Lavan, Rodgers, and Mallan, Chapter 12 in this volume). Are
these still the same under the Principate? Is the vocabulary consistent but
applied to different types of behaviour? Is being a good man in a bad period
(late Republic) the same as being a good man under a bad emperor, now
that the parameters of free speech have themselves changed?[26] And has
competition just disappeared, or is it there in new forms that may be just as
toxic?[27]

What, too, about the Roman people (Kemezis and Hellström, Chapters
1 and 9 in this volume)? This is where questions of historical interpretation
begin to overlap with those of literary technique. Does Dio use them
largely as a sounding board, secondary focalisers whose opinions provide
a useful mode of conveying his own commentary on events,[28] with public
opinion and Dio's own voice blurring into one another (Kemezis and Ash,
Chapters 1 and 4 in this volume)? Or are they treated as a genuine force
influencing events? Does their gossip not merely illuminate the atmosphere
of the reign but also affect what emperors and courtiers do (Davenport,

---

[24] Kemezis 2014: 136–9. Coudry 2016b: 296, n. 20 notes the difference of opinion here between
Kemezis and myself (Pelling 1997a: 128–31 and 2006: 261–2), as did Kemezis himself (2014: 136 and
n. 114). I stick to my earlier view.
[25] This theme starts as early as Dion. Hal. *Ant. Rom.* 1.9.4; then e.g. 2.16.1, 35–6, 2.46, 2.55.6, 3.29
(incorporation of noble Alban families into *patricii* and senate), 6.55 and 14.6. Tullus Hostilius can
justly pride the city on this policy at 3.11.4. Tarquinius Priscus is accordingly attracted to Rome when
he hears 'that the city willingly welcomes all strangers, makes them citizens, and honours them
according to their worth' (3.47.2). Cf. Poma 1989.
[26] Mallan 2016.   [27] Lindholmer 2019.   [28] cf. Millar 1964: 141.

Chapter 2)? And does that change over the course of the history as the texture of politics, especially urban politics, changes? And can we say something similar about the senate, whose role in administration is so dear to Dio's heart? Are senators seen as able to influence the Roman world more or less, or in a different way, under the new dispensation? If Dio treats Flamininus' proclamation of Greek freedom very differently from Nero's (Malik, Chapter 7), is that because one could then take it as a serious political move from a Republican senator but not now from a *princeps*? Have the times themselves changed, with a world now where cynicism and suspicion of fakery are the right responses even to apparently exemplary actions? Or is it simpler – these two are just seen as very different human beings?

Questions of structure form another area where matters of literary technique and historical interpretation come together. Millar had also already drawn attention to cases where Dio's annalistic structure breaks down,[29] and scholars continue to go thoroughly into the interpretative reasons for such breakdowns.[30] This mirrors similar work on other authors: Rich has applied the same approach to Livy,[31] and the pattern was set when Ginsburg brought out how the looser annalistic form in the later books of Tacitus' *Annals* corresponds to a change in the texture of the Principate, with the annual changeover of Republican magistracies mattering less and less.[32] The strategies behind Dio's book divisions and his organisation into pentads and decades are also matters of interpretative periodisation as well as of literary neatness (e.g. Ash, Chapter 4).

The approach to Dio's characterisation has also shifted. It is easy to find him wanting in comparison with the livelier portraits of Plutarch and Suetonius or the barbed psychological insights of Tacitus, but there is a growing tendency to see this less as a failing and more as a reflection of his interpretative priorities: his figures 'only make sense within a broad historical scheme'.[33] Is his interest then rather in characterising a reign than an emperor (Mallan, Chapter 6)? Or in linking pairs of emperors together (Davenport, Chapter 8)? Or just in evaluating how much an emperor succeeds or fails in matching up to what a *princeps* should be?[34] Maybe the individual quirks of an emperor made less difference to the empire than we might think, and Dio knew it.[35]

---

[29] Millar 1964: 39–40, cf. 56–9, 67, 70.   [30] Rich 2016; Devillers 2016b; Baron 2019.
[31] Rich 2011.   [32] Ginsburg 1981.
[33] Coudry 2016b: 300: 'Les figures, grandes ou petites, ne prennent sens que dans une interprétation historique générale'; similarly Coltelloni-Trannoy 2016b.
[34] Devillers 2016b.   [35] Kemezis 2014: 139–41.

Scholarship on the speeches has changed too. There has always been great interest in these, especially those cases where a speaker is suspected to be reflecting or projecting Dio's own views: the Agrippa–Maecenas debate of Book 52 is here particularly fascinating. For Millar, as for many since, a crucial question was whether Maecenas' hard-headed advocation of monarchy is anachronistic, with recommendations more fitted to Dio's own day than to its Augustan context. That debate continues still. Other questions could be, and were, put to the speeches, in particular those exploring where Dio drew his material from, and those could go well beyond any assumption of any single 'source' that Dio was simply copying out: take, for instance, Millar's acute observation that Cicero's orations could be echoed in Dio's own speeches but were not used to provide material for the narrative.[36] Once again similar investigations are still valuable, though the emphasis has moved more to argumentative tropes and generic affiliation. One can, for instance, track how far Antony's funeral speech for Caesar or Tiberius' for Augustus echo Greek *basilikoi logoi* or Roman *laudationes funebres* or panegyrics,[37] or in a broader sense the debt to the commonplaces and themes of Roman declamation.[38] But there is also much more readiness to regard such observations as the start of an inquiry rather than the end. Bellissime, for instance, goes on to analyse how those echoes work differently in Antony's speech and in Tiberius', and how that might illuminate the ways that history has changed: Antony's speech reflects political tumult and provokes more of it, Tiberius' marks his own position as heir in a world of relative stability.[39] And if a speaker mouths commonplace ideas, it may be a prompt to a reader to measure them against the grimier realities that emerge from the narrative: an essay on the relation to panegyric can include in its title 'the deconstruction of imperial representation'.[40]

Take, for instance, Julius Caesar's speech at Vesontio in 58 BC as war with Ariovistus threatens.[41] Caesar there gives an elaborate defence of Roman imperialism, full of fine statements about the mission of empire and Rome's care of the provinces. Millar pointed out how different this was from Dio's views of the military adventures of his own time, 'a waste of men and money and a source of future trouble',[42] but elaborated no more than to note the way this showed Dio's acquaintance with Greek philosophical justifications of empire – one of those cases, in fact, where Dio's 'sources', interpreted broadly, could still be sensed as explaining features of

[36] Millar 1964: 54–5.   [37] Bellissime 2016a.   [38] Fomin 2016.   [39] Bellissime 2016a.
[40] Schulz 2016.   [41] Kemezis 2016a.   [42] Millar 1964: 82–3.

his account. Now we might be more interested in elaborating that difference between Caesar's arguments and Dio's own views of imperial expansion, favouring a policy of restraint (Davenport, Chapter 8). Is the suggestion that history has changed, that such an idea of imperial mission was all very well as the Roman empire grew but by the time of Augustus the job was effectively done, and consolidation was better for everyone? Or is it rather that Caesar's words were all very well but already at odds with the reality, one further reason why one-man rule was a good idea? And do we sense – we probably do – that Caesar has his own self-seeking reasons for military adventurism, and they are quite different from those that he is mouthing here? If so, that is yet another case of the hypocrisy so frequent in the late Republic, also seen, for instance, in Pompey's unconvincing parade of reluctance to accept the command granted him by the *lex Gabinia*:[43] and that again leads into those questions of continuity or change when we move into the self-presentation of Augustus, and perhaps offers another reason for preferring monarchy when such damaging rivalries can be set aside.[44] Yet there can also be times when we can measure the rhetoric against the reality and find less of a mismatch. A decade later Caesar produces similar fine words when he appears in victory before the senate, in that case promising clemency (43.15–8). By then it is easy for the reader to respond with a suspicious cynicism; and yet Caesar himself has indeed been clement after Pharsalus and Thapsus,[45] and perhaps he is for once being truthful. Still, that hardly matters. If the reader is sceptical, so too will have been the senators; however merciful Caesar may be, that does not defuse their hostility. Rhetoric itself has been so devalued that it will be assumed to be a matter of gesture-politics rather than truthfulness, and that too is an important historical point.

The 'literary turn', then, has deeply affected Dio scholarship, and it has turned him into a more interesting historical thinker. That also affects the development of another major theme of Millar, the impact on Dio's writing of his own political experience. That interest remains as great as ever, but with again a shift of emphasis from Dio's political convictions to his historical interpretation. How far, for instance, has his experience under Commodus affected his presentation of Nero (Malik and Rodgers in this volume) or Elagabalus,[46] or even the early kings Tarquinius Priscus and Tarquinius Superbus?[47] How did the Severans affect his view of Sulla (Hellström, Chapter 9 in this volume, and Urso's article)?[48] And what sort

---

[43] Coudry 2016b.   [44] Bertrand 2016a.   [45] Coudry 2016a: 299.   [46] Osgood 2016.
[47] Schulz 2019b: 323–7.   [48] Urso 2016a.

of point is that? Is it just a matter of his intellectual and psychological formation, a biographical point about the man himself – no surprise that he thought like that given what he had been through, whether or not he was aware of it himself? Or is it also a matter of intratextual patterning, one that conveys to his audience that old times are returning and that Rome has always had the potential to produce such monsters or brutes?

One might still feel that that 'literary turn' has a few more rotations to go yet, especially when compared with critical developments elsewhere. Dio may suffer a little here, especially in Anglophone countries, through the lack of a recent translation (French readers are much better served by the excellent Budé editions): Earnest Cary's Loeb (1914–27) is universally used, even more so now that it is available online. Cary's revision of the translation of H. B. Foster (1905–6) was thorough and tasteful, as comparison of sample passages can show. It was rightly acclaimed on publication,[49] and has served very well. Still, a century has passed, and Robin Waterfield's new *Oxford's World's Classics* version will be very welcome.

More broadly, there is little literary theory in these recent collections, for good and/or ill, and not much use of the categories or techniques of formal narratology.[50] One could do, too, with some more pieces of straightforward literary and stylistic analysis:[51] we are too reluctant to take on the job of just showing how good a writer he can be. With other authors there is a growing interest in 'generic enrichment', with exploration of what is added by resonances of tragedy or comedy or the novel. There are some hints of that here (e.g. Malik, Chapter 7, 'the scenario quickly turns from black comedy to out-and-out tragedy', and Rodgers, Chapter 10, 'so many of this emperor's actions were stage-managed performances'), but there may be more to this than scholarly metaphor. After all, a graffito registered 'Orestes, Nero, Alcmaeon, all matricides' (61.16.2), and Nero finally came to realise that he had played Orestes and Alcmaeon in life (63.22.6) as well as on the stage (63.9.4), and with Dio as well as Tacitus we might well talk of 'amateur dramatics at the court of Nero'.[52]

---

[49] E.g. Misener 1918: 420, 'Dio has been fortunate in his translator. Dr Cary's rendering of the Greek is precise and full but free from pedantry.' Any sniffiness was aimed at the author rather than the translator: 'Caesar can be read for pleasure; Dio cannot, and the task of translating him is not one that we would choose' (unsigned, in *The Saturday Review*, 10 November 1917). Minor errors can inevitably be found: Murison 1999 noted eleven passages in Books 64–7 (helpfully collected in Damon's review, *BMCR* 2000.03.07), but one of these concerns a suggested supplement rather than a rendering and only six seem to me clear-cut. Many translations would score much worse than that.

[50] As Makhlaiuk 2017 observes, also noting Lachenaud 2016 as a partial exception.

[51] The gap here is also noted by Gotteland (2016: 379–80), who goes on to provide some good close readings of her own.

[52] Woodman 1992.

Contact with the novel may also cast light on the question how far Dio includes material that we would regard as fictional, whether we should (for instance) accept that there is a lot of unhistorical material in his accounts of games or omens (Hellström, Chapter 9) or that particular speeches were not delivered in the senate as Dio says (Kemezis, Chapter 1) or that Augustus did not really leave such testamentary advice (Lavan, Chapter 10). Would Dio's audience have taken such things literally, or would they take it for granted that historiography allowed itself a certain licence? There is room too to go back to the debate whether Dio himself would have accepted that such material was fictional or if he would have seen himself as reconstructing 'how it must have been', Augustus and Tiberius (say) being the sort of persons they were. But was it also important to keep a certain distance from the novel, maintaining historiography's dignity and essential seriousness (Ash, Chapter 4)? And if the generic boundaries are slipping more and more as Dio approaches his own day (Ash, Chapter 4), is that too a point about the history as well as about his text, with the dignity and credibility of the imperial system tottering along with the conventions of the genre? Are all expectations baffled, in literature as in life?

Intertextuality, too, figures relatively little. Several writers stress his 'Thucydideanism', particularly his taste for *logos-ergon* antitheses and his emphasis on the pervasiveness of human nature; there is little grappling with this in individual cases, exploring the ways in which memories of a specific Thucydidean original might suggest contrasts or comparisons.[53] Yet it may be that there does not need to be, that the projection of an overall Thucydidean *persona* is all that is important to build Dio's authority, a piece of what Luke Pitcher calls 'author theatre';[54] but that too needs to be argued. What, too, of other authors? Herodotus figures a little, especially his constitutions debate (3.80–2) in the background of Agrippa and Maecenas;[55] so does Plato.[56] But there is surely more to say.

We could particularly do with more on Dio's relation to those Greek predecessors who wrote about Rome.[57] Appian and Plutarch often figure in discussions, but usually in close readings comparing versions of the same events: those are immensely valuable, but is Dio assuming any knowledge of those authors in at least some of his audience, as Ash here suggests for the crossing of the Rubicon (Chapter 4)? Is he writing 'against' them in any sense? And what of Polybius, one obvious precursor as someone who comes

---

[53] I made some tentative steps in that direction in Pelling 2010b.   [54] Pitcher 2009b: esp. 34–9.
[55] Kuhlmann 2010, cf. Kemezis 2014: 131–2.   [56] Jones 2016.
[57] Fromentin (2016: 179) also notes this gap in the scholarly literature.

to be a participating observer as well as a narrator of Roman history (Mallan, Chapter 12)? Is Dio's commitment to monarchy sensed as an argument against Polybius' mixed constitution, or at least an indication that such a mixture had become obsolete a century after Polybius wrote? Or might there be a hint that the Augustan settlement was 'mixed' in a different way, with that tempering of Maecenas' autocratic reality with Agrippa's democratic façade? Is there perhaps some alignment here with Dionysius of Halicarnassus, who preferred to see Rome's greatness not just as a product of Polybius' fifty-three years but as something that had grown since its distant origins, fostered not just in one *politeia* but in a series of different ones?[58] Kemezis' concluding paragraph in his 2014 monograph suggests how much Dio and Dionysius have in common:

> Dio is an example of someone whose roots also [i.e. as well as the Severans] lay elsewhere than Rome, but more within a broader Greco-Roman mainstream. . . . [His] Bithynian antecedents are a part of his personality, but in no way hinder him from identifying not just with the Roman political structure as narrowly defined but with broader cultural traditions of the Roman elite that go back in a continuous line to the Republic . . . By entering into the previously Latin tradition of senatorial history-writing, and by reasserting his order's claim to be the interpreter of the Roman past, Dio is putting forth his own story of how the truly significant aspects of Rome have changed and not changed.[59]

Substitute 'Dionysius' for 'Dio' and 'Halicarnassus' for 'Bithynia', and a lot will fit. Of course, that reference to 'his order' marks a vital difference too, for Dio was writing as a senatorial insider; but that in itself suggests the value of plotting whether the difference this made to his narrative perspectives is really as great as we have come to think. Perhaps any affinity is just one that comes with being Greek and writing about the great city and culture that both men knew so well. But it is well worth asking whether there is more to it.[60]

There is more to do on reception too. We now understand a good deal more about the methods of the Byzantine excerptors, not merely accepting that their particular interests are colouring our impression of Dio's original,[61] but also understanding more about why those interests fit their own society

[58] Cf. esp. Dion. Hal. *Ant. Rom.* 1.8.2 with Pelling 2018.   [59] Kemezis 2014: 148–9.
[60] A good basis is laid by Fromentin 2016. As with Polybius, it should be stressed that this is not primarily a matter of Dio's 'sources'. Despite the fragmentary nature of his early books, it seems reasonably clear that his material in the early books was pretty independent of both Livy and Dionysius, though it is likely that he read both (Briquel 2016; Urso 2016a; Urso 2019). He may still be influenced by, and reacting against, their interpretative emphases.
[61] Brunt 1980, cf. Berbessou-Broustet 2016 and Bellissime and Berbessou-Broustet 2016.

(Ash, Chapter 4 and Simpson, Chapter 13 in this volume, and articles by Mallan).[62] But the history of later scholarship is also a rich and unmined field. Those living in western democracies today have little instinctive understanding of autocracy, the hazards and strategies involved in plotting a safe path, which sorts of doublespeak are essential and which are extremely unwise. Previous ages understood these things better. We may have been too overwhelmed by the bulk of nineteenth-century *Quellenforschung* and failing to look further.

So, there is still work to be done, but credit is also due to this new generation of Dio scholars for facing up to the biggest questions. The largest of all is simply put: what did it *mean*, in Dio's day, to take on this vast task of writing all of Rome's history from the beginnings (Malik, Chapter 7; and Kemezis' monograph)?[63] Is that too conditioned by any insight into conditions of his own day, any feeling that the time had come to look back on this immense temporal span as some sort of organic whole? Is there a feeling that things had changed and the future would be different? Or is it that no real future beckoned at all, that his own generation marked such an unravelling that it was time to tie together a history that was now complete? (Scholars often say something similar about the retrospect of Roman oratory in Cicero's *Brutus*, intimating a conviction that there would be no true place for oratory in any future that Rome had to offer.) And what did it mean to write it in Greek? Is that too a matter of tying the strands together, going back at the end to the language used by Fabius Pictor when Roman historiography began?[64] Is it to mark the fusion of Greek and Roman culture that was then at its peak (Millar stresses the synchronism with the massive juristic work in Latin by Ulpian of Tyre)?[65] Or is it a matter of Dio's audience (and pinning that down is a further continuing dispute), of his aiming at Greek intellectuals rather than or as well as Romans? Or a reflection of the way that the Greek historiographic tradition was now more active than the Latin?[66] Is this too a matter of intertextuality, if Greek models seemed to him now more pertinent for understanding the deepest forces at play than Roman ideas of, say, underlying distinctive virtues or long-lasting moral decline? Or are we overcomplicating, and was it simply a matter of Dio doing it because he was interested, because the distant past retained its fascination as it always had (think of the archaisms of

---

[62] Mallan 2013b and 2019.   [63] Kemezis 2014: 91–2.   [64] de Franchis: 2016: 201.
[65] Millar 2016: 9.   [66] Zecchini 2016.

the Hadrianic period), that he took his history to his own day because that was as far as history had got, and he wrote in Greek because, however much Latin he knew, he was still more comfortable in his native tongue?

Good questions. And it is hard to think that another fifty years will be enough to answer them all.

Bibliography

Aalders, G. J. D. (1986), 'Cassius Dio and the Greek world', *Mnemosyne* 39: 282–304.

Adler, A. (ed.) (1928–38), *Suidae Lexicon*, 5 vols. Leipzig.

Adler, E. (2011), 'Cassius Dio's Livia and the conspiracy of Cinna Magnus', *GRBS* 51: 133–54.

Adler, E. (2012), 'Cassius Dio's Agrippa-Maecenas debate: an operational code analysis,' *AJPh* 133: 477–520.

Adler, M. (1909), 'Zur Verschwörung des Cn. Cornelius Cinna bei Seneca und Cassius Dio', *Zeitschr. österr. Gymnasien* 60: 193–208.

Aerts, W. J. (ed.) (1990), *Michaelis Pselli Historia Syntomos*. Berlin.

Alcock, S. E. (1994), 'Nero at play? The emperor's Grecian Odyssey', in J. Elsner and J. Masters (eds.), *Reflections of Nero: Culture, History, and Representation*. London: 98–111.

Alexander, P. J. (ed. D. de F. Abrahamse) (1985), *The Byzantine Apocalyptic Tradition*. Berkeley.

Alföldy, G. (2001), '*Pietas immobilis erga principem* und ihr Lohn: Öffentliche Ehrenmonumente von Senatoren in Rom während der Frühen und Hohen Kaiserzeit', in G. Alföldy and S. Panciera (eds.), *Inschriftliche Denkmäler als Medien der Selbstdarstellung in der römischen Welt*. Stuttgart: 11–46.

Allport, G. W. and Postman, L. (1947), *The Psychology of Rumor*. New York.

Almond, G. (1956), 'Comparative political systems', *The Journal of Politics* 18: 391–409.

Alt, K. (2006), 'Der Daimon als Seelenführer: zur Vorstellung des persönlichen Schutzgeistes bei den Griechen', *Hypoboreus* 6: 219–51.

Ameling, W. (1984), 'Cassius Dio und Bithynien', *EA* 4: 123–38.

Andersen, H. A. (1938), *Cassius Dio und die Begründung des Principates*. Berlin.

Anderson, J. G. C. (1934), 'The eastern frontier under Augustus', in S. A. Cook, F. E. Adcock, and M. P. Charlesworth (eds.), *The Cambridge Ancient History. First Edition. Volume X: The Augustan Empire 44 BC–AD 70*. Cambridge: 239–83.

Ando, C. (2016), 'Cassius Dio on imperial legitimacy, from the Antonines to the Severans', in V. Fromentin *et al.* (eds.), *Cassius Dion: nouvelles lectures*. Bordeaux: 567–77.

Appelbaum, A. (2007), 'Another look at the assassination of Pertinax and the accession of Julianus', *CPh* 102: 198–207.

Arafat, K. W. (1996), *Pausanias' Greece: Ancient Artists and Roman Rulers.* Cambridge.

Ash, R. (2007), 'The wonderful world of Mucianus', in E. Bispham and G. Rowe (eds.), *Vita Vigilia Est: Essays in Honour of Barbara Levick.* London: 1–17.

Ash, R. (2016), 'Never say die! Assassinating emperors in Suetonius' *Lives of the Caesars*', in K. De Temmerman and K. Demoen (eds.), *Writing Biography in Greece and Rome: Narrative Technique and Fictionalization.* Cambridge: 200–16.

Ash, R. (2018a), 'Paradoxography and marvels in post-Domitianic Literature: "An extraordinary affair, even in the hearing!"', in A. König and C. Whitton (eds.), *Roman Literature under Nerva, Trajan, and Hadrian: Literary Interactions AD 96–138.* Cambridge: 126–45.

Ash, R. (ed.) (2018b), *Tacitus: Annals 15.* Cambridge.

Asirvatham, S. R. (2017), 'Historiography', in D. S. Richter and W. A. Johnson (eds.), *The Oxford Handbook of the Second Sophistic.* Oxford: 477–92.

Assmann, J. (2011), *Cultural Memory and Early Civilization. Writing, Remembrance, and Political Imagination.* Cambridge.

Astin, A. E. (1963), 'Augustus and "Censoria Potestas"', *Latomus* 22: 226–35.

Baar, M. (1990), *Das Bild des Kaisers Tiberius bei Tacitus, Sueton und Cassius Dio.* Stuttgart.

Baldwin, B. (1979), 'Nero and his mother's corpse', *Mnemosyne* 32: 380–1.

Baldwin, B. (1986), 'Historiography in the second century: Precursors of Dio Cassius', *Klio* 68: 479–86.

Banchich, T. M. (ed.) (2015), *The Lost History of Peter the Patrician.* London and New York.

Banchich, T. M. and Lane, E. N. (eds.) (2009), *The History of Zonaras. From Alexander Severus to the Death of Theodosius the Great.* London and New York.

Barker, E. (1957), *Social and Political Thought in Byzantium: From Justinian to the Last Palaeologus.* Oxford.

Barnes, T. D. (1974), 'The victories of Augustus', *JRS* 64: 21–6.

Barnes, T. D. (1984), 'The composition of Cassius Dio's *Roman History*', *Phoenix* 38: 240–55.

Baron, C. (2019), 'Wrinkles in time: chronological ruptures in Cassius Dio's narrative of the late Republic', in J. Osgood and C. Baron (eds.), *Cassius Dio and the Late Roman Republic.* Leiden and Boston: 50–71.

Barton, T. (1994), 'The *inventio* of Nero: Suetonius', in J. Elsner and J. Masters (eds.), *Reflections of Nero: Culture, History, and Representation.* London: 48–63.

Bartsch, S. (1994), *Actors in the Audience: Theatricality and Doublespeak from Nero to Hadrian.* Cambridge, MA.

Beagon, M. (2005), *The Elder Pliny on the Human Animal: Natural History Book 7.* Oxford.

Bellissime, M. (2016a), 'Fiction et rhétorique dans les prosopopées de l'*Histoire romaine*: les marges de liberté de l'historien', in V. Fromentin *et al.* (eds.), *Cassius Dion: nouvelles lectures*. Bordeaux: 363–77.

Bellissime, M. (2016b), 'Polysémie, contextualisation, re-sémantisation: à propos de μοναρχία et de δημοκρατία', in V. Fromentin *et al.* (eds.), *Cassius Dion: nouvelles lectures*. Bordeaux: 529–41.

Bellissime, M. and Berbessou-Broustet, B. (2016), 'L'Histoire romaine de Zonaras', in V. Fromentin *et al.* (eds.), *Cassius Dion: nouvelles lectures*. Bordeaux: 95–108.

Bellissime, M. and Hurlet F. (eds.) (2018), *Dion Cassius. Histoire Romaine. Livre 53. Texte établi par M. B., traduit et commenté par M. B. et F. H.* Paris.

Bender, F. S. G. (ed.) (1961), *Historical Commentary on Cassius Dio 54*. PhD thesis, University of Pennsylvania.

Beneker, J. (2011), 'The crossing of the Rubicon and the outbreak of civil war in Cicero, Lucan, Plutarch, and Suetonius', *Phoenix* 65: 74–99.

Bennett, J. (2001), *Trajan: Optimus Princeps*. 2nd edition. London.

Berbessou-Broustet, B. (2016), 'Xiphilin, abréviateur de Cassius Dion', in V. Fromentin *et al.* (eds.), *Cassius Dion: nouvelles lectures*. Bordeaux: 81–94.

Bering-Staschewski, R. (1981), *Römische Zeitgeschichte bei Cassius Dio*. Bochum.

Berrendonner, C. (2005), 'Les interventions du peuple dans les cités d'Étrurie et d'Ombrie à l'époque impériale,' *MEFRA* 117: 517–39.

Berti, N. (1988), *La guerra di Cesare contro Pompeo. Commento storico a Cassio Dione libro* XLI. Milan.

Bertrand, E. (2016a), 'L'empire de Cassius Dion: géographie et *imperium Romanum* dans l'*Histoire romaine*', in V. Fromentin *et al.* (eds.), *Cassius Dion: nouvelles lectures*. Bordeaux: 701–24.

Bertrand, E. (2016b), 'Point de vue de Cassius Dion sur l'impérialisme romain', in V. Fromentin *et al.* (eds.), *Cassius Dion: nouvelles lectures*. Bordeaux: 675–99.

Bertrand, E. (2019), 'Imperialism and the crisis of the Roman Republic: Dio's view on late Republican conquests (Books 36-40)', in J. Osgood and C. Baron (eds.), *Cassius Dio and the Late Roman Republic*. Leiden and Boston: 19–35.

Bethe, E. (ed.) (1900), *Pollucis Onomasticon e codicibus ab ipso collatis denuo edidit et adnotavit*. Leipzig.

Bialy, K. (2017), 'John Xiphilinos on the civil war between Pompey and Caesar in the Epitome of the *Roman History* of Cassius Dio,' in D. Słapek and I. Łuć (eds.), *Przemoc w świecie starożytnym. Źródła – struktura – interpretacje*. Lublin: 437–49.

Bingham, S. and Imrie, A. (2015), 'The prefect and the plot: a reassessment of the murder of Plautianus' *JAH* 3: 76–91.

Birley, A. R. (1981), *The Fasti of Roman Britain*. Oxford.

Birley, A. R. (1987), *Marcus Aurelius: A Biography*. London.

Birley, A. R. (1997), *Hadrian: The Restless Emperor*. London.

Birley, A. R. (1999), *Septimius Severus: The African Emperor*. London.

Birley, A. R. (2005), *The Roman Government of Britain*. Oxford.

Bittarello, M. B. (2011), 'Otho, Elagabalus and the judgement of Paris: the literary construction of the unmanly emperor', *DHA* 37: 93–113.

Blanshard, A. (2010), *Sex: Vice and Love from Antiquity to Modernity*. London.

Bleicken, J. (1962), 'Der politische Standpunkt Dios gegenüber der Monarchie', *Hermes* 90: 444–53.

Blockley, R. (ed.) (1983), *The Fragmentary Classicizing Historians of the Later Roman Empire. Eunapius, Olympiodorus, Priscus, and Malchus. Vol. II: Text, Translation, and Commentary*. Leeds.

Boissevain, U. P. (ed.) (1895–1901), *Cassii Dionis Cocceiani Historiarum Romanarum quae supersunt*, 5 vols. Leipzig.

Boschung, D. (2017), 'Jenseits des Narrativs? Kaiserporträt und Staatsrelief in der Zeit des Antoninus Pius', in C. Michels and P. F. Mittag (eds.), *Jenseits des Narrativs: Antoninus Pius in den nicht-literarischen Quellen*. Stuttgart: 53–63.

Bowersock, G. M. (1965), 'Review of Millar 1964', *Gnomon* 37: 469–74.

Bowersock, G. M. (1998), '*Vita Caesarum:* remembering and forgetting the past', in W.-W. Ehlers (eds.), *La biographie antique*. Geneva: 193–210.

Bowie, E. L. (1970), 'Greeks and their past in the Second Sophistic', *P&P* 46: 3–41.

Bowie, E. L. (1978), 'Apollonius of Tyana: tradition and reality', *ANRW* 2.16.2: 1652–99.

Bowie, E. L. (2015), 'Teachers and students in Roman Athens', in R. Ash, J. Mossman, and F. B. Titchener (eds.), *Fame and Infamy: Essays for Christopher Pelling on Characterization in Greek and Roman Biography and Historiography*. Oxford: 239–53.

Briquel, D. (2016), 'Origines et période royale', in V. Fromentin *et al.* (eds.), *Cassius Dion: nouvelles lectures*. Bordeaux: 125–41.

Brizzi, G. (2016), 'Cassio Dione e le campagne d'Oriente', in V. Fromentin *et al.* (eds.), *Cassius Dion: nouvelles lectures*. Bordeaux: 741–71.

Brunt, P. A. (1962), 'Roman constitutional problems', *CR* 12: 70–3.

Brunt, P. A. (1963), 'Review of H. D. Meyer: Die Außenpolitik des Augustus und die augusteische Dichtung', *JRS* 53: 170–6.

Brunt, P. A. (1974), 'C. Fabricius Tuscus and an Augustan *dilectus*', *ZPE* 13: 161–85.

Brunt, P. A. (1977), '*Lex de Imperio Vespasiani*', *JRS* 67: 95–116.

Brunt, P. A. (1980), 'On historical fragments and epitomes', *CQ* 30: 477–94.

Brunt, P. A. and Moore, J. M. (1973), Res Gestae Divi Augusti: *The Achievements of the Divine Augustus*. Oxford.

Budelmann, F. (2002), 'Classical commentary in Byzantium: John Tzetzes on ancient Greek literature', in R. K. Gibson and C. S. Kraus (eds.), *The Classical Commentary: Histories, Practices, Theory*. Leiden and Boston: 141–69.

Buraselis, K. (2007), Θεῖα δωρεά: *das göttlich-kaiserliche Geschenk: Studien zur Politik der Severer und zur Constitutio Antoniniana*, Vienna. (Translation of *Theia Dorea: Meletes pano sten politike tes dynasteias ton Severon kai ten Constitutio Antoniniana*, Athens, 1989.)

Burden-Strevens, C. (2015a), *Cassius Dio's Speeches and the Collapse of the Roman Republic*. PhD thesis, University of Glasgow.

Burden-Strevens, C. (2015b), 'Ein völlig romanisierter Mann'? Identity, identification, and integration in the *Roman History* of Cassius Dio and in Arrian', in S. T. Roselaar (ed.), *Processes of Cultural Change and Integration in the Roman World*. Leiden and Boston: 287–306.

Burden-Strevens, C. (2016), 'Fictitious speeches, envy, and the habituation of authority: writing the collapse of the Roman Republic', in C. H. Lange and J. M. Madsen (eds.), *Cassius Dio. Greek Intellectual and Roman Politician*. Leiden and Boston: 193–216.

Burden-Strevens, C. (2020), *Cassius Dio's Speeches and the Collapse of the Roman Republic*. Leiden and Boston.

Burden-Strevens, C. and Lindholmer, M. (eds.) (2019), *Cassius Dio's Forgotten History of Early Rome*. Leiden and Boston.

Burton, G. P. (1979), 'The *curator rei publicae*: towards a reappraisal', *Chiron* 9: 465–87.

Büttner-Wobst, T. (1890), 'Die Abhängigkeit des geschichtsschreibers Zonaras von den erhaltenen Quellen', in A. Fleckeisen (ed.), *Commentationes Fleckeisenianae*. Leipzig: 121–70.

Cameron, A. (2011), *The Last Pagans of Rome*. Oxford.

Campbell, J. B. (1984), *The Emperor and the Roman Army*. Oxford.

Campbell, J. B. (2005), 'The Severan dynasty', in A. K. Bowman, P. Garnsey and A. Cameron (eds.), *The Cambridge Ancient History. Second Edition. Volume XII: The Crisis of Empire, AD 193–337*. Cambridge: 1–27.

Carlsen, J. (2016), 'Alexander the Great in Cassius Dio', in C. H. Lange and J. M. Madsen (eds.), *Cassius Dio. Greek Intellectual and Roman Politician*. Leiden and Boston: 316–31.

Carroll, K. K. (1982), *The Parthenon Inscription. Greek, Roman and Byzantine Monographs* 9. Durham, NC.

Carsana, C. (2000), 'Considerazioni sulla fondazione di Lione alla luce di una rilettura dell'epistolario ciceroniano', *Athenaeum* 88: 203–17.

Carsana, C. (2016), 'La teoria delle forme di governo: il punto di vista di Cassio Dione sui poteri di Cesare', in V. Fromentin *et al.* (eds.), *Cassius Dion: nouvelles lectures*. Bordeaux: 545–58.

Cary, E. (ed.) (1914–27), *Dio's Roman History* ('on the basis of the version of Herbert Baldwin Foster, Ph.D.'), 9 vols. Cambridge, MA.

Champlin, E. (1979), 'Notes on the heirs of Commodus', *AJPh* 100: 288–306.

Champlin, E. (2003), *Nero*. Cambridge, MA.

Champlin, E. (2011), 'Tiberius and the Heavenly Twins', *JRS* 101: 73–99.

Charles, M. B. and Anagnostou-Laoutides, E. (2010), 'The sexual hypocrisy of Domitian: Suet., *Dom.* 8.3', *AC* 79: 173–87.

Charles, M. B. and Anagnostou-Laoutides, E. (2013–2014), 'Unmanning an emperor: Otho in the literary tradition', *CJ* 109: 199–222.

Chausson, F. (1995), 'L'autobiographie de Septime Sévère', *REL* 73: 183–98.

Chausson, F. (2000), 'De Didius Iulianus aux Nummii Albini', *MEFRA* 112: 843–79.

Chenault, R. (2012), 'Statues of senators in the Forum of Trajan and the Roman Forum in Late Antiquity', *JRS* 102: 103–32.

Chew, K. (2011), 'Eyeing epiphanies in Greek, Latin, and Sanskrit Texts', *Phoenix* 65: 207–37.

Christol, M. (2016), 'Marius Maximus, Cassius Dio, et Ulpien: destins croisés et débats politiques', in V. Fromentin *et al.* (eds.), *Cassius Dion: nouvelles lectures*. Bordeaux: 431–46.

Clauss, M. (1999), *Kaiser und Gott. Herrscherkult im römischen Reich*. Stuttgart and Leipzig.

Cleve, R. L. (1988), 'Cassius Dio and Ulpian', *AHB* 2: 118–24.

Coarelli, F. (1996), 'Fregellae, Arpinum, Aquinum: lana e fullonica nel Lazio meridionale', in M. Cébeillac-Gervasoni (ed.), *Les élites municipales de l'Italie péninsulaire des Gracques à Néron*. Naples and Rome: 199–205.

Coast, D. (2014), *News and Rumour in Jacobean England: Information, Court Politics and Diplomacy, 1618–25*. Manchester.

Coltelloni-Trannoy, M. (2016a), 'La politeia impériale d'après Cassius Dion (livres 52–59)', in V. Fromentin *et al.* (eds.), *Cassius Dion: nouvelles lectures*. Bordeaux: 559–66.

Coltelloni-Trannoy, M. (2016b), 'Les temporalités du recit impérial dans l'Histoire romaine de Cassius Dion', in V. Fromentin *et al.* (eds.), *Cassius Dion: nouvelles lectures*. Bordeaux: 335–62.

Cooley, A. (ed.) (2009), Res Gestae Divi Augusti: *Text, Translation and Commentary*. Cambridge.

Cornell, T. J., Bispham, E. H., Rich, J. W., Smith, C. J. (eds.) (2013), *The Fragments of the Roman Historians*, 3 vols. Oxford.

Cornwell, H. (2017), *Pax and the Politics of Peace: Republic to Principate*. Oxford.

Cortés Copete, J. M. (2016), 'Casio Dion 68.4 y la Autobiografía de Adriano. Íber, ítalo e italiota: a la búsqueda de una identitad imperial', *Athenaeum* 104: 545–66.

Cotton, H. M. and Yakobson, A. (2002), '*Arcanum imperii*: the powers of Augustus', in G. Clark and T. Rajak (eds.), *Philosophy and Power in the Graeco-Roman World: Essays in Honour of Miriam Griffin*. Oxford: 193–209.

Coudry, M. (2016a), 'Cassius Dio on Pompey's extraordinary commands', in C. H. Lange and J. M. Madsen (eds.), *Cassius Dio. Greek Intellectual and Roman Politician*. Leiden and Boston: 33–50.

Coudry, M. (2016b), 'Figures et récit dans les livres républicains (livres 36 à 44)', in V. Fromentin *et al.* (eds.), *Cassius Dion: nouvelles lectures*. Bordeaux: 287–302.

Coudry, M. (2019), 'The "great men" of the middle Republic in Cassius Dio's *Roman History*', in C. Burden-Strevens and M. Lindholmer (eds.), *Cassius Dio's Forgotten History of Early Rome*. Leiden and Boston: 126–64.

Courrier, C. (2014), *La plèbe de Rome et sa culture (fin du IIe siècle av. J.-C. – fin du Ier siècle ap. J.-C.)*. Rome.

Cresci Marrone, G. (1998), 'Introduzione', in G. Cresci Marrone, A. Stroppa, F. Rohr Vio (eds.), *Cassio Dione, Storia romana, V. Libri LII–LVI*. Milan: 5–36.

Cresci Marrone, G., Stroppa, A. and Rohr Vio, F. (eds.) (1998), *Cassio Dione, Storia romana, V. Libri LII–LVI*. Milan.

Criscuolo, U. (ed.) (1979), *De Creta Capta*. Leipzig.

Croke, B. (2006), 'Tradition and originality in Photius' historical reading', in J. Burke *et al.* (eds.), *Byzantine Narrative. Papers in Honour of Roger Scott*. Melbourne: 59–70.

Crook, J. (1955), *Consilium Principis. Imperial Councils and Counsellors from Augustus to Diocletian*. Cambridge.

Dalla Rosa, A. (2017), 'Quando l'epigrafia è politica. A proposito dei riferimenti epigrafici nell'opera di Cassio Dione', in S. Segenni and M. Bellomo (eds.), *Epigrafia e politica. Il contributo della documentazione epigrafica allo studio delle dinamiche politiche nel mondo romano*. Milan: 95–117.

Damon, C. (2000), 'Review of Murison 1999', *BMCR* 2000.03.07.

Davenport, C. (2011), 'Iterated consulships and the government of Severus Alexander', *ZPE* 177: 281–88.

Davenport, C. (2012a), 'Cassius Dio and Caracalla', *CQ* 62: 796–815.

Davenport, C. (2012b), 'The provincial appointments of the emperor Macrinus', *Antichthon* 46: 184–203.

Davenport, C. (2014), 'The conduct of Vitellius in Cassius Dio's *Roman History*', *Historia* 63: 96–116.

Davenport, C. (2017), 'The sexual habits of Caracalla: rumour, gossip, and historiography', *Histos* 11: 75–100.

Davenport, C. (2019), *A History of the Roman Equestrian Order*. Cambridge.

Davenport, C. and Mallan, C. (2014), 'Hadrian's adoption speech in Cassius Dio's *Roman History* and the problems of imperial succession', *AJPh* 135: 637–68.

Davenport, C. and Manley, J. (eds.) (2014), *Fronto: Selected Letters*. London.

Davies, J. (2004), *Rome's Religious History: Livy, Tacitus, and Ammianus on their Gods*. Cambridge.

de Blois, L. (1986), 'The Εἰς Βασιλέα of Ps.-Aelius Aristides', *GRBS* 27: 279–88.

de Blois, L. (1994), 'Traditional virtues and new spiritual qualities in third century views of empire, emperorship and practical politics', *Mnemosyne* 47: 166–76.

de Blois, L. (1997), 'Volk und Soldaten bei Cassius Dio', *ANRW* II.34.3: 2650–76.

de Blois, L. (1998), 'Emperor and empire in the works of Greek-speaking authors of the third century AD', *ANRW* 2.34.4: 3391–443.

de Blois, L. (1998–9), 'The perception of emperor and empire in Cassius Dio's *Roman History*', *AncSoc* 29: 267–81.

de Boor, C. *et al.* (eds) (1903–10), *Excerpta Historica iussu imperatoris Constantini Porphyrogeniti confecta*, 4 vols. Berlin.

de Franchis, M. (2016), 'Tite-Live modèle de Cassius Dion ou contre-modèle?', in V. Fromentin *et al.* (eds.), *Cassius Dion: nouvelles lectures*. Bordeaux: 191–204.

Dench, E. (2013), 'Cicero and Roman identity', in C. Steel (ed.), *The Cambridge Companion to Cicero*. Cambridge: 122–38.

Dench, E. (2018), *Empire and Political Cultures in the Roman World. Key Themes in Ancient History*. Cambridge.

Denniston, J. D. (1954), *The Greek Particles*. Oxford.

Desmond, W. (2006), 'Lessons of fear: A reading of Thucydides', *Classical Philology* 101.4: 359–79.

Devillers, O. (2016a), 'Cassius Dion et les sources pré-tacitéennes', in V. Fromentin *et al.* (eds.), *Cassius Dion: nouvelles lectures*. Bordeaux: 233–41.

Devillers, O. (2016b), 'Cassius Dion et l'évolution de l'annalistique: Remarques à propos de la représentation des Julio-Claudiens dans l'Histoire romaine', in V. Fromentin *et al.* (eds.), *Cassius Dion: nouvelles lectures*. Bordeaux: 317–34.

Di Fonzo, N. and Bordia, P. (2007), *Rumor Psychology. Social and Organizational Approaches*. Washington.

Dodds, E. R. (1965), *Pagan and Christian in an Age of Anxiety: Some Aspects of Religious Experience from Marcus Aurelius to Constantine*. Cambridge.

Duff, T. (1999), *Plutarch: Exploring Virtue and Vice*. Oxford.

Duffy, J. and Papaioannou, S. (2003), 'Michael Psellos and the authorship of the *Historia Syntomos*: final considerations,' in A. Abramea, A. Laiou, and E. Chrysos (eds.), *Byzantium, State and Society: In Memory of Nikos Oiknomides*. Athens: 219–29.

Duindam, J. (2016), *Dynasties: A Global History of Power, 1300–1800*. Cambridge.

Duncan-Jones, R. (2016), *Power and Privilege in Roman Society*. Cambridge.

Dželebdžić, D. (2005), Ἡ δημοκρατική Ρώμη στην πολιτική σκέψη του Μιχαήλ Ψελλού', *ZRIV* 42: 23–33.

Eck, W. (1984), 'Senatorial self-representation: developments in the Augustan period', in F. Millar and E. Segal (eds.), *Caesar Augustus: Seven Aspects*. Oxford: 129–67.

Eck, W. (1995), '"Tituli honorarii", curriculum vitae und Selbstdarstellung in der Hohen Kaiserzeit', in H. Solin (ed.), *Acta colloquii epigraphici Latini Helsingiae 3.-6. sept. 1991 habiti*. Helsinki: 211–37.

Eck, W. (1999), 'Elite und Leitbilder in der römischen Kaiserzeit', in J. Dummer and M. Vielberg (eds.), *Leitbilder der Spätantike – Eliten und Leitbilder*. Stuttgart: 31–55.

Eck, W. (2009), 'There are no *cursus honorum* inscriptions: the function of the *cursus honorum* in epigraphic communication', *SCI* 28: 79–92.

Eck, W. (2019), '*At magnus Caesar*, and yet! Social resistance against Augustan legislation', in K. Morrell, J. Osgood, and K. Welch (eds.), *The Alternative Augustan Age*. Oxford: 78–95.

Edmondson, J. (ed.) (1992), *Dio. The Julio-Claudians: Selections from Books 58–63 of the Roman History of Cassius Dio*. London.

Edwards, C. (1993), *The Politics of Immorality in Ancient Rome*. Cambridge.

Edwards, C. (1994), 'Beware of imitations: theatre and the subversion of imperial identity', in J. Elsner and J. Masters (eds.), *Reflections of Nero: Culture, History, and Representation*. London: 83–97.

Edwards, C. (trans.) (2000), *Suetonius: Lives of the Caesars*. Oxford.

Eisman, M. M. (1977), 'Dio and Josephus: parallel analyses', *Latomus* 36: 657–73.

Elsner, J. (2001), 'Structuring "Greece": Pausanias' *Periegesis* as a literary construct', in S. E. Alcock, J. F. Cherry, J. Elsner (eds.), *Pausanias: Travel and Memory in Roman Greece*. Oxford: 3–20.

Fantham, E. (2013), 'The performing prince', in E. Buckley and M. Dinter (eds.), *A Companion to the Neronian Age*. Chichester: 17–28.

Fargette, S. (2007), 'Rumeurs, propagande et opinion publique au temps de la guerre civile (1407–1420)', *Le Moyen Age* 113: 309–34.

Faur, J. C. (1978), 'Un discours de l'empereur Caligula au Sénat (Dion, *Hist. rom.* LIX,16)', *Klio* 40: 439–47.

Feldherr, A. (2009a), 'Delusions of grandeur: Lucretian "passages" in Livy', in P. R. Hardie (ed.), *Paradox and the Marvellous in Augustan Literature and Culture*. Oxford: 310–29.

Feldherr, A. (2009b), 'The poisoned chalice: rumor and historiography in Tacitus' account of the death of Drusus', *Materiali e discussioni per l'analisi dei testi classici* 61: 175–89.

Ferrary, J.-L. (trans. J. Edmondson) (2009), 'The powers of Augustus', in J. Edmonsdson (ed.), *Augustus*. Edinburgh: 90–136.

Ferrary, J.-L. (2010), 'À propos des pouvoirs et des honneurs décernés à César entre 48 et 44', in G. Urso (ed.), *Cesare: precursore o visionario?* Pisa: 9–30.

Fishwick, D. (1990), 'Dio and Maecenas: the emperor and the ruler cult', *Phoenix* 44: 267–75.

Flach, D. (1973), 'Dios Platz in der kaiserzeitlichen Geschichtsschreibung', *A&A* 18: 130–43.

Flower, H. (2006), *The Art of Forgetting: Disgrace and Oblivion in Roman Political Culture*. Chapel Hill.

Flusin, B. (2002), 'Les *Excerpta Constantiniens*: *logique* d'une anti-histoire', in S. Pittia (ed.), *Fragments d'historiens grecs. Autour de Denys d'Halicarnasse*. Rome: 537–59.

Fomin, A. (2016), 'Speeches in Cassius Dio', in C. H. Lange and J. M. Madsen (eds.), *Cassius Dio. Greek Intellectual and Roman Politician*. Leiden and Boston: 217–37.

Foster, H. B. (ed.) (1874–1906), *Dio's Rome: An historical narrative originally composed in Greek during the reigns of Septimus Severus, Geta and Caracalla, Macrinus, Elagabalus and Alexander Severus*, 6 vols. New York.

Fox, A. (1997), 'Rumour, news and popular political opinion in Elizabethan and early Stuart England', *The Historical Journal* 40: 597–620.

France, J. (2016), 'Financer l'empire: Agrippa, Mécène et Cassius Dion', in V. Fromentin *et al.* (eds.), *Cassius Dion: nouvelles lectures*. Bordeaux: 773–85.

François, P. (2016), 'Cassius Dion et la troisième décade de Tite-Live', in V. Fromentin *et al.* (eds.), *Cassius Dion: nouvelles lectures*. Bordeaux: 215–31.

Freyburger, M.-L., and Roddaz, J.-M. (eds.) (1991), *Dion Cassius, Histoire romaine, Livres 50 et 51. Texte établi, traduit et annoté*. Paris.

Freyburger-Galland, M.-L. (1997), *Aspects du vocabulaire politique et institutionnel de Dion Cassius*. Paris.

Freyburger-Galland, M-L. (2010), 'Dion Cassius et Suetone', in R. Poignault (ed.), *Présence du Suétone: actes du colloque tenu à Clermont-Ferrand, 25–27 novembre 2004*. Clermont-Ferrand: 147–62.

Fromentin, V. (2013), 'Zonaras abréviateur de Cassius Dion. À la recherche de la préface perdue de l'Histoire romaine', *Erga-Logoi* 1: 23–39.

Fromentin, V. (2016), 'Denys d'Halicarnasse, source et modèle de Cassius Dion?', in V. Fromentin *et al.* (eds.), *Cassius Dion: nouvelles lectures*. Bordeaux: 179–90.

Fromentin, V., Bertrand, E., Coltelloni-Trannoy, M., Molin, M., and Urso, G. (eds.) (2016a), *Cassius Dion: nouvelles lectures*, 2 vols. Bordeaux.

Fromentin, V., Bertrand, E., Coltelloni-Trannoy, M., Molin, M., and Urso, G. (2016b), 'Introduction', in V. Fromentin *et al.* (eds.), *Cassius Dion: nouvelles lectures*. Bordeaux: 11–16.

Gabba, E. (1955), 'Sulla Storia Romana di Cassio Dione', *RSI* 67: 289–333.

Gabba E. (1957), 'Note sulla polemica anticiceroniana di Asinio Pollione', *RSI* 69: 317–39

Gabba, E. (1984), 'The historians and Augustus', in F. Millar and E. Segal (eds.), *Caesar Augustus: Seven Aspects*. Oxford: 61–88.

Gavard, C. (1993), 'Rumeur et stéréotypes à la fin du Moyen Age', *Actes des congrès de la Société des historiens médiévistes de l'enseignement supérieur public* 24: 157–77.

Geiger, J. (1985), *Cornelius Nepos and Ancient Political Biography*. Stuttgart.

Gibson, B. J. (1998), 'Rumours as causes of events in Tacitus', *Materiali e discussioni per l'analisi dei testi classici* 40: 111–29.

Gill, C. (1983), 'The question of character development: Plutarch and Tacitus', *CQ* 33: 468–87.

Gill, C. (2006), *The Structured Self in Hellenistic and Roman Thought*. Oxford.

Ginsburg, J. (1981), *Tradition and Theme in the Annals of Tacitus*. New York.

Ginsburg, J. (2006), *Representing Agrippina: Constructions of Female Power in the Early Roman Empire*. New York.

Giua, M. A. (1981), 'Clemenza del sovrano e monarchia illuminata in Cassio Dione', *Athenaeum* 55: 14–22.

Giua, M. A. (1983), 'Augusto nel libro 56 della storia Romana di Cassio Dione', *Athenaeum* 61: 439–56.

Giua, M. A. (1998), 'Sul significato dei *rumores* nella storiografia di Tacito', *RSI* 110: 38–59.

Gleason, M. (2011), 'Identity theft: doubles and masquerades in Cassius Dio's contemporary history', *Classical Antiquity* 30: 33–86.

Goodyear, F. R. D. (ed.) (1972), *The Annals of Tacitus Books 1–6, Volume I: Annals 1–1.54*. Cambridge.

Gotteland, S. (2016), "Ἔκφρασις and ἐνάργεια dans l'Histoire romaine: les choix de Cassius Dio', in V. Fromentin *et al.* (eds.), *Cassius Dion: nouvelles lectures*. Bordeaux: 379–96.

Gowers, E. (2005), 'Virgil's Sibyl and the "many mouths" cliché (*Aen*.6.625–7)', *CQ* 55: 170–82.

Gowers, E. (2010), 'Augustus and "Syracuse"', *JRS* 100: 69–87.

Gowing A. M. (1992), *The Triumviral Narratives of Appian and Cassius Dio*. Ann Arbor.

Gowing, A. M. (1997), 'Cassius Dio on the reign of Nero', *ANRW* 2.34.3: 2558–90.

Gowing, A. M. (2016), 'Cassius Dio and the city of Rome,' in C. H. Lange and J. M. Madsen (eds.), *Cassius Dio. Greek Intellectual and Roman Politician*. Leiden and Boston: 117–35.

Graham, A. J. (1974), 'The limitations of prosopography in Roman imperial history (with special reference to the Severan period)', *ANRW* 2.1: 136–57.

Gray, E. W. (1970), 'The *imperium* of Marcus Agrippa', *ZPE* 6: 227–38.

Griffin, M. T. (1984), *Nero: The End of a Dynasty*. New Haven.

Griffin, M. (2000), 'Nerva to Hadrian', in A. K. Bowman, P. Garnsey, and D. Rathbone (eds.), *The Cambridge Ancient History. Second Edition. Volume XI: The High Empire, AD 70–192*. Cambridge: 84–131.

Grigoriadis, I. (ed.) (2001), Ἰωάννης Τζέτζης· Ἐπιστολαί. Athens.

Gros, E. and V. Boissée (eds.) (1845–70), *Histoire romaine de Dion Cassius*, 10 vols. Paris.

Gruen, E. S. (1974), *The Last Generation of the Roman Republic*. Berkeley.

Gruen, E. S. (1996), 'The expansion of the empire under Augustus', in A. K. Bowman, E. Champlin and A. Lintott (eds.), *The Cambridge Ancient History. Second Edition. Volume X: The Augustan Empire, 43 BC–69 AD*. Cambridge: 147–98.

Gruen, E. S. (1990), 'The imperial policy of Augustus', in K. A. Raaflaub and M. Toher (eds.), *Between Republic and Empire: Interpretations of Augustus and His Principate*. Berkeley: 395–416.

Gruen, E. S. (2005), 'Augustus and the making of the Principate', in K. Galinsky (ed.), *The Cambridge Companion to the Age of Augustus*. Cambridge: 33–51.

Gunderson, E. (2014), 'E.g. Augustus: *exemplum* in the *Augustus* and the *Tiberius*', in T. Power and R. K. Gibson (eds.), *Suetonius the Biographer: Studies in Roman Lives*. Oxford: 130–45.

Gurval, R. (1997), 'Caesar's comet: the politics and poetics of an Augustan myth', *MAAR* 42: 39–71.

Gwyn, W. B. (1991), 'Cruel Nero: The concept of the tyrant and the image of Nero in western political thought', *History of Political Thought* 12.3: 421–55.

Hagendahl H. (1944), 'The mutiny of Vesontio. A problem of tendency and credibility in Caesar's Gallic war', *C&M* 6: 1–40.

Hägg, T. (2012), *The Art of Biography in Antiquity*. Cambridge.

Hägg, T. and Rousseau, P. (2000), 'Introduction: biography and panegyric', in T. Hägg and P. Rousseau (eds.), *Greek Biography and Panegyric in Late Antiquity*. Berkeley: 1–28.

Halliwell, S. (1990), 'Traditional Greek conceptions of character', in C. B. R. Pelling (ed.), *Characterisation and Individuality in Greek Literature*. Oxford: 32–59.

Hammond, M. (1932), 'The significance of the speech of Maecenas in Dio Cassius, Book LII', *TAPA* 63: 88–102.

Hammond, M. (1957), 'Imperial elements in the formula of the Roman emperors during the first two and a half centuries of the empire', *MAAR* 25: 19–64.

Hardie, P. R. (2012), *Rumour and Renown: Representations of Fama in Western Literature*. Cambridge.

Hardy, E. G. (1906), *Studies in Roman History*. London.

Hardy, E. G. (1919), '*Lectio senatus* and *census* under Augustus', *CQ* 13.1: 43–9.

Harker, A. (2008), *Loyalty and Dissidence in Roman Egypt. The Case of the Acta Alexandrinorum*. Cambridge.

Harrington, D. (1977), 'Cassius Dio as a military historian', *Acta Classica* 20: 159–65.

Harris, W. V. (2016), *Roman Power: A Thousand Years of Empire*. Cambridge.

Harrison, S. J. (ed.) (1991), *Vergil Aeneid 10*. Oxford.

Harte, V. and M. Lane (eds.) (2013), *Politeia in Greek and Roman Philosophy*. Cambridge.

Hawkins, T. (2017), 'Pollio's paradox: popular invective and the transition to empire', in L. Grig (ed.), *Popular Culture in the Ancient World*. Cambridge: 129–48.

Hekster, O. (2002), *Commodus: An Emperor at the Crossroads*. Leiden and Boston.

Hekster, O. (2010), 'Reversed epiphanies: Roman emperors deserted by gods', *Mnemosyne* 63: 601–15.

Hekster, O., Claes, L., Manders, E., Slootjes, D., Klaassen, Y., and de Haan, N. (2014), 'Nero's ancestry and the construction of imperial ideology in the early empire. A methodological case study', *Journal of Ancient History and Archaeology* 1: 7–27.

Henderson, J. (2001), *Telling Tales on Caesar: Roman Stories from Phaedrus*. Oxford.

Henri, R. (ed.) (1951–91), *Photios, Bibliothèque*. Paris.

Hidber, T. (2004), 'Cassius Dio', in I. J. F. de Jong, R. Nünlist, and A. Bowie (eds.), *Narrators, Narratees, and Narratives in Ancient Greek Literature. Studies in Ancient Greek Narrative, Volume I*. Leiden and Boston: 187–99.

Hillard, T. W. (2011), 'Velleius 2.124.2 and the reluctant *princeps*: the evolution of Roman perceptions of leadership', in E. Cowan (ed.), *Velleius Paterculus: Making History*. Swansea: 219–51.

Hohl, E. (1937), 'Zu den Testamenten des Augustus', *Klio* 30: 323–42.

Hölscher, T. (2003), 'Images of war in Greece and Rome: between military practice, public memory, and cultural symbolism', *JRS* 93: 1–17.

Horsfall, N. (1979), '*Doctus sermones utriusque linguae?*', *ECM* 23: 79–95.

Horsfall, N. (2003), *The Culture of the Roman Plebs*. London.

Hose, M. (1994), *Erneuerung der Vergangenheit: Die Historiker im Imperium Romanum von Florus bis Cassius Dio*. Stuttgart and Leipzig.

Hose, M. (2007), 'Cassius Dio: a senator and historian in the age of anxiety', in J. Marincola (ed.), *A Companion to Greek and Roman Historiography*. Malden, MA: 461–67.

Hose, M. (2011), 'Der Kaiser und seine Begrenzung durch die antike Literatur: Betrachtungen zu Cassius Dio', in A. Winterling (ed.), *Zwischen Strukturgeschichte und Biographie: Probleme und Perspektiven einer neuen Römischen Kaisergeschichte 31 v. Chr.–192 n. Chr*. Munich: 113–24.

Hude, C. (ed.) (1927), *Scholia in Thucydidem ad optimos codices collata*. Leipzig.

Hug, T. B. (2009), 'Outwitting power: bogus kings and officials in early modern England', in B. Kümin (ed.), *Political Space in Pre-industrial Europe*. Farnham: 215–30.

Humble, N. (2013), 'Imitation as commentary? Plutarch and Byzantine historiography in the tenth century', in G. Pace and P. Volpe Cacciatore (ed.), *Gli Scritti di Plutarco: tradizione, traduzione, ricezione, commento*. Naples: 219–25.

Humble, N. (forthcoming) 'Plutarch in Byzantium', in F. Titchener and A. Zadorozhny (eds.), *The Cambridge Companion to Plutarch*. Cambridge.

Hunt, J. M. (2014), 'Rumour, newsletters and the Pope's death in early modern Rome', in S. Davies and P. Fletcher (eds.), *News in Early Modern Europe: Currents and Connections*. Leiden: 141–58.

Hurley, D.W. (2014), 'Suetonius' rubric sandwich', in T. Power and R. K. Gibson (eds.), *Suetonius the Biographer: Studies in Roman Lives*. Oxford: 21–37.

Huttner, U. (2004), *Recusatio Imperii: Ein politisches Ritual zwischen Ethik und Taktik*. Hildesheim.

Ibbetson, D. (2005), 'High classical law', in A. K. Bowman, P. Garnsey, and A. Cameron (eds.), *The Cambridge Ancient History. Second Edition. Volume XII: The Crisis of Empire, AD 193–337*. Cambridge: 184–199.

Icks, M. (2008), 'Heliogabalus, a monster on the Roman throne. The literary construction of a "bad" emperor', in I. Sluiter and R. M. Rosen (eds.), *Kakos: Badness and Anti-value in Classical Antiquity*. Leiden: 477–88.

Icks, M. (2012), *The Crimes of Elagabalus: The Life and Legacy of Rome's Decadent Boy Emperor*. Cambridge, MA.

Icks, M. (2017), 'Turning victory into defeat: negative assessments of imperial triumphs in Greco-Roman literature', in F. Goldbeck and J. Wienand (eds.), *Der römische Triumph in Prinzipat und Spätantike*. Berlin: 317–33.

Israelowich, I. (2008), 'The rain miracle of Marcus Aurelius: (re-)construction of consensus', *G&R* 55: 83–102.

Jaeger, M. (2008), *Archimedes and the Roman Imagination*. Ann Arbor.

Janko, R. (1992), *The Iliad: A Commentary. Volume IV: Books 13–16*. Cambridge.

Jeffreys, E. (1979), 'The attitudes of Byzantine chroniclers towards ancient history,' *Byzantion* 49: 199–238.

Jones, A. H. M. (1951), 'The *imperium* of Augustus', *JRS* 41: 112–19.

Jones, A. H. M. (1960), *Studies in Roman Government and Law*. New York.

Jones, B. (2016), 'Cassius Dio – *Pepaideumenos* and politician on kingship', in C. H. Lange and J. M. Madsen (eds.), *Cassius Dio: Greek Intellectual and Roman Politician*. Leiden and Boston: 297–315.

Jones, C. P. (1966), 'Towards a chronology of Plutarch's works', *JHS* 56: 61–74.

Jones, C. P. (1972), 'Aelius Aristides, ΕΙΣ ΒΑΣΙΛΕΑ', *JRS* 62: 134–52.

Juntunen, K. (2013), 'The lost books of Cassius Dio', *Chiron* 43: 459–86.

Juntunen, K. (2015), 'The image of Cleopatra in Ioannes Xiphilinos' *Epitome* of Cassius Dio: A reflection of the empress Eudokia Makrembolitissa?', *Acta Byzantina Fennica* 4: 123–51.

Kaimio, J. (1979), *The Romans and the Greek Language*. Helsinki.

Kaldellis, A. (2012), 'The Byzantine role in the making of the corpus of classical Greek historiography: a preliminary investigation', *JHS* 132: 71–85.

Kaldellis, A. (2015a), *Byzantine Readings of Ancient Historians*. New York.

Kaldellis, A. (2015b), *The Byzantine Republic: People and Power in New Rome.* Cambridge, MA.

Kaldellis, A. and Krallis, D. (eds.) (2012), *The History of Michael Attaleites. Dumbarton Oaks Medieval Library.* Cambridge, MA.

Kampianaki, T. (2017a), *John Zonaras's Epitome of History (12th c.): A Compendium of Jewish-Roman History and Its Readers.* DPhil thesis, University of Oxford.

Kampianaki, T. (2017b), 'Plutarch's *Lives* in the Byzantine chronographic tradition: the *Chronicle* of John Zonaras', *BMGS* 41: 15–29.

Kannicht, R. and Snell, B. (eds.) (1981), *Tragicorum Graecorum Fragmenta. Volume II.* Göttingen.

Kapferer, J.-N. (1990), *Rumors: Uses, Interpretations, and Images.* New Brunswick and London.

Karpozilos, A. (2009), Βυζαντινοί Ιστορικοί και Χρονογράφοι. Τόμος Γ' (11os – 12os αι.). Athens.

Kemezis, A. (2007), 'Augustus the ironic paradigm: Cassius Dio's portrayal of the *lex Julia* and the *lex Papia Poppaea*', *Phoenix* 61: 70–85.

Kemezis, A. M. (2010), 'Lucian, Fronto, and the absence of contemporary historiography under the Antonines', *AJPh* 131: 285–325.

Kemezis, A. M. (2012), 'Commemoration of the Antonine aristocracy in Cassius Dio and the *Historia Augusta*', *CQ* 62: 387–414.

Kemezis, A. M. (2014), *Greek Narratives of the Roman Empire under the Severans: Cassius Dio, Philostratus and Herodian.* Cambridge.

Kemezis A. M. (2016a), 'Dio, Caesar and the Vesontio mutineers (38.34–47): a rhetoric of lies', in C. H. Lange and J. M. Madsen (eds.), *Cassius Dio: Greek Intellectual and Roman Politician.* Leiden and Boston: 238–57.

Kemezis, A. M. (2016b), 'The fall of Elagabalus as literary narrative and political reality: a reconsideration', *Historia* 65: 348–90.

Kemezis, A. M. (2018), 'Beyond city limits: citizenship and authorship in imperial Greek literature', in K. Berthelot and J. J. Price (eds.), *In the Crucible of Empire: The Impact of Roman Citizenship upon Greeks, Jews and Christians.* Leuven: 73–103.

Kemezis, A. M. (2020), 'The romance of Republican history: narrative tension and resolution in Florus, Appian, and Chariton', in A. König, R. Langlands, and J. Uden (eds.), *Literature and Culture in the Roman Empire, 96–235: Cross-Cultural Interactions.* Cambridge: 114–33.

Kennell, N. M. (1988). 'Nerwn Periodonikhs', *AJP* 109: 239–51.

Kierdorf, W. (1980), *Laudatio Funebris: Interpretationen und Untersuchungen zur Entwicklung der römischen Leichenrede.* Meisenheim am Glan.

Kleijwegt, M. (1994), 'Caligula's "triumph" at Baiae', *Mnemosyne* 47: 652–71.

Klinger, F. (1963), *Tacitus über Augustus und Tiberius.* Munich.

Koenen, L. (1970), 'Die *laudatio funebris* des Augustus für Agrippa', *ZPE* 5: 217–83.

Kolb, F. (1972), *Literarische Beziehungen zwischen Cassius Dio, Herodian und der Historia Augusta.* Bonn.

Konstan, D. and Walsh, R. (2016), 'Civic and subversive biography in antiquity', in K. de Temmerman and K. Demoen (eds.), *Writing Biographies in Greece and Rome: Narrative Technique and Fictionalization.* Cambridge: 26–43.

Kovács, P. (2009), *Marcus Aurelius' Rain Miracle and the Marcomannic Wars. Mnemosyne Supplement 308.* Leiden.

Kragelund, P. (2012), 'Tacitus, Dio, and the "sophist" Maternus', *Historia* 61: 495–506.

Krallis, D. (2012), *Michael Attaleiates and the Politics of Imperial Decline in Eleventh-Century Byzantium.* Tempe.

Kröss, K. (2017), *Die politische Rolle der stadtrömischen plebs in der Kaiserzeit.* Leiden and Boston.

Kruse, M. (2019), 'The epitomator Ioannes Xiphilinos and the eleventh-century Xiphilinoi', *JÖB* 69: 257–74.

Kuhlmann, P. (2010), 'Die Maecenas-Rede bei Cassius Dio: Anachronismen und intertextuelle Bezüge', in D. Pausch (ed.), *Stimmen der Geschichte: Funktionen von Reden in der antiken Historiographie.* Berlin and New York: 109–21.

Kuhn-Chen, B. (2002), *Geschichtskonzeptionen griechischer Historiker im 2. und 3. Jahrhundert n.Chr. Untersuchungen zu den Werken von Appian, Cassius Dio und Herodian.* Frankfurt.

Kühnen, A. (2008), *Die Imitatio Alexandri in der römischen Politik: 1. Jh. v. Chr. – 3. Jh. n. Chr.* Münster.

Lacey, W. K. (1979), '*Summi fastigii vocabulum*: the story of a title', *JRS* 69: 28–34.

Lacey, W. K. (1996), *Augustus and the Principate.* Leeds.

Lachenaud, G. (2016), 'Récit et discours chez Cassius Dion: frontières, interférences et polyphonie', in V. Fromentin *et al.* (eds.), *Cassius Dion: nouvelles lectures.* Bordeaux: 397–414.

Lachenaud, G. and Coudry, M. (eds.) (2011), *Dion Cassius. Histoire Romaine. Livres 38, 39 et 40. Texte établi par G.L., traduit et commenté par G. L. et M. C.* Paris.

Laes, C. (2007), 'School teachers in the Roman empire: a survey of the evidence', *AClass* 50: 109–27.

Lang, D. M. (1983), 'Iran, Armenia and Georgia', in E. Yarshater (ed.), *The Cambridge History of Iran. Volume 3.1: The Seleucid, Parthian and Sasanian Periods.* Cambridge, 505–36.

Lange C. H. (2016), 'Mock the triumph: Cassius Dio, triumph and triumph-like celebrations', in C. H. Lange and J. M. Madsen (eds.), *Cassius Dio. Greek Intellectual and Roman Politician.* Leiden and Boston: 92–114.

Lange, C. H. and Madsen, J. M. (eds.) (2016), *Cassius Dio. Greek Intellectual and Roman Politician.* Leiden and Boston.

Langford, J. (2013), *Maternal Megalomania: Julia Domna and the Imperial Politics of Motherhood.* Baltimore.

Langlands, R. (2006), *Sexual Morality in Ancient Rome.* Cambridge.

Larkin, P. (1974), *High Windows.* London.

Laurence, R. (1994), 'Rumour and communication in Roman politics', *G&R* 41: 62–74.

Lavan, M. (2013), *Slaves to Rome: Paradigms of Empire in Roman Culture.* Cambridge.

Lavan, M. (2016), 'The spread of Roman citizenship, 14–212 CE: Quantification in the face of high uncertainty', *P&P* 230: 3–46.

Lavan, M. (2018), 'The foundation of empire? The spread of Roman citizenship from the fourth century BCE to the third century CE', in K. Berthelot and J. Price (eds.), *In the Crucible of Empire: The Impact of Roman Citizenship upon Greeks, Jews and Christians.* Leuven: 21–54.

Leaning, J. B. (1989), 'Didius Julianus and his biographer', *Latomus* 48: 548–65.

Leidholm, N. (2018), 'Nikephoros III Botaneiates, the Phokades, and the Fabii: embellished genealogies and contested kingship in eleventh-century Byzantium', *BMGS* 42: 185–201.

Lemerle, P. (1971), *Le premier humanisme byzantin: notes et remarques sur enseigne-ment et culture à Byzance des origines au Xe siècle.* Paris.

Lemerle, P. (trans. Lindsay, H. and Moffatt, A.) (1986), *Byzantine Humanism: The First Phase. Notes and Remarks on Education and Culture in Byzantium from Its Origins to the 10th Century.* Canberra.

Lendon, J. E. (1997), *Empire of Honour: The Art of Government in the Roman World.* Oxford.

Leone, P. A. M. (ed.) (1968), *Ioannis Tzetzae Historiae.* Naples.

Leone, P. A. M. (ed.) (1972), *Ioannis Tzetzae Epistulae.* Leipzig.

Letta, C. (1979), 'La composizione dell'opera di Cassio Dione. Cronologia e sfondo storico-politico', in L. Troiani, E. Noè, and C. Letta (eds.), *Ricerche di storiografia greca di età romana.* Pisa: 117–89.

Letta, C. (1994), 'Il "Naufragio" di Caracalla in Cassio Dione, nell'*Historia Augusta* e nei commentary degli Arvali', *ZPE* 103: 188–90.

Letta, C. (2003), 'Documenti d'archivio e iscrizioni nell'opera di Cassio Dione. Un sondaggio sulla narrazione fino ad Augusto', in A. M. Biraschi *et al.* (eds.), *L'uso dei documenti d'archivio nella storiografia antica.* Naples: 597–622.

Letta, C. (2016a), 'Fonti scritte non letterarie nella *Storia Romana* di Cassio Dione', *SCO* 62: 245–96.

Letta, C. (2016b), 'L'uso degli acta senatus nella *Storia Romana* di Cassio Dione', in V. Fromentin *et al.* (eds.), *Cassius Dion: nouvelles lectures.* Bordeaux: 243–57.

Letta, C. (2016c), 'Ritorno a Cassio Dione. Caracalla e il massacro di Alessandria', in C. Carsana and L. Troiani L. (eds.), *I percorsi di un Historikos. In memoria di Emilio Gabba.* Como: 260–72.

Letta, C. (2019a), 'Conoscenza e criteri di utilizzazione dei *senatus consulta* nella Storia Romana di Cassio Dione', in P. Buongiorno and G. Traina (eds.), *Rappresentazione e uso dei senatus consulta nelle fonti letterarie del principato / Darstellung und Gebrauch der senatus consulta in den literarischen Quellen der Kaiserzeit. Acta Senatus B6.* Stuttgart: 189–244.

Letta, C., (2019b), 'La carriera politica di Cassio Dione e la genesi della sua Storia Romana', *SCO* 65: 163–80.

Leunclavius, I. (ed.) (1606), *Ton Dionos tou Kassiou tou Kokkeianou Romaikôn Historiôn ta Heuriskomena. Dionis Cassii Cocceiani Historiae Romanae libri XLVI, partim integri, partim mutili, partim excerpti.* Hannover.

Leunissen, P. M. (1989), *Konsuln und Konsulare in der Zeit von Commodus bis Severus Alexander (180–235 n. Chr.): Prosopographische Untersuchungen zur senatorischen Elite im Römischen Kaiserreich.* Amsterdam.

Levene, D. S. (1993), *Religion in Livy.* Oxford.

Levene, D. S. (1997), 'Pity, fear and the historical audience: Tacitus on the fall of Vitellius', in S. M. Braund and C. Gill (eds.), *The Passions in Roman Thought and Literature.* Cambridge, 128–49.

Levene, D. S. (2010), *Livy on the Hannibalic War.* Oxford.

Levick, B. (1972), 'The retirement of Tiberius to Rhodes in 6 BC', *Latomus* 31: 779–813.

Levick, B. M. (1966), 'Drusus Caesar and the adoptions of AD 4', *Latomus* 25: 227–44.

Levick, B. M. (1976), *Tiberius the Politician.* London.

Levick, B. M. (1985), 'L. Verginius Rufus and the four emperors', *RhM* 128: 318–46.

Levin, S. (1989), 'The old Greek oracles in decline', *ANRW* 2.18.2: 1599–649.

Libby, B. (2010), 'The intersection of poetic and imperial authority in Phaedrus' *Fables*', *CQ* 60: 545–58.

Lichtenberger, A. (2011), *Severus Pius Augustus.* Leiden.

Liebs, D. (2012), *Summoned to the Roman Courts: Famous Trials from Antiquity.* Translated by R. L. R. Garber and C. G. Cürten. Berkeley.

Lindholmer, M. (2018), 'Cassius Dio and the "Age of δυναστεία"', *GRBS* 58: 561–90.

Lindholmer, M. (2019), 'Breaking the idealistic paradigm: competition in Dio's earlier Republic', in C. Burden-Strevens and M. Lindholmer (eds.) (2019), *Cassius Dio's Forgotten History of Early Rome.* Leiden and Boston: 190–214.

Lippold, A. (1983), 'Zur Laufbahn des P. Helvius Pertinax', *BHAC 1979–1981.* Bonn: 173–91.

Littman, R. J. and Littman, M. L. (1973), 'Galen and the Antonine plague', *AJP* 94: 243–55.

Lott, J. B. (ed.) (2012), *Death and Dynasty in Early Imperial Rome: Key Sources, with Text, Translation and Commentary.* Cambridge.

Luce, T. J. (1977), *Livy and the Composition of his History.* Princeton.

Luce, T. J. (1989), 'Ancient views on the causes of bias in historical writing', *CP* 84: 16–31.

Maccari, A. (2015), '*Quid sit pomerium*: appunti su Gellio, *Noctes Atticae* XIII, 14. Le fonti e il confronto con Festo 294 L.', *SCO* 61: 313–33.

Madsen, J. M. (2016), 'Criticising the benefactors: the Severans and the return of dynastic rule', in C. H. Lange and J. M. Madsen (eds.), *Cassius Dio: Greek Intellectual and Roman Politician.* Leiden and Boston: 136–58.

Madsen, J. M. (2020). *Cassius Dio. Ancients in Action.* London.

Magdalino, P. (1983), 'Aspects of twelfth-century Byzantine Kaiserkritik,' *Speculum* 58: 326–46.

Magdalino, P. (2013a), 'Byzantine encyclopaedism of the ninth and tenth centuries,' in J. König and G. Woolf (eds.), *Encyclopaedism from Antiquity to the Renaissance*. Cambridge: 219–31.

Magdalino, P. (2013b), 'Knowledge and authority and authorised history: the imperial intellectual programme of Leo VI and Constantine VII,' in P. Armstrong (ed.), *Authority in Byzantium*. Farnham: 187–209.

Magdalino, P. and R. Macrides (1992), 'The fourth kingdom and the rhetoric of Hellenism', in P. Magdalino (ed.), *The Perception of the Past in Twelfth-Century Europe*. London: 117–56.

Magie, D. (1950), *Roman Rule in Asia Minor*. Princeton.

Makhlaiuk, A. (2017), 'Review of Fromentin *et al.* 2016', *BMCR* 2017.12.15.

Mallan, C. T. (2013a), 'Cassius Dio on Julia Domna: a study of the political and ethical functions of biographical representation in Dio's *Roman History*', *Mnemosyne* 66: 734–60.

Mallan, C. T. (2013b), 'The style, method, and programme of Xiphilinus' *Epitome* of Cassius Dio's *Roman History*', *GRBS* 53: 610–44.

Mallan, C. T. (2014), 'The rape of Lucretia in Cassius Dio's *Roman History*', *CQ* 64: 758–71.

Mallan, C. T. (2016), '*Parrhēsia* in Cassius Dio', in C. H. Lange and J. M. Madsen (eds.), *Cassius Dio: Greek Intellectual and Roman Politician*. Leiden and Boston: 258–75.

Mallan, C. T. (2017a), 'The book indices in the manuscripts of Cassius Dio', *CQ* 66: 705–23.

Mallan, C. T. (2017b), 'The spectre of Alexander: Cassius Dio and the Alexander motif', *Greece and Rome* 64: 132–44.

Mallan, C. T. (2018), 'The historian John Zonaras: some observations on his sources and methods', in O. Devillers and B. Sebastiani (eds.), *Sources et modèles des historiens anciens*. Bordeaux: 353–66.

Mallan, C. T. (2019), 'The *regal period in the Excerpta Constantiniana* and the early Byzantine extracts from Dio's *Roman History*', in C. Burden-Strevens and M. O. Lindholmer (eds.), *Cassius Dio's Forgotten History of Early Rome*. Leiden and Boston: 76–96.

Malloch, S. J. V. (ed.) (2013), *The Annals of Tacitus Book 11*. Cambridge.

Manders, E. and Slootjes, D. (2015), 'Linking inscriptions to provincial coins: A reappraisal of Nero's visit to Greece', *Latomus* 74: 989–1005.

Manuwald, B. (1973), 'Cassius Dio und das „Totengericht" über Augustus bei Tacitus', *Hermes* 101: 352–74.

Manuwald, B. (1979), *Cassius Dio und Augustus. Philologische Untersuchungen zu den Büchern 45–56*. Wiesbaden.

Marañón, G. (1956), *Tiberius Caesar: A Study in Resentment*. London.

Marincola, J. (1997), *Authority and Tradition in Ancient Historiography*. Cambridge.

Marincola, J. (1999), 'Genre, convention and innovation in Greco-Roman histori-ography', in C. S. Kraus (ed.), *The Limits of Historiography*. Leiden: 281–324.'

Marincola, J. (2007), 'Speeches in classical historiography', in J. Maricola (ed.), *A Companion to Greek and Roman Historiography*. Oxford and Malden, MA: 118–32.

Marincola, J. (2010), 'The rhetoric of history, allusion, intertextuality, and exem-plarity in historiographical speeches', in D. Pausch (ed.), *Stimmen der Geschichte: Funktionen von Reden in der antiken Historiographie*. Berlin: 259–89.

Markopoulos, A. (2006), 'Roman antiquarianism: aspects of the Roman past in the middle Byzantine period,' in E. Jeffreys (ed.), *Proceedings of the 21st International Congress of Byzantine Studies*. Aldershot: 277–97.

Markopoulos, A. (2010), 'From narrative historiography to historical biography: New trends in Byzantine historical writing in the 10th–11th centuries', *BZ* 102: 697–715.

Marotta, V. (2009), *La cittadinanza romana in età imperiale (secoli I-III d.C.)*. Turin.

Martin, R. (2001), *Tacitus: Annals V & VI*. Warminster.

Martini, M. (2010), 'Il ruolo paradigmatico della figura di Marco Aurelio in Cassio Dione: confronto con la figura di Caracalla', *Sileno* 36: 63–77.

Marx, F. A. (1936), 'Aufidius Bassus', *Klio* 29: 94–101.

Mazzuchi, C. M. (1979), 'Alcune vicende della tradizione di Cassio Dione in epoca bizantina', *Aevum* 53: 94–139.

McDonald, A. H. (1966), 'Review of Millar 1964', *CR* 16: 318–20.

Meckler, M. L. (1999), 'Caracalla the intellectual', in E. Dal Dovolo and G. Rinaldi (eds.), *Gli Imperatori Severi: storia, archeologia, religione*. Rome: 39–46.

Mehl, A. (1981), 'Bemerkungen zu Dios und Tacitus Arbeitsweise und zur Quellenlage im „Totengericht" über Augustus', *Gymnasium* 88: 54–64.

Mendels, D. (1986), 'Greek and Roman history in the *Bibliotheca* of Photius: a note,' *Byzantion* 56: 196–206.

Mennen, I. (2011), *Power and Status in the Roman Empire, AD 193–284*. Leiden and Boston.

Meyer, P. (1891), *De Maecenatis oratione a Dione ficta*. Berlin.

Meyer, H.-D. (1961), *Die Außenpolitik des Augustus und die augusteische Dichtung*. Cologne.

Michels, C. (2018), *Antoninus Pius und die Rollenbilder des römischen Princeps*. Berlin.

Migliorati, G. (2003), *Cassio Dione e l'impero romano da Nerva ad Antonino Pio: alla luce dei nuovi documenti*. Milan.

Millar, F. G. B. (1961), 'Some speeches in Cassius Dio', *MH* 18: 11–22.

Millar, F. G. B. (1964), *A Study of Cassius Dio*. Oxford.

Millar, F. G. B. (1998), *The Crowd in Rome in the Late Republic*. Ann Arbor.

Millar, F. G. B. (2005), 'Rome in Greek culture: Cassius Dio and Ulpian', in L. Troiani and G. Zecchini (eds.), *La cultura storica nei primi due secoli dell'impero romano*. Rome: 17–40.

Millar, F. G. B. (2016), 'Préface', in V. Fromentin *et al.* (eds.), *Cassius Dion: nouvelles lectures*. Bordeaux: 9–10.

Misener, G. (1918), 'Review of Cary 1914–27: i–vi', *CPh* 13: 420.

Mitchell, S. (1995), *Anatolia: Land, Men and Gods in Asia Minor*, 2 vols. Oxford.

Molin, M. (2004), 'De l'intérêt des *Excerpta historica iussu Imp. Constantini Pophyrogenitii* pour le lecture de la dernière décade de Dion Cassius', *Ktema* 29: 209–13.

Molin, M. (2006), 'Mots, images et situations de crise dans la dernière décade de Dion Cassius d'après les *Epitomai* de Xiphilin', in M.-H. Quet, A. Giardina and M. Christol (eds.), *La "crise" de l'Empire romain de Marc Aurèle à Constantin: mutations, continuités, ruptures*. Paris: 435–53.

Molin, M. (2016a), 'Biographie de l'historien Cassius Dion', in V. Fromentin *et al.* (eds.), *Cassius Dion: nouvelles lectures*. Bordeaux: 431–46.

Molin, M. (2016b), 'Cassius Dion et la société de son temps', in V. Fromentin *et al.* (eds.), *Cassius Dion: nouvelles lectures*. Bordeaux: 469–82.

Molinier-Arbo, A. (2009), 'Dion Cassius versus Marius Maximus? Éléments de polémique entre les *Romaika* et l'*Histoire Auguste*', *Phoenix* 63: 278–95.

Mommsen, T. (1887), *Römisches Staatsrecht*, 3rd edition. Leipzig.

Moore, D. W. (2012), 'A note on *CIL* VI.1585a-b and the role of Adrastus, procurator of the Column of Marcus Aurelius', *ZPE* 181: 221–29.

Morris, J. (1965), 'Review of Millar 1964', *JHS* 85: 184–85.

Morstein-Marx, R. (2004), *Mass Oratory and Political Power in the Late Roman Republic*. Cambridge.

Moscovich, M. J. (2004), 'Cassius Dio's palace sources for the reign of Septimius Severus', *Historia* 53: 356–68.

Mratschek, S. (2013), 'Nero the imperial misfit: Philhellenism in a rich man's world', in E. Buckley and M. Dinter (eds.), *A Companion to the Neronian Age*. Chichester: 45–62.

Müller, C. G. (ed.) (1811), *John Tzetzes, On Lycophron*. Leipzig.

Murison C. L. (1999), *Rebellion and Reconstruction: Galba to Domitian. An Historical Commentary on Cassius Dio's Roman History Books 64–67 (AD 68–69)*. Atlanta.

Musurillo, H. (ed.) (1954), *The Acts of the Pagan Martyrs. Acta Alexandrinorum*. Oxford.

Németh, A. (2010), *Imperial Systematization of the Past: Emperor Constantine VII and His Historical Excerpts*. PhD thesis, Central European University.

Németh, A. (2016), 'Excerpts versus fragments: deconstructions and reconstructions of the *Excerpta Constantiniana*', in A. Grafton and G. W. Most (eds.), *Canonical Texts and Scholarly Practices: A Global Comparative Approach*. Cambridge: 253–74.

Neméth, A. (2018), *The Excerpta Constantiniana and the Byzantine Appropriation of the Past*. Cambridge.

Neville, L. (2018), *Guide to Byzantine Historical Writing*. Cambridge.

Newbold, R. F. (1975), 'Cassius Dio and the games', *AC* 44: 589–604.

Newman, W.L. (1887–1902), *The Politics of Aristotle*. Oxford.

Niebuhr, B. G. (trans. H. M. Chepmell and F. Demmler) (1875), *Niebuhr's Lectures on Roman History: Volume I*. London.

Nixon, C. E. V. and Rodgers, B. S. (eds.) (1994), *In Praise of Later Roman Emperors: The* Panegyrici Latini. Berkeley.

Noè, E. (1994), *Commento storico a Cassio Dione LIII*. Como.

Noreña, C. F. (2009), 'The ethics of autocracy in the Roman world', in R. K. Balot (ed.), *A Companion to Greek and Roman Political Thought*. Malden, MA: 266–79.

Noreña, C. F. (2011), *Imperial Ideals in the Roman West: Representation, Circulation, Power*. Cambridge.

North, H. (1966), *Sophrosyne: Self-Knowledge and Self-Restraint in Greek Literature*. Ithaca.

Nutton, V. (2013), 'Avoiding distress', in P. N. Singer (eds.), *Galen. Psychological Writings*. Cambridge: 43–106.

Oakley, S. (1997–2005), *A Commentary on Livy, Books VI–X*, 4 vols. Oxford.

Ober, J. (1982), 'Tiberius and the political testament of Augustus', *Historia* 31: 306–28.

Olson, A. (2017), 'Working with Roman history: Attalieates' portrayal of the Normans', *BMGS* 41: 1–14.

O'Neill, P. (2003), 'Going round in circles: popular speech in ancient Rome', *Classical Antiquity* 22: 135–76.

Osgood, J. (2016), 'Cassius Dio's secret history of Elagabalus', in C. H. Lange and J. M. Madsen (eds.), *Cassius Dio: Greek Intellectual and Roman Politician*. Leiden and Boston: 177–90.

Osgood, J. and Baron, C. (eds.) (2019), *Cassius Dio and the Late Republic*. Leiden and Boston.

Paillard, B. (1990), 'L'écho de la rumeur', *Communications* 12: 125–39.

Pandey, N. B. (2018), *The Poetics of Power in Augustan Rome. Latin Roman Poetic Responses to Early Imperial Iconography*. Cambridge.

Pasek, S. (2013), *Coniuratio ad principem occidendum faciendumque. Der erfolgreiche Staatsstreich gegen Commodus und die Regentschaft des Helvius Pertinax (192/193 n. Chr.)*. Munich.

Paterson, J. (2007), 'Friends in high places: the creation of the court of the Roman emperor', in A. J. S. Spawforth (ed.), *The Court and Court Society in Ancient Monarchies*. Cambridge: 121–56.

Pelling, C. B. R. (1979), 'Plutarch's method of work in the Roman *Lives*', *JHS* 99: 74–96. Reprinted with a postscript in B. Scardigli (ed.) (1995), *Essays on Plutarch's Lives*. Oxford: 265–318, and in Pelling 2002: 1–44.

Pelling, C. B. R. (1982), 'Review of Zecchini 1978', *CR* 32: 146–48.

Pelling, C. B. R. (1983), 'Review of B. Manuwald, *Cassius Dio und Augustus*', *Gnomon* 55: 221–26.

Pelling, C. B. R. (ed.) (1988), *Plutarch: Life of Antony*. Cambridge.

Pelling, C. B. R. (1996), 'The triumviral period', in A. K. Bowman, E. Champlin, and A. Lintott (eds.), *The Cambridge Ancient History. Second Edition. Volume X: The Augustan Empire, 43 BC–AD 69*. Cambridge: 1–69.

Pelling, C. B. R. (1997a), 'Biographical history? Cassius Dio on the early princi-pate', in M. J. Edwards and S. Swain (eds.), *Portraits: Biographical Representation in the Greek and Latin Literature of the Early Empire*. Oxford, 117–44.

Pelling, C. B. R. (1997b), 'Tragical dreamer: some dreams in the Roman historians', *G&R* 44: 197–205.

Pelling, C. B. R. (2002), *Plutarch and History: Eighteen Studies*. London.

Pelling, C. B. R. (2006), 'Breaking the bounds: writing about Julius Caesar', in B. McGing and J. Mossman (eds.), *The Limits of Ancient Biography*. Swansea: 255–80.

Pelling, C. B. R. (2010a), 'The spur of Fame: *Annals* 4.37-8', in C. S. Kraus, J. Marincola, and C. B. R. Pelling (eds.), *Ancient Historiography and Its Contexts: Studies in Honour of A. J. Woodman*. Oxford: 364–85.

Pelling, C. B. R. (2010b), '"Learning from that violent schoolmaster": Thucydidean intertextuality and some Greek views of Roman civil war', in B. W. Breed, C. Damon, and A. Rossi (eds.), *Citizens of Discord: Rome and Its Civil Wars*. Oxford: 105–18.

Pelling, C. B. R. (2018), 'Dionysius on regime change', in R. Hunter and C. C. de Jonge (eds.), *Dionysius of Halicarnassus and Augustan Rome*. Cambridge: 203–20.

Penzel, A. J. (ed.) (1786–99), *Des Dio Cassius Coccejanus, ehemalige Bürgermeisters in Rom, Jahrbücher römischer Geschichte*, 2 vols. Leipzig.

Pfuntner, L. (2015), 'Reading Diodorus through Photius: the case of the Sicilian slave revolts', *GRBS* 55: 256–72.

Piatkowski, A. (1984), 'Cassius Dio über den Kaiserkult', *Klio* 66: 599–604.

Pinder, M. and Buttner-Wobst, T. (eds.) (1841–97), *Ioannes Zonarae Annales*. Bonn.

Pirson, F. (1996), 'Style and message on the Column of Marcus Aurelius', *PBSR* 64: 139–79.

Pitcher, L. (2009a), 'The Roman historians after Livy', in M. Griffin (ed.), *A Companion to Julius Caesar*. Malden, MA: 267–76.

Pitcher, L. (2009b), *Writing Ancient History*. London and New York.

Pitt-Rivers, J. (1977), *The fate of Shechem: Or, The Politics of Sex: Essays in the Anthropology of the Mediterranean*. Cambridge and New York.

Pizzone, A. (2017), 'The *Historiai* of John Tzetzes: a Byzantine book of memory,' *BMGS* 41: 182–207.

Plass, P. (1985), 'An aspect of epigrammatic wit in Martial and Tacitus', *Arethusa* 18: 187–210.

Platon, M. (2016), 'Sénat et pouvoir impérial dans les livres 57 et 58 de l'*Histoire romaine* de Cassius Dion', in V. Fromentin *et al.* (eds.), *Cassius Dion: nouvelles lectures*. Bordeaux: 653–75.

Poma, G. (1989), 'Dionigi d'Alicarnasso e la cittadinanza romana', *MEFRA* 101: 187–205.

Pontani, F. (2015), 'Scholarship in the Byzantine empire (529–1453)', in F. Montanari, S. Matthaios, and A. Rengagos (eds.), *Brill's Companion to Ancient Greek Scholarship*, vol. I. Leiden and Boston: 297–455.

Possienke, H. (2011), 'Überlegungen zur Darstellung Mark Aurels im Geschichtswerk des Cassius Dio', in B. Onken and D. Rohde (eds.), in *In omni historia curiosus: Studie zur Geschichte von der Antike bis zur Neuzeit*. Wiesbaden: 43–62.

Potter, D. S. (1994), *Prophets and Emperors: Human and Divine Authority from Augustus to Theodosius*. Cambridge, MA.

Potter, D. S. (1999), *Literary Texts and the Roman Historian*. London.

Potter, D. S. (2011), 'The Greek historians of imperial Rome', in D. Woolf (ed.), *The Oxford History of Historical Writing*, vol. 1. Oxford: 316–45.

Power, T. (2011), 'Claudius' Homeric quotation', *Latomus* 70: 727–31.

Power, T. (2014a), 'Suetonius' Tacitus', *JRS* 104: 205–25.

Power, T. (2014b), 'Introduction: the originality of Suetonius', in T. Power and R. K. Gibson (eds.), *Suetonius the Biographer: Studies in Roman Lives*. Oxford: 1–18.

Power, T. and Gibson, R. K. (2014), *Suetonius the Biographer: Studies in Roman Lives*. Oxford.

Pye, L. W. (1965), 'Introduction: political culture and political development', in L. W. Pye and S. Verba (eds.), *Political Culture and Political Development*. Princeton, NJ: 3–26.

Questa, C. (1957), 'Tecnica biografica e tecnica annalistica nei libri LXII–LXIII di Cassio Dione', *StudUrb* 31: 37–53.

Rantala, J. (2016), 'Dio the dissident: the portrait of Severus in the *Roman History*', in C. H. Lange and J. Madsen (eds.), *Cassius Dio: Greek Intellectual and Roman Politician*. Leiden and Boston: 159–76.

Rees, W. (2011), *Cassius Dio, Human Nature, and the late Roman Republic*. DPhil thesis, University of Oxford.

Reimarus, H. S. (ed.) (1750–52), *Ton Dionos tou Kassiou tou Kokkeianou Romaikon historion ta sozomena. Cassii Dionis Cocceiani Historiae Romanae quae supersunt*, 2 vols. Hamburg.

Reinhold, M. (1986), 'In praise of Cassius Dio', *AClass.* 55: 213–22.

Reinhold, M. (1988), *From Republic to Principate: An Historical Commentary on Cassius Dio's Roman History Books 49–52 (36–29 B.C.)*. Atlanta, GA.

Reinhold, M. and Swan, P. (1990), 'Cassius Dio's assessment of Augustus', in K. A. Raaflaub and M. Toher (eds.), *Between Republic and Empire. Interpretations of Augustus and his Principate*. Berkeley: 155–73.

Rich, J. W. (1989), 'Dio on Augustus', in A. Cameron (ed.), *History as Text: The Writing of Ancient History*. Chapel Hill, NC: 87–110.

Rich, J. W. (1990), *Cassius Dio: The Augustan Settlement (Roman History 53–55.9)*. Warminster.

Rich, J. W. (1998), 'Augustus' Parthian honours, the Temple of Mars Ultor and the Arch in the *forum Romanum*', *PBSR* 66: 71–128.

Rich, J. W. (2011), 'Structuring Roman history: the consular year and the Roman historical tradition', *Histos* 5: 1–43. Revised version of article originally published in *Histos* 1 (1997). Revised and reprinted in J. D. Chaplin and C. S. Kraus (eds.) (2009), *Oxford Readings in Classical Studies: Livy*. Oxford. 118–47.

Rich, J. W. (2016), 'Annalistic organization and book division in Dio's Books 1–35', in V. Fromentin *et al.* (eds.), *Cassius Dion: nouvelles lectures*. Bordeaux: 271–86.

Rich, J. W. (2019), 'Speech in Cassius Dio's *Roman History* Books 1–35', in C. Burden-Strevens and M. O. Lindholmer (eds.), *Cassius Dio's Forgotten History of Early Rome*. Leiden and Boston: 217–84.

Rich, J. W. and Williams, J. H. C. (1999), '*Leges et Iura P.R. Restituit*: A new aureus of Octavian and the settlement of 28–27 B.C.', *NC* 159: 169–213.

Rives, J. B. (2003), 'Magic in Roman law: the reconstruction of a crime', *Classical Antiquity* 22: 313–39.

Roberto, U. (2009), 'Byzantine collections of late antique authors: some remarks on the *Excerpta historica Constantiniana*', in M. Wallraff and L. Mecella (eds.), *Texte und Untersuchungen zur Geschichte der altchristlichen Literatur: Die Kestoi des Julius Africanus und ihre Überlieferung*. Berlin: 71–84.

Roche, P. (ed.) (2009), *Lucan, de Bello Ciuili: Book I*. Oxford.

Rosillo-López, C. (2017), *Public Opinion and Politics in the Late Roman Republic*. Cambridge.

Roueché, C. (2002), 'The literary background of Kekaumenos', in C. Holmes and Judith Warring (eds.), *Literacy, Education and Manuscript Transmission in Byzantium and Beyond*. Leiden and Boston: 111–38.

Roueché, C. (ed.), (2013), *Kekaumenos. Advice and Anecdotes*, SAWS Dynamic Library of Wisdom Literatures. Available online at: www.ancientwisdoms.ac.uk /library/kekaumenos-consilia-et-narrationes/

Rowan, C. (2012), *Under Divine Auspices: Divine Ideology and the Visualisation of Imperial Power in the Severan Period*. Cambridge.

Rowe, G. (2002), *Princes and Political Cultures: The New Tiberian Senatorial Decrees*. Ann Arbor.

Rubin, Z. (1980), *Civil-War Propaganda and Historiography*. Brussels.

Rutledge, S. H. (2008), 'Tiberius' Philhellenism', *CW* 101: 453–67.

Saller, R. (1980), 'Anecdotes as historical evidence for the principate', *G&R* 27: 69–83.

Salmon, E. T. (1967), *Samnium and the Samnites*. Cambridge.

Salomies, O. (1990), 'A note on the establishment of the date of the Rain Miracle under Marcus Aurelius', *Arctos* 23: 107.

Scheid, J. (2016), 'Cassius Dion et la religion dans les livres 50–61. Quelques réflexions sur l'historiographie de l'époque julio-claudienne', in V. Fromentin *et al.* (eds.), *Cassius Dion: nouvelles lectures*. Bordeaux: 787–98.

Schettino, M. T. (1998), 'Perdono e *clementia principis* nello stoicismo del II secolo', in M. Sordi (ed.), *Responsabilità, perdono e vendetta nel mondo antico*. Milan: 209–38.

Schettino, M. T. (2001), 'Cassio Dione e le guerre civile di età severiana', *Gerión* 19: 533–58.

Schmidt, M. G. (1989), 'Cassius Dio, Buch LXX. Bemerkungen zur Technik des Epitomators Ioannes Xiphilinos,' *Chiron* 19: 55–9.

Schmidt, M. G. (1997), 'Die "zeitgeschichtlichen" Bücher im Werk des Cassius Dio: von Commodus zu Severus Alexander', *ANRW* 2.34.3: 2591–649.

Schmidt, M. G. (1999), 'Politische und persönliche Motivation in Dios Zeitgeschichte', in M. Zimmermann (ed.), *Geschichtsschreibung und politischer Wandel im 3. Jh. n. Chr.: Kolloquium zu Ehren von Karl Ernst Petzold (Juni 1998) anlässlich seines 80. Geburtstags*. Wiesbaden: 93–117.

Schofield, M. (2006), *Plato: Political Philosophy*. Oxford.

Schöpe, B. (2011), 'Pertinax: ein verrückt normaler Kaiser', in S. Faust and F. Leitmeir (eds.), *Repräsentationsformen in severischer Zeit*. Frankfurt: 253–69.

Schulz, V. (2014), 'Nero und Domitian bei Cassius Dio: Zwei Tyrannen aus der Sicht des 3. Jh. n. Chr.', in S. Bönisch-Meyer, L. Cordes, and V. Schulz (eds.), *Nero und Domitian: Mediale Diskurse der Herrscherrepräsentation im Vergleich*. Munich: 405–34.

Schulz, V. (2015), 'Kalkuliertes Missverstehen? Zu Störungen der Kommunikation in Tacitus' Annalen', *Philologus* 159: 156–87.

Schulz, V. (2016), 'Historiography and panegyric: the deconstruction of imperial representation in Cassius Dio's *Roman History*', in C. H. Lange and J. M. Madsen (eds.), *Cassius Dio: Greek Intellectual and Roman Politician*. Leiden and Boston: 276–96.

Schulz, V. (2019a), *Deconstructing Imperial Representation: Tacitus, Cassius Dio, and Suetonius on Nero and Domitian*, Mnemosyne Supplements 427. Leiden and Boston.

Schulz, V. (2019b), 'Defining the good ruler: early kings as proto-imperial figures in Cassius Dio', in C. Burden-Strevens and M. Lindholmer (eds.), *Cassius Dio's Forgotten History of Early Rome*. Leiden and Boston: 311–32.

Schwartz, E. (1899), 'Cassius (no. 40)', *RE* 3: 1684–722.

Scott, A. G. (2012), 'Dio and Herodian on the assassination of Caracalla', *CW* 106: 15–28.

Scott, A. G. (2015), 'Cassius Dio, Caracalla, and the senate', *Klio* 97: 157–75.

Scott, A. G. (2017), 'Cassius Dio on Septimius Severus' *decennalia* and *ludi saeculares*', *Histos* 11: 154–61.

Scott, A. G. (2018a) 'Cassius Dio's contemporary history as memoir and its implications for authorial identity', *PLLS* 17: 229–48.

Scott, A. G. (2018b), *Emperors and Usurpers: An Historical Commentary on Cassius Dio's Roman History Books 79(78)–80(80)(AD 217–229)*. New York and Oxford.

Scott, J. C. (1990), *Domination and the Arts of Resistance: Hidden Transcripts*. New Haven and London.

Seager, R. (1972), *Tiberius*. London.

Shagan, E. H. (2001), 'Rumours and popular politics in the reign of Henry VIII', in T. Harris (ed.), *The Politics of the Excluded, c. 1500–1850*. Basingstoke and Malden, MA: 30–66.

Shatzman, I. (1974), 'Tacitean rumours', *Latomus* 33: 549–78.

Sherwin-White, A. N. (1984), *Roman Foreign Policy in the East, 168 B.C. to A.D. 1*. London.

Shibutani, T. (1966), *Improvised News. A Sociological Study of Rumor*. Indianapolis and New York.

Shotter, D. C. A. (1967), 'The debate on Augustus (Tac. *Ann.* 1, 9–10)', *Mnemosyne* 4: 171–4.

Sidebottom, H. (1998), 'Herodian's historical methods and understanding of history', *ANRW* 2.34.2: 2775–836.

Sidebottom, H. (2007), 'Severan historiography: evidence, patterns, and arguments', in S. Swain, S. Harrison, and J. Elsner (eds.), *Severan Culture*. Cambridge: 58–82.

Simons, B. (2009), *Cassius Dio und die Römische Republik*. Berlin.

Sion-Jenkis, B. (2016), 'Frauenfiguren bei Cassius Dio: der Fall der Livia', in V. Fromentin *et al.* (eds.), *Cassius Dion: nouvelles lectures*. Bordeaux: 725–40.

Smith, S. D. (2004), *Man and Animal in Severan Rome. The Literary Imagination of Claudius Aelianus*. Cambridge.

Smits J. C. P. (1914), *Die Vita Commodi und Cassius Dio. Eine quellenanalytische Untersuchung*. Leiden.

Sommer, M. (2004), 'Elagabal: Wege zur Konstruktion eines 'schlechten' Kaisers', *SCI* 23: 95–110.

Spawforth, A. (1994), 'Symbol of unity? The Persian Wars tradition in the Roman empire', in S. Hornblower (ed.), *Greek Historiography*. Oxford: 233–47.

Speidel, M. A. (2017), 'Antoninus Pius, das Militär und der Krieg. Epigraphische Korrekturen zur literarischen Überlieferung', in C. Michels and P. F. Mittag (eds.), *Jenseits des Narrativs: Antoninus Pius in den nicht-literarischen Quellen*. Stuttgart: 225–68.

Spielberg, L. (2019), 'Fairy tales and hard truths in Tacitus's *Histories* 4.6–10', *CA* 38: 141–83.

Stadter, P. A. (2015), *Plutarch and His Roman Readers*. Oxford.

Steidle, W. (1988), 'Beobachtungen zum Geschichtswerk des Cassius Dio', *WJA* 14: 203–24.

Stephanus, H. (ed.) (1591), *Ton Dionos tou Kassiou Romaikon historion biblia pente kai eikosi. Dionis Cassii Romanarum historiarum libri XXV, ex Guilielmi Xylandri interpretatione*. Geneva.

Stertz, S. A. (1979), 'Pseudo-Aristides, ΕΙΣ ΒΑΣΙΛΕΑ', *CQ* 29: 172–97.

Stevenson, T. R. (2013), 'The succession planning of Augustus', *Antichthon* 47: 118–39.

Stewart, P. (2012), 'The equestrian statue of Marcus Aurelius', in M. van Ackeren (ed.), *A Companion to Marcus Aurelius*. Oxford and Malden, MA: 264–77.

Strobel, K. (2004), 'Commodus und Pertinax: "Perversion der Macht" und "Restauration des Guten"?', in H. Heftner and K. Tomaschitz (eds.), *Ad Fontes! Festschrift für Gerhard Dobesch zum 65. Geburtstag am 15 September 2004, dargebracht von Kollegen, Schülern und Freunden*. Vienna: 519–32.

Stuart, D. R. (1904), 'The attitude of Dio Cassius toward the epigraphic sources', in H. A. Sanders (ed.), *Roman Historical Sources and Institutions*. New York and London: 101–47.

Sutherland, C. H. V. (1951), *Coinage in Roman Imperial Policy: 31 BC–AD 68*. London.

Swain, S. (1996), *Hellenism and Empire: Language, Classicism, and Power in the Greek World AD 50–250*. Oxford.

Swain, S. (1997), 'Biography and biographic in the literature of the Roman empire', in M. J. Edwards and S. Swain (eds.), *Portraits: Biographical Representation in the Greek and Latin Literature of the Roman Empire*. Oxford: 1–37.

Swain, S., Harrison, S. and Elsner, J. (eds.) (2007), *Severan Culture*. Cambridge.

Swan, P. M. (1987), 'Cassius Dio on Augustus: a poverty of annalistic sources?', *Phoenix* 41: 272–91.

Swan, P. M. (1997), 'How Cassius Dio composed his Augustan books: four studies', *ANRW* 2.34.3: 2524–557.

Swan, P. M. (2004), *The Augustan Succession: An Historical Commentary on Cassius Dio's Roman History Books 55–56*. Oxford.

Syme, R. (1939), *The Roman Revolution*. Oxford.

Syme, R. (1956), 'Some friends of the Caesars', *AJPh* 77: 264–73. Republished in Badian, E. (ed.) (1979), *Roman Papers. Volume 1*. Oxford: 292–99.

Syme, R. (1958), *Tacitus*, 2 vols. Oxford.

Syme, R. (1968), *Ammianus and the Historia Augusta*. Oxford.

Syme, R. (1971), *Emperors and Biography: Studies in the Historia Augusta*. Oxford.

Syme, R. (1978), *History in Ovid*. Oxford.

Syme, R. (1979), 'Some imperatorial salutations', *Phoenix* 33.4: 308–29.

Syme, R. (1986), *The Augustan Aristocracy*. Oxford.

Tafel, L. (ed.) (1831–44), *Cassius Dio's Römische Geschichte*, 16 vols. Stuttgart.

Thomasson, B. E. (1996), *Fasti Africani: senatorische und ritterliche Amtsträger in den römischen Provinzen Nordafrikas von Augustus bis Diokletian*. Stockholm.

Timpe, D. (1967), 'Drusus' Umkehr an der Elbe', *RhM* 110: 289–306.

Toher, M. (2009), 'Divining a lost text: Augustus' *Autobiography* and the βίος Καίσαρος of Nicolaus of Damascus', in C. Smith and A. Powell (eds.), *The Lost Memoirs of Augustus and the Development of Roman Autobiography*. Swansea: 125–44.

Townend, G. B. (1961), 'Traces in Dio Cassius of Cluvius, Aufidius and Pliny', *Hermes* 89: 227–48.

Townend, G. B. (1965), 'Review of Millar 1964', *JRS* 55: 306–7.

Tränkle, H. (1969), 'Augustus bei Tacitus, Cassius Dio und dem älteren Plinius', *WS* 82: 108–30.

Treadgold, W. T. (1980), *The Nature of the Bibliotheca of Photius*. Washington, DC.

Treadgold, W. T. (2013), *The Middle Byzantine Historians*. New York.

Turkeltaub, D. (2007), 'Perceiving Iliadic gods', *HSCP* 103: 51–81.

Untila, A. *et al.* (trans.) (2000–17), *Chiliades or Book of Histories.* www.theoi.com /Text/TzetzesChiliades1.html

Urban, R. (1979), 'Tacitus und die *Res Gestae Divi Augusti*: Die Auseinandersetzung des Historikers mit der offiziellen Darstellung', *Gymnasium* 86: 59–74.

Urso, G. (2013), 'L'octroi de la citoyenneté romaine aux Latins: un anachronisme de Cassius Dion', *Erga-Logoi* 2: 73–83.

Urso, G. (2016a), 'Cassius Dion témoin de traditions disparues: les premiers siècles de la République', in V. Fromentin *et al.* (eds.), *Cassius Dion: nouvelles lectures.* Bordeaux: 143–58.

Urso, G. (2016b), 'Cassius Dio's Sulla: exemplum of cruelty and Republican dictator', in C. H. Lange and J. M. Madsen (eds.), *Cassius Dio. Greek Intellectual and Roman Politician.* Leiden and Boston: 13–32.

Urso, G. (2019), 'Cassio Dione e le fonti pre-Liviane: una versione alternative dei primi secoli di Roma', in C. Burden-Strevens and M. Lindholmer (eds.) (2019), *Cassius Dio's Forgotten History of Early Rome.* Leiden and Boston: 53–75.

van den Hout, M. P. J. (ed.) (1988), *M. Cornelii Frontonis Epistulae.* 2nd edition. Leipzig.

van der Stockt, L. (1999), 'A Plutarchan hypomnema on self-love', *AJP* 1920: 575–99.

van Minnen, P. (2001), '*P. Oxy.* LXVI 4527 and the Antonine Plague in the Fayyum', *ZPE* 135: 175–7.

van Stekelenburg, A. V. (1971), *De redevoeringen bij Cassius Dio.* Delft.

van Stekelenburg, A. V. (1976), 'Lucan and Cassius Dio as heirs to Livy: the speech of Julius Caesar at Placentia', *AClass* 19: 43–57.

Varga, R. and Pázsint, A.-I. (2019), 'The reflection of personal and collective tragedies in ancient sources 2. Tragedies in Roman epigraphy', *Journal of Ancient History and Archaeology* 6.3: 49–58.

Varner, E. R. (2004), *Mutilation and Transformation. Damnatio Memoriae and Roman Imperial Portraiture.* Leiden and Boston.

Veh, O. and Wirth, G. (eds.) (1985–92), *Cassius Dio: Römische Geschichte*, 5 vols. Zurich and Munich.

Vittinghoff, F. (1936), *Der Staatsfeind in der römischen Kaiserzeit. Untersuchungen zur „damnatio memoriae".* Berlin.

Viviani, G. (ed.) (1790–2), *Istorie Romane di Dione Cassio tradotte da G. Viviani*, 4 vols. Milan.

Vout, C. (2007), *Power and Eroticism in Imperial Rome.* Cambridge.

Wagemakers, B. (2010), 'Incest, infanticide, and cannibalism: anti-Christian imputations in the Roman empire', *G&R* 57: 337–54.

Wagner, J. A. (ed.) (1783–96), *Dio Cassius röm. Geschichte, aus dem Gr. übersetzt von J. Aug. Wagner*, 5 vols. Frankfurt.

Walbank, F. W. (1967), *A Historical Commentary on Polybius. Volume II.* Oxford.

Walbank, F. W. (1990), 'Profit or amusement: some thoughts on the motives of Hellenistic historians', in H. Verdin, G. Schepens, and E. de Keyser (eds.),

Purposes of History. Studies in Greek Historiography from the 4th to the 2nd Centuries BC. Studia Hellenistica 30. Leuven: 253–66.

Walker, S. (2000), 'Rumour, sedition and popular protest in the reign of Henry IV', *P&P* 146: 31–65.

Wallace-Hadrill, A. (1981), 'The emperor and his virtues', *Historia* 30: 298–323.

Wallace-Hadrill, A. (1982), '*Civilis princeps*: between citizen and king', *JRS* 72: 32–48.

Wallace-Hadrill, A. (1983), *Suetonius: The Scholar and His Caesars*. Bristol.

Wallace-Hadrill, A. (1996), 'The imperial court', in A. K. Bowman, E. Champlin and A. Lintott (eds.), *The Cambridge Ancient History. Second Edition. Volume X: The Augustan Empire, 43 BC–AD 69*. Cambridge: 283–308.

Wardle, D. (2002), 'The heroism and heroisation of Tiberius', in P. Defosse (ed.), *Hommages à Carl Deroux, II – Prose et linguistique, Médecine*. Brussels: 433–40.

Weir, R. (1999), 'Nero and the Herakles frieze at Delphi', *BCH* 123: 397–404.

Westall, R. (2012), 'Caracalla, *Commentarius de bello Parthico*', *Hermes* 140: 457–67.

Westall, R. (2016), 'The sources of Cassius Dio for the Roman civil wars of 49–30 BC', in C. H. Lange and J. M. Madsen (eds.), *Cassius Dio. Greek Intellectual and Roman Politician*. Leiden and Boston: 51–75.

Whitmarsh. T. J. G. (1999), 'Greek and Roman in dialogue: the Pseudo-Lucianic Nero', *JHS* 119: 142–60.

Whitmarsh. T. J. G. (2001), 'Greece is the world: exile and identity in the Second Sophistic', in S. Goldhill (ed.), *Being Greek under Rome: Cultural Identity, the Second Sophistic and the Development of Empire*. Cambridge: 269–305.

Whitmarsh, T. J. G. (2005), *The Second Sophistic*. Oxford.

Whittaker, C. R. (ed.) (1969), *Herodian: History of the Empire*, 2 vols. Cambridge, MA.

Williams, C. (2010), *Roman Homosexuality*, 2nd edition. Oxford.

Wills, J. (1996), *Repetition in Latin Poetry: Figures of Allusion*. Oxford.

Winterling, A. (1999), *Aula Caesaris. Studien zur Institutionalisierung des römischen Kaiserhofes in der Zeit von Augustus bis Commodus (31 v. Chr.— 192 n. Chr.)*. Berlin.

Winterling, A. (2011), *Caligula: A Biography*. Berkeley.

Woodman, A. J. (1977), *Velleius Paterculus 2.94–131: The Tiberian Narrative*. Cambridge.

Woodman, A. J. (1988), *Rhetoric in Classical Historiography*. London and Sydney.

Woodman, A. J. (1989), 'Tacitus' obituary of Tiberius', *CQ* 39: 197–205.

Woodman, A. J. (1992). 'Amateur dramatics at the court of Nero: *Annals* 15.48–74', in T. J. Luce and A. J. Woodman (eds.), *Tacitus and the Tacitean Tradition*, Princeton, NJ: 104–28. Reprinted in Woodman 1998: 190–217.

Woodman, A. J. (1998), *Tacitus Reviewed*. Oxford.

Woodman, A. J. (trans.) (2004), *Tacitus: The Annals*. Indianapolis.

Woodman, A. J. (2006), 'Mutiny and madness: Tacitus *Annals* 1.16–49', *Arethusa* 39: 303–29.

Wolff, H. (1976), *Die Constitutio Antoniniana und Papyrus Gissensis 40 I*, 2 vols. Cologne.

Xylander, G. (ed.) (1558), *Dionis Casii Nicaei Romanae historiae libri (tot enim hodie extant) XXV, nimirum a XXXVI ad LXI: quibus exponuntur res gestae a bello Cretico vsque ad mortem Claudii Caesaris, quae est historia annorum circiter CXXX. Nunc primum summa fide diligentiaque de Graecis Latini facti, Guilielmo Xylandro Augustano interprete*. Basel.

Zanker, P. (2010), 'By the emperor, for the people,' in B. C. Ewald and C. F. Noreña (eds.), *The Emperor and Rome: Space, Representation, and Ritual*. Cambridge: 45–87.

Zecchini G. (1978), *Cassio Dione e la guerra gallica di Cesare*. Milano.

Zecchini, G. (1987), *Il Carmen de bello Actiaco. Storiografia e lotta politica in età augustea*. Wiesbaden and Stuttgart.

Zecchini, G. (1998), 'Asinio Quadrato storico di Filippo l'Arabo', *ANRW* 2.34.4: 2999–3021.

Zecchini, G. (2016), 'Cassius Dion et l'historiographie de son temps', in V. Fromentin *et al.* (eds.), *Cassius Dion: nouvelles lectures*. Bordeaux: 113–24.

Ziegler, K. (1972), 'Zonaras' *RE* 19: 718–23.

Index

Emperors and prominent authors are indexed under the name by which they are best known (e.g. Caracalla, rather than M. Aurelius Antoninus; Plutarch, rather than C. Mestrius Plutarchus). All other Roman men are indexed by their Latin nomen, except in the cases of M. Antonius and Cn. Pompeius Magnus, who appear as Antony and Pompey, respectively, in line with the common English forms used in the book.

Lightning Source UK Ltd.
Milton Keynes UK
UKHW022223060821
388407UK00005B/96